REPORT OF
THE
ROYAL COMMISSION
ON
CORPORATE CONCENTRATION

MARCH 1978

To His Excellency the
Governor General in Council

MAY IT PLEASE YOUR EXCELLENCY

We the Commissioners appointed under Part I of the Inquiries Act by
Order in Council of 1 May 1975, P.C. 1975-999, to inquire into, report upon,
and make recommendations concerning the concentration of corporate power
in Canada more specifically set forth in Order in Council of 22 April 1975,
P.C. 1975-879,

BEG LEAVE TO SUBMIT TO YOUR EXCELLENCY THIS REPORT

_____
Robert W. V. Dickerson

_____
Pierre A. Nadeau

17 March 1978

TABLE OF CONTENTS

xi

Tables and Figures

Chapter 2

Tables

Figures

xv

Preface

Preliminary Observations

This Commission was appointed under Part I of the Inquiries Act, by two Orders in Council approved respectively on April 22 and May 1, 1975 (see Appendix A), which set out the following terms of reference:

... to inquire into, report upon, and make recommendations concerning:

(a) the nature and role of major concentrations of corporate power in Canada;

(b) the economic and social implications for the public interest of such concentrations; and

(c) whether safeguards exist or may be required to protect the public interest in the presence of such concentrations.

While this mandate contemplated a broad and wide-ranging inquiry, the origin of the Commission was more precise and identifiable. The event that led directly to its creation was the bid for control of Argus Corporation Limited made in March/April 1975 by Power Corporation of Canada, Limited, a matter upon which we comment in some detail in Chapter 7. Although the bid was ultimately unsuccessful it provoked considerable comment, since it could have resulted in a very large enterprise with significant interests in many major industries. While this result would have been achieved by acquisition rather than internal development, it was not clear whether, in this situation, existing merger laws would have protected the public interest adequately. The government concluded that it was not able to assess the full implications of such an acquisition, as there had not been, in Canada, any general review and analysis of the consequences of mergers of large, diversified firms or of the implications of concentrations of corporate ownership and power.

Thus we were not to limit our investigation to the question of conglomerate mergers. Indeed, the terms of reference do not mention either conglomerates or the Power bid for Argus. We were asked rather to venture into areas that had not been extensively explored in Canada. Although we were given broad terms of reference, we were at the same time operating under some constraints, since we had been asked to report with all reasonable dispatch. We were trying to complete our work within two years.

In constructing a framework for analyzing the problem given to us, we found that we shared a conviction regarding Canadian society. We believed that our political system, with its major role for governments as well as private business, and respect and safeguards for the freedom of individuals, was sound in its basic elements and structure and more appropriate for Canada than any other. Only a very few witnesses urged radical change. Almost all argued, or appeared to believe, that our society and our economy should function both efficiently and equitably, without a basic rearrangement of roles and relationships. This we believe also to be the view of most Canadians and we have therefore looked for improvements and made recommendations concerning the working of our institutions within the existing structure of society.

Our terms of reference, however broad, did not extend to an investigation and appraisal of the role of governments or trade unions, or of the implications of their respective activities, although there is much there that could be considered. That apart, there was little in the corporate sector that could be considered to lie outside our mandate, if such matters involved concentrations of corporate power.

We tried to approach our task without fixed views. Some of the relevant issues had not been widely discussed in Canada, while others had received some examination and analysis, mainly in academic circles. Most, we found, did not generate public enthusiasm or even great interest.

We determined early that it would be necessary to narrow the focus of our inquiry, so that we could best marshall and use the available resources. We announced that we thought it undesirable for the Commission to commence a review of competition policy generally, since qualified advisers to the government had been working on that matter for a considerable time. As expected, however, we did come upon issues touching directly on existing or proposed competition policy, and hence we make a number of observations on that subject in various chapters. We also stated that we would not duplicate the work of those responsible for reviewing and revising the Bank Act and that we did not plan to give detailed attention to the provisions of the existing Bank Act, or to the regulation of banks and bank credit. Nevertheless, there were a number of matters related to the banks as concentrations of corporate power with which we were concerned, and these are dealt with in Chapter 10. We announced that we did not intend to make a special study of foreign control of Canadian corporations or multinational corporations, since much had been written on that subject, and the Foreign Investment Review Act had been put into effect in 1974. We have considered some aspects of foreign control related to corporate concentration, and we comment on those in Chapter 8.

Many new laws were introduced during the 1960s and 1970s specifically relating to the formation and management of corporations, the securities they issue to the public, the information they must disclose, their competitive behavior, the taxation of their income and that of their shareholders, permissible investment in Canada in the case of those that are foreign-controlled, and many other related matters. In addition, new laws of general application have been introduced, which are also of considerable importance to business. They include legislation to protect the environment, to protect the consumer, to prevent discrimination in employment, and to disclose political contributions.

This extensive recent reform of the laws affecting business has confronted this Commission with a difficult task in identifying those places where the public interest may have been left inadequately guarded against the economic and social implications of major concentrations of corporate power. We have selected several areas for discussion. One subject that seemed not to have been adequately studied in the past comprised the potential implications for the public interest in the formation and conduct of large diversified corporate enterprises ("conglomerates"). These are discussed in general in Chapter 5 and a specific case is treated in Chapter 7. In addition we have reviewed in Chapter 6 the practices and laws relating to mergers, which have led to the formation of many major corporations.

We also discuss a number of other issues, to which our attention has been drawn by witnesses or briefs, or which our own studies have suggested. However we should make clear at the outset that an inquiry with the very broad terms of reference we had inevitably raises many more questions than it can hope to resolve. Therefore in many cases we simply identify possible problems that we think warrant further study.

One further preliminary point should be made. We were asked to deal with matters of public policy, not to conduct an investigation into the affairs of any specific corporation. We were not established to play the role of ombudsman; there were no "parties" before us contesting "issues" in the legal sense. It was, however, inevitable that, as an integral part of our work, we should look closely at many corporations and a number of specific events. This was almost always done as part of the process of formulating our views on the broad kinds of issues we address in the *Report*.

Documentation

Unless otherwise noted data have been brought up-to-date to 1977. Since we expect this *Report* to be of interest to laymen as well as technicians, we have avoided extensive footnotes and references. However, where appropriate, readers are directed to the thoroughly documented research studies on which part of the *Report*, especially its more technical aspects, is based.

The Work of the Commission

We went about our duties principally in four ways. These were generally distinct, although of necessity they overlapped to some extent.

Existing Material

We began by studying existing material on the subject of our inquiry. This first stage has been a continuing and intensive one, engaged in by the Commissioners, our staff, and the consultants whom we have engaged. While there is not nearly as much Canadian material on the various topics as we should have liked, there is nevertheless some, and there is a good deal more material originating in other parts of the world, particularly in the United States. We have read and discussed as many as possible of the articles, studies and other material pertinent to our work.

Submissions from the Public

The second phase of our work commenced with an invitation to the public to submit views on the matters we had been asked to consider. Within two months of the creation of the Commission, we issued a public statement announcing our plans, and concurrently advertised widely to invite all interested persons to send us their views. We repeated the invitation on several occasions, by advertising in newspapers and other journals and soliciting briefs or comments from the public.

We received more than 200 written briefs, ranging in size and scope from a few paragraphs on a single topic to complex and sophisticated submissions in several volumes touching on a large number of the subjects in which we were interested. Of the briefs, 54 came from corporations, 75 from individuals, 7 from experts whom we had asked to submit briefs or studies, 62 from associations and 3 from other organizations or persons. Included in the total for associations are the submissions we received from 5 political parties and 6 trade unions. The briefs came from every province and from the territories, from the largest cities to small villages. Roughly half came from Ontario, one-fifth from Quebec, and the remainder more or less evenly from across the country. A list of written submissions is set out in Appendix B.

These submissions will form part of our permanent papers and will be available for review and analysis by others in the future. The people who submitted briefs rendered a significant service to the Commission, and we are grateful to them.

Public Hearings

In addition to written submissions, we obtained the views of the public at public hearings. While the kinds of hearings conducted by Royal Commissions are not intended to yield scientifically accurate measurements of public opinion, they do provide a forum for the expression of views, often deeply held, and we found that the hearings (which resulted in about 8,000 pages of transcript) exposed us to a broad cross-section of opinion. The dates and places of the hearings, together with the names of the people who appeared at them, are set out in Appendix C.

We conducted the public hearings in three rounds. The first took place in November and December of 1975, and January of 1976. We visited Montreal,

Toronto, Ottawa, Winnipeg, Calgary and Vancouver and heard there testimony from people or organizations that had submitted briefs and had expressed an interest in giving oral evidence. Generally we laid down no rules as to the content of any oral presentation, and witnesses were free to discuss any topic relevant to our terms of reference. This round of hearings had two main purposes. First, it was intended that the public have a full opportunity to express its views. Secondly, it was hoped that the Commissioners could form an impression about what were likely to be the important matters to be considered. These hearings (like the others that followed) were as informal as we could make them. Witnesses were not sworn and, with only one or two exceptions, did not appear with their lawyers. Witnesses spoke on the matters of interest to them and were then questioned by the Commissioners and Commission counsel in an effort to obtain elaboration and clarification of views.

By the conclusion of the first round of hearings, and as a result of the other work we had been doing, we were able to select those issues on which we wanted to hear more oral testimony, and which could be appropriately dealt with at the next round of hearings. We had also concluded that some of the issues were best dealt with by means other than public discussion, most often through specialized research inquiries. The second round of hearings took place in April, May and June 1976. These were held in the cities of Toronto, Montreal and Ottawa because the people from whom we wished to hear were resident in one of those cities or agreed to come to testify there. In the second round of hearings we were more selective than in the first. Although the format was similar, we invited particular witnesses to discuss specific subjects. The focus of the second set of hearings was thus much more narrowly defined.

A third round of hearings was held because we thought it desirable to obtain an even wider cross-section of views of Canadians. We also thought we should do everything reasonable to encourage people without the resources for the preparation of submissions, and those who did not live in large urban centres, to come forward and give their views. Accordingly we scheduled a number of quite informal hearings at various times from May through September 1976. These were all held in the evening. They were conducted by one Commissioner, with one or two staff members (the earlier hearings had been conducted by all three Commissioners and more staff), and the Commissioners allocated and shared this responsibility among themselves. We held hearings at Halifax, Charlottetown, Fredericton, St. John's, Windsor, London, Sudbury, Thunder Bay, Sherbrooke, Chicoutimi, Trois-Rivières, Quebec City, Regina, Edmonton, Victoria, Prince George, and Yellowknife. We frequently sat well into the night, and heard both prepared and spontaneous expressions of opinion from any member of the audience who wished to come forward. In total, we had at these hearings 127 witnesses. The views expressed at the hearings were valuable to us, since they helped to define in our minds the attitudes of Canadians on a number of national, regional, and local issues. For example, one of the most difficult parts of our work has been to assess the social implications of corporate power. The evening hearings helped us to formulate our own views on this question.

Research

A significant part of our work has been conducted through a research program. Some of this was done by our staff but much of it was contracted out. The program began in the summer of 1975, and all the reports were received by 1977. It was designed to fill some of the gaps in knowledge that we found to exist, to assist us in arriving at conclusions and, perhaps most importantly, to contribute to the understanding of Canadians in several important areas. A descriptive list of the published research studies is given in Appendix D.

It did not take long before we realized that there was a lack in Canada of objective, analytical histories of the development of individual Canadian businesses. Part of our task was to report on the nature and role of concentrations of corporate power. To assess the implications of corporate activity, one must have a reasonable understanding of the facts of that activity. Thus we commissioned a number of studies focusing on the financial, operational, and corporate histories of selected enterprises. About a dozen of these are reports by investment analysts describing some of Canada's largest and most important diversified enterprises and conglomerate corporations. These are based on information that, while publicly available, has now, largely for the first time, been drawn together, analyzed and reported upon in one place. We also commissioned, from professional economists, analyses of large, but essentially non-diversified, corporations. Among these firms are a major Canadian refining and manufacturing company with extensive operations overseas, a large resource-based company selling mainly in the export market, and a large multinational company in a high-technology sector. The individual studies are of course the work of the respective authors, and do not necessarily reflect the views of the Commissioners or of the companies themselves.

A second group of research projects was more technical in nature. In this group were studies dealing with (a) the relationship, quantitatively measured, between size or other dimensions of corporate structure and corporate economic performance; (b) the causes and effects of diversification among Canadian enterprises and of the market power of large firms; (c) size and concentration in Canadian industry; (d) reciprocal buying arrangements; (e) the influence of the tax system on mergers and acquisitions; and (f) alternative assessments of networks of corporate control, as signaled by interlocking directors and officers among enterprises.

A third category of research involves studies of a less purely economic or technical kind. These have a somewhat broader, socially oriented perspective. Among these are studies dealing with (a) the impact of organization size on individual alienation; (b) the social characteristics of one-industry towns in Canada; (c) the relationship between large and smaller firms (corporate dualism) in a major Canadian industry and its implications; (d) the concept of corporate social responsibility in Canada; (e) the personnel policies and practices of very large businesses compared with those of middle-sized businesses; (f) political party financing in Canada and the law relating thereto; and (g) the relationship between corporate size and labor relations.

The research projects mentioned, and the others listed in Appendix D, are being published concurrently with the publication of this *Report*. All the research projects, some unpublished studies and internal background papers, plus all the submissions and transcripts of evidence will also be deposited in every provincial legislative library.

Robert B. Bryce

We should like to record here our deep appreciation of the significant contribution of Robert B. Bryce to the work and *Report* of this Commission. From the date of his appointment as Chairman (April 22, 1975) until his resignation because of ill health two years later, he provided the Commission with inspired and dedicated leadership.

Mr. Bryce brought to our work a unique wealth of experience gained in an illustrious career as a public servant. This career included service as Executive Director of the World Bank, Secretary of the Treasury Board, Clerk of the Privy Council and Secretary to the Cabinet, Deputy Minister of Finance and Executive Director of the International Monetary Fund.

At the time of Mr. Bryce's resignation we had completed our research work and public hearings and had made considerable progress on crystallizing our views and drafting this *Report*. However, Mr. Bryce has not participated in the work of the Commission since his resignation, and the remaining Commissioners bear responsibility for the completed *Report*.

Acknowledgements

This *Report* would not have been possible if we had not had the help of a highly competent, industrious and dedicated staff. Their names are listed in Appendix E and our thanks extends to all of them.

Conclusion

In our opinion, some of the matters upon which we have expressed a view require legislative action, but most do not. As we have discovered, much of the present legislation in some of the areas with which we are concerned has emerged gradually out of, and embodies what was previously, general practice. We hope that our observations will contribute to a similar process. We also hope that the evidence and views that have been brought to light as a result of our activities, the publication of our *Report*, and the attention thereby focused on a generally unfamiliar subject will stimulate reaction and response and will influence opinion and action in a constructive way.

Chapter 1

Introduction and Background to the Report

Large firms and concentrated industries are not new phenomena in Canada or other industrial countries. They have existed for at least 100 years. Before 1800 most manufacturing industries were composed of small firms, often one-man or family operations. With the industrial revolution, the size of the firms in most industries increased dramatically as entrepreneurs invested ever larger amounts of capital equipment to exploit new technologies and the economies of scale available in them. However, this large capital investment made these large firms more vulnerable to periodic shifts in the demand for their products over the business cycle and exacerbated these swings. To insulate themselves from these often catastrophic cyclical changes in sales and profits, firms often further increased their size by buying out competitors to control the market and to reduce what they considered to be "ruinous competition". In this way, the great increase in investment and output brought about by the industrial revolution, which has so dramatically raised our standard of living, also brought with it large firms and concentrated, oligopolistic industries. By the late 1800s this trend toward size and concentration had reached a point where the governments in Canada, the United States, England and other industrial countries had enacted legislation to curb the power of large firms. In 1889, the Canadian government enacted the predecessor to the present Combines Investigation Act, predating the Sherman Act in the United States by a year. This legislation reflected concern over both the growing size of corporations and potential abuses of corporate power, such as restrictive trade practices, by some large firms.

The level of overall concentration in the Canadian economy has almost certainly fallen in every successive decade since the turn of the century. For instance, in 1923 the Canadian Pacific Railway Company accounted for 21% of the aggregate assets of the 100 largest corporations in Canada; by 1975 the share of Canadian Pacific Limited had fallen to 6%. Concentration in most sectors and industries appears to have declined over the same period and in general, as we shall show in Chapter 2, has changed very little over the period

1

1967-76 despite the large number of mergers during that period. Many people have become increasingly uneasy over the economic, political and social impact of large firms in Canada. The sheer size of many of the firms in concentrated industries, their impact on their employees and communities and their potential economic power to administer prices and the quantity and quality of their output have caused apprehension among the public and governments, since this impact is seen to run counter to the economic and political philosophy of the free market system. This free market so eloquently espoused by Adam Smith in the eighteenth century had promised a competitive stimulus to efficiency, low and flexible prices and competition that would direct productive activity in such a way as to maximize the national income. Free markets composed of many small firms, which cannot influence the price at which their output is sold, have probably never existed in a modern, industrial economy. The Canadian economy, though widely thought to be a free enterprise one, has always been composed of large firms and oligopolistic markets in many industries and has been characterized by extensive government involvement.

Since Confederation and the "National Policy" of Sir John A. Macdonald, the federal and provincial governments have intervened in the economy through legislation, Crown corporations, erection of tariff barriers, subsidies and other direct and indirect means in support of national and provincial economic objectives and to tie Canada together as an industrial country. For instance, the railroads were built to run east and west in an attempt to change natural trade patterns and population flows, with the federal government providing cash, land grants, bond guarantees and monopoly privileges to their builders. High tariff walls were erected to protect domestic manufacturing industries from international competition and to redirect market forces from north-south to east-west trade to promote unity and national development.

From 1930 on, direct involvement by government continued or increased with the aims of promoting economic growth, establishing industries that could be internationally competitive, and regulating "key sector" industries in the public interest. World War II and the succeeding period of high demand for industrial goods gave a tremendous impetus to the growth of manufacturing in Canada. In the 30 years since World War II, Canada has gradually lowered its tariff barriers as part of the world-wide tariff reductions negotiated under the General Agreement on Tariffs and Trade. In spite of these reductions, Canada's tariffs are generally higher than those of other industrial countries, a vestige of the "National Policy", although its non-tariff barriers to trade (such as quotas) are somewhat lower. The government has continued to subsidize unprofitable transportation routes and to offer incentives for industry to locate or expand in lagging regions of the country in order to achieve a more even distribution of economic welfare among the provinces. Throughout this period the government has become increasingly concerned and involved with the transfer of income from group to group to achieve a more even income distribution. By early 1977, the portion of the economy taken out of the private sector by government ownership or direct government regulation had reached about 25% of the gross national product (GNP). Sometimes government involvement takes the form of joint projects, such as Syncrude. In a more general way, there has been increasing government regulation of pollution levels, product safety, working conditions and employment practices.

The need for government regulation and involvement in the economy may well increase in the future. There are a number of tasks in our society that may be best undertaken by government (often in conjunction with private enterprise). Some projects may be too large or risky for private firms to undertake by themselves without government support. Others may be in the national interest but not sufficiently profitable to attract private capital. For example, the development of new sources of energy that can be in place as the end of the oil age approaches is probably beyond the capacity of private Canadian industry under almost any set of market assumptions, yet it is in the public interest for Canada to develop these new sources.

Canada's Unique Economy

The economic analysis and policy recommendations contained in this *Report* reflect the distinctive characteristics of Canada and its economy. Many of these characteristics are mentioned throughout the *Report*; we summarize the most important ones here to give a background against which it and our recommendations should be viewed.

The Canadian economy is made up of small markets dispersed over a wide geographic area. Canada has a relatively small domestic market and is one of the few countries in the world whose industries do not have access to a large free trade area. Canada's small, dispersed markets often prevent Canadian producers from realizing economies of scale. A large central plant that attains efficient levels of production often faces high transport costs, while small regional plants, which reduce those costs, may be unable to achieve efficient production costs because of low volumes of production. In either case, Canadian domestic producers in many areas cannot achieve the productivity enjoyed by firms in more populous and geographically concentrated markets. Nonetheless Canada's exports as a proportion of GNP are among the highest of the major industrial countries. We are a high-wage country, facing increasing international competition both from low-wage countries and from developed countries whose industries can realize economies of scale in production and in research and development through access to large markets.

The dispersed, isolated nature of Canadian markets has also led to significant disparities in income among different regions. As well, different regions of the country have different economic bases such that their economic interests are often not congruent with and are sometimes directly opposed to one another.

Canada has a higher level of tariff protection, but a lower level of non-tariff barriers than most other industrial countries. These tariff policies partly insulate domestic business from the stimulus of foreign competition, allowing Canadian firms to operate inefficiently, by international standards, because of small scale but still to remain profitable because they can set their prices to match those of imports. Foreign firms have invested in Canada to overcome these tariff barriers; but in so doing they have frequently set up either a truncated version or a complete but scale-inefficient "miniature replica" of their larger operations outside Canada.

Canadian industry features a higher proportion of foreign ownership than does any other developed country, and the presence of foreign ownership and foreign subsidiaries in Canada contributes to Canada's dependence on capital and technology from abroad. Repatriation of dividends and interest charges at the rate of $2.5 billion per year reduces the growth of domestic pools of capital. Because of their backing by their parent firms, multinational subsidiaries are often able to obtain capital in Canada on more favorable terms than domestic companies of the same size. Technology is often imported rather than developed in Canada because it is cheaper and less risky to buy or license from foreign firms than to maintain indigenous research and development.

The State of the Economy

This *Report* has been written against the background of the present serious state of the Canadian economy. We have had persistently high inflation in Canada throughout the 1970s, somewhat constrained at times by monetary and fiscal measures and recently by the Anti-Inflation Board control program, but no solution to the problem is yet in sight. Inflation has had very damaging effects on our economy and on our ability to compete internationally. Since 1970, Canadian unit labor costs have increased relative to those of our major trading partner, the United States, although they have not increased faster than those of other developed countries. Recently, inflation has been accompanied by serious unemployment, despite large government deficit financing arising in part from measures to reduce or alleviate unemployment and to cushion its impact on unemployed workers.

The industrial sector is the weakest area of the economy. Uncertainties generated by high costs, inflation, the duration of wage and price controls, the prospective behavior of wages and prices when controls are lifted, the political future of Quebec, the increasing tendency of governments to move directly into private sector activities and the federal-provincial struggle over taxes and royalties have contributed to reducing business capital spending and new investment and induced many firms to move some of their operations south of the border. In 1976 for the first time there was a net outflow of direct foreign investment, and the indications are that this outflow continued in 1977.

Canada has been running a drastically unfavorable current account deficit with the rest of the world in recent years. From a positive balance of $96 million in 1973 the current account has deteriorated to a deficit of $4.2 billion in 1976, and an estimated $4.3 billion deficit in 1977, made up of about a $2.0 billion surplus in merchandise trade, a $0.4 billion surplus in transfer payments

and a service deficit of about $6.7 billion. Our trade surplus has also deteri-
orated since 1971 despite the fact that the prices of exports have increased
faster than the prices of imports. The book value of Canada's balance of
international indebtedness (including increases in earnings accruing to non-
residents) rose from $28.5 billion at the end of 1970 to $48.5 billion at the end
of 1976. Canada was the world's largest borrower in international markets in
1976. From 1960 to 1975, Canada's exports have increasingly consisted of
agricultural products and raw and semi-processed materials, especially non-
renewable natural resources. Manufactured goods exports have also contained
increasing amounts of non-renewable resources. The depreciation of the
Canadian dollar that started in November 1976 should eventually increase
exports, lessen imports and thus assist the merchandise trade balance but it will
also add to inflation through higher prices for imports.

The corporate sector has been seriously impaired by the troubles afflicting
the Canadian economy. With a few exceptions the real earnings of companies
in most industries are too low to generate the internal savings or to attract the
new capital required to replace, modernize and expand the plant and equipment necessary to increase output, employment and the real income of
Canadians. Reported profits fail to reveal the true picture because they do not
measure the impact of inflation on the real cost of replacing inventories and
capital investment. Over the seven years 1977-83, Canada's total capital
requirements are projected to be between $460 and $520 billion (current
dollars), which will require investment as a percentage of GNP to increase
from its past average of 22.5% to about 25% of the projected GNP over the
1977-83 period.

Operating and labor costs have increased rapidly in Canada. This is a
natural consequence of economic growth and rising wages and is found in most
advanced countries but it must be compensated for by higher labor productivity
if there is to be a rising standard of living. Canada's problems of adjusting to
production using higher cost labor are exacerbated because our work force
tends to be specialized geographically, and a large geographic displacement is
often necessary to move unemployed workers in one region to a high employment area. Employment opportunities have been increasingly centered on
natural resource exploitation in areas that are unattractive to many of the
urban unemployed. Canada's large natural resource base has also supported
the exchange level above that necessary to make many industrial sectors
competitive internationally. The fall of the Canadian dollar throughout 1977
should help alleviate this problem, however.

Canada has an abundance of natural resources, both renewable and
non-renewable. Although we are not self-sufficient in all foodstuffs, we are a
net food exporter and should remain so in the future. While we are no longer
self-sufficient in oil, our potential for future energy production is promising,
though at much higher costs than those currently incurred. We rank high in
the world in alternative fossil fuels, nuclear technology, uranium fuel supplies
and hydro power. Over the past decade Canada has undertaken a tremendous
investment in education. Its highly educated population provides a base for

Canada to expand those technology- and knowledge-intensive industries that will enjoy the highest growth in the future.

It is in the context of these problems and opportunities that we examine the economic and social implications of major concentrations of corporate power, with a recognition that, both in 1975 when the Commission was created and in late 1977 as we complete our work, corporate concentration, while important, would rank far down on any list of problems for most Canadians.

Corporate Power

The concept of "corporate power" recurs throughout this *Report* and should be defined here. Power has been defined as the possession of control, authority or influence. Judged from the briefs and testimony to the Commission, and the economic, social and political literature, the public perception of *corporate* power seems to contain two major elements, economic power and political power, and a third element, social power, which derives its existence in part from the first two. The corporation is thought to have economic power if it can control the prices at which its products are offered, control the quantity of products produced and, through its ability, due to its size, to withstand losses, influence the prices at which it purchases labor, capital and raw materials. Large corporations are thought to have political power due to the resources at their disposal and their ability to inform and persuade the politicians and civil servants who make decisions in government. They are thought to have social power because of the influence they have directly over their employees and indirectly over consumers who are affected by their decisions and, in some instances, by their ownership, or influence over the mass media.

In briefs to the Commission, many major Canadian corporations disavowed possession of power in any form. Other briefs and testimony indicated concern that corporate power of all types does exist, and that the power held by large corporations is something governments should control. Corporate economic power and its alleged or potential abuse are not seen merely as a function of absolute size or of industry concentration. Wealth and power vested in the hands of a few is argued to be inconsistent with equality and the principles of democracy. Many of the same words and analogies used to express concern about the economic power of corporations were also used in our hearings to describe their perceived political and social power.

Some indication of public sentiment toward corporations vis-à-vis other major institutions can be found in recent survey results from the Canadian Institute of Public Opinion. Its surveys consistently reveal greater concern with big unions and big government than with big business. In May 1971 and March 1976 a question was asked that reflected directly on the Commission's mandate:

> Prime Minister Trudeau has said that he believes big unions and big corporations have too much economic power, and that this power will have to be curbed if Canadians want an economy with low unemployment and stable prices. Do you think this is true or not, of either unions or corporations, or of both?

	Big Unions Only	Big Corporations Only	Both	Neither	Undecided
1971	13%	4%	55%	12%	16%
1976	16%	8%	53%	9%	14%

One question asked in 1972 and 1975 concerned the relative threat perceived from big business, big labor and big government:

> In your opinion which of the following do you think will be the biggest threat for the country in the future—big business, big labour or big government?

	Big Business	Big Labour	Big Government	Don't Know
1972	27%	36%	22%	18%
1975	20%	36%	29%	16%

(N.B. Rows add to more than 100% because of some multiple responses.)

These findings may simply reflect an overall and growing feeling of individual helplessness in a society increasingly dominated by large power blocs. While individuals may sometimes be able to deal with these power blocs, to do so is expensive, time-consuming and often ineffective. The parallels between big business, big government and big labor are not reflected in this *Report* since the mandate of the Commission is restricted to business, to "corporate concentration", but many of the problems we discuss are related to the organization of society and to all the institutions within it.

Some constraints exist to protect society against harmful exercise of corporate economic power. The most fundamental constraint, pointed out to us by many witnesses, is the operation of the market system and the readiness of competitors both foreign and domestic to increase sales, market share or profits by lowering prices or improving the quality and variety of their products. This constraint is somewhat qualified by a protectionist tariff policy and by the concentrated nature of many Canadian industries, but, on the whole, competitors are some constraint against the flagrant exercise of market power.

The second constraint on corporate economic power is the countervailing power of trade unions. This power stems from their legal right to require firms to engage in collective bargaining and their exemption from the laws against conspiracy to reduce competition and to increase prices. Unions have firmly established bargaining rights for the employees of most large non-financial corporations and government units and are increasing their membership in the financial sector. Agreements between large corporations and their unions play an important role in setting the wage and benefit patterns in the economy, and in recent years settlements involving public sector employees at times have also served as pacesetters. Although unions act as a counterbalancing force against large firms or government organizations in protecting their members, they can also reinforce the power that these organizations have over the consumers of their goods and services, since all the firms in an industry will face the same increase in labor costs and will be able to act in concert to pass these costs on to the consumer.

A third constraint on corporate power is that imposed by government and law. This constraint is probably the most complex and difficult to evaluate, and there was much discussion of its effectiveness during the course of our hearings. Witnesses from the corporate sector contended that the weight of government was already oppressively heavy for business of all sizes, while others argued that corporate power should be made subject to even greater restraints by government.

Another aspect of government as a constraint on corporate power is the demands it makes on the Canadian economy in competition with the private sector. At a time when both unemployment and inflation are severe, it is not easy to sort out the issues in this rivalry, but we have heard widespread concern about the scale of government expenditures and taxation, as well as the importance of government actions and policies in creating "excess" demand, reducing the incentives to work, entering into "excessive" wage settlements with employees and preempting a large share of the available savings to finance its deficits. Government policy currently is to limit the share of the GNP accounted for by government to its present level.

These constraints reinforce the idea that our society is one of offsetting power—business, government, labor and other. Within each of these groups there are, of course, many subgroups with varying interests and power bases. An individual often feels helpless in his dealings with these groups. If one group could exercise unchecked power, if the balance of power broke down, then our social organization would be endangered. It is probably also true that one form of power induces another, that big business will induce larger-scale labor organizations or larger-scale government. This *Report* therefore assesses the changing role and strength of corporations and makes recommendations where appropriate to improve the performance of the Canadian economy and society.

The Public Interest

Another term used in our mandate and throughout this *Report* is the "public interest". A corporation, or indeed any institution, has no single "public interest", but rather has many publics, with many competing interests. The "publics" of a corporation include shareholders, creditors, employees, customers, suppliers, governments and local, national and even international communities. There are diversities of interest within each interest group and subgroup and an individual may find himself at any one time belonging to several groups, which may have conflicting interests.

For example, shareholders have a primary concern with stock values and earnings, creditors with a high return and minimum risk and employees with the quality of their work lives, their wages and other benefits and perhaps the social value of their employment. Consumers have an interest in low prices, high-quality goods, a high level of service and product information and protection against defective or dangerous goods and services. Suppliers negotiate with the corporation on quality, price, expertise, reliability and capacity. Governments collect taxes, regulate, provide direct and indirect grants and subsidies, serve as safety and environmental controllers and promote employment.

For any corporation with finite resources, providing more to any one public usually reduces the resources available to others. Higher returns to shareholders may mean lower wages for labor. A higher level of consumer service may require more stringent rules for employees or lower profits. Better environmental protection may mean higher costs and prices and fewer jobs at a given plant.

The competing publics act through the market system and also through the political bargaining arena to achieve their goals by changing the laws and how they are interpreted and administered. We do not imply in this *Report* that there is any best allocation of corporate resources among competing publics. The questions of who within or outside a corporation should make the allocation among publics and how that allocation should be made are valid ones, but we make no *a priori* assumption that any given allocation is superior from a public interest sense.

Structure of the Report

This *Report* consists of 18 chapters. Our mandate was to investigate the social and economic impact of corporate concentration. We recognize that there is considerable overlap and interaction between the social and economic impacts of corporate concentration, but for analytical and expository purposes we have dealt with them separately. Chapters 2 through 9 deal primarily with the economic aspect of our mandate and specifically with concentration in the Canadian economy, economies of scale, the extent and implications of oligopoly, conglomerates and their performance, mergers and acquisitions and the implications of foreign direct investment. The economic section concludes with Chapter 9, which presents proposals for workable competition in the context of the existing economic structure.

Chapters 10 and 11 deal with banks and financial institutions and with the managerial, financial and other problems confronting small and medium-sized business. The five chapters beginning with Chapter 12 primarily deal with the social part of our mandate, and specifically with the special cases of corporate control, disclosure, corporate influence, working conditions and other social implications of corporate concentration. Chapter 17 discusses the role of regulated industries and Crown corporations. Chapter 18 is a summary of our general conclusions.

* * *

In Canada we have considerable corporate concentration as part of a mixed economy, and we shall almost certainly continue to have both in the future. In this *Report* we treat these as phenomena that may be inevitable for an industrial country rather than as new developments that can or should necessarily be reversed by government action. Instead we shall make proposals designed to increase the benefits to Canada from its resources using whatever forms of industrial organization and government involvement are appropriate.

Chapter 2

Corporate Size and Concentration

Introduction

As part of its mandate, the Commission was asked to inquire into "the nature and role of major concentrations of corporate power in Canada". Our first major effort in this regard was the study of several large, mostly well-known corporations, to provide some insight into the process of corporate growth and behavior of large corporations. In addition, the Commission asked Christian Marfels to prepare a manuscript on industrial concentration in Canada. This chapter summarizes and extends our earlier inquiries by examining the size and number of large corporations and groups of corporations operating in the Canadian economy and provides a descriptive background for the remainder of the *Report*, which evaluates the existence and effects of corporate power in Canada.

This chapter presents a variety of data related to the structure of Canadian industry. The major findings are summarized here before proceeding with a detailed discussion of the research that produced them.

Summary of Major Findings

The major empirical findings can be summarized as follows:

1. Aggregate concentration (i.e. the percentage of economic activity accounted for by the largest firms in Canada) decreased from 1923 to 1975; however, the greatest portion of this decrease took place before 1966. Since 1966, aggregate concentration in Canada has changed very little.

2. The average size of Canada's 100 largest non-financial corporations and the average size of Canada's 25 largest financial corporations are very much smaller than the average size of their counterparts in the United States and other developed countries.

3. Aggregate concentration is higher in Canada than in the United States.

4. Industrial concentration (i.e. the fraction of total activity in a given industry attributable to a fixed number of the largest corporations in that industry) increased in Canadian manufacturing industries from

1948 to 1972. Most of the increase took place between 1948 and 1954. Industrial concentration has remained quite stable from 1965 to 1972.
5. Industrial concentration in Canada is substantially higher than in comparable industries in the United States.

Together, these findings imply that, although Canadian firms are small when compared with the largest firms in the world, they are large relative to the overall size of the Canadian economy or relative to the sizes of individual industries. These findings illustrate a basic conundrum facing policy-makers in Canada. That is, while average firm size in many Canadian industries is below "world-scale", policies to promote larger firm sizes may exacerbate the potential problems associated with already high domestic levels of industrial concentration.

The description of Canadian industry in this chapter is the first step in considering the potential market power of firms in Canada. The remainder of the *Report* takes up the task of analyzing available evidence related to the economic and social implications of corporate concentration.

Describing Structure

No single statistic can indicate all the complex interactions, among corporations and other sectors in the economy, of interest to those studying the structure of the corporate sector. Several conventional measures are available, and will be presented here.

Description of the corporate structure of an economy can proceed on two levels. The first is the aggregate level, where the corporate sector or the largest corporations are measured against the whole economy. The second is the industry level, where the corporations are measured against their individual industry. This chapter uses both approaches.

In discussing structure at the aggregate level, two measures can be used. The first is the degree of aggregate concentration, that is the extent to which the total of economic activity is conducted by the largest corporations. The conventional measure of aggregate concentration is the aggregate concentration ratio, which is the fraction of total activity (usually assets or sales) accounted for by a group (usually numbering 100) of the largest corporations. The second measure used is simply the size of the largest corporations themselves, in relation to both the economy and other large corporations in the world.

There are several quantifiable dimensions of structure at the industry level, including degree of concentration, ease of entry into and exit from the industry, size of corporations in the industry, degree of import competition, rate of growth and rate of technological innovation in the industry. Differences in any of these dimensions have been shown by empirical studies to produce differences in the behavior of firms. While this chapter presents some data on a number of structural dimensions, it focuses primarily on the concentration ratio as a measure of industrial structure.

Our emphasis on concentration ratios derives primarily from the prominent role that they play in the administration and enforcement of competition policy in Canada and abroad. Concentration ratios have been incorporated into antitrust law in the United States and are referred to extensively in U.S. jurisprudence. Recently they have appeared in the proposed amendments to the Combines Investigation Act in Canada. Furthermore, concentration ratios have been referred to in key monopoly and merger cases in Canada and form an important part of the jurisprudence in the United Kingdom, Sweden, France and West Germany.

The entire rationale for the attempt to describe the structure of the corporate sector lies in the "market concentration doctrine", which holds that industrial structure is an important determinant of industrial conduct and performance. In particular, it suggests that the greater the concentration of economic activity in a few firms, the greater will be the likelihood of anti-competitive conduct among these firms.

Corporate Size Relative to the Total Economy

Introduction

The primary concern raised by high levels of aggregate concentration and large firm size is that decisions taken by large corporations may have consequences that extend well beyond specific markets to produce political and social as well as "purely" economic effects. Economic concerns about large absolute firm size derive from the potential for competitive abuses, such as mutual forbearance, predatory pricing, and reciprocity, which are alleged to arise from large absolute firm size (these practices are described in Chapter 5). Potential advantages of large absolute firm size are related to economies of scale in such areas as financing, research and development, management functions and risk-taking.

Corporate Groups

Some large corporations operating in the Canadian economy, while by definition separate entities, can more accurately be described as members of corporate groups bound together by common control linkages. When describing the overall concentration of corporate power, such firms should be classed not as single entities but as members of a single corporate group. The problem in such a description is to determine a definition of intercorporate control that will facilitate identification of all such groups, since effective control of one corporation by another can be achieved in a number of different ways, and since the same set of devices can indicate control in one circumstance but not in another. However, rather than undertake a case-by-case analysis of all Canadian corporations, we have adopted as a convention the definition that a corporation is effectively controlled by another when the latter owns 50% or more of the voting shares of the former.

A corporation is defined as an establishment, or group of establishments, that themselves are under common control. An establishment, as defined by

Statistics Canada, is the smallest unit that is a separate operating entity capable of reporting information. In the manufacturing sector, an establishment is approximately equivalent to a plant.

The Commission has compiled a list of the largest corporate entities in Canada. The measurement of corporate size in this context raises some problems. Since we are aggregating the various products and services that these corporate groups provide, we could measure the size of a group by the total value of all sales and services they supply (or their net revenue), the value of the total assets they employ, the number of employees for which they account or the value added of their operations. Some data constraints existed on our choice of size measure, however, which restricted us to using asset or sales measures of size. Information about large corporate complexes is useful for two purposes: to facilitate analysis of the largest corporate complexes in Canada over time and to compare the size of Canadian complexes with those in other countries.

While it was possible to aggregate corporate sales measures across most industries, financial corporations posed a problem. No comparable "sales" figures exist for financial institutions. Thus two lists of enterprises had to be compiled: a list of the 100 largest non-financial corporations and a list of the 25 largest financial corporations. In the latter, the corporations were ranked by assets.

The lists printed in Tables 2.1 and 2.2 present certain problems and anomalies. For example, because of the definition of control adopted, Argus Corporation Limited does not appear among the 100 largest non-financial corporate groups. Under the assumption that Argus effectively controls the three major corporations that now appear separately on the list and in which it has large minority interests (Massey-Ferguson Limited, Domtar Limited and Dominion Stores Limited), Argus ranks first among the top 100 non-financial corporate groups. Power Corporation is listed as the 98th largest corporate group. This, however, does not include its holdings in the financial corporations in which it has controlling interest. Several of Power's financial corporations appear on our list of largest financial groups. The exclusion of these financial corporations from the Power group accords with common practice in ranking the size of non-financial corporations.

The non-financial list understates the size of some corporate groups in that the ownership links between Canadian incorporated companies are sometimes found in the foreign parent corporation operating in another country. An example of this linkage is provided by Ford Motor Company of Canada, Limited, and Ensite Limited, both of which are subsidiaries of the Ford Motor Company of Dearborn, Michigan.

Given all these qualifications, the tables probably understate the sizes of many of the corporations listed.

Table 2.1

100 Largest Non-Financial Canadian Companies
(Including Foreign Operations[1]),
1975/76, Ranked by Sales or Revenues
(Thousands of Dollars)

Rank	Company	Sales or Revenues	Assets	Net Income (Loss) after Taxes
1.	George Weston Limited	5,046,693	1,247,681	18,723
2.	Ford Motor Company of Canada, Limited	4,437,900	1,591,100	119,800
3.	General Motors of Canada Limited**	4,335,209	1,107,212	111,230
4.	Imperial Oil Limited**	4,047,000	2,950,000	250,000
5.	Canadian Pacific Limited**	3,651,273	6,235,832	174,863
6.	Bell Canada	2,988,116	6,588,298	266,784
7.	Massey-Ferguson Limited	2,513,302	1,982,206	94,677
8.	Chrysler Canada Ltd.	2,473,547	605,470	19,471
9.	Alcan Aluminium Limited**	2,301,453	3,011,781	22,570
10.	Dominion Stores Limited	1,913,986	262,946	20,437
11.	Canada Safeway Limited	1,877,021	436,312	34,110
12.	Shell Canada Limited	1,868,375	1,549,072	144,771
13.	Canadian National Railway Company	1,846,729	4,952,538	(57,175)
14.	Gulf Oil Canada Limited	1,701,200	1,726,500	176,600
15.	Inco Limited	1,694,768	3,025,675	186,889
16.	Simpsons-Sears Limited	1,548,600	1,050,597	32,118
17.	Canada Packers Limited**	1,453,749	310,045	21,531
18.	Steinberg's Limited	1,430,195	417,674	11,460
19.	The T. Eaton Company Limited*	1,300,000	1,150,000	39,000
20.	MacMillan Bloedel Limited	1,296,689	1,197,903	(18,943)
21.	The Steel Company of Canada, Limited	1,201,756	1,678,261	88,774
22.	Hudson's Bay Company	1,178,831	821,895	22,004
23.	Brascan Limited	1,157,451	2,247,333	95,113
24.	Noranda Mines Limited**	1,156,423	1,980,117	50,525
25.	Ontario Hydro	1,070,595	8,593,301	(60,866)
26.	M. Loeb Limited	1,048,338	150,568	3,419
27.	The Oshawa Group Limited	1,023,857	254,682	7,196
28.	Moore Corporation Limited	1,005,610	737,153	69,512
29.	The Seagram Company Ltd.	977,430	1,991,314	74,120
30.	Air Canada	957,180	1,297,628	(12,473)
31.	Hydro-Québec	922,089	7,068,285	229,750
32.	TransCanada Pipelines Limited	920,389	1,572,218	66,297
33.	Texaco Canada Limited	846,543	771,722	51,135
34.	F.W. Woolworth Co. Limited	841,834	329,622	15,332
35.	Canadian General Electric Company Limited	822,134	602,435	36,232
36.	Domtar Limited	815,221	721,368	35,288
37.	Abitibi Paper Company Ltd.	764,384	870,924	13,329
38.	Dominion Foundries and Steel, Limited	738,083	944,405	55,473
39.	Canadian International Paper Co.	725,000	550,000	50,000
40.	Genstar Limited	720,100	704,608	47,156
41.	IBM Canada Ltd.	719,327	460,422	69,817
42.	International Harvester Company of Canada, Limited	713,994	488,922	22,109

Rank	Company	Sales or Revenues	Assets	Net Income (Loss) after Taxes
43.	Mitsubishi Canada Limited**	667,349	82,899	1,391
44.	Consolidated-Bathurst Limited	643,719	662,369	32,599
45.	Burns Foods Limited	622,083	135,427	4,772
46.	The Molson Companies Limited	613,632	407,052	19,620
47.	Mitsui & Co. (Canada), Ltd.**	604,532	90,849	1,529
48.	Woodward Stores Limited	596,058	251,508	11,781
49.	Canadian Industries Limited	594,908	390,226	42,638
50.	John Labatt Limited	594,191	426,150	22,176
51.	Canadian Tire Corporation Limited	561,032	358,516	25,276
52.	Imasco Limited	559,618	364,696	29,422
53.	Simpsons, Limited	547,940	562,285	22,190
54.	The Agro Company of Canada Ltd.**	522,249	14,832	1,254
55.	Hiram Walker-Gooderham & Worts Limited	509,105	913,166	50,647
56.	S.S. Kresge Company Limited	491,290	190,179	15,704
57.	BP Canada Limited	488,351	552,500	30,480
58.	Norcen Energy Resources Limited	479,102	915,754	33,408
59.	Provigo Inc.	478,139	76,644	5,585
60.	Iron Ore Company of Canada**	472,844	845,558	(696)
61.	Canada Development Corporation	469,605	1,277,537	26,050
62.	Mobil Oil Canada Ltd.**	467,160	497,716	78,832
63.	Rothmans of Pall Mall Canada Limited	464,345	403,065	15,436
64.	Dominion Bridge Company, Limited	459,316	326,994	24,442
65.	Husky Oil Ltd.	454,391	431,548	36,018
66.	Swift Canadian Co., Limited	452,467	115,467	3,456
67.	Westinghouse Canada Limited	451,642	222,572	15,703
68.	Anglo-Canadian Telephone Company	445,007	1,578,795	23,654
69.	Falconbridge Nickel Mines Limited	429,481	763,099	3,221
70.	British Columbia Hydro and Power Authority	425,270	3,556,085	3,349
71.	Westcoast Transmission Company Limited	416,677	675,189	33,019
72.	Du Pont of Canada Limited	410,219	411,048	3,714
73.	Canada Cement Lafarge Ltd.	398,919	515,669	24,337
74.	Petrofina Canada Ltd.	396,467	520,427	32,766
75.	The Consumers' Gas Company	380,077	740,679	32,634
76.	Amoco Canada Petroleum Company Ltd.**	379,831	704,175	81,622
77.	Union Carbide Canada Limited	378,172	431,852	43,136
78.	Irving Oil Limited[2]	376,905	277,716	13,815
79.	Zeller's Limited	369,891	165,260	7,078
80.	Reed Paper Ltd.	369,067	413,400	12,309
81.	Rio Algom Limited	367,382	541,115	30,032
82.	Canron Limited	365,950	182,716	13,565
83.	Hawker Siddeley Canada Ltd.	365,234	282,207	10,348
84.	Ensite Limited	363,241	204,378	14,046
85.	The Great Atlantic and Pacific Tea Company, Limited	358,536	88,032	3,146
86.	Westburne International Industries Ltd.	357,513	263,858	7,693
87.	Maple Leaf Mills Limited	354,790	148,736	10,365
88.	Ultramar Canada Limited	338,709	353,644	2,325
89.	Dow Chemical of Canada, Limited	337,000	414,000	36,000
90.	Goodyear Canada Inc.	329,229	244,938	5,187
91.	Kraft Foods Limited	320,746	111,279	11,713

Rank	Company	Sales or Revenues	Assets	Net Income (Loss) after Taxes
92.	General Foods, Limited	316,880	147,177	11,441
93.	Sun Oil Company Limited	315,018	491,118	12,396
94.	The Proctor & Gamble Company of Canada, Limited**	313,686	237,160	16,359
95.	Canadian Hydrocarbons Limited	301,200	214,101	6,860
96.	Crown Zellerbach Canada Limited	296,362	290,149	13,270
97.	Canadian Fuel Marketers Ltd.†	295,107	133,592	2,612
98.	Power Corporation of Canada, Limited[3]	293,104	579,341	32,164
99.	Pacific Petroleums, Ltd.	288,040	639,940	57,267
100.	Standard Brands Limited**	279,994	167,671	9,806

Sources: — Unless otherwise indicated (see sources listed below), the figures come from *Financial Post*, "The Financial Post 300" (Summer 1976).
* — Estimates, based on Royal Commission on Corporate Concentration (RCCC) research.
** — *Canadian Business*, "The Top 200 Plus the Next 200 of Canada's Largest Companies" (July 1976).
† — Figures come from the information given by the company to the RCCC.
— Sales and assets of Crown corporations come from the *Public Accounts of Canada*, vol. III (1976); *Public Accounts of British Columbia* (fiscal year ended March 1975); *Ontario Public Accounts, 1975-76*, vol. II; *Financial Statements of Quebec Government Enterprises, 1975-76*.
Notes: [1] Includes foreign operations of Canadian-owned companies but not non-Canadian operations of the parent companies of foreign-owned subsidiaries operating in Canada.
[2] Irving Oil Limited is controlled by the Irving family, which also controls a number of Canadian firms through holding companies. If the assets of all these firms were included, we estimate the combined Irving companies would rank among the top 30 on our list.
[3] Figures for Power Corporation of Canada, Limited, do not include financial subsidiaries.

The Largest Corporations in Canada

The lists of the largest financial and non-financial groups of corporations provide a basis for calculating aggregate concentration ratios. As already mentioned, these ratios give the percentage of total assets, sales or income in an economy that is accounted for by the largest 25, 50, 100 or 200 corporations. We then use this ratio to evaluate the size of the largest corporations relative to all domestic corporations and to similar groups of U.S. and world-wide corporations. We also examine how the relative size of these groups has changed over time in relation to domestic growth of all corporations.

For some specific comparisons between Canadian and foreign corporations, the Canadian corporations were allocated into broad fields of activity according to the Standard Industrial Classification (SIC) code. These classifications are quite broad, however, and do not allow comparisons of corporate groups in particular industrial activities or product markets.

Table 2.2

25 Largest Canadian Financial Institutions,
1975/76 Ranked by Assets

(Thousands of Dollars)

Rank	Company	Total Assets	Net Income after Taxes
1.	The Royal Bank of Canada	25,211,131	86,742
2.	Canadian Imperial Bank of Commerce	22,259,053	93,943
3.	Bank of Montreal	18,242,634	81,135
4.	Bank of Nova Scotia	16,005,998	64,702
5.	The Toronto-Dominion Bank	13,576,569	59,610
6.	Banque Canadienne Nationale	4,871,971	16,157
7.	Sun Life Assurance Company of Canada	4,699,301	N/A
8.	The Royal Trust Company	3,435,709	18,945
9.	The Manufacturers Life Insurance Co.	3,083,250	N/A
10.	La Banque Provinciale du Canada	3,059,145	8,192
11.	Canada Permanent Mortgage Corporation	2,726,390	14,358
12.	The Huron & Erie Mortgage Corporation and The Canada Trust Company (Canada Trustco Mortgage Company)	2,626,301	14,079
13.	London Life Insurance Company	2,392,256	7,422
14.	IAC Limited	2,390,847	30,450
15.	The Great-West Life Assurance Company	2,348,819	22,785
16.	The Canada Life Assurance Company	1,887,429	N/A
17.	The Mutual Life Assurance Company of Canada	1,781,723	N/A
18.	Confederation Life Insurance Company	1,485,332	6,423
19.	General Motors Acceptance Corporation of Canada Ltd.	1,308,299	9,483
20.	Victoria and Grey Trust Company	1,295,556	8,335
21.	The Mercantile Bank of Canada	1,288,163	8,902
22.	Crown Life Insurance Company	1,204,809	5,453
23.	National Trust Company, Limited	1,162,975	7,427
24.	Guaranty Trust Company of Canada	1,086,179	1,863
25.	North American Life Assurance Company	1,023,800	15,597

Source: "The Top 200 Plus the Next 200 of Canada's Largest Companies," *Canadian Business*
(July 1976).
Note: N/A = Not applicable to mutual life insurance companies.

Historical Trends in Aggregate Concentration

The earliest record of aggregate concentration in Canada that we found
was in the *Report* of the Royal Commission on Price Spreads (1937). The
Price Spreads Commission reported that the total assets of the top 100 largest
non-financial corporations (ranked by assets) were $5,096 million in 1923 and
$7,324 million in 1933. The Price Spreads Commission could not calculate a
figure for the assets of all corporations and therefore it could not compare the
assets of the 100 largest non-financial corporations with those of all corporations. Instead, they chose to compare the assets of the group of largest
corporations with (1) the assets of all corporations for which balance sheets

could be obtained, (2) total capital invested in Canadian industry and (3) national wealth. While noting the deficiency in such an approach the Price Spreads Commission reported that:

> It may be acknowledged that this invested capital figure is not at all comparable with the gross assets of corporations and it may appear, therefore, that two unlike things are being related. If the absolute percentage figures were regarded as significant, this would be a fatal criticism. But all that is desired here is to see the relative rate of growth of the large companies as compared to business generally. It is the trend that is significant, and this can be determined as the invested capital figures are comparable from year to year all through the period; the Bureau of Statistics has submitted the series as a homogeneous one for the period. Accordingly, the result has validity for the immediate purpose. (P. 22.)

While we faced no such deficiency of data for recent years (that is from 1966 onward), we still had to find a consistent basis for comparison between our data and that of the Price Spreads Commission. Definitional problems prevented our use of the Price Spreads Commission's primary statistic, "invested capital" in Canadian industries. In our analysis we compared the assets of the largest non-financial corporations to the statistic "mid-year net capital stock", which has been estimated by Statistics Canada on a consistent basis since 1926; (we estimated the figure for 1923). Since we found that non-financial assets were a reasonably constant fraction of total assets, "mid-year net capital stock" was comparable for our purpose to the statistic "total corporate assets". We, like the Price Spreads Commission, are not concerned with the absolute percentages but rather with determining whether a trend exists in aggregate concentration. We used the Price Spreads Commission's working papers to estimate the adjustment needed to make corporate assets relate only to domestic activity. Our estimates indicated that the assets of the 100 largest corporations had to be reduced by only .1% in 1923 and 2.4% in 1933 to eliminate those related to foreign activity.

The results of our analysis indicate a clear decline in aggregate concentration among non-financial corporations between 1923 and 1975 (Figure 2.1). The decline from 1933 to 1966 appears to be the most dramatic, but aggregate concentration also declined in each sample year from 1966 to 1975. When measured on as consistent a basis as possible, using the percentage of assets controlled by the top 100 firms (the most widely used measure of aggregate concentration), the clear trend seems to be toward lower overall concentration in Canadian non-financial corporations.

However, these results are not conclusive evidence that aggregate concentration has been declining continuously since 1933. Some sample year between 1933 and 1966 could have shown a lower level of aggregate concentration than did 1966, which would mean that there had been an increase between that year and 1966. On the other hand, since the war years (1939-45) probably accentuated the economic importance of large corporations in relation to medium-sized or small ones, this possibility is unlikely. One piece of supporting evidence is found in the Department of Consumer and Corporate Affairs publication entitled *Concentration in the Manufacturing Industries of Canada* (1971). The study compared the total net assets of the 94 largest non-financial corporations in 1958 and 1965. Their findings showed that the net assets attributable to the 94 largest non-financial corporations fell from 40.6% of total net assets of all non-financial corporations in 1958 to 37.6% in 1965.

Moreover, even if we allow for the fact that transport companies were unrepresentative of large corporations in the earlier years and even if we consider 1933 atypical because of the Depression's effect on smaller businesses, Figure 2.1 indicates that the historical downward trend of aggregate concentration has been maintained. The downward trend is strong enough that statistical adjustments are unlikely to change its direction.

Another criticism can be made of an analysis of aggregate concentration based on the share of assets (or sales or value added) accounted for by the top 100 firms, since over time, the number of firms in the economy has increased and hence the top 100 firms form a decreasing percentage of the total number of firms. To analyze aggregate concentration over time, a measure that keeps

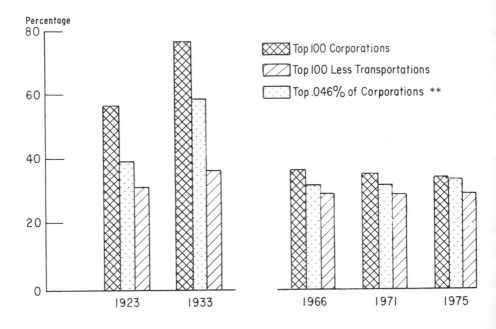

FIGURE 2.1. Assets of 100 Largest* Non-Financial Corporations as a Percentage of Total Net Capital Stock, Canada, 1923, 1933, 1966, 1971 and 1975.†
Source: RCCC research.
  Notes: *Ranked by sales.
          **This percentage was chosen for historical comparison where 100 corporations represented 0.46% of all Canadian corporations in 1975.
          †The gap between 1933 and 1966 is due to a lack of comparable data.

constant the number of corporations might be more appropriate. One such standardized measure estimates the relative amount ·of economic activity accounted for by a fixed percentage of the total number of corporations in an economy over time. We calculated this alternative measure of aggregate concentration for our sample years by determining what percentage of total non-financial corporations was represented by the 100 largest in 1975. We applied this percentage (.046%) to the total number of non-financial corpora-tions in the earlier years to determine the appropriate sample size for calculat-ing aggregate concentration ratios in those years. We determined that the top .046% of non-financial corporations represents 7 corporations in 1923, 13 in 1933, 55 in 1966, 68 in 1971 and 100 in 1975. The assets of these largest corporations as a percentage of total net capital stock were then calculated for each year.

The trend in aggregate concentration for the top .046% of non-financial corporations is similar to that for the 100 largest non-financial corporations over the entire period 1923-75. However, aggregate concentration calculated for the top .046% of non-financial corporations increased slightly over the period 1966-75, while aggregate concentration based on the largest 100 non-financial corporations decreased. In both cases, the changes in concentra-

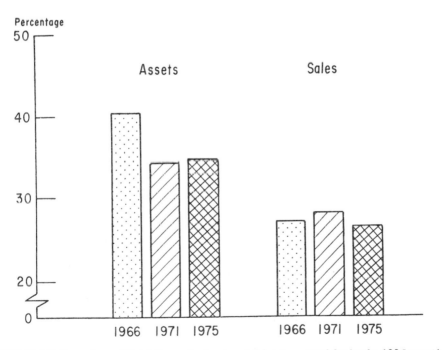

FIGURE 2.2. Percentage of Total Domestic Assets and Sales Accounted for by the 100 Largest* Non-Financial Corporations, Canada, 1966, 1971 and 1975.
Source: RCCC research.
Note: *Ranked by sales.

tion were small. The Commission therefore concludes that aggregate concentration, while decreasing over the entire period 1923-75, has since 1966 either decreased slightly or increased slightly depending on the measure used, but that whatever the measure the change has been small.

Other Measures of Recent Changes
in Aggregate Concentration

For 1966, 1971 and 1975, aggregate concentration was also calculated on sales and assets bases. During this period, asset concentration declined somewhat, while sales concentration remained almost unchanged (Figure 2.2). The decline in asset concentration is consistent with the pattern seen in Figure 2.1: a consistent but mild decline from 1966 to 1975. Sales concentration, on the other hand, first increased slightly and then declined slightly to be roughly unchanged. One possible explanation of this difference is the Commission's finding that conglomerates have, in recent years, diversified into less capital-intensive industries from more capital-intensive industries.

Data for the financial sector were limited to the period 1966-75. Comparing concentration ratios based on assets for this period (Figure 2.3) revealed

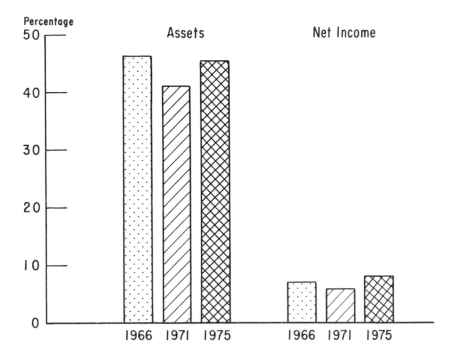

FIGURE 2.3. Percentage of Total Assets and Net Income Accounted for by the 25 Largest* Financial Corporations, Canada, 1966, 1971 and 1975.
Source: RCCC research.
Note: *Ranked by assets.

that the share of total assets accounted for by the largest 25 financial corporations decreased from 46% in 1966 to 41% in 1971 and then increased to 45% in 1975. The share of net income accruing to the largest financial corporations decreased between 1966 and 1971 from 7.2% to 5.8%. The corresponding rise between 1971 and 1975 in the share of net income by the largest financial corporations increased their share of net income of all financial corporations to 8.3%, a 15% increase over the 1966 level. Given the shorter period of time for which data are available for the financial sector and the difference in the concentration trends revealed by the asset and net income measures, no firm conclusions regarding the trend in aggregate concentration among the largest financial corporations can be drawn. However, it appears safe to conclude that any changes in aggregate concentration in the financial sector over recent years have been quite modest.

Changes in Membership
among the Largest Corporations

Some of the concern regarding aggregate concentration is based on the misconception that the firms constituting the group of largest corporations in earlier years are the same firms that make up the groups in later years, i.e. that the relative importance of specific large corporations does not change over time. This, however, is not so.

A study of the changes in membership of the 100 largest non-financial corporations (Table 2.3) revealed that, during 1967-71, 13 corporations were displaced by corporations previously too small for inclusion in the group. Also one corporation became insolvent and there were seven mergers among those already on the list. Of the roughly 46% increase in assets held by these corporations over this time period, approximately 27% was due to the entrance of new corporations. For the period 1971-75 there were 16 new entrants, accounting for approximately 12% of the increase in the assets.

Table 2.3

Change in Membership and Total
Assets of the 100 Largest* Canadian Non-Financial
Corporations, 1967-71 and 1971-75

Change in Status	1967-71	1971-75
Exits		
Replaced by larger companies	13	16
Bankruptcies	1	0
Mergers	7	6
Total	21	22
Entries	21	22
Increase in total assets ($000)	15,798,354	40,719,930
(%)	46.15	81.36
Net increase in total due to new entrants ($000)	4,237,862	4,935,041

Source: RCCC research.

Note: *Ranked by sales.

A similar pattern is found in the changes in membership among the largest 25 financial corporations (Table 2.4). There were two new entrants during 1967-71 and two during 1971-75. The net increase in total assets accounted for by these new entrants, however, was minimal (0.37% between 1966 and 1971 and 2.48% between 1971 and 1975), largely due to the predominant role of large banks.

Table 2.4

Change in Membership, Total Assets and Total Income of the
25 Largest* Financial Institutions in Canada,
1967-71 and 1971-75

Change in Status	1967-71	1971-75
Exits		
Replaced by larger companies	2	2
Bankruptcies	0	0
Mergers	0	0
Total	2	2
Entries	2	2
Increase in total		
Assets ($000)	17,951,184	53,342,849
(%)	52.25	101.99
Income ($000)	48,604	266,490
(%)	41.97	162.08
Net increase in assets due to new entrants ($000)	126,665	1,295,168

Source: RCCC research.
Note: *Ranked by assets.

International Comparison

In testimony before the Commission, several witnesses representing large corporations contended that for a variety of reasons the size of large Canadian corporations should not be measured relative to the size of the domestic market but relative to the international economy. The most frequently mentioned reason was that Canadian corporations had to adopt world-scale production units to compete effectively in international markets. Others argued that competing in the world market required corporations large enough to exploit the economies available to firms with access to world-scale financing. While we will examine some evidence on these arguments in subsequent chapters we thought it useful to compare the size of Canadian corporations with those of other countries in anticipation of those discussions.

We compared the size (both ranked and measured by sales) of the 100 largest non-financial corporations in Canada for 1975, classified by broad industrial divisions, with the 100 largest non-financial corporations in the United States and the 100 largest non-financial corporations in the rest of the world. Only four Canadian corporations (George Weston Limited, Ford, General Motors of Canada Limited and Imperial Oil Limited), were on a list of the 100 largest non-financial corporations in the world. Clearly, Canadian firms in all categories are much smaller than their counterparts in the United States and in other countries (Figure 2.4). While this difference in average size does not mean that individual Canadian firms cannot be larger than individual U.S. firms in the top 100, it does mean that, overall, the top Canadian firms generally must be much smaller than the top U.S. firms in the same industrial sector.

The largest 25 financial corporations in Canada are also quite small in comparison to their counterparts in the United States and the rest of the world. Although Canada's largest bank, The Royal Bank of Canada, ranks 23rd among financial corporations in the world, the average size of even the largest Canadian banks falls far behind the average size of those banks ranked in the 25 largest financial corporations in the U.S. and in the rest of the world (Figure 2.5). This is also true for Canadian insurance and trust corporations. The average size of the largest Canadian financial corporations is about one-tenth that of the average of the largest U.S. financial corporations.

In summary, while Canada has four non-financial corporations among the largest in the world, the corporations that make up the largest 100 non-financial corporations in Canada are (in terms of average size in assets) substantially smaller in comparison with the largest 100 non-financial corporations in the United States and the rest of the world, when classified into the same broad industrial groups. The average size of Canada's top 25 largest financial corporations was also found to be much smaller than the average size of their counterparts in the United States and elsewhere.

Statistics Canada Data
on Aggregate Concentration

Statistics Canada aggregate concentration data are compiled from unconsolidated tax return data. Their ratios therefore understate aggregate concentration even more than do our data, which include all complexes connected by majority stock ownership. However, to check on the conclusions reached in our Figures 2.1, 2.3, and 2.4 and to obtain more complete analysis of the financial sector, we have analyzed some special tabulations provided by Statistics Canada. The earliest year for which Statistics Canada data were available was 1965 and the latest was 1973.

First we examined the total number of corporations. A statistical profile of the corporate sector, provided in a report to the Commission by Marfels, shows that the number of active corporations increased from about 168,000 in 1965 to about 259,000 in 1973. For illustrative purposes, we compared the increase in the Canadian population over the same period. In 1965 there was one corporation for every 117 persons in Canada. In 1973 this ratio was one for every 85 persons.

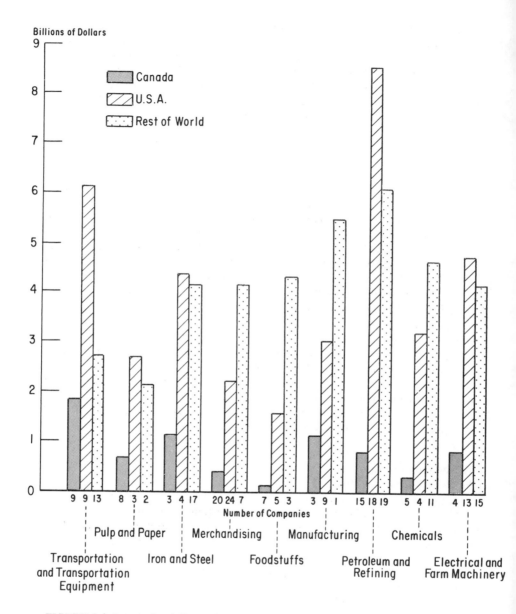

FIGURE 2.4. International Comparison of the Average Assets of Corporations among the 100 Largest* Non-Financial Corporations in Canada, the United States and the Rest of the World, Selected Industries,** 1975.

Source: RCCC research.

Notes: *Ranked by sales.
      **Seven industries have been omitted. The data for utilities, beverages and miscellaneous industries are not comparable, while the samples in the mining, construction material, rubber and tobacco industries are too small to provide statistically significant results.

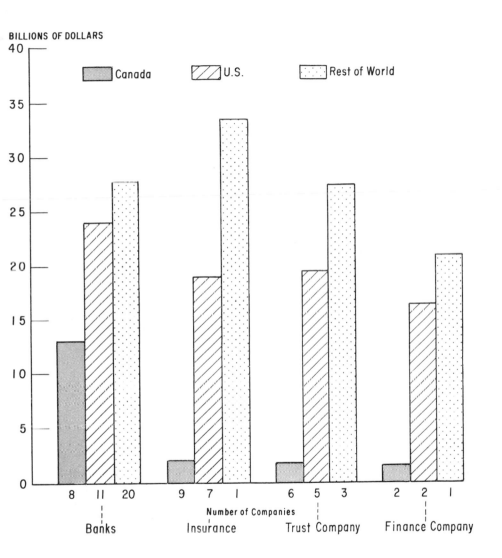

FIGURE 2.5. International Comparison of Average Assets of 25 Largest* Financial Institutions, Canada, the United States and the Rest of the World, 1975.
Source: RCCC research.
Note: *Ranked by assets.

During the same period, corporate assets grew from $145 billion to $356 billion, an average annual growth rate of 11.9%. In comparison, the average annual growth rate of the Canadian Gross National Product (GNP) was 10.2% during 1965-73. Thus, corporate assets grew slightly faster than did the GNP. Corporate sales increased from $90 billion in 1965 to $212 billion in 1973, an average annual growth rate of 11.3%.

Comparing the years 1965, 1968 and 1973, we find that about 25% of Canada's industrial resources are held by the 25 largest non-financial corporations (NFCs) and 50% by the 200 largest (Figure 2.6). The relative position of the top 25 and top 200 NFCs has changed very little between 1965 and 1973; the share of assets held by these two groups increased by 1.4 and 1.1 percentage points respectively. In absolute terms, the 25 largest NFCs had faster asset growth by 13 percentage points from 1965 to 1973 than all NFCs, while growth for the top 200 was 5 percentage points greater than the average.

In contrast to Figures 2.1 and 2.2, however, Figure 2.6 shows an increase in the level of aggregate concentration. There is a slight decline from 1965 to 1968, but a definite increase from 1968 to 1973, producing an increase over the entire period. While the period here is not exactly the same as that for the earlier figures, these results point up the tentative nature of the earlier conclusions. In short, they lead to the conclusion that the changes in aggregate concentration over the last 20 years, if any, have been very small.

For the same years the financial corporations exhibit a high degree of stability in the aggregate concentration ratios (Figure 2.7), with a slight decline from 1965 to 1968 followed by a slight increase from 1968 to 1973. These results more closely match those of Figure 2.4 and also serve to support the conclusion that changes in aggregate concentration in the financial corporations over the past 20 years have been minor.

Canadian Aggregate Concentration
Trends in International Perspective

Comparisons of aggregate concentration among countries are very difficult. Since average firm size differs from industry to industry, the different distributions of economic activity across industries in different countries will produce differences in aggregate concentration ratios. We attempted a comparison of aggregate concentration ratios only between Canada and the United States, which lessens but by no means eliminates the problem of different distributions of economic activity. Also, we attempted to ensure that only domestic activity was included in the comparisons. Even with these precautions, the most reliable, albeit somewhat distorted, comparisons we can make will be between trends in aggregate concentration in the two countries.

Aggregate concentration ratios were computed from the lists of the largest 100 NFCs ranked by sales for 1966, 1971 and 1975. Looking at assets we find that aggregate concentration in Canada is roughly twice that of the United States while the trends in the two countries are virtually the same (Figure 2.8).

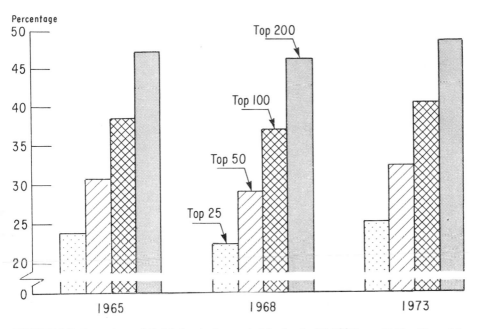

FIGURE 2.6. Percentage of Total Assets Accounted for by the 25-200 Largest* Non-Financial
Corporations, Canada, 1965, 1968 and 1973.
Source: RCCC research.
Note: *Ranked by assets.

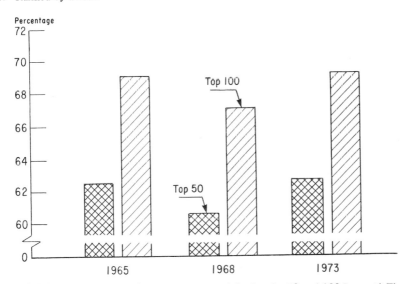

FIGURE 2.7. Percentage of Total Assets Accounted for by the 50 and 100 Largest* Financial
Corporations, Canada, 1965, 1968 and 1973.
Source: RCCC research.
Note: *Ranked by assets.

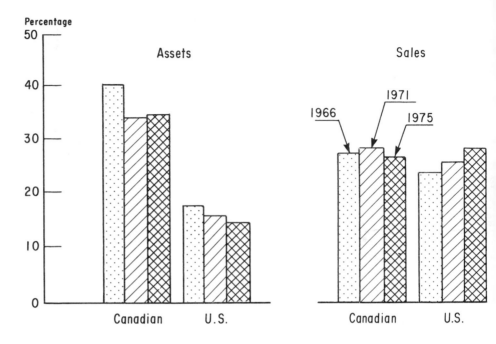

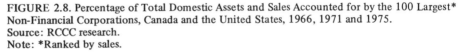

FIGURE 2.8. Percentage of Total Domestic Assets and Sales Accounted for by the 100 Largest*
Non-Financial Corporations, Canada and the United States, 1966, 1971 and 1975.
Source: RCCC research.
Note: *Ranked by sales.

For the Canadian aggregate concentration ratios to be equal to those of
the United States, the top Canadian corporations would have to be, on average,
about one-tenth the size of their U.S. counterparts. The fact that the aggregate
concentration ratios in Canada are twice those of the United States illustrates
again the basic conclusion about the size of Canadian firms. The top Canadian
firms are larger in relation to the Canadian economy than are the top U.S.
firms in relation to the U.S. economy; at the same time, they are absolutely
much smaller (these data indicate about one-fifth the average size) than the
top U.S. firms.

We also computed aggregate concentration ratios standardized for the
difference in the size of the corporate sector in the two countries. For each
sample year, we calculated what fraction the top 100 firms are of total NFCs
in the United States. We then calculated the number of Canadian NFCs which
would provide a comparable fraction of total Canadian NFCs. We then derived
Canadian aggregate concentration ratios for comparison with the aggregate
concentration ratios for the United States. The result of this modified analysis

of aggregate concentration in the two countries is presented in Figure 2.9. It shows that by this method aggregate concentration appears to be higher in the United States than in Canada. While the calculation of the ratios for both countries is based on the same percentage of their respective corporate populations, the number of U.S. and Canadian corporations involved was significantly different. For the years 1966, 1971 and 1975, the numbers of corporations in Canada comprised by the top .0049% of the total corporate population were 6, 7 and 10 respectively. The corresponding numbers of corporations in the United States were 72, 82 and 100. If we were to average the concentration ratios of this fixed proportion of the corporate population by the resulting numbers of corporations represented by the fixed percentage, Canada would again be seen to have significantly higher aggregate concentration than the United States.

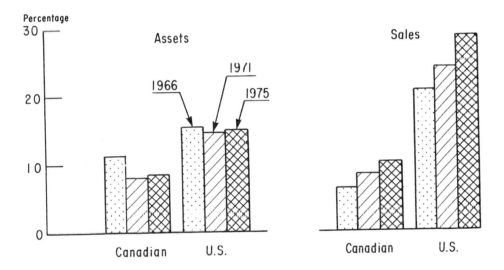

FIGURE 2.9. Percentage of Total Assets and Sales Accounted for by Top* .0049%** of Corporations, Canada and the United States, 1966, 1971 and 1975.
Source: RCCC research.
Notes: *Ranked by assets and sales respectively.
            **This percentage was chosen for historical comparison with the United States where
              100 corporations represented .0049% of all U.S. corporations in 1975.

Summary

To summarize this discussion of aggregate concentration ratios and the consideration of the size of large Canadian corporations, we have found several different sources of evidence that large Canadian corporations are large relative to the Canadian economy but small relative to other large corporations in the United States and elsewhere. We have also seen evidence of a decline in aggregate concentration in Canada in non-financial corporations from 1923 to 1966. Since the period of the mid-1960s, however, several empirical points indicate that there has been very little, if any, change in aggregate concentration either in financial or in non-financial corporations.

Corporate Size within Industries

Introduction

The previous section presented data on the size of large Canadian corporations relative to the entire corporate sector. This section presents data on the size of Canadian corporations relative to the individual industries within which they operate. As before, the purpose here is to provide a background for later sections of this *Report*. Also, as before, we are interested in both absolute levels of industrial concentration and intertemporal and international comparisons.

Our major conclusion is that market concentration in Canada is generally fairly high. In particular, it is noticeably higher than concentration in similarly defined markets in the United States. Also, concentration generally increased from 1948 to 1972, with most of the increase occurring before 1954, and with concentration roughly stable from 1965 to 1972.

Measuring Industrial Concentration

We have already pointed out that several structural characteristics of an industry are important determinants of its competitive environment and performance. While this chapter mentions most of these, it will focus chiefly on seller concentration ratios as its measure of market power. The reasons for this focus have already been discussed.

Industrial concentration ratios are the fraction of activity (output, value added, employment, profits) or of the stock of productive resources (assets) accounted for by a group of the largest firms. The group sizes most often used are 4, 8, 20, and 50, with the 4-firm ratio the most common. Other measures of industrial concentration include the inverse ratio, which measures the number of firms needed to make up a fixed percentage (usually 80%) of the industry's activity or resources, and the Herfindahl index, which is the sum of the squares of the market shares of each corporation in output or resources. Each of these latter measures has certain advantages in some contexts, but we use concentration ratios here primarily for reasons of computational convenience, ease of comprehension, historical continuity and international comparability.

This choice still presents several problems. One is in the selection of the number of firms to be included in the ratio. The choice of four is dictated primarily by census disclosure rules and the need for comparability with U.S. data. However, for reasons of confidentiality Statistics Canada is forced to withhold some 4-firm concentration ratios.

Another problem is that two industries with quite different structures could have the same 4-firm concentration ratio. For example, an industry where one firm has 50% of the sales and three others have 10%, 5% and 5%

would have a 4-firm sales concentration ratio of 70%, as would an industry where three firms each had 20% while a fourth had 10%. Clearly, these two markets have quite different structures: the first has a clearly dominant firm, while the second has a group of large but roughly equal-sized firms competing in the market.

Concentration ratios can also present problems in intertemporal comparisons. If, as is perfectly possible, the 4-firm concentration ratio decreased over a period of time, while the 8-firm ratio remained constant and the 20-firm ratio increased, it would be difficult to say whether concentration had increased, decreased or stayed constant in that industry.

These problems arise in attempting to use, as a summary measure, the concentration ratio, which ignores all the other firms in the industry. The Herfindahl index solves this problem, but suffers from difficulties in computation and data availability, which preclude its use as our major measure. However, since it is a comprehensive index, it is often used to rank industries by their degree of concentration.

Concentration ratios and Herfindahl indexes both fail to reflect the regional character of certain markets. Some products, for instance, cement, beverages and glass bottles, are not shipped far beyond the regions in which they are produced because they have high transport costs per dollar of value. For some industries, regional concentration ratios are more appropriate than national ones. A study by the Department of Consumer and Corporate Affairs concluded that "In almost all cases, the regionally weighted national concentration ratios are considerably greater than the corresponding unweighted national concentration ratios." Particularly dramatic examples of this occurred in poultry processing and stone products manufacturing.

A further problem with concentration ratios in general is that they do not reflect the degree of import competition in the industries. Since Canada is more open to international trade than most industrialized countries (foreign trade was 21.3% of Canada's GNP in 1972, compared with 16.9% for West Germany, 8.7% for Japan and 4.6% for the United States), this omission represents a possibly serious distortion. An illustration of the impact of foreign trade on concentration levels is provided for the steel industry in Marfels' study. He shows that accounting for foreign trade in the steel industry in Canada, West Germany, Japan and the United States results in a substantial reduction below published concentration levels in each of the four countries.

All these problems serve to reinforce our contention that concentration ratios are but one measure of industrial concentration and are neither a complete descriptor of industrial structure nor a perfect predictor of performance. Marfels' study indicates that potential problems associated with ignoring foreign supply and the existence of geographic submarkets do not distort available concentration ratios to the point that they provide a misleading picture of the structure of Canadian industry. Nevertheless, we wish to stress once again that other supporting evidence should be examined when drawing conclusions about the competitive environment of particular industries.

Industrial Concentration in
Historical Perspective

The dominance of a relatively small number of sellers in the marketplace is not a modern phenomenon. Economic historians argue that the early period of industrial capitalism was characterized by monopolies in many of the new industries. Competitive markets emerged only after the growth of production in factories.

The domination of industrial markets by a relatively small number of sellers began to recur with the industrial revolution and the simultaneous advances in transport and communication, which made it economically feasible and desirable to concentrate production wherever conditions of production were most favorable. This move toward increasing concentration was mainly accomplished in a series of massive merger movements. The historian Michael Bliss notes in his book *A Living Profit: Studies in the Social History of Canadian Business* that, during the merger movement of 1909-12, some 275 individual firms were reduced to 58, largely to achieve economies of scale in production and distribution. A second major wave of consolidations followed, from 1925 to 1930.

The first merger period was characterized by the formation of major firms in the heavy industries: for example, Canada Cement Company, Limited, Amalgamated Asbestos Corporation Limited, Canadian Car & Foundry Co. Ltd., Dominion Steel Corporation Ltd. Inc. and The Steel Company of Canada, Limited. Other important combinations were formed in textiles, tobacco, brewing, milling and paper. The second wave of mergers saw important consolidations in pulp and paper, canning, chemicals and dairies. The merger movements were quite widespread, so that by the end of the 1930s most Canadian industries had not more than ten important producers, and many had only three or four.

Trends in Industrial Concentration

Concentration data on individual industries in divisions of the Canadian economy other than manufacturing are spotty and are not available before 1965. The emphasis in this section is, therefore, on industries within the manufacturing division.

Several studies over a period of years have provided detailed concentration data for individual Canadian manufacturing industries. Gideon Rosenbluth's pioneering work discussed 1948 data; Max Stewart's background study for the Economic Council of Canada gave some data for 1964; a report by the Department of Consumer and Corporate Affairs presented 1965 data for both manufacturing and mining; and Statistics Canada has kept that report up-to-date biennially since 1968.

Even with these reports, intertemporal comparisons of concentration ratios are seriously hampered by conceptual and technical changes in statistical definitions and classifications. Major changes have occurred in the Standard Industrial Classification code, the definition of the enterprise as the tabulating unit and the data base covered.

Further problems in comparability arise because different studies have used different variables to compute concentration ratios. We will use concentration ratios based on employment data, from the Consumer and Corporate Affairs study, and ratios based on value of shipments data, from Marfels' study.

In this section, we define a corporation as all establishments under common control in a single industry. This is a change from the previous section, where we defined a corporation or corporate group to consist of all corporations and establishments under common control.

In his work for presentation to the OECD, R.S. Khemani of the Department of Consumer and Corporate Affairs selected a sample of 57 from 171 census manufacturing industries for which data were collected in 1972. The sample was chosen on criteria of historical comparability and data availability for the period 1948-72. This sample accounts for 52.8% and 48.3% of total manufacturing shipments and employment in 1972. It includes the major Canadian manufacturing industries of slaughtering and meat-packing, pulp and paper, iron and steel, automobiles, and petroleum refining. The rubber, electrical and chemical industries are among those omitted.

For his analysis Khemani used 4-firm concentration ratios based on employment data (chosen because of continuous availability). Industries were grouped into one of five concentration ratio classes: under 19%; 20-39%; 40-59%; 60-79% or over 80%. Then the average (weighted by the industry value of shipments, for those industries) industry concentration ratio for each concentration class was calculated and plotted, as was the weighted average for the entire sample.

Considering first all industries, industries with higher initial levels of concentration (greater than 60%) have generally had decreasing concentration ratios, while industries with medium and lower initial levels have been increasing in concentration (Figure 2.10). In particular, rapid increases in concentration have taken place in the top 4-firm concentration ratios for the class of 40-59% where the weighted average ratio went from 51.8% to 67.5% between 1948 and 1972 (Table 2.5).

In terms of the effect that these movements in the classes have on the sample as a whole, the weighted average concentration ratio for the group of industries increased from 44.3% in 1948 to 53.9% in 1965, after which it decreased, although not continuously, to 51.0% in 1972. However, most of this increase took place between 1948 and 1954. Since the early 1950s concentration in Khemani's grouped industries has remained relatively constant. This is one empirical study suggesting that concentration in individual industries did not change much from the mid-'50s to the early '70s.

Marfels classified manufacturing industries into decile percentage concentration classes. The results for 1972 are recorded in Table 2.6. The data show that the greatest percentage of sample industries had 4-firm concentration ratios between 30% and 39%. The 40-49% class had the second highest percentage of sample industries. After classifying all these industries by degree of concentration, Marfels found that 34% of all manufacturing industries in

Table 2.5

Four-Firm (Employment) Concentration in Canadian Manufacturing Industries, 1948-72
(Weighted Averages in Percentages)

CR$_4$ (Employment) Level	Percentage of Industries						
	1948	1954	1958	1965	1968	1970	1972
Class 1 80-100	89.3	83.3	81.7	86.9	83.6	86.5	82.5
Class 2 60-79	65.2	68.4	61.1	62.6	57.1	56.2	54.4
Class 3 40-59	51.8	63.8	67.9	67.2	65.8	66.0	67.5
Class 4 20-39	31.5	31.7	33.2	35.6	34.3	36.2	34.9
Class 5 0-19	10.0	12.3	11.9	13.4	14.4	16.1	17.1
	Average All Industries						
	44.3	48.7	50.2	53.9	51.1	52.9	51.0

Source: R.S. Khemani, *Concentration in the Manufacturing Industries of Canada: Analyses of Post-War Changes* (Ottawa, 1977).

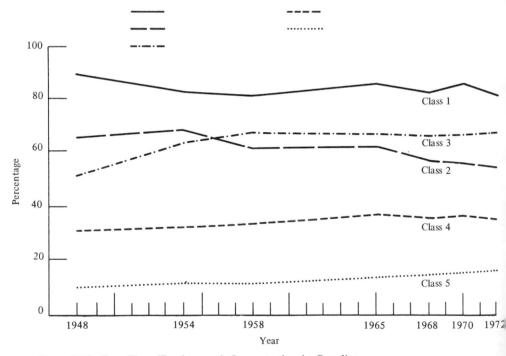

Figure 2.10. Four-Firm (Employment) Concentration in Canadian Manufacturing Industries, 1948-72.

Source: R.S. Khemani, *Concentration in the Manufacturing Industries of Canada: Analyses of Post-War Changes* (Ottawa, 1977).

Note: * — See Table 2.5.

1972 could be classified as highly concentrated, whereas 41% and 23% fell into the categories of medium and low concentration respectively.

To facilitate a quick comparison of concentration levels between 1965 and 1972 Marfels gathered the data shown in Table 2.7. He again classified industries in cumulative decile percentage concentration classes. For example, 11.6% of the industries in his sample had concentration ratios of 80% or more in 1965. The table shows that except for an increase in the number of industries registering a concentration ratio between 30% and 40% (and thus a corresponding decrease in the 20-30% class) the number of industries registering concentration ratios in the other classes has remained virtually constant.

In summary, Marfels' data confirm Khemani's findings that industrial concentration ratios remained roughly constant from the mid-'60s to the early '70s. This also tends to support the broader conclusion that aggregate concentration also was stable over a somewhat longer period from the early 1950s to the early 1970s.

Concentration in Canadian Manufacturing Industries

Having reviewed some evidence on recent trends in industrial concentration in Canada, it would be enlightening to identify those manufacturing industries which are, in fact, highly concentrated by the conventional 4-firm concentration ratio. Table 2.8 provides the industrial concentration ratios for the 20 most concentrated manufacturing industries in Canada for 1972. We reiterate our earlier proviso that concentration is only one structural measure that should be considered in evaluating the competitive environment of an industry. The limitation of the concentration ratio in this regard is illustrated by the example of the cotton yarn and cloth mills industry. Although it has the highest 4-firm concentration ratio on the list, it is an industry that is particularly open to import competition, and domestic producers could hardly be considered to enjoy a monopoly position in the domestic market.

The level of concentration in the largest manufacturing industries is more relevant to competition policy. Table 2.9 provides a summary of the concentration levels and trends for the nine largest Canadian manufacturing industries ranked by manufacturing value added in 1972. Among the largest manufacturing industries in Canada, motor vehicle manufacturers and petroleum refining are the most highly concentrated. One important point to make in this regard is that most of the sample industries in Table 2.9 experienced a decrease in industrial concentration over the period 1965-72.

Table 2.6

Four-Firm (Value-of-Shipment) Concentration Ratios in Canadian Manufacturing Industries, 1972

Industry Group	Number of Industries	Percentage of Total Manufacturing Value Added	Percentage of Industries with Ratios of										
			90 to 100	80 to 89	70 to 79	60 to 69	50 to 59	40 to 49	30 to 39	20 to 29	10 to 19	0 to 9	Not Available*
Food and beverage	18	14.3	11.1	—	16.7	16.7	5.5	16.7	27.8	5.5	—	—	—
Tobacco products	2	1.0	50.0	—	—	—	—	—	—	—	—	—	50.0
Rubber	2	3.0	—	—	—	50.0	—	—	—	—	50.0	—	—
Leather	5	0.9	—	—	20.0	20.0	—	20.0	—	40.0	—	—	—
Textiles	16	3.5	12.5	—	12.5	6.2	12.5	6.2	25.0	—	—	—	25.0
Knitting mills	3	0.9	—	—	—	—	—	—	33.3	33.3	33.3	—	—
Clothing	10	3.2	—	—	—	10.0	10.0	—	20.0	10.0	40.0	10.0	—
Wood	13	5.8	—	7.7	7.7	7.7	—	30.8	15.4	15.4	15.4	—	—
Furniture and fixtures	5	2.0	—	—	—	—	—	—	40.0	—	40.0	20.0	—
Paper and allied products	6	7.9	—	—	—	—	16.7	33.3	33.3	—	—	—	16.7
Printing and publishing	4	5.1	—	—	—	—	—	25.0	—	25.0	50.0	—	—
Primary metals	7	7.9	—	28.6	42.9	—	—	28.6	—	—	—	—	—
Metal fabricating	11	8.1	—	—	—	9.1	—	9.1	18.2	36.4	18.2	9.1	—
Machinery	4	4.1	—	25.0	—	25.0	25.0	—	—	—	25.0	—	—
Transportation equipment	10	10.8	—	10.0	—	10.0	—	20.0	10.0	10.0	—	—	40.0
Electrical products	9	6.4	—	—	22.2	11.1	33.3	11.1	—	—	—	—	22.2
Non-metallic mineral products	14	4.0	7.1	14.3	21.4	7.1	14.3	21.4	7.1	7.1	—	—	—
Petroleum and coal	3	1.9	—	33.3	33.3	—	33.3	—	—	—	—	—	—
Chemicals	11	6.3	—	—	18.2	9.1	27.3	9.1	18.2	9.1	—	—	9.1
Miscellaneous manufacturing	18	2.6	—	—	16.7	16.7	16.7	11.1	11.1	5.5	5.5	—	16.7
Total manufacturing Percentage	(100)	100.0	3.5	4.7	12.3	9.9	10.5	14.0	15.2	9.4	9.4	1.7	9.4
Number	171	($24 billion)	6	8	21	17	18	24	26	16	16	3	16

Source: Christian Marfels, *Concentration Levels and Trends in the Canadian Economy, 1965-73* (RCCC Study no. 31).

Example: Read as "11.1% of the 18 industries in the food and beverage groups have four-firm concentration ratios between 90 and 100%."

Note: *Not available because of Statistics Canada regulations with regard to confidentiality for industries with fewer than **four firms**.

Table 2.7

Cumulative Percentage of Canadian Manufacturing Industries, by Deciles of
Four-Firm (Value-of-Shipment) Concentration Ratios,
1965 and 1972

CR$_4$ Level	Cumulative Percentage of Industries	
	1965	1972
90% or more	3.4	3.9
80% or more	11.6	9.1
70% or more	21.9	22.6
60% or more	32.9	33.6
50% or more	44.5	45.2
40% or more	60.9	60.7
30% or more	71.9	77.5
20% or more	87.0	87.8
10% or more	97.3	98.1
0% or more	100.0	100.0
Total number of industries	146	155

Source: Marfels, *op. cit.*

International Comparison of Industrial
Concentration in Manufacturing Industries

Comparison of concentration levels of Canadian manufacturing industries
with counterpart industries in the United States has been a matter of long-
standing interest. Rosenbluth, in an article in the *Canadian Journal of
Economics and Political Science* (1954), found that in 50 of 56 comparable
industries Canadian concentration levels for 1948 were significantly higher
than the 1947 levels in the United States. A comparison prepared by the
Department of Consumer and Corporate Affairs of Canadian concentration
levels in 1965 with U.S. data for 1963 and 1966 revealed similar results: of the
116 manufacturing industries in the sample, 98 were significantly more
concentrated in Canada. A more recent comparison prepared by the Conference Board using 1972 concentration levels supports the previous findings that
concentration is higher in Canada than in the United States. More specifically,
roughly twice as many industries in Canada had 4-firm concentration levels in
excess of 60%.

Concentration in Selected
Manufacturing Industries

Since 1945, official concentration data for individual manufacturing
industries have been published in a number of countries on a more or less
regular basis. A sample of nine Canadian manufacturing industries with

Table 2.8

Twenty Canadian Manufacturing Industries with the Highest Four-Firm
(Value-of-Shipment) Concentration Ratios, 1972

Rank 1972*	Industry	Number of Enterprises	CR$_4$
1.	Cotton yarn and cloth mills	9	97.5
2.	Tobacco products manufacturing (6)	11	97.1
3.	Glass manufacturing	9	97.0
4.	Breweries (1)	7	96.5
5.	Fibre and filament yarn manufacturing	7	93.8
6.	Cane and beet sugar processing	7	93.7
7.	Aluminum rolling, casting and extruding (8)	55	89.0
8.	Wood preservation industries (7)	19	87.1
9.	Miscellaneous vehicle manufacturing (11)	35	86.6
10.	Abrasives manufacturing (15)	17	86.2
11.	Manufacturing of lubricating oil and greases (5)	14	85.9
12.	Cement manufacturing	8	83.7
13.	Office and store machinery manufacturing	30	82.7
14.	Copper and copper alloy rolling, casting and extruding	45	81.9
15.	Distilleries (12)	14	79.7
16.	Battery manufacturing (14)	16	79.3
17.	Manufacturing of electrical wire and cable	17	79.2
18.	Clock and watch manufacturing	18	79.0
19.	Smelting and refining	14	78.6
20.	Typewriter supplies manufacturing	11	78.3

Source: RCCC research.
Note: * — 1965 rank in parentheses where applicable.

similarly defined counterpart industries in other foreign countries was selected.
They are slaughtering and meat processing, breweries, tobacco products manufacturing, rubber tire and tube manufacturing, pulp and paper mills, iron and
steel mills, motor vehicle manufacturing, cement manufacturing and petroleum
refining. These industries are relatively easy to identify; moreover, they represent the largest Canadian manufacturing industries. We collected concentration data for these industries from several sources. The only adjustment, to
obtain at least one common measurement, was to have the calculation of
minimum estimates of the commonly used 4-firm ratios for countries that
employ 3-firm ratios.

This international comparison of industrial concentration ratios indicated
that concentration in Canada is higher than in the other countries studied
(including the United States, West Germany, France, Japan and Sweden). In
particular, concentration in Canada is higher than that in the United States for
all nine sample industries. In Germany and Sweden, the only industry with a
higher level of concentration than its counterpart in Canada is the pulp and
paper industry. In France, only the steel and rubber tire industries are more
concentrated than their Canadian counterparts. Finally, of seven comparable

Table 2.9

Concentration Levels and Trends for the Nine Largest Canadian Manufacturing Industries, 1965 and 1972
(Ranked by Manufacturing Value Added in 1972)

Industry	Year	Number of Enterprises	Number of Establishments	Manufacturing Value Added $ Millions	Manufacturing Value Added Percentage of Total Manufacturing	Value of Manufacturing Shipments $ Millions	Value of Manufacturing Shipments Percentage of Total Manufacturing	Total Employment Thousands	Total Employment Percentage of Total Manufacturing	CR_4	CR_8	CR_{20}	1965-72 Trend in Four-Firm Concentration Ratios
Pulp and paper mills	1965	56	132	1,033.5	6.9	2,104.4	6.2	69.9	4.4	36.9	57.1	86.3	Decline
	1972	65	141	1,374.1	5.6	3,127.8	5.6	79.0	4.7	34.4	52.5	80.1	
Iron and steel mills	1965	32	41	646.1	4.3	1,231.8	3.6	44.3	2.8	78.8	90.3	98.6	Decline
	1972	35	48	909.4	3.7	1,900.8	3.4	49.8	3.0	77.7	90.7	98.5	
Motor vehicle manufacturers	1965	20	20	631.4	4.2	2,120.3	6.2	42.4	2.7	93.3	98.2	100.0	Decline
	1972	17	22	906.8	3.7	4,033.6	7.2	44.0	2.6	n.a.	98.1	–	
Motor vehicle parts and accessories manufacturers	1965	149	160	326.6	2.2	755.6	2.2	32.0	2.0	54.2	64.4	80.7	Decline
	1972	171	211	866.6	3.6	1,903.1	3.4	46.2	2.7	48.8	64.8	79.6	
Sawmills and planing mills	1965	2,464	2,559	384.5	2.6	896.2	2.6	50.8	3.2	16.8	26.7	36.9	Increase
	1972	1,463	1,567	864.9	3.5	1,893.5	3.4	57.1	3.4	18.2	27.7	43.0	
Miscellaneous machinery and equipment manufacturers	1965	501	528	419.7	2.0	797.1	2.3	44.0	2.8	15.0	24.3	41.5	Decline
	1972	710	759	717.1	2.9	1,454.5	2.6	53.3	3.2	12.5	21.7	36.5	
Petroleum refining	1965	12	40	244.1	1.6	1,383.6	4.1	9.0	0.6	84.4	98.1	–	Decline
	1972	14	41	431.3	1.8	2,361.7	4.2	14.4	0.9	73.7	94.6	–	
Slaughtering and meat processors	1965	365	399	267.3	1.8	1,438.7	4.2	30.0	1.9	48.0	67.5	77.3	Decline
	1972	415	468	428.6	1.7	2,551.4	4.5	31.3	1.9	53.9	62.0	72.9	
Dairy products	1965	1,165	1,421	277.4	1.8	1,051.7	3.1	33.5	2.1	25.1	34.8	48.8	Increase
	1972	498	731	392.1	1.6	1,573.7	2.8	28.9	1.7	33.0	45.8	62.2	

Source: RCCC research.

Note: n.a. = not available.

industries in Japan, three (rubber tires, breweries, and pulp and paper) are more highly concentrated than in Canada.

These comparisons lead to several conclusions. First, it is well established, by several independent studies using data for several different years, that industrial concentration in Canada is higher than in the United States. The weight of the evidence on this point is sufficient to treat this as an established empirical fact.

Second, the trend of the evidence suggests that concentration in Canada is higher than in other industrial countries, even those with economies of roughly the same size. This conclusion is as yet tentative; it arises from a comparison of only nine industries in only one year. But that study shows a clear tendency; firmer conclusions await only further verification by more extensive studies covering more industries in more years.

Finally when taken together with the conclusions of the first section of this chapter, that large Canadian firms are much smaller than large firms in the United States or the rest of the world, this international comparison indicates that the inevitable result of expansion of the large Canadian firms to the average size of the large world firms would involve a significant increase in industrial concentration in Canada, assuming that the larger firms remained primarily oriented to the Canadian market.

Summary

This section has presented data on concentration in individual industries. It has shown that industrial concentration has generally been stable in Canada from the mid-1950s to the early 1970s. It has also presented some evidence that industrial concentration increased substantially from the late 1940s to the early 1950s. Also, although there is no direct evidence on the subject, it is probable that industrial concentration generally increased during the two early merger waves in the 1910s and 1920s.

In international comparisons, this section has established that Canadian industries are generally more highly concentrated than their counterparts in the United States, and it has presented some evidence to indicate that they are more highly concentrated than their counterparts in other industrial countries.

Chapter 3

Size and Economies of Scale

Introduction

The scale of Canadian firms and the effect of suboptimal scale on them and their component plants are central to any discussion of the structure of Canadian industry. For more than one hundred years Canada has attempted to foster a national market for Canadian manufacturers by means of a high (though lowering) tariff wall. These tariffs have encouraged both Canadian and foreign-owned firms to set up manufacturing operations within Canada, where they could compete profitably. These firms (and their component establishments) produce a much more diverse product line than firms of similar size in other countries. The small and dispersed Canadian market, combined with a policy of economic nationalism designed to aid the manufacturing and skilled labor sectors, has led to an economy whose firms and plants in many industries tend to be relatively small and unspecialized by international standards.

Small-scale operation can have a significant impact on the efficiency and international competitiveness of firms operating in Canada if their size is below what economists refer to as minimum efficient scale (MES), and if the penalties for below-MES operation are significant. MES is the point at which most economies of scale at the plant or product level are realized.

Most studies of economies of scale have focused on the product or the plant, and the recommendations stemming from them have concerned intra-industry product rationalization and concentration. This Commission in its study of large diversified firms in the Canadian economy has recognized that there might be significant firm-level economies of scale in addition to economies of scale at the product, plant and multiplant level. If such economies exist, policies that prevent this realization could affect the efficiency of the economy significantly. Consequently, we commissioned a number of studies to try to calculate the possible magnitude of firm-level, multiplant- or multiproduct-level economies. Some of this work, specifically that by Donald Mc-Fetridge and by Richard Caves *et al.*, is being published. In addition, we have consulted the work of F.M. Scherer, whose contribution to *The Economics of*

43

Multi-Plant Operation marks him as one of the leading researchers in this area, and who presented a brief, supplied data and testified before us.

Our research was directed at the question, "What economies might be related to scale at the product, plant, multiplant, and firm levels?" Special attention was directed toward determining what economies of scale might be realized by large, diversified firms. A competition policy that would break up existing conglomerate firms or impede the formation of new ones would not necessarily affect concentration levels *within* industries, but would affect the overall concentration of industrial ownership in the hands of the largest firms. Before we could make recommendations regarding such a policy, we needed accurate information on the efficiency costs involved.

In presenting our findings we begin with a short description of Canada's economic environment, the problem of economies of scale in the context of this environment and the most important economic policy measures that have been designed to deal with the problem. The next section is an analysis of the different types of economies of scale—product, plant, multiplant, and firm-level—and their relative magnitude for firms in Canada. We then describe the results of our own studies and those of other researchers, which bear on the issues before the Commission.

The Economic Environment

Canada's historic national economic policy, combined with a small, dispersed market, has often led to the establishment of relatively scale-inefficient firms and plants. This scale inefficiency is reflected in low output per man-hour in Canadian industry. The Economic Council of Canada has estimated 1974 Canadian output per man-hour at 79% of that in comparable U.S. industries. This inefficiency could also, of course, reflect inefficient organization ("X-inefficiency") brought about by high tariffs or could reflect the oligopolistic nature of many Canadian industries.

The domestic market for Canadian output is roughly one-tenth the size of that in the United States. In most industries, even from behind tariff barriers, if economies of scale are significant only a limited number of Canadian firms will be able to produce for the domestic market at prices competitive with imports. It should be noted that the distribution of the sizes of firms in Canada is not a one-tenth scale version of that in the United States. As indicated in our published research, small firms are, and have been, squeezed out of the market in Canada in industries with substantial economies of scale. Products with small-scale demand within an industry are generally not produced in Canada, since it is often cheaper to produce them abroad and ship them over the tariff wall to Canada. The distribution of firms within an industry in Canada is thus often truncated from below, leaving firm sizes in Canada much larger than one-tenth the scale of plants and product runs of the U.S. firms, but still small by international standards.

The Canadian government has had a competition policy that has tried to discourage concentration and the abuse of economic power within individual industries. The extent of discouragement is hard to gauge. The Director of Research and Investigation under the Combines Investigation Act stated in his testimony to the Commission that, although there had been only a very few, and even fewer successful, prosecutions of mergers or monopolies under the Act, firms frequently consulted the Department of Consumer and Corporate Affairs about the legality of an acquisition and were often advised not to proceed. Other observers, however, have said that in Canada mergers and acquisitions are virtually unconstrained. Leonard Wrigley, in a brief to the Commission, recommends that Canada relax its competition policy legislation even further to encourage firms to form economically efficient units, so that they are not driven to uneconomic, unrelated diversification, which forms large units but brings about few economies of scale and little synergy among the parts of the firm.

Certainly the potential conflict between realization of economies of large-scale operation and high levels of concentration, with possible anticompetitive market behavior, has been recognized by those responsible for formulating competition laws. For example, agreements that allow firms to form consortia to sell in export markets have been exempted from the conspiracy provisions of the Combines Investigation Act since 1960. The Economic Council of Canada, in its 1969 *Interim Report on Competition Policy,* proposed that its civil Competitive Practices Tribunal take into account "...the likelihood that the merger would be productive of substantial 'social saving', i.e. savings in the use of resources...."

Following this lead, L. A. Skeoch and B. C. McDonald, in their 1976 report *Dynamic Change and Accountability in a Canadian Market Economy,* recommended as part of the Stage II Combines Investigation Act amendments the following recognition of possible economies of scale arising from a merger: "but [if the Board] is also satisfied that such effect [restraint of trade] will, with reasonable probability, be on balance offset by real-cost economics...no order shall be made...."

This recommendation was incorporated into Bill C-13, which states in section 31.71 (5):

> The Board shall not make an order under subsection (3) [i.e. proscribing a merger] where after hearing the parties to a merger or proposed merger to which this section applies, it finds that the merger or proposed merger has brought about or that there is a clear probability that it will bring about substantial gains in efficiency that save resources for the Canadian economy.

In addition, the proposed amendments included provisions that would allow specialization agreements between firms in the same industry.

That Canadian firms are scale-inefficient has become a cliché both in the literature of industrial organization in Canada and among businessmen. Until 1975 relatively lower wages in Canada as compared with the United States partially masked the effect of low productivity in Canada. When the wage relationship reversed in 1975, the future of the manufacturing sector in Canada looked bleak indeed: low productivity, compounded by high costs of both labor and capital, was rapidly making large segments of Canadian industry uncompetitive internationally. One proposed solution to this predicament was the Economic Council of Canada's recommendation, in its study *Looking Outward*, that Canada move toward multilateral free trade since then all firms would be open to international competition and would have free access to world markets. They would then be forced to move toward their most efficient scale of operation at product, plant and firm levels.

In the fall of 1976, in an article in the *Financial Times*, Harold Crookell advocated an even more radical solution to the dearth of scale-efficient firms: instead of merely being permitted to make mergers that achieve economies of scale, firms should be *encouraged* by the tax system to merge into larger units.

Each commentator seems to be advocating quite different policies, all based on a different perception of the problem of economies of scale in Canadian manufacturing industry and its effect on the ability of Canadian firms to produce efficiently and to compete world-wide. Many see the inefficient size of Canadian firms as the result of two factors: a national policy of tariff barriers, which turns firms toward the domestic market and away from their natural export markets, and a competition policy that may discourage them from combining to operate at an efficient scale. By contrast, in many European countries and in Japan, the formation of large, export-oriented firms is encouraged in order to induce world-scale efficiency. These countries argue that their small market size and the imperatives of economies of scale require large firms in some industries. The rationalization is not always a success, as witness the experience of British Leyland. Where industrial rationalization occurs, competition laws may be directed toward ensuring that the benefits accrue at least in part to the public, and not only to the owners and managers of the firms involved.

The Economic Council of Canada, in its recommendation that Canada move to free trade, indicates its belief that Canadian firms, when exposed to international competition, will adjust toward most efficient scale at the product, plant and firm levels without major dislocations. Crookell, however, disputes this. He has concluded, on the basis of his research on technology and new-product generation and transfer, that most Canadian firms currently have not the scale, the resources, the organization or the skills to survive in the international marketplace or to produce goods for the domestic market at prices comparable with those of foreign manufacturers. Crookell predicts that free trade would lead to the destruction of firms in many industries, rather than to their amalgamation into larger, more efficient units. His recommendation is that the government first encourage the formation of larger firms, then reduce the tariff barriers. This recommendation has been almost universally challenged by economists and praised by businessmen.

The Analytics of Economies of Scale

Before going further in the analysis of the effects of economies of scale on the structure and efficiency of Canadian industry, we shall discuss economies of scale in manufacturing and their effect on the efficiency of production. An understanding of what is involved in the seemingly obvious term "economies of scale" is necessary before any policy alternatives can be proposed or discussed.

In spite of the amount of work that has been done on the subject of economies of scale, few firm conclusions have emerged, and for several reasons. First, there are several different economies of scale associated with the production of a given product (or group of products), and hence there are many definitions of what economies of scale are for any one industry. Second, the data to determine the economies of scale for firms in an industry are difficult to obtain, and the methodology for using this data is highly dependent on which definition of economy of scale is being used. Third, the different economies of scale associated with a specific industry interact with one another and with the other economic characteristics of the country in complex and changing ways. Even if all the economies of scale associated with an industry could be defined, untangled, and measured, the implications of these calculated values for economic policy are often unclear and probably limited to one country. Therefore researchers using one definition of economies of scale in one country may arrive at policy recommendations radically different from those of another group of researchers in another country.

We begin to unravel this tangle by listing the possible economies of scale that operate in the industrial sector. Remember, however, that these interact and overlap with one other, so that any classification will inevitably oversimplify the true situation.

Product-Specific Economies of Scale

F. M. Scherer, in his writings on the subject, places great importance on the distinctions among product-specific, plant-specific, and multiplant economies of scale. Increased volume of production of a product tends to decrease the average total costs per unit for several reasons. Economies of scale may be related to the volume of output of a product as a function of three related variables: the total expected volume of output, the rate of output per unit of time and the length of the expected run. As the total expected volume increases, management is willing to expend more time on developing cost-cutting measures and quality control in production. As the length of the production run increases, both workers and management become more familiar with the production techniques involved (learning by doing), so that production costs tend to fall over time and over the total volume of output. As the rate and the volume of production increase together, more and more of the production process can be automated, and there is an increasing possibility of line-balancing, so that the time during which machines are idle during the production run is decreased.

These three components all combine in such a way that goods whose demand warrants high-speed, long-term production runs will utilize more specialized machinery and there will be less down time for changes between products using the same machinery. Fewer line changes and more familiar products will also reduce waste and increase quality. In addition, as volume increases, the many risks associated with production, sales, and materials procurement tend to decrease, so that firms may produce closer to the expected volume of demand and at lower unit cost.

There are two major caveats to this analysis. It has assumed that neither input costs (particularly labor and materials) nor the output price is a function of the rate of production. However, to produce at a high rate of output, the firm might have to increase the wages it pays its workers or the costs of its materials, lower its selling price, and/or incur increasing transport costs to reach the larger market required to absorb its increased output. A high rate of materials demand could lead to increasing returns to scale in production and lower procurement costs or to the necessity of seeking more distant sources or to an increase in local input prices. The standard analysis shows these input and transport costs rising with volume after some output level is reached. When these additional costs are added, the average total cost per unit will eventually rise with output even if the production process itself shows increasing returns to scale. Transport costs, population density and disposable incomes are country- as well as product-specific, while market share is firm-specific. No universal optimal size plant can be calculated when these variables are included. In Canada, high unit transport costs and a dispersed market motivate many firms to construct small plants to serve a local market. Production costs from such plants will be above those from an MES plant, but total costs (including transport costs) will be minimized.

Firms such as MacMillan Bloedel Limited, Abitibi Paper Company Ltd. and George Weston Limited, in their briefs and testimony before the Commission, stressed the importance of product-level economies of scale for industry in Canada and the great disadvantage under which Canadian firms operate because they do not have access to a large domestic market. The problems of these product-level economies of scale are accentuated by the large range of products produced by Canadian manufacturers in many industries. As documented by Caves, in *Diversification, Foreign Investment and Scale in North American Manufacturing Industries*, Canadian firms (and plants) have an output of products much more diverse than that of similar-sized firms (and plants) in the United States. This diversity is a response to the demand of the market that firms in many industries either supply a full range of products or face substantial price and sales penalties. Alternatively, there may be economies of scale in marketing and distribution or fixed costs of operation, which make distribution of multiple products by one firm at large volume more efficient.

Plant Economies of Scale

Most work in the area of economies of scale has been focused on the plant. Plant economies of scale arise from indivisibilities in plant management, maintenance, repair, inventories of raw materials and construction. If the volume that exhausts a specific product's production economies of scale is greater than the MES scale of a plant, one plant will produce only one product. If the economies of scale of a product are exhausted at low volumes, a plant may produce several products, thereby utilizing its managers, engineers and machinery more efficiently. In Canada, where market conditions arising from product differentiation by firms in many oligopolistic industries demand that a firm produce a broad line of products, but where the market can absorb only small volumes of these products, firms that produce only for the domestic market can lower their total costs to some extent by producing many lines in one plant rather than in several different plants. Such larger multiproduct firms would be more efficient that many small firms, each of which produced only one product.

Multiplant Economies of Scale

In a major advance in the theory of economies of scale, Scherer *et al.* in their 1975 book, *The Economics of Multi-Plant Operation*, sought to explain what advantages accrue to firms operating a number of plants. They describe how a multiplant firm may obtain a lowest-cost allocation of production among geographically dispersed plants, by balancing transport costs against product-specific and plant-specific economies of scale. For example, a multiplant firm might obtain lowest costs by producing in short runs at small plants when transport costs are high relative to economies of scale. On the other hand, the firm may be able to specialize its plants, producing long runs in large plants, when transport costs are low. The overall lowest-cost allocation of production among plants is termed "optimal (geographically) unbalanced specialization". Scherer *et al.* contrasted these optimal costs with those that would be incurred by plants producing a full line of products in each regional plant, and concluded that "the economies attributable to optimal unbalanced specialization by multi-plant firms must be quite small in relation to total production and physical distribution costs." Multiplant operation and geographically unbalanced specialization may lead to firms producing closer to efficient scale, however, since they facilitate investment staging decisions that involve bringing on large blocks of capacity and hence lower average total costs.

In his testimony before the Commission, Scherer argued that multiplant economies of scale were probably very small for Canadian manufacturing firms. This implies that from a production point of view, little efficiency would be sacrificed in Canada if firms were broken up so that each firm had only one plant. Scherer and others were, however, primarily concerned with production and transport costs. They looked at distribution, research and development, marketing costs and profits only in relation to these production and transport costs. Consequently, many of the incentives for firms to have multiple plants, such as risk-spreading and centralized purchasing, were not recognized in their quantitative analysis.

Firm-Related Economies of Scale

For the Commission, the most interesting question is the relationship between the absolute size of the firm and the efficiency at which it can produce its products. If large firms are necessary for efficient production, product and process development, distribution, finance, advertising and export of a product, then a policy that retards or prevents the formation of such large firms would decrease the overall efficiency of the economy. Such economies might be one motivation for the formation of conglomerate firms.

In a country like Canada with a small market, firms of minimum efficient scale may imply a very high level of industrial concentration, since economies of scale at the firm level might be achieved at greater firm sizes than required to achieve MES plant economies. The expansion to MES firm size would not occur, however, in an extreme case such as refrigerator compressors, where the output from a single MES plant may well be greater than the entire Canadian market for them.

When an industry is highly concentrated, there is a serious question as to whether firms that operate at large scale are doing so to gain production efficiencies in the hope of gaining monopoly or oligopoly profits, which may result from a concentrated industrial structure and oligopolistic pricing. In Canada, this problem of motivation for large-scale production is compounded by the presence of relatively high tariff barriers and substantial foreign ownership in some industries. Both of these may serve to reduce import competition since foreign firms may not compete with their Canadian subsidiaries. In the Canadian context, therefore, economies of scale at the firm level, industrial concentration, industrial strategy, Canada's import exposure and foreign ownership are all interrelated.

The factors of production that may lead to economies of scale at the firm level (which have not already been included in product, plant and multiplant economies of scale) are generally considered to include management, finance and control, research and development (R&D), advertising and distribution, export activities and risk-taking for large projects, as well as overhead expenses such as insurance and legal services. The extent of the economies of scale associated with these factors is still a subject of some controversy. Some writers portray the top management of large firms as being inundated with a never ending deluge of paperwork and statistics, which are necessary to maintain control of their empires. Joe Bain notes in his 1968 book, *Industrial Organization*, that slow response to changing situations is almost inevitable in large organizations. He points out that decision-making in large organizations is likely to be rigid and lacking in coordination among departments. Other writers, however, extol the great efficiency of the modern manager who is able to use the latest management and computer techniques for processing and assimilating information. This latter view is supported in briefs to the Commission, by Leonard Wrigley and David Leighton, and in the testimony of the managers of many large firms, including Paul Desmarais and John McDougald.

The problem is that it is very difficult to measure the performance of firms along the dimensions of managerial effectiveness, finance, control, R&D, advertising and distribution, and export penetration, and then to plot this performance against the scale of their operations. Consider the problems of measuring the effectiveness of R&D. What variable should be used to measure it—patents, journal articles, number of significant inventions or new products and processes? There may well be different economies of scale for invention and innovation, as in the Polaroid and Xerox processes, for example. Both were invented by individuals, yet after the initial invention large organizations were required to generate the continuous innovation necessary to keep these products ahead of the market. The Polaroid SX70 camera is reported to have cost several hundred million dollars to develop, a sum not available to an individual inventor.

These then are the main areas—product, plant, multiplant and firm—through which the efficiency of the invention, production and marketing of goods could increase with scale. The next section describes the problems of measuring these economies of scale and, more importantly, reviews the Commission's main conclusions on the magnitude of these various economies of scale.

Measuring Product, Plant and Multiplant Economies of Scale

**Plant and Multiplant
Economies of Scale**

There have been several studies of the relative size of Canadian plants compared with those in the United States and other countries and the relative scale efficiencies of these plants, but a survey of the evidence does not provide an unambiguous conclusion. In Scherer's study of multiplant economies of scale in six nations, Canada was found to have the lowest mean size of plant, measured by employment (see Table 3.1).

Table 3.1

Indices of Relative Plant Sizes, Based on Average
Employment in the Largest Plants Accounting for 50%
of Industry Output

(Most comparable U.S. industry bench mark = 100)

Industry	Canada	U.S.	U.K.	Sweden	France	Germany
Brewing	50	100	77	13	23	29
Tobacco products	25	100	81	10	15	24
Cotton and synthetic fabrics	75	100	28	47	27	91
Paints and varnishes	103	100	340	121	94	162
Petroleum refining	31	100	150	28	87	n.a.
Shoes	51	100	97	27	85	103
Glass bottles	94	100	86	57	131	114
Cement	68	100	157	129	95	171
Steel	117	100	65	46	68	n.a.
Antifriction bearings	29	100	118	209	65	123
Storage batteries	34	100	n.a.	n.a.	112	426
Mean relative size	61	100	120	69	68	138

Source: Excerpted from F. M. Scherer et al., The Economics of Multi-Plant Operation (Cambridge Mass., 1975), Tables 3.3 through 3.7.
Note: n.a. = not available.

These findings were not supported by an earlier study undertaken by the Economic Council of Canada. Using employment as a measure of size, the Council reported, in its *Fourth Annual Review* in 1967, that for 1963 (the latest year then available) the average size of firms in the United States was larger than in Canada, but the average size of plants in most industries was larger in Canada. These observations led them to conclude that "the mere *size* of the establishment is probably not a dominant factor in the differences in productivity...[but rather] the size of production runs and the degree of specialization or diversification of production." The Canadian Pulp and Paper Association pointed out in their brief to the Commission that they could not fully realize potential plant economies of scale in fine papers because of the short runs of the diverse products produced.

Another viewpoint has been advanced by Caves *et al.*, who in their study for the Commission wrote that "the average-size manufacturing establishment in Canada (measured by value added) does not appear to differ greatly from that in its U.S. counterpart industry."

Paul Gorecki, in a monograph published in 1976 by the Federal Department of Consumer and Corporate Affairs and titled *Economies of Scale and Efficient Plant Size in Canadian Manufacturing Industries,* disagreed with the measure used by the Council in making its comparison. Redoing the analysis using a different measure, he found that in 69 of the 123 industries covered (or 56% of the sample), the U.S. plant sizes were larger than Canadian plant sizes by an average of 61%. For 50 industries (or 41% of the sample), however, Canadian plant sizes were larger, although the difference was only 32%.

A more appropriate comparison may be made between the size of the Canadian plant and the size of the MES plant in that industry. A comparison with this independent standard will give a better indication of how much efficiency can be improved by adopting best-practice technology (existing technology that would produce the lowest unit cost output) of an MES plant (see Table 3.2).

A number of studies have attempted to compare estimates of the MES of best-practice plants for certain industries with the actual size of plants in operation in Canada. In their study *The Tariff* (1967), H. C. Eastman and Stefan Stykolt found that in approximately one-third of the sample of 16 industries they studied no plants were of MES. In another third, less than 60% of industry capacity was optimally efficient. In only one industry was all industry capacity of the minimum efficient size. They concluded that a significant percentage of Canadian production comes from plants of technically inefficient size. This estimate should be compared with the United States, where on the average 80% of the firms in all manufacturing are above minimum efficient scale.

Gorecki calculated MES plants by the survivor method for plants in Canada and compared these estimates to MES plant sizes calculated by others using engineering and survey techniques. (An MES plant in the "survivor" sense is the plant size that most successfully competes in the market place and increases its share of industry output. Under engineering and survey tech-

Size and Economies of Scale   53

Table 3.2

Number of MES Plants Compatible with Domestic
Consumption, Canada, circa 1968 *

Industry	Number of MES Plants Compatible with Domestic Consumption, circa 1968	Actual Number of Plants, 1967	Percentage Increase in Unit Costs for Plants Operating at One-Third MES
Refrigerators and freezers	0.7	33	6.5
Cigarettes	1.3	21	2.2
Solid detergent	1.7	n.a.	3.8
Integrated steel	2.6	44	11.0
Sulphuric acid	2.7	n.a.	1.5
Breweries	2.9	48	5.0
Automobile storage batteries	4.6	24	4.6
Anti-friction bearings	5.9	n.a.	8.0
Petroleum refining	6.0	41	4.8
Paint and varnish	6.3	159	4.4
Portland cement	6.6	24	26.0
Glass bottles	7.2	n.a.	11.0
Cotton and synthetic broad-woven fabric	17.4	n.a.	7.6
Bricks	32.0	78	37.5
Bakeries	40.8	2,275	11.3
Non-rubber shoes	59.2	206	1.5

Sources: P.K. Gorecki, *Economies of Scale and Efficient Plant Size in Canadian Manufacturing Industries* (Ottawa, n.d.), Table 6.4; Dominion Bureau of Statistics, *Manufacturing Industries of Canada, 1967*, Catalogue No. 31-203 (Ottawa).
Notes: *N.B. that these data are 10 years old.
n.a. = not available.

niques, the definition of an MES plant in a given industry is based on the calculations of the engineers who design plants and machinery for that industry.) The results are set out in Table 3.3. In only one of the industries in Gorecki's sample did the estimates come close to matching (the closest was in non-rubber shoes, where the survivor technique indicated a size of 1 and the engineering technique a size of 1.7).

Gorecki's data, although not strictly comparable, give some support to Eastman and Stykolt's hypothesis that firms in Canada's oligopolistic, protected markets construct less-than-MES plants: "surviving" plants were much smaller than minimum efficient scale. The highly competitive market necessary to force firms to employ plants of at least MES is not present in Canada. In many industries in Canada, even four MES plants would supply more than the entire domestic market. The firms in Canada's tight oligopolistic industries could not construct MES plants without infringing on the market share of their competitors and precipitating a price war.

One major caveat to this whole line of analysis is the use at the plant level of engineering or survey MES estimates that do not include transport costs.

Table 3.3

Size of MES Plant Expressed as a
Percentage of Industry Size, Canada, 1967

| | Size of MES Plant | |
Industry	Survivor Estimate, 1961-66	Engineering Estimate
Petroleum refining	1.1	16.7
Non-rubber shoes	1.0	1.7
Integrated steel	0.2	38.5
Refrigerators and freezers	3.7	142.9
Automobile storage batteries	4.3	21.7
Bakeries	0.3	2.5
Bricks	1.4	3.1

Source: Adapted from Gorecki, *op. cit.*

For example, Scherer calculated that Canada's domestic market could be served by 2.9 MES breweries and 6.6 MES cement plants, yet the four largest firms in each industry operate respectively 36 breweries and 16 cement plants. If transport costs are added to the cost of production and delivered costs became the criterion, then the MES of these plants would surely decrease, especially for Canada's widely dispersed market.

The calculation of MES using engineering techniques overstates the scale disadvantage of Canadian firms and understates their relative efficiency. The studies using these estimates support the conclusion that firms in Canada have constructed plants at below MES to reduce delivered costs by serving a small market located near the plant. Many of the market areas for industries in Canada are protected from foreign competition by transport costs, and thus firms can operate small, widely dispersed plants to serve these isolated markets without fear of competition from large-scale foreign firms. On the other hand, given the geographic concentration of most Canadian manufacturing industry in Ontario and Quebec and its orientation toward purely Canadian markets, firms located in the northern United States face more or less the same transport costs to Canadian markets, but can operate at large scale, since they produce for both the Canadian and U.S. markets. The tariff structure in both the United States and Canada therefore plays a major role in creating and preserving an economic environment in which scale-inefficient firms can survive. In addition, the high degree of foreign ownership may further restrict both import competition and export possibilities and thereby encourage below-MES operation.

Scherer and researchers for the Commission were in agreement on the effects of several variables they measured in statistical studies. They found that within a given industry the percentage of firms operating at efficient scale increased with the size of the market, industry concentration, the size of cost penalties for operating below MES, and growth in demand, and decreased with transport costs. One piece of research suggested that this percentage increased with export intensity and import competition and decreased with the rate of effective tariff protection, foreign control and product differentiation.

The direction of these effects "makes sense". The larger the market size relative to MES, the more MES plants can be constructed. The higher the concentration, the greater the probability that the new capacity constructed to meet increased demand will be MES. The greater the growth rate of market size, and the greater the increment in capacity required, the greater the probability that new plants will be MES, or that existing plant capacity will be expanded to MES. The higher the transport costs, the greater the incentive to construct small, geographically dispersed plants. The greater the cost penalty for below-MES operation, the greater the incentive to construct MES plants. The greater the protection from foreign competition, the less the incentive to produce at MES. The greater the export intensity, and the larger the market, the more MES plants can be constructed in an industry.

Product Economies of Scale

In their preoccupation with plant (and multiplant) economies of scale, many observers have given only casual attention to the economies of scale of specific products. Yet these product-specific economies of scale are perhaps the most important source of production inefficiency in Canada. For example, many of Dominion Textile's plants are as large as those of textile firms in the United States and much larger than MES, but Dominion Textile Limited produces significantly more lines of textiles per plant than do U.S. textile firms. Similarly, to provide a full range of nuts and bolts, The Steel Company of Canada, Limited (Stelco), has some product runs that are much shorter than those of its competitors in the United States and Japan. The Canadian plants have much greater down time, wastage and learning costs than do U.S. plants.

These diseconomies of small-scale production at the product level have been largely neglected; yet they are often highly significant. Gorecki has made rough calculations for several industries to show the cost disadvantage of operating plants of the scale found in Canada. As indicated in Table 3.2, these cost disadvantages would be somewhat less than 10% for plants operating at only one-third MES in most industries. It should also be noted, however, that in many industries, particularly those producing a homogeneous product, a cost disadvantage of even 5% would lead to an overwhelming competitive disadvantage.

Gorecki's calculations do not include the penalties of multiproduct production within one plant. In work for the Economic Council, E. C. West analyzed both price and productivity performance in Canada vis-à-vis the United States (*Canada-United States Price and Productivity Differences in Manufacturing Industries, 1963*). His results indicated that about one-third of the variation in productivity performance between industries was associated with a scale effect: industries with a large gross output relative to the United States also displayed higher productivity relative to the United States. On the other hand, his analysis detected no relationship between relative productivity performance and relative gross output per establishment. This suggested that the economies of scale realized with large volume output most likely emanated not from differences in size of establishment, but from greater specialization within particular establishments.

A detailed industry study of Canadian productivity by the Department of Industry, Trade and Commerce, *Establishment Size and Productivity in Manufacturing Industries in Canada, 1973* (1976), suggests that plant size had no significant influence on productivity, except in a very few industries. The study does not support the view that productivity can be increased through increases in plant size alone. It does suggest that a large part of the problem may be the way production is organized *within* Canadian plants. This would be consistent with the view of the Economic Council that the cause of inefficiency at the plant level lies in the larger number of products manufactured within Canadian plants.

This certainly is not a new idea. The Royal Commission on Canada's Economic Prospects observed this phenomenon in 1957. They pointed out that if very long, standardized runs can be achieved, it may be possible to employ different production techniques using specialized machinery and to realize substantial savings in reduced idle time between runs. Scherer has illustrated how in small and medium-sized antifriction bearings operations a job-lot method was used, while those operations producing larger volumes adopted a straight-line operation. He indicated that manufacturing cost savings as high as 50% could be gained by shifting from the job-lot to the straight-line method. This illustrates an extreme case in which product-specific economies can be more important than plant-specific economies.

Scherer *et al.* go on to conclude that product-specific economies of scale in 4 and possibly as many as 7 of the sample of 12 industries examined were more important than plant-specific economies. Eastman and Stykolt found that diversity of output increased costs in such industries as rubber tires and detergents. In interviews conducted for their study on *Scale and Specialization in Canadian Manufacturing*, D. J. Daly *et al.*, found that businessmen claimed that short runs were a major factor in explaining the higher costs in Canada in a wide range of industries. Their discussions with a number of companies about what would happen to levels of output (using the same labor and machinery) if production runs could be more specialized and longer suggested that efficiency gains would be "appreciable—in some cases even dramatic".

It is the wide range of products per plant that is the main focus of the Economic Council of Canada in *Looking Outward*. On the basis of several detailed studies carried out on firms in the European Common Market, the ECC predicted that substantial intra-industry rationalization at the plant level would come about with free trade.

Before leaving the subject of plant and product-level economies of scale, one final example will be given in order to highlight the complicated nature of the whole subject of MES plants and the extreme caution that must be attached to any conclusions drawn from these calculations. In the November 1, 1976, issue of *Business Week*, Emerson Electric Company was reported to be following a strategy of being the low-cost producer in the industry. To achieve this, it had located *small* plants in rural areas where wages were low. If these plants had been observed by the researchers on plant efficiencies of scale, they would have appeared to be below MES, and hence inefficient, high-cost operations. This example is not meant to detract from the work of these researchers, but as a cautionary tale.

Firm-Level Economies of Scale

To this point the advantages of large firms and their component plants have been analyzed in terms of their production capacities. In addition to these, however, firms engage in activities that should be studied in the same light, since economies of scale might also be encountered there. Among the more important of these activities are research and development, management, finance, marketing (advertising and distribution) and risk-taking. The question to be addressed in this section is whether the economies of scale of these activities (if they exist) require a firm size larger than that required by production considerations alone.

Research and Development

Canada has one of the lowest rates of research and development expenditure, on a per capita basis, of Western industrialized nations, and Canadian research and development expenditures are concentrated in the hands of a very few large firms. Some controversy exists about the relationship between a firm's size, the amount of R&D it undertakes, and the output of that R&D. It has proven difficult to construct useful measures of R&D inputs (engineers, R&D expenditures, etc.), outputs (patents, inventions, innovations, etc.), or the relevant size to be measured (plant, division, or firm). Consequently, definitive answers to the question of the relationship between R&D and size are difficult to find.

A related question for Canada is the licensing of foreign product and process technology, rather than its indigenous generation. At present over 90% of the patents in force in Canada are held abroad.

A number of writers have concluded that big business is more conducive to innovative activity than is small business. For example, John Kenneth Galbraith asserts (without empirical evidence) that the costs of technological innovation in modern times are so great that they can be borne only by large firms. He argues further that R&D projects are risky, as well as expensive, and that only large firms can afford to maintain a balanced portfolio of R&D projects, letting the profits from those that succeed pay for those that do not. Others have observed that there are obviously some economies of scale in conducting R&D. A large laboratory can justify the purchase of specialized equipment to make experimentation easier and it can also employ specialists in many disciplines who may interact. R&D projects may also benefit from economies of scale realized in other parts of a large firm's operations. If a large firm has promotional advantages over a small firm it would be able to penetrate markets more rapidly with new products, and thus increase the profitability of developing a product. Also, because they have high volumes of sales, large firms might have an advantage in introducing process innovations, since a new process that reduces costs by a given percentage yields greater total savings to companies producing a larger volume.

The ability to license profitably may also be a function of the size of the firm and its ability to carry out its own R&D. A common form of licensing occurs through cross-licensing; i.e. two firms trade licences for different products or processes. Cross-licensing reduces the costs of technology transfer by reducing the information gap and the perceived risk of both using and selling technology. To engage in this type of activity, a firm must be able to generate its own R&D. Licensing technology instead of developing it indigenously may also place limits on the Canadian firm's export markets, in that the licensing firm will often limit the sale of the licensed products to the Canadian market.

On the other hand, it is also argued that large size can be a disadvantage in facilitating research, development and innovation. In a large corporation with a large administrative structure, the decision to proceed with R&D has to filter through a long chain of command, and this is said to increase the chance that an idea will be rejected. This may result in a bias in large firms away from more imaginative innovations. The inability to get ideas approved by top management could drive the most creative individuals out of large corporate laboratories to go it alone in their own ventures. A related problem might be a propensity for research to become over-organized in large laboratories.

To license effectively, a firm may need to be only large enough to maintain an effective listening post in the world market for technology. A small firm without a major R&D establishment may be better able to incorporate new outside technology since it has few inside researchers with a stake in their own products and processes.

Nevertheless, many briefs received by the Commission, including those from the Canadian Manufacturers' Association, Imperial Oil Limited and the Canadian Pulp and Paper Association, stressed the prevailing view among businessmen that large size is essential for creating successful R&D programs.

Canadian studies of the relationship between size and innovative activity of corporations have been particularly meager. The data source for these studies has been the Statistics Canada series, "Industrial Research and Development Expenditures". Reporting companies include all large companies and those that the Department knows or believes are engaged in research and development. These studies generally support the conclusion that companies in some size categories are more vigorous than others in advancing technology, even though the pattern is not consistent.

The bulk of the evidence indicates that, among firms engaged in research and development, R&D increases more than proportionally with scale up to a certain size and then decreases as a proportion of sales. As Scherer summarized, "relative effort tends to increase with size up to a point and then decline, with middle size firms devoting the most effort relative to their size". He drew a similar conclusion on the basis of his own research: "A little bit of bigness— up to sales levels of roughly $75 million to $200 million—is good for invention and innovation. But beyond the threshold further bigness adds little or nothing, and it carries the danger of diminishing the effectiveness of inventive and innovative performance" (*Industrial Market Structure and Economic Performance*).

Scherer's sample of firms was taken from *Fortune's* directory of the 500 largest American firms. To put his remark about "a little bit of bigness" into better perspective from the Canadian point of view, in 1964 (the closest year to that in Scherer's study for which data were available in Canada), out of Canada's largest 100 non-financial corporations, only 40 had annual sales exceeding $200 million, 49 exceeded $135 million and 68 exceeded $75 million.

Canadian studies on the relationship between innovation and size have been confined mainly to the determinants of research and development expenditures. Until very recently, these studies dealt with specific cases and with tentative statistical analyses. Research in the area was done for the Commission by McFetridge, Caves and several others. One study attempted to determine the relationship between size and R&D intensity and concluded that a company's own commitment of funds to R&D increased with size as measured by sales and employment. In two very important industries, electrical products and some chemical products, we found that R&D increased more than proportionately with size after a sales threshold was reached. This threshold was very high, in excess of $200 million. The analysis indicated that beyond a sales size of approximately $230 million, a firm's self-financing R&D would decline relative to sales. (Note that this is close to Scherer's estimates above.) Such findings do not take account of inter-industry differences in the relationship between size and innovation, or of such factors as variation in the potential for innovation in specific industries.

In 1976 in the *Canadian Journal of Economics*, J. D. Howe and D. G. McFetridge analyzed "The Determinants of R&D Expenditures" by industry and were able to account for inter-industry variations. They found that the principal determinants of R&D expenditures were current sales, cash flow and government incentive grants.

In their work for the Commission, McFetridge and his associates found that larger firms in some industries seemed able to make better use of a given R&D budget than did smaller firms. More specifically, they found that patent activity in some industries increased more than proportionately in relation to the increase in past R&D expenditures. In examining the effect of firm size on the average product of R&D in three industries, they found that an increase in firm size resulted in an increase in the number of patents resulting from a given R&D outlay as follows:

1. in the electrical industry, among the larger firms;
2. in the chemical industry, among firms with relatively large R&D budgets;

3. in the machinery industry, among firms with relatively small R&D budgets.

McFetridge concluded that it was difficult to generalize from these findings and there is no compelling evidence of a general tendency for innovative activity to rise more than proportionally with firm size.

In a brief to the Commission, Wrigley estimated the expense of a major, continuous R&D operation and the volume of sales necessary to support it: $20 million per product division.

Harold Crookell, Leonard Wrigley and Peter Killing (in a forthcoming book) have examined the ability of Canadian firms to generate R&D continuously either internally or by licensing. Instead of relying on aggregate data from a large number of firms, they conducted extensive interviews with firms in Canada, the United States and United Kingdom. Their conclusion is that Canadian firms lack the scale and the local market size to generate continuous R&D profitably. This is not to say that small firms cannot generate new products, but simply that small firms usually cannot do so on the continuous basis necessary to remain competitive internationally in the long run. This conclusion has led to Crookell's proposal that Canadian firms be given tax incentives to grow large enough to carry out continuous, profitable R&D.

These studies can lead only to very tentative conclusions. There seems to be sufficient evidence to suggest that large corporate size does confer advantages in carrying out research and development, as measured by expenditures. However, large corporate size does not seem to be a prerequisite for participation in the innovative process, and the benefits accruing to large firms seem to be confined to the later stages of the process, i.e. investment and development.

There have been no studies relating the size of the firm to its ability to license technology or use licensed technology effectively. This is an area of major importance to Canada which should be addressed in future research.

Administration
    As yet, no way has been found to measure the effectiveness of management as a function of scale. Desmarais depicts the modern manager at the control center of a diversified empire: Power has a headquarters staff of 22 to control and manage a $575 million empire. With decentralized management techniques, Desmarais sees no natural limit to the size of the modern, diversified firm. McDougald of Argus, on the other hand, sees serious dangers for operating firms that diversify beyond their areas of product expertise.

Economies of management at the firm level (for both single and multi-plant firms) may result from certain administrative and service activities requiring a staff of roughly fixed and indivisible size over a broad range of production levels. If this is true, the unit costs of these functions will decline as corporate output increases. The multiplant, multiproduct firm can average out fluctuations in demand for staff services, thus securing better staff utilization and carrying proportionally smaller reserves against its relatively flat demand peaks. Large companies can use a greater division of labour, employing specialists in such fields as linear programming and arbitration law, where small firms must do without or make do with less intensively trained personnel. The external market for these management services often does not permit their efficient use on an irregular basis.

Size may also have its disadvantages. As with research and development, the large administrative staff necessary to run big corporations may frustrate young, imaginative managers, and the added layers of bureaucracy needed to maintain control may lead to delay, mistakes and unnecessary costs.

If there are economies of management at the firm level, what impact might they have on cost and profit performance? A very rough indication of the magnitude of management costs in relation to operating costs can be made by finding what percentage the wages of administrative, office and other non-production employees formed of the total costs of production. In Canadian manufacturing as a whole, this figure was 9.8% in 1975. Studies on the relationship between size and administrative staff levels come to no firm conclusions, but Scherer et al. conclude that in only a few cases did management costs rise less than proportionally with size. For most firms, Scherer concludes that larger size brought higher unit administrative costs.

Concerning the quality of management and administrative staff personnel, Scherer et al. "perceived no obvious association between firm size and such attributes of managerial quality as dynamism, intelligence, awareness, and skill in interpersonal relations." Larger companies did display the expected tendency to maintain a wider array of staff specialists, but on the other hand, staff personnel in smaller companies had learned to wear several hats well.

The Commission received both briefs and testimony on the subject of management as it related to conglomerate organizations. Wrigley and Leighton in their briefs expressed the view that in both theory and practice there exist significant economies of scale in the use of top management which increase the efficiency of large, diversified firms. Testimony by executive officers representing such large Canadian firms as Canadian Pacific Limited, The Royal Bank of Canada and The Investors Group extolled the benefits that their subsidiaries derived from the head office staff who provided aid in such management activities as coordination, financing and long-range strategic planning. Rothman's of Pall Mall Canada Limited and Redpath Industries Limited pointed out increases in the size, employment and profitability of their subsidiaries after acquisition. However the actual performance of conglomerates in both the United States and Canada does not seem to support the contention that management economies in a conglomerate organization put the smaller non-diversified firm at a disadvantage.

A. Michael Spence, in work with Richard Caves for the Commission, showed that Canadian industries have a greater proportion of non-production workers than do comparable U.S. industries. The difference is probably a function of both the greater diversity in the output of Canadian plants and the smaller size of Canadian firms. These findings suggest that significant management savings might be forthcoming if Canadian activities were less diversified.

Richard Caves and Masu Uekusa, in *Industrial Organization in Japan,* found that administrative costs as a percentage of total costs declined for large firms.

Marketing
ADVERTISING AND DISTRIBUTION ECONOMIES OF SCALE

Does a large firm have a cost advantage over a small firm due to advantages in sales promotion? The answer is almost certainly "yes", but in answering the question one should differentiate between real and pecuniary economies of scale. The cost of advertising for the firm may decrease with size either because of the market power of larger firms in purchasing advertising or because real cost savings are achieved. Large firms may enjoy several kinds of advertising economies of scale, both pecuniary and real, over small firms. Advertising campaigns often need to attain a high threshold level to achieve their maximum effectiveness, so that there may be high absolute returns to advertising expenditures up to some high level, after which diminishing returns set in. Advertising messages are purchased from various information media, and advertiser economies are available where the price per message declines as the number of purchases increases. What percentage of these discounts reflects real cost savings to the media instead of buying power by the advertiser is not known

Large firms often create brand images for their products which introduce artificial economies of scale in marketing and thus serve as barriers to entry for small firms. For example, in many consumer goods industries, a new product must be introduced with large advertising expenditures, a substantial barrier for most small firms. Joe Bain concluded in his study (*Barriers to New Competition*) of 20 American industries that product differentiation was "of at least the same general order of importance [notably in consumer goods] ... as are economies of large-scale production and distribution" in giving established market leaders a price or cost advantage over rivals. In Scherer *et al.*'s recent work, brand image was found to confer a price advantage at the wholesale level of from 1% to 50% across their sample of eight consumer industries. Image differentiation was found to be substantially important in only two of these industries, brewing and cigarettes. A strong brand image in these two industries was found to be associated with a wholesale price advantage of from 8% to 40% in brewing and from 10% to 50% in cigarettes. Only in brewing was multiplant size essential to the exploitation of this brand image advantage. John Labatt Limited testified before us that advertising economies enabled breweries to produce a wider range of higher-quality products at a given price.

Are there systematic relationships between firm size and the profitability of advertising? Again the only measurable statistic is advertising expenditures. The results of a 1974 U.S. study by W. S. Comanor and T. A. Wilson suggest that, in most industries, larger firms spend proportionally more on advertising than do their smaller rivals. However, there were a number of industries where the data showed that large firms smaller than the industry leaders spend proportionately as much as or more than the leading firms. The latter group included most of those industries with high advertising-to-sales ratios. In both groups, however, the very small firms (those ranked below the top 20) spend little on advertising, both absolutely and in relation to sales.

Caves in his work for the Commission found that high ratios of advertising to sales are accompanied by high profits in industries that do not have substantial import competition but are accompanied by low profits in industries exposed to imports. This evidence suggests that the ability of Canadian firms to establish brand images and reap above-average profits has been decreased by foreign competition.

Another strand of evidence points to large marketing and distribution economies of scale. Canadian firms produce far more products within their industries than do firms of comparable size in the United States. This phenomenon is due to a large extent to the costs of selling and distributing products; once the brand name has been established, other products may be sold under that label at little extra cost. A salesman can sell a full line of products as easily as one product. Retail stores have large search, learning and start-up costs associated with their purchases, and so they are more likely to buy products that are part of a full line.

There are ways by which narrow-line firms can escape such preferences: for example, by seeking out that subset of dealers without broad-line preferences, by offering price discounts sufficient to induce middlemen to do their own coordination or repairs and by filling out their lines through purchases from other producers or selling their narrow line for labeling by large buyers. With any of these strategies firms may achieve viability, but at some cost disadvantage.

To what extent were smaller firms able to take advantage of different strategies to offset any disadvantage of marketing practices that were available only to the large firms, and to what extent do these advantages necessitate firm sizes larger than operations of one MES plant? Scherer *et al.* concluded that, for several industries in their study, multiplant firms enjoyed significant cost advantages in advertising over their single-plant rivals. In many industries these pecuniary and real advertising and marketing economies of scale far outweighed production economies of scale.

We think that there is quite compelling evidence of marketing and distribution economies of full-line production which impel a firm in Canada to offer a full line of products, even if it faces substantial production diseconomies of scale for some of the lines it must carry for marketing reasons.

INTERNATIONAL MARKETING

It is often argued that large firms have an advantage in exporting. In their submission to the Commission, officers of MacMillan Bloedel argued that there are great economies of scale in export marketing. Since their brief contains most of the arguments associated with this hypothesis, we quote it at some length:

> International trade...has important implications for MB's scale of operations. If MB did not have substantial size, it would not be a major exporter of Canadian

products. To be successful in international trade in commodities, a company must have large volume of its products available for sale. It must also have access to an adequate supply of raw materials, low cost manufacturing facilities, and a large marketing and transportation organization to sell to and service a variety of foreign markets.

The large volume of forest products MB sells has enabled the Company to develop a worldwide marketing system at minimum unit sales costs.

MB's network of sales agents and subsidiary companies keeps its head office in continuous contact with markets throughout the world and assists it in making long-term marketing plans in an attempt to maximize mill returns and ensure stability for both mill and customer. New markets can be opened when opportunities develop and existing markets can be expanded and services to them improved. With its existing large marketing network, MB has also been able to provide marketing services to smaller Canadian companies whose product volumes do not permit development of such a network.

The theoretical basis of this argument appears to be that there are marketing functions associated with international trade that are indivisible. That is, a certain minimum expenditure on marketing services is required to sell abroad. The small firm spreads these fixed costs over a smaller output and thus operates at a cost disadvantage. This argument assumes that the services required by a firm engaged in international trade cannot be purchased from independent suppliers in small quantities. To the extent that the small firm can obtain market research, selling effort or customs brokerage services from independent specialists in suitably small quantities, it will not necessarily face a cost disadvantage. Recognizing the disadvantages of small size in international markets, several firms (such as Interimco Company Limited) and the federal government have brought many small producers together to form export consortia to bid on large-scale international contracts. Section 32 of the Combines Investigation Act specifically exempts from prosecution agreements or combinations relating only to exports.

In research done for the Commission, McFetridge concluded that export performance was not related to size: "...holding industry and ownership effects constant, firm size exerts no effect on the proportion of sales exported. Large firms are not more 'export intensive' or 'export oriented' than are small firms."

As he pointed out, however, the data samples he used in this study, while better than those in previous studies, were not representative of the total Canadian manufacturing sector. In order to accept his conclusions, we must accept not only the premise that there are no production-cost economies of scale that make large firms more cost competitive, but also that there are no export economies of scale. Such a finding would fly in the face of the evidence in every other country and of analyses conducted by the Department of Industry, Trade and Commerce, where industrial rationalization and export consortia are seen as aids to exports.

Again the question of the relevant measure of size arises. Desmarais in his testimony used the example of Power being small and a hypothetical Power-Argus being larger and hence better able to compete internationally. McDougald, on the other hand, portrayed export performance as a function of the strength of a firm's individual components. That is Massey-Ferguson Limited can compete internationally because of its own size, not because it is part of the Argus group. The Commission concludes that probably both views contain parts of the truth. As demonstrated by the Japanese trading companies, total firm size increases ability to operate in international markets, even when diverse products and services are sold under one group. It is difficult, however, to see how a combination of Massey-Ferguson Limited, Consolidated-Bathurst Limited, Canada Steamship Lines, Limited, plus the other companies in a Power-Argus group, would increase the success of any of the component parts or the company as a whole in export markets.

In developed countries with high labor costs, manufactured exports come from innovative products and manufactured imports from standardized products. Innovation (at least continuous innovation) at the product and process level increases with scale, where scale is defined as the scale of the related product unit, not the firm as a whole. It would seem that in many industries, large scale is a prerequisite to continuous exports. In addition, for many products there is an initial size barrier that must be crossed before continuous exports can be expected. The firm must be able both to generate new products and to sustain the high initial fixed costs necessary to begin overseas operations. There are often substantial start-up costs in penetrating an export market in manufactures, which can usually be sustained only by large firms. Small firms may be able to penetrate the export market via government promotion programs, trade fairs, and participation in export consortia. In general, however, these are expensive ways to compensate for small size.

Financial Advantages of Large Firms

Large firms are said to enjoy cost or access advantages in raising capital in that they may pay lower interest rates on short- and long-term debt than do smaller establishments, they can float debt and equity issues at lower costs per dollar of funds received and they have access to sources of funds not available to smaller firms. The real economies of large size have two bases. Certain more or less fixed transaction costs are incurred in effecting a stock or bond issue. The larger the issue, the lower the cost per dollar of fixed expense incurred. In addition, investors are willing to buy the securities of large firms at interest or profit yields lower than those on securities of small firms. There are a number of reasons given for this willingness. Large firms are better known and have longer earnings records, investments in them are thought to be less risky, in the sense that earnings tend to be more stable, default rarer and the return to the equity holder more predictable. The principal reason, however, appears to be that securities of large firms have established markets and are far more liquid investments.

John Scott, in part of the Caves study for the Commission, showed that the cost of equity capital for firms in Canada decreased with size and diversity. Surprisingly, he also found that the variation in the return to stockholders was greater for more diversified firms. Scott hypothesized that stockholders may have perceived a lower risk in diversified firms and hence were willing to have both lower and more variable returns. He also found some slight evidence that the cost of debt to large, diversified firms was lower.

Commission staff studies and other empirical work indicate that large firms do in fact obtain lower interest rates on bank borrowing and that the difference is in the order of one or two percentage points. Empirical evidence also substantiates the prediction that there are economies of scale in floating stock issues. Caves testified before the Commission that there was evidence of real economies of scale in finance for firms in the United States, Japan and Europe.

On the question of whether larger diversified firms allocate their capital more efficiently than do smaller firms, the Commission was unable to detect this in the financial performance of large conglomerates. In fact, as we explain more fully in Chapter 5, our research showed that highly diversified firms had a lower return on their investment and lower returns to their stockholders than did other firms.

On the basis of the above studies the Commission concludes that large companies do have a cost and access financing advantage vis-à-vis smaller companies, but that this advantage does not seem to be reflected in better performance. In fact, larger diversified firms have both a lower return and a greater variation in this return than do non-diversified firms.

Economies of Scale in Risk-Taking

For several reasons, as its size increases, a firm's ability and willingness to take on increasingly risky projects also increase. Larger firms will have a greater number and often a greater variety of projects in which they are engaged at any one time. They can more easily "bet the averages" without as great a fear of being wiped out if any one project fails. The sum of the risky projects that two small firms are willing to undertake by themselves is therefore less than the number of risky projects that one larger firm would be willing to undertake. Put another way, for the same risky project, a small firm will usually demand a higher rate of return than will a larger one because the former requires compensation for its higher perceived risk.

Two types of projects are especially risky and usually require large firms to undertake them: research and development, and projects related to energy. R&D is risky for four reasons: (1) there is a wide variation in its possible outcome; (2) the cash outflow before a cash inflow is often very large, sometimes into the hundreds of millions of dollars; (3) the length of time between outflow and inflow is often very long; (4) the payback time is highly variable. Large firms can balance several R&D projects against one another and thereby reduce the impact of many of these risks.

By tax and other incentives, the government, of course, can decrease some of the risk perceived by firms when they undertake R&D projects. In the past, however, the government's efforts in this area have not been notably successful.

Energy and projects related to it are risky for many of the same reasons as R&D projects: they are very large, and the size of the payback is uncertain and may be delayed. Even the huge integrated oil firms feel uncomfortable about undertaking some large, risky projects and form joint ventures to do so. In several instances, the government has stepped in when it felt that insufficient investment was taking place in high-risk areas, but in neither Canada nor other countries has this course proved a complete solution to the problems posed by high-cost, high-risk projects.

The risks associated with R&D and energy projects are already large and will increase in the future. For private firms to undertake these projects, they must increase in size to realize the substantial economies of scale in risk-bearing.

Summary

A great deal has been written about the effect of scale on the efficiency of Canadian industry. Undoubtedly Canadian plants in many industries are smaller than those in other countries. But, as Scherer *et al.* demonstrate, when the low end of the plant size distribution is excluded, Canadian plants are not, in general, very much smaller. The fact that the Canadian market is only one-tenth the size of the U.S. market does not imply that industrial plants in Canada are one-tenth the size of U.S. plants as well. Plant-specific economies of scale, which have been the main focus of most of the studies, are significant in a few Canadian industries but have not, in general, imposed a major cost disadvantage on Canadian firms in serving the Canadian market.

There are two more important sources of scale inefficiency in Canada. First, to compete with imports and to satisfy consumer demand, Canadian firms in tariff-protected oligopolies produce a full line of products. Since each plant produces a much more diverse line of products than do similar-sized plants in the United States, Canadian plants employ less specialized equipment, have a higher proportion of set-up and downtime, and experience fewer of the economies of scale that arise from "learning by doing". Secondly, because of the degree of foreign ownership, the small size of firms, and high product diversity within firms, firms in Canada are unwilling or unable to undertake continuous research and development on products and processes, which is necessary to compete both at home and abroad. The cost disadvantage that this low level of R&D imposes on Canadian-owned firms is often significant but hard to quantify. Many Canadian-owned firms do not manufacture products that compete directly with foreign products or products of foreign-owned subsidiaries. With low R&D, Canadian-owned firms must compete at the price-sensitive end of the product line or purchase new products and processes on the imperfect and often costly market for licences. For firms operating in a country with high labor and capital costs, this is not an attractive position. Many of these problems can be attributed to the presence of high Canadian tariff barriers, which have encouraged both scale-inefficient production and foreign ownership in many industries.

In addition, large firms seem to be able to realize both real and pecuniary economies of scale in finance, marketing, management, and perhaps elsewhere.

These economies of scale constantly motivate Canadian firms to form larger units.

Our overall conclusion is that plant-level economies of scale, which are usually cited in discussions of size, are often of little relevance in evaluating firm size, vis-à-vis product economies, multiplant economies and economies of firm size. It is our conclusion that in many industries firm-level economies in Canada justify larger-sized businesses that do plant-level economies. How large a firm is justified depends on the industry, but it may be sizable. The major firm-level economy is probably found in risk-taking ability, in undertaking new investment, and in long-term R&D, with the largest firm sizes probably justified in high-risk sectors such as energy exploration, aerospace and similar fields. We emphasize, however, that in these areas plant-level or product-level economies are less important than past discussions of the topic in Canada have suggested.

The Commission recognizes that achieving economies of scale is only one of many motivations that may lead firms to expand. Other motivations, such as managerial empire-building and the desire to obtain market power in concentrated markets for the purpose of restraining competition, will be discussed in subsequent chapters. This chapter has dealt solely with cost considerations that encourage firms to increase their size, and serves as background to the remaining chapters on the economics of corporate concentration.

Chapter 4

Competition and Oligopoly

Our hearings and research have shown that most industries in Canada are quite concentrated: they contain a relatively few large firms, which exercise economic power in the markets they serve. This high level of concentration was discussed at length in Chapter 2. In this chapter we look at some of the implications and consequences of this concentrated structure. We look first at the objectives of the market and price systems, then at theories of competition as they apply to industries with different structures. Finally, we propose an approach to the regulation of the behavior of firms in concentrated industries.

The Role of the Market System

Each of the world's economies has to accomplish certain basic economic tasks: to determine what is to be produced, where, how and in what quantities; to allocate the goods and services produced; to replace and expand the stock of capital goods; to distribute material benefits among members of the society; and to interact with other economies through international trade and investment.

These activities may be carried out within a variety of institutional arrangements ranging along a spectrum from central planning and control (as in many Communist countries) to a system of decentralized, but interconnected markets. In Canada, economic activities take place under a mixture of arrangements, with emphasis largely on self-regulating markets, but with much and increasing resort to government intervention through regulatory boards, Crown corporations and other forms of government ownership, legislative restrictions, taxation and subsidy programs and, more recently, wage and price controls.

On the whole, although numerous constraints are placed on its operation, in Canada we continue to rely primarily on the market mechanism (also called the price system or price mechanism) to allocate resources, adjust production and consumption, distribute income and bring about economic growth. The allocation of resources through the market mechanism does not imply that firms are privately or publicly owned, nor does it say anything about the degree of competition among those enterprises. It implies only that economic units are largely autonomous with regard to the decisions they make and that they deal with one another chiefly through voluntary exchanges of goods and services.

The performance of an economic system can be measured according to the following criteria: (1) the efficiency of resource allocation: are capital, labor and raw materials used in such a way that the value of output is maximized? (2) growth: is the economy accumulating the necessary capital and technological skill to expand output and increase real per capita income? (3) stability: does the economic system provide adequate and stable employment and reasonable price stability? (4) distribution of income and output: how equitably is the output distributed among the people in the country?

In addition, in recent years public attention has focused on a set of more subjective measures of performance called social indicators. These provide measures of the quality of life rather than measures of quantity of production or efficiency of resource utilization. Examples include measures of housing, employment and environmental quality. This chapter will focus on some of the economic consequences of various market arrangements.

There are almost always significant trade-offs involved in choosing among economic policy alternatives. For example, using traditional policies, reductions in unemployment may be attained only at the cost of increased inflation; increased job satisfaction or maintenance of more "human-scale" enterprise may lead to some loss of efficiency. The fact that such trade-offs exist and that judgments tend to be highly subjective are two reasons the Commission has heard much conflicting evidence from witnesses and in briefs on what the market system and the role of large enterprises "should be". Consequently, we have had difficulty in formulating highly specific arguments and conclusions concerning the role and impact of large firms in our economy and the policies to be adopted in the presence of concentrations of economic power. In this chapter, we address the implications of concentration within individual industries for the efficient allocation of resources, for growth, and for stability.

In Chapter 2 we discussed changing industry and aggregate concentration ratios in Canada. As shown in that chapter, most industries in Canada are highly concentrated: a few firms produce a high proportion of the output of the industry. We concluded that concentration both within industries and overall has remained fairly stable in recent years. To understand how the Canadian economy functions and to make recommendations to improve its performance, we must understand the behavior and performance of firms in concentrated or oligopolistic industries.

Economists who study industry organization have developed a methodology for analyzing industries which consists of three components: the *structure* of the industry (concentration, product differentiation, barriers to entry, potential competition, cost structures, vertical integration, growth in demand, foreign competition); the *conduct* of firms within the industry (the nature of price and non-price competition and anticompetitive practices); and the *performance* of firms (efficiency in the use of capital, labor, and raw materials, profit levels and technological progressiveness).

Barriers to Entry

Before describing the four main types of market structures, a short description of the concept of "barriers to entry" is necessary. Barriers to entry are those factors that impede or prevent the entry of new firms into an industry. They can be classified into four groups.

1. Economies of scale and transport costs. If the minimum efficient scale of a firm (MES) is large relative to the demand in the industry, and if the cost penalties for below-MES operation are substantial, a new firm would have to enter the market at such a large scale that the combined output could be sold only at substantially reduced prices, perhaps below cost. High transport costs are also a barrier to entry, since they decrease the effective size of a market area and inhibit or prevent competition from firms outside the area.
2. Government-imposed or legislated restrictions such as patent protection, legal monopolies and cartels, restrictions on foreign investment and tariffs.
3. Product differentiation by existing firms through high-level and continuous advertising of brand names, company reputations or distribution outlets.
4. Absolute cost advantages arising from control of resources, technology, inability of some firms to acquire capital or raw materials, and vertical integration of firms in the industry.

The higher these barriers to entry, the more difficult it is for firms to enter the industry, the more concentrated the industry will be and the less competition there may be among firms in it. Barriers to entry have important implications for the concentration of industry, the evolution of that concentration and the conduct of the firms within various industries.

Types of Markets

On the basis of an analysis of the structure of an industry, the behavior of firms within that industry and the performance of the industry, economists classify industries into four main categories: atomistically competitive; monopolistic; monopolistically competitive; and oligopolistic. We describe, briefly, each of these market categories or models and then examine closely the oligopolistic model, which is by far the most complex of the four, but also the most relevant to an understanding of the Canadian economic system.

An atomistically competitive industry is one in which price and total industry output are determined by the market and firms have no individual discretion in setting the price of their products: firms are price-takers. Atomistically competitive industries are usually characterized as having many firms whose output is small in relation to total industry output, low barriers to entry for new firms or to expansion of output by established ones, perfect information and a homogeneous product (salt, for example). These conditions are even approximately met in only a very few industries: some sectors of agriculture and small retail establishments in service industries are the standard examples.

In atomistically competitive industries, all efficient firms are expected to earn a "normal" or competitive return on invested capital over time. If profits rise above this normal level (because of an increase in demand or a decrease in costs), existing firms will expand their output and new firms will enter the industry (since the barriers to entry are low or nonexistent), thereby lowering prices and profits.

If the markets in all industries in an economy are competitive, returns to capital will be comparable in all industries after adjustment for risk, since there are no impediments to moving these resources to another use if such a move would increase their returns. In addition, in atomistically competitive markets the marginal cost of production for any given product (including a normal return on capital) will equal the marginal value of the product to consumers, as measured by the price consumers are willing to pay for it. Thus, if all industries are competitive, resources will tend to be allocated efficiently from both production and consumption points of view. Although atomistically competitive markets are efficient in allocating resources at any one time, their effect on growth and technological progress, income distribution, and stability is not certain.

The importance of the atomistic-competition model is not that it represents reality; it does not. Rather the model and the assumption that it produces a desirable result for society are the origin of the belief by a generation of freshman economics students that many buyers and sellers are "better" than few; that "artificial" product differentiation may not be in the public interest and that more information and disclosure are always better than less. It is sometimes forgotten that all the conditions underlying the model must exist simultaneously before we can predict an outcome of efficient resource allocation. If only some of the conditions exist it cannot be assumed that firms will behave more closely to the ideal. In particular, striving for competition only in the general sense of a large number of rival producers in an industry does not guarantee that resources will be allocated efficiently.

At the other end of the spectrum, a monopoly industry is one in which there is only one firm, protected by high barriers to entry (such as large economies of scale, patents, a captive source of supply, or government regulation) and insignificant import competition. A monopolist has the power to restrict his output below that which would exist in an atomistically competitive industry in order to raise prices and profits. The price consumers pay for the product is normally greater than the cost of its production (including a normal profit). Not only does the monopolist usually make above-average profits, but productive resources are not allocated efficiently within the economy. The monopolist may also take some of his monopoly profits in an "easy life" and not produce at the optimal level of efficiency, with costs higher than they would be if he were faced with the pressures of competition. This phenomenon, which economists call "X-inefficiency", may be the most important cost arising from a monopoly.

The extreme case of monopoly is similarly of limited value in describing reality in Canada. Monopoly in the pure sense can arise only when there is no ready substitute for the monopolist's product or service. When this occurs on a large scale, government tries either to regulate the market or to place the monopolist under public ownership. Examples are found in telephone service, water supply, sewer services and railroad freight transport. Monopoly power is also constrained where there are close substitutes for the good in question. Railroads may be monopolists in transporting high-bulk commodities over long distances but, except in rare circumstances, they have no monopoly power in low-bulk or other intercity freight transport. Products such as concrete, steel, aluminium and even wood may be technically unique, but nevertheless they may be interchangeable for some purposes.

The real importance of the monopoly concept is not that pure unregulated monopoly exists in the Canadian economy; it does not. However, there are many cases of partial monopoly, characterized by an ability to set somewhat above-competitive prices, to restrict output and not to minimize costs. The exercise of such market power by firms leads, as would pure monopoly, to an inefficient allocation of resources and usually to above-average profits over time. Hence there is a feeling that society must intervene to regulate monopoly and market power, and should probably regulate businesses that seem even moderately monopolistic.

Very few Canadian industries fall into either the atomistically competitive or monopoly categories. From a structural standpoint, most industries have two or more firms and from a behavioral standpoint firms in most industries have some discretion in setting price, that is they have some market power. Economists refer to these intermediate industries as imperfectly competitive. Imperfectly competitive industries can then be further subdivided into those that are monopolistically competitive and those that are oligopolistic.

Monopolistically competitive industries are characterized by a large number of competitors, relatively low barriers to entry, price and non-price competition, and very limited monopoly power in the hands of the sellers. Representative monopolistically competitive industries are most service, most retailing and many manufacturing industries, including furniture- and garment-manufacturing and printing. Firms in these monopolistically competitive industries attempt to differentiate their products or services and are likely to follow independent pricing strategies. Some firms, as a result of locational advantages, marketing acumen or superior management and employees, may be able to earn above-competitive profits over an extended time. However, the threat of new entry into these industries is so real that it severely limits the ability of established firms to exercise monopoly power. Most important in regard to resource allocation and range of choice for consumers, the firms in these industries, as a group, will typically offer a wide variety of price, quality, design and service combinations from which to choose. If they seek it out, consumers are likely to be offered by one or more producers a price approximating that which would prevail under atomistic competition. Prices in these industries will closely approximate atomistically competitive ones and adverse effects on resource allocation and efficiency will tend to be minimal.

An oligopolistic industry is one that has only a few leading firms. These firms recognize that their pricing and output decisions are interdependent and seek to act on that realization. Firms in oligopolistic industries choose their strategy knowing that the other firms in the industry will react if their position (market share, prices, profits and growth) is threatened. Oligopolistic industries have considerable barriers to entry (economies of scale, branding, technological know-how, etc.) and often only minor import competition.

Most manufacturing and financial industries in Canada are oligopolies. The barriers to entry both natural (e.g., production economies of scale) and artificial (government regulation, advertising, control of distribution channels and vertical integration) are typically high in these industries, and firms often strive to make them higher to deter entry. Many of our recommendations for competition policy in this and succeeding chapters will be directed toward decreasing such barriers to entry in an attempt to allow industries to achieve their "natural" level of concentration, and the firms in them to behave as competitively as possible.

Structure, Conduct and Performance

For both competitive and monopoly markets the relationships among structure, conduct and performance are quite clearly defined. In competitive markets, concentration and barriers to entry are low, firms compete on the basis of price, profits are normal and resources are allocated efficiently. In a monopoly, barriers to entry are high, prices are high relative to costs, profits are usually above normal, and resources are allocated inefficiently. In oligopolistic industries, however, the link between conduct or behavior and structure is no longer determinate. There are many patterns of behavior possible (and observed) for firms within an oligopolistic industry. At one extreme, firms in an oligopolistic industry may desire and be able to collude (either explicitly, as in a cartel, or tacitly) to set near-monopoly prices and reap near-monopoly profits. At the other extreme, they may engage in cutthroat competition that drives prices and profits in the short run below even those that would prevail in a perfectly competitive industry. Thus, an oligopolistic industry may have output and prices such that profits are near normal and resources are allocated as efficiently as in a competitive industry, or have near-monopoly prices, output and profits and hence inefficient resource allocation. The essential difference among firms in monopolistic, oligopolistic and competitive industries is the discretion they have to behave anticompetitively. This varies with the degree of their market power.

The end of the spectrum nearest which an oligopolistic industry operates depends on the behavior of the firms in the industry. This behavior is strongly influenced by such structural factors as the height of barriers to entry, the threat of entry into the industry through direct investment by foreign and domestic firms, the nature of the product (the size and growth of demand, the number of close substitute products and the stage in the product life cycle) and the amount of import competition. Nevertheless it is a significant element, which, although constrained by these structural factors, has an independent dynamism of its own.

The Structuralist and Behavioralist Views

It is within oligopolistic industries with their wide range of behavior and performance that a large part of the Canadian economy operates and competition policy must address the problems these industries create. Yet economists (and regulators) have great difficulty in reaching unambiguous conclusions about the relationships among market structure, behavior and performance in oligopolistic industries, on which to base economic policy recommendations.

On the one hand are the "structuralists", who believe that market structure strongly influences performance. This structuralist view is reflected in the industrial policy of governments in many industrial countries, and is especially strong in the United States. In a 1971 study, *Concentration in Manufacturing Industries in Canada*, the Canadian Department of Consumer and Corporate Affairs set out the theory on which their analysis of industry conditions is based:

> Economic theory and actual experience suggest that the level of concentration is an important determinant of market behaviour. Other things being equal, the smaller the number of leading firms which account for a large proportion of an industry's output, the more likely it is for monopolistic practices to prevail. In highly concentrated industries, firms have considerable latitude and discretionary power in making decisions regarding price, output, and related matters. . . . when industry concentration is low, the existence of many rival firms forces each to behave independently and . . . market forces rather than individual firms determine the levels of prices and output.

If the structuralists are correct in their observations, officials in charge of enforcing competition policy have a *prima facie* justification for looking at concentrated industries. By acting to initiate change in the concentration of an industry, they may be able to remove deleterious effects on resource allocation and remedy a lack of competition. In Canada, however, government competition policy explicitly recognizes that even if high concentration brings higher prices, higher price-cost margins and profits in some industries (and hence a misallocation of resources), high concentration may also be justified in many of them by significant economies of large-scale operation at both plant and firm levels. This is most obvious in the merger, monopoly and specialization agreement provisions of Bill C-13, the proposed amendment to the Combines Investigation Act introduced in late 1977.

At the opposite end of the spectrum, there are economists and many others, several of whom also appeared before us, who disagree with the structuralist school. Their argument is that the structure of an industry provides no systematic basis to predict the nature of the performance of that industry. At the center of the anti-structuralist, or "behavioralist" approach, is a belief that there are many ever changing, dynamic factors that influence the behavior of firms in an oligopolistic industry. They conclude that the structure-conduct-performance link is not strong in oligopolies for several reasons, notably:

1. The relationship between a firm's behavior and the many elements that constitute the structure of the industry in which it operates is so

complex and industry-specific that no useful generalizations can be made. Firms in industries with the same structure can (and do) behave very differently.

2. Many of the structural aspects of an industry are constantly changing so that the system is continually being disturbed. As changes occur in these structural variables (for example, a change in technology or import competition), the behavior patterns of the industry will become less stable: the complex behavioral relationships among firms may change as they interact with one other through the marketplace even if the overall structure of the industry is unchanged. Firms that at one time had jointly attained near-monopoly prices through collusion or conscious parallel pricing may later engage in cutthroat competition. Several authors have shown that, although on average profits in oligopolistic industries are higher than in competitive ones, the variability of these profits is also higher, apparently because of frequent swings between strong competition and cooperative behavior, and the high capital intensity and unevenness of investment often found in concentrated industries.

3. The behavior of firms is personalized by their owners and managers in dissimilar, unsystematic ways so that firms will interact with one other in unpredictable ways.

Behavioralists argue that structuralists overemphasize the static elements of an industry's structure (such as concentration ratios) and underemphasize the dynamic, competitive, idiosyncratic characteristics. Some proponents of the behavioral case claim that the only really effective barriers to competition in an industry in the long run are those created by government intervention in the form of tariffs, trade programs, quotas and government regulatory bodies. The most articulate advocate of the behavioralist approach to appear before us was Donald Armstrong. On the basis of the analysis in his brief he concluded that when all the dimensions of competition are taken into account and considered in the context of interindustry competition and international trade, high levels of industry concentration as measured by production in Canada (even where such measures are relevant) are in themselves no cause to believe that competition is inadequate. In fact, he asserted that competition may be aided by the presence of large firms.

The Commission thinks that the differences between the stucturalist and behavioralist arguments may often be more apparent than real. Few advocates of the structuralist position deny the importance of those dynamic factors emphasized in the behavioralist approach, particularly in the long run. Few advocates of the structure-conduct-performance paiadigm believe that the concentration ratio is the only important characteristic of any industry's structure. Rather they see industrial structure as composed of numerous components: technology, barriers to entry, demand growth, potential competitors, import penetration, degree of vertical integration, heterogeneity of the firms within the industry, and so on. Bill C-13 recognizes that these other components of industry also influence the behavior and performance of firms and does not condemn concentration industries *per se.*

We conclude that a firm's behavior is strongly influenced by the many elements that make up the structure of its industry. Everything else being equal, as industries become more concentrated the behavior of firms changes as they become more aware of the competitive reaction of other firms in their industry to their output and price decisions, and it becomes easier for firms to coordinate these decisions among themselves. Price-cost margins and industry profits are more likely to be raised above the competitive level as the industry becomes more concentrated. "Everything else" is not often equal, however, and a competition policy in Canada that focuses solely on concentration (even if properly measured) will be misguided.

We think that frequently the market power of firms in oligopolistic industries will be undermined over time by competition or rivalry and by technological and organizational change, so long as the government does not create artificial impediments. We are not so confident that the speed of this natural development will be fast enough to be acceptable to the public. Some industries have high barriers to entry, which they can maintain for a long time. The competition policies we explore in later sections of this chapter can be used to assist or reinforce those forces at work in the economy that are likely to erode these entry barriers and to prevent existing firms from creating new barriers, thereby permitting new firms to enter oligopolistic industries and increase competition. We think government should pursue a competition policy that minimizes the undesirable economic effects of anticompetitive market structures and behavior in the short run and supports the dynamic, long-run market forces leading to more efficient market structures. Such a policy must focus on deterring the creation and maintenance of artificial barriers to entry and on facilitating innovation and adaptation in the form of new products and methods of production and distribution.

Conduct and Performance in Oligopolistic Industries

As concentration within an industry increases, the firms within it are ever more aware of their competitive interdependence in setting price and output levels and in their other strategic decisions. This section will examine some of the patterns of behavior found in oligopolistic industries in Canada and their effects on industry performance.

Pricing under Oligopoly

A wide variety of price-output combinations may exist in oligopolistic industries, ranging from those one might find under perfect competition to the same prices and quantity as in a pure monopoly. Most descriptions of pricing behavior in oligopolistic industries start with the facts that the pricing, output and other strategic decisions of one firm are made with a view to their impact on all other firms in the market and that the firms involved quickly recognize their interdependence. Managers of firms in competitive and oligopolistic industries recognize that profits will be higher when cooperative policies are pursued than when each firm aggressively seeks a larger market share through price competition. But only those in oligopolistic industries are able to coordinate their pricing and output decisions. Cooperative policies do not necessarily imply overt collusion; they may merely reflect a recognition that a price cut by one firm will be quickly matched by competitors and will not lead to significantly greater sales volume in the long run. In a price war total sales revenue for the industry may actually fall. Understandably, firms in oligopolistic industries have every incentive not to engage in price wars. As a result, economists suggest that firms in an oligopolistic industry will exhibit a tendency to maximize collective profits, will approximate the pricing behavior associated with pure monopoly and will compete primarily on a non-price basis once a "stable" price level has been reached.

To ensure any kind of industry stability and joint profit maximization, however, firms must make parallel decisions not only on price but on all major aspects of a transaction, and this is often complex and difficult. Competitors have to offer essentially the same terms of sale, delivery, transport charges, policy on free goods, sample goods and replacement goods, and have to agree on the many aspects of the quality of the goods to be offered (length of life, guarantee, after-sale service, etc.). Each of these components is an integral part of the sale, and thus may determine which firm will win market share. As an example of the difficulty of reaching agreement on even a simple aspect of competition, the International Air Transport Association (a legal cartel which fixes passenger fares on many international airline routes) had to meet in plenary sessions for two days in 1958 to define what was allowable for member airlines to serve as a luncheon sandwich on trans-Atlantic flights.

Several things strongly influence the behavior of firms in their pricing decisions and their ability to coordinate their strategies: the nature of the production and marketing of the product, technology and the rate at which it is changing, the growth in demand, the presence of a low-cost, leading firm, similar cost structures among firms, barriers to entry into the industry, the existence of potential entrants, and the degree of vertical integration in the industry. For example, general cooperation is more likely among firms that produce homogeneous products than among firms whose output is complex or can be differentiated. Thus, cooperation is likely to occur when the offerings of rival sellers are sufficiently alike in significant physical and subjective aspects that they are virtual substitutes in the minds of consumers. Salt, sugar and light bulbs are examples of such products. With perfect homogeneity, price becomes the most important and visible area in which rivalry can take place, and oligopolists can coordinate their behavior more easily and find it highly desirable to do so to avoid price wars. With such differentiated products as soft drinks, television sets and automobiles, rivalry becomes multidimensional, and the coordination problem becomes considerably more complex. Even with such heterogeneous products, however, there still is considerable parallel behavior in pricing and product decisions in which price, style, service and other components of the output package are matched by the major producers.

Within the structural constraints of an oligopolistic industry, there is still a considerable range of possible behavior patterns for firms, such as the willingness of leading firms to act as price leaders (with perhaps an erosion of their market share over time), the conflicting price and market share expectations of firms within the industry and the speed at which price cuts (and other strategic changes) will be countered by rival firms.

The degree of cooperation in strategy and particularly in pricing in an oligopolistic industry is determined by both structural and behavioral variables. Evidence of recognized interdependence among oligopolists includes fast, open response to price cuts (to indicate the inevitability of competitive retaliation), joint industry pricing based on the price level of laid-down imports rather than on costs, frequent interfirm communication (not necessarily written), and a lack of covert price-cutting (for example, the same prices offered on closed and open tenders).

The Commission has examined three types of pricing behavior often present in oligopolistic industries: price leadership, the dominant firm and conscious parallelism. These are all problem areas that have troubled economic theorists and that have been imperfectly addressed by public policy-makers in the past.

PRICE LEADERSHIP

In an oligopoly, particularly one with homogeneous products, price leadership is a common phenomenon. It occurs when one firm in the industry takes the initiative in raising and lowering prices and the other firms in the industry follow its lead. The price leader may change from time to time. Price leadership may or may not be the result of open or even tacit collusion. Rather, the firms in an industry recognize and act upon their mutual interdependence and the advantages they expect will arise from an acceptance of the prices set by the price leader as those to be charged by all the major firms in the industry.

In many industries, particularly those comprising one large producer and a number of smaller ones, the role of price leader falls to the dominant firm, the largest firm in the industry. Each small firm behaves as though it operated under conditions of perfect competition. The dominant firm chooses a price that in some sense maximizes its profits, given its assessment of the willingness of smaller competitors to follow the price move and maintain their market shares, the threat posed by imports and the likelihood of competitors entering the industry.

Occasionally the price leadership role is assumed by a firm that is not the largest or most dominant in an industry. These smaller firms seem to command respect of rivals by "expertise" in price setting and marketing or by their speed in reacting to market conditions. The leader is often the firm most disposed to cut and least disposed to raise prices. In some industries leadership changes hands from time to time. Shell Canada Limited, in their brief to the Commission, stated that their industry does have price leadership but no one overall price leader; the leader varies by geographic region and by product. In other industries the price leader remains the same over a long period. Imasco Limited stated in its testimony before the Commission that it regularly is the leader in changing cigarette prices to reflect increased costs of supplies in the industry. Thus, the reasons why a particular firm serves as the price leader for an industry may also be found in the institutional and other features which form the background to that industry's development.

The effect of price leadership in oligopoly may be the establishment of higher and more stable prices than those that would prevail under more competitive conditions. Price movements may be coordinated by the leader by sending cues (postdated price lists perhaps) to the other firms in the industry indicating an interest in higher prices in good times and a price rallying point in depressed times. Often price changes are announced in advance to the press, so that the price leader runs very little risk of its price differing from that of other firms. If they do not follow his lead, he can withdraw the change before it becomes effective.

We note two exceptions to this behavior. When the price leader in a concentrated industry has lower costs, it may hold its price below levels desired by other firms to increase its market share, deter competitive expansion, or deter entry. Second, strong price leaders may resist raising prices as a reaction to increased demand for several reasons: (1) because long-run profits (on a present-value basis) may be reduced by such behavior, (2) at the government's request, (3) to deter government competition policy actions, (4) to discourage other firms from entering the industry, and (5) to maintain the parallel pricing behavior within the industry.

In industries with price leadership, the discipline necessary to maintain similar prices among firms sometimes breaks down and there is a price war. At the retail level, the petroleum industry is particularly prone to price wars, which break out when one firm or another needs to increase its market share to absorb the production of a refinery.

In the initial stages of development, nearly every industry in Canada and the United States has been dominated by a single firm that served as a price leader: in Canada, The Steel Company of Canada, Limited (Stelco), in some steel products and Canadian General Electric Company Limited in most small appliances; in the United States, the Slater Mills in cotton textiles, American Viscose Corporation in rayon yarn, and Birds Eye, Inc. (Del.) in frozen foods. In many industries the power of the initially dominant firm was gradually reduced by industrial growth and the entrance of new firms during the period when the industry was growing and evolving. In its brief to the Commission, Stelco stated that today it has little control over prices, which "are either government controlled, or set by market forces which could not be influenced by Stelco which, although large in terms of the Canadian economy, was only a minute factor in overall market terms."

THE DOMINANT FIRM

Several Canadian industries are characterized locally or nationally by the presence of a single, dominant enterprise, which is large both in absolute terms and in relation to other firms in the industry. *Dynamic Change and Accountability in a Canadian Market Economy,* a report prepared by L. A. Skeoch and B. C. McDonald in 1976 for the Department of Consumer and Corporate Affairs, defined an enterprise as dominant within an industry if it "is capable within broad limits of choosing its rate of profits (or its share of the market) undeterred by the consideration that rivals may compete away these profits by offering better terms to customers." This is a functional definition of dominance within an industry as opposed to the statistical or market share definitions used in Britain, West Germany, Australia and the United States. Skeoch and McDonald conclude, and we concur, that for competition policy purposes, a market share definition of dominance is most useful when applied in a large economy where economies of scale are insignificant relative to demand. In the small Canadian economy, it would be difficult or impossible to choose a definitional percentage that would not be both too large in some cases and too small in others.

In the long run, more important than high industry concentration, or even the pricing behavior of the dominant firm, are the underlying factors that lead to this concentration level. If there are economies of large-scale operation, highly concentrated industries may be inevitable and may best be constrained in their behavior by tariff reductions. If dominant firms in an industry engage in "entry barrier building", then such behavior should be dealt with under the competition law.

A functional test of dominance has been rejected in most countries because it is difficult to find adequate evidence to meet it. If a statistical definition is used, and certain types of behavior are proscribed, prosecution by the government is easier and more certain, and there is far less uncertainty in the minds of businessmen about the legality or illegality of a particular business practice. Although a statistical definition reduces uncertainty, it is inevitably arbitrary and inflexible, and may lead to expensive, time-consuming investigations and prosecutions that do not make economic sense.

The dominant firm in a market is likely to be the price leader, or in any case other firms are likely to treat the prices it sets as almost unchallengeable, thereby producing a situation more akin to monopoly pricing and behavior than to price competition. The exception is in cases of "limit-entry pricing", where the price leader intentionally takes a low markup to discourage new entry. Smaller firms will be well aware of and constrained by the ability of the larger firm to outspend, outdare and outlose them, and in particular to engage from time to time in disciplinary price-cutting designed to discourage smaller firms from deviating from industry pricing and market share "standards".

The power of dominant firms is not based only on their ability to exercise price discipline. Such enterprises may have advantages based on the control of strategic resources, as in the aluminum industry; the ability to control channels of distribution or to demand preferred treatment as buyers, as seen with major department store or supermarket chains; or the ability, through vertical integration, to secure stability in the supply of raw materials and the marketing of products, as seen with some basic metals. Competition policy should be directed toward preventing the things that allow the creation and exercise of a dominant position and that, at the same time, do not give rise to real economies of scale.

This is not to suggest that the power of a dominant firm to set prices is necessarily used or misused, but the potential power is often sufficient to elicit cooperative behavior. In an industry that lacks substantial barriers to entry, a dominant firm will almost always see both its market position and its ability to maintain prices eroded by market forces, as small firms expand their market share and new firms enter the industry. This decline may take a long time, however, and consumers may find little comfort in the economists' assurances of eventual competitive behavior.

We think that in general there is a need to protect the public interest by legislation only in those cases where traditional market forces will not erode a dominant firm's position over a fairly short period. Normally this situation is thought to occur only when there are high barriers to entry or great economies of scale or where the dominant firm is protected by government policies regarding tariffs, licences, purchasing programs or patents or is located in a mature, slow-growth industry. This last case is less obvious than the others and deserves some emphasis.

Every industry in its development goes through an early formative stage, an intermediate development stage and a mature stage. In the mature stage, manufacturing, management and marketing techniques in the industry all reach an advanced stage of refinement. Markets may continue to grow, but at an orderly and predictable rate. Unanticipated or chance events are fewer as experience accumulates and statistical inference techniques are improved. Employees with the relevant experience are on hand. Established connections with customers and suppliers (including the capital market) operate to buffer changes and limit large shifts in market shares. Significant innovations tend to be fewer and are mainly improvements rather than radical changes. Entry into a mature industry by a new firm is impeded by its lack of expertise, the difficulty of upsetting established customer attachments and the absence among would-be entrants of a known performance record to present to suppliers, most notably the capital market.

A potential entrant to a mature industry must invest large amounts of capital both to finance plant and equipment at an efficient scale and also to cover high start-up costs. That investment is unlikely where the alternative exists of entering at an early stage in some other industry's development where differential experience and reputations are negligible and cost differences between new and established firms are minimal. There is also a real problem in transferring management talent and creating compatible management groups, a problem accentuated in Canada with its relative dearth of mature managerial talent.

The conclusion of this line of reasoning is that, if a firm achieves dominance during its industry's intermediate stage of development, this position is difficult to change once the industry has reached a mature stage of development. Any assumption that such dominance will be easily upset by the operation of the market is doubtful. Such firms as IBM, General Motors and Imperial Oil are unlikely to be toppled from their dominant positions, even over long periods of time. Long-term dominance has a serious effect on the economy where firms are not pushed by competition toward efficient operations and it is particularly important where a dominant position in Canada mirrors a similar one by the same enterprise in world markets.

The United States has gone furthest in limiting the behavior of dominant firms and in some cases in reducing firm size, usually through the mechanism of a decree drawn up by the Antitrust Division of the Department of Justice, consented to by the enterprise involved and then authorized by a court. One U.S. example is an agreement in the 1950s by Eastman Kodak Company to reduce its market share in the film-processing market to 50% over a seven-year period. A similar case resulted in an agreement by IBM Corporation to undertake a liberal patent licensing policy. In both these cases, the dominant firm involved agreed to stop tying the sale of its products so that smaller firms could compete against specific products in individual markets without having to produce a full line of products. Other cases include a patent licensing agreement imposed on RCA Corporation, a divestiture order against American Telephone and Telegraph Company, and an agreement by United Fruit Corporation to establish a new firm capable of serving one-third of U.S. banana import requirements, and hence break United Fruit's monopoly supply position for bananas in the U.S. market. All these cases were designed to limit the behavior of dominant firms that were trying to increase barriers to entry in their industries in order to preserve their dominant positions and profit levels. Government initiatives to limit dominance do not appear to have damaged the entrepreneurial élan of these firms over the long run. Indeed there are indications that firms like AT & T have been induced by these antitrust actions to enter new industries, often by acquiring small firms, thus stimulating competition and reducing sectoral concentration.

A review of the European, Japanese, and Australian approaches to dominant firms reveals an awareness of the problem and an acceptance of a relatively low-level definition of the market share at which domination is perceived to create a problem. In the United Kingdom a firm is regarded as a dominating enterprise when its market share is above 25%; in Japan, 30%; in West Germany, 33%; in Australia, 33%; and in Sweden, 50%. In each country the market share applies to domestic production only.

The record of experience with recent legislation in these countries is insufficient to draw general conclusions about how the laws will be administered in practice. Each country relies on an administrative tribunal possessing wide discretion. Enforcement generally focuses on a rigorous review of mergers involving dominant enterprises and an acceptance of the premise that some trade practices that might be acceptable for non-dominant firms may be abusive when used by a dominant firm. The practices that have been most aggressively attacked have involved exclusionary trade practices, price discrimination and restrictive patent licensing.

A modified approach to the problem is found in Sweden, which relies on foreign competition to restrict the ability of firms in highly concentrated industries characterized by a dominant firm to exploit their market positions. In industries such as cement, where the government has permitted mergers resulting in the virtual elimination of competition, and in which foreign competition cannot be relied upon to constrain the exercise of monopoly power, the government has taken a minority shareholding in the firm. The assumption is that a public presence in the boardroom is effective in ensuring public accountability and in constraining the exercise of monopoly power.

British legislation dealing with dominant firms is found in the Monopolies and Mergers Acts 1948 and 1965 and in the Fair Trading Act (1973). Assurances (similar to but less formal than consent agreements) are sought by the Monopolies Commission when dominant firm behavior is thought to be either anticompetitive or not in the public interest. Some of these "assurances" are in highly subjective areas. In chemical fertilizers, assurances were given not to seek "unreasonable" profits on monopolized materials. In the supply of gasoline, the principal suppliers gave undertakings dealing with the period for exclusive selling and buying agreements, full-line forcing and further acquisitions. In color film, undertakings were sought and obtained relating to a reduction in the price of films and processing charges, retailers' discounts, exclusive dealing, and tying arrangements.

The Commission has found it difficult to arrive at conclusions relating to dominant firms in the context of the Canadian economy. Ideally, we should be able to rely on foreign competition, particularly the threat of imports from the United States, to reduce the ability of dominant firms to exploit their market positions. Where Canadian tariff barriers are too high to permit this, where foreign markets are dominated by the same firms as those in Canada, or in markets such as cement where there are local monopolies, some other solution must be sought. As indicated earlier, the problem is most significant in the case of dominant firms in mature industries. Even in these industries, however, lowered tariff barriers would introduce some needed competition and reduce the sometimes considerable existence and misuse of monopoly power.

In general, and for reasons discussed at length in a later section of this chapter, we do not think that divestiture is a valid or useful approach to the problem of the dominant firm in Canada. In most cases a unilateral reduction of tariffs might prove a more acceptable alternative.

The Commission recommends that most dominant firms be treated by an approach analogous to that used in European countries. A wide range of trade practices undertaken by dominant firms should come under scrutiny even where such practices would be unobjectionable if undertaken by a firm with a relatively small market share. A civil review procedure seems a better approach than a criminal one. The decisions of the civil tribunal should be made binding and subject to judicial appeal only on points of law. Otherwise the time required to resolve finally a violation of competition law would stretch over many years and effectively neutralize competition legislation.

CONSCIOUS PARALLELISM

One of the most intractable public policy problems associated with oligopoly is the coordinated behavior of firms. This is sometimes described as conscious parallelism. It occurs when the leading firms in an oligopoly not only recognize their interdependence but are able to act upon this recognition without explicitly agreeing to do so.

If firms in an oligopoly are selling a relatively undifferentiated (or homogeneous) product, such as steel, it is likely that they all will charge identical prices or set a schedule of prices that reflects only differences in the value of services provided, including intangible services such as the provision of a dependable source of supply. In such industries, little price deviation occurs. No firm will charge more than the established industry price, and under normal circumstances no customer will pay a higher price. Producers will be discouraged from charging less because they are aware that major competitors faced with the threat of market share erosion will match the lower prices immediately. Conscious parallelism will normally produce identical list prices and usually virtually identical transaction prices. Price adjustments upward may occur almost simultaneously, entirely without any overt or covert agreement.

An example of such behavior was related in the submission in 1976 by the Automotive Retailers' Association (Alberta) to the Legislative Assembly of the Province of Alberta, regarding oil company pricing policies:

> ...the wholesale price at which dealers have to buy their gasoline, the Posted Dealer Tankwagon Price, is an "administered price". It is practically uniform, varying normally no more than a fraction of a cent between each major company. When one major company does increase its wholesale price, as Imperial did last week, others usually follow immediately by nearly identical amounts. Announcements of increases corresponding to Imperial's may be expected now at any day. ...oil industry price increases are clearly in the pattern known by economists as "conscious parallelism", common to oligopoly....

Milton Moore, in *How Much Price Competition? The Prerequisites of an Effective Canadian Competition Policy* (1970), defines the conundrum for competition policy when he states: "The key assumption in the analysis of their behaviour is that most oligopolies engage in conventional pricing practices that are indistinguishable from the tacit collusion that is almost universally disapproved." He then points out: "Formal collusion is susceptible to regulation, but conscious parallel action is extremely difficult to detect and even more difficult to prove, and it is impossible to prevent independent action on the recognition of mutual dependence. But the effects of all three are similar."

While the practice of conscious parallelism may lack all the customary elements of a formal agreement as defined by the courts in conspiracy cases, the economic effects may be just as pernicious as those associated with a conspiracy. Prices may be maintained, over a long time, at levels significantly above those that would exist under competitive conditions. Innovations and technological change may be inhibited or introduced at a slower rate. Excess capacity may continue to exist over long periods, not only constituting a burden to the consumers of the industry's output, but also acting as a barrier to the entry of new competitors. In addition, conscious parallelism may shift the major firms' cost curves upwards because of inefficiency in production and distribution in the absence of competitive pressures to be efficient. This inefficiency involves a waste of valuable resources and a loss to society as a whole.

Businessmen, and often economists, argue that parallel action by oligopolists, particularly as regards homogeneous products, is necessary and, in fact, evidence that the forces of competition are working. For example, in their joint brief to a House Committee in respect to Bill C-42 (the predecessor of Bill C-13), 12 of Canada's largest corporations stated that conscious parallelism "may be the result of acts which are completely independent and which are undertaken by persons engaged in active competition by similar means". The brief of the Canadian Pacific group of companies stated that conscious parallelism "connotes both a normal and a natural feature of competition in the market place. True competitors ordinarily seek unilaterally to meet or match as much as possible each other's prices, terms and products." The Investment Dealers' Association brief argued "competitive considerations dictate parallel policies within many oligopolies...." The brief of Imperial Oil stated: "In an oligopoly market, firms normally must recognize their mutual interdependence because of their fewness. They also are often compelled to follow 'closely parallel policies or closely matching conduct.' For example, if they are selling in the same market, any seller must match a lower price offered by a competitor or risk losing customers. If demand is buoyant and costs rising, a seller who does not follow a competitor in raising prices risks losing profits. If one seller advertises in a market, his competitors normally must do so also." Businessmen argue that parallel action or matching conduct should not be subject to competition policy legislation because it is the result of the independent decisions of the firms involved.

W. T. Stanbury and G. N. Reschenthaler conclude in a forthcoming article in the *Osgoode Hall Law Journal*, "Oligopoly and Conscious Parallelism: Theory, Policy and the Canadian Cases", that, in the context of an oligopoly, "independent" behavior by individual firms can mean only that they make their decisions without any attempt to communicate with other firms in the industry (except by their actions, which of course contain information). It does not mean that the leading firms in an oligopoly fail to recognize their interdependence. As they point out, to ask an oligopolist to behave independently in the sense of not taking into account the actions and reactions of his competitors is to ask him to behave irrationally.

In our view, to prohibit oligopolists from matching the prices of rivals is to revise significantly the established rules of the market place. It would not necessarily mean utter chaos, but it would severely disrupt the market and would not be likely to eliminate parallel behavior in any event. Prohibition orders relating to parallel behavior would be exceedingly difficult to enforce, whether standardized or differentiated products were involved. To prohibit firms from charging identical prices in an industry in which the product and service being sold is essentially undifferentiated might simply cause firms to adopt insignificant price spreads which may be offset by marginal service differentials.

Conscious Parallelism in Combines Cases. Before discussing public policy in respect to conscious parallelism, it may be useful to look at some recent cases in which it became an issue. Price-fixing and market sharing conspiracies that lessen competition unduly have been illegal in Canada since 1889. In the recent *Armco, Large Lamps* and *Atlantic Sugar* cases the defendants had argued that their behavior amounted to conscious parallelism, and that even closely parallel behavior did not constitute a conspiracy contravening the Combines Investigation Act. In the *Armco* case the firms were convicted because Mr. Justice Lerner inferred that an agreement had been made to adopt a common price list although there was no documentary or oral evidence indicating an agreement. He said: "The publication of this price list by itself was innocent conduct but common sense dictates that it would be unlikely, if not impossible, that this progressive and energetic competitor would risk another failure [of other firms to follow the prices indicated] without assurances from other members of the [industry] that, if attempted again, it would be followed by the others. The simple fact that stability was almost instantaneous makes any other inference not only improbable but unrealistic....Tacit agreement had to be the means and I find it was achieved as the results... unquestionably establish." In the *Large Lamps (Regina* v. *Canadian General Electric Company Limited et al.)* price case Mr. Justice Pennell inferred the existence of an agreement, but he did so on the basis of at least eight pieces of documentary evidence of direct communications among the three firms in respect to a common sales plan and common prices. He said he was "not able to reconcile the substantial unanimity of action taken by the accused with price conscious parallelism." To some extent, *Large Lamps* is a "traditional" conspiracy case in that the judicial determination was based on documentary or oral evidence of an agreement. While it is an axiom of the law of conspiracy that an agreement may be inferred from entirely circumstantial evidence, the criminal law requires (following the rule in *Hodge's Case*) that the inferences be consistent with the establishment of an illegal agreement and inconsistent with any other rational conclusion. This is a rigorous test, one that cannot be easily met when trying the typical case of conscious parallelism of firms in an oligopoly.

In the *Atlantic Sugar* case, involving the three largest refiners in eastern Canada, which the Crown lost at trial but is appealing, Mr. Justice Mackay stated that "Price conformity and identical price lists are characteristic of an oligopolistic industry" and that they "may well be consistent with independent competitive decisions" or be the result of an agreement. Finding no documentary evidence, and unwilling to infer the existence of an agreement, Mr. Justice Mackay acquitted the accused. With respect to the other charge that there had been an agreement as to the market share to be enjoyed by each accused, the judge found that the maintenance of traditional market shares was the result of a tacit agreement, but that competition had not been prevented or lessened unduly. It is apparent that the existing legislation is inadequate to deal with conscious parallelism.

POTENTIAL COMPETITION AND OLIGOPOLY PRICING

In many Canadian and U.S. industries with oligopolistic structures, some constraint on above-normal pricing and other uncompetitive practices exists when buyers are able to turn to alternative suppliers who are not currently producing or supplying the product in question. Existing firms in related lines of business are sometimes able to enter the new industry easily, especially if they have access to the requisite technology and financing, and are able to acquire the necessary personnel and distribution channels. Such "poised competition" is thought to come from large firms in closely related industries, or sometimes from large conglomerate firms.

The strength of poised competition and its importance in keeping down prices and profit levels in the oligopolistic sector depend upon the height of barriers to entry. Where there are patents to which a newcomer cannot obtain access at reasonable cost, brand identification, a minimum efficient scale so large as to discourage investors, large cost penalties for small-scale production or a shortage of requisite personnel, machinery, sites or raw materials, then the barriers to entry may be substantial. If the barriers to new entry are not great, however, poised competition can be a significant restraining force on the use of market power which might otherwise arise within an oligopolistic structure.

Several of those who appeared before the Commission commented on the existence of poised competition. D. G. Hartle, for example, presented the idea in a slightly broader concept:

> I do not wish to appear to suggest that the market system works so well that millions of self-seeking investors are continually searching for small potential advantages and jump upon opportunities within days. But I do believe that rates of return are held down by competition or the threat of competition. This competition can come from imports or from changes in the product lines or the pricing policies of existing firms or the entry of new firms or by the acceptance of new products and services that serve the same function but are not identical with existing products and services.

Although the Commission recognizes the competitive importance of firms poised at the edge of an industry, the limitations of potential competition must not be minimized. In Canada, the barriers to entry mentioned above are often substantial. The Commission recommends that every attempt should be made to encourage new firms to invest in concentrated industries and to discourage existing firms from raising the barriers to entry to new firms. The Commission's recommendations are intended to promote increased entry by reducing the latitude of large firms in their competitive behavior. The Foreign Investment Review Act (FIRA) has had the effect of erecting some barriers to entry by foreign firms, which are potential entrants in many Canadian industries.

Advertising as a Factor in Oligopoly

There has been a considerable controversy over whether there is a significant relationship between advertising and industry concentration, firm size and profits. Some economists argue that the theory of oligopolistic behavior predicts that advertising and concentration will interact with each other: advertising will increase the barriers to entry into an industry and thereby increase concentration; and firms in concentrated industries will compete on a non-price basis by advertising. Often firms in concentrated industries also try to prevent other firms from entering the industry by differentiating their products by marketing a broad line of similar products. Advertising is used to try to brand a product so that consumers will not switch to the products of other firms in the industry, even if these products are sold at lower prices. For example, the introduction of the yearly model change and the full-product line in the automobile industry has greatly increased the minimum efficient size of firms in that industry. Advertising is used both to differentiate the different models and to persuade consumers to buy according to yearly model changes. In addition, where there are economies of scale in advertising, larger firms may be able to exclude smaller firms from the industry. Thus dominant firms in concentrated industries often use advertising to increase barriers to entry.

Firms in concentrated industries who are aware of one another's prices and output reactions usually compete by advertising, to avoid costly price wars. Several U.S. economists have concluded that there is a direct association among advertising intensity, profits and concentration in consumer goods industries. Although there is an association among these factors, as yet there is no firm evidence as to whether there are causal links among them. U.S. economist Yale Brozen has concluded that advertising is beneficial, since it is carried out more intensively on products new to an industry and by the smaller firms in the industry, decreases brand loyalty and is associated with high- and uniform-quality goods. In his view, "advertising makes markets competitive". In a parallel study showing the benefits of advertising, Lee Benham in a 1972 article in the *Journal of Law and Economics* argued that in the eyeglass industry, "prices were found to be substantially lower in states which allowed advertising". Based on this research the Commission concludes that advertising by small firms or new entrants in a market increases competition. While advertising by dominant firms decreases it, on balance barriers to entry are lower in the presence of advertising than they would be without it.

Marketers recognize, and research supports, that brands may be classified on the basis of consumer acceptance into "major" brands and "independent" brands. Brand-switching behavior among buyers is high among brands within each group, but low between groups. Put differently, the purchaser of Kellogg's Corn Flakes may switch occasionally to the heavily advertised breakfast cereals of General Mills Incorporated, General Foods Corporation and Quaker Oats Company, but will only infrequently switch to low-priced, unadvertised or private-branded breakfast cereals. A new producer must thus either commit himself to very high advertising expenditures to overcome advertising threshold levels and compete with the giants or settle for part of the relatively small market for unadvertised cereals. The high cost of entry to the advertised sector and the high risk involved mean that virtually all new entrants stay in the low-cost, low-risk unadvertised sector. Those firms in the advertised sector can emphasize new products and other non-price features and in general act as oligopolists even though entry has not been foreclosed.

High-level advertising resulting in a joint monopoly has been recognized in some countries, notably the United States and the United Kingdom, and in recent years regulatory agencies and the courts have suggested and implemented some attempts at a solution. A charge against manufacturers of ready-to-eat cereals was made in 1970 under section 5 of the U.S. Federal Trade Commission Act. The FTC alleged that the Kellogg Company, General Mills, General Foods and Quaker Oats had adopted practices aimed at the illegal monopolization of the ready-to-eat cereals market. The FTC claimed that their intensive advertising promoted trademarks that concealed the true nature of the products and created artificial differentiation between products, which enhanced the respondents' ability to raise prices and to exclude competition.

The FTC proposed that the firms involved divest themselves of some of their production facilities, that they undertake royalty-free licensing of trademarks for a given time, that they be prohibited from acquiring other cereal manufacturers and be prohibited from offering shelf-space services to retailers. In early 1978, the case was still under litigation.

In Canada, the only case under the Combines Investigation Act resulting in an advertising restriction involved a prohibition order by consent of the parties in respect to a charge of monopoly (the case did not go to trial) against Canada Safeway Limited; it placed a ceiling on the firm's advertising and some of its promotional expenditures in Edmonton and Calgary from 1974 through 1978. Canada Safeway was also prohibited during this period from directly or indirectly stating in its advertising that its stores within Calgary or Edmonton were engaged in localized price-cutting.

In any policy decisions to restrict advertising expenditures as an aid to competition (or to prevent "waste"), the actual advertising intensity of firms in Canada must be considered. M. E. Porter (in Caves *et al.*) concluded that, in the retail consumer goods industries in Canada, the level of advertising as a percentage of sales was significantly below that in the United States.

Given this mixed evidence, the Commission sees no feasible set of laws or government policy by which government should invoke on economic grounds a general limitation on advertising for all firms within concentrated industries other than the present ones against fraudulent or misleading advertising. Limitations on high-level advertising by dominant firms in mature, oligopolistic, consumer goods industries may be an appropriate and useful remedy in some cases, however.

Oligopoly and Technological Change

One of the measures of performance listed earlier was the rate at which firms and industries develop new products and techniques of production and marketing. There have been many statistical studies that relate market structure to some aspect of innovation, but as yet no consensus has emerged.

The theory that attempts to link market structure to technological change consists of a collection of hypotheses. The arguments on one side are represented by a theory associated with J. A. Schumpeter and John Kenneth Galbraith that an oligopolistic industry structure is the best structure for inducing technological change. The essence of this argument is that market power is necessary to motivate firms to innovate and that innovation is necessary for competition, progress and growth. Galbraith advanced this argument in his book *American Capitalism* (1952). He concluded that firms needed the high profits that were available only to innovators in oligopolistic industries as an incentive for them to undertake the high risks of research and development and new product and process innovation and introduction.

The Schumpeter-Galbraith hypothesis implies that there may be a conflict between two measures of performance—efficiency of resource allocation and progress—thus raising an issue that has perplexed policy-makers and troubled this Commission. If Schumpeter and Galbraith are correct, policies designed to reduce market power or to break up oligopolies in order to promote allocative efficiency are likely to reduce technological change. As Scherer and Markham have pointed out, a misallocation of resources stemming from oligopoly may be quickly overcome by rapid technological change from innovation.

The alternative view to that of Schumpeter-Galbraith has been presented by a number of other economists over the years and was articulated by Carl Kaysen and Donald F. Turner in their book *Antitrust Policy: An Economic and Legal Analysis* (1959). This view is essentially that competition is an important, if not essential, condition for technological change in an industry and that market power is detrimental rather than helpful. Competition gives firms the incentive to innovate to defend their market positions through new products and more efficient production. It is a means to achieve at least a temporary respite from unremitting price competition.

Many empirical studies have tried to determine the relationships among market structure, firm size and technological change. To arrive at empirically supported conclusions, such research must examine the three components of technological change: invention, innovation and adoption. A careful study undertaken at the Marketing Science Institute at Harvard University and using firm-level data reached three tentative conclusions:

1. R&D efforts have significantly higher payout in profits for integrated rather than non-integrated firms;
2. R&D is more profitable for companies having large rather than small market shares;
3. The profitability of R&D is higher for large companies.

There is a general consensus among other studies that concentration aids innovation within the firm up to a threshold level, after which there is no further positive relationship. Scherer, for example, concluded that "technological vigor" increased to the point at which the four-firm concentration ratio reached 50-55%, after which increasing concentration had a depressing effect on innovation. The conclusion of Chapter 3 on returns to scale in R&D should be recalled: in many industries large firms are relatively R&D-intensive, and the output from their R&D is relatively higher than that of smaller firms. However large firms that produce unrelated products have no particular advantage in the generation of internal R&D or the adoption of innovation. Large firms are often necessary in order to undertake the very high costs and high risks often associated with large R&D projects.

In those highly concentrated Canadian industries in which price competition is low, there is less incentive to introduce new products and processes. Firms in moderately concentrated, oligopolistic industries do have a great incentive to obtain new products and processes via licensing, since licensing is unlikely to disturb the pricing structure of the industry. On the other hand, the adoption of new production process technology often makes capital plant and equipment obsolete. Firms in highly concentrated industries may attempt to prolong the life of their fixed assets by slowing the rate of adoption of new technology. This strategy will be successful only in a highly coordinated oligopoly with little import competition, in which all competitors openly or tacitly refrain from introducing innovations.

Canada may therefore be caught between the necessity of having large firms in order to have large, successful R&D programs and the fact that large firms in general imply the existence of concentrated industries. At high levels of concentration, however, firms may become insulated from competitive pressures and hence both engage in less innovative activity and also acquire fewer new products and processes by licence. Licensing often does not require large firm size to be successful; it is one way in which small firms may be able to challenge the dominant firms in oligopolistic industries.

The Commission has not been able to draw any firm conclusions about the relationship between concentration and innovation, although it is apparent that large firms are better able to undertake the risks of large-scale R&D. Transfer of products and processes by licensing seems to us to be one potential avenue by which new firms can break down the barriers to entry in concentrated industries and increase competition. We recommend, as has the Science Council of Canada, that the government make every effort to increase the rate of innovation via licensing, particularly licensing to small firms.

Oligopoly and Inflation

Popular opinion holds that large firms in oligopolistic industries are able to "pass increased costs on to the consumer" through their pricing practices, thereby increasing the rate of inflation, while firms in more competitive industries are not able to do so. This belief was expressed in several briefs and in testimony before the Commission. The Commission has not done research specifically on this relationship, and our comments here are based on the research of others, as well as on what we have been told in briefs and at our hearings. Although the relationship between oligopoly and inflation is complex, some valid generalizations can be made, although the policy implications are less clearcut.

Economic research over the past 30 years has sought both a theoretical basis and empirical data indicating the role, if any, played by market power in creating and maintaining inflationary pressures. After World War II and until the late 1950s, there was a general belief that inflation resulted from excess demand forces usually generated by government deficits financed by an expansion of the money supply. This is the so-called "demand-pull" theory in inflation. This belief was tempered by the recognition that frequently prices began to rise during an economic upswing long before full employment of labor and resources was reached.

Following the 1955-58 inflationary period, and in particular after the 1959 steel price hearing in the United States, some economists began to recognize that a combination of large corporations and unions with market power could cause a "cost-push" inflation under conditions of slack demand. According to this theory, wages, particularly those paid to unionized workers in oligopolistic industries, were pushed up faster than productivity, prices rose in response, and the monetary and fiscal authorities, who were more sensitive to unemployment than to inflation, would support the wage price spiral by following expansionary policies.

Experience in the steel industry in Canada and the United States is often cited to illustrate how an individual industry with market power, responding to the behavior of a powerful union, can bring about price increases and further inflationary pressures in the rest of the economy simultaneously with a recession characterized by falling demand. In the past, there have been several periods during which steel prices rose sharply in the presence of falling demand, stable costs and substantial excess capacity. Some of this behavior (particularly during 1953-59) has since been recognized as "catch-up" increases to restore historical profit margins. The Steel Company of Canada emphasized in its brief that steel prices as a general rule lag behind increases in the cost of production. Steelmakers, it claimed, are continually playing catch-up in their pricing policies.

This phenomenon of catch-up pricing may be partially explained by the common use of target pricing by a majority of large Canadian manufacturers, and by enterprises such as Bell Canada and Ontario Hydro in the regulated sectors. Target pricing involves setting prices for specific products, product groups or divisions in such a way as to yield a predetermined corporate average return on capital or sales (or to achieve a stated dollar amount of profit). The essence of the target-rate-of-return pricing process is that it uses sales volume to derive price, rather than price to estimate sales volume. As demand falls and capacity utilization decreases, firms that price to achieve a target rate of return will raise their prices if they believe that demand is insensitive to price. Similarly when demand and capacity utilization increase, firms using target pricing may not raise their prices immediately. If demand is steady, prices will change over a planning period only in response to changes in standard unit costs of labor and materials. This means that prices do not necessarily move downward when demand falls, but do rise when costs rise.

If firms in oligopolistic industries do not adjust their prices completely to reflect changing conditions of demand, they must either be willing to finance large changes in their inventories or be able to change the volume of production rapidly, perhaps by laying off workers. Thus a dampening effect on price swings may be translated into greater inventory or employment fluctuations. In fact, one of the hallmarks of an oligopolistic industry is that output will vary to a greater degree than will prices.

By the mid-1970s, with concurrent high unemployment and inflation visible in almost all Western industrialized countries, many economists and policy-makers had come to accept the premise that inflation could result either from excess demand or from "cost-push" forces reflecting market power or frequently from a hybrid of the two. As mentioned above, government fiscal and, especially, monetary activities have been forced by pressure from many segments of society to validate these "cost-push" cost and price increases by generally expansionary policies financed by an increase in the money supply. The initial change in prices in both concentrated and unconcentrated industries may be the same in reaction to increased costs, but in concentrated industries large firms and their large unions have the political and market power to make these higher prices stick in the face of falling demand.

Several studies have attempted to determine this relationship empirically. In probably the most comprehensive cross-sectional study of pricing behavior, Leonard Weiss found that, in the United States between 1953 and 1959, price levels rose more rapidly in concentrated industries. However, between 1959 and 1963 there was no detectable relationship between concentration levels and the degree of price increases. For 1967 to 1969, a period recognized as one of excess demand inflation, prices actually rose less in concentrated industries than in less concentrated ones. J. Fred Weston and Steven H. Lustgarten reran the analysis for the entire 1953-69 period (which contained periods of demand-pull inflation and periods of cost-push inflation) and found no *overall* statistical relationship between concentration and price behavior. The findings of Weiss and of Weston and Lustgarten, taken together, have been interpreted by many economists as showing that industrial concentration produces a "lagged", seller-induced inflation, which may exist alongside (or independently of) demand-pull inflation. Beals' survey of the empirical evidence for the U.S. Council on Wage and Price Stability in 1975 also concluded that prices in concentrated industries increased less during periods of excess demand and more during periods of insufficient demand than did prices in competitive industries, but that over a long period, price levels in oligopolistic industries increased no faster than did prices in competitive ones.

K. Dennis and D. G. McFetridge also reached the same conclusions in their work for the Canadian Prices and Incomes Commission in 1973. They concluded that there is no reason to believe that oligopoly either fosters or intensifies inflation. Dennis wrote: "it is reasonable to conclude that neither large firm size nor high concentration alone is very likely to create or intensify periodic inflationary bursts while high concentration should only limit the capacity of the economy to find a new equilibrium (at a generally lower price level) during a recessionary period." McFetridge concluded: "There is no obvious relationship between market structure as defined here, and price behavior . . . . There is, therefore, no reason to believe that a policy of market deconcentration would make the existing macro-economic policy tools more effective in limiting inflation." On the basis of these studies, the Commission has reached the conclusion that the link between oligopoly and inflation has not been established, particularly for the period before the 1975-78 "stagflation". Indeed lagged adjustment behavior in firms in oligopolistic industries may have contributed to smoothing out the rate of inflation. As yet there is no evidence aside from that based on the most casual empiricism to conclude that there is a direct relationship between oligopoly and inflation during a period of sustained unemployment accompanied by high inflation. At present, the Commission sees no reason for the government to act against firms in oligopolistic industries because of their supposed contribution to inflation.

Four major studies have been done on the relationship in Canada between industrial concentration, price-cost margins and profits. In general the results of these studies support the hypothesis that increased industrial concentration is associated with greater price-cost and profit margins, all other variables held constant. Harry Bloch in a 1974 article in the *Canadian Journal of Economics* and Richard Caves *et al.* in their report to the Commission concluded that, in addition to high concentration, high tariffs (or low import penetration) were necessary for firms to increase their price-cost margins.

A. Michael Spence (in Caves *et al.*) concluded that in general for the firms and industries in his sample, price-cost margins were higher in the United States than in Canada, despite the higher levels of concentration existing in most Canadian industries. That study concluded that price-cost margins in Canada are caught in a squeeze between high costs on the one hand and the prices of imported goods on the other. These higher costs may also be due to inefficiencies existing because of the less competitive environment in many Canadian industries. If an industry changes from a competitive to an oligopolistic one, then firms in that industry may tend to take a once-and-for-all price increase when they recognize their interdependence and act on that knowledge. An increase in the level of concentration may increase the rate of inflation, but, as we indicated in Chapter 2, there has been no overall increase in the level of industrial concentration in Canada in recent years.

Approaches to Oligopolistic Conduct

The "Joint Monopolization" Approach

In November 1977, Bill C-13, amendments to the Combines Investigation Act, was given first reading in the House of Commons. It replaced Bill C-42, which had been introduced in March. Included was a new civil provision dealing with "joint monopolization" (section 31.73). This is defined to mean a situation where a small number of persons (not all affiliated) achieve or entrench substantial control of a market by adopting closely parallel policies or closely matching conduct, and the policies or conduct have the effect of restricting entry, foreclosing a competitor's sources of supply or his sales outlets, eliminating a competitor by predatory pricing, coercing or disciplining a competitor or restraining competition by exclusionary or predatory means. The Bill provides that a finding of joint monopolization can be made "notwithstanding that the parallel policies or matching conduct... involved no arrangement or agreement between or among them". Where joint monopolization is found, the Competition Board will be empowered to issue a prohibition or remedial order or, where these would fail to restore competition, to require divestiture of assets.

The Commission is troubled by the proposals put forward in this Bill relating to joint monopolization, (although they are an improvement over what was in Bill C-42), and thinks that they go beyond what is necessary to protect the public interest. The government may still argue that the scope of its proposals would be limited to situations where parallel policies have one or more predatory or exclusionary effects, but their potential scope may be greater. We think Bill C-13 might be both fairer and more effective if it treated the "plus factors" discussed in the next section of this chapter less as consequences of parallel policies than as things that tend to accompany that kind of conduct.

Conscious Parallelism Plus

Examination of a number of the cases involving conscious parallelism or implied conspiracy in various countries suggests to us what seems a much more more workable approach to the problem of joint monopolization. In virtually every case of parallel behavior successfully prosecuted in Canada or elsewhere, some further pattern of behavior beyond the mere adoption of parallel courses of action and serving the mutual interests of the competitors was required. Such behavior has become known as "conscious parallelism plus".

As mentioned earlier, it is a natural tendency for the leading firms in an oligopoly to try to act on the recognition of their mutual dependence. It is relatively rare for the members of an oligopoly, even one producing a homogeneous good, to be able to coordinate their behavior closely *without* the use of one or more "plus factors". These factors are additional techniques over and above simple parallel action, which facilitate the coordination of interfirm behavior in an oligopoly. In their absence coordination is likely to be poorer, price and product policies less frequently identical and the industry more prone to bouts of aggressive or even "destructive" competition.

Several of these "parallel plus" situations are illustrative. In a 1914 case in the United States, parallel pricing among retail lumber dealers was accompanied by distribution by the lumber dealers' association of a list of wholesalers who also served as retailers of lumber products. Retailers, independently and individually, boycotted these wholesalers. The plus factor was publication of the list. In a 1939 case, two dominant regional motion picture exhibition chains sent identical letters to the eight major motion picture distributors stipulating "desirable" distribution rules for first-run films. Each of the letters included the names of all others receiving the letter. Each of the eight adopted the recommended rules, with the result that independent exhibitors were thereafter unable to obtain first-run films under the rules. The court inferred a conspiracy based on the plus factor that concerted action was invited by the knowledge that all distributors were aware that all others had received identical letters.

In the 1967 *Canadian Coat and Apron Supply* case in Montreal, the defendants (who accounted for 85-90% of the linen towel business on the island of Montreal) formed a trade association, the Montreal League of Linen Supply Owners. Among other things, the League hired a private detective agency to police the prices members were charging for linen supply and to report on whether members were soliciting business from other members' customers. The League also reimbursed members for losses incurred when they priced below cost to drive newcomers out of the business. The plus factors here were, quite clearly, the policing and related activities.

In several Canadian and U.S. cases, dissemination of detailed price lists and invoice information, accompanied by extensive details on actual below-list price quotations and transactions to all members of a trade association, has been adequate for the inference of conspiracy. The plus factor in these trade association cases is the distribution of detailed data on actual sales prices, accompanied by identification of the supplier and buyer sufficient to permit others to match the discounts, and thus remove the incentive for price competition. The plus factor would be important, however, only in a situation where there was close adherence to list prices in the industry. In one U.S. case, where off-list sales accounted for 25% of total industry sales and no effort was made by the association to induce members to adhere to list prices, the defendants were acquitted.

Other examples of "plus" factors that have been cited in legal cases include product standardization enforced on buyers by an industry association, with resultant increase of the cost of entry of new firms; use of absolutely uniform but artificial basing points in delivered pricing schemes, with refusal to allow f.o.b. or similar purchasing; parallel buying activity to support the price of a substitute product; uniform refusal to supply certain accounts; and the exhortation of members of the industry to avoid the destructiveness of active competition, particularly price competition. The Commission recommends that a civil (as opposed to a criminal) provision be framed to condemn joint monopolization in the form of conscious parallelism with respect to price and other policies, where one or more of such plus factors have been used to facilitate coordination of the firms involved. The remedy might take the form of an order prohibiting the use of the plus factor. The objective of such a provision is to reduce the ability of the leading firms in an oligopoly to act upon their interdependence in a tightly coordinated fashion.

To the extent that normal market competition does not erode oligopoly positions supported by economies of scale, government regulation, or other factors, then competition policy has to focus on those elements of behavior that allow firms to coordinate their policies closely. A parallelism-plus policy will not reach firms in oligopolistic industries that can act together without the use of plus factors ("those who have learned to dance together to faint music") but according to existing Canadian and U.S. jurisprudence, situations without plus factors are uncommon. A parallelism-plus policy should help to move the economic performance of many oligopolies away from the monopoly end of the spectrum. However the parallelism-plus approach is primarily useful in attacking short-term pricing behavior. Of more long-term significance are steps to speed the erosion of barriers to entry in concentrated industries, and to prevent firms from erecting additional barriers.

The Commission does not recommend that conscious parallelism, or joint monopoly, be treated as a criminal offense. We disagree with a criminal treatment of actions that may be entirely innocent in origin. Furthermore we think it wrong in principle to impose criminal penalties, including possible imprisonment, for actions that are only vaguely defined and whose criminal nature cannot be forecast in advance. On this basis alone we recommend that criminal penalties be removed completely from all competition legislation, except for very well-defined offenses such as horizontal price fixing, market division, bid rigging and false advertising.

Deconcentration of Industry

As we have seen, when industrial concentration is high, firms tend to set their prices and output in recognition of the probable competitive reaction of other firms in their industry. In concentrated industries with high barriers to entry, firms may arrive at the monopoly (or near monopoly) price, output and profit configuration through conscious parallel action or price leadership. Even under a "conscious parallelism plus" approach, well-coordinated behavior in an oligopolistic industry cannot be attacked if it has been effected without agreement or the use of plus factors. Proposals to reduce barriers to entry are long-term measures. Given this situation, it is a tempting idea simply to deconcentrate the industry by splitting large firms into a number of smaller ones, which would be expected to act more competitively.

Deconcentration of industry has been considered seriously only in the United States. The Commission does not think that deconcentration of industries by the breakup of firms that operate in them is a practical alternative for Canada. Firms in most industries in Canada are still too small to compete internationally. Canada's problem is not in decreasing the size of existing firms, but in ensuring that the large firms necessary to compete efficiently actually realize economies of scale and that they pass lower costs on to the consumer in the form of lower prices. We think, however, that a brief review of the subject is necessary for three reasons: (1) often anticombines (antitrust) sentiment felt in the United States migrates into Canada through the media and academicians and is applied to Canadian industry despite the dissimilarities between the two economies; (2) there is some sentiment among the public and some government officials that "big" is usually "bad"; and (3) it might be argued that if competition policy inhibits mergers that create more concentrated industries it should, by the same logic, deconcentrate industries that are already concentrated.

Only one group, the Communist Party of Canada, has suggested to us in a brief or in our hearings that deconcentration would be appropriate to the Canadian economy. One or two other groups, for example, the Alberta Associated Grocers, have advocated deconcentration or restrictions on growth in specific sectors. Nevertheless we have looked at deconcentration as one of the alternatives that seemed to arise from the terms of our mandate.

THE HART, NEAL AND KAYSEN-TURNER PROPOSALS

Over the past 20 years, three major proposals for industrial deconcentration have been put forward in the United States: Kaysen and Turner (1959) in their book *Antitrust Policy*, the "Neal Report" (1968) by the White House Task Force on Antitrust Policy, and the "Hart Bill" (1973) by Senator Phillip A. Hart. In the context of U.S. antitrust history, deconcentration proposals are neither academic nor utopian. Opposition to the growth of economic concentration has been found in the Congress since the passage of the Sherman Act in 1890, an act aimed at deconcentrating business structure by "breaking up the trusts". Later statutes, such as the Clayton Act (1914), Federal Trade Commission Act (1914), Celler-Kefauver Act (1950), and specialized legislation such as the Bank Holding Company Act (1956), have all agreed that economic power must be dispersed, prevented from forming or at least controlled.

The Hart Bill stems from the conclusion of its author that too much power lies in too few hands; that industry is becoming increasingly concentrated; and that market concentration results in decreased competition, price levels that are both higher and more inflexible, inefficiency, underutilization of economic capacity and a decline in exports. Senator Hart concluded that these factors combine to fuel inflation and create unemployment. He further concluded that antitrust laws were at that time inadequate and that remedies were lacking either to reduce existing concentration or to change the behavior of firms in oligopolistic industries.

The Hart Bill proposed that the Congress declare unlawful "monopoly power in any line of commerce in any section of the country or with foreign nations". The bill defined monopoly power to exist where: (1) any corporation that maintained its average rate of return on net worth after taxes in excess of 15% over a period of five consecutive years out of the most recent seven years; (2) there has been no substantial price competition among two or more corporations in any line of commerce in any section of the country for a period of three consecutive years out of the most recent five years; or (3) any four or fewer corporations account for 50% (or more) of sales in any line of commerce in any section of the country in any year out of the most recent three. The bill did not require divestiture, however, if the firms involved could demonstrate that their power was due solely to the ownership of valid patents or if divestiture would result in a loss of substantial economies of scale.

The earlier Neal and Kaysen-Turner rationales were somewhat narrower, focusing on adverse industry performance and inefficient resource allocation rather than on inflation, foreign trade or unemployment as reasons for deconcentrating oligopolistic industries. Neal and Kaysen-Turner agreed that existing antitrust laws were inadequate to restructure oligopolistic industries without a specific deconcentration statute.

We have devoted some space to these proposals because their detailed nature and the serious way in which they were received emphasize to us the attention being paid to the market concentration doctrine in the United States. Indeed, an implementation of the Hart, Neal or Kaysen-Turner proposals in Canada could require rearrangement of a significant part of the privately owned industrial sector in Canada. It is interesting to note that, although none of these proposals was ever enacted, each successive proposal is more stringent than its predecessor, possibly reflecting a growing sentiment in the United States that concentrated industries must somehow be broken up.

The issue of vertical divestiture has also been raised recently in Canada in the context of Bell Canada and Northern Telecom (formerly Northern Electric). In a 1976 report prepared for the Department of Consumer and Corporate Affairs, the Director of Investigation and Research concluded:

> The documentary evidence suggests that vertical integration in the telecommunication industry is not in the public interest. ...It is recommended that the best policy solution to the issues raised in this statement is the deconcentration of the telecommunication equipment industry. Furthermore the most effective long term method to achieve this goal is through the divestiture of Northern Electric from Bell Canada as a means of reducing existing barriers to entry into the telecommunication equipment industry.

THE COMMISSION'S VIEW

It is obvious from the U.S. discussions on vertical and horizontal divestiture that the subject is far from simple. There is, however, no persuasive evidence that structural changes would be simple in effect, pro-competitive on balance or as easily carried out as these proposals seem to assume. We therefore strongly recommend that no attempt be made to force deconcentration on the basis of a percentage of industry sales controlled by the largest firms, or on the basis of absolute firm size for diversified firms, or on the basis of the degree of vertical integration among firms. Bill C-13 emphasizes a case-by-case approach to oligopoly problems, with remedies directed at specific kinds of restrictive practices, and divestiture only as a last resort. We think this is the preferable approach.

A number of practical and significant problems would have to be worked out by any industry (or vertically integrated enterprise) facing deconcentration or dissolution. One group of problems is financial in nature. Where is the capital to come from to buy up the newly divested pieces of large firms, especially in industries where large firms dominate the world market? A second problem involves the identity of potential purchasers of spun-off sections of an enterprise. In the oil industry, for example, the most eligible purchasers (assuming that other energy suppliers would be ineligible) would be foreign energy companies with expertise in the area. The next most likely buyers would be domestic energy companies too small to come under a purchase prohibition or stronger domestic companies that lack energy expertise. Of these, how many might have the cash or financing ability to acquire and operate these divested units successfully? If the answer is, as we suspect, "very few", some serious questions arise about vendors obtaining a fair price and about the ability of a newly reorganized industry to survive and progress. These problems could be overcome, possibly by increased government ownership, but we believe the costs of such actions could far outweigh their benefits.

Closely related to financial problems are the enormous problems of disentangling contractual obligations that would have to be reformulated on the breakup of an enterprise.

Should a government body proposing divestiture be required to make up possible losses by adding their guarantees to the obligations of the newly created enterprises? The answers are far from clear, but we think it should be incumbent on anyone recommending deconcentration or divestiture to suggest how each problem might be overcome.

We have not previously mentioned another problem with a structural approach to deconcentration. Although it is difficult to know how long it would take to change the structure of a market through a legal process, the duration of major competition policy cases in Canada and the United States provides some guide. The recent *Large Lamps* case alleging shared monopoly involved conduct by three defendant companies between 1959 and 1967. The decision of the trial court was handed down in 1976, penalties announced in 1977, and the period might have been extended into 1978 or 1979 if the defendants had appealed the case to the Supreme Court of Canada. The striking feature about similar legal decisions in the United States is the degree to which conditions in the industry involved have often changed significantly by the time a final decision is reached so as to render the decision of little importance to the situation under review. The precedents set by such prolonged cases may be applied in subsequent decisions, however, and may have some cautionary effect on other firms.

The Commission is doubtful that the slow process under either the present or the proposed law will have any greater effect on concentration and competition than will dynamic processes of invention, innovation and changes in competition. This conclusion does not imply that we think that competition policy should be de-emphasized, but rather that the process should be speeded up.

Need for a Review

We would like to offer one final thought on dominant firms, and indeed on competition policy in general. The content and emphasis of competition policy and the arguments presented to us for and against aspects of such a policy are very much dependent on Canada's current economic goals, and our industrial strategy. Once adopted, there seems a great danger that a competition law will introduce rigidity rather than dynamism in industrial structure and performance. There seems, then, some virtue in recommending that competition laws be reviewed periodically, and that they be formulated as "sunset laws" and expire automatically every seven to ten years.

There is a danger of course that frequent changes in competition law would simply introduce more uncertainty into the investment and operating climate of firms, which must take a very long-run view in their most important decisions. Nevertheless we think that such a provision would stimulate continuous thinking and debate of the contents of competition policy and its relation to national economic objectives, which does not seem to happen now with this or other economic statutes. If the Bank Act review is a good analogy, and it seems so to us, a periodic re-evaluation would be worth the uncertainty it might cause.

Chapter 5

Conglomerates: Diversified Enterprise in Canada

Introduction

Diversified enterprises have existed in Canada since the late 1800s, when the Canadian Pacific Railway Company (CP) started to expand from its base in railroads to ventures in related industries: transport, mining and natural resources, communications, hotels, and real estate. Over the past 80 years, the size of CP and other enterprises in Canada that are large, relative to the size of the industries in which they operate, has been the subject of several investigations and considerable literature, which has focused primarily on the ability of these firms to set prices and constrain competition in individual markets.

Following the announcement that Power Corporation of Canada, Limited, intended to take over Argus Corporation Limited, public attention focused on the conglomerate nature of many firms operating in the Canadian economy and shifted in emphasis from the relative size, concentration and behavior of firms within one industry, to the economic and social impact of enterprises with diversified holdings in several different industries. Spokesmen from business and the business press were quick to extol the ability of diversified enterprises to mobilize and allocate capital efficiently, to rationalize industry, to prevent foreign takeovers of Canadian industry, and to compete internationally. Others were as vociferous in their condemnation of conglomerates as large aggregations of power, which seemed to them to allow a few men undue control of large segments of the Canadian economy.

In this debate, there was agreement on three points: that, potentially, conglomerates and conglomerate mergers could have a significant impact on the economic, social, and political functioning of the country; that not enough was known about their nature, scope, or importance, nor could this be readily determined from the information at hand; and that the government was unable under existing corporation and competition law to regulate either conglomerate mergers or much of the behavior of conglomerate firms. The Combines Investigation Act was enacted to deal with mergers or acquisitions that tended to create monopolies or with specific anticompetitive practices within one industry, but not with combinations of firms in several industries. Existing

103

legislation did, however, restrict the actions of conglomerate firms in using their financial subsidiaries to finance or invest in their other subsidiaries.

This Commission has investigated the characteristics of conglomerate enterprises and the mergers they undertake. We have also tried to identify the implications of the size and diversity of conglomerate firms for resource allocation and competition, to measure whether conglomerates produce an increase in overall corporate concentration, and to consider whether and how any detrimental features of conglomerate enterprises need be regulated in the public interest.

These questions were studied intensively in the United States during the middle and late 1960s, when conglomerate merger activity there was at a peak. However, with a few notable exceptions, such as International Telephone and Telegraph Corp. (IT&T) and Gulf & Western Industries Incorporated, interest in "acquisitive" conglomerates waned in the United States with the decrease in conglomerate merger activity after 1970 and with the end of the buoyant stock market, which had both nurtured and been fueled by acquisitive conglomerates. In fact by 1975, the more freeform conglomerates had almost ceased to exist entirely.

During the 1960s Canadian reactions to conglomerates were more muted, perhaps because the acquisitive conglomerate, which had so captured the public imagination in the United States, was largely absent from the Canadian economy. The lack of interest may also have been because Canadian attention was directed toward different phenomena: the takeover of Canadian firms by large foreign-owned companies and the high level of concentration within its individual industries. Whatever the reason, the Canadian public and media largely ignored the diversification process that was undertaken by firms within Canada. During this period Canada had neither the legislation with which to regulate conglomerate mergers nor the inclination to formulate any. In the United States, after ten years of study by academics, government agencies, and other groups (such as the Conference Board), a large body of data and analysis has been amassed about conglomerates, including data on their number, size, diversity, profitability, growth and stability, acquisition patterns, management techniques, financial structure and competitive behavior. The conclusions drawn from this data and analysis have been mixed and often contradictory. Perhaps reflecting the diversity of conclusions, the U.S. government has not as yet articulated a coherent policy toward conglomerates, but has resorted to a makeshift application of existing antitrust law and negotiated settlements imposed by the Justice Department to regulate conglomerate mergers.

Conclusions reached about the behavior and impact of conglomerates in the United States must be used with great care when analyzing conglomerates in Canada. There should be no presumption that U.S. government policies toward conglomerates can usefully be applied to firms in Canada. The Canadian economic, social, and governmental structure and the goals of the various interest groups differ along so many dimensions from those of the United States that the basis for analysis of conglomerate behavior and performance must differ between the two countries.

Origin and Development of Conglomerates in Canada

In the late 1800s, CP developed into not only the largest enterprise in Canada but also Canada's first large, diversified company. After completing the first transcontinental railway in 1885, CP expanded its transport operations into shipping on the Atlantic and the Pacific to offer complete service to its customers in Canada, Europe and Asia. During World War II, CP expanded first into air service and later into trucking. At present, it is investigating the possibility of entering the pipeline industry, the only major transport sector in which it does not operate (it already owns shares in TransCanada Pipelines Limited through its majority-owned subsidiary Canadian Pacific Investments Limited).

CP's major railway business led it to build a chain of hotels to house its passengers and a communications network to coordinate its rail traffic. Since much of CP's freight was raw materials and because its land holdings contained mineral deposits, it was drawn into the mining business. Its purchase of a railway property that included a lead smelter at Trail, British Columbia, led to the development of the Sullivan lead-zinc mine. The by-products of the smelting process placed CP in the fertilizer, iron and steel businesses. The land that CP acquired during initial railway construction eventually led it into the forest products, real estate, and oil and gas industries.

CP stated in its brief to us that once it had established these diverse operations, they developed in their own right without regard for their origins. Each business developed a commercial logic of its own, based not on its origins but rather on the dictates of its own marketplace and technology.

By the 1920s, as other sources of capital, management, and technological expertise developed in Canada, CP's share of total corporate assets and of the gross national product (GNP) began a long, steady decline. In 1962, recognizing that its interests had diversified to the point where their operations had no unifying logic, CP formed Canadian Pacific Investments Limited (CPI) to manage its non-transport interests.

Although the history of some of today's conglomerates goes back to the early part of the century, most Canadian companies other than CP did not begin to diversify until after World War II. Most of these firms can be classified into three groups, according to the initial base from which they began to diversify: (1) investment holding companies that increased ownership and participation in their portfolio of firms; (2) firms in declining industries or in industries regulated or expropriated by the government which were more or less forced either to diversify or to return their capital to their shareholders; and (3) firms and industries whose commercial or technological logic led to expansion into related industries. The categories are not mutually exclusive, and a firm may have passed through two or three of them. For example, Power Corporation of Canada, Limited, started as an investment holding company, which then acquired operating control of several large electric power firms. When Power's assets in this area were taken over by provincial governments, it again became a holding company. A new management then came to control the company and increased Power's participation in its investments to a point where it obtained majority control of most of them.

Diversification strategy and control policy may differ greatly among diversified firms. For example, Power Corporation, Argus Corporation Limited and Genstar Limited all have interests in diverse groups of firms and all began as holding companies. Yet each represents a distinct management and ownership philosophy. The origins and history of Canadian conglomerates do seem to have influenced their diversification strategies and the organizational structures they have used to pursue them.

Argus has followed a strategy of holding a large minority interest in each of the companies in its portfolio. By having its officers on the boards of directors of the portfolio companies, Argus provides general policy guidance and advice to each firm. Except for this managerial guidance, there is no claim of any synergy among the firms in the Argus portfolio. Each firm is helped to maximize its own efficiency, growth and profitability. In the past, when an Argus holding has had financial difficulties, Argus has come to its rescue with financial and managerial assistance.

Power Corporation seeks majority ownership to ensure control of each firm in its group. Like Argus, Power Corporation does not seem to involve itself in the day-to-day management decisions of most of its subsidiaries unless the subsidiary gets into serious difficulty.

Genstar, on the other hand, seeks 100% ownership of its subsidiaries. Through a company-wide capital budgeting process, it allocates the cash flow of all its subsidiaries to those units that it thinks have the greatest potential for growth, efficiency and long-run profitability. Genstar has tried to form its subsidiaries into groups that are coherent from a marketing and production standpoint.

For analytical purposes the distinction among Argus as a holding company, Power Corporation as an operating company, and Genstar as an "operating conglomerate" is not precise. They, and other firms such as Canadian Corporate Management Company Limited, Warnock Hersey International Limited, Federal Industries Ltd., CPI, Brascan Limited and Neonex International Limited, lie along a continuum with Canadian Pacific Securities Limited (the investment holding subsidiary of CP, which exercises virtually no management control over the firms in its portfolio) at one extreme and Genstar (which carefully monitors and controls the activities of its diverse subsidiaries) at the other. The true conglomerates in Canada are firms whose subsidiaries are of major importance to them and are not linked by any underlying marketing or technological logic.

The Strategy and Structure of Firms in Canada

A conglomerate has been defined as "a diversified firm, meaning a firm with two or more non-competing, non-vertically related products." Although this definition of a conglomerate is useful in some ways, it is too simplistic to capture the wide variety of strategies pursued by firms in Canada. For example, Power Corporation and Redpath Industries Limited would be classified under this definition as conglomerates, whereas Imperial Oil Limited and

Ford Motor Company of Canada, Limited, would not. Yet the organizational structure and operational strategies of the firms within these two groups are radically different.

The differences among firms whether in the same or different groups are in the amount of diversification of their product lines. Throughout this chapter the terms "conglomerate firm" and "conglomerate merger or acquisition" are used when there is no underlying production or marketing logic among the product lines of the firm. The terms "diversified firm" and "diversifying merger or acquisition" are used when there is an underlying production or marketing logic among the products of the firm. By these definitions Power Corporation is both a diversified firm, in that its subsidiaries within any one industry (e.g., financial, pulp and paper, communications) are related, and a conglomerate firm, in that there is no underlying logic connecting its financial subsidiaries to its pulp and paper subsidiaries to its shipping line, newspapers, etc. Similarly a merger of Power and Argus would contain elements of horizontal, vertical, diversified and conglomerate mergers. The problem then is how to measure the degree of relatedness between the product lines of a firm or firms.

As mentioned above, there are different kinds of diversified and conglomerate firms, but without a system for measuring the degree of diversification, it is not possible to distinguish precisely between one kind of firm and another, and so to draw the public policy implications of the growth, performance and behavior of one kind of firm as compared with another. In the studies of conglomerate activities in the United States in the 1950s and 1960s, the measure used by U.S. regulatory bodies and academics was based on the SIC (Standard Industrial Classification) code; on this basis, the greater the number of product lines (identified through the SIC code) of a firm, the more diversified the firm was held to be. However, two difficult problems arose in the use of this code. The first problem was that the code did not distinguish between firms such as Chrysler, which had a very large number of product lines of which one (automobiles) accounted for 90% of output, and firms such as Gulf & Western, which had many product lines, but with each broadly equal in sales. This problem has been solved by Richard Caves (in his study of the diversification of plant output in Canada and in his work for the Commission) by using more sophisticated measures of product diversification such as the Herfindahl index and the concentric measure. Essentially these give a weighted measure of the diversity of a firm's products, not simply a count of the number of different products it produces. The second and more formidable problem was that the SIC code did not distinguish between firms that diversified their output from a single production technology or marketing method, and which might have grown largely from internal diversification (such as General Electric Company and E.I. DuPont de Nemours & Company), and firms that had diversified from no common technology or marketing logic and that had grown largely through acquisitions (such as Textron Incorporated). These defects in the system of measuring diversification in the U.S. studies led to much debate and contradictory conclusions.

Another system of measuring diversification avoids these two problems altogether. It defines diversification as a departure from an original core of technology or marketing skill. The system was developed by Leonard Wrigley in 1970, at the Harvard Business School, and led to the identification of four categories of firms—single business, dominant business, related business, and unrelated business—which could be spread along a continuum of amount of diversification in product lines, with each category representing a distinct corporate strategy. Wrigley used the system to study differences among U.S. industrial corporations in their historical patterns of growth and in their organizational structures, their "way of life". Later, researchers at Harvard used the system to study the similarities and differences among the strategies and structures of large-scale enterprises in the United Kingdom, Italy, France and Germany.

The Commission has used R. P. Rumelt's elaboration of this classification system as the basis for some of its studies. According to this elaboration, the strategies of all firms can be classified into four main categories: single business, dominant business, related business, and unrelated business. Firms following a dominant business strategy can be further classified into four subcategories: dominant-vertical, dominant-constrained, dominant-linked and dominant-unrelated. The related business category is divided into two sub-categories: related-linked and related-constrained. These strategic categories essentially describe the diversity of the products that the firm has chosen to produce and their underlying sales and production relation. Definitions of each of these strategic categories appear in Table 5.1.

Using this framework, our opening definition of a conglomerate firm would include firms whose strategies can be classified as unrelated, related-linked, dominant-unrelated, dominant-linked and, perhaps, dominant-constrained and related-constrained.

These different strategies tend to be motivated by very different conditions and have very different implications for a firm's growth, return on assets and return to the investor. The Commission was able to trace the diversification patterns of firms in Canada over the period 1960-75 (Table 5.2). When these patterns are compared to those of firms in the United States (Table 5.3), we see that Canadian firms have followed a diversification pattern similar to that in the United States but at a somewhat later date.

In Canada, the United States, France, Germany, England and Italy, the percentage of the largest firms following a strategy of producing in one industry (single business) declined dramatically over the period 1950-70. In general, this decline was matched by an increase in the percentage of firms engaged in related businesses. Data assembled for the Commission using standard SIC code classifications also show an increase in diversification of firms in Canada from 1960 to 1975. These changes were accompanied by a trend toward a more divisionalized organizational structure.

Table 5.1

Definitions of Firms' Strategies

1. *Single Business*: firms that are basically committed to a single business in a single industry.

2. *Dominant Business*: firms that have diversified to some extent, but still obtain the preponderance of their revenues from a single business in a single industry.

   a) Dominant-Vertical: vertically integrated *Dominant* firms.

   b) Dominant-Constrained: non-vertical *Dominant* firms that have diversified by building on some particular strength; their activities are strongly related.

   c) Dominant-Linked: non-vertical *Dominant* firms that have diversified by building on several different strengths; activities are not closely related, but are still linked to their dominant business.

   d) Dominant-Unrelated: non-vertical *Dominant* firms whose diversified activities are not linked to their dominant business.

3. *Related Business*: non-vertically integrated diversified firms operating in several industries but whose activities are linked.

   a) Related-Constrained: *Related* firms, all of whose activities are related to a central strength.

   b) Related-Linked: *Related* firms that have diversified using several different strengths and hence are active in widely disparate businesses.

4. *Unrelated Business*: non-vertical firms that have diversified without regard to the relationships between new businesses and current activities.

Source: R.P. Rumelt, *Strategy, Structure and Economic Performance* (Boston, 1974).

In addition to a descriptive analysis of the diversification strategies of firms in Canada, this framework can be used to answer several important questions about the behavior of large firms in Canada: (1) why did firms follow a particular strategy? (2) how did they effect this change? (3) which strategies have been successful (i.e yielded high returns on assets and in the market)? (4) what has been the effect of these diversification strategies on industrial structure (and hence competition) in Canada? The following sections seek to answer these questions.

Motivations for Diversification

There has been considerable effort in Canadian and U.S. economic and business literature to try to explain why firms have shifted from a single-business strategy to diversification into other industries, either by internal growth or by merger. The motives advanced for diversification vary widely and are sometimes contradictory. Clearly firms diversify for many reasons, which may vary from firm to firm and industry to industry. Since the group of highly diversified firms in Canada is quite small, the Commission has examined these firms individually to try to reach conclusions as to their motivations for diversifying. Some firms found themselves in slow-growth, stagnant, or declining industries (e.g., beer and tobacco) because of government regulation or reduced primary demand for their product. A firm in such an industry could increase sales only by increasing its market share, a move that was difficult or

Table 5.2

Strategy of Top 200 (1975) Publicly Held
Firms in Canada, 1960-75

(Estimated Percentages)

Strategy	1960		1965		1970		1975	
Single business	31		18		14		13	
Dominant business	51		52		47		41	
Dominant-vertical		24		23		20		13
Dominant-constrained		17		17		12		8
Dominant-linked		10		11		8		10
Dominant-unrelated		0		1		7		10
Related business	13		22		25		28	
Related-constrained		8		12		9		8
Related-linked		5		10		12		20
Unrelated business	5		8		14		17	

Source: Royal Commission on Corporate Concentration (RCCC) research.

Table 5.3

Strategy of U.S. Firms, 1949, 1959 and 1969

(Estimated Percentages)

Strategy	1949		1959		1969	
Single business	34.5		16.2		6.2	
Dominant business	35.4		37.3		29.2	
Dominant-vertical		15.7		14.8		15.6
Dominant-constrained		18.0		16.0		7.1
Dominant-linked		0.9		3.8		5.6
Dominant-unrelated		0.9		2.6		0.9
Related business	26.7		40.0		45.2	
Related-constrained		18.8		29.1		21.6
Related-linked		7.9		10.9		23.6
Unrelated business	3.4		6.5		19.4	
Unrelated-passive		3.4		5.3		8.5
Acquisitive conglomerate		0.0		1.2		10.9
Total number of firms used to derive the estimates		189		207		183

Source: R.P. Rumelt, *Strategy, Structure, and Economic Performance* (Boston, Mass., 1974), p. 51.

Table 5.4

Financial Characteristics of U.S. Firms in Different Strategic Categories, 1970

(Percentages)

Strategic Category	Financial Characteristics			
	Growth in Sales per Share	Growth in Earnings per Share	Return on Investment	Return on Equity
Single Business	5.84	3.92	10.81	13.20
Dominant-vertical	5.26	5.14	8.24	10.18
Dominant-constrained	7.93	7.60	12.71	14.91
Dominant-linked and dominant-unrelated	5.23	6.11	8.69	10.28
Related-constrained	7.93	8.56	11.97	14.11
Related-linked	6.29	5.57	10.43	12.28
Unrelated-passive	4.67	5.96	9.40	10.38
Acquisitive conglomerate	10.48	9.46	9.56	13.13

Source: Rumelt, *Strategy, Structure, and Financial Performance of the Fortune 500* (DBA dissertation, Graduate School of Business Administration, Harvard University, Boston, 1972).

impossible because of the reaction of firms in its own oligopolistic industry and because of possible government response. The profits of firms in this group were often satisfactory, but their growth rate in sales and profits was not.

Richard Caves, in his work for the Commission, found strong support for the hypothesis that firms in Canada such as Redpath Industries Limited, Jannock Corporation Limited, The Molson Companies Limited, Rothmans of Pall Mall Canada Limited, John Labatt Limited and Imasco Limited have diversified out of concentrated slow-growth industries so that they could continue to grow. These firms have followed the dominant-unrelated strategy, which, as already noted, has not usually been successful in either Canada or the United States.

Action by the U.S. government to block horizontal mergers and improve competition in concentrated industries has been widely cited as an incentive for some firms to diversify out of such industries. In Canada, however, enforcement of the Combines Investigation Act has been ineffective in discouraging mergers that increase concentration within an industry, and it seems to us that this incentive to diversify has not been important in Canada.

Firms in slow-growth, concentrated industries could gradually decrease in size, but managements have usually refused to accept this alternative. Tax laws in Canada give firms an incentive to reinvest their cash flow rather than to pay large dividends, which will be heavily taxed. Reinvestment offers shareholders the prospect of profits in the form of capital gains rather than as regular income.

Diversification through mergers and acquisitions is one means by which a firm may continue to increase the value of its shareholders' investment, while at the same time shifting the investment to other uses, which it hopes will prove more profitable. A contrary, but not inconsistent, argument is that managers are willing to sacrifice the returns to their shareholders to pursue asset and sales growth through diversification. This is the argument most strongly advocated by John Kenneth Galbraith and is supported by evidence that executive salaries increased with the size of the firm. The difficulties encountered by Redpath, Imasco, Molson, and Rothmans in their initial diversifying investments in Canada also lend some credence to this argument.

In research for the Commission, Caves has concluded that firms in concentrated industries in Canada have tended to diversify into less-concentrated industries, industries where there was greater scope for growth in market share and where there tended to be fewer foreign-owned firms, smaller firms, and a lower dependence on export sales. Firms also react to inbound diversification into their base industries by diversifying into other industries. These firms were seeking to reduce their risks of operation as well as increase their growth and profitability by merging or taking over firms in "safer", less oligopolistic industries whose products did not have to compete on the world market. Risk reduction was thus a powerful motivation for firms to enter new markets through mergers and aquisitions.

In briefs to the Commission, Leonard Wrigley and David Leighton emphasized the important role played by the developments in managerial techniques, which may enable management to coordinate effectively the activities of diversified and geographically separated subsidiaries. In their view modern managers can use these techniques to increase the efficiency of diversified firms regardless of the industries in which they operate. Such techniques can be applied to financial planning and capital budgeting, accounting and control systems, production scheduling and inventory control, marketing research and analysis, long-range forecasting and business-government relations. The evolution in data handling and analysis through the extensive use of computers may have augmented management's power and effectiveness even further. These economies of scale in management and control were discussed in Chapter 3, "Size and Economies of Scale". The overall effect of economies of scale in management will be examined in a later section of this chapter, "Performance of Diversified Firms".

Research and development appear to have shaped the strategies of those U.S. companies, such as General Electric, Du Pont and American Telephone and Telegraph Company, which have diversified into related products. These companies have moved beyond dependence on a single market to multimarket strategies. They are characterized by an institutionalized research and development effort, that is the systematic search for new products, to gain the high profits of products in the early stages of the product life cycle. The success of this strategy is reflected in the high profit and return figures for related American firms shown in Table 5.4. As noted above, the nature of the base industries from which many Canadian firms have had to diversify has discouraged this type of diversification in Canada, or at least made it unprofitable. This point will be discussed later in this chapter.

Methods of Diversification

Firms can diversify either through internal expansion or by acquiring another firm in a merger or acquisition. This latter activity has been erratic, but increasing over the period 1945-75 (see Chapter 6, "Mergers and Acquisitions").

As already described, the definition of a "conglomerate merger" presents several problems. For the purposes of its work, the Commission has defined a "conglomerate merger" as one in which the products of the acquired firm were not the same or closely related in production or marketing to those of the acquiring firm. If the acquired firm was itself diversified, and if some of its major subsidiaries operated in industries in which the acquiring firm did not operate, the merger was considered to be conglomerate. By this definition, not all mergers by a conglomerate can necessarily be classified as conglomerate mergers.

Since 1900, the absolute and relative number of conglomerate mergers has increased, as has the total number of mergers. However, the percentage of domestic companies engaging in mergers decreased over the period 1969-76. Comparable figures for conglomerate mergers in the United States indicate that the conglomerate merger trend peaked in that country in 1967, but in late 1977 there was a resurgence in the number of conglomerate mergers in the United States.

A random sample of 91 mergers in Canada by 10 conglomerate firms during the period 1960-75 was examined in terms of the market share and industry structure of the acquired firm (see Tables 5.5, 5.6). The firms in the sample tended to acquire firms by making "toehold" acquisitions in unconcentrated industries (sometimes because all major firms in the industry were already subsidiaries of foreign-controlled multinational enterprises and not for sale). If the acquired firm's industry was concentrated, the acquired firm tended to be intermediate in size. (See Table 5.6.)

An alternative way to diversify is through internal expansion using the firm's existing management and workers, research and development facilities, and sales force. From 1960 to 1975, growth in assets of Canadian firms appears to be related to the strategy of the firms: the greater the degree of diversification the greater was the proportion of growth due to mergers (Table 5.7).

How did firms whose strategy was to diversify by merger finance their acquisitions? For the period 1960-75, diversified firms were more likely to use stock to pay for their acquisitions than were single businesses, which tended to use cash already on hand (Table 5.8). It should be noted that, unlike the practice in the United States, there has been little use of unusual securities given in exchange for acquired companies. In particular, the possibility of using stock traded at high price/earnings (P/E) multiples to buy firms with lower multiples has been greatly reduced by Canadian regulations governing accounting for mergers, and the relatively low P/E multiples assigned by stock markets to conglomerate enterprises.

Table 5.5

Market Share of a Sample of Firms Acquired by 10 Conglomerates,* Canada, 1960-75

Market Share	Percentage of	
	Firms	Assets
20% or more	5	25*
10-19.9%	15	32
5-9.9%	27	23
1-4.9%	24	15
Less than 1.0%	24	5

Number of firms in sample 91

Source: RCCC research.
Notes: *Argus Corporation Limited, Brascan Limited, Canadian Pacific Investments Limited,
          Imasco Limited, Jannock Corporation Limited, John Labatt Limited, Neonex
          International Ltd., Power Corporation of Canada, Limited, Redpath Industries
          Limited and Warnock Hersey International Limited.
          **Read as "5% of the firms had 20% or more of their relevant market and accounted for
          25% of the assets of all acquired firms in our sample".

Table 5.6

Market Position and Level of Industry Concentration for a Sample of Firms Acquired by 10 Conglomerates* Canada, 1960-75

	Type of Industry			
Market Position of Acquisition	Concentrated (CR$_4$ over 60%)	Intermediate (CR$_4$ 40-60%)	Unconcentrated (CR$_4$ less than 40%)	Total
Leading firm (Market share 10% or more)	5	9	4	18
Intermediate (Market share 5-9%)	9	7	9	25
Toehold (Market share less than 5%)	5	14	29	48
Total	19	30	42	91

Source: RCCC research.
Note: * See Table 5.5 note.

Table 5.7

Type of Growth in Assets of Top 200* (1975) Publicly Held Firms in Canada, 1960-75

(Percentages)

Strategic Category of Firm	Type of Growth	
	Internal	Merger
Single business	91	9
Dominant business	72	28
Related business	68	32
Unrelated business	57	43

Source: RCCC research; estimates based on annual reports.
Note: *Ranked by sales.

Table 5.8

Methods of Financing Acquisitions by Publicly Held
Canadian Firms, 1960-75

(Percentages)

Method of Financing	Strategic Category of Acquiring Firm			
	Unrelated Business	Related Business	Dominant Business	Single Business
Working capital	2	15	55	53
Long-term debt	34	21	8	19
Convertible debentures	8	9	2	3
Preferred stock	4	18	6	14
Common stock	52	37	29	11
Total	100	100	100	100

Source: RCCC research: annual reports on mergers by publicly held Canadian firms in the top 200 (1975), ranked by sales.

On the other hand, some Canadian enterprises have been able to acquire subsidiaries by using the acquired firm's own dividends or unused debt capacity. The acquiring firm borrows the money for its acquisition and repays the loan from the cash flow of the acquired firm, or from a subsequent debt issue of the acquired firm. This financing method has on occasion allowed small aggressive firms to take over large, unleveraged, high pay-out firms.

Performance of Diversified Firms in Canada

Capital Allocation

One of the major claims of diversified firms such as Genstar and Canadian Corporate Management in their submissions to the Commission was that diversified firms are a more efficient means of transferring capital from one industry to another than is the imperfect capital market in Canada. In research done for the Commission, D. G. McFetridge tested this claim. For the period 1961-70 he found no difference in a sample of 205 Canadian firms between returns on internally reinvested funds and those on externally raised capital.

The lack of ready capital for small and medium-sized business in Canada has often been cited as a primary cause of the takeover of Canadian firms by foreign bidders. Canadian firms taken over in the 1968-73 period tended to be more highly leveraged than those which were not, and thus more in need of infusions of new equity capital. More significantly, R. F. Hinchcliff and D. M. Shapiro in work done for Statistics Canada in 1975 found that firms acquired by foreign firms were less liquid, more highly leveraged, and more profitable than were firms taken over by Canadian firms. On the other hand, parallel research in the United States has concluded that acquired firms there had lower leverage ratios than firms in the same industry that had not merged. This finding supports the general belief that capital for expansion is more easily available to small businesses in the United States than it is in Canada.

Profitability, Risk and Efficiency

The controversy over the relative profitability and risk of large diversified firms is widely reflected in the economic literature. If, as several witnesses testified before the Commission, a strategy of conglomerate diversification allows firms to achieve economies of scale in finance and management, they should be more profitable and give a higher return to their investors at lower risk than do firms with otherwise identical opportunities which have followed other strategies.

A growing body of evidence, however, throws into doubt the theory that a strategy of conglomerate diversification is either a profitable one for investors or a good use of the firm's assets. Rumelt concluded in *Strategy, Structure and Economic Performance* that unrelated-passive firms (firms that were conglomerate holding companies) had the lowest rate of sales growth, very high variability in earnings per share, and next to the lowest return on capital. The U.S. Federal Trade Commission in 1972 stated that from their research they could find no significant change in the post-merger profitability of those firms acquired by diversified firms. As indicated in Table 5.9, there seems to have been no clear direction to the changes between pre-merger and post-merger profitability for a sample of the firms acquired by highly diversified firms in Canada in the 1960-73 period. In his Ph.D. thesis, "An Analysis of Financial Performance and the Level of External Growth through Merger", S. N. Laiken found no correlation between the diversification of firms in Canada and their growth in either earnings (or sales) per share or their profit performance. Caves and his associates support these conclusions. They found that return to the investor in Canada may indeed have decreased, and risk increased, with diversification. McFetridge also concluded that, contrary to his expectation, as the diversity of a firm increased, its profitability decreased.

Table 5.9

Change in Profitability after Acquisition of
Manufacturing Firms Acquired by Sample
Conglomerates, United States and Canada,
1960-73

	Total Number of Firms Acquired	Change in Profitability	
		Increase	Decrease
United States	43	23	20
Canada	24	13	11

Source: U.S. data: Federal Trade Commission; Canadian data: RCCC research.

This failure of conglomerates to increase the profitability of their new acquisitions may be due to a necessary gestation period during which acquiring firms learn how to manage their newly acquired subsidiaries, and to realize the many synergies that may be inherent in the merged firm. Given time, it has been argued, even highly diversified firms with no marketing or technological

Table 5.10

Comparison of 10 Conglomerates*
with Simulated Portfolios, Canada, 1960-75
(Percentages)

	Conglomerates	Simulated Portfolios (1)	(2)***
Return to stockholders	9.4	12.7	10.0
Return** on total assets	6.7	10.3	8.1
Growth rate of earnings per share	4.3	6.8	5.3

Source: RCCC research.
Notes: *See Table 5.5 note.
       **Based on earnings before interest and taxes.
       ***Column (2) includes an average acquisition premium of 27.5% above market price.

link between their subsidiaries will be able to increase profits because of the synergy of the various components. This synergy is most often thought to come from the ability of modern managers to transcend the skills required in any one business and to achieve economies of scale in management time and effectiveness through modern management techniques.

An impressive rebuttal of the synergy argument for highly diversified firms was given by R. H. Mason and M. B. Goudzwaard in the *Journal of Finance* (1976). They constructed 22 portfolios of stocks that duplicated the initial assets and acquisitions of 22 U.S. conglomerates over the period

Table 5.11

Performance of Publicly Held Firms in
the Top 200* (1975), Canada, 1960-75
(Percentages)

Strategic Category of Firm	Growth in Earnings per Share	Growth in Sales per Share	Return on Equity	Return to the Investor
Single Business	2.1↓	6.8	10.5	8.9
Dominant-vertical	3.7↓	6.5	7.1↓	8.3↓
Dominant-constrained	5.2↑	8.3↑	11.2↑	19.1↑
Dominant-linked	4.3	6.1	8.9	16.3
Dominant-unrelated	2.0↓	4.2↓	7.5↓	10.2↓
Related-constrained	7.5↑	8.7↑	11.2↑	20.3↑
Related-linked	3.7	6.0↓	6.9↓	12.2
Unrelated business	3.1↓	5.2↓	7.1↓	8.1↓

Source: RCCC research.
Notes: * Ranked by sales.
       (↓) = significantly below average at the 10% level of significance.
       (↑) = significantly above average at the 10% level of significance.

1962-67. Of the 22 "mirror portfolios", 19 had a higher return on investment and return to the stockholder than did the actual conglomerate firm. This result was totally unexpected by the authors and is even more surprising since the period was one when the conglomerate firm in the United States was very popular.

Our research replicated this study for ten highly diversified firms in Canada over the period 1960-75 and showed similar results. Firms that followed a strategy of unrelated diversification were less profitable in sales, grew less quickly and returned less to their stockholders in dividends and stock appreciation than did a portfolio of stocks that duplicated the acquiring firm's diversification pattern (Table 5.10). As well, of the 100 largest publicly held firms in Canada, those that followed a strategy of unrelated diversification (dominant-related, related-linked and unrelated business) had a significantly lower return on equity and return to their investors over the same period (Table 5.11).

The Commission considered this conclusion sufficiently important to warrant replicating the research, to check whether the outcome was consistent given different assumptions, portfolio selections and benchmarks. In this research, Jerome Baesel and Dwight Grant looked for a measure of performance that did not rely on accounting statements, in order to eliminate the problem of conceptual or measurement error in the preparation of those statements.

The first part of the research was designed to investigate whether long-term market performance of the common stock of acquisitive companies was significantly different from long-term market performance of a diversified portfolio of common stocks. They measured the annual rate of return on the common stock for five groups of firms: the Toronto Stock Exchange (TSE), a random sample of firms on the TSE, a group of 35 firms that made five or more acquisitions over the period 1960-75, the ten conglomerate firms in the Commission's earlier study, and a group of mutual funds. Performance was measured on both an unadjusted basis (return above the risk-free rate) and a risk-adjusted return (as measured by the Treynor index). The study again covered the period 1960-75, which we think adequately reflects both good and bad periods of market performance.

The results of this study were mixed. In the period 1960-69, during which the TSE performed well, both the acquisition-oriented firms and the ten firms that pursued a strategy of conglomerate diversification significantly outperformed the firms in the other groups. During the period 1970-75, a period of poor market performance, the market performance of the acquisition-oriented and conglomerate firms was worse, although not significantly so, than those in the other samples. Over the entire period, there were no significant differences in the performance of any of the samples. The results of these two studies are not necessarily contradictory. The population of firms in each strategic category (as displayed in Table 5.11) changed over the period 1960-75. Thus many of the firms that followed a strategy of unrelated diversification fell into that category only in the late 1960s or early 1970s, a time when Baesel and Grant found that such firms were not performing well on the stock market.

Why have Canadian firms been largely *unsuccessful* in their diversification strategies? As stated earlier, Canadian firms appear to have followed U.S. firms in a strategy of increased diversification. While U.S. firms have tended to diversify into related industries, however, Canadian firms have diversified largely into unrelated industries. There are still a greater proportion of single businesses and dominant businesses in Canada than in the United States, but within the dominant-business category a greater proportion of firms have diversified into unrelated industries in Canada than in the United States. Similarly, Canadian firms that have followed a strategy of related diversification are more diverse than U.S. firms within that category, i.e. they have followed a related-linked strategy.

For firms that followed a strategy of unrelated diversification in Canada the problems of low profits and low returns to their investors have been particularly acute (Table 5.11). J. T. Scott in research for the Commission also found that these lower returns were accompanied by higher risks. It should be noted that the firms in each group have changed over the period. For example, Redpath, Jannock, and Labatt have changed their strategies from single business to dominant-unrelated; Imasco has changed from a single business to related-linked. The returns in each strategic category are only for firms in that category during that year. Table 5.11 indicates that the performance of firms differed significantly according to strategy.

In an effort to test Wrigley's conclusions concerning the relative unprofitability of the diversification strategies followed by Canadian firms, Caves and his associates placed 58 of the firms in their sample into Wrigley's four strategic categories: single, dominant, related and unrelated. They found that the base industries of firms in each category had distinguishing characteristics and that once the structural characteristics of the firms' base industry were taken into account the strategic categories had no significant influence on profits. Caves' conclusion implies that Canadian firms have not followed a strategy of unrelated diversification in error, with resulting low return, but that given the industries in which they were operating originally, they had no alternative but to follow a strategy of unrelated diversification. For example, Redpath could not diversify into a high-growth, high-profit industry related to sugar refining because, in all likelihood, no such industry existed. Caves concluded on the basis of the firms in his sample that there are a large number of firms in Canada whose base industries allow them little scope for related diversification (e.g., brewing, tobacco, mining and textiles). For these firms, diversification may have been a better strategy despite its low returns than remaining solely in the base industry. It has also been suggested to the Commission that unrelated diversification may also be caused by a miniature replica effect for the subsidiaries of foreign firms: i.e. Canadian-owned firms may imitate the diversification they observe at home and abroad as a competitive response.

The Commission decided to expand this study and took a sample of the 100 largest, publicly held Canadian firms and classified them into the eight strategic subcategories described earlier. The growth in earnings per share, sales per share, return on equity, and return to the investor were then calculated for the firms in each group.

Our results partly support Caves' conclusions. Many Canadian firms did diversify out of concentrated, capital-intensive, low-growth industries. Only for those firms that followed a diversification strategy into related products was there an improvement in the efficiency of the firm (measured by return on equity) or in return to the investor. Firms that diversified into unrelated businesses performed significantly worse than their base industries. Firms that diversified into related industries improved their performance over other firms in the economy and over their base industry performance. These firms seem to have been able to realize both economies of scale and some synergy in their related diversification. One explanation for this finding is that only firms that diversified into related industries could realize economies of scale from their larger operations.

Another explanation for the lack of increased profitability of highly diversified firms has been proposed by a number of writers who have argued that owner-managed firms are more profitable than firms managed by delegates of the owner, because of lower motivation among such delegates and greater difficulties in control. Similarly, it has been argued that managers of firms controlled by an absentee dominant shareholder may be less likely to take risks to increase profits. If a diversifying firm acquires owner-managed firms, it may be decreasing both the profitability and the incentive to innovate in its new subsidiaries despite achieving real economies of scale in management and finance.

Another plausible explanation for our finding is offered in research by Michael Gort and T. F. Hogarty in the 1970 *Journal of Law and Economics*. They suggested that firms that diversify by merger pay such a large premium over the market value of the firm's equity for their acquisitions that they are unable to recoup their money from future operations. In a study of tender offers for publicly held firms in Canada from 1960 to 1975, the Commission found that acquiring firms paid an average premium of 27.3% over market price at the time of the offer for the firm they acquired.

The existence of this premium means that if actual return on assets of the acquiring firm is used as a measure of efficiency, we cannot easily draw conclusions as to whether there is synergy in mergers as a whole, even though diversified companies as a group have not performed as well as their "mirror portfolios". It is possible that there is considerable synergy involved in mergers, but that the acquisition premiums paid were so high that an acquiring firm could not thereafter achieve the industry's average return on investment, and thus give shareholders a normal return, even though it had increased the efficiency and profitability of its acquisition.

In an attempt to correct for this bias, the asset bases of the acquiring firms in our sample were deflated by the amount of the merger premiums. Although the returns on assets and to investors improved for highly diversified firms, they were still significantly below those for firms that diversified into related industries.

From our research, the general conclusion can be drawn that firms that have diversified into unrelated industries have not increased their return on investment, their return to their shareholders, or their growth in sales per share. For some time such firms have exhibited very low price/earnings ratios, a reflection of the market's current opinion of their growth prospects and the trend of their earnings.

In a brief to the Commission, Wrigley has suggested what seems to be a crucial factor in Canadian firms' lack of success in diversification strategy: their lack of sufficient size within related product groups. In Canada, both the diversifying enterprise and the firms it acquired were usually far smaller than such firms in the United States. Even with diversification and increased enterprise size, many Canadian firms were still at a considerable disadvantage in their ability to undertake research and development, and in particular to innovate. As was described in Chapter 3, R&D was found to increase with scale up to a very large size, particularly the scale of output of the related products produced by the firm.

These problems of low expenditures on research and development and low productivity have become almost cliché in Canada. In addition to the high degree of foreign ownership (*Foreign Direct Investment in Canada* [Gray Report], 1972) and poor business-government relations (Science Council of Canada, 1971), major impediments to sustained innovation in Canada are simply the relatively small size, the great diversity of products and the organizational structure of Canadian enterprises.

Until Canadian firms have a larger market either through specialization agreements between firms, industry reorganization, or trade into foreign markets, they will be largely blocked from attaining sufficient size to undertake continuous innovation. Unrelated diversification has not helped to solve this problem. As a consequence of unrelated diversification, the size of the enterprise has increased, but the size of its basic economic marketing, technological and production units has not. It is the size of the related product units that is crucial to achieving economies of scale and the minimum size for continuous process and product innovation. We say this while recognizing that any attempt to resolve the problem must include safeguards against the potential anticompetitive results of monopoly or oligopoly.

Even though firms in Canada that have diversified into unrelated industries have not increased either their efficiency or their return to their shareholders, they could still be seen as a potentially efficient means of allocating resources in the economy and as an attractive investment if they had been able to reduce their risks even though they lowered their profits. Established financial and economic theory holds that diversified firms should be less risky, that is they should have a lower variation on sales and earnings than do undiversified firms. However a major finding of Scott in the Caves study for the Commission is that the variation in sales and earnings in Canada increased with the diversity of the firm.

Recognizing some of these problems, some enterprises in Canada that have followed a strategy of unrelated diversification in the past have recently begun to try to focus their products and new acquisitions into more closely related product groups (notable examples being Genstar and Imasco). Such enterprises seem to have concluded that purely financial control of unrelated subsidiaries does not lead to higher profits and more efficient operations, as the acquisition logic of the 1960s argued that it would.

Unsound Capital Structures

Concern has been expressed in the United States that the financing of mergers with debt has led to less-conservative (debt-heavy) capital structures in acquiring firms. While there is little good evidence on this point even in the United States, the Commission did undertake a limited investigation of the financial ratios of net income to total liabilities, working capital to total debt, net cash flow to total debt, total debt to long-term debt, and the current ratio in several Canadian enterprises that had undertaken debt-financed diversification since 1965. The analysis was complicated by the fact that virtually all Canadian business showed some deterioration in these ratios during the period 1970-75. While not claiming that our research was either extensive or definitive, we were unable to find evidence of deteriorating capital structures due to debt-financed expansion that would warrant either more extensive research on our part or any expression of concern. In some instances, such as Power's takeover of Consolidated-Bathurst Limited or the takeover of The Price Company Limited by Abitibi Paper Company Ltd., diversified firms have tapped their unused borrowing power to acquire new subsidiaries or aid existing ones. In these cases, however, although total debt increased, the size, diversity and earning power of the enterprise could carry the new debt without increasing the risk of default.

Competition with Foreign Firms

Two important international aspects of the Canadian economy affect Canadian firms. One is the significant percentage of Canadian industry controlled by foreign-based multinational enterprises; the second is the size and scope of Canada's international trade.

The question of the relationships among economies of scale, size and exports has already been covered in Chapter 3. In that chapter we concluded that there probably was a very weak relationship between the size of the firm and its ability to export. A stronger relationship probably exists between the size of the output of related products within the firm and its exports. No relationship was found between the size of highly diversified firms and the exports of their products.

It was suggested to the Commission that a diversified firm such as Power Corporation could function much as some of the huge, diversified Japanese trading companies do in encouraging exports from components of the group. It is difficult to see, however, how financial and media interests could help the export of pulp and paper products or computers.

Many briefs have argued that when Canadian enterprises diversify by taking over smaller firms, these firms are saved from foreign takeover. If correct, this is an important factor in considering corporate diversification. If takeovers by foreign firms are restricted or generally discouraged by the Foreign Investment Review Agency (FIRA), and if venture capital firms, banks and the stock market are unable or unwilling to provide sufficient equity or loan capital, a misallocation of resources might arise in the Canadian economy unless Canadian-controlled firms were willing to acquire small, growing firms. Without such nourishment the incentive to invent and invest in new products might well decrease even further from its current low level.

Competition

Many of the fears regarding diversified firms stem from a belief that somehow, as a result of the diversification process, they will reduce competition, increase industrial concentration, raise prices, reduce quality, decrease output and slow innovation. We might then ask what, if any, relationship exists between diversification and market concentration. That is does diversification increase concentration within the sector of which the acquired or acquiring firm is a member? In the United States, recent research has concluded that when conglomerate firms diversified into an industry (inbound diversification) the market position of leading firms was weakened, especially where the market was concentrated and the entering firm was large. C. W. Berry reached similar conclusions for the United States in *Corporate Growth and Diversification*, based on studies of changes in concentration in industries with a high rate of inbound diversification. Caves, in his research for the Commission, concluded that firms in Canada diversify out of concentrated industries and into less-concentrated ones instead of trying to increase concentration in their base industry either internally or by merger. He also found both that inbound diversification tended to occur in industries with moderate barriers to entry and that lower profits were found in industries with high inbound diversification. These diversification patterns might thus be beneficial in the long run to the Canadian economy.

In the United States, conglomerate acquisitions of leading firms have been blocked by regulatory agencies on the presumption that a large, acquisitive, diversifying firm could enter the industry through internal expansion or by acquiring a smaller firm, and thus its entry by a large acquisition decreases potential competition in the industry. In addition, if a firm's acquisition is blocked by the courts, it may be forced to expand via internal growth. The focus for expansion in virtually every enterprise studied by the Commission has been on either internal growth or acquisition, but not both. Single businesses grew mostly by internal expansion, whereas unrelated businesses grew mostly by merger. When a firm diversified into a new business, it almost always did so by merger or acquisition, not by internal expansion. Once a firm has diversified into a new industry by acquisition it sometimes greatly increases the size of its new subsidiary by allocating funds to it from its other operations. We conclude that a potential-entry argument that conglomerate acquisitions reduce competition would not be a valid reason for forestalling conglomerate mergers in

Canada, except perhaps in very unusual circumstances, and that the reducing-potential-competition argument should probably not be extended to apply to conglomerates.

In testimony before the Commission, John Narver concluded, on the basis of U.S. experience, that if a diversifying firm enters an industry by acquiring a leading or dominant firm, overall competition will probably decrease. If the diversifying firm makes a toehold acquisition, however, competition within the industry will probably increase. As described earlier, over the period 1960-75 conglomerates in Canada tended to diversify by toehold acquisitions into unconcentrated industries. In general, firms that made toehold acquisitions tended to expand the market share of their new subsidiaries, whereas firms that acquired leading firms did not (Table 5.12). These results are similar to those of L. G. Goldberg in a 1973 article in the *Journal of Law and Economics*. He concluded that concentration ratios did not increase for industries that experienced considerable inbound conglomerate diversification. In Canada, when diversifying firms actively increased their subsidiaries' market shares, not only did their profits increase but the efficiency of the firms as measured by return on equity frequently increased as well. On the basis of this evidence, the Commission concludes that conglomerate mergers have not in general decreased competition within industries by increasing their concentration or by ceasing to be potential competitors by means of internal expansion.

Potential Restraints to Competition

Discussions of anticompetitive practices associated with conglomerate enterprises have usually cited the potentials for such practices inherent in large corporate size, or have illustrated abuses by reference to scattered examples. The ones cited most commonly are the following: reciprocity, tying agreements, exclusive dealing, predatory pricing, cross-subsidization, mutual forbearance and increasing barriers to entry.

RECIPROCITY

Reciprocity occurs when two or more firms agree to buy one another's products at preferential prices. Certainly as the number of products a firm produces increases, the potential for reciprocal dealings with other firms increases. B. T. Allen in a 1975 article in the *Journal of Law and Economics* concluded that the greater the number of closely related products a U.S. company made the more opportunities for reciprocity it had *and used*. He also found that reciprocity was inversely related to market share, leading him to conclude that reciprocity was practised by companies as a device for cutting prices and hiding the evidence from larger rivals. On the other hand, J. W. Markham, in *Conglomerate Enterprise and Public Policy*, found that reciprocal dealing decreased diversification. Allen concluded: "Genuinely *diversifying* mergers are unlikely to produce any reciprocity potential." Allen went on to state: "The practice [reciprocity] evidently does enhance competition within concentrated industries by adding an element of sub rosa price cutting." In any event, so long as markets for the products of both firms are competitive, there

Table 5.12

Post-Acquisition Changes in Market Positions
of Firms Acquired by 10 Conglomerates,*
Canada 1965-75

Changes in Market Position

| Market Position of Acquisition | Type of Industry | | | | | | Subtotals | | Total |
| | Concentrated (CR$_4$ over 60%) | | Intermediate (CR$_4$ 40-60%) | | Unconcentrated (CR$_4$ less than 40%) | | | | |
	Increase	Decrease	Increase	Decrease	Increase	Decrease	Increase	Decrease	
Leading firm (Market share 10% or more)	3	2	4	5	2	2	9	9	18
Intermediate (Market share 5-9%)	3	6	3	4	3	6	9	16	25
Toehold (Market share less than 5%)	3	2	6	8	8	21	17	31	48
Total	9	10	13	17	13	29	35	56	91

Source: RCCC research.

Note: *See Table 5.5 note.

is no misallocation of resources or loss of efficiency even if reciprocal dealing does occur. This observation is not much consolation for the small, single-product firm, which is foreclosed from selling its products to major markets or buyers because of the existence of reciprocal buying arrangements. Such an excluded firm does not even have recourse to Canadian courts under the Combines Investigation Act, since reciprocity is not presently considered to be an offense under the Act or under proposed amendments to it. Companies or individuals may, however, bring civil suits for damages suffered from other restrictive practices such as refusal to deal or exclusive dealing.

Caves, in *International Trade and Finance: Essays in Honour of Jan Tinbergen*, cites historical and contemporary evidence of the extent of reciprocity in the United States. He shows that reciprocity is most likely to exist when large firms have market power and when a large part of their business consists of inter-company transactions of semi-processed goods or components. When reciprocal dealing occurs in such imperfectly competitive markets it may reduce economic efficiency if the effect is to raise supplier prices and enhance the profitability of an existing monopoly position. William Stanbury examined reciprocity in a report for the Commission and pointed out that existing estimates of the extent of reciprocal dealing the United States are very rough, and that there is virtually no evidence on the economic significance of this practice either there or in Canada. The Commission recognizes that persistent reciprocity at other than market prices is socially objectionable. However, it has not been able to uncover evidence that reciprocity is practised to any significant degree in Canada by diversified firms.

Often what is seen as reciprocal dealing is simply the result of long-term, historical buying and selling relationships between two firms. In a world of uncertainty and high search costs, firms may be minimizing their total costs even when they do not purchase from the supplier with the lowest price. The expected costs associated with searching for a lower-cost good or service, testing it, adapting to its requirements and forming a new buyer-supplier relationship may be greater than any expected gains. Uncertainty about future supply or the financial stability of the supplier further reduces incentives to seek and switch to a lower-cost supplier.

The Commission concludes that whatever dangers may be inherent in reciprocal dealing among diversified enterprises do not deserve additional legislative treatment at this time.

TYING AGREEMENTS AND EXCLUSIVE DEALING

Concern has been expressed that diversified enterprise will be more likely to engage in tying agreements and exclusive dealing than will firms in a single line of business. A tying arrangement occurs when a supplier makes the sale of one good conditional upon the buyer's agreement to take as well a second, unrelated good. For example, in the United States, Procter & Gamble Company was forced to divest itself of Clorox Company in part because the court held that Procter & Gamble's wide range of related products enabled it to coerce stores to stock Clorox to the exclusion of other bleach products.

However, it is also agreed that if Procter & Gamble had been maximizing its profits by using all its monopoly power before its acquisition of Clorox, one must conclude that the company would have no further leverage to force stores to expand their purchases of Clorox. Thus, to conclude that conglomerate diversification will increase the propensity of firms to engage in tied selling, we must believe either that these firms have unexercised monopoly power, or that the diversification process somehow confers additional monopoly power on them in the individual markets for their products. It seems to us that neither of these two situations are likely to exist.

Exclusive dealing occurs where a supplier insists that his dealers agree to stock or sell no other directly competitive lines of goods. This may occur because an exclusive territory is offered the dealer as a quid pro quo or because the seller has some unexercised market power permitting him to make such a demand. In either case, the supplier must both have unexercised monopoly power and face constraints on its exercise.

The Commission concludes that existing law is probably sufficient to treat those cases of tying arrangements and exclusive dealing that may arise. The Commission similarly concludes that no case exists for a general presumption against diversified enterprises on the basis of their increased ability to use tying arrangements or exclusive dealing in unfair competition.

PREDATORY PRICING

One persistent fear about conglomerate enterprises, which is not felt about large, single-product, single-market firms, is their latent power to employ predatory pricing to penetrate new markets. The argument is that, temporarily, a conglomerate may use the profits from one product to subsidize the price of another product below the level of long-term total cost, and thereby capture market share from single-product sellers who are unable to subsidize their sales. A single-product firm cannot follow this strategy unless it is willing and able to sustain short-term losses, or unless it can practise price discrimination.

Unless an increased market share for the new product can be maintained, however, and above-normal profits derived from its sales, the diversified firm trying to maximize profits has no incentive to engage in predatory pricing. If the market is competitive or there are relatively low barriers to entry, the firm that gains market share by predatory pricing will not be able to recoup its lost profits by eventually raising prices, since if it raises prices its competitors will recapture their lost markets.

However, in some consumer-goods markets where heavy advertising expenditures create strong brand preferences and high barriers to entry, predatory pricing could be used by a diversified firm to increase its long-term profits. For example, after IT&T acquired Continental Baking Company in 1968, it rapidly expanded the market share of Continental's Wonder Bread by pricing the bread below its long-term average cost. The company presumably hoped to gain a large share of the bread market, and eventually to be able to raise its prices, but, because of brand loyalty, without losing customers. In 1975, IT&T

was found guilty in the United States of predatory pricing, fined and enjoined from continuing to employ that pricing policy.

In Canada, the Combines Investigation Act gives the government power to attack predatory pricing, although there is virtually no jurisprudence on the issue. The basic problem with enforcing predatory pricing legislation comes from the difficulty of distinguishing between predatory pricing and normal rigorous competition. A firm with a modern, efficient plant and equipment may very well be able to price below older firms in an industry.

On balance, we believe that a strong and well-enforced competition law is probably the best deterrent to a feeling that predatory-pricing practices are either possible or likely.

CROSS-SUBSIDIZATION

Cross-subsidization to allow pricing below full cost is similar in effect to predatory pricing. A firm may use profits from one of its product lines (or subsidiaries) to subsidize another product temporarily to enhance its market share. Again, if the firm is motivated solely to maximize its profits, it will not engage in cross-subsidization unless it thinks that in the long run the subsidized product can be profitable on its own. It will not engage in cross-subsidization in the sense of allocating corporate resources to uses where they will earn below normal returns.

In briefs to the Commission, diversified firms had very different responses to the issue of cross-subsidization. The Chief Executive Officer of Argus Corporation denied that Argus has ever cross-subsidized any of the firms in its group. Molson has subsidized losses of Beaver Lumber Company Limited for several years. Similarly, Power Corporation has shifted resources to several of its subsidiaries when they have run into difficulties; it put fresh money into Dominion Glass Company Limited when that firm ran into temporary financial and operating difficulties, and it provided financial assistance to Laurentide Financial Corporation Limited when that subsidiary was in trouble. Thus, in emergencies, Power Corporation and other diversified firms have provided funds for their subsidiaries by using their general corporate financial strength.

Genstar, on the other hand, actively pursues a second, quite different, kind of cross-subsidization, using the cash flow of subsidiaries in slow-growing but still profitable industries to subsidize the cash flow of subsidiaries in fast-growing, cash deficit, but potentially more profitable, industries. Genstar has created an internal allocation system designed to allocate its resources to their most efficient use. Genstar stated in its brief that one of the virtues of a diversified enterprise is precisely this ability to transfer resources from one industry to another more efficiently than does the financial sector.

From an economic point of view, this short-run, cash-flow cross-subsidization, which may lead ultimately to more efficient use of capital and employees, may be beneficial to both the firm and the economy. Of course, cash-flow cross-subsidization can lead to an inefficient allocation of resources if a firm continues to subsidize the long-run production of a product that cannot be made efficiently or sold at a profit. In this connection, it is interesting to note that Michael Porter in a 1976 article in the *California Management Review* concluded that highly diversified firms were more likely to retain losing subsidiaries than were other firms.

In his recent books Galbraith has concluded that managers of firms in the "planning sector", the large firms in the economy, seek growth and stability by sacrificing profits, which are simply maintained above some minimum acceptable level. According to this view firms seeking to maximize growth would have every incentive to use cross-product subsidization, predatory pricing and tied sales (up to a point) even if these practices reduced the firm's long-run profits. The Commission has observed several instances where non-profit-maximizing objectives have been pursued by some diversified firms. These practices do not lead to efficient resource allocation, nor do they encourage innovation and competition within industries. As with some of the other problems of diversified firms already described, the solution to this problem is elusive. Eventually the investors should reflect dissatisfaction with such growth strategies by giving these firms very low price/earnings multiples and threatening the management with takeover raids (however, conglomerate firms can hide these indicators of poor performance for significant periods and thereby cause serious resource misallocation). Government-owned enterprises have been guilty of the same distortion of resource allocation by subsidizing inefficient ventures, often without even the minimum profit constraint that acts as a partial check on large firms in the private sector.

Diversified enterprises offer managers alternative uses for the funds generated by uneconomic subsidiaries besides that of reinvestment in the declining industry or returning the funds to the shareholders. Redpath, Molson, Imasco and others have all diversified to transfer resources out of their base industries by initially subsidizing diversification into other industries through merger or acquisition or by setting up a new plant.

The question then is not whether subsidization occurs within diversified enterprises in Canada, but whether it has beneficial, neutral, or harmful effects on the efficiency with which resources are allocated within the economy. The conclusion of the Commission is that the effects of cash-flow subsidization do not in general appear harmful, nor is the incidence of inefficient cross-subsidization common enough, to suggest a need for legislative constraints on diversified firms beyond those existing in the present Combines Investigation Act. The most overt example of inefficient cross-subsidization of long-term losses which the Commission has encountered occurs among chain newspapers, where groups systematically subsidize losing papers, as a matter of policy, over long periods of time. This cross-subsidization is usually applauded inside and outside the newspaper industry as creating a more competitive press, and has been described as one of the benefits of chain operations for newspapers.

MUTUAL FORBEARANCE

As the operations of conglomerates spread throughout the economy, their subsidiaries will come to operate in the same industries more and more often.

The potential thus exists for a few conglomerates to agree, tacitly or overtly, to restrict competition in an industry, even an unconcentrated one. Thus mutual forbearance could take two forms: subsidiaries of conglomerates in the same industry could collude to set and maintain prices above a competitive level while at the same time accepting static market shares, or a conglomerate could refrain from entering an industry dominated by the subsidiary of another conglomerate. Both these forms of mutual forbearance would reduce competition in the specific industry and in the economy as a whole.

So long as entry into an industry is unrestricted, however, mutual forbearance is not a preferable long-run practice. If the subsidiaries of conglomerate firms do not compete in their overlapping industries or if they collude to maintain high prices, other firms will simply price below the conglomerates and take away market share. If subsidiaries of conglomerates are the only potential entrants, however, mutual forbearance between conglomerates may be a practicable strategy. Its use would lead to substantial misallocation of resources.

In Canada, where conglomerates tend to make toehold investments in unconcentrated industries, there seems little scope for mutual forbearance. The Commission concludes that while the problem of mutual forbearance is potentially important, it is in reality a special multimarket example of the oligopoly problem discussed in Chapter 4. The solution to mutual forbearance lies, we think, in more disclosure, lowered barriers to entry, availability of equity and debt capital and constraints on predatory practices, rather than in any special legislation. These measures would better ensure that opportunities for high profits would be recognized and that independent firms would tend to move into those industries where those opportunities existed, thereby increasing competition and lowering prices and profits.

INCREASING BARRIERS TO ENTRY

The entry of a large, diversified enterprise into an industry may serve to increase barriers to entry into it, even without any overt anticompetitive action by the enterprise. If other firms in the industry and other potential entrants believe that the diversified firm is able and willing to engage in anticompetitive behavior, they may curtail the scope of normal competitive activities so as not to antagonize what they perceive to be a stronger adversary. In this way, a subsidiary of a conglomerate may become the "barometer" firm in a shared oligopoly, since other firms in the industry perceive it to be most able to engage in a price war for market share.

If conglomerate firms were able through any of the practices described above to erect barriers to entry, we should expect to find that industries with a high proportion of diversified firms would have high price-cost margins. Yet research by S. A. Rhoades in a 1974 article in the *Review of Economics and Statistics* on U.S. firms has come to the opposite conclusion. Also, as mentioned above, McFetridge found that corporate profits declined with diversification. Firms in Canada do not seem to have been daunted by conglomerate diversification.

While again recognizing that increased barriers to entry are a continuing potential danger, the Commission is not able to propose a solution to what is basically a problem of smaller firms believing that larger firms have an unfair advantage that ensures their victory in a competitive situation.

Loss of Information

As formerly independent, single-product firms whose sales and profits were made public are acquired by diversified enterprises that consolidate the operating statements of their subsidiaries into their own financial statements, information is lost to direct investors, firms within the industry, the stock market and society. Firms within the industry and, more importantly, potential entrants no longer have information about sales, profits, costs and growth rates by line of business to use in evaluating the desirability of shifting resources into or out of the industry. Similarly, investors are less efficient in their allocation of resources to various industrial sectors and firms, since their evaluation of the investment potential of firms and industries is more subject to error.

This problem exists both in the evaluation of single-product firms in an industry in which subsidiaries of conglomerates operate and in the evaluation of conglomerates themselves. One researcher for the U.S. Federal Trade Commission spent two months trying to construct profitability figures by product line for one conglomerate firm using all available public documents. He failed completely. In research done in the United States, D.W. Collins in a 1975 *Journal of Financial Economics* article argued that his evidence supported the conclusion that information loss has caused investors in the stock market to make incorrect, inefficient selections for their portfolios.

The problem of loss of information is not so acute in the case of a firm whose subsidiaries have public shareholders and must issue annual reports; however, often these subsidiaries produce a wide range of products about which information is not available. On the other hand, companies that seek 100% ownership of subsidiaries can consolidate their statements and so not reveal their profitability.

This loss of information is not confined to conglomerate firms. Provincially chartered or private firms are not subject to the same disclosure requirements as are federally chartered firms. We address this problem in a more general context in Chapter 13, "Disclosure of Corporate Information".

Conclusion

In its recommendations concerning the economic impact of conglomerate enterprises, the Commission has two objectives in mind: (1) to increase the efficiency of resource allocation in the Canadian economy, and hence the ability of Canadian firms to provide goods at low prices to Canadians and to compete on a world basis; and (2) to inhibit anti-competitive practices that might permit large firms to achieve an unfair advantage over their competitors and to gain monopoly returns. Our recommendations are also made in the context of the realities of the Canadian economy.

The level of sectoral concentration has not changed appreciably over the past decade, nor has the growth of large firms increased the share of the economy controlled by the top 50 or 100 firms. If large firms in Canada had not pursued a strategy of diversified growth, aggregate industrial concentration might well have declined, but sectoral concentration might also have grown. In general, the diversification process does not seem to have led to increased concentration or reduced competition in specific industries. Indeed the large size of conglomerate enterprises does not imply that their subsidiaries are large in their individual industries. By definition, a conglomerate firm has subsidiaries in several sectors, so that a large conglomerate may be composed of diverse units, none of which necessarily has any appreciable degree of control in its own market. The argument was made earlier that, in general, conglomerates in Canada have diversified into such unrelated industries that they have not been able to take significant advantage of economies of scale within their components, or to find any significant synergies among their components. In particular, they have not been able to form a common basis for continuous technological innovation. Conglomerates may even be blocking the formation of firms that could diversify into related products, since firms in a given industry are much less likely to merge into one efficient firm if they are controlled by different conglomerate firms than if they are independent firms. Even if one conglomerate firm were willing to sell its subsidiary in an industry to a rival, the combines authorities might not be anxious for such a merger to take place. In the Power-Argus controversy, critics pointed to the potential increase in concentration in forest products and communications media as a reason for blocking the merger. Yet it may be that such large concentrations within industries are necessary if increased efficiency is to be achieved.

A similar problem would arise if George Weston Limited and Argus attempted to merge, this time with possibly increased concentration in the retail food industry. This line of reasoning, if valid, in effect reverses the usual argument against conglomerates. Conglomerate firms may thus be detrimental to the economy if their overall size tends to inhibit formation of economically efficient units in their subsidiaries through horizontal mergers at the industry level.

On the other hand, diversification into unrelated sectors has helped allocate resources from old, static industries to newer, more dynamic ones. Acquisition activities by diversified companies have almost certainly improved the efficiency of the market for firms in Canada, thereby increasing the incentive to form and develop new products and processes, while decreasing the number of such firms that are taken over by foreign firms. On balance, however, conglomerate diversification has probably decreased the efficiency of resource allocation in the Canadian economy, although not seriously. Firms that have followed a strategy of conglomerate diversification have, in general, given their shareholders and given their investors below-average returns in the market. Over a long period, therefore, the practice of unrelated diversification is likely to cease through the force of competition. Indeed, many conglomerate firms are already rationalizing their subsidiaries in an effort to increase their efficiency and returns on assets and to their stockholders.

The Commission concludes, therefore, that there is no need for any general prohibition against conglomerate mergers or a general review for conglomerate mergers. In *general*, conglomerate mergers and acquisitions do not decrease competition or seriously misallocate Canada's resources.

Chapter 6

Mergers and Acquisitions

The subject of corporate mergers and acquisitions is obviously relevant to the task of this Commission, and indeed to any consideration of the process of corporate growth and concentration. As a result, it has been the subject of considerable research by the Commission. Our interest does not, however, imply that we consider mergers and acquisitions to be exceptional phenomena but rather that they are an integral and normal part of commercial life. In this chapter we discuss only their economic and legal aspects. The social influence of the resulting large corporate groups is dealt with later in this *Report*.

Mergers and acquisitions tend to be discussed under different names depending on the context of the discussion. In law, the name varies with the form of the transaction: takeover bid, purchase of shares, amalgamation, purchase of assets, or reorganization. In accounting, the usual term is a "business combination", while in economics the term "merger" refers to an amalgamation between firms, and "acquisition" generally refers to a takeover of one firm by another. Since these terms encompass the same general concept, any transaction as a result of which (1) two firms amalgamate into a third one either by an agreement or a reorganization defined in statutes, (2) the assets of a firm or a substantial part thereof are transferred to another firm, or (3) the voting control of a corporation is transferred to another one, will, throughout our discussion, be referred to as either a merger or acquisition.

Legal Aspects of Mergers

The concern of the law with the different methods of acquisition is based, in part, on their potential effect on the interests of minority shareholders, protection of whom is germane to our mandate. Minority shareholders enhance the liquidity and marketability of corporate shares, contribute to the vitality of secondary markets and are necessary to the financing of most public corporations. For these reasons, we consider that in a merger it is important that

135

minority shareholders be well informed and have a mechanism by which to participate in decisions.

There are three basic methods of effecting a merger or an acquisition:

1. by an amalgamation under the corporations acts of Canada or one of the provinces, the effect of which is to continue the merging corporations as a single new one having all the property and rights and subject to all the liabilities of the previous ones;
2. by one corporation purchasing a substantial part of the assets of another for cash or securities, following which the vendor corporation may be wound up and the consideration received distributed to its shareholders;
3. by one corporation purchasing the shares of another either by private agreement or in a takeover bid or sometimes both.

The form of the transaction is generally not determined by corporate constraints (votes required, number of meetings, approvals, etc.) but by considerations related to the state of capital markets or taxation implications (the latter are discussed in a background report commissioned by us from Stikeman, Elliott, Tamaki, Mercier & Robb, *Corporate Concentration and the Canadian Tax System*). In an amalgamation, a purchase of assets and a private agreement to purchase shares, the rules under which the transaction takes place are usually found in the statute under which the corporation has been created and the civil law of the province where the contract is made. In takeover bids, additional applicable provisions are found in the securities legislation of most of the provinces and, if the target corporation is a federal one, in the Canada Business Corporations Act.

Amalgamation

All the corporation statutes in Canada provide that any two or more corporations may amalgamate. The corporations enter into an agreement under which a new corporation emerges with a legal identity separate from the preceding ones. The agreement usually specifies the name of the proposed new corporation, its directors, share capital, the terms of the exchange of the shares of the previous corporations for shares of the new one, the bylaws, and so on. It is not effective until it has been approved by a certain majority of the shareholders of the amalgamating corporations. This majority may vary from two-thirds to three-quarters depending on the jurisdiction. Under some statutes (the federal one, for example) approval of every class of shareholder is needed. If the amalgamation changes the rights or priorities of a class of shares of one of the former corporations, the agreement must be approved by the holders of that class of shares.

One difficulty facing corporations that contemplate amalgamating is the fact that no corporation statute in Canada allows for the amalgamation of a corporation created under it with a corporation created under a different statute (e.g., a Quebec corporation with a federal one). The federal act and some provincial statutes do provide, however, that a corporation constituted in one jurisdiction may apply to be continued in another. Through the use of these provisions an amalgamation is possible between firms in different jurisdictions. For example, an Ontario corporation could emigrate to the federal jurisdiction or a federal corporation could apply for a certificate continuing it under the Ontario act. Afterwards, as both corporations would be under the same act, the amalgamation could proceed. This procedure is based on reciprocal legislation which exists in Ontario, Manitoba, Alberta, Saskatchewan, New Brunswick and British Columbia, and in the Canada Business Corporations Act.

Takeover Bids

Takeover bids are the most dramatic form of acquisition, as illustrated by the terms employed: the acquired company is known as the target corporation; when the bid comes as a complete surprise to the management of the offeree company, it may become known as "raid". Takeover bids are most often used when a prospective purchaser seeks to acquire a controlling interest from a large number of small shareholders. In the typical case, the target company's shares are listed on a stock exchange, and the bidder offers to purchase from all holders at a stated price. Managers of corporations with many small, unrelated shareholder interests thus often fear takeover bids.

Takeovers provide the greatest source of concern about minority share-holder protection. The Commission thinks that so long as takeover legislation ensures that shareholders receive full and timely information and have a reasonable time to consider it, takeover bids encourage vitality and competition in the management of public corporations. The possibility of a takeover partly replaces shareholders' supervision and surveillance, which are often lacking.

The securities laws of Quebec, Ontario, Manitoba, Saskatchewan, Alberta and British Columbia regulate takeover bids addressed to shareholders residing in their jurisdictions. If the target corporation is federally incorporated, the takeover bid must also comply with the federal act. In most legislation a takeover bid is defined as an offer to purchase voting shares of a corporation, which together with the voting shares owned by the purchaser will, in the aggregate, exceed 20% of the outstanding voting shares of the target corporation (in several jurisdictions the figure is 10%).

Some offers are excluded from the application of the acts:

1. an offer to purchase shares by way of private agreement with fewer than 15 shareholders and which is not extended to shareholders in general;
2. an offer to be executed through a stock exchange or in the over-the-counter market;
3. an offer to purchase shares of a private company; or
4. an offer exempted by a court or the administrator of the act.

A Premium for Control
Under a Private Agreement

The acquisition of control by way of private agreement with a small group of shareholders is a common occurrence, and the offer will be exempt from statutory takeover bid provisions when there are fewer than 15 solicited shareholders. For example, had Power Corporation of Canada, Limited, been able to bid for and acquire the shares of Argus Corporation Limited held by The Ravelston Corporation Limited, no public offer to the other shareholders of Argus would have been necessary, and no statutory provisions would have applied.

Often such an agreement for the acquisition of effective control of a corporation precedes a takeover bid for the remaining shares. Sometimes the price offered for the controlling shares will exceed the purchase price offered to the minority shareholders because control commands a premium. If the purchaser wants only effective control he may not make a full offer, or any offer at all, to the other shareholders. If an offer is made to them, the remaining shareholders have the choice of retaining their shares or selling them at a lower price than that paid for the controlling shares. These practices have been attacked as unfair and discriminatory.

Canadian statute law does not prohibit a control premium in a private agreement. In the United States there are no statutory provisions concerning control premiums, but courts sometimes intervene in favor of minority shareholders. The City Code, which governs takeover bids in Great Britain, requires a general offer to be made to all shareholders at the same price. Under the City Code the same requirements apply when control is acquired in a "creeping takeover" when control is bought gradually.

Concern has been expressed about the fact that a share worth one price, if it is sold by a minority shareholder, can be worth a higher price if it is sold as part of a block of shares carrying control of the corporation. Some argue that each share in a company is the same as every other share of the same class and should command the same price in a sale. The risks and burdens of corporate ownership are not always equal on a per share basis, however. Owners of controlling equity interests in corporations assume greater liquidity risks than do minority shareholders, particularly in thinly traded issues. No proposals have been made to share "blockage discounts" with minority holders. A law forcing the acquirer to make the same offer to all shareholders may reduce the number of potential buyers and the price paid for the controlling shares. It could also decrease the motivation of entrepreneurs who see the prospect of a premium for their controlling shares as a strong incentive to assume the risks of starting a business. Thus an obligation to make a general offer raises a possibility that many privately (as well as socially) beneficial reallocations of corporate equity may be thwarted.

A control premium becomes questionable if it represents the price a purchaser is prepared to pay for the opportunity to take unlawful advantage of minority shareholders. For example, sellers of control may attempt to take all or part of a control premium in the form of an excessively favorable employment contract from the new controller or in some other "side benefit". However, the courts in the United States have been able to characterize such conduct as wrongs to the corporation or its other shareholders and to order payment to it, or them, of the benefits improperly received by the seller.

To the extent that the law provides remedies to minority shareholders against directors and others who abuse their authority, the improper component of a control premium will be minimal. We think that, for the most part, the law is already adequate to deal with whatever harm can arise out of transfers of controlling interests in corporations. More effective examination and disclosure of transactions between corporations and their directors and other insiders (such as we propose in Chapter 13) would supplement existing legal remedies significantly. For these reasons we are unwilling to endorse the idea (contemplated in Ontario) that purchasers of shares should be required either not to pay a control premium or to pay it even to those who do not have a controlling interest to sell.

Trading by Insiders

One of the preoccupations of the securities administrators has been the fact that the management and controlling interests of a corporation have access to confidential information that could be used to the detriment of the minority shareholders in connection with a trade in securities. Accordingly, directors, senior officers and those controlling over 10% of a corporation are required to report trading to the appropriate securities commission, which in turn makes the information public. Provisions have been enacted to penalize insiders who make use of pertinent confidential information to trade in securities.

Suggestions have been made that present measures are too narrow in application and too limited in scope and do not remove the possibility of abuse of minority shareholders. In our opinion there is no need for new legislation if the present requirements for timely disclosure of material facts are followed and enforced.

Takeover bids raise a special set of issues. If, for instance, an offer is for less than 10% of the voting shares, the insiders of the offerer are not considered to be insiders of the target corporation. Conversely, if there have been negotiations between the offerer and the shareholders of the target corporation, the insiders of the target corporation are not insiders of the offerer. To treat these conflicts of interest along the lines of insider liabilities, the federal act contains provisions under which the liability extends to the directors and officers of each corporation during the six months preceding the date on which a corporation acquires the shares of another. The Commission thinks that such safeguards are consistent with the rationale of insider trading provisions and that they should be available to all Canadian shareholders and incorporated in all provincial statutes.

Statistics on Mergers

Number of Mergers

The principal source of information on Canadian mergers is a study relating to the years 1945-61, which employed a questionnaire survey conducted under the Combines Investigation Act. It covered all companies subject to that Act that were known or thought to have acquired other companies. These data were analyzed by Grant L. Reuber and Frank Roseman in a study published by the Economic Council of Canada in 1969 (*The Take-Over of Canadian Firms, 1945-61: An Empirical Analysis*). Subsequent data have been collected by what is now the Bureau of Competition Policy of the Department of Consumer and Corporate Affairs. These data are compiled from published sources, principally financial newspapers and magazines in Canada. As a consequence, it is likely that unpublicized mergers are often unnoticed. These are most likely to be mergers involving small companies. On the other hand, premature reporting of merger transactions may lead to the inclusion of some acquisitions that were never, in fact, consummated. On balance, the data collection process for merger activity probably understates the number of mergers in Canada. These data have been analyzed by the research staff of this Commission. In addition, Samuel Martin, Stanley Laiken and Douglas Haslam in a study for the Canadian Institute of Chartered Accountants undertook a detailed analysis of mergers entered into by companies listed on the Toronto Stock Exchange during the years 1960-68. Their study focused primarily on the accounting and financial aspects of mergers. A related study by Laiken, which appeared in the *Antitrust Bulletin* in 1973, evaluated the financial performances of merging and non-merging companies in Canada over the period 1960-68.

The Commission's focus on merger activity in Canada after 1945 is dictated, in part, by the fact that most of the available data are for this period. In addition, conglomerate mergers, which constitute an important part of the Commission's inquiries, are primarily post-World War II phenomena. Our analysis concentrates on the number of mergers, although alternative measures of merger activity, such as the value of total assets acquired, are also relevant. Unfortunately, consistent data on measures of merger activity other than number of mergers are unavailable for the period not covered by Reuber and Roseman.

There have been distinct cycles in merger activity in Canada since 1945 (Table 6.1, Figure 6.1). The periods of relatively high activity were immediately after the war in 1945 and 1946, the boom years 1955 and 1956, the recession years 1959 to 1961, and the years 1968 to 1972, which include the final phases of the boom of the late 1960s and the recession and bear-market period of the early 1970s. The percentage of mergers that were acquisitions of Canadian businesses by foreign-controlled companies fluctuated between about 20% and 45%, being generally higher during the 1954-62 period than in the earlier or later periods. The number of mergers each year has been only a small percentage of the total number of Canadian companies. We note, however, that the number of mergers reported in Table 6.1 exclude acquisitions of service

Table 6.1

Summary* of Canadian Mergers, 1945-74

Year	Total Number of Active** Domestic Companies	Mergers		Number of Domestic Acquisitions	Foreign Acquisitions	
		Number	As a Percentage of Active Domestic Companies		Number	As a Percentage of All Mergers
1945	27,229	74	0.27	51	23	31.1
1946	30,442	79	0.26	64	15	19.0
1947	34,087	45	0.13	32	13	28.9
1948	35,960	53	0.15	39	14	26.4
1949	37,467	38	0.10	27	11	28.9
1950	40,545	45	0.11	36	9	20.0
1951	43,365	80	0.18	61	19	23.8
1952	45,777	76	0.17	59	17	22.4
1953	49,745	93	0.19	68	25	26.9
1954	54,434	104	0.19	61	43	41.3
1955	59,773	134	0.22	78	56	41.8
1956	67,480	135	0.20	81	54	40.0
1957	73,823	103	0.14	68	35	34.0
1958	80,770	140	0.17	80	60	47.9
1959	88,806	186	0.21	120	66	35.5
1960	97,549	203	0.21	110	93	45.8
1961	106,309	238	0.22	148	86	36.8
1962	115,082	185	0.16	106	79	42.7
1963	118,597	129	0.11	88	41	31.8
1964	126,813	204	0.16	124	80	39.2
1965	152,818	235	0.15	157	78	33.2
1966	164,410	203	0.12	123	80	39.4
1967	176,210	228	0.13	143	85	37.3
1968	185,816	402	0.22	239	163	40.5
1969	199,994	504	0.23	336	168	33.3
1970	212,192	427	0.20	265	162	37.9
1971	228,458	388	0.17	245	143	36.9
1972	236,431	429	0.18	302	127	29.6
1973	258,501	352	0.14	252	100	28.4
1974	276,157P	296	0.10	218	78	26.4

Sources: All data for 1945-61: G.L. Reuber and Roseman, *The Take-Over of Canadian Firms, 1945-61: An Empirical Analysis* (Ottawa, 1969), Table 3.1. Data for all other years: *Combines Investigation Report* (1976); *Corporation Taxation Statistics* (1974).

Notes: * – The merger data reported in the table do not include all mergers undertaken in Canada. Most notably, they exclude mergers among companies in service businesses, which are not covered under the provisions of the Combines Investigation Act. As a result, the percentage that total mergers represent of the total number of companies in each year is less than the percentage that would be obtained if all mergers in Canada had been reported. Furthermore, the divergence between the two percentages is probably larger for the later years, because of the relatively faster growth of the service sector since 1945.

   ** – Excludes Crown corporations, cooperatives and personal corporations.

   P – Indicates projected value based on continuation of average annual growth rate from 1970 to 1973.

businesses. Such mergers are not included in the records compiled by the Bureau of Competition Policy, and clearly would increase the merger intensity ratios if they were included in the total number of Canadian mergers.

Canadian and U.S. merger cycles have been quite similar (Figure 6.1). One apparent difference is that the high level of merger activity reached in the late 1960s relative to base year 1955 was sustained longer in Canada than in the United States and has declined relatively less in the early 1970s. Of course, the absolute number of mergers in the United States has been consistently higher than that in Canada over the postwar period.

The broad similarity in overall merger patterns suggests that a common set of factors has influenced the pace of merger activity in the two countries.

Reuber and Roseman in their study of Canadian mergers concluded that for the 1945-61 period:

Our "best" estimate in some respects is that variations in foreign mergers in Canada [i.e. Canadian firms coming under foreign control] can be explained by variations in the number of mergers in the United States, the number of commercial failures in Canada and the supply of internally generated funds in Canada's corporate sector. In effect, this can be interpreted as saying that foreign mergers in Canada are governed by the same factors governing domestic mergers in the United States, conditioned by the level of activity in Canada and Canadian credit conditions.

Variations in the number of domestic mergers in Canada, according to our evidence, can best be explained by variations in stock market prices in Canada, reflecting business expectations, and internally generated funds in Canada's corporate sector, reflecting Canadian credit conditions.

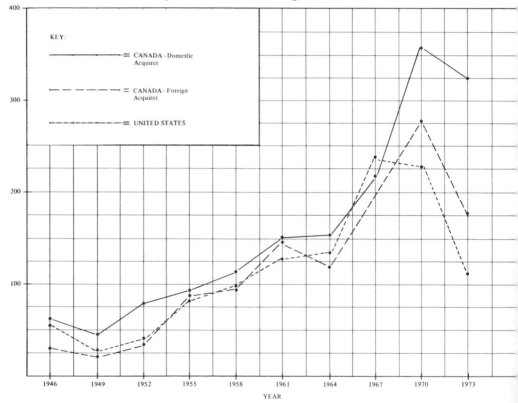

FIGURE 6.1: Variations in the Number of Mergers, Canada and the United States, 1945-74 (Three-Year Moving Average Index, 1955 = 100).
Sources: Canada: Table 6.1.
United States: 1945-70, *U.S. Historical Statistics* (1975); 1971-74.
U.S. Department of Commerce, *Statistical Abstract of the U.S.* (1976).

Commission staff found that over the entire period 1947-74, the rates of change in the number of mergers in Canada and in the United States were directly and significantly related to the rates of change in Canadian and U.S. stock prices respectively. However, the relationship between changes in merger activity and stock price changes, while still positive, was statistically insignificant for Canada during the subperiod 1947-63 and was statistically insignificant for the United States during the subperiod 1964-74. Furthermore, the overall level of real economic activity, as measured by the rate of change in industrial production, was not significantly related to merger activity in either subperiod for Canada, and was significantly (and directly) related to U.S. merger activity only for the 1947-63 subperiod.

While our results appear to differ from the findings of Reuber and Roseman, our statistical model was not identical with theirs and hence the results are not strictly comparable. It is worth noting that Christopher Maule, in an unpublished doctoral thesis, concludes that, while cyclical movement in Canadian merger activity was similar to the cyclical behavior of stock prices during the period 1948-63, after 1959 the relationship was, if anything, inverse. He further concludes, on the basis of earlier work on Canadian mergers done by J. C. Weldon, that Canadian mergers and stock prices do not show any consistent relationship with each other over the period 1900-63. Maule also found that the cyclical relationship between merger activity and industrial production is weakly inverse when both stock prices and industrial production are employed simultaneously to explain Canadian merger patterns.

The Commission concludes that, while capital market conditions are related to aggregate merger patterns in North America for specific periods after 1945, the relationship is not uniform. Furthermore, capital market conditions do not provide a satisfactory explanation of the broad similarity in merger activity patterns in Canada and the United States since 1945; nor do overall economic conditions in the two countries explain the broadly similar merger experiences of the two countries. A complete understanding of the merger process requires more than consideration of macroeconomic conditions.

Distribution of Mergers among Industries

The Commission analyzed Canadian data for 17 broad manufacturing industry groups. The distribution of acquisition activity over time and across manufacturing industries, as depicted in Table 6.2, was tested for similarity between Canada and the United States. Potential difficulties in such a comparison are introduced by the possibility that differences in the relative sizes of the various industries in the two countries will contribute to observed differences in merger intensities. Furthermore, the time periods for the Canadian and U.S. data are not identical. Comparisons of the data in Table 6.2 must, therefore, be treated with caution. The 17 industries were ranked in order of relative merger intensity, and the rank orders for the Canadian and U.S. series were compared. Statistical tests show that the rank orders for the series are quite similar, lending some support to the general conclusion that the distribution of merger activity across manufacturing industries has been quite comparable in Canada and the United States.

Table 6.2

Distribution of Manufacturing Companies Acquired by Industry of Acquired Firm, United States and Canada, Ranked by Percentage of Acquisitions

Percentage of Acquisitions in Manufacturing

Industry	United States 1948-68	1973	Industry	Canada 1945-61	1973
1. Machinery	13.2	12.7	1. Food	26.3	8.5
2. Food	8.7	15.0	2. Paper	8.2	3.9
3. Chemicals	8.5	11.0	3. Chemicals	7.9	15.5
4. Electrical machinery	7.6	14.6	4. Fabricated metals	7.8	12.4
5. Paper	7.1	4.6	5. Printing	6.9	13.2
6. Primary metals	6.8	4.9	6. Non-metallic minerals	5.9	10.4
7. Fabricated metals	6.7	7.2	7. Electrical products	5.2	6.4
8. Textiles	5.9	3.6	8. Wood	5.1	6.2
9. Transportation equipment	5.7	7.9	9. Machinery	3.7	4.7
10. Non-metallic minerals	4.3	4.5	10. Textiles	3.5	2.4
11. Petroleum	4.2	1.7	11. Transportation equipment	3.2	3.8
12. Printing	3.1	3.8	12. Leather	3.1	0.1
13. Wood	2.6	3.1	13. Primary metals	2.5	2.3
14. Rubber	1.9	2.7	14. Petroleum	1.6	1.6
15. Furniture	1.0	1.3	15. Rubber	1.1	0.0
16. Leather	0.9	0.8	16. Furniture	0.9	7.0
17. Tobacco	0.4	0.5	17. Tobacco	0.4	0.8

Sources: Canada: for the years 1945-61, the data were derived from Tables 4-8 and A-7 of Reuber and Roseman, *op. cit.*; for 1973, Royal Commission on Corporate Concentration (RCCC) analysis of the Department of Consumer and Corporate Affairs' record of mergers.

U.S.: for the 1948-68 data, Table 1.7 of the Federal Trade Commission, *Economic Report on Corporate Mergers* (Washington, 1969); for the 1973 data, *ibid., Statistical Report on Mergers and Acquisitions* (July 1974).

Note: The Spearman rank correlation coefficient for the U.S. (1948-68) and Canadian (1945-61) series is 0.67.

To investigate merger activity in Canadian manufacturing industries further, we made a statistical analysis paralleling that used for U.S. mergers and reported by Michael Gort in a 1969 article in the *Quarterly Journal of Economics*. Inter-industry differences in merger activity (measured by acquired firms as a percentage of the total number of firms, Table 6.3) were related to sectoral concentration ratios and other explanatory variables for 17 industry groups. The results indicated, among other things, that merger intensity in an industry is directly related to concentration in an industry, employment growth in an industry and growth in the average firm size in the industry. The relationship between merger rates and growth in the number of firms in the industry is inverse.

The finding that merger intensity is directly related to growth in average firm size in Canada is consistent with the notion that mergers, at least in part, are undertaken to secure real and/or pecuniary economies of scale. Further evidence is provided by the observation that mergers are undertaken relatively

Table 6.3

Merger Activity in Canadian Manufacturing Industries,
1945-61 and 1972-73

Industry	Acquired Firms as a Percentage of Total Number of Firms		
	1945-61	1972	1973
1. Food and beverages	0.88	1.27	0.37
2. Tobacco	0.85	0.00	4.76
3. Rubber	1.03	0.00	0.00
4. Leather	0.42	1.13	0.56
5. Textiles	0.40	1.31	0.29
6. Knitting mills	0.31	0.00	0.00
7. Clothing	0.07	0.23	0.58
8. Wood	0.22	0.61	0.44
9. Furniture	0.11	0.79	0.89
10. Paper	1.24	0.42	1.06
11. Printing, etc.	0.30	0.50	0.60
12. Machinery	0.26	2.16	0.65
13. Transport equipment	0.52	1.86	0.62
14. Electrical products	0.84	1.60	1.16
15. Non-metallic mineral products	0.59	0.71	1.32
16. Petroleum and coal products	1.58	4.00	4.00
17. Chemicals	0.51	2.19	2.19

Sources: Number of acquired firms: 1945-61, Reuber and Roseman, *op cit.*, Table 4A-3; 1972 and 1973, RCCC analysis of Department of Consumer and Corporate Affairs' record of mergers.

Total number of firms: *Corporation Taxation Statistics.*

more frequently in industries having above-average ratios of salaried employees to total employees. The latter ratio might be taken as a crude proxy measure of the "managerial intensity" of an industry. Many people have suggested that managers are scarce in Canada; hence firms could be expected to try to economize on managerial talent by taking advantage of available economies of scale in managerial functions. It should be acknowledged, however, that concentrated merger activity in managerially intensive industries is also consistent with the argument that mergers are undertaken to fulfill managerial objectives for firm growth.

It is difficult to place an unambiguous interpretation on the finding that merger intensity is directly related to concentration. This observation is consistent with the hypothesis that mergers are undertaken by firms in concentrated industries to acquire more market power, by both increasing their market shares and absorbing smaller firms that may have posed a threat to parallel pricing behavior in the industry. However, industry concentration may be an indirect measure of the firm-level economies of scale in an industry as well as an imperfect measure of market power. Therefore, since the empirical variables used in the research described above provide rather crude tests of the underlying theoretical relationships, interpretations of the statistical results must be tentative.

Distribution of Mergers by Type

In addition to looking at mergers in general, we also analyzed the mergers in Canada by type: horizontal, vertical and conglomerate (Table 6.4). Horizontal mergers are essentially those between businesses competing in the same industry. Vertical mergers are those between actual or potential customers and suppliers in the same industry. Conglomerate mergers are those between businesses in different industries. Horizontal mergers can be further divided to show those which involve an extension of the business after the merger into a different geographic area or into a different product within the same general industry.

Canadian data for the years 1972, 1973 and 1974 were compiled by Commission staff from information in the Department of Consumer and Corporate Affairs' record of mergers. The classification of mergers by type for those years relied for the most part on the description of merging companies in that record. If companies were producing the same or related products or services the merger was classified as horizontal. If the companies were linked by different stages in a common production process, the merger was classified as vertical. All mergers involving largely unrelated production processes or acquisitions by a holding company were classified as conglomerate. Given the imprecisions in our classification procedure, we did not attempt to distinguish different categories of broad horizontal mergers in the years 1972-74. Furthermore, the U.S. distributions are based upon large acquisitions in manufacturing and mining, while the Canadian distributions are based upon all recorded industrial mergers. Once again, comparisons must be taken to indicate general rather than exact relationships.

Table 6.4

Percentage Distribution of Types of Mergers,
Canada and the United States

Country	Type of Merger	Percentage of Total Mergers			
		1945-61	1972	1973	1974
Canada	Broad horizontal	68.25	68.9	68.9	67.7
	Horizontal	40.23			
	Geographic market extension	12.71			
	Product extension	9.71			
	Other	5.60			
	Vertical	22.43	12.3	12.5	9.2
	Conglomerate	9.31	18.8	18.6	23.1
United States		1948-63			
	Broad horizontal	67.02	58.6	56.2	62.9
	Horizontal	23.21			
	Geographic market extension	5.64			
	Product extension	38.17			
	Vertical	19.89	17.2	11.0	4.8
	Conglomerate	12.74	24.1	32.8	32.3

Sources: Canada: 1945-61, calculations by the staff of the Commission from Table 5-3 of
Reuber and Roseman, *op. cit.*, 1972, 1973 and 1973, RCCC analysis of the
Department of Consumer and Corporate Affairs' record of mergers.
U.S.:   1948-68, Federal Trade Commission, *op. cit.* (1969), p. 673; 1973 and
1974, *ibid., Statistical Report on Mergers and Acquisitions* (1974).

The data show that about 68% of Canadian mergers have been of the
horizontal type, both in the 1945-61 period and in recent years. In the United
States, about the same proportion were horizontal in the 1948-63 period, but
less so in recent years, with a substantially higher percentage of conglomerate
mergers. Our classification of U.S. merger activity has been made comparable
with the Canadian classifications. As a result, product extension and market
extension acquisitions in the United States have been classed as horizontal
mergers, whereas the U.S. Federal Trade Commission includes such acquisitions within a broader conglomerate category. In Canada the proportion of
conglomerate mergers in recent years was about double the 9% that they
formed in the 1945-61 period and half again as high as the 12% reported by
Martin, Laiken and Haslam for the period 1960-68, but it was still significantly short of the proportion of conglomerate mergers in the United States in
recent years. Similarity in the distribution of mergers by type between Canada
and the United States further supports the conclusion that broadly similar
factors have influenced merger patterns in the two countries.

Characteristics of Merging Firms

The size of Canadian firms acquired was studied in detail by Reuber and Roseman for the 1945-61 period, and by Statistics Canada for 1970 and 1971. It is more difficult to determine the size of an acquiring firm when it is foreign-owned. However, it is generally true that the acquiring firm is substantially larger than the firm acquired. Over the period 1945-61 as well as in the years 1970 and 1971, acquiring firms were consistently larger than acquired firms (Table 6.5).

Perhaps more surprising is that the firms acquired are usually as profitable as the firms acquiring them, although the detailed study of the 1945-61 mergers showed that a much higher proportion of the acquired firms had suffered losses. The study of 1970 and 1971 mergers showed more mixed rates of profitability, on average not differing much between acquired and acquiring firms.

Similarities in merger patterns between Canada and the United States and, in particular, the fact that merger-intensive industries tend to be the same in the two countries suggest that the underlying motives for merger activity may relate strongly to market structures and production conditions for individual industries in the two countries. More specifically, Canadian and U.S. industries tend to have similar if not identical characteristics: highly concentrated industries in Canada tend to be highly concentrated in the United States; high-technology industries in Canada are also high-technology in the United States. Similar demand conditions imply that faster growing industries in the two countries will tend to be the same. In short, the marked similarity in Canadian and U.S. merger patterns could have an explanation in common microeconomic characteristics of industrial organization and performance in the two countries.

Economics of Mergers

Motives for Merging: Theory and Evidence

The Commission received considerable information concerning mergers in the briefs submitted to it, in testimony at its public hearings and in its own studies. This material identifies numerous motives for merging, both on the part of companies acquiring control of other companies and on the part of those willing, and often seeking, to sell control of their companies. We note at the outset that a large percentage of mergers may not, in fact, live up to the expectations of the acquiring companies. Furthermore, we should not expect to find pursuit of enhanced market power cited in the public record as a merger motive. Nevertheless, the possible importance of such a motive in specific mergers must be considered in evaluating alternative policies toward mergers.

The motives of the acquiring companies or, strictly speaking, those who control them, are varied and frequently mixed. We cannot always be sure that stated motives are true motives, and we list cautiously the stated motives. Readers should note that some of the motives brought to the Commission's attention are closely related and that several motives on both buyers' and sellers' sides may be involved in any one merger transaction.

Table 6.5

Relative Size and Profitability of Acquired to Acquiring Firms before Merger,
Canada, 1945-61 and 1970-71

	Average Assets		Average Sales		Profit Rate	
	Acquired	Acquiring	Acquired	Acquiring	Acquired	Acquiring
	(Millions of Dollars)		(Millions of Dollars)		(Percentage)	
1945-61	3.46	45.65	4.24	53.54		
1970	4.72	37.57	2.39	25.95	4.74	7.07
1971	3.45	91.97	3.04	40.73	5.97	4.77

Sources: Average assets and average sales, 1945-61, calculated from Reuber and Roseman, *op. cit.*, Tables 4.3, 4.4; profit rates, 1945-61, calculated from *ibid.*, Table 4.11; other calculations based on data from "Pilot Project on Statistics of Corporate Takeovers in the Canadian Economy", *Canadian Statistical Review* (Feb. 1976).

MOTIVES TO ACQUIRE

The simplest motive for acquisition is that of a holding company, or less frequently an active operating company with cash or credit to spare, which finds, or is presented with, what it considers on examination to be an attractive investment at a reasonable price. The company to be acquired may be in a business quite unrelated to that of the buyer, or it may have related production and marketing activities that make it attractive. We have encountered several instances of quick acquisition decisions apparently not part of a preconceived plan in which favorable price or prospects appeared to be the buyer's main motive.

More complex are the motives of a group that sets out to rationalize an industry, as has happened in Canada on several occasions. An acquirer may set out to achieve various economies of size or scale, or may desire to establish or extend market power. Such cases have potentially significant economic consequences and their impact may require careful appraisal to determine whether they are beneficial or harmful to the public interest. An example of a series of mergers undertaken apparently to achieve operating economies occurred when Voyageur Inc. acquired several small carriers.

Less complex but also of potential economic importance is the motive of a group (or company) that wishes to enter an industry or to expand in it, and which finds that acquiring control of an existing company is cheaper or quicker than assembling its own facilities. This is a common phenomenon in a depressed securities market, where many firms have a market value well below their asset value. The acquisition by Abitibi Paper Company Ltd. of control of The Price Company Limited was based in part upon that consideration. Such acquisitions also enable firms to acquire experienced employees and management and established relationships with customers and suppliers.

We have also encountered many vertical mergers in which an active business has acquired control of one or more of its customers or suppliers to obtain more secure markets or more reliable sources of supply or for reasons of improved product quality and scheduling. George Weston Limited is an example of a Canadian firm that has become vertically integrated to a high degree through mergers.

Another motive, which might be expected in the oligopolistic industries common in Canada, is the desire of an aggressive company to acquire one of its competitors to increase its share of the market without creating excess capacity or upsetting the established price structure. Such mergers may lead to increased concentration in the industry concerned, but may also permit greater efficiency in the use of existing plants or their ultimate replacement with more economic plants. They may also permit economies at the firm level in management, financing and various staff functions. However, such mergers may lead to greater dominance by one firm in the industry and a reduction in competition.

Some companies have acquired others that provided complementary products or services, which enabled the acquiring company to offer a more complete line of related services or products. While this objective could be achieved partially by agreement, it was thought that control would result in better marketing. It was stated that the acquisition of a 50.1% interest in The Great-West Life Assurance Company by The Investors Group in 1969 was motivated at least in part by the marketing advantages that would result from Investors' expansion into a related service. Corporations selling products outside Canada have acquired foreign affiliates to market their exports or to produce in foreign countries behind trade barriers. Alcan and Massey-Ferguson Limited have penetrated foreign markets in this way.

There have been cases where companies seem clearly to have been acquired to use their liquid assets or borrowing capacity for the purposes of the acquiring company, including the making of further acquisitions.

Another motive is to acquire a business to use in it special technical or commercial abilities of the acquiring firm. Marketing skills appear to have led to diversified acquisitions in some conglomerate mergers, while technical expertise seems to be a more common motive in vertical or horizontal mergers. Both Imasco Limited and the Molson Companies Limited have achieved a high degree of diversification predicated on exploiting their marketing abilities more fully.

The explicit purpose of a number of Canadian corporate groups has been the acquisition of control of independent and relatively small but promising companies in order to provide financing and management that they could not otherwise obtain. Testimony given us by some of those who sold control of such independent businesses, but who continued to operate them with a considerable degree of autonomy, has led us to believe that this can be a constructive and profitable means of growth without the formation of really large corporate control groups. Canadian Corporate Management Company Limited and Hugh Russel Limited are firms that have grown in this way.

We have been told of cases of deliberate diversification by mergers to provide more stable earnings and to utilize more fully the capacity of management and other corporate level staff personnel. These hopes have not always been realized.

As mentioned in Chapter 5, we have received briefs and testimony from some who have had carefully planned programs to use profits and cash flow from profitable but relatively slowly growing operations to acquire and develop businesses in more dynamic industries. This was the motive behind Molson's several acquisitions in the latter part of the 1960s and in the 1970s, and Genstar's acquisitions as well. A related motive is to acquire controlling interests in businesses in Canada for the purposes of reinvesting in Canada funds available from operating profits or divestiture in other countries. Brascan Limited and John Labatt Limited are two examples of firms that have repatriated capital or profits.

Sometimes a greater degree of shareholding control has been acquired to rehabilitate a business in which the acquiring company already had a substantial equity, and this has on occasion involved the infusion of additional capital and/or the replacement or reorganization of top management. Argus and Power have thus extended their share control in Standard Broadcasting Corporation Limited and Consolidated-Bathurst Limited respectively. As the history of Canadian financial institutions illustrates, mergers are often arranged to rescue a failing business. Unity Bank of Canada was a financially troubled firm when La Banque Provinciale du Canada took control of it in 1977.

Acquisitions are sometimes made by companies under the control of confident and dynamic men motivated by the desire to grow and to create a corporate empire. Indeed, given the types of men who succeed in business and the kinds of opportunities that arise, it would be surprising if there were not cases of this kind, especially when there are available businesses under the control of others who appear less dynamic and venturesome. If such acquisitions do result in transferring resources to more aggressive and innovative managers, they help to promote greater economic efficiency. On the other hand, we have seen examples where unrelated acquisitions have led to deterioration in efficiency and performance.

In concluding this list, we should mention that there are other considerations that are contributory rather than primary motivations. One of the most widespread is the exemption from taxation of dividends received by one corporation from another, while dividends going to individuals enjoy only a tax credit. This exemption encourages retention and reinvestment of earnings by the corporation as opposed to the paying out of corporate earnings for reinvestment by shareholders. While the tax treatment of dividends should not, by itself, influence the decision of a firm toward external rather than internal growth, it encourages the retention of earnings within the corporate sector, thereby facilitating corporate acquisitions.

MOTIVES TO SELL

Our investigations have revealed that the initiative for merging usually comes from those who wish to sell control of a business. There are many reasons to sell. Commonly those controlling a relatively small independent business are unable to finance its expansion without selling control. Whether this is because of some remediable gap in the capital market, other reasons relating to the behavior patterns of financial institutions, or the economics of corporate control is a subject we discuss in Chapter 11.

Frequently the motive to sell is simply a natural desire on the part of an owner-manager to retire from active business and to get the best price he can. A related motive arises from the difficulties that managers of small but growing companies may have in adjusting to the type of management functions undertaken in larger firms. Owners wishing to dispose of a business concern find that their tax burden can be substantially reduced by selling to another corporation instead of liquidating the firm's assets. Some witnesses emphasized to us the difficulties encountered by small firms in complying with the numerous government regulations affecting all businesses as a reason to sell out.

In some cases, and it is hard to judge how many, the owners of a controlling interest in a business desire to diversify their holdings into marketable assets at the time when they retire or plan their estates. The desire for a more liquid portfolio to pay estate taxes at some future date provides an incentive for owners of closely held businesses to sell. In other cases, heirs who come into possession of controlling interests in such businesses may have no taste for the risks and responsibilities of such an investment and will seek to sell.

Often those who control a losing or troublesome business decide to cut their losses and sell the business.

We have noted the sale of minority controlling shareholdings when another strong interest becomes a major shareholder with either an immediate or probable dominant position in the company. We have also seen cases in which two dominant shareholders in a number of companies will exchange holdings to give each party controlling interests in particular companies.

Finally, sometimes owners may sell simply because they believe that the offered price exceeds the underlying value of the business.

We have compared our observations on stated merger motives with other published reports on this subject. The most extensive review was made by Reuber and Roseman in their 1969 report to the Economic Council on the results of the government survey of mergers. The most common reason for merging given by the successor merged company was the desire of the owners of the acquired company to sell. The next most common reason was that it was "cheaper and less risky to buy rather than build", and in the text it is emphasized that mergers were most often favored because they were "faster". A significant number of respondents gave as a motive for merging the acquisition of something unique to the acquired firm (or to other firms like it). Other reasons included the desire to expand capacity, the desire to reduce costs, or reasons directly related to the competitive situation. The desire to diversify into new fields, or into related or complementary products, or into new territories was also frequently mentioned. Broadly speaking the reasons given in this survey taken 14 years ago were similar to those we found in the briefs presented to us, although efficiency motives for merging were more frequently cited in the briefs than in Reuber's and Roseman's survey.

Some recent evidence on the declared motives for merging is provided in annual Foreign Investment Review Agency (FIRA) reports. They apply to foreign acquisitions requiring FIRA approval and, thereby, suggest caution in using the results, since firms may provide those reasons they think are most likely to win FIRA approval. The applications for approval emphasize, on the part of the acquiring businesses, desires for horizontal integration and expansion or for vertical integration. Other mergers result from acquisitions outside Canada of foreign parents of Canadian businesses. About 8% of the total gave diversification as the primary motive. About 23% of the sellers of businesses gave the poor financial position of the business as the reason, while about 18% stated inability to finance expansion as their primary reason. Desires of the parent company to divest itself of a Canadian subsidiary to raise capital or for other reasons was given as the cause in about 18% of the cases.

An international list of reasons for merging was given in a 1974 report of the Organisation for Economic Co-operation and Development (OECD) on mergers and competition policy. The report listed a dozen reasons, nearly all of which we also encountered in Canada. The report concludes that several motives will be present in most mergers and that there can be no overriding presumption in favor of or against mergers. Some smaller U.S. surveys found that synergy was expected in sales administration and research and development, while management considerations played an important role in a large proportion of mergers.

Economic Effects of Mergers

Mergers do not always achieve their purposes and the reasons given are not an entirely satisfactory guide to the probable effects of mergers in particular industries or cases or to their effects in general. Also, it is unrealistic to expect respondents to merger surveys to cite anticompetitive motives for undertaking mergers, although they may exist. The Commission has had an opportunity to review the financial results of many companies that have made frequent acquisitions and has set forth in Chapter 5 those results for a number of conglomerate groups; however, we have not been able to make a comprehensive survey of the effects of mergers in Canada. Because of the inadequacy of public information in this area, such a study would have necessitated fairly large-scale surveying efforts of the type undertaken by Reuber and Roseman (which took almost four years to complete).

Numerous studies in the United States have attempted to determine whether identifiable gains from mergers are realized by acquiring companies. The studies provide no unambiguous conclusions as to how acquiring firms have fared after mergers, inasmuch as some studies show that mergers apparently are not profitable, while others show that there are gains to both the acquiring and the acquired companies. The various studies, to a greater or lesser degree, are subject to the methodological reservations that the time period of analysis may not have been long enough to capture the effects of possible efficiency gains and that the procedures to hold constant all other factors besides acquisition activity were imperfect.

The major evidence for Canada is included in the Reuber and Roseman study based on a survey of mergers from 1945 to 1961. Those companies that had merged were asked to describe "the economies, if any, secured by the merger which were not otherwise obtainable". While the results of answers to such a questionnaire must be interpreted with caution, of the approximately two-thirds of the respondents who answered this question, about 46% said there were no economies or only negligible ones, about 25% cited the rather vague "administration and management" category and about 30% cited more specific economies in buying, selling, transport and production. Only about 15% of the mergers were said to have brought economies in the integration of plants and the use of materials.

In his 1973 study, Laiken analyzed the financial performance of a sample of 369 Canadian-based firms listed on the Toronto Stock Exchange during the period 1960-70. The firms were classified into groups based on their use of mergers for expansion during the period. He concluded that a weak direct association between increased merger activity and the ratio of operating income to total income provides a very slight indication of increased efficiency in the allocation of capital funds from mergers. As well, the lack of a strong inverse association in the ratios of operating income to total capital, and of net income to common equity may be taken as some evidence that merging firms were not consistently less efficient in their use of capital. However, the available evidence on conglomerate mergers in Canada, discussed in Chapter 5, suggests that diversified mergers did not generally prove profitable for acquiring firms. Moreover, there is some evidence to support the conclusion that conglomerate acquisitions increase the variability of the earnings of acquiring firms.

The available studies indicate that there is insufficient evidence to conclude that most of the mergers taking place in Canada add very much to real efficiency in production and distribution. The evidence does suggest that productive mergers do take place, although the effects of the size of an enterprise upon its efficiency are complicated and vary with circumstances. The Commission did receive numerous briefs from companies suggesting that economies of scale, particularly in overhead, managerial functions and cash management, are attainable through the acquisition process. The managerial functions most often centralized within the head office of the acquiring company include financial management, accounting, legal and insurance services, employee benefits and public relations.

In several briefs, management of the acquired companies indicated that assistance in some of the above-mentioned functions was an important reason favoring the acquisitions. For example, the management of Progresso Foods Corp. (formerly Uddo & Taormina Corp.), acquired by Imasco, claimed that the Imasco takeover brought substantial improvements in the company's accounting techniques, legal knowledge, inventory control and management information systems. The management of another company taken over by Imasco, Grissol Foods Limited, cited improvements and cost savings in the legal counselling and insurance functions after integration of these functions into the parent's operations. In these cases, it may have been more difficult or costly to obtain assistance by alternative methods, such as hiring management consultants.

Concern about potential competitive effects of mergers has centered, in part, on the relationship between merger activity and subsequent changes in industrial concentration. In the previously cited study, Laiken concluded that higher levels of merger activity in Canada were not associated with increases in profit margins or with increased price/earnings ratios. On this basis, he suggests that mergers did not increase the market power of acquiring companies. Recent evidence on patterns of industrial concentration in Canada was assembled for the Commission by Christian Marfels. Employing special tabulations by Statistics Canada, he constructed various measures of aggregate concentration. In one exercise, aggregate concentration ratios for the 25, 50, 100 and 200 largest non-financial corporations in Canada were compared for 1965, 1968 and 1973. Modest increases in asset concentration were evident for the first 25 and the first 200 non-financial corporations from 1965 to 1973, while sales concentration showed a slight decrease. In another exercise, a measure of industrial concentration was constructed, specifically a Herfindahl index for 129 manufacturing industries. Detailed analyses of the indices by industry group showed that concentration trends had a tendency to decline during 1965-72. Analyses of concentration trends in nine large manufacturing industries support this conclusion. Six of the nine industries showed declines in both enterprise and establishment concentration for various measures of concentration. Thus, aggregate industrial concentration in Canada did not generally increase during a period in which merger activity was quite intense.

Some admittedly rough analysis by our staff also contradicts the notion that merger activity was associated with a significant increase in concentration at the industry level. Specifically, the percentage change in the number of largest firms accounting for 80% of industry employment between two discrete years, 1948 and 1965, was calculated for a sample of 10 industries. The industries were ranked in terms of this measure and in order of their merger intensities over the period 1945-61, from highest to lowest values. The rank orders of the two series were compared and found to be unrelated; however, since complete data on which to calculate the 1948 concentration ratios were unavailable for several of the sample industries, this result might be subject to error.

Critics of the evidence cited above might argue that in merger-intensive industries (which are generally characterized by faster than average growth) concentration, rather than staying the same, might have decreased if the mergers had not taken place. On the other hand, it is also possible that market shares of acquiring companies would have been larger had they devoted their efforts to internal growth in their primary industries and diversified less. Moreover, the impact of mergers on industrial concentration will be overstated if mergers are in fact an alternative to exit for the absorbed companies.

In summary, while individual mergers may have the effect of increasing concentration in some instances, the Commission thinks that no long-run general relationship between merger activity and concentration can be identified in Canada during the period since 1945. This was also the conclusion reached by Lawrence Skeoch and Bruce McDonald in their 1976 report to the

Minister of Consumer and Corporate Affairs, *Dynamic Change and Accountability in a Canadian Market Economy*:

> To revert to the Canadian situation: in terms of (1) relative merger numbers (and their limited effect in bringing together the leading firms) in the post-war years as against the earlier merger movements, (2) the large post-war increase in the number of firms, and (3) also keeping in mind the dimensions of merger and joint venture activity in Sweden and the United States, it would appear that the *general* merger movement in Canada has not given rise to any important consequences for the economy. At the same time, there have undoubtedly been a significant number of mergers that the Canadian economy would have been better off without. It is not so much the *number* ["perhaps half a dozen mergers in the last two decades that I would rather have seen not take place," Skeoch told us] of mergers that gives cause for current concern as the nature of the comparatively small number of those that have occurred.

Competition Law and Policy Concerning Mergers

Competition Law in Canada

One of the economic implications of large corporate groups and of the mergers sometimes used in forming them are their effects, or possible effects, on competition in various Canadian industries and markets. Since 1923 there has been a section in the Combines Investigation Act that makes it an indictable offense to form a merger (or a monopoly) by which competition in an industry (or trade or profession) is lessened, or is likely to be lessened, to the detriment of or against the interests of the public, i.e. consumers, producers or others. Nevertheless, there is concern as to whether this law and its application constitute an adequate safeguard to the public interest. Two features of the law must be noted. The first is that, for constitutional reasons, it was thought in the past that Parliament could legislate in this field only by using criminal law. This requires cases to be tried in the courts and to be proven beyond a reasonable doubt under strict rules of evidence. In mergers it is important to prove conclusively that competition is likely to be lessened "in the future", and to prove this "beyond a reasonable doubt". It must also be shown that the effects of a merger in lessening competition will likely be to the detriment of or against the interest of the public, essentially a matter of economic appraisal.

The *Proposals for a New Competition Policy for Canada, Second Stage* (1977) conclude that:

> Although there has been a section in the [Combines Investigation] Act since 1923 which makes it an indictable offence to be party to a merger which has operated or is likely to operate to the detriment of the public, its enforcement has not been successful. Before World War II there was only one prosecution for a merger offence, the Western Fruits and Vegetables case, and it resulted in an acquittal. Following this, there were no further prosecutions until the *Canadian Breweries* case in 1959 and, shortly thereafter, the *Western Sugar* case. Both of these prosecutions also ended in acquittal. The Electric Reduction Company of Canada Limited pleaded guilty to a merger charge in 1970 and K.C. Irving Limited was convicted of merger charges by the trial court in 1974 but the decision was reversed

on appeal. In another case an order was issued against Anthes Imperial Limited in 1973 which prohibited it from acquiring Associated Foundry Limited. There has never been [in Canada] a conviction after a full trial which was not reversed on appeal.

Since monopoly, monopolistic pricing, supply reduction and related practices are all violations under other sections of the Combines Investigation Act, there has been little scope for action under the merger section. The Director of Investigation and Research charged with administration of the Combines Investigation Act did, however, testify before us that the merger provisions of the Act have some deterrent value. Some parties contemplating mergers are dissuaded as a result of consulting with the Director and his staff, and it is possible that others have been deterred by advice of legal counsel. Nevertheless, the Director stated in his brief to the Commission, referring to the provisions of the law relating to mergers and monopolies, "I believe it is fair to say that these sections of the competition law have not been effective enforcement tools to date, and thus competition policy in Canada has not been as effective as might otherwise have been the case".

It is difficult to assess how much the public interest in Canada has been harmed by the weakness of the Act in regard to mergers. In Chapter 2 we presented statistics suggesting that concentration in specific Canadian industries did not generally increase from 1965 to 1972. Of course, evidence gathered for such a short period must be treated with caution. Furthermore, one can point to periods of merger activity in the early part of this century when concentration increased substantially across a broad range of industries. In Chapter 4 we examined the nature of competition in relatively concentrated industries and markets and concluded that while a significant amount of "conscious parallelism" exists with respect to pricing decisions, competition frequently occurs along non-price dimensions in these industries. In Chapter 5 we examined some competitive practices of diversified "conglomerate" corporations and found no evidence of serious anticompetitive practices. In this chapter we have seen that the overall postwar merger movement in Canada does not appear to have given rise to widespread anticompetitive consequences for the economy.

However, we are aware that many observers, including Skeoch and McDonald, believe that the anticompetitive effects of a small number of mergers have indeed been significant. William Stanbury, in a paper prepared for the Commission, argues that several acquisitions provided acquiring companies with substantial positions of market power in relevant markets. The Commission agrees with the view that for a small number of mergers in Canada, there may be reasonable cause for concern that harm might occur to competition and to the public interest.

Considerations Regarding
the Application of Law to Mergers

The Commission's responsibility regarding competition law and its administration is to assess to what degree it represents an adequate safeguard to the public interest. Before attempting an assessment, we briefly outline the relevant considerations in framing merger policy.

On competition policy generally we agree with those who say that competition law should not be framed as criminal law if it is constitutionally possible to express it otherwise. We also agree with Skeoch and McDonald that the proper focus of concern of a competition law should be on the misuse of dominant market power or the attempt to increase or entrench a dominant position by anticompetitive means. Examples of such abuses, according to Skeoch and McDonald, are:

> preclusive acquisiting [sic] or ownership of resources and facilities; deliberated exclusion; reinforcing a dominant position by exclusive dealing and tying arrangements, or by refusal to deal; predatory discrimination; a design to forestall competition and to hold its monopoly position by other than the achievement of real-cost economies; the use of reciprocal buying-selling advantages, and the like.

Under existing competition law a corporate merger is not in itself an abuse of market power; it is only a technique by which two or more firms can become, in effect, one. However, a merger could create a situation in which the merged firm may acquire and abuse market power. As well, a merger can in some circumstances reduce competition even if the merged firm does not actively engage in anticompetitive conduct.

Few would disagree that a competition law must deal with mergers or their consequences in some way. The difficult question is how far a competition law should seek to go in preventing the consummation of mergers that may threaten competition, and to what extent the law should operate, after the fact, against whatever anticompetitive consequences are seen to flow from a completed merger.

The question is essentially one of emphasis, but the decision as to where to put the emphasis is a matter of judgment on which reasonable people may legitimately differ. To the extent that the law is left to operate after the fact, dealing with traceable consequences, there is a risk that the law may not be able to apply effective sanctions against the parties to a completed merger, since it is not always possible to assign to a particular merger any deterioration of competition that may occur. Even if the anticompetitive effects of a completed merger can eventually be traced and stopped, an unacceptable amount of damage may have been suffered in the meantime by customers or suppliers of the merged firm. On the other hand, if the law scrutinizes all proposed mergers so as to stop those that may be competitively harmful, it may have such unsettling effects on normal commercial activity that beneficial mergers may be deterred.

In addition to the cost of maintaining an agency to screen potential mergers there are the out-of-pocket costs and the costs of uncertainty and delay that will be imposed on the parties to a proposed merger. Moreover, a law that requires some form of official consent or permission before people may do something (in this case complete a corporate merger) raises an important philosophical question. The matter is not simply one of economics.

We think there should be a high burden of proof on those who advocate a law requiring official or even quasi-judicial consent before a particular course of action is undertaken. There should be several essential preconditions to justify any law that is permissive instead of prohibitory. Foremost among these would be a high probability of substantial and irreversible harm to the community. Also, the standards upon which the permission will be granted or withheld should be clear and capable of being related to facts that can be determined and demonstrated at the time permission is sought. Permission should not depend on unverifiable predictions of what the applicant might or might not be able to do at some time in the future nor should it be conditional on future events beyond an applicant's control.

The evidence that we have seen does not suggest that industrial concentration has increased significantly even during a period of high merger activity. In our view the law should not be biased against mergers because their benefits cannot be clearly and indisputably demonstrated in a pre-merger screening procedure. The law should act preventively only when there is a clear likelihood that harm will result if it does not. The evidence does not suggest that corporate mergers generally tend to be harmful in competitive terms; rather it suggests that the danger is slight. In our opinion, therefore, there is no justification for an elaborate preventive law and a correspondingly expensive screening apparatus with which to enforce it. If it is difficult to assess the economic consequences of a completed merger, it is far more difficult to predict the outcome of a proposed one. Any mechanism designed to predict which mergers will be beneficial and which harmful will be enormously cumbersome and prone to error.

Finally, there is the question of timing. There is a marked lack of confidence today in at least the short-term economic future of Canada. It does not seem prudent at this time to launch new and untried schemes of general economic regulation of the kind that would be implicit in a preventive merger law. The risk that a new merger law might further depress business confidence might be worth taking if there were strong evidence of harmful anticompetitive practices and if there were a reasonable prospect that the law could improve conditions significantly at an acceptable cost. Neither of these conditions obtain.

For all these reasons, we think that the competition law should deal in a prohibitory way with proven anticompetitive conduct and, correspondingly, that corporate mergers should not be subject to a review process or require official approval or consent before they are completed. Our conclusion carries with it a risk that, if there is a merger that has a significantly harmful effect on competition, the law will be able to deal with it only after the fact. We think this risk is slight. We recognize, however, that some people are not willing to accept this risk and demand, instead, a preventive measure. The government, implicitly, has acceded to this view by introducing Bill C-13. We think it is right, therefore, for us to expand on our argument by reference to this Bill so that people will be better able to judge the merits of the two opposing points of views.

BILL C-13

THRESHOLD STANDARDS

Assuming that a preventive merger law should not reach all mergers, but only those that may have significant implications for competition, the statute should first establish criteria by which the mergers most likely to be harmful can be identified.

The criteria set out in subsection 31.71(2) of Bill C-13 do not meet these standards because they are too vague and because they seem likely to subject far too many potential mergers to review. If a review process is desirable at all, we should prefer a threshold that uses the size of the merging firms (measured, for example, by assets or sales). A threshold of this kind can be criticized for arbitrariness, but it does bring certainty into the law, and that is an important consideration. We suggest the following criteria, which combine a size standard with a market-share test:

horizontal mergers: a horizontal merger between parties who sell in the same market, in which the parties would have at least a 50% share of the relevant market after the merger, and where each party has at least $50 million of sales or assets before the merger, would be subject to review and could not be completed without the approval of the reviewing tribunal;

vertical mergers: a vertical merger where one party is a customer of the second, in which one party has at least a 50% share of a relevant market, and where each party has at least $50 million of sales or assets before the merger, would be subject to review and could not be completed without the approval of the reviewing tribunal;

conglomerate mergers: a conglomerate merger with horizontal or vertical market dimensions should be reviewed against the criteria above; a conglomerate merger where there is no horizontal or vertical aspect raises few issues relevant to a competition law and should be treated in the way we recommend in Chapter 7 for a merger like the proposed Power-Argus one.

REVIEW STANDARDS (COMPETITION BOARD)

If a proposed merger does exceed the threshold limits, so that it must then be examined and approved before the parties are allowed to complete it, the next question is by what standard is it to be judged? Bill C-13 sets out an elaborate list of factors in subsections 31.71(4) and (5) against which a proposed merger could be tested. Many of these factors are disturbingly vague, but our chief criticism is that too many of them depend on the "likelihood" of future events.

In an advance appraisal process the decision-maker is necessarily examining promise, not performance. It is difficult enough for anyone to identify, isolate and weigh the consequences (to the public as well as to the parties) of a completed merger several years after it has occurred. It is far more difficult to do so when the merger is merely a prospect, at the point where its consequences are in the indeterminate future. Any judgment of a proposed merger against standards like those described in Bill C-13 will be at best an inspired guess.

It would be possible to test proposed mergers against standards less elaborate than those contained in Bill C-13. In the United States, for example, proposed mergers are examined in terms of the merged firm's resulting market share. The U.S. Department of Justice has published specific guidelines indicating market shares that will ordinarily be challenged. Courts in the United States have generally refused to consider offsetting benefits that arise from reduced costs, increased efficiency and the like when deciding whether a proposed merger should be approved.

In *Dynamic Change and Accountability in a Canadian Market Economy,* Skeoch and McDonald criticize this exclusive concern with market share and say that, whatever its suitability in the United States, it would be inappropriate in Canada:

> A small economy does not enjoy the same elbow-room in policy making. A few bad merger decisions may strengthen monopolistic elements unduly or they may inhibit the development of firms of sufficient size to undertake production and marketing effectively in a world context, and to participate, at least as a partner, in the complex process of innovation.

They urge that mergers should be evaluated against broader criteria.

We acknowledge the force of this criticism, but it does not follow that Canada should therefore subject proposed mergers to a more sophisticated examination than that attempted in the United States. In our opinion, the ideal described by Skeoch and McDonald and carried into Bill C-13 is simply not practical in this country. The criteria set out in the Bill are far too complicated to interpret and time-consuming to apply. The tangible and intangible costs, including risk and uncertainty, of the examination they would require would far outweigh the benefits.

We suspect that the merger law in the United States works as well as it does because the courts in that country have tested mergers largely by reference to anticipated market shares. They have recognized that any other consequences are too speculative, especially if those other factors pull in opposite directions and the judge has to consider how far one unmeasured and unmeasurable factor offsets another. An appraisal process operating on this basis is a chimera, creating an illusion of profundity.

In sum, although it should be relatively easy to establish a threshold by which to select those mergers that should be reviewed in advance, we are not convinced that any review process would produce results reliable enough to justify the costs of the review. The forecasting process is the Achilles heel of a merger law.

APPEALS

The extensive powers to be vested in the proposed Competition Board quite naturally give rise to a feeling that there should be some right of appeal so that mistaken decisions can be corrected. We assume that the decisions of the Competition Board, like those of other regulatory tribunals, would be appealable to the ordinary courts on questions of jurisdiction and procedural fairness. The more difficult question, however, is whether there should be a right to appeal on the merits, that is should the substantive decisions of the regulatory tribunal be reviewable by the courts.

Regulatory tribunals, like the proposed Competition Board, are usually created because of an understandable belief that the ordinary courts are not equipped to handle the kind of questions that arise under "economic" laws. If that is true, it would be pointless to allow the decisions of the Board to be reviewed, on their merits, in the courts. In addition, the long time that would elapse if decisions of the Competition Board could be carried through the courts might weaken the competition law fatally.

Although we can agree with the drafters of Bill C-13 that the substantive decisions of the Competition Board should not be appealable to the courts, we cannot agree with section 31.91, which gives the federal Cabinet power to annul the Board's orders. If anything, this alternative is worse because it displaces open standards with hidden discretion. It will stultify the development of the law and it will create suspicion about the integrity with which it is administered.

There is a valid case for government intervention to vary or rescind regulatory decisions that go contrary to decided government policy. The dangers of this kind of lawmaking are so great, however, that some kind of parliamentary supervision should come into play when government uses such a power.

In our opinion, the concern about appeals, and the mistaken response to that concern in Bill C-13, stem from a fundamental misconception of what a tribunal like the Competition Board should be. The Competition Board should be more of a legislative body than an adjudicatory one. A broad regulatory scheme like that foreshadowed in the Competition Bill is a complex area in which Parliament cannot be expected to legislate in detail. The Competition Board's primary function should be to create the necessary legislative infill, using all the techniques of what in the United States is called "rule-making". It will not be enough to leave this task to case-by-case adjudication. That is only one rule-making technique, and not the most useful one. In the merger area particularly, history suggests that there will be few cases indeed and, as we have said, there should be especially few involving an advance assessment of proposed mergers. This means that the inescapable uncertainty in even the best-drafted statutory provisions will not be clarified in a reasonable time by case decisions.

We resist the temptation to digress to a more extensive discussion of the lawmaking functions of the Competition Board or regulatory tribunals general-ly, because that raises other important questions of accountability and parliamentary control, which go beyond our terms of reference. We wish only to make the observation that we think Bill C-13 places too much emphasis on the Competition Board as an adjudicatory body, and to record a doubt about the usefulness of trial-like proceedings in the development of economic policy.

CLEARANCE PROCEDURE (COMPETITION POLICY ADVOCATE)

Bill C-13 provides for another kind of review process, which may have been designed to resolve some of the problems we have raised above. The parties to a proposed merger can inform the Competition Policy Advocate (the official who is given a kind of prosecutorial function in Bill C-13) of their plans. If the Advocate is satisfied that the merger would not be an undesirable one he can issue a certificate to that effect, and he is thereafter barred from attacking the merger before the Competition Board. This could be a useful procedure in many cases, particularly if the Advocate takes advantage of the opportunity given him in section 27.2 to issue interpretative opinions. These interpretative opinions would be a form of rule-making.

The other consequences of the Competition Policy Advocate's "clearance procedure" are less easy to predict. On the one hand, the availability of the clearance procedure may mean that few corporations will be content to act on the advice of legal counsel as to whether any merger being contemplated will be subject to the statute. The Advocate's certificate could become an item on the checklist of every corporate solicitor. If that were so, the Competition Policy Advocate could be asked to rule on almost every proposed merger in Canada, including those that would have no conceivable effect on competition. It is impossible to tell how much of a burden this might impose on the Competition Policy Advocate, and what staff he will need to discharge this "insurance" function for the private sector.

On the other hand, the Advocate's examination may be seen as a further impediment to corporate mergers. Often it will take a considerable time to collect and explain the "material facts" the Competition Policy Advocate will need to study before he can issue a certificate. Section 31.71(22) of Bill C-13 obliges the Advocate to give his decision within six months after he receives the information, although he can ask a member of the Competition Board to extend this time to twelve months. These time limits are deceptive, however, because they do not start to run until the Competition Policy Advocate has received *all* the necessary information, and many months could pass during which the parties will be responding to requests from the Competition Policy Advocate for information additional to that supplied initially. The parties may not have all the information relevant to the Advocate's examination and may have to do research of their own to obtain it. Information supplied may suggest the need for additional information; the Competition Policy Advocate may feel obliged to verify some of the information he receives, and so on.

It would be impossible, of course, to specify completely and precisely in the statute the information the Competition Policy Advocate should have before he makes his decision. Presumably the information would be broadly that which would be put before the Competition Board if the merger were to be reviewed by the Board. The Advocate will be doing informally essentially what the Board would do formally.

It is important to the integrity of the competition law that the Competition Policy Advocate's examination be thorough, but it is only reasonable to expect the Advocate to be cautious before issuing clearance certificates. The potential embarrassment to him and to the government if he approves a merger that experience later shows to be competitively damaging will always be present in his mind. However unconsciously, the Advocate's bias will be to deny approval and thus keep open the opportunity to attack the merger later before the Competition Board.

A clearance procedure of the kind contemplated in Bill C-13 requires an escape provision, if only to deal with situations in which the Competition Policy Advocate's certificate may have been based on incomplete, incorrect or misleading information. Thus, Bill C-13 provides that, if the Competition Policy Advocate can convince a member of the Competition Board that he was not given all the relevant information, then, notwithstanding his clearance certificate, the merger is not immune from later attack. However, the Bill also provides that any six people can apply for, and the Minister of Consumer and Corporate Affairs may direct, the Competition Policy Advocate to carry out an "inquiry" into the merger, whether or not it has already been approved by the Advocate. On the conclusion of the inquiry the Advocate can decide that there are grounds to attack the merger after all, and there is apparently no way in which his determination could be challenged, notwithstanding that it was inconsistent with his earlier decision and the clearance certificate.

However justified these "let out" provisions may be, the point for our purposes is that they qualify the finality of any clearance certificate issued by the Competition Policy Advocate in respect of a proposed merger. The usefulness of the advance review procedure by the Advocate is correspondingly qualified.

The Competition Policy Advocate's responsibility under the merger clearance procedure of Bill C-13 is heavy, especially where the merger is an important one. It is only right that he has all the available relevant evidence before him, and that he has adequate time to study it before he makes his decision. Although we are sympathetic to the idea behind the clearance procedure, which we think is intended to facilitate desirable mergers, we fear that the unavoidable costs and delays in that procedure, the possibility that the Competition Policy Advocate may give an unfavorable ruling at the end of it and the uncertainty overhanging even a favorable ruling may destroy much of its value in the minds of corporate executives.

CONSENT ORDERS

Section 31.79.1 of Bill C-13 provides for "consent orders" where the Competition Policy Advocate and the parties can agree on the disposition of a case without a hearing before the Competition Board. If the competition law is to include a preventive provision of the kind set out in Bill C-13, we think the consent order provision will be useful. But it should be accompanied by some safeguards.

In some of the more serious matters with which the competition law is concerned, little can be expected from case-by-case adjudication by the Competition Board. In cases involving mergers and joint monopolization, for example, the relative weight of the several factors is so uncertain, the circumstances so complex and the nature of the Board's orders so unconfined that few businesses will be able to bear the uncertainty (to say nothing of the delay and cost) of a hearing before the Board. These and many other possible cases will almost always be settled by consent between the Competition Policy Advocate and the parties.

The consent order provisions of Bill C-13 therefore invite a kind of plea bargaining on an unprecedented scale. Plea bargaining is coming to be recognized as a problem in the administration of the criminal law, but it is more serious in regulatory law because its direct consequences reach far beyond the interests of the immediate parties. It is not clear from section 31.79.1 that the Competition Board will review and approve all case settlements; it should have this duty and power because of the overwhelming power of the Competition Policy Advocate to put pressure on businessmen who cannot afford to fight. Moreover, these settlements should be fully reported by the Board, so that everyone will be able to see how the law is working in practice. The process of review, approval and publication will serve as a check on the Competition Policy Advocate and it will also tend to allay suspicions about secret and perhaps politically inspired "deals".

Conclusions

We expressed the opinion earlier that competition was not seriously threatened by corporate mergers, and also that the costs of a review process by the Competition Board were not justified by the unsatisfactory results that may be expected from it. Our examination of Bill C-13, including the provisions for advance clearance by the Competition Policy Advocate, Cabinet appeals and consent orders, has not caused us to alter that conclusion. It is not that a process requiring a prediction of the economic effects of mergers cannot be made to work; it is that the process can operate only at what we think will be a prohibitive cost and that the results of the process will not be sufficiently worthwhile.

This conclusion reinforces the view we stated earlier: that competition law should deal with abuses or further entrenchment of market power. The law should act in the traditional prohibitory fashion: if facts are established showing that a firm is guilty of proscribed conduct, the court or responsible tribunal makes an order designed to stop the practice and, possibly, to compensate those who have been injured by it. In extreme cases, the tribunal could of course order dissolution of the offending firm or divestiture of some of its assets and operations. Indeed, the law should make it abundantly clear that sanctions as severe as dissolution and divestiture will be applied, where necessary, to companies who abuse market power. Ideally, the responsible tribunal should have a rule-making function under which, among other things, it could indicate the circumstances in which such severe remedies would probably be applied. This would do much to ensure that objectionable practices did not occur. In particular, it would impel parties to a merger to make sure that the new firm did not take improper advantage of increased market power resulting from the merger.

Chapter 7

Power/Argus

Introduction

In the spring of 1975, Power Corporation of Canada, Limited, launched a bid to acquire control of Argus Corporation Limited. Power's attempt to take over Argus prompted considerable comment in business and other circles and, although it is not mentioned specifically in our terms of reference, it led directly to the establishment of this Commission.

While we are examining and appraising a number of issues from a broad perspective, we have also studied many specific cases, of which Power's attempted takeover of Argus is the most prominent. As a general rule we have looked at these cases only to improve our understanding of corporate activity, to apply theories and concepts to real situations, and to determine whether, or to what extent, patterns of behavior occur. To some extent, our consideration of the Power bid for Argus is an exception. Because the takeover bid was the reason for this Commission, and because it is quite clear from questions asked in the House of Commons that Parliament wishes our views on it, we decided to examine Power and Argus in particular and to assess the implications of a possible merging of control of the two firms. We also thought it might be useful to have a fairly detailed analysis of this case when our general conclusions of wider application are being considered.

We received detailed submissions from both Power and Argus, and also conducted public hearings at which their chief executive officers gave evidence. In addition, we received submissions and oral testimony from several of the companies affiliated with the two corporations. We also commissioned studies of each corporation and its major affiliates. These studies, which are published concurrently with this *Report*, focus on the financial affairs of the two companies and contain considerable historical and topical detail. Readers who are interested in more information about Power and Argus than is found in this chapter should refer to the studies.

Power Corporation of Canada, Limited

Power Corporation was founded in 1925 by members of the investment firm Nesbitt, Thomson & Company Limited. For many years its holdings were

169

largely in the electrical generating industry, but in the early 1960s most of its assets were either sold or expropriated. Over the next decade it made investments in transport, pulp and paper, financial services, and communications. In 1968 control of Power was effectively acquired by Paul Desmarais and his associate, the late Jean Parisien. As of June 30, 1977, Desmarais and the Parisien family interests owned about 18% of the equity stock of Power (through their holding company, Gelco Enterprises Ltd., in which Desmarais has a 75% and the Parisien family a 25% interest). This holding includes 97.6% of those shares carrying multiple voting rights, so that in the aggregate they have about 53% of the total votes that can be cast at a Power shareholders meeting. They have both effective and legal control of Power.

Power has controlling positions in a number of large and important Canadian companies (the most significant of which are the subject of separate sections within the study on Power Corporation referred to above). Its ownership and degree of control of the major investments it held at the time of the takeover bid are shown in Figure 7.1.

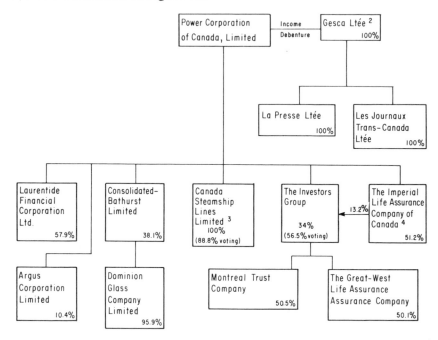

FIGURE 7.1. Power Corporation of Canada, Limited. Major Investments, March 25, 1975.[1]
Common shares.

Source: Royal Commission on Corporate Concentration (RCCC) research.

Notes

1. This table illustrates the size and diversity of the Power interests on the date Power announced its intention to take over Argus. There have been changes since then but none are significant for the purposes of this *Report*.

2. The shares of Gesca are owned by Gelco Enterprises (the Desmarais-Parisien holding company).

3. Subsequent to March 25, 1975, Power increased its ownership of Canada Steamship Lines to 100% voting. As a result of its bid for Argus, and subsequent thereto, it increased its interest in Argus to 25.3% voting and 52.9% equity.

4. In 1977 Power sold its holdings in Imperial Life to a life insurance company based in Quebec City, for about $10 million, and it has since purchased, through its wholly owned subsidiary, TransCanada Corporation Fund, Imperial's 13.2% interest in Investors.

The relationship between Power and the companies in which it has interests (with the exception of Argus) is one of active and interested supervision over broad policy matters and of important activities such as the selection of a chief executive officer and board nominees. While Power is represented on the executive committees of these affiliates, the committees are not crucial to the maintenance of its control. Representation on the boards of the affiliates is important, and Power influences them mainly in this way. Except for Consolidated-Bathurst Limited, over which it has effective (but not legal) control, and Argus, over which it has no control whatsoever, Power owns (or controls through other affiliates) sufficient shares to give it over 50% of the votes in all its affiliates.

Power is a large company, at least by Canadian standards. In our list of Canada's largest non-financial firms for 1975, Power ranked 98th by sales ($293 million), 45th by assets ($579 million) and 38th by net income ($32 million). Its financial affiliates administer billions of dollars of assets, some of which are owned by the companies in question and some of which they merely administer. Whether the assets are owned, as by life insurance companies, or are merely administered, as by trust companies, Power's ability to deal with them is carefully limited and constrained by law.

Argus Corporation Limited

Argus Corporation was founded in 1945 by a group of Toronto business and investment men led by E. P. Taylor and the late W. Eric Phillips. Its original philosophy, stated in the 1946 annual report, was to invest in a relatively few enterprises, mainly for long-term growth, and it has adhered to this approach. It is a closed-end investment company, which has been controlled since its inception by a small group of people, the composition of which has occasionally changed. This group now holds its interests through The Ravelston Corporation Limited, a holding company. Since 1971 J. A. McDougald has been Chairman and President of Argus.

At the end of 1977, McDougald and his associates, through Ravelston, owned or controlled, directly or indirectly, about 61.5% of the common (voting) shares of Argus, giving them legal control. They also owned or controlled about 23% of the Class C (non-voting) shares which were distributed to the common shareholders on a 4-for-1 basis in May 1962. They had in the aggregate about 31% of the equity stock of Argus. Power in mid-1977 held about 25% of the common shares and sufficient Class C shares to give it almost 53% of the equity stock of Argus, apart from the senior Class A and Class B preferred shares. The Jackman interests (who have an informal arrangement with the Ravelston group) hold 8.6% of the common shares and the remaining 5% is in the hands of the public.

At the time of Power's bid for control, Argus held (and still holds) large, but minority, positions in five major Canadian companies in the following industries: merchandising; pulp, paper and packaging; mining; manufacturing; and communications. Its major investments as at March 25, 1975, are shown in Figure 7.2.

Several of these companies are important in the Canadian economy in their own right. For example, in our list of large Canadian non-financial firms, Dominion Stores ranked 10th by sales ($1.9 billion), and Domtar ranked 36th by sales ($815 million). In addition Massey-Ferguson, which ranked 7th by sales, is a multinational corporation of significant stature, with sales outside Canada of over $2 billion.

Argus has held its investment in these companies for many years (on a weighted basis, the average time that each investment has been held ranges from about 12 years to about 29 years). This factor, among others, has permitted Argus to play a significant role in their affairs while holding only a minority interest. Argus representatives constitute a majority on each executive committee (Standard Broadcasting Corporation Limited does not have such a committee), and these committees do, in fact, have and exercise power. Argus is also represented on the boards of all five companies, its representatives constituting from one-third to one-half of the membership. No other shareholder holds as much as 10% of the voting shares of these companies.

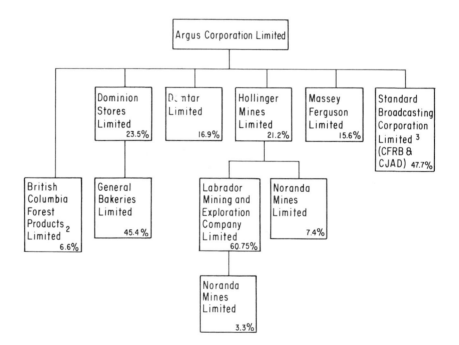

FIGURE 7.2. Argus Corporation Limited. Major Investments, March 25, 1975.[1]

Source: RCCC research.

Notes

1. This table illustrates the size and diversity of the Argus interests on the date Power announced its intention to take over Argus. There have been some changes since then but none that are significant for purposes of this *Report*.

2. Interest disposed of July 5, 1976.

3. On March 13, 1975, Standard Broadcasting received approval from the CRTC to purchase a 52% interest in Bushnell Communications Limited. The purchase became effective April 28, 1975. In October 1976 it increased its interest to 62.2%.

Argus is careful to say that it does not "control" these companies. It readily acknowledges, however, that it influences their affairs. The influence is such that no major transaction is undertaken by any of the companies without the approval of the Argus representatives on the boards. Because Argus does not have legal control, its investments in the companies are carried on the Argus balance sheet at quoted market value. Power carries its Argus investment on a cost basis (with market value indicated), but its wholly owned subsidiaries are consolidated, and other subsidiary and affiliated companies are accounted for on an equity basis.

Argus, like Power, is an important company that influences the affairs of other major corporations. Because it has less than a 50% interest in, and therefore does not legally control, its associated companies, it is not included in most lists of Canadian firm rankings by size. However, its 1975 balance sheet indicated assets of $204 million and net income of $12.1 million.

Relationships with Affiliates and Associated Companies

From the foregoing, it will be apparent that there are some significant differences between Power and Argus. Certainly their origins and their business activities and strategies seem to be sufficiently divergent to limit the usefulness of comparisons between them. One of the most striking differences is the perception each corporation has of its relationships with its affiliated companies. Power monitors the performance of its affiliates and, because of its legal control, seems to accept some degree of residual responsibility for them. Power considers that having a controlling interest is good for its own shareholders. Desmarais told us, "If you have control of something, it is usually worth more than just a passive investment."

Argus is adamant on its interpretation of the question of control of its associated companies. Argus has a large, but minority, interest in the five companies and has always taken the position that it does not control them and cannot speak for them. McDougald told us that "Argus Corporation is not a conglomerate. Argus has not subsidiaries and does not manage any other companies in which it holds shares...and does not advance funds to or purchase debt instruments of the companies in which it holds shares."

These may not be real differences between the two firms, however, only differences in style or perception. Desmarais, when asked, thought that "They [Argus] probably have the same amount of direction, and the same amount of control that we have, but that is an historical control and was spelled over a period of time. . . ." Recognizing, and subject to, the very important constraints upon Argus that might arise in some circumstances where it does not have over 50% of the votes in a company, we are inclined to agree that, as a practical matter, there is no important difference in the influence exercised by Power over its affiliates and that exercised by Argus over its associated companies.

The Takeover Bid

In the spring of 1969, Power acquired about 10.4% of the Argus common shares. Most of these were bought from Gelco (Messrs. Desmarais and Parisien) and the rest were bought in the open market. Power has subsequently stated that this original acquisition was made because of the strength of Argus and its importance as a pool of capital. In June 1969, two Argus shareholders, Ravelston and Windfields Farm Limited, pooled the voting power of their combined shares, for a minimum of five years. Between the time of its original purchase and the spring of 1975, Power did not increase its investment in Argus.

On March 25, 1975, Power announced that it proposed to make a bid to acquire all Argus common and Class C (non-voting) shares. The offer was $22 for each common share and $17 for each Class C share. In the six preceding months the common shares had traded within a range of $13 to $17, and the Class C shares had traded within a range of $8.25 to $13. The offer, made on April 3, was more successful in obtaining Class C shares than in obtaining common shares.

Argus shareholders were informed that Ravelston would not accept the Power offer. Because Ravelston held 50.9% of the common stock, this meant that the Power bid for control had failed. Although the Power offer for common stock was conditional upon an 80% or greater acceptance by Argus shareholders, Power accepted all shares tendered. Shortly after the offer closed Ravelston increased its holdings in Argus to 61%. Although control of Argus did not change hands, Power has continued to buy common shares of Argus whenever they become available. At the end of 1977 it held about 53% of the Argus equity stock and about 25% of the votes.

Power has stated that it attempted to buy control of Argus because "it was considered to be a good investment opportunity" for Power's shareholders, and because Power could then broaden its earnings and assets base and expand into new areas. The study commissioned by us refers to the bid as "mystifying" and suggests that, had Power acquired control of Argus, some or all of Argus' investments would likely have been sold, and the proceeds used to acquire control of other companies. Desmarais has indicated that if the Argus controlling stock becomes available, Power would still like to acquire it, although at the present time it seems clear that, as he told us, "the doors have been slammed pretty firmly."

If the takeover bid had been totally successful the cost to Power would have been about $148.5 million. This sum was committed to Power by The Royal Bank of Canada and the Canadian Imperial Bank of Commerce, on a temporary basis. The amount that had to be provided to Power to pay for the shares that were tendered was about $70 million, which was raised by Power through its sale to three banks of income debentures of varying maturities.

The Commission's Assessment

In the Canadian context a merged Power-Argus would be prominent among major concentrations of corporate power. Even though Power does not at the present time control Argus, we offer our comments on the implications for Canadians of a successful takeover of Argus by Power.

Financial Aspects

While a change in control of Argus would not immediately alter the size or composition of companies in the merged group, it is nevertheless useful to draw a picture of what a Power-Argus corporation would look like. After the acquisition was completed, and before any disposition of assets, the combined firm would have had assets (at balance sheet values) of $783 million. This would have placed it about 37th (in terms of assets) in our 1975 list of large non-financial firms. On an earnings basis it would have ranked about 24th. In these calculations we are not including the assets administered by the financial companies in the Power group.

Dollars alone may not be an adequate measure or satisfactory indicator for a complete evaluation of potential impact. A Power-Argus corporation would have a substantial influence over major firms in many important industries (see Table 7.1). Except for the interests in pulp and paper, and

Table 7.1

Power and Argus,

Combined Major Investments, March 25, 1975

(Common Shares)

Financial Services		Pulp, Paper and Packaging	
Investors Group	34.9%	Consolidated-Bathurst[3]	38.1%
	(56.5% voting)		
Great-West Life[1]	50.1%	Domtar	16.9%
Montreal Trust	50.5%	British Columbia	
		Forest Products	6.6%
		Communications	
Imperial Life[2]	51.2%	Standard Broadcasting	47.7%
Laurentide	57.9%	La Presse[4]	100%
		Les Journaux Trans-Canada[4]	100%
Manufacturing		*Mining*	
Massey-Ferguson	15.6%	Hollinger Mines[5]	21.2%
Transport		*Merchandising*	
Canada Steamship	100%	Dominion Stores[6]	23.5%
	(88.8% voting)		

Source: RCCC research.

Notes
1. Owns 9.5% Investors voting shares.
2. Owns 13.2% Investors voting shares and 7% equity.
3. Owns 95.9% Dominion Glass.
4. Owned by Gesca Ltée. All income and gains accrue to Power until 2020.
5. Owns or controls directly or indirectly, 10.7% Noranda Mines.
6. Owns 45.4% General Bakeries.

possibly communications, a joining of the two firms would produce essentially a conglomerate merger. As we said in Chapter 5, our research indicates that firms that have diversified into unrelated industries have decreased their return on investment, return to their shareholders and growth in sales per share. We assume for these purposes that, while a merger of Power and Argus would create a single large enterprise there would not be any material increase in the size of its component economic and technological units. We see nothing to indicate that a merged Power-Argus would be an exception to the general conclusion drawn from our research, although the merged firm might realize gains in financial flexibility, an increased ability to raise capital in international markets and returns to scale in management. Although the probable financial performance of the merged firm does not raise issues of important public interest, it might well be of considerable importance to shareholders.

The possibility of a Power-Argus combination does, however, raise some issues that touch upon the public interest more directly. These issues arise within the context of competition policy and the broad social impact of such a merger.

Competition Policy Aspects

Canadian competition policy is found in the Combines Investigation Act. If Power and Argus controlled, directly or indirectly, or had significant interests in, corporations that competed with one another in particular product markets in Canada, and in addition jointly accounted for a substantial proportion of those markets (i.e. in the range of 60%), then their merger might violate the Act. A possible violation of the Act would also occur if any of the firms were significant actual or potential customers or suppliers of one another and if there were serious doubt as to whether firms outside their group would be hampered in selling to or buying from firms within the group.

In the Power-Argus situation such questions do not generally arise. Only with Consolidated-Bathurst and Domtar, and then only in the pulp and paper sector, would there be any reason to consider whether competition law might be violated by the merger. We have reviewed this part of the hypothetical transaction, and in doing so have focused on the structural impact of the joining together of Consolidated-Bathurst and Domtar under the Power-Argus parentage. We assume here that Argus' direct holdings in British Columbia Forest Products Limited at the time of the bid would have been sold, as was Argus' intention at the time.

The nature of the pulp and paper industry requires that competitive impact be assessed within the context of individual product markets and carefully defined geographic markets. Our review, based on a market share evaluation, indicates that in the product categories of paperboard and corrugated boxes, and possibly fine papers, the merged organization could have a significant impact. In the areas mentioned, but probably in no others, the joining of Consolidated-Bathurst and Domtar would, we believe, have an impact significant enough to warrant those responsible for the administration of the Combines Investigation Act investigating the facts.

The only other field where there might be issues relevant to competition policy is communications. Standard Broadcasting cannot be said to compete in any significant way with either the newspapers or the broadcasting companies in the Power group. Even if it did, there is little likelihood that the merger would lessen competition to the detriment of the public. While other issues are raised by this aspect of the merger (and we shall refer to them below), there is no reason to think that it would offend competition law.

It is our conclusion that, judged according to our view of the general effects of conglomerate mergers, there is no reason to think that the Power bid for Argus, had it been successful, would have resulted in a situation adverse to the public interest because of a lessening of competition.

Other Aspects

Shortly after the takeover bid was announced, the *Financial Post* referred to the combined firm as one that would comprise "a dazzling collection of some of the country's largest companies". Certainly a successful bid would have seen a number of very significant companies in some major industries fall within the control of one parent company (and ultimately one individual). Even though competition law might not be violated, would this accumulation of corporations within one group constitute a danger to the public interest? Should this concentration of ownership, which was probably at the root of most public apprehension regarding the takeover, be a matter requiring public action?

INTERNATIONAL TRADE

Power has suggested that the takeover would be beneficial, since a combined Power-Argus would "create a Canadian company of size capable of operating more effectively on a world scale". McDougald commented, regarding this statement, that "Most of (our companies) are...fairly good on the world scale as it is and we don't need anyone to help us."

We have seen nothing to suggest that the present affiliates of Power or the associated companies of Argus are too small to function effectively. It is likely that the individual companies would not benefit in the way suggested from the change of ownership and control resulting from the merger, unless there were significant divestment of some companies and subsequent investment of the proceeds in assets capable of being profitably used by the companies still held.

On the evidence we have heard, the Commission accepts that in some international markets, large corporate size may be of some assistance in doing business successfully. A successful takeover of Argus might therefore improve some customers' perceptions of Power's ability to participate in world-scale transactions. Canada certainly needs firms that can mobilize the capital and other resources required to do business in competition with foreign corporations. A Power-Argus merger holds out to some observers the prospect of increased Canadian investments abroad, or greater exports by the merged enterprise. After reviewing the probable consequences of a merger, we conclude that any benefits to the Canadian public in increased international trade from a combination of the two enterprises are likely to be negligible.

FINANCIAL INSTITUTIONS

The presence in a merged Power-Argus of some large financial institutions is not, of itself, a matter of concern. The common ownership of Investors, Great-West Life, Imperial Life, Montreal Trust and Laurentide has had little observable effect on the operations or performance of those companies, or of their competitors. Even if they were part of a larger group and related to other major firms, they would still be governed by laws that effectively eliminate any significant risk of misuse of funds.

COMMUNICATIONS

We have said that the merging of the communications interests of Argus and Power would not appear to violate the Combines Investigation Act. Because of the relationship between Desmarais and Power, however, it would certainly constitute a significant concentration of ownership of media interests. As of mid-1976, Gesca (owned by Gelco, but with income accruing to Power) owned five daily newspapers in Quebec, which accounted for over 50% of the circulation of French-language dailies in the province. Of the five, *La Presse* was the most important and had the largest circulation of any French-language daily newspaper in Canada. Three of the others are the only daily papers published in their respective cities (Sherbrooke, Trois-Rivières and Granby). Gesca also owned indirectly a radio station in Granby. Power Corporation held a $7.25 million debenture of, and 2.1 million participating, non-voting preferred shares in, Beau-dem Ltée. Beau-dem owned three television stations, seven AM radio stations and three FM radio stations. Of these CKAC, Montreal, is the largest French-language radio station in the province. Desmarais (who indirectly owns 75% of Gelco) also has a 33.3% interest in Prades Ltd., which operates a small radio station in Shawinigan and a television station in Carleton, Quebec, which in turn has a number of rebroadcast stations.

Standard Broadcasting, controlled by Argus, operates CFRB, Toronto, the radio station with the largest audience in Canada, and CJAD, Montreal, which has the largest English-language radio station audience in Quebec. Since the Power Corporation offer, Standard has acquired a 62.2% interest in Bushnell Communications Limited. Bushnell operates CJOH-TV, the largest television station in Ottawa, and has 75% of one Ottawa cablevision company and 44% of another. Approval for the purchase by Standard of a 52% interest in Bushnell was given by the then Canadian Radio-Television Commission on March 13, 1975.

A takeover by Power of Argus would constitute a change in effective control of Standard Broadcasting. That aspect of the transaction would have to be specifically approved by the Canadian Radio-Television and Telecommunications Commission (CRTC), which has authority to revoke a broadcast licence if it does not approve a change in effective control of a broadcast licensee. The CRTC has in the past expressed concern about the accumulation of significant ownership interests in broadcasting (especially where ownership of newspapers may also be involved), because of the potential influence of owners of communications interests. For example, in January 1977, the Chairman of the CRTC said that it "has no real hang-ups about size of broadcasting undertakings. Its concerns are rather that there should be no undue concentration of media control, particularly in any given location. . . ." We understand and share that concern.

We see no advantage to the public interest in the common ownership of the Power-Argus communications interests, and there is a potential detriment to the public interest if enough important instruments of communication, in different media fields, are owned or controlled by one person or group.

SIZE AND INFLUENCE

Among the factors that should be considered in evaluating the contemplated takeover from a more general perspective are the merged firm's overall size, probable behavior and likely degree of influence. Of course, it is difficult to measure such implications of corporate size as impact upon the public or ability to influence various kinds of actions. The activities of large companies may have positive effects, negative effects, or a complex mixture of both. To the extent that large corporations do have them, such impact and ability (actual or potential) probably increase (although probably not proportionately) with size. This is so whether the measurement is the greater number of employees in the merged group, the greater opportunities for contact with government representatives at many levels or any one of a number of other possible factors.

Desmarais himself (with the Parisien family interests) would effectively control many important firms. We know of no standards by which to state that this would be "excessive power", but it would certainly be substantial. It is true, however, as the Power brief indicated, that ownership or control is only one of a number of "levers of power that are used to influence decisions and shape events". Yet because it is such an important factor, Desmarais would be able, potentially, to exercise, or to attempt to exercise, very considerable influence, even with the many legal and other constraints that would be present. We must ask whether such potential influence is harmful to the Canadian public interest.

That question requires a difficult and delicate judgment of public policy. We do not think there would be substantial economic gains or losses from a Power-Argus merger. The social costs are probably minimal. Since Argus has not been active in acquiring other companies, its absorption into Power would have no effect on the market in the buying and selling of businesses. In our view, the overall consequences of such a merger are relatively neutral. In such circumstances, should the paramount consideration be one of maximizing the decentralization and diffusion of whatever power exists in corporations and corporate groups, or should we tolerate whatever happens in this particular market unless, according to legislated standards (such as those expressed in competition law), the public interest is harmed?

As we indicated in Chapter 6, it is our view that there is probably some point between these two positions at which Parliament should intervene to review an acquisition or merger. It is, of course, impossible to specify precisely where that point lies. Threshold limits, beyond which a person or group would be prevented from proceeding, should be avoided, because they would inevitably be arbitrary and would be a serious damper on initiative and action. The possibility of intervention could arise only in rare situations like the present one involving several very large and important firms with many interests in several significant and sensitive sectors of the economy. Canada does not have many firms like Power and Argus. In most acquisitions, competition law would protect most aspects of the public interest.

In those few instances where undesirable concentration of ownership, influence, or control would arise, the Cabinet should undertake an appraisal of that specific case. Ultimately, the decision whether or not to intervene will have to be made by Parliament, and it will reflect political and social concerns. Because of the implications of intervention, or non-intervention, we think it is appropriate that the responsibility for these judgments be placed with the Cabinet.

Conclusion

Our analysis of the Power-Argus situation leads us to think that the power resulting from a merger of the two firms is not likely to have an adverse effect upon the public interest. Had Power acquired Argus, it would not thereby have significantly increased its market power in any industry. There are no other factors in the Power-Argus situation that lead us to conclude that the merged firm or those controlling it would act in a way that would be detrimental to the public interest.

Chapter 8

Foreign Direct Investment

Long-term foreign direct investment has an important impact on the structure and behavior of Canadian industry and hence on the economic power exercised by large firms in Canada. An understanding of this impact requires a brief review of the size, nature and causes of foreign direct investment in Canada, but, since the impact of foreign direct investment is manifested in social as well as economic activities, a wider framework encompassing its social and political as well as economic consequences must be used.

Long-term foreign direct investment is basically the transfer of a package of assets from a foreign-domiciled corporation through corporate channels into an enterprise in Canada, either by acquisition of an existing firm or the creation of a new enterprise, which thereafter becomes a subsidiary of the foreign corporation and subject to its control. The assets transferred in the package may include capital, a licence to use a brand name and preferred access to markets and sources of raw materials. The most important part of the package, however, is usually a distinctive technology, the "core skill" of the parent corporation. This core skill, as defined by Leonard Wrigley, is the "collective knowledge, skills, and habits of working together . . . required to enable the firm to survive and grow in a competitive market." The core skill (or know-how) is "information not just of a technology or of a market, but of one in relation to the other", and, because it is a collective skill, it can usually be transferred most efficiently within the administrative channels of the corporation, rather than between corporations through the market by arm's length transactions between independent firms. In making investments outside their base countries, multinational enterprises are maximizing the rent they can obtain from their core skills. This process has the potential for increasing the economic growth of the host country, but it may also lead to a different level and diversity of output both within the host country and across the countries in which the multinational enterprise operates.

This raises a fundamental dilemma for Canadian society. Although it is difficult to quantify its social, political and economic impact on Canada,

181

foreign direct investment, by bringing into Canada technology, management skills and capital, raises the productivity of Canadian industry, accelerates the rate of industrial growth and promotes economic prosperity. In the longer run, however, it may atrophy or limit the ability of Canadian firms to develop indigenous research and development, entrepreneurial expertise or export capacity, decrease the amount of upgrading of Canada's natural resources before export and cause a reverse flow of dividends, interest and capital. In addition to these potential economic problems, foreign ownership may not be compatible with Canadian political sovereignty. Foreign laws and directives reach into Canada through multinational enterprises. For example, in the case of the uranium cartel, the Canadian subsidiary of a U.S. firm was reluctant to comply with the wishes of the Canadian government for fear of U.S. antitrust laws.

Before World War II, direct investment by foreigners represented only 33% of total foreign investment in Canada. The remaining 67% was portfolio investment in the stocks and bonds of Canadian companies and governments. There was little public awareness of attempts by foreign governments to apply their legislation in Canada along with direct investment originating in their country.

Since the 1950s there has been growing concern in Canada about the political, social and economic implications of direct foreign investment. In part, this concern arose because of the increasing amounts of such investment after the war. By 1950, direct foreign investment in Canada amounted to $3,975 million, or 45.9% of total foreign capital invested in Canada. By 1960, it amounted to $12,872 million, or 57.9% of such foreign capital. About 1960, the U.S. government began to pass and implement legislation that applied to the activities of Canadian subsidiaries of U.S. firms. Such legislation restricted the application of Canadian public policies in respect of Canadian subsidiaries of foreign companies. Also, during this period Canadian nationalism began to emerge as a political and social force. The dilemma of how to reconcile prosperity and sovereignty thus became acute.

It is clear from the briefs and oral evidence submitted to us that there is concern about long-term foreign direct investment in Canada. It is also clear that while many people hold strong views on the subject there is no unanimity among them. The subject presents a problem for which the solution under present circumstances can be only an untidy, flexible and ambiguous compromise.

This chapter describes the historical dimensions of foreign direct investment in Canada, the public issues it has raised and the government's responses to these issues. We then present a number of ideas originating with our briefs and hearings on the effect of foreign investment on corporate concentration and conclude with suggestions for alternative ways to resolve the Canadian problem of foreign investment.

The Nature and Level of Foreign Investment in Canada

Over the past 100 years Canada's major economic goal has been to develop its economy through broadly based industrialization covering a wide range of manufacturing and resource development activities. To achieve this Canada has looked to foreign direct, portfolio and debt investment for about 30% of the capital required. From 1900 to 1914, two-thirds, on average, of foreign investment in Canada came from Britain although the British share was declining. From 1918 to 1939 the United States was the major source of foreign capital. The total amount of foreign capital rose over the years from $1.2 billion in 1900 to $3.8 billion in 1914, and $7.6 billion in 1930. Portfolio investment constituted about two-thirds of total foreign investment in Canada in 1926 and continued to make up over 60% of the total until World War II. This investment was mostly in the form of non-resident holdings of railway securities and government bonds.

Since the end of World War II, foreign investment in Canada has undergone two major changes (see Table 8.1). The first was a great increase in total amount from $8.7 billion in 1950 to $68.6 billion in 1975. Even allowing for inflation of 140%, an increase of that amount is without precedent in any major industrial country, with the possible exception of Australia. The change in the nature of foreign investment from portfolio to direct investment was equally important. The direct investment component (comprising the total of equity investments, undistributed retained earnings and long-term debt owed to the parent firm) of foreign capital invested in Canada rose from 39% in 1946 to 46% in 1950 and to 58% in 1960. Since 1966 it has hovered between 58% and 61% with no particular trend. (By contrast, in the past most Canadian investment abroad has been portfolio rather than direct investment.) This change in the nature of the major proportion of foreign investment corresponded with a change in source. Since World War II the major source of foreign investment has been corporations, primarily the 500 largest U.S. industrial corporations. Of the $39.8 billion of direct foreign investment in Canada by 1975, $32.2 billion had been invested by U.S. corporations. The impact of this change toward direct investment by the largest corporations can be seen in the ownership of the 200 largest Canadian industrial corporations: 91 are the subsidiaries of firms numbered among the 500 largest U.S. corporations.

Before proceeding, it should be mentioned that direct investment is a two-way flow. Some Canadian firms (for example, Moore Corporation Limited, Massey-Ferguson Limited and Inco Limited) have made extensive overseas investments. This flow has increased in the last few years until in 1976 the outflow of funds for Canadian direct investment abroad was greater than the flow of foreign direct investment into this country.

Foreign Direct Investment

Foreign direct investment tends to be one of two quite different kinds: either an investment made to take advantage of opportunities in the market of the host country or an investment made to exploit resources available in the

Table 8.1

Contributors to Change in Book Value of Foreign Direct and Long-Term Investment[1] in Canada, 1945-75
(Billions of Dollars and Percentages)

Foreign Direct Investment Flows	1946-50	1951-55	1956-60	1961-65	1966-70	1971-75
Net capital inflow for direct investment	0.49	2.00	2.86	2.15	3.63	3.55
Net increase in undistributed earnings	0.71	1.40	1.69	2.21	4.24	10.63
Other factors[2]	0.06	0.35	0.59	0.12	1.13	0.70
Net increase in book value	1.26	3.75	5.14	4.48	9.00	13.48

	1945		1950		1955		1960		1965		1970		1975	
	$	%	$	%	$	%	$	%	$	%	$	%	$	%
Stock of Foreign Direct Investment by Source														
U.S.	2.30	84.9	3.43	86.2	6.51	84.3	10.55	82.0	14.06	81.0	21.40	81.2	32.19	80.8
U.K.	0.35	12.8	0.47	11.8	0.89	11.5	1.53	11.9	2.03	11.7	2.50	9.5	3.72	9.3
Other countries	0.06	2.3	0.08	2.0	0.33	4.2	0.79	6.1	1.26	7.3	2.45	9.3	3.93	9.9
All countries	2.71	100.0	3.98	100.0	7.73	100.0	12.87	100.0	17.36	100.0	26.36	100.0	39.84	100.0
Total Foreign Long-Term Investment, by Source														
U.S.	4.99	70.3	6.55	75.6	10.30	76.1	16.72	75.3	23.39	79.0	34.91	79.3	52.94	77.1
U.K.	1.75	24.7	1.75	20.2	2.38	17.6	3.36	15.1	3.51	11.9	4.02	9.1	5.67	8.3
Other countries	0.35	5.0	0.36	4.2	0.85	6.3	2.13	9.6	2.70	9.1	5.10	11.6	10.04	14.6
All countries	7.09	100.0	8.66	100.0	13.53	100.0	22.21	100.0	29.60	100.0	44.04	100.0	68.65	100.0

Foreign Direct Investment
as a Percentage of Total
Investment in Canada by
Source

Source							
U.S.	46.2	52.3	63.3	63.1	60.1	61.3	60.8
U.K.	19.9	26.7	37.3	45.7	57.9	62.3	65.5
Other countries	17.3	22.2	38.3	36.9	46.8	48.1	39.1
All countries	38.3	45.9	57.1	58.0	58.6	59.8	58.0

[1] Foreign long-term investment as recorded in these series consists of all long-term claims on residents of Canada held by non-residents, except for investments in Canadian companies reinvested abroad. This net stock of foreign-owned long-term capital employed in Canada comprises direct investment, portfolio investment (including foreign investment in Canadian government securities) and miscellaneous investment. Foreign direct investment comprises equity, retained earnings and long-term debt.

[2] New issues, retirements, borrowing, investment abroad, etc., affecting the total value of foreign direct investment in Canada, and other factors including revaluations, reclassifications and similar accounting adjustments.

Source: *Canada's International Investment Position 1971-1973*, Statistics Canada Cat. No. 67-202, pp. 86-89 and 103, and *Statistics Canada Daily* of January 10 and 30, 1978.

host country. The nature of the assets transferred from the parent corporation to the subsidiary varies accordingly.

When an investment is made to exploit the market of the host country, the distinctive core skill of the foreign-domiciled corporation is transferred to the subsidiary. In addition to the core skill, there is the right to use the corporate name, which can be a valuable asset both to raise capital in the host country and to secure consumer acceptance of products. These two assets, core skill and corporate name, are such that their use abroad need not again require the same costs associated with their original development, while their use by the corporation in its home market is not appreciably reduced.

Resources acquired in the host country are usually either raw materials or labor (but in some instances they include technology and other core skills). Investments to exploit raw materials may represent no more than backward integration of a foreign corporation anxious for assured raw material supplies. Exploitation of a raw material such as oil is likely to represent an extension of a multinational enterprise's core skills to a new geographic region. Firms also make direct investments in exploration, development and marketing in countries to obtain access to cheap factors of production (for example, cheap labor). Investments to exploit both material and labor resources tend to be made in countries where capital is costly, and usually the investment package has to contain the necessary capital as well as the firm's core skills.

In industries characterized by rapid change and advancement in the level of core skills such as marketing, production, technology, research and development (R&D), finance and management, the market for these core skills is often imperfect and inefficient, so that they will only rarely be transferred from firm to firm by a sale of licensing rights, management consulting, or "turnkey" projects. Instead a firm will have to make a direct investment to maximize the profit deriving from its core skills. In stable industries, competition reduces these profits from direct investment and makes the external market for core skills more efficient and thus reduces the incentives to make direct foreign investment. The present level of world-wide direct foreign investment may indeed represent the peak of multinational enterprise because many of the industries (for example, processed foods) in which it has occurred in the past are becoming more stable. We expect that where continuous technological innovation is important transfer of the core skill will be largely within the corporation and that industries reflecting these conditions will tend to be characterized by direct foreign investment.

Firms whose core skills include product differentiation by branding and associated marketing expertise also have a high propensity to make direct foreign investments. They often erect substantial barriers to entry to new, local firms because of the scale of marketing efforts necessary to obtain a viable market share and the uncertainty of the success of such an effort. Unlike technological skills these skills in marketing are difficult to duplicate or erode by potential competitors.

The core skills of a multinational enterprise often give it a competitive advantage over those domestically owned firms that have no foreign operations themselves. In addition, the subsidiary of a multinational enterprise often also has greater access to both international and local capital markets than have domestically owned firms of similar size. A multinational enterprise may invest in a country to obtain economies of scale or a reduction of risk for the firm as a whole, which are not available for a domestic firm operating in only one market. Thus it can make new investments or sustain previously established positions under conditions that would be unattractive to domestically owned firms.

Analysis of the characteristics of foreign-domiciled corporations that make direct investments abroad must begin with reference to the characteristics of the 500 largest industrial corporations in the United States ("Fortune 500"), because this group is responsible for $140-$150 billion, or about 60%, of total, world-wide, direct foreign investment outside the Communist countries. Corporations in the "Fortune 500" tend to be in industries characterized by continuous technological innovation, capital intensity, product differentiation and income-elasticity of demand (for example, automobiles, chemicals, electronics, petroleum and convenience goods).

It has been said that these large U.S. firms are extremely profit-oriented and seek their profits by exploiting those of their core skills that cannot easily be duplicated by other firms. From that view, growth and diversification are incidental by-products of the pursuit for profits. Such firms also tend to withdraw quickly through divestiture of tangible assets when markets prove unprofitable or when a government demands access to their core skills for local investors through joint ownership.

To the extent that the economic activity in different national markets is uncorrelated, direct investment can reduce variations in a firm's income stream. Multinational enterprises also try to invest in several markets to ensure that they have operations in whichever market grows the most quickly. Risk reduction as well as profits can therefore motivate international diversification.

Until the mid 1960s, the largest U.S. corporations had a comparative advantage over firms from other developed countries because of their size, which allowed them to enjoy the large economies of scale available in generating core skills in finance, management, R&D and marketing and in their access to the largest, highest income market in the world. But a comparison of the 100 largest U.S. corporations with the 100 largest non-U.S. corporations suggests that the relative size advantage, while still great in 1965, has been gradually eroded from 1965 onwards until by 1975 there was no significant size difference: in 1975 the average sales of the 100 largest industrial corporations were $5,600 million while those of the 100 largest non-U.S. corporations were $4,900 million. Robert Rowthorn and Hymer Stephen in *International Big Business* have concluded that the growth of large multinational corporations is linked to the growth of their base national markets. As the growth of the U.S. economy has fallen relative to that in some other developed countries, U.S. multinational corporations have begun to lose their dominant international position. Robert B. Stobaugh in an article in the *Journal of International Business* (1977) observed that U.S. multinationals are facing increasing competition from larger multinationals domiciled in other countries. This comparison of changes in relative size is significant because foreign direct investment in Canada tends to be made by large corporations. In the decade ahead the relative U.S. presence in Canada probably will not be so large as in the past decade; non-U.S. corporations will form a higher proportion of the foreign direct investment in Canada than they have in the past.

The probability of a decline in the level of U.S. foreign direct investment is strengthened by recent data on divestitures by U.S. corporations that in the past have made large foreign direct investments. Of the 500 largest U.S. corporations, some 180 have been classified as multinational enterprises, in that they have subsidiaries in six or more foreign countries, or have obtained 25% or more of their sales from foreign subsidiaries. Some of these U.S.-based multinational enterprises have recently been withdrawing their direct investment at about the same rate as others have been making it. A 1977 unpublished study undertaken by Brent Wilson at the University of Virginia found that complete divestitures of U.S. overseas subsidiaries totalled 1,459 during the 1971-75 period, nearly four times the number divested from 1961 through 1965, and that the increase in the number of divestitures coincided with a decline in the number of new foreign subsidiaries being formed. In 1971, there were 3.3 new investments for each disinvestment; by 1975, that ratio was 1.4 new investments for each disinvestment. According to *Fortune,* most of the disinvestments were motivated by inadequate earnings rather than by pressures from the host countries.

In research for the Commission, Richard Caves found evidence that foreign firms make direct investments in Canadian industries with both high concentration and moderately high barriers to entry. When attention is focused on disinvestments, Caves' conclusion seems to be reinforced. Comparatively few divestitures have taken place in highly concentrated industries like automobiles, tobacco products, office equipment, chemicals and pharmaceuticals. By contrast, a relatively high percentage of disinvestments has occurred in such unconcentrated industries as apparel, beverages, furniture and leather goods. Multinational enterprises divest their holdings in these unconcentrated industries because of low profits caused by local and international competition.

In considering the degree of foreign ownership and control of Canadian industry, however, it is important to begin with aggregate data. From 1954 to 1974 the total capital employed in Canada in the non-financial sectors increased from $28.2 billion to $129.7 billion (Table 8.2). Of this, the proportion under domestic control throughout the entire period varied between 64% and 72%. The degree of foreign ownership and control of economic activity in Canada throughout the 15 years 1960-1974 has been high but quite stable (33%-36%). The indications are that this degree of overall stability has continued to the present.

However, important structural changes did take place from 1954 to 1972. The degree of U.S. control rose slightly while that of non-U.S. foreign control rose more significantly. Non-U.S. foreign control was 4% in 1954, 8% in 1969, and 9% in 1971 and 1972. It should be noted, however, that these are

Table 8.2

Estimated Book Value,[1] Ownership and Control[2] of Capital Employed
in Non-Financial Industries,[3] Canada, 1954-74

Year	Total Capital Employed	Percentage of Capital Employed Owned in		Percentage of Capital Employed Controlled in		
		All Foreign Countries	U.S.A.	Canada	U.S.A.	Other Foreign Countries
	(Billions of Dollars)					
1954	28.2	33	25	72	24	4
1955	30.4	33	25	69	26	5
1956	34.0	34	26	69	26	5
1957	37.6	34	26	68	27	5
1958	40.5	34	26	68	26	6
1959	43.6	34	26	68	26	6
1960	45.6	34	27	67	26	7
1961	47.6	35	27	67	26	7
1962	49.2	35	28	66	27	7
1963	51.8	35	29	66	27	7
1964	55.3	35	29	66	27	7
1965	60.0	35	29	66	27	7
1966	65.7	35	29	66	27	7
1967	71.6	35	29	65	28	7
1968	77.5	35	29	65	28	7
1969	85.2	35	29	64	28	8
1970	90.9	35	29	64	28	8
1971	98.0	34	28	64	27	9
1972	104.9	34	28	65	26	9
1973	115.9	34	28	66	26	8
1974	129.7	34	27	67	25	8

Source: Statistics Canada, *Canada's International Investment Position, 1926-27* Cat. 67-202,
pp. 148-49; *Statistics Canada Daily*, Cat. 11-001E (Aug. 27, 1976, and Dec. 16, 1977).

Notes:
[1] The book value of long-term debt and equity (including retained earnings) employed in enterprises in Canada.
[2] The ownership series measures the proportion of foreign-owned capital (both portfolio holdings of non-residents and direct investment) to total long-term capital employed.
The control series classifies enterprises by country of control by majority ownership of voting rights, i.e. data on "foreign-controlled investments" may include de investments by Canadians and investors from third countries in enterprises controlled abroad.
[3] Non-financial industries include manufacturing, petroleum and natural gas, mining and smelting, railways, other utilities, merchandising and construction.

book-value figures, which may understate the size of the older U.S. investments. The change has been gradual; the trend for both U.S. ownership and U.S. control of the total capital employed in the non-financial industries of Canada reached its peak during the late sixties. A comparison of the increase in foreign investment (debt, equity and retained earnings) from U.S. and non-U.S. sources (Table 8.3) confirms the dominant U.S. investment presence over this long-term period.

Table 8.3

Source of Net New Investment* in Non-Financial Industries, Canada,
1955-74
(Billions of Dollars)

| Year | Net New Investment | | |
	By Residents	By All Non-Residents	By U.S. Residents As A Percentage of Total Non-Resident Investment
1955	1.5	0.8	62
1956	2.1	1.6	69
1957	2.2	1.4	86
1958	1.9	0.9	89
1959	2.1	1.0	80
1960	1.1	0.9	67
1961	1.2	0.8	100
1962	0.7	0.9	78
1963	1.7	0.9	100
1964	2.3	1.3	92
1965	3.0	1.6	87
1966	3.5	2.2	95
1967	4.0	1.9	89
1968	3.8	2.1	81
1969	5.2	2.5	80
1970	3.9	1.8	78
1971	5.4	1.8	67
1972	4.6	2.3	74
1973	7.3	3.7	81
1974	9.5	4.2	76

Source: Statistics Canada, *Canada's International Investment Position, 1926-67* and *1971-73*;
Statistics Canada Daily (Dec. 16, 1977).
Note: *Though representing changes in foreign investment, this figure does not reflect actual
capital inflows because of the role of retained earnings arising from Canadian operations,
and capital outflows of foreign interests.

Significant sectoral changes in the degree of foreign ownership have taken place over the period 1967-74 (Table 8.3). There have been increases in the mining and service sectors, and in the tobacco, textile, paper, food, beverage, furniture and non-metallic industries within the manufacturing sector. But decreases were recorded in utilities, finance, wholesale and retail trade sectors and for the petroleum and coal products, chemicals and chemical products, transport equipment, primary metals, metal fabricating and machinery industries in the manufacturing sector.

Foreign direct investment in Canada has not been spread evenly or randomly across all industrial sectors. It is especially low and a decreasing percentage in those sectors that, under law, hold large elements of public enterprise, such as public utilities and transport, or where foreign ownership is restricted, as in the communications and financial industries. It is also low in sectors characterized by many small firms, such as construction, wholesale trade and retail trade, in which the scope for transferring unique core skills is low. In general, the industry segments with a very high degree of foreign ownership in 1967 were the same in 1974. Correspondingly, those with a low degree in 1967 tended to be low in 1974.

Foreign ownership is particularly high in manufacturing and non-renewable resources (petroleum and mining). In 1974, the total capital employed in these two major sectors was $62 billion, nearly half of the $129.7 billion of capital employed in the major industrial sectors of Canada. Of the $44.1 billion in foreign-owned investment in the non-financial sectors in Canada in 1974, $33.6 billion (76%) was in manufacturing and non-renewable resources. Over the period 1967-74 the foreign-owned share of these sectors has been quite stable. (See Tables 8.4 and 8.5.)

Table 8.4

Degree of Non-Resident Majority Ownership
of Corporations* in Canada as Measured by Assets,
1967 and 1974

Industry	Assets of Foreign-Controlled Corporations as a Percentage of Industry Assets	
	1967	1974
Agriculture, forestry and fishing	8.2	9.8
Mining		
Metal mining	42.0	55.1
Mineral fuels	81.7	74.0
Other mining	50.0	58.4
Total mining	60.0	63.0
Manufacturing		
Food	35.7	38.8
Beverages	17.6	21.9
Tobacco products	83.6	99.8
Rubber products	92.4	93.7
Leather products	21.9	22.6
Textile mills	49.6	60.2
Knitting mills	18.8	23.5
Clothing	12.0	15.5
Wood industries	25.8	27.0
Furniture industries	15.8	18.5
Paper and allied industries	38.8	43.7
Printing, publishing and allied industries	11.6	11.5
Primary metals	55.6	37.9
Metal fabricating	44.4	38.3
Machinery	71.9	67.6
Transport equipment	86.2	79.6
Electrical products	65.7	65.1
Non-metallic mineral products	47.1	62.4
Petroleum and coal products	99.6	94.4
Chemicals and chemical products	83.0	76.6
Miscellaneous manufacturing	48.7	47.1
Total manufacturing	56.7	56.6

Table 8.4—Continued

Industry	Assets of Foreign-Controlled Corporations as a Percentage of Industry Assets	
	1967	1974
Construction	14.0	12.6
Utilities		
Transportation	–	8.5
Storage	6.0	3.7
Communication	–	0.5
Public utilities	7.3	2.4
Total utilities	6.2	4.3
Wholesale trade	28.5	27.8
Retail trade	20.4	18.2
Finance	12.1	10.7
Services	17.3	23.4
Total all industries	26.0	22.1
Total non-financial industries	38.0	32.8

Source: Statistics Canada, *Corporations and Labour Unions Returns Act,* Annual Report, 1967, pp. 50-103, and 1974, pp. 116-17.

Note:

*Assets of corporations having 50% or more of their voting rights owned by non-residents as a percentage of total assets in the industry. A corporation is considered to be foreign-controlled if 50% or more of its voting rights are known to be held outside Canada or are held by one or more Canadian corporations that are themselves foreign-controlled.

Also included are corporations that are exempt from the provisions of the Corporations and Labour Unions Returns Act (CALURA) but that report under other federal legislation.

To determine whether the level and direction of change for foreign ownership for each segment was random or the outcome of economic forces in the market, the four-firm concentration ratio for 1972 and the average size of the firms accounting for 50% of the output of the industry were noted for each industry segment (to the extent the classification system matched). There was a strong direct correlation between the degree of foreign ownership and the degree of concentration and the presence of large firms. The degree of foreign ownership is very high in those industry segments where an oligopoly of three or four firms account for a high proportion of total sales in the industry. By contrast, the degree of foreign ownership is low in those industry segments where there are many small firms in the industry and no firm has a significant share of the market. The direction of change in the degree of foreign ownership from 1967 to 1973 is directly related to the concentration ratios of 1972. There have been, on the one hand, divestitures by foreign corporations in those industries marked by low concentration and strong competition and, on the other hand, increased direct investments in industries marked by high concentration or oligopoly. Changes in degree of foreign ownership within industry segments were not random and are related to the advantages such investments have in oligopolistic industries and the advantage of possessing core skills that

Table 8.5

Estimated Book Value and Ownership of Total Capital Employed in
Manufacturing and Non-Renewable Resources,* Canada, 1967 and 1974
(Billions of Dollars)

Ownership	Book Value						Percentage of Total Capital Employed in Manufacturing and Non-Renewable Resources	
	Manufacturing		Non-Renewable Resources		Total Amount			
	1967	1974	1967	1974	1967	1974	1967	1974
Canadian	9.8	16.8	5.7	11.5	15.5	28.4	44	46
Foreign	10.7	18.4	9.1	15.2	19.8	33.6	56	54
Total	20.5	35.2	14.9	26.8	35.4	62.0	100	100

Source: Statistics Canada, *Canada's International Investment Position, 1971-73; Statistics Canada Daily* (Dec. 16, 1977).

Note: *Petroleum and natural gas, plus mining and smelting.

could be developed only with large expenditures. The difficulties new firms
face in acquiring these core skills, especially brand names, marketing skills and
R&D, contributed to the high concentration in these industries and the high
level of foreign investment. This analysis is supported by Thomas Horst who
found that the larger firms in an industry in the United States had higher
propensities to invest abroad than did their smaller competitors.

The high degree of foreign control of non-government-owned manufacturing industry (59% in 1975) can be partially explained by economic factors. The
manufacturing industry of most other advanced, industrial countries has access
to a market of at least 100 million people. The United States has a free trade
area of over 200 million people, and the same is true of Western Europe. By
contrast, tariff walls abroad seriously reduce the incentive for Canada's
manufacturing industry to be scale-efficient and largely confine it to a domestic market of 23 million people. Foreign firms are encouraged to invest in
Canada to overcome the Canadian tariff walls and often construct small,
scale-inefficient plants to serve only the domestic market.

Multinational enterprises based in the United Kingdom or the United
States also have had easy access to large pools of capital, which was available
at much lower cost than capital in Canada. When the Canadian subsidiary of a
multinational firm chooses to raise its capital in Canada, Canadian financial
institutions are more willing to make loans to it than to domestic firms of
similar size and often at more attractive rates.

Domestic manufacturers, both Canadian and foreign-owned, in many
Canadian industries do not have the promise of high sales to justify the costs of
developing new process or product technology to match that in the foreign

corporations. Foreign subsidiaries have access to their parents' technology, however. Domestically owned manufacturers often cannot compete against foreign subsidiaries in that part of the domestic market where continuous technological innovation is essential for success. In many industries, Canada's domestic market is too small to enable Canadian-controlled firms to be efficient and to compete against foreign subsidiaries who have access to their parents' core skills. Because of this access foreign subsidiaries often enjoy a significant competitive advantage over Canadian-owned firms. In research done for the Commission, Caves concluded that although there was no systematic decrease in the proportion of value added accounted for by Canadian controlled establishments in large size classes, their productivity was 19% below that of foreign-controlled subsidiaries, mainly because of this technological gap.

Effect on Industrial Structure and Behavior

Often the oligopolistic market structure developed abroad has been transplanted to Canada by the direct investments of firms involved in the oligopoly. When a dominant firm in an oligopolistic industry makes a direct investment abroad, it is common for other firms in the oligopoly to follow it to protect their market share and market power and to reduce the risk that the foreign operation of one of their competitors will give it a competitive advantage. It is this propensity by firms in oligopolistic industry to "follow the leader" that has been a major factor in the creation of the "miniature replica" effect that characterizes so many Canadian industries. In addition, many of the same underlying economic factors (economies of scale, advertising, R&D, productivity, capital costs, etc.) that influence the degree of concentration in other countries also exist in Canada. Some countries have encouraged foreign investment to increase exports and to have world-scale plants. Except in a few instances, Canada is not one of them. Indeed, the foreign direct investment that has come to Canada did not come to "look outward" through exports. Once such an inward looking industry has been developed, it is difficult to reorient it, but success is possible, as is demonstrated by such firms as Dominion Engineering Works Ltd. and the diesel operation of General Motors of Canada Limited, which compete with their parents in export markets.

Foreign direct investment does not seem to have increased the concentration of industries in Canada. No general relation has been observed between inbound foreign direct investment and changes in the level of concentration, nor are Canadian industries with high foreign ownership relatively more concentrated than industries in other countries with lower foreign ownership. In fact, when a follow-the-leader oligopolistic response prompts foreign direct investment, it often has lead to an overpopulation of both foreign-controlled and domestic firms in the particular industry in Canada, all of which operate below efficient world scale and have excess capacity. In such industries, foreign subsidiaries are at a competitive advantage since they have access to their parents' technology and marketing skills. Several authors have concluded that foreign direct investment increases product differentiation and promotional behavior in host countries and thereby increases barriers to entry by domestic firms. On the other hand, it may decrease the market imperfections in the movement of capital and core skills and may make an industry more competitive and progressive. John Dunning, in an article in the *Journal of World Trade Law* (1974), concluded that if foreign direct investment is undertaken to secure sources of raw materials for a vertically integrated multinational enterprise, it will become more difficult for new investments to take place in downstream industries because new firms will be excluded from those sources of raw material.

Foreign direct investment can also affect the behavior of firms in Canada even when it does not affect the level of concentration or average size of the firms in the industry: the size of any one foreign-owned subsidiary will be an understated measure of its competitive strength if there are any economies associated with multiplant, multimarket operation or the acquisition and utilization of core skills. A multinational enterprise can smooth its sales and profit streams by taking advantage of different cost and demand structures in the countries in which it operates. If a subsidiary in one country runs into difficulties from competitive pressures or inadequate demand, its operations can be sustained by other units of the multinational either by transfers of funds and by diverting production to it. A multinational enterprise will therefore be better able to deal with risk than will domestic firms operating in a single market and hence it will be in a better competitive position. The subsidiary of a multinational enterprise may also gain an advantage by engaging in a number of anticompetitive practices that have little to do with its relative efficiency: predatory pricing, use of its "deep pocket" in finance, technology and marketing, and manipulation of transfer pricing. Some of these practices can be employed by a domestic conglomerate firm, although they may be illegal under the Combines Investigation Act, but they are harder to identify and prosecute when undertaken by a multinational enterprise. Others, such as transfer pricing to reduce taxes, are possible only for a multinational enterprise. Transfer pricing is monitored and regulated by the Department of National Revenue (Revenue Canada) under the Income Tax Act. Nevertheless, multinational enterprises still have considerable latitude in setting transfer prices to enable their subsidiaries to compete effectively, to transfer money in and out of Canada and to reduce their total corporate taxes.

The firms in an industry with high foreign ownership are aware of the resources behind foreign subsidiaries. This awareness may increase the effectiveness of price discipline and parallel pricing and discourage price competition through price cutting. Even in industries largely populated by Canadian-owned firms, the incentive to engage in price wars is decreased by the real possibility of foreign takeovers of firms weakened by the price war. The classic example of such a chain of events was the takeover of the Canada & Dominion Sugar Company, Limited (now Redpath Industries Limited) by Tate and Lyle Ltd. in 1959. For the same reasons, new domestic firms may be deterred from entering an industry in the face of competition from firms having access to resources and competitive techniques unavailable to themselves.

Public Concern

Since the 1950s, there has been widespread concern in Canada about the immediate and long-term social and economic implications for the public interest of the high degree of foreign ownership and of the potential foreign control of Canadian economic activity. This concern increased in intensity during the 1960s, with the belief that foreign control of economic activity was increasing and the identification in the public mind of foreign subsidiaries with both big business and U.S. foreign policy. (There is, however, considerable variation in the attitudes among the provincial governments toward foreign direct investment. Some have been far more eager to have foreign direct investment and far more hospitable toward it than others have been.) In this period as well a rising standard of living and a rising level of education combined to promote greater public concern over social issues. One of these was the threat to national sovereignty posed by foreign direct investment. Interdependence in political and economic matters between Canada and other countries, therefore, was more likely to be interpreted as infringement of Canadian sovereignty.

Over the years, the Gallup Poll has asked the question: "Do you think there is enough United States capital in Canada now, or would you like to see more United States capital invested in Canada"? The responses over the nine years 1964-72 show a strong shift of opinion toward the belief that increased United States investment in Canada should be discouraged (Table 8.6).

Table 8.6

Canadian Public Attitudes toward
U.S. Investment in Canada
(Percentages)

| | Attitude | | |
Year	Enough Now	Like More	Undecided
1964	46	33	21
1967	60	24	16
1970	62	25	13
1972	67	22	11

Source: *Gallup Report* (Feb. 12, 1972).

At the same time, the significance of this shift of opinion can easily be exaggerated. When Canadians have been polled over the last decade to determine the issues of greatest concern to them, unemployment, inflation and other economic issues always topped the list, while foreign control ranked quite low.

The federal government responded to this concern in part through a number of investigations and reports, including the *Final Report* of the Royal

Commission on Canada's Economic Prospects (the Gordon Commission, 1957); the Report on *Foreign Ownership and the Structure of Canadian Industry* (the Watkins *Report*, 1968); the *Report* of the House of Commons Standing Committee on External Affairs and National Defence (the Wahn Committee, 1970; and *Foreign Direct Investment in Canada* (the Gray *Report*, 1972). It also increased the required reporting of foreign ownership under the Corporations and Labour Unions Returns act (CALURA) in 1962. In addition, there have been several investigations of foreign ownership at the provincial level.

A central finding of these reports was that foreign direct investment in Canada was increasing, and that this increase was leading to increasing foreign control over Canadian industry. The reports treated foreign direct investment as a problem of how to "maximize the benefits or minimize the costs" of such investment, that is as a problem solvable at least in principle by a set of plans and regulations. Since each report focused on a different aspect of the problem, the dilemma posed by the existence of conflicting economic, social and political goals was avoided.

While there were differences in focus and coverage between the various reports, there were also similarities, particularly as regards the following two areas:
1. administrative relationships between a Canadian subsidiary and its foreign-domiciled parent, which raised the issues of non-disclosure of financial and operating information by the subsidiary; determination of taxable profits in Canada, associated with the problem of transfer prices on intercompany sales and purchases; location of research and development facilities, and the development of indigenous technology; and the autonomy and nationality of the managers of subsidiaries in Canada;
2. political affiliation of the foreign-owned subsidiary, which raised the issues of the extraterritorial application of foreign antitrust, labor and securities law and laws relating to exports to particular countries and application of balance-of-payments guidelines to the financial operations of subsidiaries in Canada.

In addition, the reports were concerned with the sale of equity shares in a foreign-owned subsidiary to the Canadian public, corporate citizenship in terms of social responsibility of the subsidiary, and the marketing and purchasing policies of the subsidiary that discriminated against exports and in favor of imports from the foreign parent corporation. A summary of the more important ideas in these reports follows.

The Gordon Commission (1957)

The mandate of the Gordon Commission was the economic development of Canada, but its *Report* highlighted the nature and degree of foreign control of Canadian industry. After enumerating the benefits to Canada of foreign investment, the *Report* stated:

> The benefits of foreign investment that we have mentioned are very real and tangible. It is more difficult to state in similarly precise terms what the dangers are

in the present situation and what conflicts might occur between the interest of Canadians and the interests of the foreign owners of wholly-owned subsidiaries of foreign companies operating in Canada.

The *Report* was especially concerned with the possibility that the managers of U.S. subsidiaries in Canada, if faced with a conflict between U.S. and Canadian interests, would elect to support the U.S. position. The major recommendations included the issuing of a sizable minority of equity stock in foreign-controlled subsidiaries to Canadians; appointment of Canadians to boards of directors; disclosure of financial data on the operations of subsidiaries in Canada; staffing of senior positions with Canadians; purchasing supplies from local firms; and increased attention to export markets. A key recommendation, subsequently implemented, of the Gordon Commission was that financial intermediation (banks, trust companies, insurance companies, etc.) should be in Canadian hands.

The Watkins Report (1968)

The next major investigation into foreign ownership was made by a task force headed by Melvin Watkins. The task force originated in friction between the U.S. and Canadian governments over the extraterritorial application of U.S. laws to U.S.-owned subsidiaries in Canada. The specific instance was the publication by the U.S. government of its guidelines for U.S. direct investment abroad in 1965 and 1966 to encourage the repatriation of foreign earnings to improve the U.S. balance of payments. As a result, Canadians who previously had seen foreign direct investment in Canada as a major economic benefit became concerned that U.S. subsidiaries would have to make their decisions in the light of official government policies to the detriment of Canada.

However, the Watkins *Report* was concerned also with other instances of extraterritoriality: application of U.S. legislation on trading with Communist countries, U.S. antitrust law and U.S. labor law. Central to the *Report* was the idea that "The major deficiency in Canadian policy has been not its liberality towards foreign investment *per se* but the absence of an integrated set of policies, partly with respect to both foreign and domestic firms, partly with respect only to foreign firms, to ensure higher benefit and smaller costs for Canadians from the operations of multinational corporations."

The major recommendations of the Watkins *Report* were to create a government agency to survey multinational activities in Canada; to compel foreign subsidiaries to disclose more of their activities in Canada; to encourage rationalization of Canadian industry; to subsidize research and development and management education in Canada; to form the Canada Development Corporation; and to forbid the application of foreign laws in Canada.

In contrast to the Gordon Commission, which sought to alter the ownership of subsidiaries, the Watkins Task Force sought to alter their behavior. The question of whether it is better to reduce the degree of foreign ownership or to "improve" the behavior of foreign subsidiaries is of great importance.

The Wahn Committee (1970)

The third major investigation of foreign control of Canadian economic activity was conducted in 1970 by a Parliamentary Standing Committee chaired by Ian Wahn. This committee had as its terms of reference the examination of "Canada-United States" relations. U.S. direct investment in Canada became a central element in its *Report*. The Wahn Committee based its views on the work done by the Watkins group, some of whom testified before the Committee. However, a distinctive recommendation of the Wahn Committee was that, over a reasonable period of time, all foreign-owned firms in Canada would allow for at least 51% of their voting shares to be owned by Canadian citizens, and that the Canadian share of members on the board of directors should reflect the Canadian share of equity participation.

The Gray Report (1972)

The fourth investigation of foreign control of Canadian economic activity was *Foreign Direct Investment in Canada* (the Gray *Report*) in 1972. This report sought to determine both the economic forces that promoted this foreign investment and to measure its benefits and costs. Although the *Report* covered a wide range of topics, it gave the greatest attention to the factors affecting the development and transfer of technology for Canadian industry.

The *Report* saw the major benefit of foreign direct investment as access to foreign technology, with resultant increased productivity in Canada and the introduction of new or improved products to the Canadian market. A close relationship was seen between technology and economic progress. Technology itself was treated as the outcome of corporate research and development. Hence, the question of where this research and development was conducted was viewed as important.

The fact that most of the technology used by foreign subsidiaries in Canada was developed abroad in the research and development facilities of the parent corporation led the Gray *Report* to use the term "truncation" to describe the situation and condition of the subsidiary as a business enterprise. The assumption was that the functions conducted by a national firm would cover a wide range, including research and development. Since subsidiaries in Canada did not cover such a range, they were seen as truncated. This situation is illustrated by the fact that over 90% of all patents in use in Canada are held by foreign corporations or individuals. The Gray *Report* raised a host of other issues, including taxation, transfer prices, "stultification" of Canadian entrepreneurship and extraterritoriality.

Three policy alternatives were considered: Canadianization (in the sense of 51% of equity being held by Canadians), exclusion of foreign subsidiaries from "key sectors" of the economy and a foreign investment review agency to maximize the net benefits to Canada from foreign direct investment. The Gray *Report* recommended the third alternative and listed six categories of investments that could be reviewed.

Debate on the Issues

These reports have been criticized both for their analysis and conclusions on the economic issues and for the narrowness of the viewpoint taken. It has been argued for example, that the differences among foreign-owned subsidiaries in Canada are so great that it is not possible to make valid generalizations for the total population. It has also been said that the reports were relevant to only one segment of the total population (and not necessarily the largest or most important one), that where the subsidiary followed exactly the strategy of the parent corporation.

Another critic attacked the reports from quite a different direction. He examined the uses of licence agreements by Canadian-owned firms to determine whether manufacturing under licence was a sound corporate strategy, as had been suggested in the Gray *Report*. He found that it was sound for firms licensing to strengthen existing areas of business and those carrying out a program of closely related diversification. For a sizable number of firms trying to enter an area of business not closely related to existing businesses the use of licensing agreements was judged to be entirely unsuitable. Licensing by Canadian firms on a broad scale was not considered to be a reasonable alternative to direct foreign investment, which may, therefore, be the only way to gain access to new technology.

Harry Johnson made a more general attack. He argued that the nation-state has no necessary enduring value and that it exists for the convenience of the people. He stated: "The subsidiaries of foreign based corporations tend to be viewed with considerable suspicion...just as the local branches of national corporations were viewed with considerable suspicion in an earlier era which witnessed the rise of the national corporation in competition with the local corporation or family business."

Other, more broadly based criticisms of the reports concluded that they were overly concerned with the behavior of foreign-owned subsidiaries in Canada and not sufficiently concerned with the impact of the visibility and magnitude of the presence of these subsidiaries on the development of all aspects of Canadian society, social and political as well as economic. Such investment it is argued "dwarfs the people, and stunts and distorts the development of distinctive Canadian identity". The problem is stated to be that, in relation to the magnitude of foreign direct investment in Canada, there is not enough domestic-controlled enterprise, not sufficient "champions of industry", to enable Canadians to develop a sense of participation and to have confidence in themselves. This has in turn contributed to the inward-looking nature of much of Canadian manufacturing industry and its deep-seated pessimism about its ability to compete on an international scale.

Government Responses

Since the 1950s, the federal government has responded in a variety of ways to public concerns about the social and economic implications for the public interest of foreign direct investment in Canada. At the same time provincial governments have responded to concerns particular to the provinces. As a result, by 1977 the powers available to government to control foreign direct investment appear to us adequate in the light of the concerns articulated:

1. key sector policy and public ownership: the exclusion of foreign direct investment from or the limitation of the activities of foreign subsidiaries in sectors of the economy deemed critical in relation to Canadian public policies or the development of a distinctive Canadian culture;
2. significant benefit to Canada: the establishment of the Foreign Investment Review Agency to encourage significant benefit to Canada from new foreign direct investment; and
3. political sovereignty: the establishment of machinery to provide countervailing power to attempts of foreign governments to apply their laws in Canada.

Key Sector Policy

Federal and provincial governments have passed legislation excluding or limiting foreign ownership in certain industries deemed "key sectors" in the economy: transport, finance and communications. Foreign ownership and control is effectively excluded or sharply restricted in Canada in the airline, railroad, commercial banking, radio, television and other industries.

In addition to these "key sectors", the federal and provincial governments have, since the mid 1970s, come to the view that some "non-renewable" or "exhaustible" resources should also be protected one way or another from foreign control. This has led to the creation of federal and provincial Crown corporations to undertake new investments in the natural resources sectors, the nationalization of some potash firms in Saskatchewan and the formation of a variety of agencies to monitor and control exploration, extraction and marketing of many resource products.

Significant Benefit to Canada

The concept of significant benefit to Canada underlies measures recognizing that a foreign subsidiary in Canada has an administrative relationship with its parent corporation abroad and that therefore market relations and market forces do not operate to differentiate the economic activities of the subsidiary from that of its parent. Although there is a general consensus that multinational enterprises increase the efficiency of resource allocation and increase world output, they can and do make decisions that adversely affect the interests of a particular country in the interests of the system as a whole. Naturally each nation wants to maximize the benefits to itself of any foreign subsidiaries operating within its borders. This goal may place it in direct conflict with other countries over the diversion of the benefits that accrue to a multinational enterprise as a whole. The multinational enterprise is often caught in the middle in these conflicts. In an attempt to increase the benefits flowing to it from the substantial foreign presence in its economy, Canada set up the Foreign Investment Review Agency (FIRA) to screen new foreign investment in Canada.

FIRA is supposed to ensure that significant benefits accrue to Canada from "new foreign direct investment." It screens two forms of foreign investment:

(1) most acquisitions of control of Canadian businesses by non-Canadians, and
(2) the establishment of new Canadian businesses by non-Canadians who either do not already have any business in Canada, or do not have any business in Canada to which the new business is or would be related.

Five general criteria are employed to assess a reviewable investment:

1. the effect of the level and nature of economic activity in Canada, including employment, processing of resources, reduction of imports and increase in exports, purchasing of Canadian goods, and other such "spillovers";
2. the level of participation by Canadians as managers, shareholders, and directors;
3. the effect on industrial efficiency, technological development, and product innovation and variety;
4. the effect on the competitive behaviour of firms already in the industry; and
5. the compatibility of the investment or acquisition with government industrial and economic policies.

FIRA then attempts to increase the net benefits that Canada receives from foreign direct investment (rather than attempting to exclude or limit it). FIRA's role is more than a screening agency that simply accepts or rejects applications placed before it. It bargains with the foreign firms or their subsidiaries who have made an application before it to increase the benefits and decrease the costs that Canada will realize from each new investment or takeover.

FIRA itself is not directly concerned that proper taxation is paid on income generated in Canada. The issue is extremely complex in relation to subsidiary operations, but it is also extremely important, and hence must be considered here if only in summary fashion.

When a subsidiary of a foreign multinational enterprise buys or sells goods or services with its parent or another unit of the enterprise, the potential for manipulation of the transfer price of these goods and services is always present. Firms will try to set transfer prices to reduce their burden of taxes and tariffs in one country or systemwide, to transfer money out of a country or to gain a competitive advantage in a particular market. Such motivation exists for all multinational enterprises in all countries.

For the subsidiaries of foreign-based multinational enterprises in Canada, Revenue Canada requires that transfer prices for goods be at "fair market value". Some internal transfer prices can be checked against external market prices for comparable goods, or at least against internal data on direct costs and allowance for overhead, even though checks are difficult in a complex multinational system. Cooperation between U.S. and Canadian tax authorities has reduced the latitude for manipulation of transfer pricing, but it is still an important problem. It is even more difficult for Revenue Canada to check that licence fees royalties and management fees reflect the real costs of transferring technology into Canada: such royalties can be above or below the real costs depending on the strategy of the firm. Of the $2.1 billion dollars that U.S. firms received in total fees and royalties in 1972, only $0.7 billion was received from unaffiliated foreigners. The opportunity for manipulation is thus substantial. Royalties can be a method of transferring taxable income out of Canada into another country, either to be taxed in that country or "stored" in a tax haven for several years. Thus, multinational corporations have a definite advantage over purely domestic corporations in regard to taxation of income generated by technology. The motivation of foreign firms to manipulate transfer prices may be reduced by several factors, however: the similarity of business tax rates in the United States and Canada, the credit of foreign income taxes against U.S. tax liabilities, and the distortions that artificial transfer prices build into a firm's information and control systems. G. F. Kopits in an article in the *Economic Journal* (1976) concluded that the tax incentive to manipulate transfer prices has decreased for firms in Canada. Nonetheless, multinational enterprises in Canada still have considerable latitude and incentive to manipulate transfer pricing to reduce reported profits in Canada. More study of transfer pricing is necessary to identify more exactly where the problems lie, their magnitude and how they can be minimized.

Multinational enterprises may transfer to their foreign subsidiaries components of the core skills they have developed in their home markets at prices based on anticompetitive considerations: low prices to allow the subsidiary to capture market share; high prices to keep profits low and thereby to discourage potential entrants. The profit element in licence fees and royalties and the potential for anticompetitive behavior using technology developed by the parent were not seriously explored in the three major reports mentioned above.

Political Sovereignty

To provide some offset to the application of foreign laws in Canada, the federal government has undertaken a number of specific measures, each related to specific instances of extraterritoriality.

Section 31.6 of the Combines Investigation Act prohibits any restriction of exports in compliance with the laws of foreign governments. The United States (under the Trading with the Enemy Act) has in the past attempted to ensure that U.S.-controlled subsidiaries in Canada did not export goods to specified Communist countries. Under section 31.6, subsidiaries are not allowed to restrict exports solely because of U.S. legislation. The impact of the section is to attempt to allow the manager of subsidiaries in Canada greater autonomy vis-à-vis the government of the country in which the parent corporation resides. Similarly the Canadian government through an Order in Council has prohibited subsidiaries of foreign firms from supplying additional information to the

U.S. government concerning the uranium cartel that was in operation during the early 1970s.

In addition to these measures, in 1975 the government of Canada tabled a set of "Principles of International Business Conduct", which replaced earlier guidelines introduced in 1967. Fourteen principles were enumerated, which were intended to have the effect of fostering in the foreign-owned subsidiary in Canada a measure of independence in decision-making in relation to its foreign parent and also to encourage the subsidiaries to be "good corporate citizens".

Development of Domestic Enterprises

Foreign direct investment has often been achieved by acquisition of an existing domestically owned business. It has been stated to us that many of these foreign acquisitions of Canadian-owned companies occurred because there is a lack of large Canadian diversified firms with a specific interest in acquiring existing domestic firms. In part to deal with this concern, the government established the Canada Development Corporation (CDC) in 1971. Over the long run, CDC is intended to be mainly a widely owned corporation, with government ownership limited to 10% of equity shares. CDC has a threefold objective: (a) to develop and maintain strong, Canadian-controlled corporations in the private sector of the economy; (b) to widen the investment opportunities open to Canadians; and (c) to operate at a profit. The management of CDC has inferred from these objectives that it should compete with foreign corporations for the acquisition of Canadian firms and, through share purchases, establish a Canadian interest in foreign firms with subsidiaries in Canada. For example, CDC has acquired a 30% interest in Texasgulf Inc.

Current Issues and Policies

We now turn to several current issues and policies raised by witnesses who appeared before us during our hearings and by others in briefs submitted to the Commission. The following seem to us particularly relevant: the buying and selling of companies in Canada; Canadian technological capability; and the performance of foreign-controlled subsidiaries. The issue here is twofold, the reduction in competition for corporate assets and the lower income-generating potential of these assets.

The Market for Firms in Canada

Hugh Russel Limited told us that because of the existence of FIRA it was able to buy two domestic firms at a discount below the price that would have existed prior to FIRA, because FIRA had greatly reduced competition from foreign-owned companies. While this discount probably applies to a limited number of firms, it indicates that FIRA has a potentially significant impact on the value of small Canadian firms.

Canada is not alone in requiring a review of foreign investment. Many other developed countries, with the notable exception of the United States, do so too, either explicitly through a review process or local equity participation requirements or implicitly through work permits, exchange controls on foreign capital or government purchasing policies.

In Canada, the market for corporate assets is far from perfect in any segment of industry. The existence of FIRA serves as a restriction of entry to the market for foreign firms. Under the Act, the government has turned down about 10% of the applications that were submitted to it and not withdrawn. Approximately another 10% of the initial applications were withdrawn before a decision was handed down. It is impossible to know how many applications were never made. The existence of FIRA has introduced uncertainty into the market for firms. As a result, the seller of a business has faced a buyer who was in a stronger position to drive down the price. This effect was particularly evident during the first year of FIRA's operation and has decreased as potential foreign investors (and foreign subsidiaries) have learned more about FIRA's procedures and operations, and as FIRA has increased the speed of its processing and become more lenient toward foreign investment during 1977.

With transfer of an appropriate core skill from another enterprise, income-generating potential of an existing business may be increased without adding to the cost (since the cost to transfer the core skill is usually very low). The skills required to effect this potential increase in income often exist in a foreign-controlled rather than in a domestically owned firm. Under ideal conditions the assets required from abroad could be transferred via the market. But, as already described, the market for these assets is highly imperfect. FIRA may have impeded the transfer into Canada of core skills that could improve the productivity of existing assets.

The mobility of multinational corporations in their investment and production decisions also poses a difficult problem for Canada. A cyclical downturn or a change in tax rates may lead a multinational to shift its investment or operations elsewhere, whereas a locally owned firm without subsidiaries in other countries would be less mobile and more likely to continue investing in Canada. The very efficiency with which multinational corporations transfer capital to the area of highest return and production to the area of lowest cost may have severe negative effects on the countries in which they operate if the economic environment reduces profits or raises costs.

Canadian Technological Capability

Many firms compete on the basis of continuous technological innovation requiring costly research and engineering facilities. While costs may be low at the early stages of new product or process innovation, expenditures tend to increase substantially as a new product approaches the stage of test marketing. Canadian firms with a domestic market of 23 million people find it difficult to spread costs over enough sales to undertake such expenditures and, given their generally inward-looking nature, many of them do not consider export markets.

There have been suggestions that Canada should seek "technological sovereignty" in certain key sectors so that all the technology required by Canadian firms in those sectors is developed in the country. Once produced, however, technology is not costly to transfer, at least within the administrative channels of a multinational enterprise. To replicate in Canada the technology developed abroad would waste resources, the more so because of the small size of the Canadian market where such technology could be exploited and the difficulty many Canadian firms find in going abroad through trade and investment. Some Canadian firms, however, such as Northern Telecom, have been highly successful in developing technology in Canada and exporting and investing abroad.

Attempts by the Canadian government in the past to foster domestic R&D, either by private firms or by the government itself for eventual transfer to industry, have been generally unsuccessful. U.S. firms, because of their access to a large, high-income market are organized to develop and transfer technology; most Canadian firms are not. There may be some scope for the government to foster the development of new technology in Canada through incentives aimed at specific sectors to increase the amount of R&D undertaken by firms in those sectors. Often the subsidiaries of foreign firms have been able to take advantage of Canadian government programs to develop R&D while their domestically owned competitors have not.

Performance of Foreign-Controlled Subsidiaries

There have been several studies on the performance of subsidiaries in Canada relative to their parent corporations abroad and to domestically owned firms in Canada. Such studies have focused on labor or capital productivity, costs, the range or type of output, exports and technological innovation.

Obviously, if a subsidiary is established in Canada merely for domestic production of goods previously imported across tariff barriers, its labor and capital productivity is likely to be lower and its costs higher than in the parent corporation established in a larger market. Although Caves in his research for the Commission found that labor productivity was 19% lower in domestically owned firms than in foreign-owned subsidiaries, when other variables such as capital intensity, size, factor costs, technological opportunities and industry mix are taken into account, this productivity differential disappears. That is Canadian-owned firms as such are not less productive; however, they do not have easy access to the core skills such as technology and marketing and hence are generally less productive than foreign-owned subsidiaries in the same industry.

D. G. McFetridge in his work for the Commission concluded that subsidiaries of foreign firms export slightly more than domestically owned firms, but that a large percentage of their exports goes to other units of the multinational at the direction of the head office. Even exports by foreign-owned subsidiaries to unrelated firms abroad are often at the direction of the multinational's head office and not at the initiative of the local subsidiary. Many foreign-owned subsidiaries thus fail to develop export potential or expertise in exporting, since either they are restricted to the Canadian market or their export activities are handled by their parent or at its direction. This type of extraterritoriality is much more difficult to deal with than that imposed by foreign law. On the other hand, Caves concluded that subsidiaries of multinational firms exported more than similar domestically owned firms because of economies of scale in international transactions and the informational economies available to multinational firms. Foreign ownership, by providing efficient access to the expertise of the parent firm, enables small subsidiaries in some industries in Canada to export even though they are not themselves large enough to mount an export effort.

Conclusions

Most public concern about the social and economic implications for the public interest of foreign direct investment in Canada was predicated on the belief that such investment was leading to an increasing degree of foreign ownership and control of economic activity in Canada. In fact, the overall degree of such foreign ownership and control in the non-financial sectors has been fairly stable at about 34% since 1960. Part of the dilemma posed by foreign direct investment is the location in foreign-domiciled corporations of economic power over Canadian affairs. Over the years, the government of Canada has taken a number of steps to reduce the dimensions of the problem of extraterritoriality.

There is no irreconcilable conflict between the desirability of foreign direct investment as a vehicle for prosperity and the impact of such investment on the social, economic and political milieux in Canada. In considering how to resolve this conflict four alternative sets of action have been suggested:

1. buy back control over the presently foreign-owned subsidiaries;
2. increase the number of key sectors, and buy back control of foreign-owned subsidiaries in them;
3. develop criteria for FIRA that would extend its scope to include the expansion of established foreign-controlled business within their existing or related lines of activity; or
4. retain the system of government responses as it has developed but improve the method of administering them.

In considering each of these alternatives, it is necessary to bear in mind the fact that, historically, foreign direct investment has brought major economic benefits to Canada as well as some economic and social costs. The benefits include the acquisition of technology, capital, access to markets, employment and increased levels of competition among firms. In addition, the major part of the profits of foreign-controlled subsidiaries has not been remitted abroad, but has been reinvested in the country.

The costs include truncation of our export and R&D capability and strengthened oligopolistic structure and behavior in many industries. On balance, however, the economic benefits seem to outweigh the economic and social costs, especially in the short run. There is cause to be concerned about the economic performance of enterprises in the manufacturing sector, but the concern, we believe, should relate to the question of the appropriate commercial policy for all firms in Canada not to new policies designed to place further constraints on foreign investment.

Our argument against the first alternative is threefold:

1. capital needs: to buy back the subsidiaries would require the export of Canadian wealth abroad for years and preempt the capital market for new domestically owned firms;

2. acquisition of technology: subsidiaries operate on the basis of open-door access to the technology of their parent corporation; if subsidiaries become Canadian-owned, such access may be denied them or would be much more costly; and

3. national sovereignty: the challenge is for Canadians to develop their own industrial corporations using national savings and, if necessary, foreign borrowing to enter new sectors and new ventures.

We believe that the second alternative, the "key sector" concept, has been pressed as far as it should go. We have the same objection to any extension of that idea as we have toward the "buy back Canada" concept.

In rejecting the first two alternatives we recognize that foreign ownership may prevent Canada from following a strategy of rationalization and technological advance in some of its industries. At present, there are many disincentives to prevent firms from rationalizing their production by mergers or by production-sharing agreements. As tariffs are reduced and as foreign competition, especially from low-wage countries increases, there will be greater pressure toward rationalization. However, rather than buying back foreign-owned companies, it would be preferable to provide incentives for the merger of both foreign and domestically owned firms in an industry into larger, more efficient units and to use laws that will override any antitrust objections in the United States and other countries.

The argument for the extension of FIRA's scope to all foreign-owned firms is that at present a large percentage of the investment of foreign-owned and controlled subsidiaries does not come before FIRA because these firms do not try to expand into new areas or to acquire other firms. An expansion of FIRA's jurisdiction to cover all expansion would require a substantial increase in its size to administer this screening. More important, it would put Canadian industry in a turmoil at a time when it is already in a troubled state. Given this, we set aside the third alternative.

We think the fourth alternative is the best, that is to keep the system of government responses as it has developed but to improve the method of administering them. Canada now has enough laws relating to foreign control of various types of enterprises. These laws arm the government with adequate powers to deal with foreign direct investment in Canada. We do not see the need for additional regulations to deal with existing firms and we cannot justify a case for new laws to deal with hypothetical issues that might or might not arise in the future. What seems to us essential at this time is efficient, sophisticated and firm administration of existing laws. Special attention should be directed by the Department of Consumer and Corporate Affairs toward the subsidiaries of multinational enterprises to ensure that they do not misuse their competitive powers to the detriment of Canadian-owned industry. Bill C-13 will permit the competition Policy Advocate to bring foreign investment proposals before the Competition Board to assess their competitive implications. Presumably FIRA and the Cabinet will take the Board's decision into account when considering the overall effect of an investment. Revenue Canada can also have a substantial impact on both the level of taxes collected on profits made by multinational enterprises in Canada and on their competitive tactics.

The objective of the system should be first to attract, retain, and expand beneficial foreign-controlled enterprises willing to compete and operate in the marketplace within the framework of Canadian laws and policies; and second to secure from these enterprises a significant benefit for Canada. Over the past decade multinational enterprises have become increasingly subject to pressures from the governments in the countries in which they operate. Each country wants to extract "fair" (which they often equate with the maximum) benefits from the multinational. These goals place countries in direct conflict with each other and the multinationals in the middle. More local processing, exports and R&D in one country often mean less in another. The most demanding countries can often extract the greatest benefits to the detriment of others. This lesson is learned quickly and the demands on the multinationals are increased. Two examples are illustrative of these problems: (1) pressure is developing in the United States to restrict multinationals from transferring "U.S." technology abroad; (2) when Inco announced in late 1977 that it planned to lay off a large number of workers in Canada, a cry was raised to lay off Inco workers abroad first. Since Canada has such a high level of foreign investment, it is particularly exposed to these pressures. For this reason, Canada must formulate policies to work with multinational corporations and the countries in which they operate to achieve an equitable distribution of the benefits they generate.

Chapter 9

Workable Competition: An Approach to the Economic Implications of Corporate Concentration

Observers of the Canadian economy over the past few years have described many of its deficiencies, from inflation and unemployment to an apparent failure to be competitive and efficient, which is reflected in high domestic production costs and weak export performance. Many people have concluded that the private sector of the economy is not working effectively to deliver goods and services in a manner consistent with the public interest. The most severe critics say that we require substantially more government intervention to correct market and other imperfections.

We do not agree that further intervention in the economy by government would help any of these problems or that major rearrangements of the economy are necessary. Certainly problems exist, but we think that under certain circumstances, which we discuss below, the performance of the private sector can be improved.

In this chapter we briefly review the characteristics of Canadian markets, and the organization and strategy of firms in those markets. We discuss a proposal for progress toward a goal of greater competition in sectors of the Canadian economy and outline a framework of conditions that seem to us necessary to achieve that goal.

Characteristics of Canadian Markets

As we showed in earlier chapters, the structure and conduct of firms and industries in Canada differ greatly from the assumptions of the economic models of pure competition. The Canadian economy is not composed of industries in which there are large numbers of competitors in a laissez-faire marketplace with price as the only significant competitive variable. Rather it is characterized by a mixture of sizes of enterprises, substantial foreign ownership with Canadian competitors fearing the "deep pockets" of foreign parent

211

companies, barriers to import competition in some industries and an openness to imports in others (sometimes in spite of tariff barriers). In many industries, the market is dominated by a single large firm or has an oligopolistic structure in which prices and other terms of sale are arrived at through consciously parallel behavior.

Substantial barriers to both entry and exit are widespread in the economy. These are of three kinds: natural barriers stemming from economies of scale and the cost penalties of operating below minimum efficient scale (MES) in the small Canadian market; artificial barriers erected by firms already established in an industry, such as product differentiation through heavy advertising; and legislative, regulatory or traditional barriers erected by government with the intent or effect of limiting entry to an industry. While these barriers tend to restrain potential entrants to an industry, they are particularly effective against small and medium-sized firms whose management generally lacks the knowledge, expertise or money to overcome them. Research based on Statistics Canada data and comparable figures for other countries suggests that in many industries Canada has a lower proportion of small firms and, particularly, medium-sized firms relative to larger firms, than most other western industrial countries (this conclusion is supported whether measurement is by asset size or by size relative to the leading firms in the industry). In part, because they do not have competitive stimulus from small and medium-sized firms, larger firms in our economy in general have poorer economic performance in many areas, including innovation and cost reduction, than do firms in other industrial countries.

Canada's small and geographically fragmented domestic markets help to inhibit potential competition, especially when there is only enough demand to justify a small number of plants. The few firms that do build efficient-scale plants may behave as classic oligopolists, limiting entry by setting prices that are high in relation to their own costs but not high enough to cover the costs of a new entrant at below minimum efficient scale or to permit import competition over existing tariff barriers. Such oligopolists may make it known that they are willing to drive out new entrants (even those who may wish to construct MES plants), by cutting prices in the short run so that the new entrant is unable to attain a breakeven level of sales. As part of their recognition of interdependence with competitors, oligopolists may collectively accept market shares that do not justify construction of MES plants for any firm in the industry. A firm wishing to build a larger, more efficient plant cannot do so without infringing on the market shares of fellow oligopolists and risking either a price war or other forms of retaliation. In sum, our small domestic markets may simultaneously foster oligopolistic behavior, deter firms from growing to more efficient size and, as we saw in Chapter 3, discourage firms from specializing their production. The historically high effective tariff in manufacturing and the geographic dispersion of the Canadian market have also encouraged inward-looking industries that tend to perceive market size as being restricted to national or regional areas.

Over the past 15 years Canada's largest corporations have declined in size relative to those in the same industries in other countries. Even in export-oriented industries, or industries with substantial import competition, Canada has never had more than a few companies ranking among the largest in their respective world industries, and our representation is declining. A study done initially for the U.S. Department of Commerce and extended by this Commission compared 13 different industries in 15 industrial countries. Canadian membership among the 10 largest companies (measured by sales) in the 13 industries dropped from 7 in 1960, to 2 in 1974. Neither of the latter (Massey-Ferguson Limited in the general machinery industry and Alcan Aluminium Limited in mining and metals) was in the largest 5 in its industry. From 1960 to 1975 Japanese and European companies grew about two and a half times faster than comparable large Canadian companies.

From 1960 to 1974 no new Canadian company reached the top-ten rank in any of the 13 industries examined, and these included industries with substantial firm-level economies such as aerospace, pulp and paper, chemicals and commercial banking. The five companies that dropped out of the top ten in their respective industries were Canada Packers Limited, International Nickel Company of Canada, Limited, The Royal Bank of Canada, Canadian Imperial Bank of Commerce and Bank of Montreal. While the comparison does not imply that big is automatically better, there is some evidence that Canadian firms have been characterized by inadequate research and development, innovation, export performance and perhaps risk-taking compared with firms in the same industries in other countries, and that this poorer performance may be related to an inability to achieve firm-level economies of scale.

Characteristics of the Canadian economy such as high concentration, small market size and high effective tariffs produce a series of basic dilemmas in the formation of public policy. Even without consciously parallel oligopolistic behavior, solutions to problems of efficiency would be difficult in a small domestic market. Efficiency in many industries could be improved by permitting or encouraging firms to expand their operations to more efficient size or to merge, but this might also result in higher industry concentration or, in some industries, absolute monopoly control. If larger size and higher concentration levels occurred in markets with tariff or other barriers to entry, most cost savings from improved efficiency would probably not be passed along to consumers either through lower prices or through higher-quality products or improved service. Similarly, if firms were encouraged to become more efficient through specialization arrangements, but the entry of new competitors was constrained, consumers might end up with a narrower range of products from which to choose, without any cost savings passed on to them.

Workable Competition

The oligopolistic nature of many industries leads to competition among large firms based not on price alone but on a complex mixture of price, product quality, service, technology and innovation and the promotion of real and artificial product differences. Smaller firms within these oligopolistic industries are generally unable to match their larger rivals in terms of advertising and product proliferation or to innovate or copy innovations quickly. Instead they compete on price or on the basis of a narrow product line, geographic coverage, or expert service. Of these, the major differentiating factor available to smaller firms is price. In competing in this way the smaller firms help to "fill in" the principal missing variable in competition among large, interdependent oligopolists. Recent U.S. research by Howard Newman suggests that price-cost margins and profits tend to decrease (a sign of competition) as the heterogeneity of size of firms in an industry increases.

In Canada, with the dual problem of a relative lack of small firms and the existence of major firms perhaps not large enough or sufficiently specialized to compete internationally, a realistic goal may be an economy many of whose industries are composed of firms of different sizes and following different corporate strategies, with law and enforcement adequate to prevent overt restrictive trade practices or the building of artificial barriers to entry in concentrated industries. In a mixed-size, mixed-strategy industry, leading firms might be able to expand to MES through internal growth and through mergers and acquisitions, even if this expansion resulted in higher concentration levels. Existing smaller and medium-sized firms in each industry might be able to compete on bases different from those of the leading firms (primarily price and specialized market segments) and would have the opportunity to expand and profit if successful. Smaller and medium-sized firms in each industry, plus import competition, might then intensify competition and keep larger or dominant firms from abusing market power or denying consumers the benefits of competition.

The question arising from this discussion is how a small or medium-sized firm operating below conventional MES, or at MES but without all firm-level economies, can compete on price with larger firms. It is done by specializing narrowly in a technology or production process with different MES characteristics, competing in specialized markets or competing with unique skills but without the full range of functions or support services of larger firms. Examples of smaller-scale firms are cited in Rein Peterson's *Small Business: Building a Balanced Economy* (1977).

Our concept of a workably competitive Canadian economy depends on the deliberate encouragement of mixed-size, mixed-strategy industries to move economic performance in the direction of the efficiency and range of price-service-quality-promotion values that are generally seen to flow from a competitive economy. There are, of course, no guarantees that this would happen in all industries. In some industries, economies of scale occur at such large volumes, and costs for below-MES operation are so great, that small firms cannot survive. Even a large number of small competitors in a given industry might choose not to compete aggressively on price or service. However, it appears to us that, if restrictive trade practices and behavior that maintain and build barriers to entry can be minimized, the incentives to competition will be substantial.

Conditions for Workable Competition

The following pages describe the more important conditions necessary to promote workable competition in Canada. Many of them are discussed in more detail in later chapters of this *Report*.

The first and probably most important condition is that small and medium-sized firms must not be unfairly prevented from operating and expanding and must not face artificial barriers in entering new industries. New entrants must have the opportunity to get into a market without handicaps other than the normal ones arising from the fact that existing competitors will have well-established ties with customers or a stable technology and skilled employees. A major impediment to this degree of "ease of entry", and thus to a viable mixed-size business sector, is that most new and growing Canadian firms are effectively excluded from access to equity and debt markets and to medium-term lending. These problems are discussed at length in Chapter 11 and to a lesser extent in Chapter 10 of this *Report*.

Also, to lower barriers to entry dominant firms holding patent and trademark rights must not be allowed to foreclose whole markets to new entrants. While we have done no research and heard little testimony on patent and trademark policy, this requirement follows from our general assumption that new entrants must face no artificial impediments to entering a market. Several suggestions have been put forward in the literature on this problem, usually in the form of conditions for compulsory negotiated entry to existing patent pools where such access is essential to operation in a particular industry. The federal Department of Consumer and Corporate Affairs published a major discussion paper on the subject of the revision of the patent law in June 1976 and has indicated that further material will be forthcoming.

A second condition necessary for workable competition is selective reductions in the tariff and non-tariff barriers that protect most Canadian manufacturing industries. In small markets, firms must be encouraged to expand to efficient scale and to specialize, and to pass the benefits of greater efficiency on to consumers. The need to achieve economies of scale is particularly important in industries having potential export markets. The necessary encouragement could be provided by lowering tariff barriers, as advocated by recent studies such as the Economic Council of Canada's *Looking Outward: A New Trade Strategy for Canada* (1975). This study argues that there are greater economic benefits to free trade than to a high tariff policy in some if not all industries and that on balance Canada would gain from a move toward free trade.

We would certainly support tariff reduction if it were accompanied by government sanction of specialization agreements. Under a specialization agreement competitors in a market would be allowed to allocate production among themselves to achieve longer production runs and resulting economies, but with the *quid pro quo* of progressive lowering of Canadian tariff levels to ensure that savings are passed on to the public by way of lowered prices. While it is usually argued that tariff reductions should follow specialization agreements, the opposite sequence also has much to be said for it. As a response to an industry which is fragmented in structure and operating behind high tariff barriers, a negotiated or unilateral reduction in those barriers might be accompanied by an invitation to the firms affected to initiate specialization agreements, or to consider mergers as a way of achieving economies of scale. Caution would have to be used when moving toward free trade to ensure that the social costs of such a policy are not so high that they outweigh the economic benefits. In any policy of negotiated or unilateral tariff reductions the government would have to stand prepared to assist injured industries and workers in reallocating capital and manpower to newly vigorous and efficient sectors.

A third condition is that there must be disclosure of accounting and profit information such that it is more difficult for conglomerate firms to hide areas of rapid growth or high profitability behind a protective shield of consolidated reporting. This is a central consideration in reducing barriers to entry. The basic force attracting new investment into an industry is the promise of economic profits, i.e. profits higher than those offered by alternative investment possibilities of similar risk. Consolidated accounting procedures permit corporations to hide areas of high profitability over extended periods so as not to encourage new competing investment. Corporate disclosure is discussed in Chapter 13 of this *Report* and in a study by John Kazanjian published as part of our research series.

The fourth condition is that competition policy must be strong and vigorously enforced, particularly in the areas of restrictive trade practices, attempts to build or maintain barriers to entry and attempts by dominant firms in mature industries to monopolize markets. We emphasize the need for an approach to conscious parallelism such as that of "parallelism-plus" (see Chapter 4). Elsewhere in this *Report* we have been critical of some of the proposed amendments to the Combines Investigation Act. These represent specific concerns, however, and should in no way be taken to indicate that we think competition policy is unimportant. On the contrary, a strong and vigorously enforced competition law is necessary to prevent dominant firms from entrenching a monopoly or quasi-monopoly position or exploiting tariff protection, to provide a check on abuses of market power, and to increase the likelihood of entry and competition from small and medium-sized firms. In this context particular attention should be paid to the competitive practices of the subsidiaries of foreign multinationals since, potentially, they can exercise a disproportionate influence on the competitive environment in Canada.

A final possible condition necessary for workable competition is that the proportion of the Canadian economy constrained by government regulation or ownership should be reviewed and possibly reduced.

We are not opposed in principle to government ownership or regulation of business, and we recognize that it is often necessary and beneficial. We do think, however, that in a significant number of cases government intervention may have created and sustained inefficiencies in the economy and monopoly profits by some firms, and that government ownership or regulation has either prevented or deterred competition.

Once established, there is typically little or no government review of the regulatory process itself. We know of no case since 1950 of any Canadian regulated industry ever being completely deregulated as conditions changed, or of any major Crown corporation being returned to private ownership. We discuss the regulated sector at greater length in Chapter 17 of this *Report*, and recommend that a critical study of that sector be undertaken.

For a workably competitive society, we thus conclude that at a minimum the necessary conditions comprise active encouragement of small and medium-sized firms, minimizing of existing barriers to entry, a review of the utility of government regulation, reconsideration of tariff and non-tariff barriers to import competition, disclosure of accounting and profit information, and vigorous enforcement of competition law against restrictive trade practices and attempts to build artificial entry barriers. This set of conditions may well be incomplete, but it encompasses those requirements that we think are most basic and necessary to reduce the detriment to the public interest that may result from concentrations of corporate power in Canada.

As well as being necessary conditions for workable competition in the economy as a whole, these may also be viewed as potential remedies when there are extended signs of poor economic performance in a single concentrated sector vis-à-vis observed performance in comparable sectors in Canada or in the same sector in other countries. For example, one indication of poor performance (or lack of workable competition) might be prices in Canada that were persistently higher than prices for similar or identical products in the United States, when price differentials were not justified by differences in federal and provincial taxes, freight and insurance, the exchange rate or additional costs of raw materials or labor.

A similar indicator of poor performance might be continued lack of new entry in an industry dominated by one or more very large enterprises, where long-term profits were substantially above the rate of return earned by firms in industries with similar risk characteristics, and where production or other economies of scale were not sufficient to deter entry. However, above-average, short-term profit levels in themselves should not be taken as sufficient evidence of lack of competition or of poor performance. Other indicators of poor performance would include evidence of the systematic maintenance of excess capacity not justified by seasonable fluctuations or reasonable standby needs, a persistent lag by firms in adopting cost-reducing technological changes or the suppression of product changes.

Discussions of the conditions under which workable competition can exist have appeared in the economic literature for many years beginning with the writing of J. M. Clark in the late 1930s. Since that time the concept of workable competition has developed in a number of directions in attempts to provide appropriate leads for policy to help society attain the substance of the advantages promised in more traditional economic models, but as attainable, performance-oriented goals.

We have not cited or attempted to summarize this literature here. While the objective of attaining workable competition is common to all discussions, the means suggested differ markedly from one to the other and, in some, from our own discussion. We have attempted only to outline the most important areas. The focus of our recommendations is on increasing dynamic market forces in the economy such that industries move toward greater efficiency, greater specialization, and concentration levels that are determined by market forces. These are the same objectives sought in the Skeoch-McDonald *Report* (*Dynamic Change and Accountability in a Canadian Market Economy,* 1976), which we have cited in several earlier chapters. We think the concept of workable competition is one that is sufficiently flexible to meet the many economic constraints peculiar to the Canadian economy and that recognizes the myriad business organizational forms and characteristics of firms and markets found in our economy.

Chapter 10

The Banks and Other Financial Institutions

Introduction

It was recognized in Parliament at the time this Commission was established that the larger chartered banks were "major concentrations of corporate power" within the mandate of this Commission. They are familiar institutions, known at first hand to most Canadians, and were a principal subject of the massive *Report* of the Royal Commission on Banking and Finance (the Porter Commission) in 1964. Most recently they have been the focus of a 1976 study by the Economic Council of Canada on deposit institutions. We have received substantial briefs from four of the five largest banks and from the Canadian Bankers' Association, and senior officers of these banks appeared at our hearings. We have also heard and read a number of criticisms of these banks' operations. As well we have reviewed many of the briefs submitted to the Minister of Finance concerning the revision of the Bank Act. We have studied a number of aspects of the operation of the banks, including the banks' role in the financing of new and expanding medium-sized business and the structure of their interest and other charges. We have also studied carefully the proposals made by the Government in August 1976 in the *White Paper on the Revision of Canadian Banking Legislation* (the *White Paper*). In view of the extensive material on Canadian chartered banking already available, we have not contracted outside research studies on matters relating specifically to the banks.

In this chapter we consider first the legislation governing the banks and the substantial changes made in the Bank Act in 1967. Then we present some background material on the banks, their sources of funds and the ways they use them, with some comments on their profits and efficiency. We go on to describe the principal institutions that compete with the banks, the markets in which they compete, and the nature of the competition among banks themselves. This leads us to certain conclusions about this competition and how it might be increased. We also make some observations about the boards of directors of the banks and make some recommendations about directors.

219

Banking Legislation

The British North America Act gives to the federal Parliament exclusive power to legislate in regard to "Banking, Incorporation of Banks, and the Issue of Paper Money" as well as "Savings Banks". The essential legal meaning of "banking", as we have been told, and the *White Paper* confirms by implication, is the acceptance of deposits that are transferable to third parties by cheque or similar instrument. Parliament has not permitted any companies other than those incorporated by Parliament to call themselves banks. However it has not interfered with, or as yet sought to regulate, activities of other companies or cooperatives (e.g., trust companies and *caisses populaires*) that carry on banking services in the constitutional sense. The proposal in the *White Paper* to require such institutions to be members of the "Canadian Payments Association" and to be subject to certain obligations as such is the first proposal to exercise this broader power of Parliament over "banking", whether carried out by banks or by other institutions created under either federal or provincial law.

It has been the practice in the past for Parliament to incorporate new banks by a separate act for each. Existing banks are "rechartered" by the decennial bill to amend the Bank Act. With occasional exceptions of detail, all banks are required to conform to the terms of the Bank Act, which governs in great detail the powers, organization and obligations of the chartered banks, taking the place of the general corporations acts and also providing the essential elements of regulation of their activities. While the Bank Act governs most of the powers of the banks, they are responsible to provincial legislation for matters under provincial jurisdiction so long as there is no conflict with the Bank Act.

The 1967 Revision of the Bank Act

The last revision of the Bank Act was passed by Parliament early in 1967 and came into effect (with some lags in certain provisions) on May 1 of that year. This revision was a very important one, following consideration of the *Report* of the Porter Commission, one of the most comprehensive reviews ever made of any industry and field of policy in Canada. The basic thrust of the legislation was to try to make banking business more competitive and to reduce the degree of regulation and restraint upon its operations. The banks were prohibited from entering into agreements concerning the interest rates they charged or paid (as they had been free to do and had done in the past) unless these were specifically requested or approved by the Minister of Finance. The statutory ceiling of 6% on the interest rates they could charge was also removed. The banks were also permitted to make conventional mortgage loans on real property up to a gradually increasing limit and, in addition, unlimited mortgage loans under the National Housing Act (NHA).

In keeping with earlier federal legislation in 1965 affecting trust and loan and insurance companies, the 1967 Bank Act limited ownership of chartered banks in order to prevent or remove foreign control. In the case of banks the general limitation of ownership by one person or group of associated persons (or corporations) of not more than 10% applied to Canadian as well as to foreign shareholders, both because this appeared feasible (with one notable exception) and because a general discrimination against foreign control was felt potentially to endanger the position of Canadian banks in foreign countries. There was also introduced a general 10% limitation (with minor exceptions) on the voting shares of other Canadian corporations that a bank might own. If the value of the bank's holding did not exceed $5 million, the permissible limitation was as high as 50%. These restrictions on share ownership of banks and by banks have meant that a bank could not be part of a group of affiliated companies subject to a single control, nor could it form such a group itself (except for some defined types of subsidiary companies in related activities in Canada or subsidiaries in other countries).

There were several clauses in the 1967 Act relating to directors of banks. No one was to be appointed or elected a director who was a director of another bank or of a trust or loan company that accepts deposits, or who was a director of another Canadian company of which other directors of the bank already constituted one-fifth or more of the directors of that corporation.

The 1967 revision of the Bank Act did not implement all the proposals of the Porter Commission. In particular, it did not authorize, and regulate the operation of, agencies of foreign banks in Canada as banks. It did not, however, prevent subsidiaries of foreign banks in Canada from engaging in certain types of business that Canadian banks are not allowed to undertake, as well as business normally done by Canadian banks. Moreover there was no legislation, such as the Commission had recommended, to bring within federal control the activities of other institutions carrying out functions that the Commission considered to be essentially the business of banking.

The Business of the Banks

The leading Canadian banks are large by any standard: large in Canada, large in terms of their international reputations and operations, large in the number of their branches throughout the country, and large in their physical presence in the buildings with which they are identified in major Canadian cities. The salient facts about the size of each of the chartered banks (except the most recent, which have only just commenced operations) are given in Table 10.1. Total assets (the usual measure of size) are also given for December 1967 for comparison. In 1976 the five largest banks had about 90% of the assets of all the banks, compared with 93% in 1967. The share of the five largest has been in the 80–90% range since the late twenties.

The five largest banks, with Canadian branches ranging from 891 to 1,660 in number in 1975 (Table 10.1), all provide retail banking services in urban

Table 10.1

Characteristics of Chartered Banks in Canada

(Millions of dollars)

	Assets		Revenue	Balance of Revenue (Deficit) 1976*		Branches in Canada	Canadian Employees
	1967	Oct. 1976	1976	Before Tax	After Tax	1975	1975
The Royal Bank of Canada	7,810	28,832	2,437	267.4	157.4	1,432	28,655
Canadian Imperial Bank of Commerce	7,516	26,104	2,208	273.9	145.9	1,660	27,855
Bank of Montreal	6,345	20,492	1,799	174.8	95.9	1,243	25,770
Bank of Nova Scotia	4,303	18,181	1,508	213.5	116.9	924	18,430
The Toronto Dominion Bank	3,568	16,192	1,298	170.3	92.2	891	14,766
Banque Canadienne Nationale	1,281	5,675	498	45.1	24.5	479	7,304
La Banque Provinciale du Canada	627	3,624	316	31.8	17.0	324	4,573
The Mercantile Bank of Canada	198	1,708	150	20.6	13.9	12	483
Bank of British Columbia	**	844	77	5.9	3.1	30	888
Unity Bank of Canada	**	180	18	(3.5)	(3.5)	23	303
Canadian Commercial & Industrial Bank	**	16	–	–	–	–	–
Total	31,648	121,848	10,309	1,199.8	663.3	7,018	129,027

Sources: Brief submitted by Canadian Bankers' Association (December 1975); *Canada Gazette*; Royal Commission on Corporate Concentration (RCCC) research.

Notes: *Before appropriation for losses.
**Chartered subsequent to 1967.

and suburban, country and frontier areas, as well as wholesale banking services for large businesses and governments in the major cities and in many centres outside Canada. They are heavily involved in both domestic and foreign banking. Below the biggest five, the banks tend either to do retail business like the major banks but on a regional basis, or else to concentrate on wholesale transactions. The focus of wholesale operations is to obtain funds by securing large term deposits or selling short- and medium-term paper in money markets and to lend to large or medium-sized businesses without incurring the costs of operating branches.

Sources of Funds

More specific information about the role of the banks is summarized in Table 10.2 which sets forth details of the Canadian assets and liabilities of the banks collectively. The banks secure their funds primarily by way of deposits from their customers, for which they provide services, interest, or a combination of both. Demand deposits (lines 18 and 19) typically carry no interest but involve considerable personal service in handling transactions, for which some service charges are levied. Demand deposits are held by businesses and individuals for carrying out transactions and to have immediately available working balances. The banks compete for these largely by the convenience of the branch location, but also by the extent and quality of services offered, including financial services to businesses (for example, automated cash management and payroll handling).

The second item to note is chequable personal savings deposits (line 20), on which some interest is paid and some free services rendered. These are the working accounts of many individual Canadians. The third item is non-chequable savings deposits and term deposits of individuals (lines 21 and 22). These are pure savings accounts on which the banks pay interest in competition with one another and with other institutions. Other, "non-personal" deposits are mainly fixed-term deposits held by businesses, on which interest is paid, generally at publicly posted rates, or, when large sums are involved, at negotiated and highly competitive rates. The Government of Canada deposits are shown separately in line 24. These are the government's working balances, and are distributed among the banks by a formula. Most carry a rate of interest just below the market rate on treasury bills.

We shall not endeavor to comment on all the other items, but would note the figure of $1,169 million for debentures (line 28). These are the banks' means of supplementing their own capital funds by borrowing in the form of medium-term debentures, which are subordinate to deposits as claims on the bank and are sold in the bond market. Line 31 shows the shareholders' equity in the banks, including paid-up capital and accumulated profits. Line 32 is the accumulated total of appropriations for losses. It is a part of the past revenues of each bank set aside as a prudent estimate of what may be expected by way

Table 10.2

Assets and Liabilities of Chartered Banks in Canada, 1967 and 1976
(Millions of Dollars)

Line No.		December 1967	October 1976
	ASSETS		
	Liquid assets		
1	Bank of Canada deposits and notes	1,547	3,893
2	Canadian day-to-day loans	306	344
3	Treasury bills	1,725	4,177
4	Government of Canada direct and guaranteed bonds	2,904	4,349
5	Call and short term loans	336	1,273
	Loans in Canadian dollars		
6	Business loans	6,929	27,553
7	Personal loans	3,594	16,834
8	Other loans	3,327	6,987
9	Mortgages insured under NHA	749	4,954
10	Other residential mortgages	91	3,727
	Canadian securities		
11	Corporate	554	2,602
12	Provincial and municipal	646	1,135
13	Canadian dollar items in transit	1,190	1,630
14	Customers' liabilities under acceptances, guarantees and letters of credit	819	5,006
15	All other Canadian currency assets	484	1,968
16	Total foreign currency	6,470	35,417
17	Total[1]	31,669	121,849
	LIABILITIES AND SHAREHOLDERS' EQUITY		
	Canadian dollar deposits		
	Demand deposits		
18	Personal deposits	366	2,761
19	Other deposits	6,120	10,031
	Personal savings		
20	Chequable	⎫	6,679
21	Non-chequable	⎬ 11,760	18,579
22	Fixed	⎭	14,184
23	Other notice deposits	3,255	18,005
24	Government of Canada	618	1,934
25	Provincial governments	309	986
26	Other banks	235	1,015
27	Acceptances, guarantees and letters of credit	819	5,006
28	Debentures	40	1,169
29	Other Canadian liabilities	106	304
30	Foreign liabilities	6,309	36,135
31	Shareholders' equity	1,310	3,332
32	Appropriation for losses	424	1,090
34	Accounting adjustment[2]		639
	Total[1]	31,669	121,849

Source: Bank of Canada *Review*.
Notes: 1. Totals may not add exactly because of rounding.
2. Accounting adjustment is added because in the 1976 personal savings figures are understated by $639 million because the breakdown was available only in the weekly rather than in the monthly series.

of losses on the loans and securities carried on the bank's books. How, and indeed whether, this should be shown in the bank's accounts has been a controversial issue in past revisions of the Bank Act, as have the limits on what may be added to such reserves as a deductible expense for tax purposes. The present Bank Act does not require that annual loan losses be reported to shareholders. However, for the year 1976, most banks made this information available by reporting both their average five-year losses and the difference between actual 1976 losses and their five-year averages. We expect this practice to continue.

In addition to accepting and managing deposits and making loans and investments, the banks perform a variety of services for businesses and individuals, including the sale or purchase of foreign exchange, the acquisition and sale of securities for their customers and the provision of safekeeping and some accounting services. It does not seem necessary to go into these for the purpose of this *Report*.

Uses of Funds

What the banks do with the funds they borrow as deposits or otherwise is illustrated by their Canadian asset items in Table 10.2. The biggest item is business loans (line 6), details of which are published monthly by size and quarterly by industry and region. These extend all the way from the smallest business loans right up to the largest loans to the biggest business enterprises. The next category (line 7) is personal loans, including those secured by claims on various types of assets (for example, automobiles) as well as unsecured loans and certain guaranteed loans (notably student loans). The "other loans" (line 8) include Canada Savings Bonds and loans to governments, institutions, finance companies, farmers, and grain dealers. Lines 9 and 10 show residential mortgage loans (as distinct from business loans) of which 57% are insured under the NHA. Since the 1967 revision of the Bank Act the banks have been active lenders in the housing mortgage field. The other major item to note is the holdings of securities other than Government of Canada securities (lines 11 and 12); about one-third of these are provincial and municipal securities, and two-thirds are corporate securities.

The liquid assets of the banks (lines 1-5) yield less return than do other assets but are readily marketable to meet cash requirements. The largest part of these are treasury bills and other Government of Canada securities (lines 3 and 4). The most important part consists of deposits at the Bank of Canada plus statutory note holdings (line 1). These are the "primary cash reserves" of the banks, on which no interest is paid and which the banks are required by law to hold as a specified fraction of their deposits. The chartered banks also hold a large proportion of their liquid assets in the form of secondary reserves as required under the Bank of Canada Act. It is through the creation or reduction in these reserves that the Bank of Canada controls the aggregate volume of bank deposits and influences credit conditions.

Regional Flow of Funds

The Canadian branch banking system facilitates the flow of funds from geographic areas with surplus deposits to geographic areas whose demand for funds exceeds their savings in the form of bank deposits. Since the Bank of Canada began reporting assets and liabilities of banks by geographic areas in 1974, the figures show that Ontario and Saskatchewan have been exporters of banking funds to the rest of Canada, with Ontario providing much the largest share. It should be noted, however, that these data have limitations because of the exclusion of the *caisses populaires* and other financial intermediaries in looking at flows of funds and because such assets as government securities, corporate securities, day-to-day loans, Bank of Canada notes and deposits, Wheat Board loans and deposits by the government of Canada must be allocated on a somewhat arbitrary basis. The allocation is also somewhat biased because of the effect of the location of head offices on the "booking procedure" for loans to large companies that borrow through their head offices but actually spend the money in another province. As well, money market deposits originating outside Ontario are often booked in Toronto.

Our research also indicates that the structure of deposits and loans in Canadian chartered banks is in general determined by the economic profile of each province. Thus on a per capita basis, a high level of demand deposits tends to be associated with high average income, notably in Ontario, British Columbia and Alberta. Savings deposits are highly correlated to income province by province, except for Quebec, where the chartered banks' share of savings deposits is low. Corporate deposits, which make up the majority of non-personal term deposits, are concentrated in centres of corporate and manufacturing activity.

Loan demand is also primarily determined by economic factors. Mortgage loans are highest per capita in provinces that have a high rate of population growth, notably Alberta and British Columbia. Small business loans are highly correlated with retail sales per capita. Farm loans are highest per capita where agricultural activity is highest.

Profitability

After the 1967 revision of the Bank Act the profitability of the chartered banks increased quite substantially, as of course was expected. The 1976 Economic Council of Canada study shows an increase in the after-tax rate of return on equity of the seven largest banks from an average of 8.1% in the 1963-67 period to 12.9% in 1968-73. The study notes that this latter figure is higher than that for all U.S. insured banks in the same period. The *White Paper* notes that the 1963-67 rate of return on equity of the banks was below that of other industries, while in the 1968-73 period it has been higher than that of other sectors. The Canadian Bankers' Association, in its brief to this Commission, dealt at some length with the rates of return on assets of the chartered banks, and their relation to the spread between the banks' borrowing and lending rates for the years 1967-75. Over this period, the balance of revenue of the banks as a percentage of total assets increased sharply from 0.96

in 1967 to 1.25 in 1969, then declined to a lower level for 1971-73, dropped sharply to 1.04 in 1974 and rose to 1.24 in 1975. Balance of revenue is the figure normally used as a measure of profits, and includes a provision for losses on loans at an average rate over a five-year period. For the years 1970-75, the Association compared this ratio for international business with that for domestic business for the five largest banks (Table 10.3). While it shows a lower rate of profit on international assets, 0.79% over the six years as compared with 1.33% on domestic, it also shows a very sharp rise in 1975 to 1.05%, when the rate of domestic assets also returned from a depressed level in 1974 to the level of the preceding years. Several banks commented in their briefs to this Commission on their rates of return on equity, noting the need both to build up their capital by retaining earnings and to demonstrate sufficient profitability to raise new capital for expansion.

While two of the banks in their briefs compared Canadian bank profits with those of U.S. banks and of other industries, we think the best up-to-date comparison is that given to the Montreal Society of Financial Analysts in December 1976 by the president of the Canadian Bankers' Association. These figures compare the seven largest Canadian chartered banks with a large number of industries as represented by companies reported in the Financial Research Institute Service. These are large non-financial companies most of which are publicly traded. This comparison shows that chartered banks had an average after-tax return on equity from 1968 to 1975 of 13.6%. Over the same period the average after-tax return on shareholders' equity for the 30 non-financial industries was 10.3%. The highest non-financial sector return was 17.5% for office equipment companies, and the lowest was 4.3% for electric utilities. Other industries of interest are: auto and auto parts (15.5%), metal mining (14.0%), printing and publishing (13.3%), oil and gas refiners (11.9%), broadcasting (9.9%), and transport (6.4%).

The same presentation compared the seven largest Canadian banks with the five largest U.S. banks. It covered only the years up to 1973, but we have also obtained the comparison for 1974 and 1975. Together they indicate that over the years 1968-75 the average after-tax rate of return on shareholders' equity for the seven Canadian banks was 13.6%, while that of the five largest U.S. banks for the same period was 12.6%. After-tax return during this time ranged from 18.3% to 11.2% for the Canadian banks and from 14.8% to 10.3% for U.S. banks. In all years but two the rate of the Canadian banks was higher. There are substantial differences between the accounting practices of U.S. and Canadian banks, and real difficulties in finding a set of U.S. banks that are properly comparable to the Canadian banks, but in spite of these problems we think these comparisons indicate the general state of Canadian bank profitability in recent years.

In comparing profits of the banks with those of other industries since 1970 one must bear in mind that the profits of other industries would be less if proper allowance had been made for the distorting effects of inflation in calculating them. One must also consider that industrial profits as a whole have generally been very low in comparison with the high rates of interest

Table 10.3

Domestic and International Business, Five Largest Canadian Banks, 1970-75

(Percentages and Millions of dollars)

Year	Assets[1] Domestic Amount	Percentage	International Amount	Percentage	Total Amount	Balance of Revenue[2] Domestic Amount	Percentage	International Amount	Percentage	Total Amount	Balance of Revenue as a Percentage of Assets Domestic	International	Total
1970	28,616	71.0	11,667	29.0	40,283	414.8	84.3	77.4	15.7	492.2	1.45	0.66	1.22
1971	32,354	71.9	12,654	28.1	45,008	418.4	81.0	98.1	19.0	516.5	1.29	0.78	1.15
1972	38,174	73.6	13,724	26.4	51,898	515.2	82.4	110.0	17.6	625.2	1.35	0.80	1.20
1973	44,189	72.0	17,175	28.0	61,364	592.1	82.6	124.2	17.4	716.3	1.34	0.72	1.17
1974	53,176	69.4	23,474	30.6	76,651	628.6	78.2	174.7	21.8	803.3	1.18	0.74	1.05
1975	63,330	70.0	27,102	30.0	90,432	851.8	75.0	284.1	25.0	1,135.9	1.35	1.05	1.26

Source: Canadian Bankers' Association, Brief to the RCCC (December 1975), p. 71.
Notes: 1. Average monthly assets calculated on a 13-month-end basis.
2. As at October 31.

prevailing during the last decade. A return of 13% or less for non-financial institutions over a period of years has proven inadequate to bring forth new equity investment in a period when return on government guaranteed debt is close to 10%. By way of comparison, the rate structure of the proposed Kitimat pipeline was set to return 14.5% on equity to investors, and with guaranteed purchase agreements this investment is fairly low risk. The historical premium of low-risk equity over guaranteed debt is at or just above 3%.

So many assumptions must be made in comparing Canadian and foreign bank profitability, or in making comparisons with non-financial institutions, and the differences in profit rates are sufficiently small, that after doing extensive work ourselves we are unable either to support or to refute the conclusion reached by others that the chartered banks are earning excessive profits on their Canadian operations. Possibly non-financial institutions in Canada have been earning too little return on equity.

One thing that should be mentioned in a discussion of bank profitability is the unique feature of commercial banking: banks have a built-in stabilizer, which produces profits in good times or bad while industrial corporations do not. Bank profit performance over the past decade has not been exceptional in good times, but has been much better than average in bad times.

In normal times, the cost of short-term money to the banks is considerably less than the return from longer-term investments and loans. The difference between the cost of capital and its return is called the banking spread. When the economy threatens a downturn, the relation of interest rates will usually reverse itself. Businessmen try to keep their borrowings short-term, expecting to be able to refinance when interest rates drop. Investors want to take advantage of longer-term, higher-interest investments to avoid or minimize the expected drop in rates. In this situation, the banking spread narrows, and short-term rates may even rise above long-term rates, as happened in 1973-74.

Even when the spread decreases sharply, however, banks are saved by their core of low-cost chequing and savings deposits. At the crest of a boom, the banking spread gets smaller, but loan volume increases to offset the drop in profit margins. Bank leverage ratios (the ratio of total assets to equity) rise dramatically under such circumstances, to 28:1 in Canada in 1975, as high as 34:1 for U.S. institutions such as Bank of America in 1975.

When an economic slowdown comes, as in 1974-75, demand for loans falls and loan losses rise to high levels. The banks' borrowing and lending rates fall, but the borrowing rate falls more sharply than does the lending rate, which is determined in part by yields in the commercial paper and bond markets. The basic bank spread thus grows wider at exactly those times when loan volume is decreasing and losses are highest.

Thus there is a self-correcting mechanism. In a bouyant economy the banks make money on volume. In a declining or stagnant economy they make money on spread. The industry is essentially self-stabilizing with or without favorable Bank of Canada or government actions, and can be expected to show stable earnings simply because it can be expected to show losses very seldom. In late 1975 the Bank of Canada adopted a "monetarist approach" under which interest spreads changed less markedly than in the past, but the historical pattern of stabilization is still operative.

Another explanation for observed bank profit figures was suggested by The Royal Bank of Canada in its brief:

> ... during periods of unanticipated rapid inflation (as occurred in 1975) most banks will experience a temporary acceleration in their percentage return on shareholder capital. This situation arises because annual profits tend to rise in proportion to the volume or stock of loans oustanding—which has the almost automatic tendency to swell during periods of high inflation. However, there is no similar automatic tendency for the banks' stock of capital to rise or swell, in immediate response to inflation. Thus, shareholder return—measured as the percentage of profits to capital—will increase.

Efficiency

The major banks have been profitable in recent years. Have they also been efficient? The banks themselves have told us in their briefs that their large size and diversified services contribute to their efficiency, through specialization of staff functions, spreading overheads across a variety of services and the use of computers and other techniques.

Our own work and the Canadian research of which we are aware have not been able to discover substantial economies of scale in banking when the number of branches is held constant. It may well be that most economies of scale are exhausted at some asset size and that beyond this level what a bank acquires by increased size is flexibility, diversity of expertise and credibility in national and international financial markets.

BRANCHING

There seems little doubt that the very large scale of the major Canadian banks does provide them with strength, stability and a good reputation, which enable them to extend diversified banking services throughout Canada and to secure profitable international banking business. However, there are some criticisms of their overall efficiency. In 1964 the Porter Commission discussed the possibility of there being excessive branching in the system as a whole:

> Indeed, some would argue that far from suffering from a lack of bank branches, we have more than are needed to provide the community with adequate banking service. If this is true, the result can only be to increase the cost of bank services or to reduce the bank shareholders' return. Since the opening of unnecessary branches is a wasteful form of competition, the American authorities have attempted to control bank branching in a variety of ways. However, such controls are always difficult to administer equitably, may result in some communities being poorly served, and might well impede healthy development by preventing efficient banks from expanding as rapidly as they might to provide better service to the public. We think it best to retain the branching freedom which has been part of our legislation, although we believe that there are tendencies in some areas to excessive expenditures on branching. The banks have clearly done a remarkable job in serving Canada's newer communities and their loss of competitive position cannot be

ascribed to a shortage of outlets either in those or other centres. They might in future make more use of other forms of competition rather than adding to the density of branches in urban and suburban areas.

The Bank of Nova Scotia dealt with this point in its brief to us, pointing out that Canada has 42% more deposit-taking offices per capita than did the United States in 1973. The bank suggests, however, that comparison with the United States is not an adequate yardstick (though it was used by the Porter Commission and others) and that there are several geographic and economic factors that have resulted in and justify the large number of branches. They argue that branches in small towns and frontier settlements provide reliable and important services, which have a social and geographic value that may warrant their operating at a loss financed by profits elsewhere.

This Commission considers that there are probably more urban and suburban branches than is optimal from the point of view of the efficiency of the system as a whole, as indeed is true of many kinds of retail business. On balance, however, we see no practical way of reducing the number other than through gradual rationalization.

RATIO OF NET INTEREST REVENUE TO TOTAL ASSETS

The Economic Council in its study of deposit institutions has compared the efficiency of the Canadian banks with that of U.S. banks by comparing the difference between all domestic interest revenues and all domestic interest expenditures (that is net interest revenue expressed per dollar of domestic assets). In this comparison, they found that after deducting income taxes (which are much higher on banks in Canada because U.S. banks hold tax-exempt state and local securities that do not exist in Canada), the net interest revenue per dollar of assets in Canada was about 5% more than that in the United States. This would be consistent either with a higher profit rate on equity in Canada or with higher costs per dollar of assets (that is with some lower efficiency), or some of each. However, the Council concludes that the differences between the two systems are so numerous and substantial that a significant conclusion about efficiency on that basis would not be warranted. The Council also compares the difference between the average rate of interest on loans and that on deposits (that is net yield) after making a number of adjustments because of the larger proportion of non-interest bearing deposits in the United States, but apparently without adjusting for other differences between the two systems. On this basis the Council concludes that Canadian costs of banking are higher than those in the United States partly because of higher income taxes and partly for "other reasons". We think that the differences between the two systems make it difficult or impossible to separate these "other reasons" meaningfully and to draw conclusions about them.

International Banking Activities

The largest Canadian chartered banks have engaged in international operations for over a hundred years, primarily in New York, London and the

Caribbean. During the past 10 years the nature of these international operations has changed dramatically. In the late 1960s, Canadian banks began a major expansion of their international activities, largely as a result of the rise of the Eurodollar market and multinational corporations. Banks have expanded from overseas branches and agencies to include representative offices, foreign affiliates and subsidiaries.

Just how successful they have been in expanding international operations is indicated by the fact that at the end of 1966 their foreign-currency assets amounted to 25.1% of their Canadian assets, while by the end of 1976 they had increased to 42.4%. Foreign currency liabilities as a proportion of Canadian dollar liabilities in the same period rose from 24.7% to 43.5%. Total foreign-currency assets and liabilities of the chartered banks increased by 667% and 688% respectively from December 1966 to December 1976, while Canadian dollar assets grew at a much slower rate, increasing by 394% and 390% respectively over the period. Foreign-currency operations have made a major contribution to the overall asset and liability growth of the Canadian banks over the last decade.

Much of this growth can be attributed to the development of the Eurocurrency system, where Canadian banks compete with foreign banks for large U.S. dollar deposits on the Eurocurrency market. They relend these deposits to residents or non-residents (including foreign banks), or invest them in U.S. dollar-denominated securities.

About 25% of the balance of revenue of the five largest Canadian chartered banks comes from foreign-currency operations. This performance is not spectacular in view of the fact that foreign-currency assets account for almost 30% of total assets. Margins (loan yield minus deposit yield) are low in foreign wholesale operations, although volume is very large.

The composition of the foreign-currency assets and liabilities of the chartered banks also changed significantly with regard to residency, type of holder and place of booking during the 1966-76 period. Interbank activities have become much more common. Deposits with other banks have risen from 26.9% of the total foreign-currency assets in December 1966 to 51.34% in December 1976, whereas deposits of other banks with Canadian banks have increased from 22.8% of total foreign-currency liabilities to 54.2% over the same period.

International activities by Canadian banks are not closely monitored by Canadian authorities and are not specifically regulated under the Bank Act. Canadian banks do not have to hold cash or liquidity reserves against foreign-currency deposits. The Inspector General of Banks does have broad supervisory powers over the foreign-currency operations of the chartered banks, and does collect data on many of the international activities of the banks.

Table 10.4 indicates the geographic distribution of Canadian bank branches, agencies, representative offices, and branches of subsidiary companies as of May 31, 1977.

Table 10.4

Location of Canadian Chartered Banks outside Canada,
May 31, 1977

Location	Number of Branches
United Kingdom	28
United States	70
France	8
West Germany	7
Bahamas	52
Barbados	26
Guyana	11
Mexico	4
South and Central America	26
Dominican Republic	22
Virgin Islands (British and U.S.)	7
Puerto Rico	16
Trinidad and Tobago	33
Jamaica (and Cayman Islands)	93
Other West Indies	31
Other Europe	16
Asia (including Middle East)	42
Australia	5
Total	497

Source: Canadian Bankers' Association.
Note: Chartered banks are represented by branches, agencies, representative offices and/or branches of subsidiary companies.

Competition

The Financial Institutions Competing with Banks

A variety of classes of companies and other financial institutions compete with the banks in one market or another. The more important of these are listed in Table 10.5, which shows the aggregate assets held by each class and by the largest single institution in the group (where that is available). In this section we shall describe briefly the nature of the business carried out by each institution.

TRUST AND MORTGAGE LOAN COMPANIES

Both trust and mortgage loan companies have been specifically recognized in the Bank Act as competitors of the banks, by the provision banning interlocking directors. Taken together (because they are similar and often affiliated) their aggregate assets (excluding estate, trust and agency funds administered by them) are about $27.7 billion and the largest single company involved has assets of about $3.4 billion (Table 10.5). These companies offer chequable deposits, non-chequable savings deposits and term deposits in the one- to five-year range, together with a number of related services. They

Table 10.5

Major Financial Institutions in Canada
(Millions of Dollars)

	Total Assets			Annual Revenue, 1975	Largest Institutions by Asset Size, December 1975
	December 1967	Latest	(Date)		
Private Sector					
Chartered banks	31,669	121,849	(10/76)	10,309i	28,832[h]
Trust and mortgage loan companies	7,125	27,667	(12/76)	2,308	3,436[a]
Trusteed pension funds	8,068[b]	21,572	(3/76)	3,863	1,296
Life insurance companies	12,912[b]	25,908[b]	(12/76)	N/A	2,542
Caisses populaires and credit unions	3,382	14,987	(9/76)	616	—
Sales finance companies	4,501	10,073	(12/76)	1,436	2,391
Property and casualty insurance companies	2,304	6,679	(12/76)	N/A	—
Mutual funds	2,229	2,774	(9/76)	161	364
Foreign bank affiliates	n.a.	2,402	(12/76)	n.a.	n.a.
Commercial paper[e]	187[d]	1,796	(12/76)	—	—
Quebec savings banks	506	1,118	(12/76)	115	—
Public Sector					
Canada Pension Plan	681 (3/67)	9,770	(3/76)	2,129[g,j]	N/A
Central Mortgage and Housing Corporation (CMHC)	—	9,191	(12/76)	799 [f,g]	N/A
Caisse de Dépôt et Placement du Québec	419[f]	5,340[f]	(12/76)	318[f,g]	N/A
Federal Business Development Bank	305	1,454	(12/76)	116	N/A
Government savings institutions[c]	241 (3/67)	1,067	—	n.a.	777

Sources: Bank of Canada *Review*; Statistics Canada, *Financial Institutions*, 61-007; Annual Reports of CMHC, Caisse de Dépôt, Superintendent of Insurance; Statistics Canada, *Quarterly Survey of Trusteed Pension Plans*, 74-001.

Notes:
a. As most trusteed funds do not publish their total asset figure, it is not possible to determine the largest fund. The figure given represents the CNR's fund, the largest fund for which data is publicly available.
b. Canadian assets only.
c. Deposits only. Excludes provincial government deposits.
d. December 1968.
e. Only that portion issued by non-financial corporations.
f. Includes funds under management.
g. Includes contributions.
h. October 1976.
i. Year ended October 31, 1976.
j. Year ended March 1976.
n.a. = not available.
N/A = not applicable.

invest most of their funds in mortgage loans on residential properties, but they also hold longer-term securities as investments and shorter-term securities (as well as bank deposits) as liquid assets. They put about 2% of their assets into personal and business loans. Under various provincial statutes they are subject to "basket clauses" that limit their combined consumer and business loan portfolio to 5-7% of assets. Their leasing portfolios are quite large, however. The trust companies also administer many billions of dollars' worth of assets held in estate, trust and agency funds under their fiduciary powers, on which commissions and fees of approximately $178 million were earned for the year ended December 1976. As well they are very active in real estate and derive a significant proportion of their earnings from real estate commissions and services connected with the housing industry.

CAISSES POPULAIRES AND CREDIT UNIONS

By far the largest numerical group of institutions competing with the banks in deposit business and certain types of loans to individuals is that comprising the *caisses populaires* and credit unions, of which there are thousands of "locals". These are normally associated in each province with one or more "centrals", which assist them in holding reserves and providing services. The locals are cooperatives in which the membership is normally limited to certain areas or the employees of a particular employer. Their aggregate assets as of December 1976 were approximately $15 billion. They receive deposits as well as share capital from their members. Their total chequable deposits amount to about $3 billion, their non-chequable demand savings deposits to about the same, their term deposits to about $5 billion and their share capital to $3 billion. Thus they compete for the retail banking business on a widespread and decentralized basis. They make personal loans and mortgage loans to their members, and, to the extent of about $0.5 billion, business loans to cooperatives and commercial enterprises. They are organized and regulated under provincial laws. The revised credit union acts emerging in several provinces (Ontario and Manitoba are the latest) vastly expand the business powers of credit unions. The Ontario act, in particular, has a general "enabling" clause permitting credit unions to carry out a broad range of lending activities currently engaged in by chartered banks.

LIFE INSURANCE COMPANIES

The life insurance companies are the largest financial intermediaries, next to the banks. Their business overlaps that of the banks primarily in the investment of funds in bonds and mortgage loans. They also deal actively in the private placement market and purchase substantial quantities of securities directly or through an investment dealer. Such a purchase competes with a bank making a term loan to a business corporation. Insurance companies make loans to individuals against existing insurance contracts but do not pursue such business, as it is unprofitable. The aggregate assets of the life insurance companies held in Canada at year end 1976 were about $26 billion, about 39% of which is mortgages and 36% bonds.

TRUSTEED PENSION PLANS

The next largest group of financial institutions, and the most rapidly growing one, comprises the trusteed pension plans, which in 1976 amounted in aggregate to about $25 billion. Their individual sizes and investments are not disclosed, but at least one, that of the Canadian National Railways, amounts to over a billion dollars in value. The majority of these aggregate assets are invested in the bonds and stocks of larger and more established companies and in mortgages, all of which overlap the investments of the banks.

FINANCIAL CORPORATIONS

The sales finance and consumer loan companies (now termed "financial corporations") had aggregate assets in 1976 of about $11 billion, the largest individual company accounting for about $2.4 billion. They obtain the bulk of their funds by selling short-term paper in the money markets and by selling bonds and debentures. They normally have substantial lines of credit with Canadian and U.S. banks. They finance retail sales to consumers ($2.3 billion outstanding), make personal loans ($1.8 billion outstanding) and provide financing for industrial and commercial customers and wholesalers. In recent years they have rapidly increased their activity in financial leasing and mortgage lending.

FOREIGN BANKS

There are several smaller classes of institutions that invest funds in bonds or shares, such as the non-life insurance companies and mutual funds, but these need not be described in detail here. One category of potentially greater importance is that comprising Canadian corporations that are financial subsidiaries or affiliates of foreign banks, which operate in Canada outside regulation under the Bank Act (although, if they incorporate as financial institutions of a type covered by a statute, for example, the Trust Companies Act or the Loan Companies Act, they are subject to that statute). The Bank of Canada publishes (in its *Review*) statistics on all those they can identify as being Canadian corporations owned by foreign banking institutions and primarily involved in commercial lending or the money market (it excludes trust and venture capital companies as well as financial institutions affiliated with foreign companies other than banks). These statistics show foreign bank assets in December 1976 at about $2.4 billion. There are 22-25 major and very active foreign bank affiliates, 2 of which have Canadian assets exceeding $500 million. Foreign bank lending is financed primarily by borrowing in the money market and by funds from parent or affiliated companies. Foreign bank affiliates use their funds for making business loans and financial leasing of equipment. While still small by comparison with the banks and some other Canadian companies, they are often subsidiaries of very large foreign banks, enjoy a strong credit rating and are sophisticated competitors of the Canadian banks in wholesale and commercial lending.

The increasing penetration of the Canadian market by foreign banks has to be viewed in the context of the changing role of Canadian and U.S. banks, and particularly in the context of the increasing involvement of U.S. banks in the private placement of debt securities, an activity that Canadian banks are prohibited from undertaking. The biggest and most powerful of the U.S. banks have gone far beyond taking deposits and offering short- and medium-term loans to business. If a company wants to expand its financial base, a bank like Citicorp, J. P. Morgan, Chase Manhattan, or First Chicago will undertake normal short- and medium-term commercial lending, advise the corporation on possible acquisition or divestiture (at a fee), help it structure and organize a new issue of equity or debt, and also arrange for private placements of these securities with institutional investors. U.S. banks are prohibited by U.S. legislation (the Glass-Steagall Act) only from actually underwriting or distributing securities. In 1976, U.S. banks placed about $700 million in debt and $225 million in equity. The largest single placement through a bank was made in 1975, for $200 million. U.S. banks have also syndicated and underwritten Eurobonds for private placement to replace or refinance their own Eurocurrency term lending to North American customers.

The Commission does not think that it would be desirable in Canada to have the melding of commercial banking and underwriting functions that is occurring in the United States, because of the very real dangers in concentrating so much financial and economic power in one set of institutions. The U.S. trends do have an impact on Canada, however. U.S. banks with Canadian affiliates can offer underwriting and related services based on U.S. money and security markets that competing Canadian banks cannot offer, to a market of medium-sized companies that do not already have relationships with other financial intermediaries.

The U.S. banks also have a special advantage in that they can take business from subsidiary firms in Canada whose parent firms do business with the banks' parents abroad. Such captive business is found extensively in the advertising and insurance fields with U.S. subsidiaries in Canada, in relationships analogous to those in banking.

The vulnerability of Canadian banking business to foreign competition is apparent in bank loan figures. Total bank business loan volume at the beginning of 1977 was about $28.2 billion, of which $16.6 billion was in about 6,400 loans of $1 million or more. Thus 2% of the business loans made by Canadian banks account for almost 58% of dollar lending activity. These are presumably the loans for which foreign bankers compete. Such competition is not usually on price, as interest spreads for loans of this size are already narrow and lending rates virtually identical. If the competition is based on the range of services offered, then Canadian banks are at a disadvantage in comparison with U.S. banks in the underwriting aspects of financial services excluded under the Bank Act and possibly in leasing and factoring.

We have no recommendations to offer on correcting this competitive imbalance, or on the overall issue of participation by foreign banks. Recommendations on these issues will be extensively discussed and debated as part of the 1977-78 Bank Act amendments. The resolution will depend at least in part on assumptions as to whether banking is indeed a key sector of the Canadian economy, and as such should be subject to special regulation or protection vis-à-vis foreign competition.

Public Sector Financial Institutions

We will not endeavor to set forth details of the size of all the various types of governmental agencies that supplement privately owned financial organizations. The largest, yet the most restricted in its investments, is the Canada Pension Plan Investment Fund, which amounted in 1976 to about $10 billion, virtually all invested in provincial government securities issued at interest rates equivalent to those on federal government long-term bonds. The next largest is the Central Mortgage and Housing Corporation, whose total 1976 assets of $8 billion were almost wholly invested in various types of mortgage loans, about one-third of the outstanding loans having been made at market rates but most of them having been made at rates below the market for various public purposes. The current practice is to emphasize the latter almost entirely.

One of the largest and most diversified institutions is the Caisse de Dépôt et Placement du Québec, in which the funds of the Quebec Pension Plan and other Quebec government accounts, amounting to $5.3 billion in mid-1977, are invested in government, municipal and corporate bonds and in stocks and mortgages. The Province of Alberta Treasury Branches and The Province of Ontario Savings Office are essentially small government banking operations, but their public deposits of $777 million and $287 million respectively are too small to affect the competitive position of the privately owned institutions, except perhaps in local markets in Alberta. In more specialized fields, the Farm Credit Corporation, financed by the government of Canada and with assets of $2 billion, is the main institution in Canada making farm mortgage loans. The Export Development Corporation, with assets of about $1.2 billion, finances export credits, as well as insuring and guaranteeing such credits provided by suppliers, banks or other institutions.

The Federal Business Development Bank (FBDB) is a new Crown corporation that came into being in 1975, taking over the operations of the Industrial Development Bank (IDB). The IDB provided mainly financial assistance to smaller businesses unable to obtain financing from regular sources. FBDB was set up to expand IDB services, specifically to provide proportionally more equity financing and more comprehensive management counselling services. Total assets of the FBDB at March 30, 1977, were $1.43 billion.

In 1967, the federal government created the Canada Deposit Insurance Corporation (CDIC), Ontario, the Ontario Deposit Insurance Corporation (ODIC) and Quebec, the Quebec Deposit Insurance Board (QDIB). Deposit insurance, by protecting depositors against financial loss due to bankruptcy of the institution holding their deposits (a term broadly defined by CDIC), reduces the risk of a "run" on the institution and thus the risk of bankruptcy due to uncertainty. In Canada, the branch banking system ensures that a run on any one branch will most probably not bankrupt the entire institution. The trust and mortgage loan companies, however, whose deposits from the public were increasing, neither had extensive branch systems nor were required to hold reserves. Hence, additional protection for the public was needed. The CDIC may also act as a lender-of-last-resort to member institutions (all federally incorporated, private, financial institutions taking deposits). It can obtain up to $500 million from the federal government to make loans to members temporarily in financial difficulties and unable to obtain funds elsewhere.

Other public sector financial institutions include the Ontario Housing Corporation, Quebec Housing Corporation, Alberta Municipal Finance Corporation, Alberta Housing Corporation, Saskatchewan Economic Development Corporation and other government bodies that lend money to individuals and private enterprises.

Competition in Deposit Markets

In judging the nature and the extent of the competition between these various institutions and the banks, it is necessary to look at the particular markets in which they compete. There are three basic types of deposits: personal savings, nonpersonal term and notice deposits and demand deposits with chartered banks. The last category will not be discussed because the portion of demand deposits attributable to the personal sector is not considered to be part of savings. The banks are the only institutions required to hold non-interest bearing reserves on demand deposits, and, as a result, demand deposits in chartered banks bear no interest. Demand deposits made in chartered banks, whether personal savings or not, tend to be minimum amounts (although they do vary substantially with the level of interest rates), and represent funds intended for use in financial transactions of the depositor.

PERSONAL SAVINGS

The personal savings or "retail" market share held by the major deposit-taking institutions are shown in Table 10.6. As expected, the chartered banks have the greatest share of this market, about 55% as compared to 25% for trust and mortgage loan companies and 19% for *caisses populaires* and credit unions. The *caisses populaires* and the credit unions have increased their share of these deposits since 1967, while the chartered banks' share has declined from 57% to 55%. Although the banks' share declined between 1967 and 1976, in absolute amounts deposits grew from about $12 billion to $39 billion.

If Canada Savings Bonds are considered as being equivalent to personal savings deposits, then the banks' share of total deposits increased slightly, while the Canada Savings Bonds' share declined from 24% to 18%. The removal in 1967 of the ceiling on the interest rates the banks could charge on loans, together with the lower reserve requirements on notice deposits and greater freedom to invest in mortgages, has enabled the banks to remain competitive for these savings deposits.

Table 10.6

Canadian Retail Money Market, 1967 and 1976
(Millions of Dollars)

	December 1967		June 1976	
	Amount	Percentage	Amount	Percentage
Banks[1]	11,760	57.3 (43.7)	39,051	54.7 (45.1)
Trust and mortgage loan companies[2]	5,286	25.7 (19.7)	17,919	25.1 (20.7)
Caisses populaires and credit unions	3,039	14.8 (11.3)	13,332	18.7 (15.4)
Quebec savings banks	456	2.2 (1.7)	1,034	1.5 (1.2)
Personal savings market	20,541	100.0 (76.5)	71,336	100.0 (82.4)
Canada Savings Bonds	6,319	(23.5)	15,212	(17.6)
Total	28,860	(100.0)	86,548	(100.0)

Source: Bank of Canada.
Notes: 1. Personal savings in chartered banks plus, in 1976, term deposits of one year or more in bank mortgage subsidiaries. Personal demand deposits are excluded as it is assumed that only amounts sufficient to cover current expenditures are kept in demand accounts.
2. Includes all demand deposits plus all term deposits with original term to maturity of over one year. In 1976, term deposits of one year or more in bank mortgage companies are excluded.

"WHOLESALE" DEPOSITS

The banks have the largest share of "wholesale" deposits, i.e. large non-personal term and notice deposits. While trust and mortgage loan companies do compete with the bank for these funds, the main competition in this field comes from traders in the market in the sale and purchase of short-term notes, "commercial paper" and treasury bills (Table 10.7).

Major borrowers in the money market, apart from the banks themselves and their "acceptances" (that is guarantees) of notes issued by others, include the sales finance companies, Canadian financial subsidiaries of foreign banks, major non-financial companies with a high credit standing and provincial governments and municipalities. This commercial and financial short-term paper, amounting to about $8 billion, provides volatile and sensitive competition to large bank certificates of deposit for short-term business balances.

Competition in Loan Markets

CONSUMER CREDIT

There are three major lending fields in which the banks compete with other institutions. In the field of consumer credit, the 1967 change in the Bank Act resulted in a substantial increase in consumer lending by the banks, a substantial reduction in the interest rates charged on consumer loans relative to

Table 10.7

Canadian Money Market Funds,
December 1976

	Millions of Dollars	Percentage
Chartered banks		
Non-personal term and notice deposits	18,887	48.4
Foreign currency deposits of residents	6,984	17.9
Trust and mortgage loan companies		
Fixed term deposits with original term to maturity of less than 1 year	1,841	4.7
Government of Canada[1]		
Treasury bills	1,429	3.7
Bonds with less than 3 years to maturity	1,760	4.5
Provincial and municipal governments		
Treasury bills and other short-term paper	556	1.4
Paper		
Sales finance	3,158	8.1
Commercial	4,022	10.3
Bankers acceptances	1,135	2.9
Less bank holdings of paper[2]	(795)	(2.0)
Total	38,977	99.9

Source: RCCC research.
Notes: 1. Excludes holdings of government accounts, the Bank of Canada and the chartered banks.
      2. This amount is excluded from the overall total but, because it cannot be allocated among different types of paper, it is included in the individual amounts.

other interest rates, and more uniform rates across Canada. The brief to this Commission from the Bank of Nova Scotia contains detailed information concerning the impact of the banks on this market. The latest figures on consumer credit outstanding, as reported regularly by the Bank of Canada, show the banks have provided about 59% of the total of about $27 billion (which compared with a total of about $8 billion in March 1967), the *caisses populaires* and credit unions about 14%, the sales finance and consumer loan companies about 11%, and the retail dealers 11%, while smaller shares have been provided by the life insurance companies' policy loans, the trust and mortgage loan companies, and the Quebec savings banks. In December 1966 (before the Bank Act revision) the share of the banks in outstanding consumer credit was about 32%, while that of the sales finance and consumer loan companies was about 30% and that of the retail dealers about 20%.

MORTGAGE LENDING

In the field of mortgage lending the situation is quite different. Here too the importance of the banks' role has increased since 1967, when the Bank Act first permitted them to lend on conventional first mortgages. Under the previous Act, they had been permitted to lend only on National Housing Act mortgages. In this market there are many large lenders and a very large number of borrowers. The largest source of funds, especially for mortgages on residential property, are the trust and mortgage loan companies. Second come the life insurance companies (who were earlier the largest source but now prefer long-term commercial mortgages rather than the shorter-term residential loans). As well there are a variety of other institutional and corporate lenders, including government agencies. The share of the banks in the outstanding mortgages at December 31, 1976, as reported by Statistics Canada, was about 14%, the same share they held at the end of 1975. The banks have proven to be aggressive participants in this large, growing market, which is relatively unconcentrated on both the supply and demand side. The same can also be said of the other deposit-taking institutions, the near-banks, whose share in the mortgage market has also been rising since the 1967 revision of the Bank Act, notwithstanding the competition of the banks.

BUSINESS LOANS

The third and main lending field in which the banks operate is that of business loans. This is a large and varied category about which the Economic Council report states the following:

> The commercial lending market differs from other lending markets in that, among the deposit institutions, only chartered banks play a significant role. This market is also distinctive because the alternative sources of funds for businesses are numerous and varied—including the issue of short-term paper, bonds, and equities; the use of accounts payable and government assistance; and reliance on internal funds. The range of alternatives varies substantially, however, by size of firm. Larger firms have access to direct, as well as international markets; smaller firms depend more on accounts payable and on chartered banks for their external funds.

> The commercial loan market is extensive. Outstanding business loans of Canadian chartered banks amounted to $18.2 billion at the end of March 1974—an amount nearly equivalent to total consumer credit outstanding. Thus business loans represented 53% of all Canadian-dollar loans made by chartered banks. The share of business loans as a proportion of bank assets rose steadily from 25.1% in 1961 to 34.3% in 1974.

The business loan market is difficult to delineate. The lenders include all chartered banks, finance companies and the Federal Business Development Bank. The borrowers include businesses of all kinds, industry, public utilities, construction contractors and merchandisers. The market also includes "capital leasing" by leasing companies and sales finance companies. At the end of the first quarter in 1975, the total outstanding of such financing amounted to $27 billion. In addition, the business loan market is served by affiliates of foreign banks and, to a small extent, by trust and mortgage loan companies, credit unions and *caisses populaires* and by finance companies, which purchase commercial paper. Because of inadequacies of data as well as double counting problems, a total for business loans is not available. However, Table 10.8 shows

Table 10.8

Business Loans — Outstanding Balances of Selected Holders [Canada], 1975[1]

	Bank	Sales Finance & Consumer Loan Companies	Finance Leasing Companies	Industrial Development Bank	Total
$ Million	20,960	4,388	528.3	1,087.3	26,963.6
As % of Total	77.7	16.3	2.0	4.0	

	Affiliates of Foreign Banks	Trust & Loan Companies	Credit Unions & Caisses Populaires	Commercial Paper
$ Million	1,515	226.2	80.4	7,345

1. First quarter-end 1975.
   Note: Some of the balances held by foreign bank affiliates are already included in figures pertaining to sales finance and finance leasing companies. For this reason, their outstandings could not be included in the total figure. Balances of trust and loan companies and credit unions are rough estimates done by DNS and, therefore, are also excluded from the total.
Source: Bank of Nova Scotia, "Corporate Concentration and Banking in Canada", mimeo. brief to RCCC (Feb. 1976), Table 8.

estimates of the various segments made by the Bank of Nova Scotia in their brief to this Commission.

The chartered banks have played an important role in expanding the flow of funds to their customers, not only by generating funds within the banking system, but also by giving them access to the money market by guaranteeing their commercial paper in the form of bankers' acceptances. The amount of bankers' acceptances outstanding is generally over $1 billion.

While the chartered banks have been by far the largest suppliers to the business loan market, they have not been growing as fast as the leasing companies, the subsidiaries of foreign banks and indeed the money market generally. Corporate bonds should also be considered to be competitors for parts of the business loan market as maturities on bank loans lengthen, while those on bonds decrease. At the end of 1975, the outstanding corporate bond debt in Canadian currency was $19.2 billion, and an additional $5.2 billion was outstanding in foreign currency bonds. It can be seen that this compares in size with the $27 billion shown for the traditional sources of business loans.

The standard delineation of the business loan market also excludes receivables of non-financial companies. At year-end 1974, receivables of industrial corporations amounted to nearly $33.5 billion, comparable in dollar volume to the business loans outstanding of chartered banks, sales finance companies, finance leasing companies and the Federal Business Development Bank combined.

It is evident that the banks are the dominant institutions making business loans but are subject to the constraint of the money and bond markets when competing for large borrowers with good credit standing. There is also some competition from other institutional lenders and financial lessors for loans of all sizes. The extensive branch system of the banks gives them an accessibility advantage in lending to small businesses. Small and medium-sized businesses are more reliant upon the banks for credit lines and terms than are larger borrowers.

In the briefs and our hearings we were supplied with information concerning certain special types of loan arrangements. Consortium financing has become common on very large international loans in the Eurocurrency markets during the past 15 years and it is now becoming increasingly common in Canada. It is particularly necessary for large-scale projects, such as those in the energy field, and indeed several Canadian banks have developed particular expertise in arranging large-scale consortium lending. At the other extreme have been specialized loan and financial services for farmers and the few "store front" banks for low-income urban areas.

Nature of Competition among Banks

OLIGOPOLISTIC CHARACTERISTICS

In Canadian markets the major Canadian banks compete with one another as oligopolists. That is, as sellers having a large share of a market with relatively few competitors, they must take into account the effect of their actions on their competitors' reactions. At the retail level and to a lesser extent in wholesale transactions, banks normally emphasize competition in the services they provide and in other non-price factors. There are occasional changes in prices (usually in interest rates) initiated by one or another of them to which the others react and out of which a new level of price emerges. However, the banks are subject to competition from other institutions, particularly in the fields of mortgage and large business loans. It should be recalled that it has been only in the past ten years that the banks have been prohibited from entering freely into agreements among themselves about interest rates on loans and deposits. Only since 1976 have they been prohibited from agreeing to fix service charges.

Banks are subject to another peculiar condition in this respect because it is the central bank, on public policy grounds, which acts as price leader in changing the levels of interest: changes in the bank rate are always followed by the chartered banks. In times of strong competition this may result in changes in spread as well as changes in levels of interest rates.

On two occasions between 1967 and 1976 the chartered banks in consultation with, or at the request of, the central bank and with the approval of the Minister of Finance, worked out agreements to limit interest rates. The first agreement came about in 1969, when the Bank of Canada's monetary policy was to reduce liquidity of the banking system as part of a restraint program while interest rates were rising. The major banks, at the request of the Bank of Canada and with the approval of the Minister, agreed not to compete aggressively for large Canadian dollar deposits. As a result, the rate of interest on these deposits rose less than on other short-term notes. Again in 1972, after consultation with the central bank and approval of the Minister, an agreement among the banks lasting until January 1975 was worked out to limit the rise in interest rates on large dollar deposits that was then taking place.

From the above review of the markets in which the banks compete, their share of those markets, and their size vis-à-vis competitors, it is evident that the major banks are very substantial institutions. Their widespread network of branches, their strong position in both deposit and lending markets, their profitability and their international reputation all contribute to this position. The major banks are also active participants in international banking. The largest Canadian banks have ranked in the 20 or 25 preferred first-tier banking institutions in the world in recent years, when confidence in many foreign banks was shaken by foreign exchange crises and the problems of financing recurrent, large, international deficits. This first-tier status allows them to borrow in major international money markets at the best possible rate, and thus to relend to customers around the world at rates competitive with those of other major international institutions.

INTEREST RATES

Deposits. The behavior of interest rates on personal deposits and smaller non-personal term and notice deposits appears to follow the normal patterns of price behavior among oligopolists: that is one or another takes a lead in changing the rate, often following a change in the bank rate, and others follow fairly quickly. On rare occasions a bank may choose to reduce or reject the lead bank's change and set a pattern by its own action. On the largest deposits, interest rates are negotiated according to the state of the market and the bargaining powers of the depositor vis-à-vis alternative short-term investments.

Loans. On the lending side, the rates charged on standard, unsecured personal loans have been relatively stable, increasing only twice since 1967. With regard to mortgages on residential properties the situation is more complicated because of the presence of other large lenders, and non-price rationing and a preference for established customers when funds are short.

On business loans, the "prime" rate for the best customers is published and usually changes when the central bank rate changes. The prime rates charged by all banks tend to equalize quickly after a central bank change, whoever first responds to it. The rates on most other business loans are determined by adding a margin to the prime rate, a margin that rarely exceeds 3%, for the normal type of nominal demand loans. On rare occasions a bank will lend to a major customer at less than the prime rate.

The Bank of Canada collects quarterly a sample of rates charged on new demand business loans, and publishes the average rate, weighted by dollar volume, in its *Review*. Figure 10.1 compares the prime rate on bank loans, the average rate on new demand loans and the money market rate for three-month finance company paper. The last is normally below the prime rate, but is much more volatile. The weighted average rate on new demand loans ranges between 0.5% and 0.75% above the prime rate.

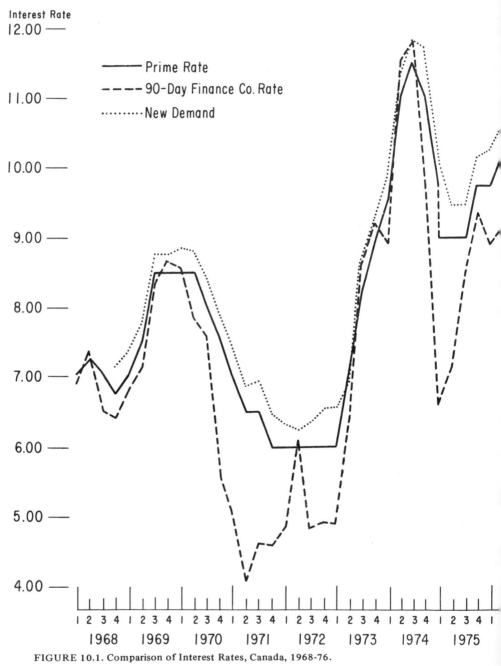

FIGURE 10.1. Comparison of Interest Rates, Canada, 1968-76.

Source: Bank of Canada *Review.*

In 1964 the Porter Commission said:

> At present there is a strictly limited amount of price competition among banks in their lending business. Banks may differ in their view of whether a particular customer merits prime rate or not, but their rates are subject to agreed minimum levels. Price competition has been further restricted in periods of credit restraint by agreements among the banks to the effect that no bank will take over an account from another by offering a better rate or a larger line of credit. The "no raiding" pacts have not survived for long but while they do, the borrowers' main negotiating weapon, the threat to go to another bank, is effectively spiked.

Since that time, the Bank Act has outlawed such agreements on rates. Representatives of the banks appearing before us indicated that borrowers could, and not infrequently did, go to other banks in search of better terms. In their "retail" business at branch level bank managers generally have an incentive to compete for business loans below certain size limits but are restrained by formula lending or by guidelines in the margins they charge over prime rate.

COMPETITION FOR LARGE ACCOUNTS

There quite clearly is active competition among the banks for the accounts, or shares of the accounts, of the largest corporations. This only infrequently takes the form of price competition on the effective interest rate charged; indeed most large customers already borrow at "prime rate" or very close to it. Competition more frequently takes the form of larger (or small but sophisticated) customers negotiating for lines of credit, lending conditions, security covenants, or other aspects of the loan package. It is noteworthy that the ratio of size of credit lines in relation to the amount actually used is consistently higher for larger authorized credit lines, both over time and across various industries, than it is for the smaller ones. While this may be due to a variety of factors, it would be consistent with some negotiated advantage for large and valued clients.

It should be noted that, at times when money is tight and credit must be rationed, the banks say they give priority to smaller customers rather than to their large corporate customers. The Chairman of one bank told us, "We give priority [under these circumstances] to mortgage lending, to consumer needs and to the requirements of small businesses, which often have no other source of financing but their chartered bank .... Major corporations have access to many other sources of credit, including the money markets in Canada, parent companies abroad, the Eurodollar market, foreign banks operating in Canada, and so on." Such a system of priorities is in line with the strong suggestions that have been made by the Bank of Canada to the chartered banks at times when credit availability has been tightened.

Cross-Subsidization

An issue considered by the Commission in Chapter 5, "Conglomerates", was the existence of cross-subsidization among activities of an organization, particularly where one activity was carried on at a loss over a long period and subsidized by other activities on which the organization was able to earn above-average returns.

Banking is one of the few areas where we have observed a form of long-term cross-subsidization. The chartered banks, and indeed all Canadian deposit-taking institutions, charge a price well below cost for personal chequing accounts, for servicing utility bills and for a few other services. Some trust companies perform these services at no charge. The purpose of such cross-subsidization is quite clearly to use personal chequing accounts as a "loss leader" for savings accounts, and for general banking business.

The Commission has no recommendations to make concerning such practices. Banks subsidize an important service for individual customers but the effect does not seem highly detrimental to other institutions.

Entry into the Banking Business

The 1967 amendments to the Bank Act were in large part intended to increase competition by prohibiting agreements in interest rates, by removing the ceiling on rates, by banning some interlocking of directors, by permitting lending on conventional mortgages and by altering the formula for reserve requirements to encourage a greater variety of deposits. On the other hand they did nothing directly to ease entry into the banking business and in fact restricted severely the possibility of foreigners setting up a chartered bank, or of a Canadian company establishing a bank as a subsidiary. While five new banks have been incorporated, and some of the smaller banks have grown more rapidly than the larger ones (La Banque Provinciale du Canada in part by merger with the Banque Populaire in 1970 and with Unity Bank of Canada in 1977), the fraction of the total Canadian assets held by the five largest banks has declined very little.

General Conclusions Regarding Competition

We have concluded that the general situation of the banks does not call for substantial further regulation. However, the oligopolistic nature of competition among the banks (which is similar to that in many other industries), makes it desirable to promote by whatever means are practicable a greater ease of entry into the business of banking itself, and a greater degree of competition between other financial institutions and the banks.

The prohibition of agreements on interest rates and the removal of the statutory ceiling on rates charged by the banks have permitted the strong growth of the banks in the past decade and the shift from what had been something like a cartel operating subject to a statutory ceiling on rates to the present situation of competition among the leading banks constrained by competition from other markets and institutions. There has been relatively little competitive pressure from new banks, although the smaller banks in aggregate have grown slightly faster in relation to the established banks.

The economic barriers to entry of new banks into the retail branch banking business, which are noted in the study of the Economic Council, appear to us so formidable that easing of the legal and procedural barriers would not be enough to bring any early increase in competition sufficient to permit a new bank to rival one of the big five. The regional banks, which might be taken to include the Bank of British Columbia, together with the two much older and larger Banque canadienne nationale and La Banque provinciale du Canada, seem unlikely to make serious inroads on the national market share of the big five.

COMPETITION BY OTHERS IN THE RETAIL BANKING FIELD

The trust companies can be expected to grow in the retail banking field, but the rate will depend on whether legal and institutional circumstances are favorable to them. They are still small by comparison with the banks, but the competition they provide seems to have improved somewhat the retail services available to depositors. The credit unions and *caisses populaires* collectively have been growing more rapidly than the banks, particularly in their share of chequable deposits, and may well continue to do so. In our view, the trust and loan companies on the one hand and the *caisses populaires* and credit unions on the other are the only existing and potential competition for the banks in the retail branch business and should be encouraged to continue in that role.

We are therefore concerned that proposals in the *White Paper* would require these institutions to become members of the Payments Association and hold non-interest-bearing reserves. We believe that in the long run they should belong to that Association and should hold reserves adequate for the purposes of the clearing function. However, we think at this time it is unwise to weaken the competitive ability of these institutions vis-à-vis the larger banks in order to accomplish long-term objectives. We think it would be desirable to permit these existing institutions (trust and mortgage loan companies, *caisses populaires* and credit unions) to decide themselves whether they wish to become members of the Payments Association now or to wait until later when its advantages would be more important and the current objections less serious.

We think it desirable that the trust and mortgage loan companies be explicitly permitted to enter more fully into the business of making personal loans in competition with the banks, perhaps by legislation expanding the permitted limits of their basket clauses. Their growth in the past ten years has come about to a large degree from the abnormal demand for residential mortgages, arising in considerable part from demographic changes that will certainly slacken during the next decade.

While it is less essential in terms of competition that trust and mortgage loan companies enter the commercial lending field, because it is already competitive, we think it desirable that they be permitted to make commercial loans to smaller businesses. Already several trust companies are getting involved in commercial lending through wholly owned subsidiaries and others have explored incorporation as "savings banks". While we recognize the important potential conflict of interest for trust companies between their trustee services and commercial lending, we do not believe this can be convincingly resolved in the way that the Economic Council proposes by "the separation of intermediary and fiduciary activities over time." We would suggest, however, that the possibility be explored of restricting the class of borrowers to whom trust companies may make commercial loans to businesses that have neither issued securities to the public nor are subsidiaries, parents or affiliates of such public companies. In this way' their competition with the banks might be directed usefully toward smaller, private companies, where the potential conflicts of interest with fiduciary duties would be relatively small and might be prevented by specific restrictions against lending to companies whose shares or debt are held in fiduciary accounts.

COMPETITION FROM NEW BANKS

A major potential source of competition for the large banks in the commercial or wholesale sector appears to be from new specialized banks. We support the establishment of such new banks whether or not controlled by foreign banks (or bank holding companies), subject, of course, to whatever limitations are established by Parliament under the Bank Act. This should introduce additional effective competition on a controlled scale and perhaps some valuable innovation.

We would also recommend that new Canadian-controlled banks be permitted to start on as favorable a basis as possible to compete with new foreign-controlled banks and the existing banks. To get the initial strength for a successful start against this competition, it may well be necessary that they be permitted to commence under the firm majority control of a strong corporate or other associated group able to retain majority control of the bank for a substantial number of years before beginning to reduce its shareholdings down to the 10% limit applying generally under the Bank Act. We think this type of additional domestic competition will be possible only if there is a clear policy defined in the legislation giving the necessary assurance to potential Canadian entrants that they can have sufficient time to become profitable and to have something valuable to sell when the time comes. As long as there is a controlling shareholder or group of associated shareholders, "self-dealing" provisions should apply to that bank, as they now apply to other financial institutions, to prevent it lending to or investing in related companies under essentially the same control (with the exception, of course, of specified bank subsidiaries).

The Commission has indicated its strong support for easier entry to the Canadian banking sector, both at the retail and wholesale banking levels. But we feel that, while there is an important role for small and medium-sized banks to play, this will supplement rather than duplicate that played by the major Canadian chartered banks. There have almost certainly been economic as well as regulatory reasons for the lack of small and medium-sized domestic Canadian banks. As Canada achieves a more advanced industrial economy, the role of specialized or local banks filling other roles may become more important, but it will not soon replace that filled by the existing major banks.

One great advantage of the size and strength of the Canadian banking sector is seen in its ability to compete in international financial markets. The largest Canadian banks have also gained considerable expertise in the type of consortium financing necessary to develop the largest of our energy and resource projects during the rest of this century. It would be difficult or impossible to undertake consortium financing of major projects without very large banks.

Finally, our system of large national banks provides major borrowers such as the provinces access to major capital markets in Canada and abroad, an access that would be much more difficult without the presence of these large banks and the confidence engendered by their size.

MERGERS

The *White Paper* proposes that the law relating to mergers of banks be part of the general competition law relating to mergers, but that the Minister of Finance have the power to authorize "such mergers which, in his view, are in the interests of the stability of the financial system." We see no objection to the application of the competition law in this respect, although we also see no necessity to shift the administration of a power that comes into play so infrequently and on which it will be necessary in any case to consult the Minister of Finance. Successive federal governments in the past 15 years have not announced any policy in regard to bank mergers, and only two mergers involving relatively small banks have been approved. Our study of the situation leads us to observe that no mergers among the five largest banks would appear to us to be necessary or desirable in the medium-term future but that if two or more smaller banks wished to merge to be more competitive with the big banks such a proposal should be sympathetically considered on its merits. In addition, we recognize the continuing possibility that from time to time a small bank in serious financial difficulties may have to be taken over by one of the stronger banks as a means of protecting the public interest, including the good reputation of the Canadian banking system as a whole.

DISCLOSURE

The general subject of disclosure of corporate information is discussed later in this *Report*. Here we wish only to mention some aspects of disclosure that pertain particularly to the banks (and to other financial institutions not subject to the general corporations or securities acts). The Bank Act itself sets forth many of the financial statements that must be made by the banks, either to their shareholders or to government for publication or for the purpose of regulation or compilation of statistics. The 1976 *White Paper* indicated in general terms that further disclosure would be required regarding bank activities, changes in accounting practices and other areas. The proposed changes do not seem to go as far as the breakdowns in aggregate figures proposed by the Association of Canadian Bank Analysts in their brief to the Department of Finance in November 1975. We think that the bank analysts' proposals would be very useful to investors and others in assessing the business performance of individual banks and that the information requested could be provided in the annual statements of each bank at little expense.

The banks are greatly increasing the numbers and range of their subsidiaries and affiliated companies both in Canada and abroad. While some information on these is published, we think it is in the public interest that the banks should clearly identify their subsidiary and affiliated companies even where they are jointly owned or controlled by that bank and other financial institutions. The information given should include the type of business in which the subsidiary or affiliate is engaged, its total assets, the investment in it by the bank and other affiliates of the bank and the percentage of voting shares held. We also support the proposal in the *White Paper* that the statements of each controlled subsidiary whose accounts are consolidated into those of the bank should be published separately. For each subsidiary and affiliate so reported, the banks should also indicate where applicable their policies on their charges to their subsidiaries for banking services provided to them.

We also think that the banks, as corporations, should be required to circulate management proxy circulars like those business corporations are generally required to circulate under section 144 of the Canada Business Corporations Act. The form and content of such circulars should be established by regulations under the Bank Act and should include that information required of other corporations unless there are good reasons to the contrary.

One aspect of the circular that might differ from that for corporations generally concerns indebtedness of directors, and those nominated to be directors, and officers of the bank. In the case of the banks this would normally involve relationships that exist in the ordinary course of business, and we think they need not be disclosed. However, the aggregate of loans outstanding to directors and to persons nominated to be directors should be disclosed in the proxy circular, and also the aggregate of loans to companies of which the directors or nominees are officers.

We suggest these as a minimum standard in addition to the financial disclosure already required of Canadian chartered banks. The level of bank disclosure in Canada is currently somewhat below that existing in the United States and very substantially less than the voluntary disclosure code announced in November 1976 by BankAmerica Corporation (see Chapter 13). This disclosure policy reverses the usual bank policy of considering all information confidential and requiring justification for individual disclosure, assumes that the "right to know" is paramount and requires justification for imposing limits on the right to know. As part of that policy, and with only minor exceptions, BankAmerica makes available to the public all information it files with government agencies. While this goes far beyond what is proposed for Canadian banks, or required for U.S. banks generally, and beyond what we think Canadian law need require, it is a good example of what a very large and responsible corporation judges to be desirable in its own and the public interest.

Directorship

The Banks' Boards of Directors

The Bank Act has a number of special provisions applying to boards of directors that differ from those in the general corporation acts. There has been considerable public interest in the size and composition of these boards and the extent to which bank directors are directors and executives of other corporations and may be regarded as part of a network of corporate influence throughout Canada. In addition, the composition and functioning of boards of directors form a part of the relations between the banks and their major corporate customers. The Commission has therefore given some special attention to this subject and asked questions about it in its public hearings.

The boards of the banks are typically much larger than those of the great majority of commercial and industrial companies. While this had led us to question whether they are unwieldy, and therefore perhaps less effective than they should be, and whether the large size dilutes the sense of responsibility of individual directors, we cannot assert that the reassuring answers to these questions given us by bank witnesses were wrong or that the size of the boards is harmful to the public interest. The bankers in their briefs and testimony to us have stressed the importance of having representation on their boards from all regions of Canada and all the major industries to provide a source of informed advice and good business judgment. The banks have not shown an equivalent desire to achieve a correspondingly balanced diversity in occupational experience, age, sex, language or social background among their directors. This has exposed them to criticism as a recognized central circle of the "corporate elite".

In regard to the functions of their boards of directors, bankers have stated that, while it is necessary for the boards or their committees to approve loans above specified sizes as part of an effective managerial system, in fact directors rarely intervene in questioning or changing the decisions of lending officers and senior management. The essential duties of the directors are to advise and guide management in regard to policies of the bank, including lending policies, to monitor the performance of senior management and, if and when necessary, to appoint new chief officers. The bankers have also confirmed to us that they expect directors to assist in obtaining or retaining the accounts of major customers.

There seems no doubt that senior executives of important Canadian businesses and leading lawyers regard it as an honor and a valuable experience to serve on the board of one of the well-established banks. These boards are composed largely of the chief executives of major corporations that are customers of the bank (though not necessarily of only that bank), and that will usually borrow from that bank. Another element of the board is usually composed of leading members of legal firms who serve the bank in various parts of Canada. To some degree, therefore, most members of the board have important business relations with the bank in addition to their fiduciary duties as directors.

This nature and role of the boards of banks is traditional and certainly well known. The directors are, as far as we can judge, persons of ability and integrity. So we mean it as no personal reflection on incumbent bank directors when we express our concern about the situation where the boards of our major lending institutions are composed almost entirely of persons who have an additional relationship with the bank, usually as the chief officer of a borrower. Inevitably this creates the possibility of a conflict of interest, collective as well as individual, where the directors' obligations to the bank may clash with their duties elsewhere. Regardless of the degree of integrity and good faith that exists, in such a situation circumstances may cloud judgment. At present only a small number of directors on the boards of the major banks can look at and evaluate the policies, management and activities of the bank free of any complication that might arise from their own business connections.

Given these circumstances, and recognizing the important role of the chartered banks in the Canadian economy, we recommend that the law require that a bank's board of directors always include a reasonable proportion of members who have no direct business relationships with the bank as borrowers or advisers, or indirect relationships by being officers or members of corporations or firms that are borrowers or advisers. These persons might be academics, lawyers or business people unconnected with the particular bank or others who might have non-corporate backgrounds. A director in the other group (e.g., an operating officer of a borrower) who found himself faced with an actual conflict of interest would be governed by the present provisions of the Bank Act relating to non-participation in decisions. Because of the very high regard in which bank directorships are generally held, we think it would not be difficult for the banks to find eminently qualified people without business connections with the bank to serve on their boards. Many chief executives of corporations are prepared to serve on the boards of other large companies that appear quite unrelated to their own company.

Interlocking Directorates

We have also given serious consideration to the subject of interlocking directorates between banks and other corporations, since some writers have attributed suspicious importance to these highly visible connections. There is no doubt that many of our most prominent business people serve on the board of a bank and also on the boards of other companies. Banks and other companies certainly look for the same sort of board members, people with senior business management experience or experience in corporation law. However we are satisfied from our study of the situation that the banks do not use these outside directors in common as a source of confidential information on their client companies. The banks can and do obtain and rely upon confidential reports and financial data obtained directly from their borrowers.

For this reason we see no need to extend to others the ban on directors of trust or mortgage loan companies, or of other banks, serving as directors of banks. Indeed it seems to us that the limit set by section 18(7) of the Bank Act on the number of directors of another company who may be elected or appointed directors of a bank is an unnecessary nuisance. Its origin seems to have been in a recommendation of the Porter Commission that would have applied to "any other single banking institution" when that Commission was proposing that trust and mortgage loan companies be treated as banking institutions. Since separate provision was made in the Act for a complete ban on such interlocks (which had been frequently and deliberately used as a connection), the inclusion of section 18(7) cannot be justified on the basis of the Commission recommendation. All we have found in justification of it were some rather general remarks by the Minister of Finance to the Senate Committee on Banking and Commerce about the desirability of less interlocking, spreading the distribution of the directorships and securing more variegated boards. We think it is not effective in attaining these purposes and that the measure we have proposed above is more important.

Since we hope that the trust and mortgage loan companies will continue to be effective competitors of the banks in the fields of service to depositors and personal loans, we would not suggest eliminating the ban on their directors' serving on the boards of banks and of such competing companies. Indeed, as other institutions become stronger competitors of the banks in future, it may be desirable to extend this ban to them in a later revision of the Bank Act, as well as to the boards of any recognized non-bank banking affiliates of foreign banks.

Shareholdings of Directors

The Bank Act requires a director to be a substantial shareholder in the bank on whose board he sits. This provision has been in the law for many years, as had an earlier provision for double liability of shareholders, which was dropped in the 1930s when the banks' rights to issue currency notes were terminated on the setting up of the Bank of Canada. While we found some senior bank witnesses who thought a more moderate shareholding would still be desirable, we believe that in principle directors need not be shareholders, and that token shareholdings would serve no useful purpose. The requirement for a large shareholding even though financed by a loan from the bank, as is often the case, may deter some otherwise desirable directors from serving because of the financial risk involved in the vicissitudes of the stock market. The Canada Business Corporations Act and other modern corporation law does not require that directors of companies in general be shareholders at all, and we cannot see why the directors of Canadian banks need be subject to this requirement. We recommend that it be dropped. In the establishment of new banks it will be necessary to ensure that they are adequately financed and have responsible and competent directors and top management, but that is a separate question.

Senior Bank Officers as Directors of Other Companies

On another but related subject, we have noted the following brief and somewhat cryptic observation of the Porter Commission (it follows a section dealing with bank holdings of the stock of non-financial businesses):

> In a related area we believe it unwise and undesirable for the executive officers of banking institutions to serve as directors of other commercial concerns, with the exception of subsidiaries or affiliates, but we do not feel that this practice warrants a legislative prohibition.

No reason was given for this advice and it does not appear to have had much effect. The most senior officers of three of the five largest banks are directors of a dozen or more apparently unaffiliated other businesses, and the senior officers of the other banks have a few such directorates. We questioned some of these senior bankers on this subject. One of them, with many directorships, said he had never agreed with the Porter recommendation and that he thought both the bank and the other company benefited from having "someone from the financial world on their board". Another with many directorships said in his bank's brief that while the senior officers of the bank could gain valuable experience on the boards of other companies, the bank had to be very careful not to let its senior officers become so involved in the affairs of other companies that their primary responsibility to the bank might suffer. He added ". . . I do it for competitive reasons and because I think the bank gets the benefit." A third senior banker, with only a few outside directorships, said, in response to a question about a possible conflict of duty, "No, this is certainly part of the reason (for restricting outside relationships). The problem that you have raised we have concerned ourselves with long and hard and discussed and worried about it. There is no doubt that the potential problem is there."

This Commission recognizes that there is some risk that having many outside directorships, for competitive reasons, may take up too much of the time and efforts of the chief officers of banks, and that conflicts of duty to the bank and to the other company involved may arise. It may also be that the subordinate management and lending officers of the bank could be affected in their judgment of a company's credit if the president of the bank is on its board. We think these considerations should be appraised by the boards of the banks concerned and that in each case the senior officers of a bank should accept an outside directorship only with the prior consent of the board. The capacity of the individual and the circumstances of each case are likely to vary so much that legislation on this matter is not appropriate. As we say in Chapter 12, our study of other types of companies as well as banks, and of the increasingly heavy legal responsibility of directors as a result of statutory changes and judicial interpretation, leads us to believe that no one with another full-time occupation should serve on more than a few outside boards of directors. A gradual restraint exercised in this respect would assist in bringing a wider diffusion of the responsibility of directing Canadian business and a more diversified character to corporate boards.

Chapter 11

Investment and Business Growth

This chapter discusses the environment for investment in the Canadian economy, particularly that for investment in dynamic small and medium-sized businesses. We discuss the need for greater aggregate supply of investment capital, the institutionalization of investment, the impact of the tax system, and other environmental factors reflected in the supply of investment and the viability of smaller businesses. We conclude with a brief discussion of two ideas for tax changes that might help to solve the aggregate savings and risk-return problems in the Canadian economy.

Many roles are filled by dynamic smaller firms in our economy. In some oligopolistic industries where economies of scale are not important, they can increase price competition. As indicated in the discussion of workable competition in Chapter 9, although in many industries smaller firms are unable to match the variety of product offerings of large firms in oligopolistic markets or their overall invention or innovation, they can compete on price, service and location or in individual segments of a market. In some industries in which large firms follow parallel price and service policies, dynamic smaller firms competing on price or service may increase the range of alternatives available to customers. In this way consumers may have available the whole spectrum of price-quality-service choices, although not necessarily from any one supplier.

Several definitions are used to distinguish among "small", "medium" and large firms. Although a definition based on size (whether of assets, revenue or employment) is necessarily arbitrary, it is frequently necessary for administrative purposes. For instance, the Department of Industry, Trade and Commerce uses a working definition, which defines a "small business" as an independently owned firm "with fewer than 100 employees in the manufacturing sector, and fewer than 50 employees in other sectors". Other definitions of small business are less concerned with absolute size as such and instead emphasize the owner-managed aspect of enterprise and the relative share of the market. Using this approach, the Canadian Federation of Independent Business accepts the U.S. Small Business Administration's definition of a small business as a

257

firm that "is independently owned and operated, and which is not dominant in its field of operations". In this chapter, the term "smaller" is used to include both small and medium-sized firms, although we are aware of the importance of making the distinction between independently owned and managed small businesses and branch plants. As well, we are concerned with the relatively young or new firms that are not dominant in their markets and with innovative firms in technologically new industries.

We are particularly interested in the most dynamic of the smaller businesses, those that can both challenge the entrenched positions of the dominant firms in their industries and provide the nucleus for rapid future growth of the economy. Such firms typically have both higher risk and higher returns (in the long run) than older, better-established firms, both large and small. It is commonly believed that conventional lenders in Canada are generally unwilling to provide capital for high-risk firms, whose growth is often stunted as a result (sometimes they fail entirely).

Other reasons have been suggested to us for generally encouraging smaller firms. One is their social and cultural importance. For example, strengthening the base of small and medium-sized business in smaller towns or in less industrialized areas of the country may help in stemming the migration to major urban centers, which in spite of our large land areas has made Canada the most urbanized society in the industrialized western world. An increase in the number and variety of smaller enterprises would be of great value to smaller centers that are currently one-industry towns. Smaller businesses are often more sensitive to regional differences and more aware of regional requirements than are larger firms. Smaller businesses also have a considerable impact on employment. Of the more than one million businesses in Canada, the majority are small and privately owned. In 1973, 90% of all Canadian firms employed fewer than 100 people each, and collectively these firms accounted for 60% of total employment. As indicated in Chapter 9, in comparison with almost every western industrial country, Canada has a lower ratio of small and particularly medium-sized firms to larger firms in many industries. This is true in spite of the fact that the largest establishments in Canada do not themselves compare in asset size, sales or growth rates with the largest firms world-wide. Even where ratios of small and medium-sized firms in Canada are comparable with those in the United States, it appears that smaller firms have not grown relative to growth rates of larger ones to the same extent as they have in the United States.

The lower ratio of small businesses in some industries suggests either substantial barriers to entry or an anticipated risk-return ratio that does not attract new investment in those industries. The lack of medium-sized firms suggests either impediments to the growth of smaller firms or a risk-return relationship that provides inadequate incentive to such growth. In any case, there are the questions of where dynamic, new small businesses are to come from and whether conditions exist to enable them to grow.

In our briefs and hearings and in discussions with many investors, we heard evidence that there were managerial, financial, technical and scale barriers to entry and to growth in Canada and that returns were inadequate to make investment in smaller ventures attractive. We did not find agreement on the relative importance of these factors. Some investors argued, for example, that the main deficiency was in the overall quality of Canadian management; that an adequate supply of proposals for new, well-managed projects would bring forth appropriate financing. Others argued that there was an adequate flow of proposals but a lack of capital to finance them. Other investors argued that, even if there were adequate projects and financing available in Canada, the much superior risk-return ratio available in the United States and elsewhere would severely limit investment in Canada. Problems exist in all these areas, but perhaps most dramatically in the provision of financing. We begin by discussing the developing shortage of investment capital in Canada and then focus on the situation for risk capital.

The Supply of Investment Capital

The financial problems of small and medium-sized companies must be viewed in the context of the developing shortage of investment capital in Canada and, as part of that problem, the need for increased business profits. In the seven years from 1970 to 1976, Canadians invested $214.6 billion in machinery and equipment, other business investment, housing and government construction. Stated in 1977 dollars, this is about $280 billion. It is currently estimated that in the seven years beginning in 1977, Canada will require between $460 and $520 billion (current dollars) of investment. About 30-35% of the projected investment will be in energy and transport; part of this has already been committed and much of the remainder would be difficult to postpone without adversely affecting our standard of living. The projected total investment requirement represents an increase of 2-3% (over the 1970-76 average of 22.5%) of the gross national product (GNP) that must be saved and invested. Though there exists considerable "slack" in the economy at present, there is some concern that the real growth rate of the economy may fall short of what is required to call forth the necessary volume of savings to finance the projected capital requirements. Investment in the basic industries in Canada from 1974 to 1976 tended to be for replacement, pollution control and adaptation to alternative energy sources rather than for new facilities to add additional productive capacity. In part, this occurred because Canadian industry was operating at 84-88% of capacity over this period. However, this capacity figure is increasingly suspect, since what is listed as unused capacity includes facilities too inefficient to be used and facilities that pollute and cannot be used.

Table 11.1 indicates the sources of funds that were available for investment over the 1970-76 period. The statistics suggest that Canada will have to find incentives other than a very large rise in interest rates to increase the amount of its GNP saved. In recent years, the largest share of funds have come from depreciation allowances, which do not represent a net addition to our stock of capital assets. In any case, depreciation allowances are a declining

Table 11.1
Sources of Gross Saving, Canada, 1970-76
(The Finance of Gross Domestic Capital Formation)
(Percentages)

	1970	1971	1972	1973	1974	1975	1976
Personal saving[1]	16.7	17.6	21.2	24.6	26.5	30.3	29.5
Government[2]	15.4	12.4	11.0	13.0	15.9	0.3	0.7
Corporate savings[3]	16.0	14.8	15.1	16.5	12.5	11.9	13.2
Capital consumption[4]	55.2	51.7	49.0	45.3	41.5	44.7	44.3
Non-residents saving[5]	-5.2	-0.9	2.9	0.8	5.4	13.2	10.4
Residual error	1.9	4.4	0.8	-0.2	-1.8	-0.4	1.9
	100.0	100.0	100.0	100.0	100.0	100.0	100.0
Total savings Billions of dollars	$17.8	$20.3	$23.4	$29.5	$38.0	$40.0	$45.6
As percentage of GNP	20.7	21.5	22.2	23.9	25.8	24.2	24.0

Source: Statistics Canada, *National Income and Expenditure Accounts*, First Quarter 1977.
Notes:
1. Persons and unincorporated business (personal saving plus adjustment on grain transactions).
2. Total revenue less total current expenditure of the federal, provincial and local governments, the hospitals and the Canada and Quebec Pension Plans.
3. Corporate and government business enterprises (which equals undistributed corporation profits plus undistributed profits of government business enterprises plus capital assistance plus inventory valuation adjustment).
4. Capital consumption allowances and miscellaneous valuation adjustments (of persons and unincorporated business, government, and corporate and government business enterprises).
5. Non-residents saving equals the surplus (−) or deficit (+) of Canada on current transactions with non-residents and indicates savings made available to the economy by non-residents.

source of total investment capital. The decrease from 55% in 1970 to 44% in 1976 is largely due to inflation and it indicates the degree to which productive assets have had to be replaced at higher prices.

Another striking change is the net contribution of government. Government savings are the difference between total revenue at all levels of government and the total current spending of those governments. Over the period 1970-76, government invested about the same proportion of the GNP (ranging from 15-17%), but did so in the latter years almost totally by way of borrowed funds, bringing its net investment close to zero. The investment from non-Canadian sources since 1970 has been substantial, but it peaked in 1975 and is projected to decrease slowly for the rest of this decade.

The rate of personal savings seems to have peaked during 1975. The major factor in this is the maturing of pension plans, part of personal savings. When a pension plan is new, it has many contributors but few pensioners and so accumulates funds rapidly. As the fund matures it grows more slowly and ceases to be a net provider of new investment money. Canada's pension funds (excluding Registered Retirement Savings Plans) are at various stages of maturity, but over the next seven years can be expected to provide a lower proportion of new capital than they have over the last seven years.

The number of alternatives available to maintain or increase saving as a percentage of GNP are limited. One alternative would be to permit Canadian interest rates to increase to a higher level (well above rates in the United States) over a long period, which would raise the flow of personal savings and the inflow of non-resident capital but at a high cost in overall economic dislocation and a further and perhaps dramatic increase in the level of external debt. In mid-1977, Canada's foreign debt was $49.7 billion, a doubling in a decade. Another alternative would be for federal, provincial or local governments to reduce their current expenditures and their reliance on debt financing.

The only other alternative that seems feasible is a substantial increase in corporate after-tax profits. Because of the relative openness to imports of some sectors of the economy, and the high labor costs in the manufacturing sector, there is little scope for widening profit margins so that returns on capital improve sufficiently to induce new investment. Some other way must be found to improve the risk-return ratio and thus to increase the proportion of GNP flowing to savings and investment.

The Supply of Equity Capital

One important aspect of the shortage of capital has been the decline in the number and aggregate value of new equity issues in Canada since 1969. There was a buoyant market for equities in the late 1960s, a collapse in 1970 and some recovery in 1975 for preferred issues, but with net new common issues remaining at depressed levels (Table 11.2). The increase of net new issues of preferred shares and of debt in 1975 and 1976 has been partly attributed to a "rush to the market" by some large Canadian firms as a result of the announcement by the Securities and Exchange Commission in the United

Table 11.2

Net New Issues of Corporate Bonds and Shares, Canada, 1964-76

Year	Bonds[1] Payable in Canadian Dollars[2]	Payable in Canadian and Foreign Currency[3]	New Equity[4] Preferred Shares	Common Shares	Total	Number of New Public Common Equity Issues[5] by Companies of Less than $1 Million	$1 Million to under $2 Million	$2 Million to $3 Million	Gross Value of New Equity Issues by Companies of Less than $1 Million	$1 Million to under $2 Million	$2 Million to $3 Million	Total
	(Millions of Dollars)					(Numbers of Prospectuses)			(Thousands of dollars)			
1964	573	787	38	269	307	n.a.	n.a.	n.a.	n.a.	n.a.	n.a.	n.a.
1966	404	970	177	388	565	4			1,323			1,323
1968	436	734	122	436	558	13	7	4	6,077	9,100	10,060	25,237
1969	451	833	143	851	994	29	34	7	15,957	46,541	14,098	76,595
1970	1,131	1,494	101	251	352	14	3	1	5,241	3,900	2,406	11,547
1971	1,786	1,834	111	230	341	16	2	3	7,085	2,769	7,687	17,541
1972	1,551	1,623	199	420	619	7	12	8	3,602	16,205	18,535	38,342
1973	1,578	1,555	84	527	611	8	8		3,503	12,602		16,105
1974	1,551	1,778	434	304	738	5			1,274			1,274
1975	2,293	2,917	743	486	1,229	2			520			520
1976	1,239	4,244	631	569	1,180	1	1		375	1,815		2,190

Source: *Bank of Canada Review* (Aug. 1977), *Financial Post Record of New Issues*, Ontario Securities Commission and Royal Commission on Corporate Concentration (RCCC) research.

Notes:

1. Includes secondary offerings and debt portions of combination debt-equity offerings.
2. Net new bond issues payable in Canadian dollars only (excludes issues placed in overseas markets).
3. Net new bond issues payable in Canadian and foreign currencies (includes Canadian dollar issues placed in overseas markets).
4. Net new preferred and common stock issues payable in Canadian and foreign currencies.
5. Excluding issues by mining (or exploration) companies and all issues that are privately placed. Also excludes combination debt-equity and rights (or combination shares-warrant) offerings in addition to all debt, finance and secondary issues.

n.a. = not available.

States in early 1975 that firms reporting under SEC rules would also have to report inflation-adjusted earnings for the 1976 operating year, thus indicating lower earnings levels and much higher price-earnings ratios than had previously been reported. The attraction to the chartered banks of new types of preferred shares may also have contributed to the increase.

Private placements of new equity appear to have declined in number but increased in dollar volume from 1969 through 1975. Most of the dollar volume of private placements is in larger companies in more mature industries rather than in smaller companies in high-risk areas. Given the high rates of inflation in the past few years, equity requirements for all firms have certainly risen, making the comparison between levels of new issues in the late 1960s and recent levels more dramatic.

Even when new issues of equity returned to their 1969 levels, the aggregate figures conceal the fact that recently the issues have been largely in the form of preferred shares rather than common shares and primarily for larger enterprises (as small and medium-sized companies are generally foreclosed from this kind of financing). To raise equity in the form of common shares requires a much better environment in the stock market than does preferred share financing. The percentage of preferred to total new equity financing has risen from 32% in 1972 to 60% in 1975 and to 53% in 1976 (Table 11.2).

For both small and large companies, the substantial dollar amount of debt and preferred shares combined with relatively small amounts of new common stock has produced escalating corporate debt-to-equity ratios over the past seven years. The leveraging of debt, with its resultant higher-risk capital structure must inevitably stop somewhere, thus curtailing the growth of firms. At some point there must be either new equity or increased corporate retained earnings before growth through debt financing can continue.

A related issue raised before the Commission on several occasions was the tremendous difficulty faced by small, privately held companies in going public through a securities issue. If a company cannot get past the small, privately held stage, there is much less incentive to start or invest in new ventures with the intention of taking a profit as they develop and mature, and there is much less liquidity in such an investment. Over the past several years virtually no new equity issues under $3 million have been underwritten in Canada. There were 5 issues in 1974, 2 in 1975, and 2 in 1976 (Table 11.2).

Table 11.3 indicates the average costs of issue for recent public securities issues in Canada. We include these figures because they do not support the commonly held belief that fixed costs for small equity issues are prohibitive. Also, the smallest companies could raise money either through debt or preferred shares at rates not more than 3 percentage points above the rates charged to the largest companies. A small issuer encounters both higher issue costs for either debt or equity and higher proportional legal, audit, printing and perhaps translation costs than would a large issuer, other things being equal, but the differentials are not prohibitive themselves although they act as a disincentive. What prevents access to public debt and equity markets for small firms is not cost but a lack of buyers at rates of return similar to those that bring forth capital in other countries.

Table 11.3

Costs of Issue of Public Securities Issues (Excluding Mining Issues), Canada, 1974-77

	Cost of Issue*		
Size of Issue	Debt Issues	Preferred Shares	Common Shares
$1–3 million (issuer has no previous securities in market)			10–12½%
About $5 million (issuer has no previous securities in market)	up to 7%		10–12½%
$1–5 million (issuer known, good credit rating)	3–4%	5–6%	up to 8%
About $10 million (good, well-recognized credit)	2%	4–5%	up to 8%
$25 million and over (good, well-recognized credit)	1½–2%	3–4%	up to 8%

Additional Expenses

Legal, audit and printing costs for a public issue are $50,000 minimum. If the issuer has no previous securities in the market, costs are $75,000 minimum. Maximum legal, audit and printing costs for a very large issue are about $150,000. If offered in more than one language, translation and printing costs would add to the cost.

Source: Investment Dealers Association of Canada, and RCCC research.

Notes: Some private placements may have been made through facilities provided by firms or institutions not part of the Investment Dealers Association or the major Canadian stock exchanges, and therefore not covered in this sample. The underwriting spreads reflected here may not be strictly comparable even on similar types of issues by the same issuer. For example, some parts of issues may be placed privately, some issues may be placed on a best-effort agency basis. Also, underwriting fees vary depending on the terms and characteristics of issues such as term options, heavy sinking funds, and so on. Thus while the information is fairly representative of costs of transactions, there may be individual transactions which for a number of reasons are above or below the ranges stated.

* – Variable costs associated with an issue of public securities as a percentage of the total amount of the issue.

Most saving by Canadians is done through institutions: bank deposits, guaranteed investment certificates, Registered Retirement Savings Plans (RRSPs), Registered Home Ownership Plans (RHOSPs), pension funds and life insurance. These institutions have concentrated their funds in bonds, mortgages, equities of the largest Canadian companies and the debt of the federal and provincial governments. The institutionalization of savings has come at the expense of a shift away from personal investment in equities. National income statistics show that dividends as a percentage of individual investment income have declined from 40% in 1966 to 19% in 1975, while bond and bank interest payments have increased from 40% to 72% and mortgage income and other investment income have remained relatively stable at 10%.

The institutionalization of investment and the trend away from personal investment in equities seem in large measure a result of the 1971 taxation changes in Canada. The impact of these changes has been to shift emphasis from seeking capital gains to investment in tax-sheltered or tax-free situations. We indicate below the kinds of tax shelters being used and the degree to which funds are diverted away from risk investment.

The most important individual tax shelter is the exemption of one's principal place of residence from capital gains tax. A priority for many Canadians today is the purchase of as large a home as can be financed in the short run. Another priority for many Canadians is to invest in an RRSP or an RHOSP, both tax-sheltered. Most of these plans are administered by large institutions and run conservatively, their funds being invested largely in debt instruments or large enterprises. The flow of personal funds to tax-sheltered investments is illustrated by the growth in RRSPs and RHOSPs from 1970 to 1976 (Table 11.4).

Table 11.4
Investment in Registered Pension Funds, RRSPs and RHOSPs,
Canada 1970-76
(Millions of Dollars)

	1970	1971	1972	1973	1974	1975	1976
Registered pension funds	728	817	964	1,093	1,310	1,416	1,605
RRSPs	225	318	655	923	1,244	1,725	2,100
RHOSPs					194	395	460
Total RRSPs and RHOSPs	225	318	655	923	1,438	2,120	2,560

Source: Statistics Canada, *Pension Plans in Canada,* Cat. No. 74-201; Bank of Canada; Dept. of National Revenue.

A partial solution to the problem of institutional conservatism might be to encourage self-administered, tax-sheltered RRSPs. Several trust companies in Canada currently offer self-administered plans, but they are expensive to operate and require a great deal of paperwork to meet government requirements.

The next priority for an individual is to make an investment that will return a tax-free $1,000 per year for the lowest possible investment. Over the past few years this has meant debt instruments of large institutions or Canada Savings Bonds, but virtually never equity, and certainly never equity of small and medium-sized companies with low dividend payouts.

There is evidence that when an industry is seen to be profitable, or where tax advantages exist, there are a great many Canadians who become active investors even though the risks have not changed. For example, shortages of start-up and expansion capital have not occurred in the construction industry. New builders and suppliers have continuously entered the field, and had no difficulty in obtaining funds to begin or expand operations in an industry that has been blessed in the recent past by favorable tax legislation. A great deal of money became available for Canadian movie production and for natural gas exploration in the mid-1970s when these high-risk activities were given special tax status.

Nevertheless, a much higher proportion of funds flow through the institutional investment process in Canada than in the United States, and it is in part the domination of markets by institutions that creates the overall appearance of conservatism. The reasons that the institutions themselves do not reinvest a high proportion of these funds in equities seems due to the nature of the institutions and their liabilities and to their internal organization and reward systems which minimize any incentive to invest in the equity of smaller companies.

The Supply of Term Debt

Many people have told us of a gap in the supply of term debt to medium-sized firms. Term debt is usually defined as that issued for a one-to-twenty-year period but it is most common in the five-to-ten-year range. There are also substantial differences in the compositions of debt and equity of corporations of various size. The bulk of debt raised by large corporations is in the form of bonds. The principal source of long-term debt to small and medium-sized corporations is mortgage debt, which accounts for about half of all long-term debt they raise. Smaller corporations do not have access to the corporate bond market in Canada, although they may manage to place bond issues privately. Smaller firms also make more intensive use of long-term debt in the form of loans from suppliers.

The reason for the gap in the provision of debt to smaller firms is not clear, however. The income streams of smaller firms may be more variable than those of larger firms or they may not have a "track record" and hence appear more risky to lending institutions. On the other hand, Canadian banks may earn satisfactory profits without making higher-risk loans to smaller firms, as they do in the United States.

Over the past few years an increasing number of intermediaries have been willing to supply term funds to medium-sized firms. Roynat, companies like Permanent Capital Corporation in Toronto, the Federal Business Development Bank, venture capital companies and financial leasing companies are serving segments of this market. Life insurance companies have contributed to the supply of term capital through mortgages on non-residential buildings, although in mid-1977 only one life insurance company held a significant number of non-mortgage securities of medium-sized companies. Two new banks, the Canadian Commercial and Industrial Bank and Northland Bank, argued in their charter applications that there is a real need in Canada for term loans to small and medium-sized businesses, which they intended to meet. Affiliates of foreign banks are increasingly moving into this sector, especially through specialized leasing.

Since 1971 there has been a significant increase in the role of established banks in term lending, as reflected in the percentage of term loans to all business loans made. Most of this growth has come in loans to corporations with assets exceeding $25 million, but some has been in the $10-$25 million category. It is likely that the real number of term loans to business of all sizes exceeds that reported by banks, because many term loans appear on bank books as demand loans but with an understanding that the loan can be rolled over for a longer period.

We do not consider the gap in the supply of term capital as important a concern as the other capital gaps we discuss in this chapter. We point it out as an illustration of one more problem that has faced medium-sized businesses seeking to finance rapid growth.

The Supply of Risk Capital

It was suggested to us in several briefs and in our hearings that a deficiency in the availability of risk capital in Canada is a factor in the relative shortage of small and medium-sized business in this country. Risk capital is sometimes referred to as venture capital; we use the terms interchangeably to refer to the provision of capital where the loan or equity investment is neither secure nor liquid, a situation that may of course prevail at many stages in a company's development, and with large as well as small enterprises. Risk capital or venture capital may be in the form of equity, debt, convertible debt or combinations of these. The shortfall in Canada is not only in the supply of equity, but includes all capital for high-risk, high-return investments. The shortfall seems, however, to be most pronounced in the lack of money for startup situations, particularly when compared with the United States.

Before World War II, virtually the only source of risk capital in Canada outside the mining sector was wealthy individuals who made personal investments in companies not suitable for traditional bank lending or for institutional portfolios. After the war, some of these individuals organized small staffs of professional managers with pools of funds intended for venture investment. Typically, these prototype venture capital firms were focused on areas of particular interest to the individuals. Canada Overseas Investments and Helix Investments in Canada and Rockefeller Brothers Inc. in the United States began as family investment capital operations. The success of these professionally managed venture firms brought others into the field, some subsidiaries of large companies or financial institutions, some representing capital pools that had not before been involved in this type of investment. We discuss next the role of venture capital companies, chartered banks, individuals and government agencies in providing risk capital.

THE ROLE OF VENTURE CAPITAL COMPANIES

Venture capital companies are important, not because of the total dollar volume of their investments, but because they have in the past been one source of risk capital for small and medium-sized businesses and could expand that role in the future with the right incentives. The venture capital industry in Canada has operated somewhat differently from its counterparts in the United

States and the United Kingdom, with the difference being partly a result of the smaller size of Canadian venture capital companies.

To the best of our knowledge there are only seven venture capital companies in Canada with capitalization of $10-$15 million, the minimum capitalization necessary to carry a diversified investment portfolio from startup to maturity. Some of the existing venture capital companies have had to tailor their investment strategy to overcome the shortfall. One way is to seek investment opportunities that can be realized in a short time. Another is to invest in less risky investments by avoiding startups or other investments that will require subsequent rounds of financing. The most common strategy is for a venture capitalist to use debt investments as well as equity, with an interest flow to help the venture supplier over the early years and equity participation that can then be held at low cost and sold if a suitable opportunity arises. This approach favors investment in more mature companies, as a new venture usually has no capacity to service debt in its initial stages of growth.

Once a company in which a venture capitalist has invested reaches a mature, profitable stage the investor looks for a way to divest the holding and recycle the capital into new investments. The traditional way of doing this has been for the company to "go public". The Canadian equities market has not been favorable for the equity of new small companies since the late 1960s.

The second way of divesting is to arrange for the acquisition of the whole company, or at least the venture capitalist's holdings, by another company or investor. The Foreign Investment Review Act has limited this alternative and by reducing the competition of foreign buyers has somewhat reduced the market value of small, privately held businesses. After the initial uncertainties surrounding FIRA, however, its effect on the market for small firms has decreased in importance.

A third way of divesting is to sell the venture capitalist's holding back to the principals of the company or to the company itself. This possibility is sometimes written into the investment from the beginning but it has the shortcoming that it is not usually in the company's best interest to redeem its shares by the expenditure of scarce, internally generated capital. The same shortcoming applies to realizing an investment by taking large dividends out of the company.

The difficulty of divesting in Canada has contributed to what is a natural tendency in every country: that over a short life cycle many venture capital companies evolve to become closed-end investment trusts, operating companies or holding companies. The natural attrition accentuates the need in normal times for new venture capitalists to come into the industry.

The number of venture capital companies in Canada and the dollars invested by them declined markedly from 1970 to 1976. In 1970 there were about 45 major venture capital companies (with funds available for invest-ments over $2 million each) active in Canada, making about 120 investments a year. In 1976 there were 23 major venture capital suppliers (not including the Federal Business Development Bank), with 56 investments made by 33 companies or consortia of companies. Some of the more significant venture capital companies that have or are withdrawing from Canada include Charterhouse Canada Limited, Guardian Venture Group, Citicorp Venture Capital Canada Ltd., Merban Capital Corp., International Capital Corp., Nevron Capital Corp., and MacMillan Bloedel's venture capital division. The only significant recent new sources of active venture capital in Canada are the four companies to which the Canada Development Corporation has committed funds plus newly formed affiliates of Brascan Limited and Inco Limited. The companies that have left the industry have cited the deteriorating risk-reward relationship for investment, the difficulties of divesting and the tax situation in Canada vis-à-vis the United States.

The total amount invested by major venture capital companies in 1976 was approximately $17 million, compared with $6.5 million in 1975 and about $40 million in 1970. These figures exclude natural resource investments, which vary widely year by year depending on the tax status of the individual investments. By way of comparison, major venture capital companies in the United States are estimated to have invested about $670 million during 1976 (not including the investments by Small Business Investment Corporations, which are discussed below).

The composite picture we have is one of a shrinking Canadian industry, both in terms of number of companies and dollars invested, with those who remain in the industry putting an increasing proportion of their assets into tax-haven natural resource industries, and into investments outside of Canada.

THE ROLE OF THE CHARTERED BANKS

In Chapter 10 of this *Report* we discussed the operations of Canadian chartered banks. The chartered banks are not generally in the business of providing risk capital. Canadian banks do occasionally make use of flexible and innovative lending techniques such as income debentures or retractable preferred shares, but these are usually directed to firms with more than $10 million in sales or assets. Specialized lending techniques are generally available only in larger, commercially oriented branches of the banks or at their head offices. To make use of them a borrower must be sophisticated enough both to know to go beyond his local branch for assistance and also to convince his bank of his ability to service the debt. He must be able to prepare cash flow, interest and debt service coverage projections and to explain the various assumptions and supporting rationale behind those projections.

Several chartered banks either have chosen to provide capital through small venture capital divisions, or to participate in ownership of venture capital companies to provide risk capital to small and medium-sized businesses. The bank's preference in such financing is usually for an interest-bearing instrument to achieve current income, but financing also takes the form of subordinated debt or preferred shares, often with overrides to achieve a minimum rate of return.

Section 76 of the Bank Act places a constraint on banks in that they are prohibited from holding more than 10% of the outstanding voting shares of a company if their investment is over $5 million, but with an investment under $5 million they can hold up to 50% of the shares. Under a proposal in the government's 1976 *White Paper*, the chartered banks' participation would effectively be restricted to 10% of any venture investment, rather than the 50% for investments under $5 million now permitted. This would restrict venture participation by banks since it prohibits them from taking a position that allows them to assume control either to protect an investment in a company that is being badly managed, or to purchase the interest of another participant who wishes to withdraw. The Commission finds the *White Paper*'s recommendations unduly restrictive and recommends that section 76 be amended to raise the $5 million limit to $10 million.

THE ROLE OF INDIVIDUAL INVESTORS

Another source of venture capital is individuals who make personal, high-risk investments. There is no information available on the aggregate of such investments nor any formal clearing mechanism to put suppliers and users of such capital together. Some informal "matching" is done by members of the legal profession, investment consultants, accountants, bankers and others, but the process is an imperfect one. We have been unable to determine the degree to which individuals fill the need for risk capital investment, but indications from investment advisers and others are that with a few exceptions this source is limited to relatively small amounts of capital.

THE ROLE OF GOVERNMENT AGENCIES

The shortage of risk capital available from the private sector is reduced by numerous government agencies, federal and provincial, which offer financial assistance to small and medium-sized businesses. We have identified 97 separate federal and provincial government assistance programs available to smaller businesses, and undoubtedly there are others. The programs range from loan agencies and guarantors to assistance with training programs, pollution abatement and other individual expenditures. For example, the federal Department of Finance guarantees business loans up to $75,000 to businesses whose gross annual revenues do not exceed $1.5 million for the purchase, installation, renovation and improvement of equipment or premises or the purchase of land. The Federal Business Development Bank (FBDB) provides loans or loan guarantees. However, most government agencies concentrate their lending on low-risk types of business (although they may involve high-risk individuals or geographic areas). The FBDB is an exception to this lending pattern. It entered the venture capital field in 1976 and in the first 18 months of operating in this area made 51 investments for a total of $6.3 million. The Department of Regional Economic Expansion has also been a major source of funds to both small and large businesses in some regions of the country.

It is difficult to classify federal or provincial assistance programs because their objectives are so clearly different from those of other suppliers of capital. Governments' objectives may include creating local employment, increasing exports, replacing imports into a region or the country, introduction of new technology, regional economic growth and creating new employment skills. Often a prerequisite for much government funding, particularly from federal agencies, is evidence that the funds cannot be obtained from other sources and that the project is unlikely to go ahead without government assistance. The wide range of criteria other than profitability leads government agencies, particularly provincial agencies, to take considerable time to approve applications. Despite these initiatives by government and the private sector, there is a shortage of risk capital in Canada to finance the small, dynamic businesses necessary to increase competition and lead growth in the economy.

SMALL BUSINESS INVESTMENT CORPORATIONS

The United States has not had the same problems as Canada with the supply of risk capital, partly because the environment for enterpreneurship has been seen to be better, partly because the risk-return ratio in the U.S. has clearly been better, partly because the tax system has been more favorable. One example reflecting the more favorable environment and tax system in the United States is the Small Business Investment Company (SBIC) created under the Small Business Investment Act of 1958.

At March 31, 1976 there were 325 SBICs in operation in the United States, with assets totalling $1,100 millions (43% of which was borrowed). During 1976, SBICs invested in 2,200 small and medium-sized firms, 1,225 of which were first-time investments. Half these firms had been in existence less than three years. The annual sales of these new firms averaged $2.1 million, and they employed an average of 62 people each. For the six years ended December 31, 1976, the successful SBIC-financed firms grew at an average rate of 22%, while the average growth rate for the U.S. economy was 5-7% over the same period.

Proposals for a Venture Investment Corporation (VIC) in Canada, similar to the SBIC, have come from many sources in the past several years, including a report by Robert Grasley to the Ministry of State, the Investment Dealers Association, and the Association of Canadian Venture Capital Companies. At the provincial level, Ontario and Quebec have passed legislation giving provincial tax relief for those corporations making *bona fide* risk capital investments in those provinces, and Alberta, New Brunswick and Nova Scotia have either proposed or indicated strong interest in similar legislation. However, provincial solutions to a national problem have a limited impact and they raise the possibility of provincial competition over tax concessions. An effective tax-based solution for this national problem of risk capital must come at the federal level.

In their brief to the Commission, the Association of Canadian Venture Capital Companies recommended the federal licensing of special Venture Investment Corporations to invest capital in startups and small business in Canada. They suggested that amounts invested in shares in such a company be fully deductible from the taxable income of the shareholder. This would be an extraordinarily generous tax provision. "Flow-through" provisions would tax the income of the company only in the hands of shareholders but not in the hands of venture capital intermediaries. Further recommendations include extending the loss-carry-forward period to ten years from five for small and medium-sized companies.

Solutions of this kind might encourage large corporations with capital and managerial talent to enter the risk capital field, and perhaps expose their younger executives to the management problems in it as part of their training. However, VICs are not the answer for rapidly growing medium-sized companies, which would quickly outgrow the funds available in VICs not financed by institutions.

Nevertheless, the SBIC concept in the United States is one indication of how quickly and effectively tax changes can attract capital and entrepreneurs to the market. If the federal government wants to increase the flow of funds to startups and high-risk, high-return areas very quickly, a plan similar to SBICs might be equally effective in Canada. Problems of definition and equity would no doubt arise, and it would be necessary to guard against abuse of the plan. However, such problems could presumably be solved by statutory amendments, as they have been with RHOSPs and similar programs in recent years.

Management and Technical Expertise

As we pointed out earlier in this chapter, it is sometimes argued that the lack of dynamic, smaller businesses may reflect a shortage of sound projects. This shortage is said to arise from a lack of entrepreneurship, management skills, engineering and other technical expertise, or a "critical mass" of highly skilled managerial and technical people in one location in the country.

Such a claim is obviously difficult to prove or to disprove. The relatively low level of formal business education in Canadian management has been the theme of considerable research and writing over the past decade. It has been argued that Canadian management has a traditional decision-making style that emphasizes neither entrepreneurship nor scientific approaches to decision-making; that there are insufficient trained, experienced managers who can supplement their intuitive decision-making with analysis; or that the high degree of foreign ownership of Canadian industry has produced many individuals trained in only one narrow, functional area of business such as marketing or finance, but few with experience in overall business strategy and planning or in making large-scale entrepreneurial decisions.

Some evidence of a "managerial gap" comes from comparative statistics on education and other characteristics of middle and upper management in Canada and the United States. Studies have concluded that the typical Canadian senior executive is older than his U.S. counterpart, has received less formal education, has risen through the ranks more slowly and is more likely to have been selected on the basis of experience rather than formal professional background or training. Based on 1975 statistics, the managerial group in Canada had a smaller proportion of university educated people and, perhaps more relevant, a much smaller proportion of people with graduate qualifications in business administration, administrative studies or related fields, than was true in the United States. There were in the United States three and a half times as many Master of Business Administration graduates per 100,000 people in 1975 as there were in Canada. Statistics on graduate business education may not be an accurate indicator of entrepreneurship and business expertise but they are indicative of the relative importance placed on management skills and entrepreneurship in a society.

In comparing proposals to venture capital suppliers submitted in Canada and the United States, the Commission has found considerable differences in quality and depth of presentation. At the risk of oversimplication, the typical Canadian submission is made by an individual entrepreneur or a small group with what appears to be a good proposal backed by strength in one or two functional areas but with no expertise in others and no well-developed idea of where such expertise is to come from or of long-term business strategy. The Canadian venture capital supplier is then placed in a position of having either to turn down the proposal or to become involved in finding additional management people or expertise to fill the management team. Those U.S. proposals we have seen were much more fully developed, contained not only a proposal but short and long-term development plans and seemed to originate with entrepreneurs who had a considerable range of background and skills.

Within our general concern about management and technical expertise is the difficult problem of maintaining a healthy climate for new, high-technology enterprises. These deserve special attention for several reasons. Certainly these are the enterprises most sensitive to a lack of management or technical expertise or a "critical mass" of highly skilled people. They are particularly important in the context of our proposals for workable competition because new or innovative technology represents one way in which new firms can compete in markets characterized by an oligopolistic structure and mature firms. Less related to our mandate, but no less important to the problems facing Canada, is the fact that rates of sales growth and job creation in innovative and high-technology companies are very much greater than they are in more mature companies.

We raise the problem of managerial and technological gaps because they are both important problems and constraints in considering the financial gaps discussed earlier. The managerial gap may tend to close as management skills become more broadly distributed through the economy and as younger managers with formal training in business administration mature and gain more experience. The management problem is complicated by the degree of foreign ownership, government ownership and regulated industry in the economy, none of which are conducive to the development of rounded entrepreneurial skills, and by the relatively small resources being devoted to management training.

Taxation

It is abundantly clear from what we have said in this chapter that savings over the next few years will be inadequate to finance the necessary business investment and that current and expected risk-return ratios will be inadequate to induce risk capital investment. This and the other serious problems of the Canadian economy which we reviewed briefly in Chapter 1 concern us deeply.

We think there must be more questioning of things that have heretofore been accepted as unchangeable. If the problems we face are as deep-seated as we think, then their solutions probably require equally fundamental changes in some of our economic arrangements. Mere tinkering with effects will not come to grips with basic underlying causes. All of us must be prepared to think about the unthinkable.

It seemed to us, therefore, that we might be able to stimulate this kind of thinking if we could ourselves throw a provocative proposal into the arena. For several reasons, we decided that the tax system was an appropriate candidate for discussion.

First, experience shows that the economy does respond to tax changes. We have pointed out several examples in this chapter. Second, we believe that major changes to the tax system will be necessary to raise the supply of savings and to improve the expected return sufficiently to attract those savings to business investment. It is appropriate to discuss the tax system in this chapter because a healthy, small business sector is one of the most realistic antidotes to the economic concentration that is inevitable in the Canadian economy, and which is a constant threat to competition. The health of small business depends, more than anything else, on a vigorous economy. In addition, the measurement of taxable income and the system to collect tax on it are particularly severe problems for smaller businesses. A tax on profits is disproportionately burdensome on a small business because retained earnings are often its principal source of capital. Finally, the complexity of the tax system creates a compliance cost that the small business is least able to afford.

In making suggestions in this area, we are aware that there is disagreement about the impact of tax changes on savings and investment. Most observers agree that investment is determined by perceptions of future risk-return relationships rather than by short-term tax changes. We also recognize the argument that changes to spur investment may be less effective when applied to an industrial economy that from 1975 up to at least the first quarter of 1977 was operating at less than 85% of capacity. However, we view tax change as a long-term attempt to alter permanently the risk-reward balance rather than to cure short-term problems. For this reason, our remarks are directed to possible changes in the basic structure of taxation and, in particular, to changes that will reverse the existing bias against equity investment and toward the institutionalization of savings. Several of the witnesses we heard made suggestions for new deductions or allowances designed to encourage or stimulate either small business or business generally. As our opening remarks in this section indicate, however, we think more is required. We decided, therefore, to invite a reconsideration of two fundamental features of the tax system. Specifically, we ask whether capital gains taxation is worthwhile and also whether it is appropriate to tax business income at the time it is now taxed.

We acknowledge that the two ideas discussed here are radical. They would have far-reaching economic effects, including possibly profound consequences for government revenue, which would have to be compensated for by reductions in expenditure or new taxes, or both, some of which would be extremely painful. We realize that the recommendations that follow may not be the best way to meet the shortfall in investment or may not be feasible for a variety of reasons. Nevertheless, we think the problem is so important that study and debate on the issues must be started so that changes of whatever nature are effected as soon as possible. We do not regard these recommendations as definitive but as an attempt to highlight the issues involved and to give our best efforts at a solution to them. If there is critical reaction to these proposals, we hope that it will not be so much to refute or criticize them as to propose alternative solutions to this important problem.

Capital Gains Taxation

Canada began to tax capital gains in 1972 because Parliament accepted the argument that it was unfair to tax ordinary income fully and exempt capital gains. This is a perfectly reasonable argument on grounds of equity, although it was not carried to its logical conclusion, for only half of capital gains are taxable. In addition, the kind of capital gain that most people expect to enjoy at some time (that realized on the sale of a "principal residence") is exempt altogether.

Estimated yields from the tax on capital gains rose from $54 million in 1972 to $235 million in 1976, slightly less than half of which was paid by corporations. These are very modest sums indeed, especially when compared with the total federal tax revenues of $32.4 billion in 1976/77. It is true that the stock market has been depressed for most of the period in which the capital gains tax has been in existence and that the yield from the tax should increase if the market becomes more buoyant (the extent to which the existence of the capital gains tax is responsible for the depressed market is a matter for considerable argument). However, amendments to the Income Tax Act, including the decision to exempt the first $1,000 of capital gains, dividend and interest income (previously the exemption applied only to dividends and interest) will erode the capital gains tax base further.

In exchange for a relatively small sum in tax revenue and a partial move toward more equity, Canada's tax system was made much more complex and expensive to operate. The question is, was it worth it? We do not think so. There is no reason to expect that the capital gains tax will ever make a significant contribution to the government's tax revenues. It certainly will not do so while the Canadian economy remains in its present depressed state, and the existence of the tax is one depressing factor that the economy can ill afford at this time. The design of the capital gains tax ensured that it would do little in terms of equity, and the most recent amendments to the tax law are a further step backward in this sense. The result is a complicated and costly addition to the tax system and a disincentive to business investment, with little compensating benefit.

Abolition of the capital gains tax would be worthwhile because it would simplify the tax system at a small cost in revenue and equity and, in addition, contribute to a better investment climate in Canada. That the latter is desirable, indeed necessary, cannot be doubted.

Taxation of Business Income

Business income, it should be noted, is not the same as corporate income because many businesses are not incorporated. Also, many corporations have income, such as investment income and capital gains, which is not business income. The distinction between business income and corporate income is important conceptually, though perhaps less so quantitatively. We will return to the distinction later but for the moment will discuss corporate income as though it is the same as business income.

If corporate income is taxed, a tax system must face the problem of whether and, if so, how to tax dividends because, of course, dividends are distributions of corporate income. If dividends are also taxed in the hands of the shareholders who receive them there is double taxation of the same income because the corporation is only an intermediary.

Before 1972 Canada ameliorated this double taxation in several ways. First, although dividend recipients were required to take dividends into income and to calculate tax at the appropriate personal rates on total income, they were then allowed to deduct from tax payable a dividend tax credit amounting to 20% of the net dividend. Secondly, corporations were allowed to pay a special additional tax of 15% or 20% on certain amounts of corporate income that had already borne the usual corporate tax at the time it was earned. The remaining 80% or 85% of these amounts could then be distributed without any further tax in the hands of the shareholders. Dividends paid by one corporation to another were generally not taxed at all but were of course taxed in the usual way when eventually paid out to individual shareholders. In this rough and ready fashion, shareholders receiving dividends were compensated for the tax that had been paid by the corporation at the point where the income was first earned.

Among other changes, the reform of the Canadian tax system in 1972 attempted to make the dividend tax credit system more precise, so that corporate income was taxed in the hands of individual shareholders at their appropriate personal rates, with a full credit for the tax paid by the corporation at the time the income was earned. The special 15% and 20% tax elections were abolished or confined to corporate income earned before 1972. The corporate tax system is more complicated than this brief explanation implies, partly because it must also deal with the problem of capital gains earned by corporations and subsequently distributed as dividends. The point of interest in terms of this discussion is that there is not really any longer a tax on corporate income as such. Corporations do indeed pay tax on income as they earn it, but this tax is really an advance payment on behalf of the shareholders. As a corporation pays dividends the corporate tax previously paid is, in effect, refunded or credited against the tax that those shareholders resident in Canada are then required to pay on the dividends. Non-resident shareholders are subject to an additional withholding tax of 15% or 25%, but they are normally able to credit this withholding tax against the tax they will pay in their own countries on their total income, including their Canadian dividends.

It is worth observing at this point that the "gross-up and credit" procedure by which corporate tax is passed through to dividend recipients has steadily become both more arbitrary and more generous to shareholders. Originally, a dividend recipient would "gross-up" his dividend by one-third, include that enlarged sum in his income, calculate his personal tax, and then deduct from tax payable the amount by which he grossed up the dividend, that is, one-third of the net dividend he received. On the assumption that the corporation had originally paid a tax of 25% on the income it earned, the gross-up and credit formula was thought to be very close to neutral; the aggregate of the credits to resident shareholders neither exceeded nor fell short of the amount of tax paid by the corporation on the income out of which the dividend was paid.

To the extent that combined federal and provincial corporation tax rates were more or less than 25%, the gross-up and credit procedure either failed to return to shareholders the total tax paid by the corporation or it returned too much. The credit is about right to the extent that the dividend is paid out of income that is taxed at the lower or "small business" rate of 25%, for example. The 5% reduction of tax on corporate profits earned from manufacturing or processing operations can result in an excess credit to shareholders of such companies.

The amendments to the Income Tax Act made in 1977 increased the gross-up and credit of one-third to 50%. Under this revision in the formula, resident shareholders other than those in the very highest personal income tax brackets will recover more through the dividend tax credit than the corporation will have paid in the first instance on their pro rata share of the corporation's income. Thus Canada has moved since 1971 from a position where there was some relief from the double taxation of corporate income to one where corporate source income may well be taxed less heavily than most other kinds of income.

We make no observations on what the proper level of taxation of corporate source income should be or on whether that kind of income should be taxed more or less heavily than other kinds of income. We ask only whether the *timing* of corporate taxation is appropriate. Should the tax system, as it does now, tax corporate income as it is earned and give that tax (or a somewhat greater or lesser amount) back to resident shareholders as they receive and pay tax on dividends? Or should corporate income perhaps be exempt from tax so long as it is employed in the business, with the tax becoming payable only as that income is distributed?

We favor the latter alternative for several reasons. For one thing, taxation on this basis should greatly assist small business because, if the retained earnings that are its chief source of expansion capital are not reduced by taxation, the aggregate amount available for reinvestment will be increased substantially. Secondly, and this applies to the profits of large as well as small businesses, profits are not properly available for either private or public consumption so long as they are productively employed in business. The figures we reported earlier in this chapter show dramatically the need for increased investment, and that the share that should be provided by retained corporate profits will simply not be available. A change in the tax system to alter the timing of the taxation of retained corporate profits would meet the problem squarely.

In addition, inflation has undermined in a most fundamental way the art of income measurement. Because reported profits in many industries are illusory, the effective corporate tax rate is very much higher than the apparent rate. We do not believe that the accounting profession or anyone else will be able to devise a means of discounting for inflation that will produce a fairer figure for taxable income, if only because inflation affects different businesses in different ways. The problem is not one of accounting, as many seem to assume. Rather, the problem is that the unit of measurement, money, which is what the accountants have to work with, has become an unreliable indicator of value. Recognizing, in a very limited way, the inflation problem, the 1977 Income Tax Act amendments granted a 3% inventory deduction to compensate, in some degree, for the effects of inflation and illusory inventory profits. This approach, in our opinion, is a mere palliative as well as a further complication in the income tax system.

The fundamental point is that it is no longer possible to measure business income with sufficient precision for tax purposes and, equally important, in a way that can be applied fairly to all businesses. There can be no equity in a tax system when the concept that is at the root of the system, income, means different things depending on the kind of activity that gives rise to that income.

Another reason for arguing for a tax deferral for business income is that the income tax provisions determining what business income is, combined with those applying to corporations as such, are by far the most lengthy and complex in the Income Tax Act. If it is possible to devise a tax applying instead to corporate distributions it should be possible to simplify the statute. We do not pretend that we have foreseen and worked out solutions to all the technical problems that would be encountered in such a change. There is no doubt that the change would be difficult, at least in the transition stage.

All the same, anyone with an understanding of the present Income Tax Act will acknowledge that it is easily the most complex of any on the statute books. The resources devoted by businessmen and their professional advisers to understanding and complying with it have never, to our knowledge, been calculated, but there can be no doubt that the compliance cost is formidable. In addition, the bulk of the administrative burden and cost to government of operating the law surely derives from those parts of the Act that deal with the taxation of business and corporate income. The costs are not confined to the costs of operating the Departments of Finance, Justice and National Revenue and the salaries and fees paid to tax advisers in the private sector. There is also the cost that society incurs in having so many of its best minds engaged in the sterile and unproductive task of tax compliance. In addition to the other reasons for reconsidering the way in which business or corporate income is taxed, we think that the probable savings in compliance and administrative costs would make such a reform worthwhile.

There are some serious problems in any revision of the tax system along the lines we suggest, and we will describe briefly the most obvious of them.

First, if corporate income tax as we now know it were abolished there would be a severe effect on government revenue. Revenue from the corporation income tax was $6.42 billion for 1976/77, or nearly 20% of total federal tax revenue. This figure is overstated to the extent that the offsetting dividend tax credit reduces the revenue from the personal income tax.

We do not know of any way to predict what effect abolition of the present corporate tax would have on dividend payments. Since abolition of the tax would roughly double the amount of profits available for dividends, one could reasonably expect some increase in dividend payments, and this of course would mean an increase in personal tax, which would tend to offset the loss of revenue from the corporate tax. An increase in dividend payments, together with the fact that the corporate tax had been abolished, would almost certainly produce a marked improvement in business and investment prospects, and this would be reflected in higher stock values and an increase in returns from the capital gains tax (if that tax were retained).

As against this, business could see the abolition of the present corporate tax principally as a source of expansion capital and also as a way of reducing prices. Both objectives are highly desirable in themselves, especially now when investment capital seems to be shunning Canada and when Canadian industry is becoming less and less competitive. If the tax savings were employed chiefly in these ways, however, government revenue would probably drop sharply.

While it is easy to say that it is impossible for a government suddenly to reduce its tax revenue by 19%, it is worth recalling that total federal tax revenue *increased* by more than 350% in the ten years from 1967 to 1977. The immediate revenue loss that would result from even a sudden change in the manner of taxing corporate income does not look quite so unmanageable when it is viewed against the rate at which the government's total tax revenue has increased in recent years. Nevertheless, any replacement of the present tax on corporate income with one on corporate distributions would have to be phased in gradually. At the same time, reform of the corporate tax on the lines we suggest may well justify reduction or elimination of some other tax concessions.

Taxation has been described as the art of plucking the largest amount of feathers from the goose with the least amount of hissing. A tax on corporations is much more attractive politically than one on individuals because, in our electoral system, corporations have only a limited ability to hiss. But the political attractiveness of a corporation tax may well be one of the strongest reasons for doing away with it. Many people are saying that the state's appetite for tax revenue will have to be curbed if the economy is to thrive. If that is so, a good way of injecting a necessary and healthy discipline into government finance may be to make tax collection politically more painful than it has been.

A tax on corporate distributions could not be expressed as a withholding tax because the rate of tax would have to be considerably higher than the 15% rate now provided for in the international tax treaties to which Canada is a party. It is not realistic to expect a wholesale and early revision of those treaties. The distribution tax would have to be imposed on resident Canadian corporations, but be based on amounts distributed or deemed to be distributed to shareholders, not on income earned by the corporations. This would not preclude the granting to resident Canadians of a tax credit (with or without a form of "grossing-up") based on the amounts received by them from such corporations.

The gain in simplicity we hope for would be lost if dividend distributions had to be analyzed according to the kind of corporate income out of which the dividends were paid. For this reason, we think the tax should apply simply to corporate distributions. But this would mean, for example, that capital gains of corporations would be fully taxed on distribution (even if the capital gains tax were otherwise abolished). All corporate distributions to shareholders (probably including stock dividends, but not true repayments of capital) would provoke the distribution tax, and all distributions would carry the right to whatever dividend tax credit was decided upon. The system suggested here is somewhat less symmetrical than the present one, but we frankly prefer simplicity to symmetry. The price of a tax deferral on retained profits is a certain roughness round the edges.

The kind of tax change discussed here would stimulate a search for avoidance techniques, in particular, ways to "strip" corporate surplus without incurring the distribution tax. In all probability, however, any such avoidance techniques would be new variations on an old theme. The tax authorities conquered the "surplus stripping" problem even before "tax reform" in 1972. We are not therefore worried about tax avoidance. Indeed, the simplicity of a distribution tax system may well make it easier to deal with the kind of schemes that might be devised to escape the tax. There would no doubt have to be a number of rules "deeming" corporations to have distributed profits in certain circumstances.

Income other than business income received by at least some, if not all, corporations would have to be taxed as received rather than as distributed; otherwise there would be excessive tax deferral through the use of holding companies. The law may have to "deem" an amount equal to corporate non-business income (including capital gains) to be distributed in the year it is received. An alternative would be a tax on all or most corporate non-business income at a rate high enough to ensure that it was in fact distributed in the year it was received.

Distinction between corporate income earned from active business and that earned from a passive investment by a corporation creates problems of definition and also requires an allocation of expenses between at least those two categories of income. These are by no means insignificant problems but, again, many of the difficulties could be sidestepped through "rough justice" rules. For example, if a corporation's gross non-business income did not exceed, say, 10% of total income, its total income could be treated as business income. Most corporations in active commercial or industrial business with only small or occasional amounts of rental or interest income, for instance, would not have to concern themselves with the provisions designed to force distribution of non-business income.

Although a tax credit, combined with a technique to force distribution of investment income, should work well with many holding companies and other intermediaries, it may be necessary to restrict the credit in some cases. For example, tax-exempt intermediaries such as pension and retirement funds could be denied the tax credit so that they would, in effect, be taxed on their dividend income. It seems clear from the figures we cited earlier in this chapter that the tax system has been generous to these plans, with the result that investment flows have been distorted. If it is desirable to reduce the attractiveness of these investment vehicles, a denial of a tax credit may be a better way of doing it than a restriction on the deductibility of contributions made to those funds. It might also be necessary to restrict or deny the tax credit to some other financial intermediaries such as mutual funds and insurance companies. Selective restrictions of this kind would also reduce the revenue loss to government.

The income of unincorporated businesses in Canada is not large in aggregate (7.4% of total reported personal income in 1974), because most business, large and small, is carried on through the corporate form. The question arises as to how non-corporate business income is to be taxed if corporate income is exempted. One alternative would be to let it be taxed as income in the hands of the proprietors and partners, as it is now, reasoning that most of the remaining unincorporated businesses would then go through the relatively simple step of incorporation to take advantage of the new corporate tax regime. Another alternative would be to allow unincorporated business to elect to have the corporate tax rules apply to them even though they did not actually incorporate. Again, it might be simpler if professionals and farmers, for example, were allowed to compute their income on the cash basis, as they could do before 1972. Provisions designed to put unincorporated businesses on a footing roughly equivalent to corporations would be preferable to elaborate ones that attempt to obtain a very precise equality of treatment.

Chapter 12

Corporate Ownership, Control and Management

Introduction

In this chapter, we look at some of the features of large corporations as legal entities. Among the matters discussed are the legal structure of the corporation, the roles played by the shareholders and directors and assigned to them by law, our views on these roles, various suggestions for structural reform of corporations, and conflicts of interest within the corporation.

Three fundamental statutory elements—shareholders, directors and officers/managers—form the framework of major Canadian corporations. These components are generally distinct, but they can overlap. Within the corporation, each group has both a legal role and a role that has evolved through custom and practice and is somewhat different from that implied by the legal model. The lines between the theoretical and the practical are not clear, however, and at both levels there are some links among the three groups. Each group will be examined, particularly from the aspect of corporate control, which we consider to be central to any realistic discussion of corporate concentration.

The comments that follow should be considered mainly in relation to the major Canadian corporations, as it is there we find the "major concentrations of corporate power in Canada". While some of what we say may well be appropriate to most other widely held corporations, we concentrate on the very large firms.

Shareholders' Rights

The holders of voting shares in corporations are granted by statute certain rights regarding the corporation's business and affairs. In the large, widely held Canadian corporation, it is difficult for an individual shareholder (except one with a significant or controlling position in the company) to exercise his rights in a meaningful way, because the voice of any single shareholder is normally so faint as to be inaudible. In this context major corporations are very much like other large institutions: their very size and structure seems to induce, or at the least contribute to, a feeling of alienation, powerlessness and apathy on the part of the individual.

It has long been recognized that small shareholders rarely assert their rights in most major corporations. They do have certain rights, however, some of which are relevant to the question of control of the corporation, in particular, the right to elect the directors. The outcome of the election is invariably predetermined, because the process of nomination is in the hands of the incumbent management and board, as is the proxy machinery. Those in control have a great advantage over any other shareholder because they are required by law to solicit proxies, and these are almost always returned in management's favor. A 1976 American study entitled *Constitutionalizing the Corporation* (by the Corporate Accountability Research Group) analyzed directorial elections from 1956 through 1973 in companies that were required to file data with the Securities and Exchange Commission. The elections of directors that went unopposed, and where the slate proposed by the incumbent management and board was automatically elected, ranged from 98.1% in 1958 and 1961, to 99.7% in 1973. The elections (the vast majority were uncontested) in which management retained control of the board ranged from 99.7% in 4 of the years, to a high of 99.9% in 10 of the years. While to our knowledge no comparable statistics for Canada are available, we believe a Canadian survey would reveal similar results.

The individual shareholder's other management-related rights are in some cases novel and largely untested; in other cases they are of longer standing but generally unused, and in almost all cases they are unlikely to be exercised without some support from other interested shareholders. These other rights vary from the relatively new opportunity to make a "shareholder's proposal" to the right to request the appointment of an inspector to investigate the company's affairs. But these and other rights would be exercised only in unusual situations: they cannot be considered so central to the regular government of the corporation as to permit, encourage or lead to a serious level of shareholder participation. The undeniable (and generally undenied) fact is that management usually holds the power in the corporation, save where there is a large or controlling shareholder, who will then wield power (often through the board) to a degree determined by both his investment and his inclination.

Types of Shareholders

The three principal types of shareholders in public (by which we mean widely held) companies are individuals, institutions and corporations. Each of these types of shareholders will normally have different interests and objectives, and therefore may be expected to act differently as shareholders.

Individual Shareholders

Individual shareholders are people who hold direct investments in public companies beneficially. The size of their holdings may vary from just one share to many, although generally most individual shareholdings are small. For example, Bell Canada has about 250,000 shareholders, more than any other Canadian corporation. Almost two-thirds of these shareholders hold fewer than 100 Bell shares each.

As a rule, when an individual has large holdings in a company, they are held through an intermediary, such as a holding company, or through a trust arrangement. This may be done sometimes because of a concern for continuity in the event of the death of the holder, sometimes because of tax or other financial considerations. Since individuals with large blocks of stock in public companies behave very much like corporate and institutional shareholders, the remainder of this section will refer only to investors holding small amounts of stock.

Individual shareholders do not normally take an active part in the affairs of a company. Their function in the company's internal processes is limited to voting their stock, usually by proxy and usually in support of management. They cannot easily influence either the directors or the management of a company to a course of action contrary to that proposed. Their power is exercised in the form of proxy votes solicited by and delivered to management, and in this sense is clearly biased in favor of management. Effective action for individual shareholders who disagree with management's proposed actions may involve a proxy fight, and this requires adequate financing. As a result, therefore, while support of management by these shareholders is expressed by the delivery of proxies, lack of support tends to be expressed simply by the sale of the stock. If management has committed an act that the shareholder alleges is improper, there may be some recourse at law, if the shareholder chooses, and is able, to exercise his or her rights.

Although institutional shareholdings have been increasing, individual shareholdings are still substantial. From April 1975 to March 1976, Toronto Stock Exchange trading for individual investors made up 77.29% of all orders and 48.59% of the total dollar value. Institutional investors were responsible for 14.19% of the total but 43.31% of the dollar value traded. (The balance was accounted for by transactions by member firms of the TSE on behalf of another member, affiliate or broker.)

Trading completed for institutions tended to concentrate on the 100 most active stocks to a greater extent than did trading for individuals: 59.23% of the dollar value for institutional trading, compared with 35.96% for individuals, was directed toward the 100 most active stocks. It might be concluded, therefore, that the individual investor makes a significant contribution to the liquidity of less active stocks (generally the smaller companies).

Concern has been expressed by some that the level of aggregate individual shareholdings is dropping (to some extent this is confirmed by the T.S.E. statistics). One of the results of individuals holding a greater proportion of shares would be less concentration of ownership of corporations by large or institutional shareholders. Some corporations have established stock purchase plans to encourage their employees to acquire an equity interest in the firm. One common type requires the company to make a contribution to the plan in an amount equal to that made by any employee who wishes to participate. Shares of the company are either purchased on the open market by the plan's trustee or issued afresh and held for participating employees. Our impression is that generally such arrangements have been of very little interest to the great majority of the employees of companies which have established such plans.

A number of proposals have been advanced to permit the use in Canada of some kind of "Registered Employee Stock Ownership Plan". The United States has adopted such a plan, sometimes known as the Kelso Plan, involving a trust for all employees which purchases newly issued stock from the company at current market value. The stock is paid for with money borrowed by the trust from a financier, such as a bank, and the company guarantees the repayment of the loan. The company then makes periodic payments (which, for the plan to be successful, must be tax deductible) to the trust, which repays its loan with those funds. Periodically the shares held by the trust are allocated to the employees.

It is argued that a plan of this kind would produce more widespread ownership of corporations by their employees, and, assuming shares were distributed only to Canadians, would thereby decrease the amount of foreign ownership. It is clear that the plan as proposed would have many implications, not least on tax revenue, since its efficacy depends on participating corporations being able to deduct for tax purposes contributions which are not now deductible from income. The plan involves a dilution of the equity of non-employee shareholders (who, unlike the employees, will have paid for their shares) and requires the general public to subsidize a portion of the contributions to the employees' trust by permitting corporate payments to be tax deductible. It also discriminates in favor of employees of public corporations vis-à-vis employees of unincorporated businesses, which cannot participate, public sector employees and employees who wish to put their savings elsewhere. For these reasons, and also because we do not discern any appreciable interest on the part of employees in those plans now in operation, we are not prepared to recommend that this new plan be adopted in Canada.

Institutional Shareholders

Institutional shareholders include insurance companies, pension funds, mutual funds, banks, credit unions, trust companies and other organizations acting either as trustees or as owners in their own rights. Institutions are becoming important participants in the equity market and they hold a substantial number of the shares of many large Canadian companies. The size of their holdings naturally varies, but is normally much larger than the average individual holding. Some institutions, such as banks, are constrained by law to a maximum percentage beneficial holding of the common stock of any single corporation. In addition, their purchases of shares of corporations may be legally limited depending upon the dividend record and other performance measures of the corporations in question. But these legal constraints do not have as significant an influence on investment policies or on the practices and the activities of institutions as shareholders, as do their investment objectives. Most institutions prefer to hold assets that are readily marketable, although because the size of Canadian markets is limited, they often accept lack of liquidity in their holdings.

Institutional investors are almost always inactive shareholders. They usually give management their proxies, but if they disapprove of management or of corporate decisions, and their expressed concerns go unanswered, they may well sell their stock rather than oppose management, for a proxy fight involves risk, inconvenience, considerable cost and bad publicity. The least costly action is to sell where possible, and, when the controversial issue has passed into history, to make a fresh judgment as to whether the shares of the particular corporation are again an acceptable investment.

We have not considered seriously the idea of imposing on registered, but non-beneficial, shareholders statutory obligations that would require all discretionary rights attached to the shares to be passed through to the beneficial owners, because we do not think the idea is practical. One of the results of such a provision would be a significant cost of communication that would inevitably be borne by the beneficial owner. At present an interested shareholder can make such arrangements and the ordinary laws of trusts and contract will apply. With some institutions, such as pension funds, it is extremely difficult even to identify the "beneficial owners", let alone have them exercise discretionary rights. Some fund managers or trustees now insist on acting only on the direction of the beneficial owner (e.g., in some takeover bids). We have found no evidence that professional managers are abusing the trust placed in them by their investors, and for that reason, as well as for the other reasons noted, we think it unnecessary for us to recommend new regulation in this area.

Corporate Shareholders

Corporate shareholders (other than institutions) may be operating companies, or investment and holding companies, and they may be private, or public companies. Both operating companies and holding companies tend to act as shareholders in similar ways, their behavior depending largely on the nature and the size of their investment. The distinction in the present context between a public corporate shareholder (such as Argus or Power) and a private one (such as Ravelston or Gelco) is that a public company is owned by a large number of investors, while a private company is owned by a very few people (See Chapter 7). Private companies tend more to be the alter egos of individual shareholders.

Often when a corporation makes a large non-portfolio investment in a company it will seek representation on the board of directors, and may take an active interest in management. Disagreement with management decisions does not automatically result in an attempt to dispose of the investment, for a number of reasons. The investment may be sufficiently large to give ultimate control to the investor and thereby permit it to effect management changes. The investment may be sufficiently large that it is difficult to find a single buyer, and large holdings usually cannot be put on the market without having some effect on the market price. Even where an investment is not large enough to provide control, it might secure support from other shareholders; the corporate investor can provide a rallying point for dissident shareholders. Finally, the investment may still look better than available alternatives.

Types of Corporate Control

The legal rights of shareholders, and the different kinds of shareholders we have described, must be considered in the context of corporate control. Control may be considered and analyzed from several points of view. Our concern here is with the ways in which different categories of shareholdings may affect control of major publicly held corporations. Some examples are given to illustrate the different categories, but it must be remembered that corporate life is not static, and circumstances may propel a company from one category of control to another.

Absolute Control

The first category, absolute control, describes the corporation controlled by one person, corporation or institution (or a group of persons acting in concert) through ownership of all or virtually all the voting stock of the corporation. In the absence of any arrangements made to the contrary, the owners would have total influence and control over the operations of the corporation. This is a situation common to major Canadian corporations. For instance, most of the companies on our list for 1975 of the 100 largest non-financial corporations (See Chapter 2) have wholly owned subsidiaries. As well, 22% of the corporations on our list are wholly owned subsidiaries of foreign-owned corporations.

An illustration of a large Canadian firm wholly owned by a foreign firm would be Chrysler Canada Ltd. (8th on our list), owned by Chrysler Corporation of Detroit. Examples of the large Canadian firm with a large wholly owned subsidiary would be Genstar Limited and its subsidiary, BACM Limited, or The Molson Companies Limited and its subsidiary, Beaver Lumber Company Limited. In those situations, the parent can exercise total control over the subsidiary, although the subsidiary may be a major corporation in its own right. The parent can select the board of the subsidiary, arrange its financing, and control its business activities by selecting its management. Subject to any other relevant considerations the parent could transform the legally separate but operationally integrated subsidiary into a division of the parent and the subsidiary, as a legal entity, would vanish.

Majority Control

The term "majority control" is used when a corporation is controlled by one person (or a group of persons acting in concert) owning over 50% but less than all of the voting stock of the corporation. This majority control situation signifies virtually the same degree of dominance and influence over the operation of a subsidiary as does total ownership of stock. The presence of outside minority interests (supplemented sometimes by corporate policy considerations) imposes some legal restraints on the freedom and flexibility of the parent in dealing with the subsidiary's affairs. There will normally be found in this case constraints imposed by the legal requirements involving the rights of minority shareholders. Many large Canadian firms are in this category: 26% on our list of the 100 largest non-financial firms are controlled in this way by corporate parents. As with the first category, many Canadian corporations themselves have subsidiaries that are partly, but not wholly, owned.

An example of majority control is that exercised by Power Corporation of Canada, Limited, over the affairs of Laurentide Financial Corporation Ltd. Power Corporation controls, directly or indirectly, about 58% of the voting stock of Laurentide (itself one of Canada's major sales finance corporations). The board of directors of Laurentide is selected with the tacit approval of Power, and although Laurentide arranges its own financing, major transactions are subject to the approval of the parent. While Laurentide has its own separate and independent authority on day-to-day operations, broad policy is determined in conjunction with Power.

Minority Control

In a "minority control" situation a corporation is "controlled" by one person (a group of persons acting in concert) owning less than 50% of the voting stock, but owning more voting stock than any other single shareholder or group of shareholders acting together. This situation is inherently less stable than that of majority control, since control depends upon the continued relative passiveness of other shareholders and on the controller's ability to obtain their proxy support. The length of time the minority block has been held and the force of personality of the controller may also be important factors contributing to effective minority control. Minority shareholding situations involving Power Corporation and Argus Corporation Limited are discussed in detail in Chapter 7.

Some new information on the extent and significance of minority control of corporations is provided by a research report prepared for the Commission by S. D. Berkowitz, Yehuda Kotowitz, Leonard Waverman *et al.*, and entitled *Enterprise Structure and Corporate Concentration*. Analyses were made of data relating to the connections among 5,305 companies, all of which were connected in one way or another to 361 leading Canadian corporations. Intercorporate ownership, direct and indirect, was identified and traced, as well as connections through directors and officers of the "owning" firms serving on the boards of directors or executive committees of corporations which their firms owned in whole or in part. After testing the effects of various degrees of direct and indirect ownership and of the number of directors and officers serving on subordinate boards, the authors assembled tables of interrelated firms which made possible comparison of "enterprises" of groups of companies under a common control by the usual 50% ownership definition of control, and then by alternative definitions based on 25% or more ownership, or 15% or more ownership, plus 3 interlocking directors or officers as described above.

The most important results of the study are stated as follows:

The most striking result of our study is the low degree of leverage in Canadian intercorporate ownership: very few corporations appear to control others by holding minority shares. Moreover, most ownership ties emanating from non-financial institutions involved 100% ownership. By contrast, fairly extensive ownership leverage is shown by two large conglomerates, Argus Corporation Ltd.... and Power Corporation of Canada... as well as financial institutions (e.g., trust companies) which frequently have significant, though less than a 50%, share of holding companies. The owned holding companies, in turn, do not generally exhibit high leverage and appear to own at least 50%—and in many cases 100%—of the shares of the companies controlled by them.

Even in those cases where minority share ownership is associated with control by our definition, relatively little ownership leverage is used.... Very little difference... in the composition of enterprises is exhibited when their definition is broadened from 25% to 15% ownership.... This is true whether the management tie is defined by directorship/officership or by executive board membership. In fact only very few substantial changes in major enterprises occur in either of these cases.

We were also interested in the extent to which the concentration ratios of enterprises in different manufacturing industries were increased by extending the usual 50% ownership test of control to include minority control as identified above. The general result may be summed up in two sentences. Changes in ownership definitions affected at most only 8 out of 153 manufacturing industries. Secondly, the weighted average of the percentage of total sales made by the top four firms in each of the 153 manufacturing industries was increased only from 50.35% to 50.66% by taking these selected definitions of minority control into account.

From the specific cases we have examined and the general analysis in the Berkowitz *et al.* study, we conclude that, while minority control is conspicuous in some large corporate groups, such as Argus, it is not very important in increasing the extent of major concentrations of power within Canadian industries.

We have described three kinds of control situations, but it must be pointed out that these categories are not exhaustive. The ingenuity of businessmen and their advisers ensures that there will be mechanisms for controlling corporations other than those listed above. The use of intricate capital structures, voting trust arrangements, pooling agreements, shareholder agreements, loan agreements, supply contracts, complex debt instruments, and other devices adds to the variety of the ways and means by which corporations may be controlled.

Voting Rights

There is one variation on the mechanisms of control that does deserve some brief comment here. The use of non-voting or multiple-voting stock gives more influence or control to the holders of certain stock than would be true if each share carried the right to only one vote. While new issues of multiple-voting stock are now uncommon, the relatively widespread existence of non-voting stock has prompted some criticism. Argus and Power are, again, good examples:

1. Argus equity stock is made up of voting common shares and non-voting participating preference shares. The Ravelston Corporation's holding of Argus stock consists almost entirely of common shares, which though representing only about 31% of total equity carry 61.5% of the total votes attached to shares of Argus and thus give Ravelston majority control.

2. In contrast, Power Corporation owns about 53% of the equity stock of Argus (apart from the senior class A and class B preferred shares). However, most of its stock is non-voting: in fact, Power has only 25% of the total votes attached to Argus shares. While this is a substantial percentage, it does not give Power even minority control since majority control is held by Ravelston.

3. As of June 30, 1977, the Desmarais and Parisien family interests (through intermediaries) owned only about 18% of the equity stock of Power Corporation. However, this holding included 97.6% of the participating preferred shares, which carry 10 votes per share (as a result of a decision in 1928). As a result they had about 53% of the total votes attached to the shares of Power.

4. Power owns or controls, directly or indirectly, about 40% of the equity stock (composed of several classes of common shares) of The Investors Group. Some of the Investors equity stock carries no votes, but most of the shares held by Power and its affiliated companies do, so that Power controls about 70% of the total votes attached to the shares of Investors.

The use of non-voting and multiple-voting stock has been examined from time to time by authorities responsible for administering corporate law in Canada as well as by the stock exchanges and securities commissions. The consensus of these groups seems to be that the presence of non-voting or multiple-voting stock is not a danger to the investing public.

We are content to accept their judgment in this matter. If minority and institutional shareholders have confidence in the management and in the controlling interest and wish to acquire non-voting equity stock, they are frequently able to do so at a price substantially below that of the voting stock. Public companies are required to disclose the voting rights attached to particular classes of shares. Such disclosure satisfies concerns for the interests of purchasers of non-voting shares.

The Role of Directors

We alluded earlier to the role that directors perform in the management of large Canadian companies. Their activities should be considered in relation to their legal powers and responsibilities. While there are some minor differences in wording, most Canadian company law statutes are similar to the Canada Business Corporations Act, which stipulates that "the directors shall manage the business and affairs of a corporation". (However, the newly passed Manitoba Corporations Act states that "the directors of a corporation shall (a) exercise the powers of the corporation directly or indirectly through the employees and agents of the corporation; and (b) direct the management of the business and affairs of the corporation.")

In practice, the directors of most large Canadian companies are selected by senior management in consultation with the board (or by the controlling shareholder, where there is one), and the shareholders at the annual meeting almost invariably ratify that selection by electing those persons as directors. The directors then re-appoint the senior management of the company, and, of course, it is the senior management and its staff that supervise day-to-day business operations. In a large corporation that is itself wholly owned by another firm, it is the parent organization that selects the board and appoints management. The board in that situation is almost always composed entirely of employees, and rarely exercises any independent power.

No one expects the directors of a large, modern corporation to "manage the business" in the way in which directors of a small or closely held company might, but the extent of their legal duties is not yet altogether clear. The courts in Canada have not had many opportunities to comment upon the precise nature of the obligations of directors of large corporations to "manage the business", but it is reasonable to expect that the scope of their legal mandate encompasses the supervision of the broad direction of the business, and that they normally accomplish this by appointing and overseeing senior management.

We do not suggest that directors are without any real power themselves, either legally or in practice. They perform the useful function of rendering advice and counsel to senior management, and the infrequent (but when the occasion arises, important) act of replacing a chief executive officer. In addition, the law vests in the directors control of a number of important functions, the exercise of which the directors cannot delegate. For example, under the Canada Business Corporations Act, only the directors have the power to submit to shareholders matters legally requiring their approval, to fill a vacancy in the office of auditor, to settle the manner and terms of an issue of securities, to declare dividends, approve takeover bid circulars and approve financial statements.

Canadian corporate statutes, in describing the role of the board, are worded in a very general way. Judicial decisions in this area, at the senior court levels, are infrequent and it is difficult to deduce general principles from cases turning on particular facts. We recognize, however, that with our complex society and the growing awareness by groups in society of the impact that corporations have on them, there may be more frequent opportunities for the courts to assess and comment upon the functions of directors. In the 1974 *Canadian Aero Service* case Chief Justice Laskin of the Supreme Court of Canada, in remarking upon the fiduciary aspect of a director's duty, stated that "the general standards of loyalty, good faith and avoidance of a conflict of duty and self-interest to which the conduct of a director or senior officer must conform, must be tested in each case by many factors which it would be reckless to attempt to enumerate exhaustively."

The Canada Business Corporations Act and other Canadian statutes now impose upon directors a higher standard of diligence and care than existed at common law, and we expect that there will be a growing body of corporate jurisprudence, defining and delineating more fully the duties and the rights of directors.

In the course of our hearings, we have studied and read much about boards of directors of major Canadian corporations. Naturally it is not possible to talk definitively about what all boards do or do not do, because circumstances among corporations differ, and there are, within a certain range, varying degrees of activity by boards. Boards may "do" something by just existing; their very presence can be a check on an overzealous management. Boards have been known to act firmly in crises. Subject to these observations, it is possible to generalize that many Canadian boards, and certainly those of large corporations, fulfill mainly an advisory and confirmatory role. They do not normally "make" decisions but confirm and ratify the decisions made by senior management, and they are a source of advice and counsel when it is sought by management. They also perform the tasks the law has delegated only to them, even though the initiative for the performance of the task may come from management. Typically, Canadian directors spend only a modest amount of time on the corporation's affairs: most have their own businesses to run and many serve on several boards, thus limiting the time they can devote to any one corporation's business. Where a director "represents" a controlling shareholder, however, he usually exhibits a much higher level of activity than he would otherwise.

Changes in the Directors' Role

We are conscious of a growing recognition by senior management and others that the contribution that might be made by boards and the significance to public corporations of the composition of boards are matters that have not been sufficiently considered in the past. There is a shift in attitudes: some corporations are beginning to expect more activity and responsibility from their directors. We view this trend as highly desirable, and we think it will be reinforced by several phenomena.

First, more and more people are becoming aware of the impact that corporations have on their lives. They will continue to demand that corporations be ever more responsive to legitimate public and shareholder needs. The board can be a valuable instrument in helping the corporation to be responsive.

Second, the public perception and understanding of big business could stand some improvement. Since the board of a corporation is very visible, some corporations, partly in their own self-interest and partly to broaden the sources of advice at the board level, are now taking steps to obtain more diversity of interests and backgrounds among the people serving on their boards.

Third, board members are coming to realize that failure to fulfill, in a meaningful way, the responsibilities vested in them by law may result in direct, personal exposure to law suits.

Fourth, managements, in their own self-interest, are seeing that the board can be a useful source of aid and assistance, and that more of the burdens of directing major corporations should properly be shared by the directors.

The Commission thinks that the board should not be expected to duplicate the role of the officers of the corporation: the board is not intended or designed to be, and should not try to be, a second level of management. But that does not mean that the board should be totally divorced from the function of management, or totally dependent on management for information. Directors are given the right and the responsibility of managing the business of the corporation, and, by practice and convention, this means directing the management of the corporation's business. To fulfill this obligation adequately, directors must be sufficiently knowledgeable about the corporation's affairs to ask management the right questions, and to be able to judge whether or not they are receiving the right answers. The role of the board should include the initiation of and participation in active discussion on issues of corporate policy (especially those that might reasonably be expected to come under some later public scrutiny). The role of the individual director should also include the initiation of and participation in such discussions, even though that may appear unsettling and unnecessary to management.

In short we see an expanded role for directors. Directors must monitor management: this is their duty in the interests of the corporation, and it will be in the best interests of all affected by the corporation. The responsibility flowing from the proper exercise of this function will require directors to spend more time on the affairs of the corporation than they normally do now. To advance the concerns of the corporation (and its shareholders) in a manner consistent with the interests of the community in which it functions, directors will have to be concerned with, and cognizant of, matters beyond those brought to the board's attention by management. The board should act as a check on the executive, be fully informed of the company's affairs, and be able to monitor the actions of management. Any other role for directors will be inadequate and will result in their being the "captives" of the management that selects them.

Recommendations

Several conclusions may be drawn from these comments:

First. Given the expanded role we envisage for directors, we think that boards and some board committees should be composed largely of persons drawn from outside the company. These "outside" directors would be persons who are not present or former officers or employees of the company or its parent or affiliates, and who are not closely related to any of the senior management. Also, they should not have a close contractual or advisory relationship with the company (including parent and affiliates) or management, such as would be the case with the company's outside counsel or its underwriter. They would then be much more likely to bring to the director's job a more independent critical and objective attitude than it is fair to expect from "inside" directors.

However, underwriters and legal counsel are frequently well qualified to fulfill the monitoring role of a director, even when they also act professionally for the company on whose board they sit. For one thing, financial and legal matters are subjects often dealt with at the board level. Secondly, underwriters and lawyers in active practice tend to develop a valuable critical sense and they are well placed to observe problems and situations comparable with those they will see as directors of a company. Finally, they will seldom be as dependent upon one company as a company officer will ordinarily be. It could sometimes be detrimental to treat underwriters, legal counsel and other professional advisers as "insiders" in the full sense, even though they are not truly "outsiders" either.

One way to resolve the problem would be to acknowledge that, while professional advisers will often be highly suitable as directors, they should not sit on the boards of companies with which they have a professional relationship. Companies should seek such directors not from the underwriting, legal and other firms which act for them, but from firms with which they do not normally deal. We hesitate to be categorical about this because many professionals may not be willing to serve as directors unless they can combine those duties with ordinary professional work for the company.

We are content to make the point that if professional advisers are not truly independent they cannot satisfy the ideal criteria of an outside director. In the inevitable balancing of "outside" and "inside" components of a board of directors, the anomalous position of professional advisers should be recognized. Where a substantial proportion of the directors are truly outsiders, there need be less concern over the presence of a director who is also in a professional relationship with the company. Where, however, the board is dominated by company officers or other insiders, more effort should be made to ensure that any professional advisers on the board do not also act for the company in a substantial way.

Because we believe the board should become a more meaningful institution, we disapprove of the practice (which, although slowly diminishing, is still very common) of placing large numbers of "insiders" on boards of large public companies. The board is readily able to obtain all the benefits of an officer's or adviser's knowledge and experience without also having him sit on the board, and the board is better able to perform its function with fewer of these "insiders" as part of the formal structure. On the other hand there is a real benefit in having a direct and continuous liaison between the board and management, and there should be no objection to the president's sitting on the board. For the same reason, and also to provide continuity and exposure, some companies may wish to have one, or perhaps two, other senior officers on the board. But beyond two or three at the top, we can see no advantage from having insiders on boards.

If a company is a wholly owned subsidiary there is much less reason for concern about the composition of its board. Many such subsidiaries operate, in effect, as branches or divisions of the parent company and, where such subsidiaries are small, then boards of directors are little more than a formality.

Where subsidiaries are sizable, and in particular when they are also foreign-owned, we think, however, that such boards should have outside members for the same reasons that apply to other large corporations.

Second. We believe that individuals should not sit on the boards of more than a very few publicly held companies. Directors usually have a full-time occupation, and we do not see how it would be possible to carry out the duties of a normally senior position while also performing the serious duties of director in more than a very few companies. There are exceptions, however, in the case of those people who are "professional" directors, or those who for some reason have the time to devote to more companies than might otherwise be considered reasonable.

Third. We see an augmented role for the audit committee of the corporation, in connection with transactions involving potential conflicts of interest among the directors, officers, major shareholders and the company. Audit committees were first introduced legislatively in Canada in the late 1960s, largely as a result of a series of well-publicized corporate failures, but many companies had established such committees before the law compelled them to do so. These committees are intended to fulfill a specific and somewhat limited role, but we think that they can properly be asked to do more. We return to this point later in this chapter.

Fourth. The directors should increase the direct contact they have with the corporation's independent auditors and its outside counsel for two reasons. First, the directors could obtain from these advisers additional information and clarification of factual aspects of corporate activities (and the auditors and lawyers should have no difficulty in participating in that kind of communication). Secondly (but only if the auditor or lawyer is not thereby placed in an untenable position of potential breach of duty to the corporation), a director could obtain the adviser's views and advice about corporate policies and transactions undertaken or proposed. In both cases this would be contact independent of management, and it should enhance the director's understanding of the implications of his or her part in the decision-making process. Access to the independent advisers should be direct, confidential if the director so chooses, and at the corporation's expense. If an adviser is unable, because of a potential conflict of duty, to provide the advice sought, the corporation should reimburse the director for any reasonable expense then incurred in seeking outside guidance.

A major consequence of these recommendations is that directors will have to devote considerable time to their duties, and that they will have to be paid enough to ensure that qualified people will accept the job. We recognize that many of the rewards of board membership are non-monetary but suggest that greater monetary rewards will be necessary if individuals are to perform the expanded duties expected of them.

It was suggested to us that directors should also have the assistance of some expert staff of their own. These would be employees of, and paid by, the corporation, but would be selected by and be responsible to the directors. The purpose would be to supplement the directors' knowledge of technical or complex matters, and to do so by a mechanism divorced from corporate management itself, so that the directors would not have to rely entirely on the explanations provided by management. We think that our recommendations can be implemented without such a change. In any case some experience should be accumulated with other changes before consideration is given to this more far-reaching idea.

Diversity on Boards of Directors

If, as we suggest above, individuals in future should accept significantly fewer directorships of public companies than is common now, many companies would have to select some directors who are new to the role. Companies would be able to choose directors with different backgrounds and viewpoints from those which are typical today. In any case we consider that diversification of this kind among directors would be highly desirable, and would help major corporations to understand better the impact their activities have on society. We also believe that it is quite feasible, for although some argue that there is a scarcity of qualified Canadians to serve on boards, that view is based on too narrow a concept of the qualities required in a director.

We understand the desire of the chief officers of major corporations to have on their boards people who have had experience themselves as chief officers of other corporations, and we would not suggest that most directors should not have these qualifications. But we think that more directors with the necessary intelligence and good judgment could be found among those who have had experience elsewhere than in business. An effort is now made by many companies to diversify their boards on geographic lines; we suggest the same in terms of occupational backgrounds and viewpoints. We do not suggest tokenism in this respect; those selected should expect, and be expected, to participate actively in discussions at the board on many subjects, and they should have sufficient stature and ability that their views will carry weight with their colleagues who have business training and expertise. Good directors should be expected to question and debate corporate policies and plans, which should then develop along lines that reflect the various views of and contributions made by the board. We think that diversity of this kind will help corporations to confront at the highest level, and to understand the problems they face in the turbulent economic and social setting in which they must now operate.

It has been argued by some that corporate reform should go further: that directors should be given by law, individually or collectively, specifically defined areas of authority (e.g., to supervise and be responsible for product safety), and that this will foster greater personal and corporate responsibility. However, we think that the law is now fashioned broadly enough to allow directors to exercise authority for those corporate acts over which, under any system, they could reasonably be expected to have control.

The suggestions we have made are not recommendations for legislation. We think the results will be better if these views are adopted voluntarily rather than being imposed by law upon an antagonistic group, and then observed only with reluctance and formality. The final result might then be tokenism or cosmetic "window dressing". These are ideas that must work "not only in the courtroom but also in the boardroom". We hope that major Canadian companies will respond to these suggestions in a positive way, and will incorporate them into their formal operating activities.

"Public" Directors

It has been suggested to us that "public" or "public interest" or "ombudsman" directors should be appointed to the boards of major Canadian corporations. These would be people who would not be elected by the shareholders, and whose mandate would be to represent the "public interest". There are a variety of proposals put forth along this line, all in response to the question: "Since corporations have such a great impact on so many groups within the community, why is it only the shareholders who have the right to select directors, and why is it only to the corporation and to its shareholders that the directors are, in normal circumstances, legally accountable?"

The argument has been put effectively and clearly by Abram Chayes in an article in *The Corporation in Modern Society*:

> It is unreal, however, to rely on the shareholder constituency to keep corporate power responsible by the exercise of franchise....Of all those standing in relation to the large corporation, the shareholder is least subject to its power. Through the mechanism of the security markets, his relation to the corporation is rendered highly abstract and formal, quite limited in scope, and readily reducible to monetary terms. The market affords him a way of breaking this relation that is simple and effective. He can sell his stock, and remove himself, qua shareholder, at least from the power of the corporation....A concept of the corporation which draws the boundary of 'membership' thus narrowly is seriously inadequate....
>
> A more spacious conception of 'membership', and one closer to the facts of corporate life, would include all those having a relation of sufficient intimacy with the corporation or subject to its power in a sufficiently specialized way. Their rightful share in decisions on the exercise of corporate power would be exercised through an institutional arrangement appropriately designed to represent the interests of a constituency of members having a significant common relation to the corporation and its power.

The proponents of the many different models put forward suggest that if the public is in some fashion represented on the board, if there is a change whereby groups other than shareholders have a franchise, the problem of the legitimacy of power of the directors and of the corporation is answered. And once the constituencies that have a rightful "membership" in the corporation also participate, through institutionalized processes, in the government of the corporation, then the central question of accountability of the directors and the corporation is also substantially solved.

We have given serious consideration to these proposals, for they touch a question central to our mandate: whether large corporations are adequately aware of and responsive to the interests of the communities in which they function. We do not think it practical to recommend any of the structural changes proposed. There are two basic problems with the many proposals for a so-called public director. One relates to the role such a person would play in a business organization. It is not clear whether he should be a social auditor, an ombudsman, a spokesman for the "public interest", or a representative of all groups, except shareholders, concerned with the corporation. It is equally uncertain whether he would be a voting or non-voting board member; whether he would share the same responsibilities as other directors; whether he would owe the same duties as other directors to the corporation, and to the shareholders; how he would obtain any effective power and authority, and how the many conflicts that would inevitably arise in such a situation would be resolved. We have not seen any prescription that answers these questions satisfactorily.

The second problem is even more fundamental. The critical question that has not been satisfactorily answered by any of the proponents, or any of the authors whose work we have studied, is this: "Who should be entitled to select the public director, and by what process should he be selected?" If the idea is to provide an answer to an alleged lack of legitimacy, it is mandatory to have an acceptable and workable selection arrangement; otherwise the public director will be no more "legitimate" than any other director.

Chayes recognized the importance of this question, and the difficulty inherent in it: "It is not always easy to identify such constituencies nor is it always clear what institutional forms are appropriate for recognizing their interests." We go further and say, after careful study of many proposals, that it is *never* easy to identify the appropriate constituencies, and the appropriate institutional forms are *never* clearly definable. Even if it were possible to select special interest groups, balancing the extent of their participation relative to one another and to shareholders would inevitably be completely arbitrary. Even Ralph Nader considers the idea of a "public interest" director unworkable, and would have only the shareholders elect the board albeit by an expanded electoral procedure. The difficulty with this question is that the potential "appointing groups" are amorphous and transitory. In one year a particular group may appear to have a legitimate interest to be recognized, and in the next year it may have ceased to exist. There will, in addition, be as many potential constituencies striving for the right to participate in the election of a director as there are interpretations of what is truly in the "public interest".

We agree that the activities of the major Canadian corporations do affect many "publics" and that they have a significant impact on, and responsibility to, people other than those traditionally understood to be its sole constituency—shareholders (of course, much the same could be said of other major groups, such as trade unions). We conclude, however, that the only practical and equitable method of selecting directors is one whereby the shareholders (a group that most commentators agree should participate in corporate government) elect or ratify management's choice of directors. The only workable scheme to ensure greater responsiveness to society's legitimate demands is to reform the board and its workings along the lines we describe in this chapter.

All the proposed schemes we have examined have as many defects as those in the present system (and some have more). A diversified and more diligent board should reduce the significance of the present defects considerably. If the interests of the general public or any particular group are still ignored by a corporation, there may be recourse of one kind or another available to protect the aggrieved parties. If not, the way to protect the complainant is to provide that recourse at law, not to graft onto the corporate structure a clumsy and impractical appendage.

Much the same kind of problem arises when considering the suggestion that Canadian corporations should have on their boards consumer directors, environmental protection directors or other directors legally and specifically charged with representing and being responsible to a certain "interest group". The selection process would usually be difficult or impossible to devise in a fair and workable way. Moreover, we think such directors would invariably, and frequently, find themselves in an irreconcilable conflict among duties to the special interest group, to the shareholders and to the corporation. We believe our earlier suggestion, to have some board members with special knowledge of pertinent areas, without placing special legal responsibility on them, is by far the most sensible approach.

Worker Directors

The idea of worker, or employee directors, is much more difficult and complex.

Other countries have varying arrangements featuring a degree of worker involvement at some level in the decision-making process. These schemes range from joint consultation (where management makes the decisions but permits worker representatives to be heard) to worker control (where final authority rests in the workers' representatives), with a wide variety of plans between those two extremes. In Britain the Committee of Inquiry on Industrial Democracy (Chairman, Lord Bullock) made an extensive analysis of this question. The Committee divided on its recommendations, and its *Report* has created considerable controversy in Britain. One of the most highly developed Western European arrangements, and probably the best known in Canada, is the German system of co-determination. This involves a two-tier board system, with equal representation of workers and shareholders on the supervisory board (corresponding roughly to a Canadian board of directors), but primarily management representation on what corresponds to the executive Committee of a Canadian board of directors.

These plans exist for different reasons, including the hope of alleviating worker alienation, increasing productivity, distributing power and authority more equitably, and contributing to industrial harmony. These are all admirable objectives, but most observers have concluded that a scheme of worker participation, at the board level or elsewhere, will by itself do little to accomplish these ends, and above all will not produce industrial peace. In Germany, the machinery of participation is distinct from that of wage determination, but the processes work together and have a reciprocal influence. In

Canada, however, without a shift toward such an orderly system of collective bargaining, and perhaps the introduction of works councils along the lines of the German model, we are doubtful that worker participation itself will lead either to the greater satisfaction of any group concerned or to greater industrial harmony. Furthermore, the danger of co-option is present: "participation" may become a device by which management obtains the support of workers without any significant participation on their part.

If Canadian unions or management do think worker participation or worker directors is a good idea it should be made clear that such an arrangement could now become the subject of an understanding between union and management. No change in the law would be necessary for management to agree to include the union's nominees on the slate proposed for election to the board. With share ownership no longer a prerequisite to directorship, there would be no financial obstacles in the way of a worker director. We do see the possibility of occasional conflict of interest on the part of a worker director, between the objectives of the employees and those of the shareholders, but some practical solutions to that problem may be found in particular cases.

However, the notion seems somewhat remote and academic at present, since neither Canadian labor nor Canadian management generally advocates or appears to support the idea. We conclude that at the present time, and in the context of our industrial relations history and current practice, the idea of worker directors in major Canadian corporations does not offer great promise, but the subject will undoubtedly be a matter of continued public discussion and deserves further study in the light of European experience.

Interlocking Directorates

Some have argued that interlocking directorates are indications of the existence of social and economic networks that permeate the upper echelons of Canadian business and thus serve further to concentrate power. Others have said that, since board members in practice tend to lack any really substantial amount of decision-making power, the concern about interlocks is exaggerated.

Throughout our hearings, and in many of the submissions we received, there were expressions and comments on the question of interlocking directorates. As well, we commissioned the aforementioned study of corporate interconnections by Berkowitz et al.

The presence of the same individual on the boards of directors of several or even a dozen or more companies is well known and is easily identified in the Directory of Directors and other public sources. We have not endeavored to count these interlocks or to interrelate them. We have found no real evidence that individual interlocks are significant in themselves. Many large companies are looking for the same type of person as a director, and these individuals are apparently willing to serve on a number of boards.

The significance of the phenomenon lies in the relatively limited group from which companies select directors, and the similarity of background and outlook that this frequently implies. For example, the major banks seek many of the same people for outside directors as are selected by major industrial companies. We are satisfied, based on the evidence we have heard, that banks do not rely on interlocking outside directors as a source of information about their clients. Undoubtedly they hope their directors will bring business to the bank, subject to their fiduciary obligations as directors of other companies, but that is a different connection from that usually discussed.

Some have offered, as a partial explanation for the existence of so many directors-in-common, the view that there is a scarcity of qualified Canadians available to serve as directors. Most of these already sit on one or more boards, and (the argument goes) it is therefore inevitable that these highly qualified individuals will be sought after, with the result that there will be many overlapping or cross-directorates. Others attribute the reason for the pervasiveness of interlocks to the common class within society from which the directors have sprung or to which they have risen, to the homogeneous ideological and cultural attitudes of such people, and to the natural human tendency to seek out the familiar and friendly as companions.

The law is generally silent on the question of interlocks. The most notable statutory provisions are sections 18(5) and 18(6) of the Bank Act, which provide that a person may not be a bank director if he is a director of another bank, or of a trust or loan company that accepts deposits from the public, or of a bank under the Quebec Savings Bank Act. While these provisions have been criticized as being easily avoidable, we have found no instances of avoidance and think the law has accomplished the intention of Parliament.

The courts in Canada have not yet had many occasions to deal with the legal difficulties that might arise in an interlocking situation. The Supreme Court of Canada, in the 1974 *Canadian Aero Service* case, placed renewed emphasis on the fiduciary obligations of people in senior corporate positions. Stanley Beck interpreted that judgment as placing directors who are on boards in certain kinds of interlocking situations in a "tenuous legal position" and in "constant danger of being in breach of their duty to either, or both, of their masters".

In their 1976 Report *Dynamic Change and Accountability in a Canadian Market Economy*, for the federal Department of Consumer and Corporate Affairs, L. A. Skeoch and B. C. McDonald discussed interlocks within the context of competition policy. They stated that they were not aware of any reliable evidence that interlocks have "harmed competitive processes in Canada in any generally significant way". Neither have we discovered any such evidence, although there is reason, *a priori*, to be concerned about the situation where one person sits on the boards of two companies, each a significant force in its market, that compete with each other in any market that is material to either company.

After giving the matter consideration, we are not prepared to recommend further restrictions on interlocking directorates. We see little justification for regulation in this area, and the undesirable effects of such action might well outweigh any benefits. The cost would indeed be real, measured in terms of the disruption and dislocation of both personal and corporate activities.

There is one case where, in our judgment, the social and economic benefits of action regarding interlocks exceed the costs. That case relates to bank directors and officers, and we have dealt with that in Chapter 10.

We have also considered the situation of a person serving as a senior officer or director of two companies that are competitors in a market that is material to both companies. The access to information that such an individual has, and the obligations to both companies inherent in the nature of his role, place him in a difficult position and pose dangers to both companies. Perhaps the greatest danger is the possibility that there will be less vigorous rivalry and competition between the two firms than would occur if there were no interlock. There are few situations in Canada like that, too few to warrant a prohibition in law. We have seen no positive evidence of detriment resulting from horizontal interlocks, although the danger is always present. If detriment did arise, the common law provides some degree of protection to an aggrieved corporation, although not to the competitive process.

The proposed amendments to the Combines Investigation Act give the Competition Board power to prohibit specific horizontal interlocks, and we see this as sufficient protection for the competitive process and the public interest. For these reasons, and while we are not at all in favor of horizontal interlocks, we do not recommend a prohibition of them per se.

Management Control

We described earlier the major categories of stock ownership relevant to the question of control of corporations. In each of the cases mentioned, the controlling shareholder normally exercises control partly by ensuring that the board members are persons acceptable to him and partly by arranging for the appointment of senior management compatible with his views and objectives. The management is ultimately replaceable at the will of the controlling shareholder and this is understandable, since the controlling shareholder has the largest direct financial stake in the company's prosperity and is naturally anxious to ensure that senior management is acceptable to him.

There are many corporations where no one person or group of persons acting in concert owns a significant percentage of the voting shares. In those situations control of the corporation comes to be exercised by those who manage the corporation.

Management depends for its continued control on its influence over the proxy machinery. So long as no substantial shareholder becomes interested in the company's affairs, and recognizing that the presence of the board is always a factor, management is able to perpetuate itself and the board, mainly through its control over the proxy process.

In the banking industry, one of the most visible and highly concentrated in Canada, Parliament has acted to ensure that no person or group can acquire control of a bank. It has done this by limiting the maximum percentage of bank shares that can be beneficially owned by any one person or group. One of the principal consequences of this legislation is that (subject to the presence of the board, as we have noted) the management of a bank will always effectively control it.

Another conspicuous case of management control in Canada is that of Canadian Pacific Limited. The company has no person holding a significant block of voting stock, and control of the corporation is exercised by senior management. Directors and senior officers of CP own less than 0.28% of the equity stock. It should be noted that one of the effects of the 1971 offer by CP to exchange high-yield non-voting stock for the outstanding voting preferred stock was to consolidate further the control position of management.

Control by incumbents, including management, may also be buttressed by the application of provisions in the law relating to "constrained shares". The ability of a public company to constrain shares (that is to restrict in some way the issue or transfer of its shares) was first created by the Canada Corporations Act in 1970. The purpose of this provision was that companies in certain businesses, such as broadcasting, could impose conditions on the issue or transfer of their shares to ensure that a minimum percentage of the shares remained in Canadian hands, and that more than a maximum percentage did not fall into the hands of "non-Canadians" and thus jeopardize a right or licence held by the company.

In 1976 one of the largest Canadian companies, Brascan Limited, passed a bylaw constraining the transfer of its shares. John Labatt Limited, about 29%-owned by Brascan (through a wholly owned subsidiary), passed a similar bylaw. These were the only firms, of those that appeared before us, to have taken such action. The reason given to us by Brascan for the passage of its bylaw was that the company wanted to ensure that it did not inadvertently become a "non-eligible person" for the purposes of the Foreign Investment Review Act, since that would impose serious limitations on Brascan's ability to act quickly in certain situations. By virtue of the bylaw, people who are "non-Canadian" will be members of a constrained class. A transfer of a share of Brascan will not be entered in the registers of Brascan and a subscription for a share of Brascan will not be accepted if the result of entering the transfer or accepting the subscription would be that the shareholdings (registered, beneficial or associated) of the members of the constrained-class or any member thereof would, in effect, exceed certain stipulated limits. One of the results of this kind of bylaw is to provide a further layer of insulation for the incumbent controlling group (in Brascan's case, the management) against any potential bidders for control.

Further Recommendations

Our reading and research on corporate control lead us to conclude that an effort should be made to achieve a better balance among the relative positions of management, the board and the shareholders, and many of our recommendations in this chapter are directed to that end. Most shareholders apparently do not seem to want to participate more fully in "corporate democracy". However, the present system is such that it is difficult to judge whether, if the system were altered, shareholders would take a greater interest in the corporate process. Certainly it is clear that at present if a shareholder wishes to participate in an effective way he has little opportunity to do so. We think that some modification of the internal corporate processes would be desirable, and would be in the best interest of both corporations and their shareholders.

The Proxy Process

We make two recommendations here. The first deals with the proxy information circular which precedes the election of directors. Shareholders would benefit by having more information than is given to them at present. By way of example, shareholders should be advised as to the amount of director's fee and other compensation paid by the corporation to each nominee who is already a director, a summary of the amount of time spent and the nature of the activities in which the nominees who are directors have been engaged on company business, any material interest of nominees in any transaction with the company (whether or not material to the company) in the period since the last proxy information circular, a brief account of the business experience of each nominee during the preceding five years indicating the nature of his responsibilities, and a statement as to any material criminal convictions and civil judgments against the nominee.

A shareholder wishing to exercise his franchise in an informed way would be in a better position to do so if he had such information. Corporations could also consider including a statement of the reasons why each particular nominee is proposed for election. There may still be no "contest" (assuming the continuation of the current practice of proposing only as many nominees as there are places on the board) but the shareholder who is so inclined could vote for some nominees (or withhold his vote) on a more informed basis.

The Nominating Process

The second recommendation relates to the process by which people are selected for board membership. In most companies senior management (in conjunction with the controlling group or key board members, where applicable) proposes individuals for election to the board. This often creates a situation where the board member feels that he owes his position (as indeed in many cases he does) to the chief executive officer. It is anomalous to have the chief executive officer, who, in management theory and in law, is responsible to the board, participating so substantially in its selection. We have earlier urged that boards be composed almost entirely of outsiders, but this would be meaningful only if the outsiders were as independent as possible, and by that we mean having the ability to counsel and monitor without subservience to the management or the controlling group. This state is fully consistent with a harmonious working relationship between the outside director and management, but, insofar as possible, the director must not owe, or believe he owes, his position and his continuity in the company to the chief executive officer. It will help in fostering an independent attitude on the part of outside directors if they are chosen, not by the chief executive officer or senior management, but by a nominating committee composed entirely of outside directors. This committee would be selected by the board, and might be headed by the chairman of the board (assuming he was an "outsider"). It would seek suggestions for board nominees from other members of the board and from senior management, including the chief executive officer; where there was a major shareholder, its views would, of course, be obtained (remembering that the nominees, once elected, owe a duty to all the shareholders, not just the controlling group). The proposed slate would also have to be approved by the board as a whole. The nominating committee itself, however, would be ultimately responsible for determining the names that would go before the shareholders. The result, over a period of time, should be to inculcate and foster in outside directors a more independent attitude.

Conflicts of Interest

We now turn to a consideration of the difficult question of conflicts of interest. In some major corporate groups in Canada there are companies whose shares are wholly owned by one person or group of persons (or companies). In those situations the interests of the subsidiary are normally identical with the interests of the parent shareholder. Transactions may be carried out between the parent and the subsidiary (and due regard will usually be paid to the provisions of the law, including income tax requirements), but the shareholder need be concerned only with its own interests because there are no other shareholders. For example, assets may be transferred back and forth with relative ease. It is clear that this situation provides (subject to creditors' rights) great flexibility to the parent in dealing with the subsidiary, its business and its assets.

Many major companies in Canada, however, are not wholly owned subsidiaries of other companies, nor are the subsidiaries of many major companies wholly owned by them, so that there are other, outside or minority shareholders. When these other shareholders are present in a corporate structure, the possibility of a conflict of interest may arise. The conflict might be between the interests of the majority and the minority shareholders or between the interests of the management and the company itself.

In the case we are discussing here, the shareholders who are not part of the controlling or management group will normally take very little part in company activities. Their knowledge of company affairs will be limited to whatever information they obtain from the company in the annual report, the proxy information circular and interim reports, such matters as may be commented upon in the press, and information that may be given to them by or through their financial advisers. The minimum quantity and quality of information received by them is prescribed by law; anything beyond is gratuitous and is determined by the company (which normally means the management). If a transaction occurs or is proposed that might result in a conflict of interest, the outside shareholder can, if aware of it, determine whether there is some legal recourse available to protect his interests.

Directors of corporations are, of course, subject to legal rules and constraints, including their obligation to abide by what has come to be known as the "corporate opportunity doctrine". Simply put, this doctrine states that where a director of a company learns of an opportunity that may be usefully exploited by the corporation, he has an obligation, before availing himself of the opportunity personally, to advise the corporation of its existence and to permit it to take up the opportunity. The doctrine is in the process of development in Canada, and it is not possible to say what its precise limits are. It confirms and is consistent with the fiduciary obligation of the director, and with the view that directors should be assiduous in their duty to the corporation and to all shareholders.

Other rules also provide safeguards. A director or officer who is directly or indirectly a party to or materially interested in a material contract with the corporation must disclose that fact to the corporation. Any such director must also generally abstain from voting on the transaction. Each annual proxy information circular must disclose to shareholders details of any material interest in any such transaction in the past year if the transaction has had a material effect on the company. In addition, insiders are now subject to stringent rules relating to buying and selling their corporation's securities, and to their use, or abuse, of confidential information. A prompt report to a securities commission is now required regarding such "insider trading".

There are specific provisions in certain statutes governing financial institutions relating to what might be called "self-dealing". As early as 1910 Parliament passed laws relating to "self-dealing" or "self-trading" in the life insurance industry. The laws were periodically revised and in 1970 they were revised substantially. The general effect is to provide that a company subject to the authority of the Superintendent of Insurance may not make loans to or investments in a corporation that is a substantial shareholder of that company, or to any corporation in which one of the company's substantial shareholders has a significant interest. There are also other provisions intended to restrict and limit potential diversion and misuse of corporate funds. The Superintendent of Insurance has told us that these provisions have been effective for the purposes intended.

During the course of our study we examined some transactions that illustrate the difficult problems that can arise where there are minority shareholders or where persons in management enter into transactions with the company. In these situations the interests of the minority shareholders must be protected. The first level of protection exists within the management of a company. The second level of protection is at the board. The third exists with the minority shareholder himself. We think that shareholders should have more complete, and more timely, information about transactions involving insiders than they do at present. They would then be in a better position to ensure that their rights were not being abused.

There is room for improvement in the procedures that now exist at the board level in this area. We think the present rules as to declaration and abstention should remain, but in addition the audit committee should become involved. The audit committee of a major corporation now has the duty of reviewing the financial statements of the corporation before the board approves them, and in the course of doing so normally meets with the corporation's auditor. The audit committee must include a majority of outside directors. We think that all transactions or matters (subject to a *de minimis* exception) proposed to be undertaken by the corporation that may involve any potential conflict of interest, such as those we have described where management, directors, or major shareholders have an interest that is material to them (even if not material to the company), should be considered by and be subject to the approval of such a committee. The audit committee already exists in major corporations and, with its function of critical evaluation, is an appropriate body to perform this task. The auditors (and other advisers, where suitable) would participate in such a review. The audit committee should report to the board, and we think that the board should then send this report to the shareholders as part of its regular contact with them.

This procedure would be a welcome improvement in the communications between a corporation and its shareholders, since under current practice the rights of minority shareholders may be materially weakened by their lack of knowledge. The best way in which we can illustrate the need for this is by recounting our own experience in one situation. In analyzing a transaction we had recourse first to the same documents that a minority shareholder would receive (in this case, he would have received them many months after the transaction occurred). From these documents we were able to determine the basic nature of the transaction.

However, we could not determine from these documents the corporate rationale for the transaction, and therefore we could not determine whether the transaction was motivated primarily because of the fact that insiders were involved. We could not determine what facts were disclosed to the board or what independent analysis, if any, the directors might have taken. We could not determine whether any member or members of the board opposed the transaction and, if so, for what reason. We could not determine the method of calculating the price to be paid for the asset in question and whether that price was objectively fair. We consulted a financial analyst, knowledgeable about the affairs of the company, but he was not able to enlighten us much more. It was only when we discussed the transaction with senior representatives of the company that we obtained sufficient information for our purposes.

Of course, a minority shareholder would not have opportunity to engage in the kind of discussions that we conducted. A minority shareholder, once he learned of the transaction, would have to decide whether his interests had been neglected, or whether the transaction was fair and reasonable and in the best interests of the corporation. This places the shareholder in a very difficult position, and may be a factor contributing to the apathy of smaller shareholders. For shareholders to be able to make a proper and informed judgment in this kind of case, they should have additional information of the kind described above.

This is not to say that the lack of full and prompt information is the only difficulty faced by a minority shareholder. Enforcing rights is expensive, and major corporations and insiders normally have greater resources than the individual shareholder. But recent statutory changes in the Canada Business Corporations Act and other statutes have introduced remedies, and lowered procedural hurdles, and ought to help shareholders who wish to bring action to correct abuses. The effectiveness of these changes remains to be fully tested, but we are optimistic that they will prove to be valuable to shareholders. While there has been some criticism of some parts of the provisions, they seem to us to be substantially adequate and clearly desirable. The recommendations we have made will complement these remedies and make them more useful.

We said earlier that the public interest on an issue such as conflict of duty will coincide with private interests. While private and proprietary rights are chiefly involved here, in the broadest sense there is an overriding public concern. It is in the public's interest that the internal activities of our major corporations, and our other major institutions, be conducted on an orderly and equitable basis, and as far as possible be seen to be so conducted. The public's perception of corporations influences its confidence in the workings of our economic system and affects its willingness to invest. We think it desirable that the interests of all concerned with corporations be, and be seen to be, fairly protected.

Chapter 13

Disclosure of Corporate Information

Introduction

Corporations generate, accumulate and sometimes disseminate vast quantities of data. The nature and range of corporate information is as varied as that of corporate activity itself. Early in our work we decided that one of the main issues facing us was to determine whether, in the face of major concentrations of corporate power, the public interest would be better protected if more of this information, or better information, were required to be made public.

Much has been written about disclosure of corporate information, and we do not propose to discuss more of the various views and arguments than is necessary. To obtain a perspective as neutral and objective as possible, we commissioned an independent research study on disclosure, which we are publishing separately. This study, by John Kazanjian, is quite thorough, and readers who are interested in pursuing the subject in more detail than we are able to provide here are referred to it. As part of its analysis, the study makes the point that most of the various disclosure requirements are found in different places, not by accident but because they are intended to accomplish different purposes and satisfy the needs of different segments of society. There is not, nor do we think there can be, one totally comprehensive disclosure regime in Canada. Because information about corporations is needed for different purposes it is not easy to devise one practical scheme that will satisfy all requirements.

The most difficult problem is not how to make corporate information available, but to decide what should be disclosed. It is easy enough to pile one disclosure requirement upon another; indeed that is what the law has tended to do, creating in the process a mixture of the significant and the trivial, with overlapping and duplicated collection systems and filing requirements. The result is an enormous mass of undigested data, which is often inaccessible and incomprehensible to those who might want to use it.

In the following discussion we refer to both corporate disclosure and corporate reporting. We intend the former phrase to refer to information that

311

is communicated, either directly or through an intermediary (such as a governmental agency) to some person in the public domain, such as an investor or shareholder. Communication of this kind is the same, for large corporations, as disclosure to the public at large. Corporate reporting, on the other hand, denotes the delivery of information by corporations to government, to be used by government for its own purposes. Such information is not necessarily further conveyed to the public, and sometimes statutes forbid it. We will discuss both of these concepts and their practical implications.

To put corporate disclosure in perspective, we will segregate the mandatory disclosure and reporting obligations of large Canadian corporations into three broad categories. We will then give a brief overview of these requirements, having in mind the largest Canadian companies (and assuming where necessary that they are governed by the Canada Business Corporations Act). While there may be some overlapping within these categories, particularly in the investor and shareholder areas, generally the requirements and the purposes are distinct.

Current Disclosure and Reporting Obligations

Disclosure to Investors

The provincial securities commissions (particularly the Ontario Securities Commission, which has led the others) regulate trading in corporate securities. In a practical and important way, stock exchanges also have some power. For example, both the Ontario Securities Commission and the Toronto Stock Exchange have certain disclosure requirements. Each is concerned, but in different degrees, with disclosure of information relating to both the primary issue of securities and trading in secondary markets. Rules on disclosure are found both in the Securities Act and Regulations and in the policies of the Securities Commission and the Stock Exchange. In the case of the widely held, public company, the reporting or filing of material by it with one of these authorities constitutes disclosure to the public, since any person who is interested in the affairs of a particular company is able to obtain much of the information held by these agencies (except that in private files). The delivery of most information by companies to these bodies is, therefore, tantamount to the disclosure of it to any interested creditor, supplier, medium of public communication or member of the general public.

A brief summary of some of the principal disclosure documents may be helpful. These include prospectuses, takeover bid circulars, insider trading reports, financial statements, and other documents containing significant information concerning a company's affairs. One of the primary disclosure instruments is a prospectus, which is pre-cleared with a securities commission and delivered to the purchasers of securities when a company offers its securities to the public. The prospectus contains general information, plus particulars relating to such matters as the securities being offered, dividend payments, options, directors' and officers' interest in transactions with the company and principal holders of the corporation's securities. Certain financial statements are also included in a prospectus. Prospectuses are thus a source of considerable corporate information, but since they are prepared in connection with a particular sales effort they have a very short useful life. Some companies offer securities infrequently; others do so regularly. A current prospectus can provide timely and useful information whereas one that is some years old is likely to be unreliable for many purposes.

Takeover bids and the documents accompanying them contain some information on the bidding company and its key individuals. If a bid involves payment in securities, then it must contain information equivalent to that required in a prospectus.

As well, insider trading reports must be filed by certain persons (directors, senior officers and persons owning more than 10% of certain kinds of shares) when they trade in the securities of the company. The reason the law requires insider trading reports to be filed is not primarily because there is a great public interest in the information contained in them. The principal purpose of the law is to deter trading in corporate securities by insiders using confidential information. The law presumes that the very fact that trades have to be disclosed publicly will deter those who might otherwise engage in improper transactions.

Comprehensive audited financial statements must be filed annually by publicly held companies, which are also obliged to file interim unaudited financial statements for the six-month period that commences after each fiscal year end. These statements are substantially the same documents usually sent to shareholders. The Toronto Stock Exchange also requires quarterly publication of unaudited financial statements.

Public companies are also required to make prompt disclosure of all significant information about their affairs. This information would include changes in corporate control, acquisition or disposition of material assets, takeovers, changes in capital structure, unusual changes in earnings, or any other material change that might substantially affect the market value of a company's securities. These "timely disclosure" rules are an important element in the investor disclosure system.

The rules of these authorities have been devised to accomplish specific purposes. Each separate component in the disclosure scheme is thought to have an identifiable function in attaining the objectives. Collectively these rules are intended to protect investors, to act as a deterrent against fraud in securities dealing, and to facilitate the orderly working of the capital markets. Protection of investors by disclosure is a well-accepted policy in Canada, as it is in the United States and other Western countries. While the securities commission and stock exchange rules are not a general disclosure system, the information that corporations divulge under this regime constitutes one of the major repositories of corporate data available to the public.

In fact, the public makes little direct use of this source of information; studies show that almost nobody reads prospectuses and other information in the files of the Ontario Securities Commission. Undoubtedly, the same is true of the similar information filed with the other provincial securities commissions and with the Department of Consumer and Corporate Affairs in Ottawa. This, however, is not an argument against public filing. Analysts, financial journalists and other expert commentators do use this information, and they disseminate it to the public in a distilled and understandable form.

Disclosure is not static. Disclosure for investor purposes is under constant review by securities commissions and other regulatory bodies. There have been, and will continue to be, many suggestions for changes in disclosure to investors. The federal Department of Consumer and Corporate Affairs is also studying the regulations of the securities markets in Canada, and disclosure of information to investors will be an important part of that study.

Disclosure to Shareholders

As with disclosure to investors, any information that is reported by very large companies to their shareholders is, in effect, in the public domain. Shareholder reporting requirements are found in corporate law (the Canada Business Corporations Act and its provincial counterparts), and to some extent in securities law, and constitute one of the principal methods by which the managers of corporations account for their stewardship to the owners of corporations.

One of the main shareholder disclosure instruments prescribed by law is the proxy information circular, which must be given to shareholders before any meeting where their proxies are solicited. It contains information that government has determined is likely to be useful to the shareholder whose proxy is sought. The information may also be of value to others. For example, we found proxy information circulars very helpful in our study of corporations. These circulars, which are issued at least annually, must contain, for example, information about financial assistance that may have been given by the corporation to certain persons, management remuneration, indemnification of directors or officers, changes in corporate control and the material interest of certain persons in transactions with the company.

Financial statements are another principal source of information, and they must also be sent to shareholders. In addition, although corporate law does not specifically require them in the form now common (except for the financial statements), custom and convention dictate that companies send annual reports to their shareholders.

It is generally recognized that the ordinary shareholder does not read these documents carefully (as most individual investors do not read prospectuses with any great care), although the annual report probably receives more attention than other material. Most of the shareholder (and investor) documents are necessarily legalistic, partly because they are prescribed in considerable detail in the law, but chiefly because they can create far-reaching legal obligations and liabilities if they are not drawn with the utmost care. This inevitably gives a legal tone to the documents, which in turn undoubtedly contributes to the recipients' disinclination to read them. They do, however, provide another source of publicly available data that cannot be overlooked when examining the question of corporate disclosure.

Disclosure to Governments

It is our impression that major corporations do not quarrel much with the disclosure obligations placed upon them under the two systems mentioned above, although there is some disagreement with certain details and considerable apprehension about new requirements. On the whole, there is a state of relative resignation toward the requirements of disclosure to investors and shareholders but, at the same time, some doubt that all the requirements are absolutely necessary. In the area of disclosure (or reporting) to governments, however, there is widespread dissatisfaction among corporations, for reasons to be discussed shortly.

This part of the disclosure system is by far the most complex, and it is possible for us only to outline in quite general terms some of the main requirements at the federal level (there are other requirements at other governmental levels). Considerable quantities of corporate information are collected by the federal government, either sporadically or regularly, and, if regularly, on an annual, semi-annual, quarterly, monthly, or even daily basis. It may cover financial status and activities, production activities, sales and export activities, employment data and practices, payroll information, research and development activities, basic identifying data, ownership data, taxation information or an infinite number of other things. Information and statistics reported to the government may be used for statistical, regulatory, law enforcement, policy and administration or other purposes. Sometimes the information collected is used exclusively within the particular department requesting it (often because either a statute or an express or implicit understanding with the provider requires such confidentiality). Sometimes the data is exchanged among several departments, and sometimes it is made available to the public at various levels of aggregation. While there are several possible methods of cataloguing government's corporate data collection work, we will divide the system into four broad categories.

LAW ENFORCEMENT OR INVESTIGATIVE PURPOSES

Data collected for these purposes range from information obtained by the Royal Canadian Mounted Police, to data seized under warrant by the Combines Investigation Branch, to financial and wage settlement data filed with the Anti-Inflation Board. The law usually requires this data to be kept confidential by the collecting department, because it is considered that the dissemination of it within the government or to the public could be unfairly prejudicial to legitimate private interests.

STATISTICAL PURPOSES

Another important category is the collection of corporate information in statistical form. A great deal of data is collected by Statistics Canada from individual companies. To prevent commercially sensitive information from being exploited by competitors or others, the data are not made available to other government departments, or the public, on an individual firm basis. Only aggregated data are published. It must be said that aggregated industrial data are used by many businesses and are quite important to them for planning and other purposes.

POLICY AND ADMINISTRATIVE PURPOSES

General. To examine the implications of policy alternatives, to judge the effectiveness of current policies and to administer existing programs, federal departments and agencies request information from corporations. Data collected under this category range from those obtained by regulatory agencies like the Canadian Transport Commission to ad hoc departmental surveys of selected firms in specific industries. Information collected is usually kept confidential within the department, but partially for a reason different from the one mentioned earlier. Here confidentiality is the rule (usually as a matter of policy but not of law) because it is felt that disclosure might cause harm, and also because the concept of ministerial responsibility as it is practised requires it. Release of information other than through the appropriate minister is thought to be a potential source of jeopardy to the neutrality of public servants. If any information collected under this category is not to be kept confidential, the policy requires such a decision ultimately to be made by the appropriate Minister, who is then accountable to Parliament for that decision.

Most corporate information, and particularly that collected unsystematically, is provided under this category. While there are occasional shared collection efforts by departments, and some interdepartmental data exchanges, this part of government's program is dependent mainly on decentralized collection with a policy of quite limited interchange of data. Each department is free to request whatever it chooses, even if the information has already been collected in substantially the same form by another department or agency. There is no central coordinating unit in government that maintains an index of material requested and received by the various government departments. There is nothing in the law requiring governmental data requests to be compatible with existing data series in Statistics Canada or elsewhere. Indeed, even Statistics Canada produces series that cannot be linked to other series because of definitional, sample or timing differences. So in this area there is less than adequate coordination and, inevitably, some duplication of requests.

CALURA. One of the principal instruments used by the government in collecting data from business sources is the Corporations and Labour Unions Returns Act (CALURA), which was passed in 1962. CALURA is administered by the Chief Statistician of Canada under the authority of the Minister of Industry, Trade and Commerce. Its purpose is "to collect financial and other information on the affairs of certain corporations and labour unions carrying on activities in Canada. Such information was considered necessary to evaluate the extent and effects of non-resident ownership and control of corporations in Canada and the extent and effects of the association of Canadians with international labour unions."

Part I of CALURA deals with corporations whose gross revenue during a reporting period exceeds $500,000 or whose assets exceed $250,000. Bill C-7, introduced in October 1977, proposes to raise these amounts to at least $10 million and $5 million respectively. Crown corporations and corporations operating under such federal statutes as the Canadian and British Insurance Companies Act, the Trust Companies Act, the Loan Companies Act, the Small Loans Act, the Radio Act and the Railway Act are exempt to avoid duplication of returns where substantially the same kind of information is available under other federal legislation.

CALURA (when amended) will apply to every corporation incorporated in Canada and also to every corporation doing business in Canada regardless of the jurisdiction within which it is incorporated unless it is exempted by legislation. There are a number of corporations that are incorporated outside Canada but, because of their operations in Canada, are reporting corporations under CALURA. At present, the exempt corporations are generally those that provide similar information under federal regulatory legislation or that are government-owned, non-profit, or smaller than the minimum size specified in CALURA. The principal reporting exclusions are the more than 350 Crown corporations and their subsidiaries in Canada.

Corporation returns are divided into confidential and non-confidential sections. The non-confidential section (Section A) includes information on the incorporation, officers and directors, and ownership of the corporation's issued shares. The confidential section of the return (Section B) includes financial statements similar to those required under the Income Tax Act and a schedule of selected payments to non-residents. The data base under CALURA is very broad, but the non-confidential information at least is very limited in scope. If the range of the Section A information were to be expanded significantly, it would be desirable to reduce the number of reporting corporations by setting higher threshold criteria as proposed in Bill C-7.

The returns are made to the Chief Statistician of Canada. CALURA provides that the non-confidential part (Section A) shall be kept on record in the Department of Consumer and Corporate Affairs to which one copy is forwarded by the Chief Statistician of Canada. Anyone is permitted to inspect these copies upon payment of a nominal fee. Section B of the corporation return remains in the control and custody of the Chief Statistician of Canada and is not available to anyone other than an official or authorized person.

One of the inevitable results of this confidentiality is that companies have to supply to other government departments information they have already supplied under Section B of CALURA. Part of the price that is thus paid (in this category as well as others) to maintain confidentiality of data is limited departmental exchange of data and some duplication and inefficiency.

TAX COLLECTION PURPOSES

Tax returns are a separate category in our analysis. Since government revenues emanate from taxation, it is obviously essential that the returns filed by all taxpayers, including corporations, be as accurate and complete as possible. It is generally believed that confidentiality of tax returns will help to produce accurate reporting of income. There is a tradition (certainly perceived as such by the general public) that tax returns are confidential documents, and statutes such as the Income Tax Act have elevated that concept to a statutory requirement. That Act, for example, stipulates that, except in narrowly described cases, it is an offense for any official to communicate to any other person any information collected under the Income Tax Act. Further, as a matter of practice, access to all tax data, corporate or otherwise, is severely restricted, since tax returns are required for the collection of revenue, not information.

* * * *

While there may be other kinds of information-gathering by government, such as the Canada Business Corporation Act's requirement that certain information regarding federal companies be filed with the government and be open for public inspection, the principal categories have been listed here. It is clear that, considering all information included in the investor/shareholder documents, and that made available through government, there is in the public domain considerable data on major companies. Indeed, most corporate information used by us consisted of such publicly available details. These information bases are supplemented by commercial sources such as the various Financial Post services.

Some corporations disseminate information to the public voluntarily. Since this consists primarily of commentary on and interpretation of publicly available data, there is a substantial public relations aspect to the information produced. One reason why some corporations do this is their concern that lack of cooperation or initiative will lead to further compulsory disclosure.

Arguments for and against More Disclosure

Some observers might conclude that there is now adequate information in the public domain about major corporations. However, many witnesses came before our public hearings to urge that large corporations be required to make much greater disclosure of their affairs. It is useful to summarize the principal arguments made by the proponents of more disclosure.

Arguments for More Disclosure

The arguments for greater disclosure rest on the proposition that major corporations command such considerable material and human resources, and have such an impact on people and public policies, that they should be made to account for their use of these resources. Since the present public disclosure regime is based mainly upon the corporation's legal obligations to investors and shareholders (whose interests are relatively narrow), the rest of society has insufficient information about them. The "public" (by which is usually meant the many interest groups in society) needs information to make sound judgments about corporate actions. Among the groups alleged to be touched and affected in a material way by major firms are consumers, employees, suppliers, creditors, present and potential competitors, the media, residents of communities where the corporation is active, in short (especially when one includes investors and shareholders) all groups in society.

Accountability to diverse groups is impossible unless an adequate base of information, different from that now disclosed to investors and shareholders, is available. Many corporations acknowledge that there is an information gap and that the information disclosed by them is not sufficient for broad public purposes. We have been told by several very large corporations that there has been insufficient information revealed about corporations. While some firms recognize the existence of this gap there is no agreement on how to solve the problem.

Some proponents of fuller disclosure also argue that if the size and nature of our economy are such that we will inevitably have a high degree of corporate concentration, the adverse effects of this can be ameliorated in part by making more information about large firms available to the public.

Many advocates of further disclosure are quite general in their approach, while others are specific. To illustrate areas of corporate information some argue should be disclosed, we quote from a brief we received from the Taskforce on the Churches and Corporate Responsibility urging that major corporations be required to disclose publicly the following data "to make citizens aware of the extent of concentration, power and influence of corporations". We offer no comment on this particular list, except to point out that it is similar to many of those compiled by various other groups.

a) a full list of subsidiaries, domestic and foreign, including companies over which, through partial ownership, some aspect of control is exercised;
b) a record of all other directorships and/or management positions held by each director and officer in any other corporation or public authority;
c) earnings of each senior management officer;
d) record of numbers of shares owned, directly or beneficially in any one corporation by each director and officer of that corporation;
e) international intra-corporate transfer payments;
f) ownership of land and of natural resources;
g) taxes paid and to what country as well as nature and amount of tax concessions and from what authorities;
h) financial and other contributions and/or gifts made to political parties, individual politicians and senior civil servants in Canada and abroad;
i) government export guarantees and export insurance arrangements;
j) developmental ventures, at the initial stages of planning.

That same brief argues that corporations be required to disclose to their shareholders on request (which would have the effect of public disclosure) the following additional information:

a) personnel policy and practice relating to employment conditions, equal opportunities, labour relations, wage structures, in-service training and accident prevention;

b) operating policy and practice relating to environmental protection and community impact;

c) product quality and safety; and

d) military contracts.

Those who support fuller disclosure point to other jurisdictions and suggest that Canada emulate them. For example, companies whose shares are traded on stock exchanges in the United States (including some large Canadian companies) must file periodically with the Securities and Exchange Commission many documents (such as an annual Form 10-K, discussed below), some of which contain more information than companies are required to disclose in Canada to investors and shareholders. Further, the Organisation for Economic Cooperation and Development (of which Canada is a member) has recently issued guidelines for multinational enterprises which suggest the disclosure of more information by such enterprises than is now legally required of large Canadian firms. We comment later on the OECD guidelines.

Some advance the proposition that Canada is more likely to avoid corporate scandal, and the serious difficulties experienced as a result, if more is known about corporate activities. This is not a new idea. In 1913 Mr. Justice Louis Brandeis of the U.S. Supreme Court argued that "Publicity is justly commended as a remedy for social and industrial diseases. Sunlight is said to be the best of disinfectants; electric light the most efficient policeman." This philosophy underlies many of the disclosure requirements in our present securities laws. So public disclosure, it is said, is not only correct in principle but may also be an effective deterrent to harmful conduct.

Finally, those who argue for disclosure of more information suggest that it is in the corporations' own interests as the best alternative to greater governmental or institutional intervention.

Arguments against More Disclosure

There is much opposition to these arguments for more disclosure, mainly from companies that might be expected to be subject to any additional requirements, although not all of them are opposed to broader rules. We will summarize here the principal arguments against more disclosure. It is argued that, while corporate activities obviously affect many groups in society, only the investor and shareholder groups are readily identifiable, and only they have a clear and measurable connection with the company. It is suggested that there is no public consensus that corporations have a general responsibility to other segments of society (such as environmentalists or consumers) and it is therefore an untenable argument that the corporation should be accountable to a multitude of interests. If there are corporate obligations to other groups, such obligations should become the subject of explicit legal provisions, and not be camouflaged as disclosure rules. The corporation should (and can only) be held "accountable" to those with a direct financial investment in it (the shareholders and investors) because corporations are not, as some suggest, political institutions. They are instruments comprising essentially private capital formations whose object is to foster the interests of the proprietors. Requiring disclosure for some nebulous public purpose is an unwarranted intrusion into corporate privacy.

One of the main objections relates to the vast amount of information that corporations are now required to report (principally because of the proliferation of demands by governments) and to the lack of coordination of the many requirements. It is urged that, if any significant new disclosure burden is imposed, there must first be a major rationalization of present requirements to eliminate duplication and reduce cost.

It is also argued that because disclosing information may be costly, those who advocate more disclosure should be obliged to demonstrate that there will be a resulting benefit greater than the cost. This is particularly true in those many cases where the demand for disclosure is being made by some "activist" group, since the cost will usually be borne not by the group but by the shareholders or the purchaser of the corporation's products.

A similar argument is that since most information likely to be of any benefit to anyone is already disclosed in one way or another, the onus ought to be placed on those insisting on more information to establish that it will satisfy a legitimate and unfilled need. A related argument is that too much information can obscure understanding.

Finally it is said that further disclosure requirements should not be created without a precise identification of the intended recipient of the information, for disclosure is not an end in itself, and the nature and quality of the information provided is determined by the position and purpose of the end user. For example, if the user is an investor or shareholder, a certain level or standard of disclosure (such as "prospectus level") is generally expected, and corporations are well aware of the legal implications that flow from such standards. If the user is a competitor, care must be taken or competitive harm, rather than benefit, may result from more disclosure. If the recipient is government, the precise purpose should be identified; otherwise the corporation will find it very difficult to determine what information should be provided and exactly how far to go in providing it. If the intended user is the general public, then it will be very costly and time-consuming to provide specific information unobscured by large quantities of less useful data. As well, it is argued, because the needs and interests of the public are so diverse, there are no adequate analytical and dissemination techniques through which the information could be made useful to the public.

The Commission's View

After considering all these arguments and studying much of what has been written, we have concluded that the disclosure question is best resolved in two stages and, in a sense, at two levels. Our mandate includes a consideration of whether safeguards may be required to protect the public interest in the presence of major concentrations of power. The fundamental and central disclosure issue before us is the degree to which the Canadian public should have knowledge and information about large Canadian corporations. Much of this information is already in the public realm (although not centralized for ready access). The question remaining to be settled is whether there should be more or at least more useful, disclosure.

We think the public does have a right to know more than it does now, but, as well, that many of the present disclosure requirements should be clarified and simplified. It is important that we make clear that the view we have reached, and which we will explain in some detail, is applicable only to the very largest Canadian companies, and should not be seen as applying to small or medium-sized enterprises.

We have in mind two categories of firms: financial and non-financial. In the financial area, which would include banks, insurance companies, trust companies and sales finance companies, our comments apply only to those firms with assets of $1 billion or more. Assets are the most useful measurement of a financial firm's significance. The figure we have suggested would mean that, out of the 1976 *Financial Post* list of 35 large financial enterprises, 26 firms would qualify. In the non-financial area we would lower the asset figure to $250 million, and would also apply, as an alternative, a sales figure test of $250 million per year. The non-financial group would include manufacturers, merchandisers, some Crown corporations, real estate companies, natural-resource-based companies, holding companies and other firms. In 1975/76, 114 non-financial firms had sales, and 78 had assets, exceeding $250 million. In both financial and non-financial areas each firm's subsidiaries and affiliates are included: thus the levels we suggest are on a consolidated basis.

Our conclusion that more relevant (and less irrelevant) information should be in the public domain is not related to any specific objective, such as investor protection or consumer knowledge. There are so many constituencies in the community, and their relationships with any particular corporation are so complex and fluid, that it is neither possible nor necessary to classify them. Rather we think that large enterprises should focus their disclosure policy on making information available to the public in general, so that all constituent groups can be better informed. Most of the corporate information now open to the public has been made available as part of the process of the operation of capital markets. While this is, naturally, an essential feature of our economic life, the focus on this market has strongly influenced the disclosure rules. We think that all segments of society should have a broad base of information upon which to found rational judgments about the activities of major corporations. The general public, which is made up of diverse constituent groups, should have the opportunity to know more than it does at present about the structure, the workings and the impact of major corporations.

We have come to this conclusion because we are convinced that openness is fundamental to confidence, and it would be in the public interest if there were more understanding of our major business enterprises. That is often lacking. We do not suggest that openness guarantees confidence, but we do think that lack of openness inhibits it.

The Royal Bank of Canada, in a special brief to us on disclosure, put the issue clearly: "There is growing recognition that in the post-capitalist society which is now evolving, major corporations will have multiple responsibilities and multiple accountabilities. Fuller disclosure of information about all facets of corporate activity will be an inevitable concomitant of these developments". In our view disclosure of information to the general public (and not just to, or for the benefit of, any particular component of the public) is an integral part of a large corporation's social responsibility.

Approaches to Further Disclosure

Importance of a Sectoral Approach

We will elaborate on the kinds of items we think should be disclosed, but we will not do this in great detail, for specific reasons. First, and most importantly, we are more concerned to indicate here our general attitude and our position on the question of openness than to delve into the intricacies, benefits and problems raised by the disclosure of particular items. Secondly, it will be apparent that differences among industries mean that the significance of some areas of disclosure will vary from industry to industry. Appropriate disclosure of a particular item will vary among manufacturing companies, service corporations, utilities, holding companies and banks. To illustrate, disclosure of loss ratios by borrower size, or where directors or other insiders are borrowers, may be significant for lending institutions but not for other kinds of firms. The particulars of the operations of land developers, such as those relating to land assembly, current asset values, development plans and other items uniquely related to that business, are not applicable in other industries.

We think that, with very large firms, better disclosure will result only from a process of detailed, sectoral analysis. This should be done industry by industry, so that the disclosure requirements affecting the large firms in each industry are determined by reference to that industry. In each case (and so far as practical, with each particular item) the benefits and costs of requiring or not requiring the disclosure will have to be considered. The premise on which each decision should be based should be that of openness, unless it can be shown that disclosure in any particular instance would be unfairly prejudicial in terms of cost or competitive harm.

For an illustration of the possibilities of specific sectoral disclosure, reference may be made to the disclosure code voluntarily adopted in November 1976 by BankAmerica Corporation and mentioned by us in Chapter 10. Among the many items the bank will disclose are an analysis of its loan portfolio, data on problem loans, loan loss experience by major categories, loans and credits to affiliated organizations, geographic distribution of loans and investments, standard terms and conditions of consumer loans, consumer credit policies and practices, and aggregate loans made to board members and their companies.

U.S. Form 10-K Requirements

Consideration should be given to disclosure requirements in other countries. As in Canada, most of these have developed in response to a need to satisfy requirements of the capital markets. But even in the United States, where disclosure rules are quite involved and precise, some of the particular requirements are only peripherally related to investor protection. In the course of our work on this subject we examined several of the "Form 10-Ks" filed with American authorities by certain Canadian corporations. Form 10-K is a continuing disclosure document that must be filed annually with the Securities and Exchange Commission in the United States by each company whose securities are traded on stock exchanges or are required to be registered for trading in the United States (whether or not the firm is "going to the market" with a fresh issue of securities). That form contains information that is not normally or regularly disclosed by corporations in Canada although a good deal of it is discussed as a matter of convention in annual reports and some must be disclosed when a prospectus is issued. For example, Form 10-K requires a disclosing company to make annual public disclosure of the following items, which relate to its specific business activities and the environment in which it operates:

1. The business done and intended to be done by the company and its subsidiaries.
2. Competitive conditions in the industry or industries involved and the competitive position of the company. If several products or services are involved, separate consideration is given to the principal products or services or classes of products or services. An estimate of the number of competitors is included, and, where material, the particular markets in which the company competes are identified. Where one or a small number of competitors are dominant, they are identified.
3. If a material part of the business is dependent upon a single customer or a few customers, the loss of any of whom would have a materially adverse effect on the business of the company, the name of the customer or customers, their relationship, if any, to the company and material facts regarding their importance to the business of the company.
4. The sources and availability of raw materials essential to the business.
5. The importance to the business and the duration and effect of all material patents, trademarks, licences, franchises and concessions held.
6. The estimated dollar amount spent during each of the last two fiscal years on material research activities relating to the developments of new products or services or the improvement of existing products or services, indicating those activities which were company-sponsored and/or those which were customer-sponsored.
7. The material effects that compliance with federal, state and local provisions which have been enacted or adopted regulating the discharge of materials into the environment, or otherwise relating to the protection of the environment, may have upon the capital expenditures, earnings and competitive position of the company and its subsidiaries.

8. The number of persons employed by the company.
9. The principal methods of competition (e.g., price, service, warranty, or product performance) and positive and negative factors pertaining to the competitive position of the company, to the extent that they exist.
10. The location and general character of the principal plants, mines and other materially important physical properties of the company and its subsidiaries, whether owned or leased, and, if leased, the expiration dates of material leases.
11. A list or diagram of all parents and subsidiaries of the company and, for each entity named, an indication of the percentage of voting securities owned, or other basis of control, by its immediate parent, if any. The list or diagram includes the company submitting it and shows clearly the relationship of each entity named, both to the company and to the other entities named.

We are not able to say that from the perspective of the Canadian investor or shareholder it is essential that large Canadian firms provide this kind of information annually. We recognize that, even from the point of view of the security holder, the present 10-K requirements are not flawless. But we do think that the regular publication of such information about major companies would be in the public interest, and would contribute significantly to the public's ability to comprehend and evaluate corporate activity. The Form 10-K information listed above would probably be appropriate for disclosure in industries where the major Canadian firms are found. Certainly the production of such data (which are already disclosed in the United States by more than 100 Canadian firms) would not be harmful to corporate interests, and the cost of its disclosure is clearly tolerable for the very large corporations. The Canadian Manufacturers' Association has told us that their "information generally suggests that corporations having experience of this type of disclosure have little objection to it". We can see no valid objection to a similar kind of disclosure in this country.

We have not included in our list the controversial 10-K requirement of disclosure of remuneration paid to each of the three highest paid corporate officers, and each director who received more than $40,000. Personal information like this should remain confidential.

OECD Guidelines

Another approach to a consideration of specific items is found in the recommendations of the Organisation for Economic Cooperation and Development (OECD) briefly referred to earlier. Its "guidelines" for multinational enterprises, while not binding, further illustrate the kind of detail on corporate activity that it would be useful for the public to have. As with the Form 10-K data, some of the OECD information is now already disclosed by Canadian firms in annual reports, prospectuses or other documents. When considering the OECD guidelines, the focus should be on the Canadian corporation. Many of our large firms are themselves subsidiaries, and while we would impose the disclosure obligations on the Canadian firm and its own subsidiaries, we would require it to file information about its parent organization only to the extent such information is available to it, or available in the foreign parent's country.

As with the examples from Form 10-K, the OECD guidelines would apply in most of our major industries. Where the guidelines refer to "geographical area", we have substituted "province". OECD suggests annual disclosure of at least the following:

   i) the structure of the enterprise, showing the name and location of the parent company, its main affiliates, its percentage ownership, direct and indirect, in these affiliates, including shareholdings between them;
   ii) the provinces . . . where operations are carried out and the principal activities carried on therein by the parent company and the main affiliates;
   iii) the operating results and sales by province and the sales in the major lines of business for the enterprise as a whole;
   iv) significant new capital investment by province and, as far as practicable, by major lines of business for the enterprise as a whole;
   v) a statement of the sources and uses of funds by the enterprise as a whole;
   vi) the average number of employees in each province;
   vii) research and development expenditure for the enterprise as a whole;
   viii) the policies followed in respect of intra-group pricing;
   ix) the accounting policies, including those on consolidation, observed in compiling the published information.

The OECD and 10-K examples are two sets of rules that we think would be useful as starting points, although some modifications might be necessary to suit Canadian circumstances. For example, import and export statistics would be of some value here. Also, there should be appropriate criteria to preclude the publication of trivial data. Considerable experience has been gained in the United States with the 10-K requirements. Each item would be applicable in most, if not all, Canadian industries. However, there would still be a need, as we have mentioned, for an analysis of this applicability and effect, and to determine what further disclosure might be required in specific industries.

Minimum Standards

Some large corporations are presently exempt from even minimal disclosure requirements. For example, federally regulated financial institutions are not subject to the provisions of general corporate law, including those relating to financial and other disclosure. The government's *White Paper on the Revision of Canadian Banking Legislation* (August 1976) recognizes this as a deficiency, and proposes that it should be remedied. In our view, similar action should be taken regarding other regulated corporations, including Crown corporations, so that all very large firms, regardless of the nature of their business, are generally subject to the same minimum disclosure requirements.

Possibility of Competitive Harm

One of the considerations that bears on the question of disclosure is the competitive harm that might result, and this would certainly have to be examined when industrial analyses are made. Public disclosure of certain kinds of information would cause serious competitive harm. If such harm would be industry-wide (for example, where foreign imports provided significant competition), then none of the firms should be required to make public disclosure of that particular information. If individual firms would suffer competitively there ought to be an exemption procedure, similar to that now found in the Canada Business Corporations Act.

However, in assessing general or specific justification for exemption it should be borne in mind that the public interest is often served when competitors exploit the information contained in financial statements. For example, the disclosure of large profits can bring more competitors into a market and lead to the efficient allocation of productive resources. While the disclosing firm may suffer some decrease in profits because of the greater competition, this is no more than the play of market forces responding to the proper signals. To define it as competitive harm resulting from disclosure is inconsistent with a private enterprise economy since, as Kazanjian has said, "it would insulate competitors from normal market forces and allocate resources not to the most efficient producer but to the most efficient concealer".

Cost

Although we are conscious of the cost of disclosure, we do not suggest that the public should have more information only if there is no incremental cost attached to its disclosure. The issue is too important for that to be paramount. Moreover, with very large firms, virtually all the information that might be disclosed to the public, following the lines of our approach, is already reported in some fashion to government, or, at any rate, is readily available. This includes such diverse items as inter-corporate transactions, processing of raw materials, exports, sources of financing, advertising expenditures, pollution control costs, plant-specific figures and a long list of other items. Since under one or more of the governmental data collection systems we have described most, if not all, of these details are already reported to government, it would not involve the corporations in much additional cost to make them publicly and regularly available.

Government Handling of Business Information

Opposition to further requirements for information for internal government use is hardening. There is no doubt that governments now make many demands on business for information. Both large and small businesses are affected, and the latter have more difficulty in complying with such demands (we are glad to see that demands on them have recently been reduced). Yet the opposition is not just a reflex reaction to problems that might arise from a requirement for more reporting; it is more subtle than that. Corporations on the whole have been content with disclosure rules relating to investors and shareholders because they see a direct and legitimate link between these groups and the company. A growing number of corporations, however, are refusing to accord the same legitimacy to some governmental requests for information. They are not persuaded that there is much benefit to anyone in complying with certain requests for data, even though many businesses make use of data collected and disseminated by government and generally understand the government's need for corporate information. Contributing to this attitude is the variety of different collecting processes and the duplication that inevitably results from an emphasis on confidentiality and limited interdepartmental and intergovernment access to data.

We are not experts in the precise needs of government for corporate information, nor in the best methods of collecting, distributing or disseminating data. The following comments are thus necessarily tentative suggestions for consideration only.

We said earlier that large firms should be more open about their activities, and that government has a central role to play in achieving that goal. We believe that the time has come for a review and possible reform of the system of government handling of certain business information.

There are three aspects to this question. We defer briefly our consideration of one of them, the matter of government's collection of business information, but we will now discuss the other two parts: distribution within government and dissemination outside government of information collected from business, particularly from the largest and economically most significant companies in Canada.

Major Firms and Confidentiality

Government should move away from rigid adherence to the rule of confidentiality. Major corporations cannot be treated in all respects as private institutions. For the reasons we have given earlier, much of the information these firms report to government already has a quasi-public character. There could be some benefit if more of it were freely interchangeable among government departments (except Revenue Canada and the Bureau of Competition Policy). For example, most, if not all, the data reported by these firms on the present Section B of the CALURA form could be distributed or available within government with no detriment to the company concerned. For these major corporations we are suggesting a significant shift in emphasis: the rule regarding their data would be one of open access within government subject to necessary exceptions such as data related to law enforcement. One of the principal results of this policy should be a reduction in aggregate information demands upon such firms. With a freer interchange of information, requests from different sources for similar data should be less common. Any company that has filed data once should not have to file substantially similar data with another federal government department.

Recognizing what has happened in the past, it would probably be desirable to do more than merely discourage the tendency in government to proliferate and duplicate data collection. If, for example, a corporation has filed an information return containing information of the kind we have suggested, government departments should not be allowed to demand the same or similar information again. Corporations should be required to file only whatever supplementary information is properly required by a particular department.

Need for a Central Repository

To complement the freer distribution of major corporate data within government, and to help achieve greater openness, an effective method of disseminating data on these large firms to the public is needed. It would be desirable to establish a central repository for corporate data intended to be made available to the public. The additional information we have discussed earlier would be included in this category. With the aid of modern copying and computer techniques the logistics of this should not be a serious problem. The advantage is that all data and all documents that these major corporations provide to shareholders, investors, the press and government agencies, and that should be open to the public, would be accumulated, centralized and readily accessible. Because housing this data in Ottawa, while necessary, is not convenient for most Canadians, arrangements should be made to make the data accessible in other centres also, for example, the regional offices of the Department of Consumer and Corporate Affairs.

This central repository should be flexible enough in its structure and workings so that companies could, if they wished, also deposit there copies of documents they give to investors, shareholders, stock exchanges and securities commissions. To the extent that corporations disclose in such documents matters that would be required to be disclosed under the proposal we have made, the deposit of the documents would thereby relieve the corporations of having to make a separate disclosure report on those matters. (If desired, additional material, such as that given by the firms to the media or financial analysts, could also be deposited.) We do not suggest an alteration in the nature of these documents, which are primarily intended for investor or shareholder purposes. A great deal of work and care goes into their preparation, and they have all come to be regarded as "public" documents. Their deposit in the central repository would merely accord some official recognition to this fact, and make them continuously available.

Under this proposal, there would in time be developed a truly comprehensive collection of important corporate information, to which all those concerned with one or other aspect of corporate activity would have ready access. The cost to the companies should be nominal. CALURA is already used for the purposes of collecting certain kinds of corporate data, and we think that Act, and the facilities established pursuant to it, can be adapted to the purpose we have suggested. The benefit to the public should justify the costs.

While we favor the concept of differential disclosure (a system where the data requested of the largest corporations and made publicly available is more detailed and extensive than would be the case with other firms), the system should be flexible enough to permit other public corporations to participate if they wished to do so. They would then be accepting the fact that most of the data reported to government would be interchangeable among departments and deposited in the public repository. In addition, they would be subject to the extended disclosure requirements applicable to the very large firms. On the other hand, any information filed by them should come within the rule prohibiting individual government departments from requesting it again.

Periodic Review

Since large quantities of data are collected from the hundreds of thousands of businesses with which we have not been directly concerned, we think we should comment on the collection process itself, not only in reference to the very largest companies but to all Canadian businesses. As indicated earlier, although we have not conducted a detailed analysis of the multitude of data requests made by government to business, we have seen and heard enough to reach some conclusions.

We think it would be a productive process—and a healthy discipline—for there to be a periodic public review of the broad issues involved in government's collection of business data. Those issues would include the general processes by which information is collected. the degree of coordination of data requests within government, the problems of duplication and confidentiality (clearly related), the integration of federal requests with those made by other governments, and related general questions. The reviewing body could also consider things such as the difficulties created when a branch of government that has determined it needs certain data for a particular purpose succumbs to the bureaucratic tendency to allow that practice to become entrenched permanently. This kind of analysis and evaluation should be conducted regularly, perhaps every five years, but it does not require a permanent body. Indeed some argue that CALURA itself should become a "sunset law", either renewed or allowed to die at regular intervals (say, every five to seven years).

However accomplished, the law should create a public review committee of people from within and outside the public service, with a majority of members and a chairman from outside government. We think qualified people from outside government should and would participate in this kind of review, particularly since there would not be long time commitments involved: a few weeks should suffice to conduct the kind of critical evaluation and analysis we think would be desirable.

Permanent Control Mechanism

This procedure is not intended to be a substitute for effective control in the implementation and handling of government's collection efforts. The periodic review will necessarily concern itself mainly with broad principles, and will examine details only as an aid in coming to general conclusions. It is equally important that there be a continuing and permanent control mechanism so that the policies and principles established by government following the report of the review committee are realized in practice, and in the most efficient manner. To achieve that it is necessary to require specific departmental data requests to be approved by a review committee to ensure that the broad guidelines are adhered to in practice. For it is in the implementation process that duplication and lack of coordination may result.

We think there should be a body drawn largely from within government to perform a continuous review, between the periodic reviews, of the information-collecting process. Since we see this as a permanent job it is not practical to expect outsiders to participate full-time; but outsiders may agree to examine specific situations for short periods, and we suggest that they be asked to do so. This body might perform the task (to a certain degree now performed by the Treasury Board) of approving specific data requests to be made by government of businesses, both large and small. It would act as a central, co-ordinating agency, responsible for ensuring that there is no duplication, that the data have not already been provided to another department, that the request and the manner of its implementation conform to the policies established by the review committee. This agency should also pay close attention to the difficulties smaller businesses have in reporting information to government, and should make every attempt to reduce the burden upon those firms. This agency and the work it will perform are necessary complements to the periodic review committee.

Those of our recommendations requiring legislative action can probably be implemented by amendments to the Corporations and Labour Unions Returns Act. The implementation of these ideas need not interfere with the work of other authorities (such as securities commissions), which will continue to examine possible innovations in their own disclosure regimes.

We cannot leave this discussion, however, without mentioning that the aim of reducing the multiplicity of information collection requirements will not be achieved unless there is better federal-provincial coordination. Much of the present duplication exists because information that must be filed under federal law must also be filed, for example, under the securities legislation of one or more provinces. Often, we are told, there are trivial differences in forms and the like, which prevent the filing with one agency of a copy of a document filed with another, even though the information is in all important respects identical. There is no easy solution to this problem because it is a problem of federalism itself. Nevertheless, governments should be more conscious than they are of the cost of disclosure.

It should be possible for the review committee to include provincial government representatives, and for the central information repository to include much of the information that would otherwise be collected individually by provincial governments and agencies.

Private Companies

Companies whose shares are closely held ("private" companies) do not rely on the capital markets for equity funds in the same way as widely held, public companies. For this reason it had long been considered that their financial affairs were of concern only to their own shareholders and creditors, and that the public had no legitimate interest in such a firm's financial statements. In 1970 the Canada Corporations Act was amended to require any private firm incorporated under that Act whose annual revenues exceeded $10 million or whose assets exceeded $5 million to make public its annual financial statements by filing them with the government. Firms above the stipulated size level (an admittedly arbitrary one) were presumed to have a sufficient public impact to warrant their financial statements being publicly available. However, provincial legislatures have not yet implemented similar rules applicable to provincially incorporated firms.

We have two comments to make on this subject. Public disclosure of financial statements by some closely held companies above an appropriate size, wherever incorporated, seems to us valid in principle. It is certainly justified where they receive grants, subsidies, loans or assistance from the federal or other governments. It seems to us correct in principle that any such firm, regardless of the place of its incorporation or its share ownership, that receives public funds or assistance, should be required to make the same public filings of its financial statements (and those of its affiliated companies) as is now required of all large private federally incorporated firms. This information would be useful to Parliament and others when considering such matters as trade and industrial policies. Most importantly, if public funds are going to be used to aid a large private company, it should be on the condition that the public receives certain financial information about it.

The Irving Group of Companies

Virtually all the companies we examined in the course of our work are very large organizations with impact in many regions of Canada. Indeed, a good many are significant nationwide, and some are important outside Canada as well. There are probably very few firms in Canada that are active within only one particular geographic area but that are nevertheless so important to that area as to be truly a "concentration of corporate power". The most significant such regional corporate force is the Irving group in New Brunswick.

Founded by K. C. Ivring in the 1920s and now headed by his three sons, the Irving group consists of about one hundred companies. The group is one of the predominant forces in the Maritime region in oil refining and distribution, pulp, paper, timber products, shipbuilding and newspapers and is a powerful influence in the life of the region. Collectively, it probably employs more than ten thousand people and may have aggregate annual revenues exceeding a billion dollars. By any measure it is a major concentration of power and within the context of the Atlantic provinces it is especially significant.

A good deal has been written about the Irving group, although most of it has been based more on educated guesswork than on fully reliable facts. This is so because the Irving companies do not make public any information about their size, scope of activities or financial affairs unless required to do so by law. The law (particularly provincial law) at present imposes very few requirements of public disclosure on privately owned firms such as the Irving companies.

As we have done with a number of other firms, we commissioned a study of the Irving group. These studies are intended to describe in some detail the nature and role of these major corporate concentrations. All the other studies include considerable financial and corporate information because the shares of the various firms are widely held, and so the firms make public their financial statements (and generally much other data). Since this was not so with the Irvings, we requested them to provide us with some basic financial information for the purposes of the study. Concurrently we compiled a corporate chart, which is as accurate as public information permitted (and which is published in the study).

Through their counsel the Irvings said that they would not provide us with the basic financial information needed for a study which would be made public. We gave considerable thought to the matter and also engaged New Brunswick counsel to advise us on local procedure in case we decided to attempt to obtain the information by legal process in that jurisdiction. Our assessment of the situation was that, while any legal process we initiated would likely be successful eventually, we would probably be embroiled in a protracted, distracting and expensive contest. We concluded that the circumstances did not justify such a diversion from the more important task of compiling this *Report*. The study on the Irving group, while not as complete as the others we have commissioned, is being published along with the rest because it does add somewhat to the public knowledge about this important group of companies.

This experience is a vivid illustration of the deficiencies in the law upon which we have commented in this section and which, as we have said, should be remedied.

Line-of-Business Reporting

One of the other issues we wish to discuss is whether some advanced form of "Line-of-Business" (L.O.B.) financial reporting should be required of large companies. L.O.B. reporting, or segmented reporting, would apply to a diversified firm operating in more than one industry, or producing many products, and would require that firm to report its financial results by major product lines. Some people suggest that this will highlight profitable opportunities for potential competitors, provide additional information for investors, and lead to a better allocation of economic resources. As we said in Chapter 9, we also think it is important to workable competition.

The Canada Business Corporations Act, in force since December 1975, requires corporations coming under it to produce financial statements in conformity with the Regulations under the Act. Regulation 47, which applies to a corporation that carries on a diversified business, requires from federally incorporated companies a form of L.O.B. reporting. The regulation requires that the financial statements of such corporations disclose separately a summary of financial information for each class of business the revenue of which is 10% or more of the corporation's total revenue. The directors must determine the classes of businesses, usually in accordance with the Statistics Canada

Standard Industrial Classification Code. However, the directors can select a different classification if they think that would be more appropriate. The Ontario Business Corporations Act also requires L.O.B. reporting, and the Ontario Securities Commission has published a draft regulation under which L.O.B. reporting will be required.

The U.S. Securities and Exchange Commission requires companies to include segmented financial information in their annual 10-K reports. The requirements as to line-of-business reporting are similar to those in Ontario, the determination of the particular lines of business being left to the directors of the company.

The most controversial and far-reaching proposal for L.O.B. reporting is that of the U.S. Federal Trade Commission, which in 1974 began a program requiring large firms to report to the FTC income statement and balance sheet information on some 275 different categories. The program is quite complex, and was explained to us in testimony by F. M. Scherer, who was at the time the director of the Bureau of Economics of the FTC, and one of those responsible for the implementation of the program.

Scherer pointed out that the L.O.B. data are aggregated, so that individual company data are not identifiable in any report by the FTC. His testimony contains details of the uses to which L.O.B. data will be put, and the benefits that are expected to flow from the program. These benefits are related in part to the role played by the FTC in the U.S. antitrust enforcement program. The program is intended to assist the FTC in its analysis of competitive market performance; long-term above-average profits in any line of business are regarded as evidence of high barriers to entry in that sector.

Scherer told us about the difficulties in the program, and the strong objections that have been raised. A number of firms refused to comply, resulting in legal proceedings between them and the FTC. One of the serious problems is the necessity of defining categories of product on a somewhat arbitrary basis, leading some opponents to argue that the data produced are bound to be "contaminated" and therefore unreliable. Opponents of the program argue that no reliable conclusions could be drawn from information about sales or profits in a category which includes (as is the case with one FTC category) aircraft seats, church pews and blackboards. A further problem arises in vertically integrated firms. Since different firms will use different methods of pricing products transferred from one division to another, it is argued that there is bound to be too much inconsistency of practices to permit comparisons of results. Another major problem is in allocating common costs to separate categories of product. With different allocation methods among firms, widely varying results are bound to occur.

In our view the new federal requirements (supplemented by the Ontario rules) should provide all the benefits to Canada that might reasonably be expected of a segmented or line-of-business reporting program. We cannot, of course, comment on the utility of the FTC's program for the United States, but we do not believe that as detailed a program should be introduced in Canada.

Inflation Accounting

The lack of an adequate method of accounting for inflation almost certainly produces the single most important gap in financial disclosure by Canadian enterprises. During an inflationary period the financial statements of corporations, prepared using generally accepted accounting principles based on historical cost figures, contain serious distortions. For example the rate of growth in sales and profits is overstated. Actual profits are overstated, because expenses such as depreciation and cost of goods sold are understated. Return on investment is overstated because profits are overstated and invested capital is understated. Management of capital is distorted, because management has paid income taxes and dividends based on illusory profits. Balance sheets lose much of their meaning as mixed dollar balances are accumulated. In these and other ways, the usefulness and relevance of information provided by historic cost accounting is greatly reduced in periods of high inflation.

The problems raised by historical accounting practices are more pronounced in Canada than in the countries with which it competes in export markets, because Canada is one of the few countries where industry currently receives no allowance for inventory replacement through use of the LIFO (last in, first out) method in the calculation of taxable income although the tax law grants a small deduction. LIFO accounting is permitted in the United States, Great Britain, Japan, and other countries.

The difficulties confronting Canadian companies are, of course, not solely the result of current accounting practices; they are caused by inflation itself. But the accounting problem is pressing, and a good deal of concern has been expressed to us about it.

There are further implications. The recording of artificially high profits may accelerate demands from various segments of society, such as shareholders and employees, for a larger share of profits, when in reality profits are less than they appear to be. Clearly the fall in the real rate of return on investment, coupled with the distribution of what may be excessive dividend payments, has made it more difficult for many firms to acquire or retain the funds needed for expansion.

These and other implications are discussed in a May 1976 study, *Inflation: Its Impact on Business,* by Touche Ross & Company, chartered accountants. The Touche Ross study indicates, for example, that annual depreciation charges against earnings by Canadian business, based on the historical costs of existing assets, are far below the actual annual outlays of capital needed to replace this productive capacity. In the two-year period 1974-75, depreciation calculated on the basis of replacement cost of assets was said to exceed the historical depreciation charged against earnings by $5.7 billion.

Various methods have been proposed for recognizing and reflecting the reality of inflation in financial statement presentation. These are being reviewed and analyzed by many groups in this country. The accounting profession, several large accounting firms and individuals in several disciplines have produced and published discussion papers on LIFO inventory accounting, price-level accounting and current value accounting, which are the three variations to current practice under most active consideration. The federal government is now participating with the Canadian Institute of Chartered Accountants in its study of the various methods that might be utilized to alleviate the problem. An Ontario Select Committee has also looked at this problem.

We are not proposing to do more than draw attention to this difficult problem. This is a technically complex issue, and must be studied in considerable detail. Skills of a number of disciplines must be applied to an analysis of the implications of alternative proposals. We believe that the appropriate groups and public authorities in Canada are properly aware of the problem, and are addressing it. We hope a solution is reached soon, so that the public may have a better understanding of the true economic position and performance of Canadian business.

General Comment on Disclosure

This chapter would not be complete unless we expressed our view on a further aspect of disclosure. We have a bias in favor of openness, and its healthy effects. We have dealt here with corporate openness, but the approach we have suggested would apply equally to other major organizations in Canada. Other examples would be trade unions, pension funds and government. Little is known by the public about the structure or financial significance of trade unions and pension funds. Some pension funds have assets in the many hundreds of millions of dollars and, as we said in Chapter 10, at least one, that of the Canadian National Railways, exceeds a billion dollars. They are becoming large concentrations of corporate ownership. Their beneficiaries should receive information about their activities and investments in much the same way as shareholders of corporations do.

It is beyond our mandate to do more than draw attention to this situation and to say that the same approach to disclosure that we have suggested apply to large and important companies is also appropriate for other large institutions.

In a democratic society dominated by large institutions it is natural that there should be as much demand for accountability and openness regarding government's activities as there is from the corporate sector. Yet there are many implications in the policy of allowing the public more access to and knowledge about government and its actions. It is not for us to consider this complex and controversial issue, and we have not been asked to appraise it. But we are urging more openness, and we must say that it would be consistent with what we have proposed for corporations if there were effective laws providing for disclosure of government information. Public confidence in government is even more important than public confidence in corporations, and disclosure of information is central to the maintenance of that trust.

Chapter 14

Corporate Influence

Among the potentially most important social implications of major concentrations of corporate power is the influence exerted by corporations upon public authorities and public opinion. For the purposes of this chapter, influence may be thought of as both "the capacity or power of persons or things to produce effects on others by intangible or indirect means", and the capacity to persuade.

Most theories of the contention of competing interests in society assume both that the process of contention is good ("democratic pluralism") and that the powers possessed by the legitimate contending interests will not be so disproportionate as to render the contest a ritual. If, however, as some argue, unequal contests arise when knowledgeable, well-financed, and well-organized corporate interests enter the debate in the formation of public policy, the prospect of corporate concentration raises the possibility that this reputed advantage will be enhanced.

While corporate influence is described extensively in the literature, beliefs about its nature differ widely. At one extreme, the view is held that because of the nature of class power and the power of the purse, big business molds public opinion largely as it desires and controls government actions by some form of conspiracy with ruling members of the federal and provincial governments. At the other extreme, the view is expressed that lobbying does not exist in Canada, that the mass media are dominated by radical writers and broadcasters, that governments are so dependent for votes on popular measures that their economic and social policies are invariably antibusiness, and that this produces an economic environment in which private enterprise and investment cannot continue to provide growth and prosperity.

Clearly, both extremes misrepresent the reality. This Commission has relied on information gathered from a wide variety of sources in reaching an opinion on the subject, including the briefs and testimony presented to us, previously published research and research studies commissioned by us.

337

Corporate Involvement in Government Decision-Making

We are here concerned with the influence of major corporations upon public authorities: governments at the federal, provincial and municipal levels and their regulatory agencies. In general, as the size of jurisdiction decreases and the constitutional field of responsibility narrows, the large corporation might be expected to become a more dominant force in decision-making. Put differently, the larger the corporation and the smaller the government unit, the more influence that corporation is likely to have. The one-company town is the extreme example of this phenomenon.

Many of the gaps in research on corporate influence in Canada exist because of the form of government we have in this country. The cabinet and parliamentary form of government and the lesser importance of committees and their chairmen in Parliament as compared with the U.S. government do not give rise to nearly the amount of publicly recognized lobbying activity as that evident in the United States. Moreover, the traditions of cabinet and public service confidentiality hide the most important parts of the process by which many interest groups and important individuals may influence the decisions of governments in Canada. At the local level the process is more open but probably less important to an understanding of the implications of major concentrations of corporate power.

Two separate issues must be considered. The first is the question of access to those engaged in policy-making and administration, and the second is whether, given access, the representatives of major corporations have an undue share of influence.

Access to public authorities is an essential part of the democratic process. It is available in principle both through members of Parliament (and of the provincial legislatures), including members of Cabinet and their personal political staffs, and through the various departments and offices of the public service. This access is less than satisfactory for many people, particularly those living away from Ottawa and the provincial capitals and those who do not normally deal directly with government and so have not developed expertise or contacts. Also the information upon which to make a case is often not in the public domain and is too expensive to produce independently.

There is little doubt that the representatives of major corporations can and do have greater access to both politicians and public servants than do other individuals through trade associations, their own professional representatives and, perhaps most effectively, private conversations between corporate officers and those involved in the policy-making and legislative process. This type of access is achieved not only by business but also by farm and labor groups and by many others with special interests who have organized themselves and acquired the knowledge necessary to achieve such access.

Contacts between leaders of government and business can be very close and personal, though this is by no means general. It is not surprising that there should be close contact between many businesses and the governments of Canada and the provinces in which they operate, for there is a comon concern with a wide variety of economic and social problems and legislative and regulatory measures. The success of government measures requires knowledge of how they may be expected to affect particular industries or companies, while the success of business projects will require a knowledge of the laws and public policies that will apply to them. It is in the public interest that there should be consultation in these matters.

It seems to this Commission, however, that not only should the public authorities be making some serious efforts to provide information to, and access for, early consultation with other interests affected by the same kinds of policies and measures that are the subject of consultation with businesses, but also they should make public the policy alternatives and background materials that underlie proposed bills. In this way those who are not knowledgeable about the ways of government will have a better chance to identify and promote their interests in these matters. Already some steps along these lines have been taken in Ottawa and some provincial capitals, but more seem to be needed to counterbalance the substantial organizational and financial advantages that businesses have in consulting with governments. There is the much greater availability of background studies and data in the U.S. congressional system and in relation to U.S. regulatory agency decisions.

When we turn from the question of access to consider whether it results in effective influence, we are on more difficult ground. Under our parliamentary system, important decisions are basically made by ministers, either in Cabinet, or Cabinet committees, or in their offices in discussion with their senior officials. Generally the discussions are not made in public, nor are the final papers underlying them usually published. The decisions are proposed to Parliament or the legislatures for action or announced publicly and are then usually debated and defended at length. Those who make the decisions take responsibility for them and must defend them with arguments but need not say who or what influenced them (although they frequently will). The consequence is that evidence is usually lacking on who really influenced a decision. Even when the result coincides with the views of major businesses it should not be assumed that undue influence rather than the facts of the situation and general government policies led to the decision.

Some writers, such as Wallace Clement, have observed the extent to which the corporate "élite" and the government "élite" (political and bureaucratic) spring from similar classes and have concluded that "it appears the alliance between government and business is not an alliance of equals but one dominated by the interests of corporate capitalism".

On the other hand, two sociologists, Donald P. Warwick and John G. Craig, who testified before us, reported in their brief:

None of the élite studies in Canada has been able to establish that the large or concentrated corporations, or their related interest group associations, have a disproportionate influence on political decision-making at the federal or provincial level when compared with unions, parties, consumer organizations, or other lobbies. This is not to deny that such influence exists, but to point out that research to date has not supplied convincing evidence on the political influence of corporations. Presthus (1973) has carried out the most intensive study to date. At the empirical level his research attempted to trace the interactions among interest group directors and two other groups: federal and provincial legislators; and federal and provincial higher civil servants. While this study provides useful information about the resulting interactions, it permits no generalizations about the relative influence of large or concentrated corporations. Needless to say, research in this area is extremely difficult. The Gray Report (Government of Canada, 1972) faced similar difficulties in assessing the political impact of foreign-controlled corporations.

One of the most detailed and well-documented case studies of the efforts of major corporations to influence public policy in Ottawa was the study by Ronald Lang (*The Politics of Drugs*) on the efforts of the international pharmaceutical industry between 1961 and 1969 to influence policies and legislation directed to reducing drug prices in Canada. This case illustrates both the various means that can be used to influence policy and how they can be overcome by determined effort. Lang compares the effectiveness of the lobbying techniques of the Pharmaceutical Manufacturers' Association of Canada (PMAC) and the Association of British Pharmaceutical Industries (ABPI). The ABPI was successful in its efforts in Britain to maintain drug prices, but the PMAC in Canada was not. The reason why the PMAC's efforts did not meet with more success in Canada than they did rests at least in part with the fact that it employed American congressional lobbying techniques, which were unsuited to the parliamentary system. The imported tactics served to alienate both parliamentarians and media alike. Lang describes the PMAC's lobbying techniques as intensive, ineffective, and highly inappropriate in contrast to the highly organized and credible ABPI efforts in Britain.

Published references to corporate influence in connection with revisions to the combines legislation include the picture H. G. Thorburn has given us (in the *Canadian Journal of Economics and Political Science*, 1964) of a campaign in which business groups undertook to persuade the government to change proposed anti-combines legislation through the "personal influence of prominent business leaders and elaborate briefs prepared by skilled lawyers". Thorburn concluded that, in that instance, the government "gave in to interested parties to such an extent that its most important amendments could not be defended by rational analysis". William Stanbury, in *Business Interests and the Reform of Canadian Competition Policy, 1971-75* (1977), has presented a similar picture of a more recent attempt to revise the same legislation. This literature conveys a picture of substantial and effective business influence on competition policy.

The history of tax reform between the publication of the *Report* of the Royal Commission on Taxation in 1967 and the passage of legislation in

December 1971 was another example of the process by which business attempted to influence policy and highly technical legislation. In this case much of the action took the form of published briefs and statements and the proceedings of the Standing Committee on Finance, Trade and Economic Affairs of the House of Commons. It was complicated by the active participation of the provincial governments, most of whom argued both in private and in public in favor of certain business views in preference to the initial position of the federal government. Some business views ultimately prevailed on detailed points and certain major issues pertaining largely to business-related aspects of taxation. Certainly though, the principle components of tax reform were put into legislation in a form that led most business commentators to feel they had lost the battle.

Business leaders have told us in public and in private, singly and in groups, that their views on the country's economic and social needs are not being taken into account by governments. This is consistent with their public statements during the last few years, and with the decisions that numerous businesses have taken to defer capital projects or to invest outside Canada. Among other issues businessmen have cited the rush for increased royalties and tax revenues from petroleum and other minerals in 1974, the way government borrowing has affected capital markets, "excessive" wage increases, particularly in the public sector, the rapid growth in public expenditures and taxation, the increasing encroachment by government in the marketplace by agencies such as the Foreign Investment Review Agency (FIRA), the nature and confusion of the Anti-Inflation Program and the suggestions that the controls may be followed by basic changes in business-government relations.

Formal collective consultations between government and business (and between trade unions and government) have not been particularly productive for many years. Therefore, the importance of the governments' contacts with individual industries and companies on particular issues has increased. Some efforts are now being made to bring about more formal consultations of government leaders with both labor and business leaders and with others such as farmers' and consumers' representatives. Perhaps, in new circumstances, these may achieve some success and reduce the widespread suspicion and concern. But until they do, governments should be as frank as possible about their consultations with particular industry groups and individual businesses and make efforts to have consultations on the same subjects with other interested and informed groups who may have a different perspective.

The close relations between many members of the Senate and major corporations, which are usually quite open and well known, have given rise over the years to a concern about conflicts of interest. This concern would probably have been greater if people thought the Senate wielded more effective power vis-à-vis the House of Commons. Possible means to deal with these conflicts of interest were studied and reported upon by the Standing Senate Committee on

Legal and Constitutional Affairs during 1976. This Commission does not believe that its mandate extends to making further suggestions for parliamentary reform.

Corporate Contributions to Political Parties

Public perceptions of the influence of corporations upon governments have been reinforced in the past both by the contributions made to the financing of political parties and the election expenditures of candidates for political office and by the secrecy of these contributions. This problem has been well known in Canada since the famous "Pacific Scandal" of 1872. What is less well known is the role that contributions by businessmen and corporations have always played in sustaining the political process in Canada and the increasing need for contributions from various sources as the costs of communication and campaigning have increased.

There has been a good deal of serious study and action on this subject, commencing in Quebec in 1960. To bring the information and analysis up to date we commissioned a research report on the subject by Khayyam Paltiel, and his report is being published separately by the Commission. It analyzes the federal and provincial election laws in Canada and includes a summary survey of political finances and their control in the United States, Britain, France, Germany, Sweden and Japan.

The principal federal legislation on the subject is the Election Expenses Act of 1974. It gives legal status both to political parties and to candidates and imposes on them responsibilities for controlling and reporting their expenses and for disclosing both the contributions received from various types of givers (individuals, trade unions, associations, and corporations) and the identity of all those giving more than $100. The Act sets limits, related to the number of electors in the district in which he runs, on the amount of a candidate's campaign expenditures. There are also limits on the amount of broadcasting time that may be purchased by political parties; half the cost of this time is reimbursed from public funds. Candidates who gain at least 15% of the votes cast in their ridings are reimbursed from public funds for part of their election expenses. A carefully defined tax credit is allowed under the Income Tax Act to taxpayers for contributions to federal or provincial parties or candidates.

There is a wide variation among provincial laws, which it is impractical to review here. Quebec has been the leader in reform as well as in the recognition of the problem. The following paragraphs from Paltiel's study sum up his review of legislation:

> The legal accountability of parties, candidates and their agents, for their financial practices is an essential first step in any reform program, but the efficacy of the legislation has yet to be tested in the readiness of responsible officials to prosecute

and the courts to punish violations; a complaisant or coopted control body, no matter its formal authority, can well undermine the intent of any law. Much has been done to remove the mystery surrounding party funds through the enactment of detailed reporting and disclosure provisions, but only Ontario and Saskatchewan have tackled the problem of funds from non-domestic sources and only Manitoba has sought to eliminate the influence of corporate gifts. The federal law attempts to inhibit the swamping of the electorate by advertising on the electronic media but the Ontario ceilings on advertising expenditures simply invite wealthy parties and candidates to outshout their competitors. Subventions to candidates have introduced a measure of equity to the political process but apart from Quebec no jurisdiction provides direct aid to parties between elections and they remain crippled as formulators and communicators of policy and programs, and the electorate remains largely ignorant of alternative options. Tax incentives may encourage giving in Ontario and the federal level, but it has yet to be shown that the older parties can organize mass fund-raising and abandon their dependence on business sources. Publicity and disclosure are helpful but the control bodies appear to take an accounting rather than an analytic or scholarly approach to the data at their disposal. A plethora of facts can confuse as well as illuminate if represented in undigestible form.

Probity, openness and equity have been fostered but significant reductions in campaign costs have yet to be achieved in Canada and its provinces. Solutions must yet be found to stimulate greater participation in the electoral process which is the only substitute for the tactics of violent confrontation.

Since the completion of Paltiel's study, the National Assembly of Quebec has passed an Act that bars outright all contributions by corporations to political parties and candidates. Manitoba also bans such contributions and Ontario limits them (but at a high level). Under federal, Ontario and Saskatchewan laws, corporate contributions must be disclosed both by parties and candidates if they exceed $100.

Corporate contributions may lead to some sense of obligation and conflict of interest, as well as suspicion, even though the companies involved often contribute to two or more rival parties or candidates and neither ask nor expect any *quid pro quo*. In the short term, we think suspicions can be diminished and potential conflicts of interest revealed by requiring disclosure of contributions from organizations as well as individuals. This should be supplemented by annual corporate disclosure of aggregate political contributions. This seems to us where the detailed and comprehensive obligation should lie. Canada can control and require disclosure of contributions from Canadian corporations whether foreign-controlled or not, and we think that no distinction should be made among them at present as long as the parties and candidates are required to give in detail the identity of all donors of substantial amounts and the corporations make the disclosure we have mentioned.

We do not propose that Canada seek to prohibit political contributions made in other countries by Canadian corporations or their officers or subsidiaries. We do think, however, that they should be disclosed in Canada. The permissibility of such donations is a matter for the foreign countries to control and Canada should not seek to legislate extraterritorial behavior, as we have objected to other countries doing in regard to Canada.

Corporate Influence on Charitable Organizations

Another way in which corporations affect their environment is through their general policies regarding donations to, and participation in, charitable organizations. The number of requests for corporate donations, tax laws that allow deductions for charitable donations up to 20% of net income before tax, and general acceptance by corporation executives of the desirability of making donations indicate that we can expect this practice to continue.

Since 1958 there has been a general upward trend in Canadian corporate donations both in absolute amounts and as a percentage of individual donations. This emphasizes the growing reliance by organizations seeking money on continuing donations by corporations. On the other hand, corporate donations as a percentage of total corporate net income before tax declined from 1958 through 1967 and were stable at around .7% from 1969 to 1974. Canadian corporations contribute a considerably smaller percentage of net income before tax (a weighted average of .67%) than do their U.S. counterparts (a weighted average of 1.1%). (See Table 14.1.)

Statistics Canada figures based on taxation statistics and reporting the ratio of charitable donations to profits by major industry groups for 1969-74 show relatively unconcentrated industries like knitting mills, clothing industries, furniture manufacturing and leather products as having consistently high ratios of donations to profits. At the other extreme, with consistently low ratios, are found more concentrated industries such as public utilities, communications and mineral fuels. This suggests some support for the hypothesis that the more concentrated the industry, the lower the relative level of charitable contributions. Available data is really inadequate to draw such a general conclusion however, nor are data available that will allow us to obtain unambiguous results in comparisons of contribution levels by asset size of contributing industry. The figures in Table 14.1 do not include company-paid staff time donated by employers, or the use of corporate facilities by charitable groups.

Whether various community functions should have to be supported by voluntary contributions at all is an important question, but one beyond our mandate. Nevertheless it must be recognized that corporate donations are and will continue to be an important factor in the continuation of many of these services. At present the donations policies of large Canadian corporations remain largely hidden. We think corporations should disclose in their annual reports their aggregate donations, plus detail by category of recipient. In addition we think the tax authorities should provide aggregate statistics on both corporate and personal donations as shown in returns submitted to them. Some rational assessment of the donations process is required and this would be facilitated by such disclosure.

Table 14.1

Corporate and Individual Charitable Donations,
Canada and United States, 1958-75
(Millions of Dollars and Percentages)

Year	Canada				United States	
	Individual Donations	Corporate Donations			Corporate Donations	
		Amount	As a Percentage of Individual Donations	As a Percentage of Net Income before Tax	Amount	As a Percentage of Net Income before Tax
1958	$326	$38	11.6	1.31	$395	.96
1959	358	42	12.0	1.20	482	.93
1960	n.a.	39	n.a.	1.20	482	.99
1961	302	38	12.6	1.10	512	1.05
1962	298	40	13.4	.89	595	1.11
1963	308	42	13.5	n.a.	657	1.14
1964	326	46	14.1	n.a.	729	1.13
1965	299	64	21.4	.97	785	1.04
1966	224	64	28.6	n.a.	805	1.00
1967	243	74	30.5	.96	830	1.07
1968	251	73	29.1	n.a.	1005	1.17
1969	260	67	25.8	.70	1005	1.26
1970	268	69	25.7	.80	797	1.11
1971	281	74	26.4	.70	865	1.05
1972	345	93	26.9	.85	1009	1.05
1973	393	118	30.0	.72	1174	1.01
1974	440	170	38.6	.70	1250	.98
1975					1175	1.03

Sources: Canada: 1958-59, Dept. of National Revenue, *Taxation Statistics* (1960, 1961); 1960-75, Institute of Donations and Public Affairs Research, *Corporate Giving in Canada* (1971-1975); net income before tax, Statistics Canada, *Corporate Financial Statistics*, Cat. 51-207.

United States: Conference Board in Canada, *Annual Survey of Corporate Contributions* (1975).

Note: n.a. = not available.

Corporate Activities Abroad

Any discussion of the influence of large corporations must at least touch some of the issues confronting Canadian corporations doing business internationally.

Corporations encounter practices in other countries which would be offensive or illegal if carried out in Canada. We live in a world where payments of one kind or another are both common and expected in many countries and are often not specifically prohibited under the laws of those countries or are sanctioned by general practice. Apparently such payments are routinely made by corporations competing with those from Canada. Under such circumstances answers can never be simple nor can they be uniform across all situations and all countries. We do not think that Canada should attempt to dictate morality or business practice to other countries. If international codes of conduct are desirable, they should originate in international bodies such as the Organisation for Economic Cooperation and Development.

A distinct but related situation is that in which Canadian firms operate in areas of the world where social conditions are not to the liking of Canadians: Canadian banks and mining corporations in South Africa are examples. Here again the situation is not simple. While some have argued that such a presence supports and legitimates the government involved, others argue that foreign corporations that practise non-discriminatory hiring and treatment represent the leading edge of change in many areas of the world.

Several Canadian corporations testified before us that their policy was to consider business operations in each individual country on their own economic and social merits unless it was explicit Canadian government policy that they not participate. This seems to us the proper approach to this problem.

Corporate Advertising

The most visible way that major corporations endeavor to influence opinion is by advertising their products and, on occasion, their political, social or economic views. Each year corporations spend large sums in Canada on advertising: about $800 million in 1976, of which $240 million was spent on television advertising alone.

Advocacy Advertising

Apart from product advertising, large businesses can influence public opinion through the resources they devote to presenting their political, social or economic views to the public through paid media advertising. This is referred to as advocacy advertising, a term that has been defined by Claude Thompson, a lawyer for the Association of Canadian Advertisers, in the following way:

> ...it is something more than advertising directed to improve a corporate image, it attempts to inform and persuade the public about matters that are not directly related to the sale of a product or a service. It reacts and retaliates against unfair

attacks upon such of the free enterprise system as remains. It attempts to influence government and the public at election time....

Most print and broadcast media in Canada will accept advocacy advertising from commercial clients. A partial exception is the Canadian Broadcasting Corporation whose commercial acceptance policy says:

The CBC does not sell time for controversial or opinion broadcasting...

and goes on to say that:

Institutional advertising must avoid offering a point of view on a subject that is controversial or urging the audience to adopt a particular attitude or course of action on economic, social or political subjects.

We characterize this as a "partial exception" in noting that the CBC found no violation of this code in running the 1976 Imperial Oil Limited advertisements with the slogan: "Each year Imperial spends hundreds of millions of dollars on the big, tough, expensive job of developing petroleum supply.... If Imperial is to continue to help Canada lessen its oil dependence on other countries the company will have to put even more money to work." This was an advertisement that many advertisers and agencies in Canada viewed as a political statement dealing with an area of public controversy, and which an executive of Imperial's own advertising agency classified as "a prototype of advocacy advertising of the future." Critics of the Imperial Oil advertisements argued that Imperial claimed a profit of only 6 cents on the sales dollar, which is not the way a company would normally report its profits. In 1975, Imperial's rate of return on invested capital was about 12% and on shareholders' equity about 16%, and this is what they reported in their 1975 annual report. Critics further point out that Imperial spent $74 million on exploration in 1975, the same amount they spent in 1972 when their profits were only about 60% of the 1975 profits.

The CBC has refused to run other advocacy advertising, for example the 1976-77 "Lets Free Enterprise" campaign of the Insurance Bureau of Canada, which was carried on the CTV network and by independent stations.

It has been drawn to the Commission's attention by those who lack the resources to present views contrary to those of corporations that such advertising is unfair, and that an opportunity to reply in a form and manner comparable with that of the original message should be available. It seems to us that advocacy advertising is becoming more common and that rules to govern its use are needed.

It is the issue of the right to reply to advocacy advertising, to counter-advertise, that we wish to emphasize here. The issue of what advertising a medium should accept is a complex one but unrelated to corporate concentration. The decisions reflect a weighing of factors by the media involved, and we have no reason to believe that they are being made in a biased or irresponsible way.

A concern does arise when a controversial message is run, and when members of the public or organizations with another view are denied access to the media to reply, not because of lack of funds, or because all available time has been purchased by other advertisers, but because media do not wish to offend larger advertisers by permitting counter-advertising. This last appears to be the case in Canada with broadcast media, but not with print media. Most, and perhaps all, radio and television stations in Canada currently refuse to sell or supply broadcast time for counter-advertising under any circumstances, primarily, we have been told, because of concern about the possible commercial repercussions from their regular advertisers.

Since the Canadian Radio-Television and Telecommunications Commission (CRTC) is studying the question, we make only general recommendations here. It seems to us necessary to guarantee the rights of those with opposing points of view to purchase broadcast time for the airing of their views. To allow the unopposed selling of economic or political philosophy in the guise of product advertising by dominant firms is patently unfair, and an abuse directly related to the financial "clout" of the advertiser.

However, it is difficult at times to separate advocacy advertising from general non-product advertising, or to decide where it stands with reference to the important principle of freedom of expression. An acceptable approach might be to emulate the fairness doctrine found in the United States. We think that when a paid message representing one side of a significant social, political or economic issue is broadcast, and where there is some issue of truth or interpretation involved, then opposing parties should have the right to reply.

This right should be one of access to the media. Media should not be able to refuse to sell substantially equal time if they have broadcast the initial message. The right of reply need not involve free time, which was during one period an important source of friction in the United States. We recommend that at this time the doctrine apply only to broadcast media, as we are not aware of any cases in which groups have been systematically prohibited from placing counter-advertising in the press. Each broadcaster should indicate in an annual report to the CRTC how much time has been requested, on what issues, and the nature of its response not only as an element in the licence renewal process, but also as a basis on which to evaluate the need for revisions in the application of the principle.

General Product Advertising

Some economists say that heavy advertising expenditures by dominant firms increase product (or seller) differentiation in an industry and thus raise barriers to entry. The alternative view is that heavy advertising is a competitive activity, which aids a new firm entering an industry and thus reduces barriers to entry. Those who argue that heavy advertising is not a barrier to entry, but rather the most successful means of new entry, cite behavior that is said to support this view. For example, new products are observed to be advertised more intensively than are old products. Commonly smaller firms in an industry advertise more intensively than does the firm with the largest market share.

A more obvious criticism of product advertising arises where oligopolists selling essentially homogeneous products try to differentiate them with offsetting advertising in the pursuit of market share. While advertising is an important source of product and purchase information for consumers, it is neither an objective nor a balanced source. We see a real need to improve the information available about alternative prices and sources of products. Publications such as *Consumer Reports*, organizations such as the Consumers' Association of Canada and innovations such as transmission of comparative supermarket prices by cable television are commendable efforts in this direction. However, the need is still largely unfilled, and further initiatives are needed to provide diversity in the product-price-service mix available to consumers, and lessen dependence on advertising as a source of information.

General product advertising has also come under attack from critics for its tastelessness, exploitation of children, perpetuation of stereotypes and fostering of unrealistic expectations. Much criticism has surrounded lifestyle advertising and the possibility that it may inaccurately reflect or even change the values of society. A review of one week of television advertising in North America led the distinguished analyst Erich Fromm to conclude that the major message implied in what he had seen was that ". . . we must all strive to have more, rather than to be more."

The other side of the advertising issue is that product advertising provides the main support of newspapers, magazines and private broadcasting, for which no socially or politically acceptable alternative has yet been found. Privately supported media are essential to the kind of society Canadians seem to want. While these can apparently survive some selective restraint upon certain types of advertising, general restraints could be very damaging and might threaten the country's traditional multiplicity of news and information sources. Restraints might also hinder the advertising of new products and services and thus raise the barriers to entry protecting existing products and firms. Thus while high-level product advertising by major firms has serious implications, particularly when a "life style" is being promoted or implied, we do not see any easy or fair way to restrain it.

Corporate Influence on Public Opinion

In studying conglomerate groups of companies, the Commission has heard a particular concern with regard to the influencing of public opinion. This arises when the control of newspapers or broadcasting stations is in the hands of companies or individuals who own other industrial or commercial enterprises. In these cases there is said to be a potential interest on the part of those who control the media to influence the opinions expressed or the selection of news to be published. We shall discuss three examples of this danger, each with special circumstances.

Particular Cases

The first relates to Power Corporation of Canada, Limited, and more particularly to Paul Desmarais and the companies through which he controls Power Corporation and the newspapers *La Presse* and *Montréal Matin* (Montreal), *Le Nouvelliste* (Trois-Rivières), *La Voix de L'Est* (Granby) and *La Tribune* (Sherbrooke). In addition, as we mentioned in Chapter 7, he has some financial connections with companies and individuals controlling other newspapers and broadcasting stations in Causapscal, Carleton, Shawinigan, Kingston, Peterborough and elsewhere. The most important connection, however, is that with *La Presse*. Control of that newspaper was transferred to him under special legislation of Quebec in 1967.

Desmarais' control of newspapers has been the subject of some controversy in Quebec and special scrutiny by a committee of the Quebec Assembly. He testified to this Commission about his role in regard to *La Presse* and the measures taken to safeguard the independence of the publisher and the journalists. The Commission is aware of the views on this situation in Quebec expressed by Claude Ryan, publisher and editor of *Le Devoir*, who testified as an expert witness in court on a quite separate case and before a Senate Committee. We have also commissioned a special study of *La Presse*, which we are publishing separately. The study suggests little cause for concern, except that potential editorial bias is created by any kind of concentrated ownership.

The second case relating to newspapers is the control of the five English-language daily newspapers in New Brunswick by K. C. Irving and the Irving family interests, who also control a large number of industrial and commercial companies in that province. Certain Irving companies were charged under the Combines Investigation Act with creating and operating a monopoly, throughout New Brunswick, of the business of producing and selling English-language daily newspapers and were found guilty by Mr. Justice Robichaud of the Queen's Bench Division of the Supreme Court of New Brunswick. This verdict was subsequently reversed by the Court of Appeal for New Brunswick and the reversal was upheld by the Supreme Court of Canada.

Many facts of the case and the potential conflicts of interest were brought out in detail in the trial. Although the judge found that the accused had established a monopoly, he stated his belief that Irving and his family did not interfere with the editorial or news policies of the papers and either retained the previous publishers or appointed successors who were qualified and not obviously biased. As in the *La Presse* case, however, the potential for abuse is present.

The third case relates to broadcasting and concerns the control by Argus Corporation Limited of Standard Broadcasting Corporation Limited, in which Argus acquired a major interest in 1946. As we pointed out in Chapter 7, Standard owns a major Toronto private radio station, CFRB. In 1960 it acquired a major English-language radio station, CJAD, in Montreal, and shortly thereafter established FM radio stations in Toronto and Montreal, with the approval of the Board of Broadcast Governors. By way of background it might be mentioned that persons associated with Argus had made an unsuccessful attempt to acquire control of the Toronto *Globe and Mail* newspaper in 1955. A separate attempt was made in 1956 to acquire control of the Toronto *Star*, but it too was unsuccessful.

Attempts by Argus, through Standard Broadcasting, to acquire a television licence in Toronto were withdrawn when approvals were delayed by the CRTC, and an attempted purchase of two radio stations in Hamilton was denied by the CRTC, in accordance with its policy of discouraging the concentration of media ownership. However in 1974 the CRTC approved the acquisition of control by Standard Broadcasting of Bushnell Communications Limited, which controlled television station CJOH in Ottawa and two relay stations in Cornwall and Desoronto, as well as a cable television system in Ottawa and neighboring areas. The CRTC eventually forced the divestiture by Bushnell of the cable television systems, in accordance with its regular policies, though this move was strenuously opposed by the minority shareholders. The CRTC decision exhibited no concern over Argus Corporation's expanding control of important broadcasting stations in spite of its substantial other industrial and commercial holdings.

CRTC Policy

The CRTC states that it has followed an active policy of preventing what it regards as undue concentration of ownership and control of the mass media. It has stated that "the ownership and control of broadcasting undertakings should be separate from the ownership and control of newspapers except in special circumstances". It is also opposed in principle to the ownership and control of cable television systems by those controlling television broadcasting stations. Within the broadcasting field itself, the CRTC has endeavored to promote local ownership and participation, to prevent control by the same interests of more than one station in a network and generally to discourage dominance in an area by multiple station ownership by one company or group of related companies. In carrying out these policies it has encountered some difficulties arising from the need, in accordance with government policy under the Broadcasting Act, to transfer ownership and control from foreign-controlled corporations, since it has been necessary to find buyers qualified to provide satisfactory standards of service.

The CRTC announced in a statement of policy in August 1968 that among the points to be considered in approving ownership of broadcasting outlets was the "extent of ownership of other commercial undertakings which might influence the performance of broadcasting stations". There have been very few cases where this point seems to have been given much if any weight in decisions. The clearest case seems to have been the denial of a proposal by the Campeau Corporation in 1974 to acquire control of Bushnell Communications with its television station in Ottawa. In this case the CRTC "also took note of the concerns expressed by the intervenors regarding the possible conflicts of interest that might arise between the objectives of a company engaged in the development and management of real estate and the responsibilities imposed on broadcasters by the Broadcasting Act" and went on to say, "In the opinion of the CRTC the representatives of Campeau failed to respond adequately to these concerns." In this case the possible conflicts of interest were specific and local. For this reason they were given second place to the CRTC's view that the Campeau company had not given adequate consideration to, or made specific plans and provisions for, carrying out the obligations and responsibilities inherent in the operation of the various broadcasting undertakings they were proposing to acquire.

We have not explored extensively the concentration of corporate power represented by ownership of chains of newspapers, although we did carry out some research. The subject was thoroughly examined in a 1970 *Report* of the Special Senate Committee on Mass Media (the Davey *Report*), which concluded that the case for (or against) newspaper chains was finely balanced. The Committee went on to recommend a Press Ownership Review Board to approve or disapprove mergers or acquisitions of newspapers and periodicals and suggested that all transactions that increase the concentration of ownership in the mass media should be regarded as contrary to the public interest unless shown to be otherwise.

The *Report* concluded that of the 116 daily newspapers in Canada in 1970, 77 were controlled or partially owned by chains. Our research indicated that in 1976 there were 115 daily newspapers in Canada of which 80 were owned or controlled by chains. The trend to chain ownership of major city daily newspapers in Canada seems to be virtually over, largely because of the economic unattractiveness of many of the relatively few remaining independent papers. The long-term trend to chain ownership of small city daily and weekly newspapers will almost certainly continue, largely because of the economies of scale in chain operation and the easier access to financing of acquisitions by existing chains.

The trends in newspaper ownership must be viewed against a background of some of the trends in the industry. The number of cities with two or more separately owned daily newspapers in Canada has decreased steadily since the 1920s.

Another characteristic of many Canadian newspapers, particularly large city dailies, is that they are profitable enterprises. The Davey *Report* concluded that for the pre-1970 period, the "daily-newspaper and broadcasting industries make profits that are, on the average, *very* generous". At the same time, the *Report* commented that these profits were apparently not transformed into improved performance. The *Report* was especially critical of this lack of quality.

The most important challenge to the daily newspaper industry is the technological one from cable television and its ability to deliver many forms of advertising and news to a household faster and more cheaply than a newspaper can. One possibility is that within the next decade cable will replace newspapers in many major cities as the principal carrier of classified advertising, which accounts for about 30% of all daily newspaper revenue. If this happens, it is estimated that a third to a half of all daily newspapers in those cities might become unprofitable. This technological challenge at least partially explains why the principal merger and expansion trend by large city daily newspapers in Canada today is an attempt to expand in a quasi-conglomerate way into non-print communication.

The CRTC cases indicate that it is carrying out a coherent policy under the Broadcasting Act to restrain the concentration of corporate power within the media field, subject to the need to find owners with the capital and inclination to provide an adequate quality of broadcasting service. The CRTC appears to have been satisfied that conflicts of interest on the part of controlling owners who also owned substantial equities in commerce or industry were not serious enough to exclude them from control of broadcasting outlets. We have no knowledge of any behavior on the part of such owners that would justify a general exclusion. It is the trend of one medium expanding into other media areas and of ownership of media interests by industrial or commercial interests that seem to us the most significant to the public interest at this time and the areas where greatest concern should be focused.

Although we do not support the idea of a Press Ownership Review Board, consideration should be given to permitting the CRTC, where appropriate, not only to constrain print media from controlling broadcast or electronic media, as it now does, but also to prevent broadcast media from acquiring or controlling major print media, which the CRTC currently can do only by indirect means if at all.

Chapter 15

Business Size and
Working Conditions

In this chapter we look at five major issues related to employment and discuss the relation between them and corporate concentration. We believe most Canadians would agree that these are the most important problems today in the world of work, except of course for unemployment. However, the relation between size or concentration and rates of unemployment has already been extensively studied in Canada and elsewhere without conclusive results. While there is general agreement on the existence and importance of the problems we shall be discussing, there is much less agreement on their causes and possible solutions. Where competing theories exist, there is frequently insufficient systematic information to support recommendations on one side or the other.

The first issue considered is that of equal opportunity in employment. What is the nature and extent of discrimination in seeking employment or in achieving promotion within an organization? It has been argued that in Canada there is a lack of equal opportunity for women, Francophones, native people and those with particular ethnic, racial or religious backgrounds. Such individuals are thought to have a more difficult time finding work, to obtain less desirable work when they do, to be paid less for the same work, to have less chance of being promoted and to be the first to be laid off. We look at some of the evidence in this area and in particular whether the largest enterprises seem any more of less prone to discriminate than other private and public sector employers.

The second issue is that of level of earnings and other benefits. Is there any difference related to size of firm in the compensation and fringe benefits offered to employees?

The third issue is that of employment-related health and safety. In recent years Canadians have become increasingly aware of many threats to health inherent in certain types of employment. Are larger employers more or less likely to identify and correct unsafe and toxic conditions? Do they lag behind or lead other employers and interest groups in dealing with health?

The fourth issue is alienation from work. Obtaining and keeping employment, earning a fair wage and achieving some financial security have traditionally been what most people ask and expect from employment. It is perhaps a mark of the progress of industrial societies that these are no longer sufficient. Rather than being only a means to the end of obtaining money and security to enjoy life away from the job, many workers also expect the job itself to produce satisfaction and non-monetary rewards. At the same time, many social critics maintain that work in modern societies is intrinsically alienating; that workers feel no sense of pride, involvement or commitment, but rather feel that they are objects to be used according to the impersonal demands of the market and of technology. We attempt to evaluate the evidence available on this difficult question.

The fifth issue is that of power and influence in the work environment. For some critics, the issues we have identified so far are less important than the process by which they are decided. They argue that however satisfactory the conditions of work, if they can be changed unilaterally by the employer, then the system is inherently unfair to workers. Such critics emphasize the need for countervailing power, which has traditionally meant labor unions and government intervention. We consider briefly several of the complex questions raised in this context. Does big business dominate unions, as several of those testifying before us have charged; is the reverse true or is there a reasonable balance of power? We look at several issues made more important by the fact that in 1975 and 1976 Canada had the greatest proportion of time lost through strikes in the industrialized Western world. Are larger companies more prone to strikes than smaller ones? Are strikes longer or shorter in duration in larger companies? Does our record of labor discontent appear to be related to the degree of corporate concentration?

To assist us in understanding the relation between size and human resource policies, the Commission had four studies undertaken on topics of particular interest. The studies, by John W. Gartrell, Victor V. Murray and David E. Dimick, Terrence H. White, and The Niagara Institute, are described below and are being published. In addition to these we also commissioned a brief from Donald P. Warwick and John G. Craig. The brief, which was presented at our public hearings, undertook an identification of the most important social issues associated with corporate concentration, an explanation of the most commonly presented themes and hypotheses related to these issues in the Canadian literature and an analysis of the quality of research and data currently available testing these themes and hypotheses.

Distribution of Employment

In our research we attempted to identify the proportion of employees in enterprises of different sizes or areas of high economic concentration. If size or concentration (however defined) had some bearing on work-related issues, how much of the labor force would be affected?

While this seems an obvious question, it is difficult to obtain relevant data. Statistics Canada breaks down labor force statistics only by industry and

occupational classifications and not by employer size or concentration measures. The best available figure is for the 1973 distribution of employees by
establishment (or plant) size. While there is certainly a relation between size of
plant and size of enterprise or degree of control of an industry by a given firm,
it is by no means exact. Hence the table that follows (Table 15.1) is at best
only suggestive of the proportion of employees working in the largest firms.

In 1973, about 17% of employees in manufacturing industries in Canada
worked in establishments with more than 1,000 employees, while about 46%
were in establishments with fewer than 200 employees (Table 15.1). Since the
1950s, there has been a slight trend for the proportion of employees in the
smallest and largest establishments to diminish slightly and in the middle-size
establishments to increase slightly. Although we do not have firm-level data, it
is probably accurate to say that only 15% or fewer Canadian employees in
manufacturing industries work for private sector firms employing more than
5,000 people.

Table 15.1

Distribution of Employees in Manufacturing Industries,
by Establishment Size, Canada, 1949-73

(Percentages)

Size of Establishment	Percentage Distribution of Employees						
	1949	1955	1961	1964	1968	1970	1973
1–49* employees	23.0	22.2	21.2	19.6	18.2	17.8	16.6
50–99	11.3	11.1	12.4	11.7	11.5	11.6	11.2
100–199	13.3	12.6	13.9	14.0	14.4	15.2	15.4
200–499	18.2	17.6	19.1	19.4	19.9	19.9	21.9
500–999	33.4	12.9	12.4	12.7	12.0	12.4	13.0
1,000 or more		22.5	17.1	18.5	19.5	18.4	17.3
Head office sales offices, and auxiliary units	0.8	1.2	4.0	4.1	4.5	4.7	4.3

Source: Statistics Canada, Cat. 31. 210.
Note: * — Bias may exist in 1949 and 1955 data for this size group because of the inclusion
         of working owners and partners.

It is tempting to conclude from the figures that whatever the largest
employers do vis-à-vis their employees is not highly relevant, that it is what the
smaller, private firms and organizations in the public sector do that matters.
However, large private sector employers lead in influencing employee relations
practices in their specific industries and in the country as a whole. With their
usually large plants in several locations, private sector employers often exert a
major influence on the quality of life in particular communities and regions.

Equal Opportunity in Employment

Regarding the world of work two values are widely shared. One is that
ability to do a job should be the only criterion considered in hiring, compensat-

ing and promoting an employee. The converse is that it is wrong to withhold a job or promotion or to pay lower wages because of a person's race, sex, ethnic group, religion or other characteristics that in themselves have nothing to do with the ability to work satisfactorily. (In many collective agreements there are clauses that stipulate that seniority will be used to determine promotions. Here seniority is used as a surrogate for ability; unions argue that the most senior worker is usually the most able.)

In spite of these values it is widely documented that discrimination in employment has been and is still widespread in our society. Specific references may be found in the brief by Warwick and Craig. It is not the function of this *Report* to document these statistics and studies. We merely assert here that it can be statistically documented that historically the following has occurred:

> Women in general have been paid less for the same work, and have been less likely to be selected for upper-level managerial jobs. This is substantiated by the statistics in *Women in the Labour Force (1976)*, published by the federal Department of Labour. Royal Commission research by Murray and Dimick found only 7 women among 483 members of the top three levels of management in the 20 large and middle-sized Canadian companies that they studied.

> Francophones in Anglophone-controlled companies in Quebec have been under-represented in upper levels of management and in the more skilled and technical occupations.

> Recent immigrants, especially those not from the United Kingdom or northern European countries, have a lower probability of obtaining secure steady employment, suffer wage discrimination and are less likely to rise to upper management. The same holds true for native peoples. Though doubtless not as common now as it was, there is evidence of continuing discrimination against Jews and members of other minority religious groups.

> People who are physically or mentally handicapped find their chances of finding employment lower, even when the job sought is unrelated to their condition.

The low representation of certain groups in the work force is often argued in the literature to be due not to overt discrimination against specific groups but to the cultural backgrounds and expectations of members of such groups, to their educational backgrounds and to their lack of exposure to a range of life experiences and activities, with differences in background combining with the employer's commitment to hiring and promotion on the basis of training and job experience. The limited evidence we have seen suggests that most "discrimination" is probably of this nature.

Our own research and reading of the literature found no persuasive evidence that very large employers are more or less likely to discriminate than others. Walter Haessel and John Palmer have studied the relation of discrimination to concentration in the United States. They contend that the more a firm approaches monopolistic control of the markets in which it competes, the more it will discriminate against disadvantaged people in its employment practices. Their argument was that all employers will discriminate if they have the chance, but that the more a firm gets into a dominant position the more it can afford to do so. Haessel and Palmer present evidence in support of their model from U.S. census data, where they find a negative relationship between four-firm concentration ratios for various industries and percentages of women and black Americans in selected occupations. They recognize that the correlation found between industry concentration and discrimination could have occurred for reasons other than the posited combination of power and the sexual or racial prejudice of employers. For example, Haessel and Palmer do not consider the variable of technology and the possibility that more concentrated industries are technology-intensive. The dominant technology of an industry strongly influences the skills and knowledge required by employers. Insofar as women or black Americans may not have acquired requisite job skills because of discriminatory social values outside the workplace, they will not be qualified to work in that industry.

If one accepts the contention that members of disadvantaged groups do not have equal opportunity in employment because their preparation for some jobs is inadequate, then the primary responsibility for improving equality of opportunity clearly lies with institutions like education and government, with the communications media to encourage the disadvantaged to break their stereotyped work patterns and to create concomitant supportive attitudes in the general population and of course with the minority individual himself. Large corporations, however, even if not a disproportionate cause of employment discrimination, have a special opportunity to assist in correcting such situations. Because they employ large numbers of people, the effectiveness and visibility of large corporations' employment practices are likely to be greater than are those of smaller companies. In those industries where they are leaders in business practice, large corporations' personnel policies are also likely to be followed.

The role of larger businesses was illustrated in several of the research studies prepared for the Commission. Murray and Dimick undertook a study of similarities and differences in personnel practices between ten very large companies with 6,000 or more employees, and ten smaller firms with 450 to 5,500 employees, with larger and smaller firms paired in industries ranging from mining to manufacturing to retailing. Interviews were conducted with 150 personnel managers, line managers and union stewards. Simultaneously, The Niagara Institute undertook a study on broad issues of attitudes and actions in the realm of corporate social responsibility. The Institute used a mail survey sent to 1,083 corporations with at least $10 million in annual sales, from which 284 usable responses were obtained. Questions were asked about a number of issues related to employee relations, as well as issues related to the larger society. Responses were analyzed by number of employees and annual gross revenues of employers.

The Murray-Dimick and Niagara Institute studies, and several corporate briefs submitted to us, indicated that efforts are being made to increase the number of women in management, to increase the use of French in Anglophone-controlled businesses in Quebec and the number of Francophone employees in management, and in some cases to provide opportunities for handicapped people. However, only one company studied by Murray and Dimick (a large chartered bank) had instituted a special training program for young people from backgrounds of chronic poverty and unemployment. An attempt by that bank to expand the program by getting the participation of other banks and financial institutions failed.

In summary, existing material on equal employment opportunity suggests that discrimination is widespread but may be based primarily on differing cultural and educational backgrounds and expectations. There is no evidence that large employers are more or less likely to discriminate than smaller ones. Efforts are being made by some large corporations to rectify some kinds of discrimination but such efforts do not have a high priority in the spectrum of corporate activities.

Earnings and Other Benefits

The level of earnings and other benefits received from employment is a basic concern for most employed Canadians. The most recent information on this subject comes from Statistics Canada's survey of employer labor costs for 1976 (Table 15.2). It makes available for the first time an all-industry tabulation based on a survey of 6,975 reporting plants or establishments. Again we have the problem of the nonavailability of data by size of enterprise; so the results may only in a general sense be attributed to large employers.

In general, enterprises with over 200 employees pay more per capita in total compensation, particularly in vacation and holiday pay, pension contributions, and private life and health insurance than employees in any other size categories. The biggest differences are between large and middle-sized establishments on the one hand and small establishments on the other. (Units of 19 and fewer employees in this survey should not be seen as representative of the smallest businesses, as this subgroup contains a large proportion of units which are themselves part of larger employment units.)

These general findings are supported by breakdowns by job classification, which also indicate higher total compensation packages in larger establishments than in smaller. In virtually all the 30 job classifications measured, workers in establishments employing fewer than 100 people earned less than those in establishments of 100-499, who in turn earned less than those in establishments of 500 or over, in each case for similar work. Examples from 5 of the 30 industries measured are given in Table 15.3.

The findings are supported at the firm level in the study of personnel policies in large and medium-sized firms undertaken by Murray and Dimick. They examined the relationship between firm size and wages paid in eight common occupational categories between ten pairs of larger and smaller firms in different industries. They found wages paid by the large firms to be slightly higher in six of the seven comparable occupations and a tendency for larger firms to have formal policies of paying above-average compensation.

Table 15.2

Employee Compensation, All Industries,* by Size of Establishment, Canada, 1977

	Overall Average	Number of Employees in Establishment									
		5000 and Over	2500 to 4999	1500 to 2499	1000 to 1499	500 to 999	200 to 499	100 to 199	50 to 99	20 to 49	19 and Under
Pay for time worked											
Basic pay for regular work	$10,845.00	$11,451.00	$11,782.00	$12,086.00	$11,671.00	$11,186.00	$10,410.00	$10,369.00	$9,945.00	$9,598.00	$9,770.00
Commissions, incentive bonuses	257.02	75.58	29.46	119.65	140.05	201.34	294.60	293.44	484.32	528.54	626.26
Overtime pay	412.11	433.99	450.07	646.60	414.32	560.42	460.12	349.44	303.32	192.99	164.14
Shift premium pay	40.13	48.09	58.91	72.52	38.51	58.17	48.92	24.88	18.90	11.64	2.93
Other premium pay	37.96	65.27	55.38	65.26	36.18	38.03	43.72	28.00	8.95	12.61	16.60
Sub total**	11,592.22	12,073.93	12,375.82	12,990.02	12,300.06	12,043.96	11,257.36	11,064.76	10,760.49	10,443.78	10,579.92
Paid absence											
Paid holidays	488.02	550.79	563.18	584.96	560.21	513.44	462.20	446.90	411.72	382.10	361.48
Vacation pay	712.52	894.32	812.96	836.76	847.31	741.63	667.28	598.29	552.94	537.27	539.30
Sick leave pay	136.65	258.79	177.90	202.04	180.90	144.30	97.85	75.69	64.64	55.28	60.57
Personal or other leave	22.77	50.38	25.92	33.84	14.01	21.25	18.74	13.48	10.94	9.70	11.72
Sub total**	1,359.96	1,754.28	1,579.96	1,660.60	1,602.43	1,420.62	1,246.27	1,134.36	1,022.24	984.35	973.07
Miscellaneous direct payments	245.10	161.46	195.58	300.94	190.23	336.69	251.92	256.11	268.52	262.82	231.55
Gross Payroll**	13,197.28	13,989.67	14,151.36	14,951.56	14,092.72	13,801.27	12,755.55	12,455.23	12,051.25	11,690.95	11,784.55
Employer contributions to employee welfare and benefit plans											
Workmen's Compensation	159.42	75.58	119.00	201.84	157.56	196.87	180.09	184.57	175.03	162.93	175.86
Unemployment Insurance	174.60	178.63	190.87	189.75	176.23	184.57	171.77	169.01	165.09	160.02	159.25
Canada Pension Plan and Quebec Pension Plan	130.14	127.11	134.31	135.36	131.88	135.35	131.17	123.58	127.30	123.16	123.10
Private Pension Plan	472.84	1,045.48	695.14	802.51	436.50	465.34	361.23	200.12	172.05	139.65	180.75
Quebec Hospital Insurance Board	39.04	35.50	20.03	54.39	61.16	49.22	38.52	36.29	32.82	32.00	30.29
Private life and health insurance	148.58	158.02	167.30	224.74	150.56	177.86	153.03	126.50	112.38	104.73	100.63
Supplementary unemployment benefits and other	24.94	13.74	22.38	71.31	28.01	32.44	24.98	22.81	16.90	16.49	19.54
Sub total**	1,149.56	1,634.06	1,349.03	1,679.90	1,141.90	1,241.65	1,060.79	867.88	801.57	738.98	789.42
Total Compensation**	14,346.84	15,623.73	15,500.39	16,631.46	15,234.62	15,042.92	13,816.34	13,323.11	12,870.82	12,429.93	12,573.97
Number of reporting establishments	6,975	51	63	108	132	318	826	1,000	999	1,774	1,644
Employment (Thousands of employees)	5,658.0	907.6	375.6	314.1	489.2	719.6	876.6	705.5	595.7	538.0	136.2
Percentage	100.0	16.0	6.6	5.6	8.6	12.7	15.5	12.5	10.5	9.5	2.4

Source: Compiled by K.J. Harwood, Labour Division, Statistics Canada, 1977.

Notes: * – including non-commercial sector.

    ** – Columns do not add because of rounding.

Table 15.3

Hourly Wage Rates by Establishment Size,
Selected Industries, Canada,
October 1, 1975

| | Hourly Wage Rates in Establishments of | | |
| | 500 Employees | 100-499 Employees | 1-99 Employees |
Industry/Occupation			
Industrial chemicals-Operator, Class A (male)	$6.95	$6.25	$5.57
Industrial chemicals-Welder, maintenance	7.01	6.79	6.77
Petroleum refineries-Burner operator (male)	6.62	6.49	n.a.
Petroleum refineries-Truck driver, light and heavy (male)	5.84	5.76	n.a.
Iron and steel-laborer non-production (male)	5.51	4.33	4.33
Bag manufacturing-Bag machine operator (female)	4.39	4.47	3.44
Bag manufacturing-Box maker, paperboard (male)	6.12	4.85	4.43
Sawmills-Lumber sorter (male)	n.a.	5.50	5.05

Source: Royal Commission on Corporate Concentration (RCCC) research.
Note: n.a. = not available.

There is little research relating wage rates to the degree of product market concentration. Comparisons of selected concentration ratios and average annual earnings for comparable industry definitions compiled by our research staff reveal a weak but positive relationship between degree of industry concentration and average annual wage in 1970. However, this may be explained by capital intensity as an intervening variable. Thus, it may be that the higher the capital intensity the higher the wage rate.

J. C. H. Jones and L. Laudadio of the University of Victoria, using Canadian data for 1965 and 1969 in studying of wage differentials and market imperfections, indicated that the presence of unions causes a variation in wage rates. They argued that it is a combination of the presence of unions and high concentration which best explains the level of wage rates. They hypothesized that union power and market power will increase the wage rates higher than average wage rates (the value of marginal product of labour) for the industry or occupation. Commission staff attempted to test this hypothesis, but existing data in Canada on unionization is reported in such a way that unambiguous conclusions are impossible. Thus in looking at the relation of size to earnings and other benefits, all we can safely conclude is that the largest businesses do appear to have higher total compensation packages than do smaller or medium-sized businesses, with the causes and the relationship to industry concentration uncertain.

Employees' Health and Safety

Acceptable levels of work-related risk, along with societal values regarding employers' responsibilities for maintaining employees' health, are constantly being redefined. The traditional attitude of the 19th and early 20th centuries was that of "employee beware". While the concept that an employer must take responsibility for his employees' safety began to gain support in Canada with the introduction of workmen's compensation legislation about 1910, awareness of threats to health from many chemicals, gases and other materials and work procedures not previously suspect dates only from about 1960. For example, until recently the feeling seemed to be that materials could be used until proven dangerous. There now seems growing support for the idea that materials should not be used until they have been first tested and proven safe. We do not intend here to document or discuss at length the range of threats to employee health and safety, but rather to consider the question of the influence of size or concentration on the incidence of such threats.

Unfortunately the data available on health and safety are very sparse. The recent Report of the Ontario Royal Commission on the Health and Safety of Workers in Mines (1976) provides some information on mine size and the frequency of fatal accidents. The fewest fatalities, 0.312 per million man-hours, occur in mines with more than 1,000 employees underground. Mines with 200 to 1,000 employees were next (0.411 per million man-hours) with the smallest mines having the highest rate of fatalities (0.944 per million man-hours).

A 1974 U.S. survey of over 800 companies by the Conference Board estimated the proportion of employees exposed to health hazards as perceived by responding companies. As indicated in Table 15.4, the highest proportion of employees judged to be exposed to health risks occurred in the next-to-largest size category (10,000-49,999 employees). The highest proportion of employees judged not to be exposed to risk occurs in the smallest size category. No explanation is offered as to why these categories should relate as they do to perceived health hazards. Additional U.S. data from the American Health Association for 1973 examines the relationship among size, type of industry and incidence of injury and illness and indicates that the largest and smallest firms are "safest" in most industries, while the highest incidence of injury and illness occurs in the middle-sized categories, especially the 100-249 employee group.

Table 15.4

**Proportion of Employees Judged To Be Exposed To
Health Hazards, United States, 1972**

Number of Employees in Responding Companies	None	1-24% Employees Exposed	25% or More Employees Exposed
under 1,000	65%	25%	10%
1,000–2,499	45	42	13
2,500–4,999	45	47	8
5,000–9,999	49	34	17
10,000–49,999	34	33	23
50,000 or more	40	38	16

Source: Conference Board, Industry Roles in Health Care (New York, 1974).
Note: Read as "65% of the responding companies with fewer than 1,000 employees judged that no employees were exposed to health hazards."

As with employment discrimination, about all that can be concluded from such fragmentary data is that the largest firms are no different from other employers in matters of health and safety. There is no *a priori* reason to think that large size itself creates hazard. Findings such as those in the American Health Association study may arise because of a sampling bias in which firms in the comparatively safe sectors of trade and services are more heavily represented among the smallest employers.

Nevertheless, Canada's largest corporations can lead in creating safer, healthier work environments. Certainly smaller businesses are unlikely to assume the cost of more stringent health and safety standards if their larger competitors do not or will not. Some large firms have led in cooperation with unions, governments and independent agencies in carrying out research and implementing remedies for health hazards. For instance, the Saskatchewan government and business enterprises in that province have created joint employee-management safety committees, and the federal government has proposed an industrial safety and health centre to undertake research into health hazards and to assist in developing standards and educational programs.

Bureaucracy and Alienation

A frequent criticism in the sociological literature is that modern technological society is characterized by work that is increasingly specialized, impersonal and separated from people's total lives; that it occurs in large bureaucracies, which allow little expression of individuality and inhibit relationships with others based on anything but task-oriented demands. The net effect of these conditions is thought to create a society in which the majority of people feel no sense of deep commitment, community, or power; in short, an alienated society.

Critics in the Marxist tradition see the roots of alienation in the capitalist system, with its characteristic values of private property, materialism and emphasis on individual competition in all areas of life. Critics in the tradition of the 19th-century French sociologist Emile Durkheim see the root of our modern ills in the emergence of mass society and the development of highly specialized jobs, which break down the close-knit, supportive communities of preindustrial society. Finally there is a school of thought stemming from the work of the early German sociologist Max Weber, which sees size and the growth of bureaucracy rather than capitalism or industrialization as the more general cause of alienation.

It is not our intention to enter into the continuing discussion of the validity of the different schools of social criticism. We did look at the available evidence on the proposition that organizational size is linked to "bureaucracy" and that the two together give rise to the phenomenon of alienation. The results of research into the effects of organizational size have been rather mixed, chiefly because of the difficulty of defining and measuring size. The most common definition is number of employees, although asset size is also sometimes used. Few sociological studies consider measures of economic concentration. There is also the question of what is "big". Some studies look at size categories ranging from 25 or fewer to 500 or more employees. Others involve categories up to 5,000 employees, but seldom above. The biggest variation in research lies in the definition of the unit studied; is the critical aspect of size the enterprise, the plant or workplace or the administrative unit or group within which the employee works?

Size and Bureaucracy

It is commonly argued that as an organization increases in size, it becomes more bureaucratic in the sense that it develops more levels of hierarchy, more activities are governed by formal rules and regulations and there are more paperwork, committees and specialization. Some believe this evolution creates the red tape, buck-passing, featherbedding and carelessness that the average person thinks of when he talks about bureaucrats and bureaucracy. The corollary of this belief is that if big organizations could somehow be made smaller these disadvantages would vanish.

Richard Hall of the University of Minnesota has worked extensively on the effects of size on organizational structure and effectiveness. In a 1976 review of the literature on this subject he concluded that "there is a slight tendency for larger organizations to be both more complex and more formalized but only on a few variables does this relationship prove to be strong. On others there is little, if any, relationship". Some of the studies he cites even argue a relationship in which large organizations as they grow beyond a certain point start to show structural characteristics more resembling smaller firms, with the greatest amount of bureaucratization thus found in middle-sized organizations. However, much of the reported research is based on plant rather than firm size or does not include examination of very large firms.

It is clear that insofar as size affects organization structure and performance, it does so primarily through interaction with other variables such as technology or the managerial style of the organization's leaders. For example, the degree of decentralization of authority has been found to vary independently of size. Thus a small organization run with strong centralized control may be in certain respects more bureaucratic than a large one run with a high degree of delegated authority. If solutions to the problems of bureaucracy are required, they would appear to lie largely in finding ways to bring about decentralization of authority, greater clarification of results to be achieved and improved ways of deciding how such results will be measured. More research remains to be done on this subject, particularly in regard to the very largest public and private organizations (e.g., those with 10,000 or more employees).

Size and Employee Alienation

To improve our understanding of the nature of alienation from work and its possible relation to corporate concentration, we commissioned a study of this topic by John W. Gartrell. His study focuses on a reanalysis of the results of two of the largest and most recent empirical studies of the subject, the *Canadian Work Values* study (1975) carried out by the federal Department of

Manpower and Immigration in 1974, and *The 1972-73 Quality of Employment Survey* (1973) carried out for the U.S. Department of Labor and the National Institute for Occupational Safety and Health by the Survey Research Center of the University of Michigan. Both the U.S. and the Canadian studies were based on questionnaires related to job satisfaction. Gartrell singles out specific items that, in his opinion, relate to four different dimensions of alienation; from these he argues that it is possible to make statements about alienation in general.

The study from the Department of Manpower and Immigration concluded that most Canadians had a strong motivation to work and indicated overall satisfaction with their jobs. Work was seen to play a "principal role in the attainment of important life goals"; nearly 90% of the more than 1,000 respondents said their jobs provided some degree of satisfaction. The degree of satisfaction varied depending on how it was measured. While 87% said that "all in all" they were "very" or "somewhat" satisfied with their jobs, 39% would have second thoughts or would definitely not take the same job if they could choose again; 41% would have doubts about advising a good friend to take their jobs; 39% would not stay in their present job if they were free to go into any type of job they wanted; and 53% felt their jobs were not very much like the sort of job they wanted when they first started.

It was found that interesting work, having enough information, having enough authority, and opportunity to develop abilities, were rated on average to be the most important characteristics of an ideal job in a rank ordering of 34 characteristics of work. However, in their current employment, promotional opportunities, challenge and growth were the elements of work with which respondents were the least satisfied, suggesting that some of what is most desired in work is not often found.

Gartrell concludes that while there is some direct relationship between size and alienation in each of the two data sets, it is a weak one. The size of the immediate work group was "relatively unrelated" to alienation (less so than the size of the organization). Many characteristics were more strongly related to alienation but in an inverse direction: the lower the age, education, income or job complexity, the higher the level of alienation.

In another study conducted for the Commission, Terrence H. White undertook an examination of the relationships among organizational size, job satisfaction and labor-management relations in a sample of 552 hourly rated production workers in 11 plants ranging in size from 100 to 1,400 employees. His questionnaire sought employees' attitudes toward their work, pay, opportunity for promotion, supervision and fellow workers as well as their perception of the quality of labor relations at the plant level. He also reviewed the literature relating strike data to organizational size, and reanalyzed data on this question gathered for the *Report* of the Royal Commission Inquiry into Labour Disputes (1968).

White found that in the sample of 11 plants, there was a direct relationship between size of plant and all the satisfaction variables measures. On the other hand, when analyzed statistically with other variables such as the respondents' work autonomy, opportunity for promotion, supervisory style and personal characteristics, size explained only one to three per cent of the variance in job satisfaction. Many other variables, particularly opportunity for promotion and opportunity to use one's skills, accounted for much more. Thus White reaches virtually the same conclusion as Gartrell that in the studies carried out to date size alone is relatively unimportant as an explanatory variable with regard to employees' work attitudes.

G. K. Ingham of the University of Leicester, in his *Size of Industrial Organization and Worker Behaviour* (1970), comments on other studies attempting to relate size and employee attitudes and actions at work. He acknowledges the considerable paucity of research in this area but like Gartrell and White he concludes that size alone is not a critical factor.

It is clear that much additional research and study into the factors that influence work experience would have to be done to reach well-supported conclusions on these issues. Recently, the federal Department of Labour announced plans to create a quality of working life centre and a Canadian Council on Quality of Working Life to support and conduct research into this field. Canada's largest firms have an opportunity to support and contribute to such an endeavor. Although there is no evidence that large enterprises result in increased employee alienation and dissatisfaction as a result of their size, large firms are the ones that have the resources and that can take the lead in studying and experimenting with new forms of work environments.

Power and Influence

We turn now to the issue of who has power or influence in shaping working conditions. The power relationship most relevant here is that between business management and organized labor.

Organization of Labor

Does the growth of a business in relative or absolute size tend to be accompanied by a tendency for its employees to join labor unions? We found a fairly weak relationship between 4-firm concentration ratios in 1970 and the percentage of non-office employees under contract in Canada (Table 15.5) while that between the percentage of employees in plants of more than 200 employees and the degree of unionization was stronger (Table 15.6).

One explanation frequently offered for the direct relationship between size and unionization is that the larger the enterprise, the greater the degree of work-related personal dissatisfaction, and hence the greater the attraction of unionization. However, this explanation is not supported by the findings on the relationship between size and work-related satisfaction, discussed in the previous section on alienation. Also, a large proportion of union members in Canada work for organizations smaller than 200 employees (as does most of the total labor force).

Another explanation is simply that employees in large organizations are more efficiently reached by union organizers and can develop the necessary

Table 15.5

Four-Firm (Value Added) Concentration and Degree of Unionization, Canadian Manufacturing Industries, 1970

Industry	4-Firm Concentration Ratio	Percentage of Non-Office Employees under Contract
Women's clothing	6.4	51
Children's clothing	10.2	27
Men's clothing	13.6	59
Sawmills and planing mills	17.8	69
Pulp and newsprint	36.3	98
Wire and wire products	37.5	78
Small electrical appliances	49.0	75
Iron and steel mills	78.6	73
Smelting and refining	82.4	98
Petroleum refineries	84.1	89
Motor vehicles	94.0	100
Tobacco products	97.0	97

Sources: Statistics Canada, *Industrial Organization and Concentration in the Manufacturing, Mining and Logging Industries,* Cat. 31-402 (1970); RCCC research.

Notes: The correlation coefficient between industrial concentration and unionization over all manufacturing sectors was .52.

The industries represented are those for which both 4-firm concentration ratios and unionization figures were available.

Table 15.6

Plant Size and Degree of Unionization, Canadian Manufacturing Industries, 1970

Industry	Percentage of Employees in Plants of More than 200 Employees	Percentage of Non-office Employees under Collective Bargaining Agreements
Children's clothing	11	27
Men's clothing	47	59
Dairies	25	61
Petroleum refineries	38	89
Pulp and newsprint	89	98
Iron and steel mills	91	73
Smelting and refining	80	98
Motor vehicles	86	100
Household radio and TV	90	91
Electrical industrial equipment	59	84

Source: RCCC research.

Notes: The correlation coefficient between the percentage of workers under collective bargaining agreements and the percentage of employees in plants with 200 employees or more was .71.

The industries represented are those for which both plant size data and unionization figures are available.

collective strength to confront management and undertake proceedings for recognition without fear of retaliation. This also seems overly simplistic; it may be that the observed relationship between size and unionization is explained by intervening variables like technology, or by more complex interrelationships not yet examined.

Another important question is whether there is disproportionate power on one side or the other of existing collective bargaining relationships. This is an issue on which there is much heated opinion but very little systematic theory or data. Several business firms testifying before the Commission, notably the Steel Company of Canada, Limited, professed to be highly constrained by the power of their labor unions. Stelco stated its belief (disputed by the United Steelworkers of America) that many large international unions develop their contract demands at the national level or even at U.S. headquarters, put the resources of the whole union into backing these demands and restrict local unions from any modification of such demands no matter what the economic circumstances facing the particular company or plant. While this certainly occurs in some instances, we have found very little research into the extent or impact of the practice.

Unions argue that multinational and conglomerate enterprises have an unfair advantage in resisting union demands, in that they can threaten to or actually shift production from one location to another to influence the bargaining process or to avoid union and government demands. It is also argued that conglomerates, multinationals and other large corporations have sufficient diversity in their sources of income that they can take a strike in one area but carry on operations financed by their earnings in other operations. The brief from Power Corporation of Canada, Limited, cited its ability to withstand strikes as one of the advantages of conglomerate diversification. It appears to us that systematic research on the extent or impact of such practices is only beginning to take place and that as yet few firm conclusions are available.

One possible offset to the actual or apparent power differences between large and small employers and large and small unions is the trend toward bargaining by associations, in which industry-wide contracts within provinces are negotiated by associations of employers and unions of various sizes. This trend is particularly marked in British Columbia, where bargaining by associations already takes place in the forest, metal fabricating and food retailing industries. While some critics believe that the concentration of power represented by employer and union associations is too great, others see it as an improvement over the fractionated system where unions can engage in whipsawing tactics and single large employers can dominate an industry. It is argued that multi-employer bargaining promotes maturity in the process in that it encourages the employment of full-time negotiators and provides them with the time and resources to do more research and carry on discussions on a day-to-day basis rather than only at contract time.

We did not think it within our terms of reference to try to research claims of the adequacy or inadequacy of labor relations law. Our concern was with the relation of these laws to corporate concentration. In that context, we could see no particular advantages or disadvantages that apply primarily to large versus smaller units in labor relations. No general case can be made that either the employer or the union has undue power in collective bargaining where large employers in the private sector are concerned.

In many industries, the managers and owners of smaller businesses see collective bargaining between big business and big labor as similar to that which takes place in the public sector and equally damaging. In an oligopolistic industry dominated by a few employers, collective bargaining takes place but the pressure to settle at the lowest possible level is reduced because both employer and union know that the employer may ultimately be able to pass increased costs on to consumers. Smaller competing businesses are confronted by the same unions making similar if not identical demands. In this situation (of large unions in an oligopolistic industry), it is sometimes argued that while there is some bargaining and occasional strikes, in the end both parties gain at the cost both of inflation and of pressure on smaller firms.

Industrial Conflict

One indicator of whether one side or the other in a collective bargaining arrangement has undue power is the nature of industrial conflict. Where business has dominant power, few strikes will tend to occur because the union realizes it cannot win. If strikes do occur out of sheer frustration they will be of short duration, because the union cannot hold out.

We were particularly concerned to ascertain if the incidence or length of strikes was influenced by corporate concentration. Some evidence was provided by the study by Terrence White. Reviewing four previous reports of research in Britain and the United States, White concludes that even in a single dimension of industrial conflict, such as the frequency of strikes, there is no clear pattern. Some research indicates a direct relationship with size; other studies suggest an inverse relationship. White himself reanalyzed the data from the Royal Commission Inquiry into Labour Disputes on 800 out of 1,786 strikes in Ontario between 1958 and 1967. These data show a clear direct relationship between size of establishment and frequency of strikes, with the frequency particularly marked for plants of 1,000 employees or more. With regard to duration of strikes the relationship is the reverse: the larger the plant, the shorter the strike, again with the result particularly marked in plants of 1,000 or more employees. These conclusions are substantially supported in a related study of the incidence of strikes and their duration in British Columbia and Ontario in 1975.

In approaching the question of why a relation between size and strikes might exist White concludes that:

> Negotiating behaviour is a very, very complex process and in view of our earlier findings on the relative unimportance of size as an explanatory variable, explanations of strike patterns as related to bargaining unit size and alienation are unlikely to prove enduring when more systematic analyses are performed. Without reference to multivariable, longitudinal analyses there are no data-based explanations that we may relate to with any degree of confidence.

Others have been less hesitant about advancing explanations for such findings, suggesting that greater strike incidence in large plants reflects the "growing impersonality of the labor-management relationship" while the greater duration of the strikes in smaller plants is a reflection of the common-sense observation that "family quarrels are often the most long-lasting".

While there may be some validity to this latter position, we tend to concur with White that much more research on the matter is needed before such a conclusion could be supported. Size enters the picture as only one of several factors that can influence power positions. Its general importance and specific role remains to be established.

Chapter 16

Business and Society

The Social Consequences of Corporate Concentration

As our terms of reference make clear, questions about the social implications of corporate concentration contributed to the concerns that led to the creation of this Commission. The submissions to us, our hearings, and commentary in the press leave little doubt that issues such as the accountability of corporations, fears of undue corporate power, and a general unease about institutional bigness concern many Canadians, sometimes more than the economic aspects of concentration and competition do.

We found the social area the most difficult part of our mandate. Seldom is there the kind of evidence that a Royal Commission would like as a basis for recommendations. There are formidable obstacles to social research, in part because of the complex and amorphous nature of the issues, in part because of the limited amount of existing behavioral research in Canada. A complicating factor is the wide variety of meanings attached to the term "corporate concentration" in behaviorally oriented writing. Many people argue that the greater the degree of economic concentration and the greater the size of a single corporation, the greater the social, economic and political risks to the country. However, seldom do they specify the precise form of concentration under discussion: within an industry, a province, a town or city, relative to the size of other employers in an area or something else.

Social issues also go beyond the business sector. Several submissions to this Commission expressed fear about the growing concentration of government power, particularly in the form of regulatory and investigative agencies. Other submissions discussed the power of trade unions. These concerns suggest that the social consequences of size of power might be more profitably treated in the broader context of a study of institutional concentration of all kinds.

Shortly after our appointment we prepared a list of the possible social consequences of corporate concentration, the available evidence for each, and the alternative remedies available in areas where further protection of the public interest might be warranted. In undertaking this task we reviewed the sociological and related literature on corporate concentration in Canada and

373

interviewed and received recommendations from a several sociologists and behavioral scientists. We commissioned an expert brief from Donald P. Warwick and John G. Craig, two sociologists who listed the social themes that appear most frequently in the Canadian literature and to evaluate the available evidence about the relation of these concerns to corporate concentration. Warwick and Craig produced a series of hypotheses as to possible relations between concentration and particular social consequences and rated the overall evidence and plausibility of each hypothesis. To this list we added our own thoughts, and those raised in briefs, and prepared discussion questions on social issues, which we put to some witnesses at our hearings. In addition, we undertook research projects on topics that we thought might produce data soon enough to be useful in our *Report*.

In their brief, Warwick and Craig looked at social consequences under 12 major themes: equality of opportunity, political decision-making, the media, regional disparity, responsiveness to local communities, innovation, corporate accountability, potential social crises, alienation of workers, citizen participation, social and philanthropic institutions and Canadian foreign policy. Of the 37 general hypotheses relating these themes to corporate concentration, they categorized the evidence underlying 10 as "solid" (for at least part of the hypothesis), 6 as "persuasive but not empirical", 5 as "inferential", 7 as "impressionistic or anecdotal", 5 as "weak or fragmentary", 3 as "difficult to assess", and 1 as "no evidence". Many of these topics appeared to us simply too elusive and difficult to be studied in the time available. For example, Warwick and Craig suggested a hypothesis that "The development of large, Canadian-based multinational corporations will undercut the ability of the government to implement foreign policies which may conflict with corporate goals." While there is considerable documentation of individual cases where multinational firms operate independently of the foreign policies of their home governments and appear to engage in activities directly opposed to those policies, the concern stems largely from U.S. experience, and particularly from the actions of the International Telephone and Telegraph Corporation in Chile. In Canada, the evidence is even more sketchy and anecdotal. In an article in the *Canadian Review of Sociology and Anthropology* (1974) Craig suggested that during the 1960s Canada's foreign policy called for condemnation of apartheid in South Africa, and for foreign aid to increase the standard of living in the Caribbean region; but during this period the sugar industry in Canada switched its procurement of raw sugar from the Caribbean countries to South Africa. However, there has been no systematic study of the problem, no indication that the individual cases took place without the knowledge of the Canadian government and no publicly available information about other considerations that may have been seen by government as offsetting the implied "harms". In addition, it is often difficult to say what the foreign or any other "policy" of the Canadian or any government is, and even more difficult to test particular conduct or action against it. A government "policy" is often no more than the expression of a hope or sentiment, and a particular policy or an aspect of it frequently conflicts with another. It will seldom be possible to draw useful conclusions about corporate social responsibility by weighing a corporation's actions against government policy.

The four preceding chapters have discussed most of what we considered the manageable topics from our list of social consequences. For example, many writers have examined the degree to which boards or managers exercise control over corporate decisions and the degree to which boards of directors operate corporations without significant challenge. Chapter 12, "Corporate Ownership, Control and Management", reviewed the legal and actual roles of shareholders, directors, officers and managers. We looked at the principal types of shareholders in public companies and their different interests and objectives, and we discussed the idea that boards of directors and executive committees should be composed largely of people drawn from outside the company, the need for a nominating committee composed entirely of "outside" directors, and the view that persons should not sit on the boards of more than a few publicly held companies.

In terms of disclosure, Warwick, Craig and others have advanced the general proposition that the larger the corporation, the more difficult it is for an investigator unfamiliar with the corporate structure to dig out relevant information. They argue both that there should be less secrecy of information within the corporation, especially one with many subsidiaries, and that there should be more disclosure of corporate information to government and the public at large. Chapter 13, "Disclosure of Corporate Information", discussed the current disclosure and reporting obligations of large Canadian corporations to investors, shareholders and governments. We considered the need for sectoral disclosure and the costs involved, and discussed the handling of business information by goverment.

Virtually every study of elites and influence in Canada has argued that "The greater the degree of corporate concentration in an industry, or the larger the size of a single corporation, the greater the influence of the corporation on governmental decision-making." The evidence of this to date (considering the importance of the topic) has been sparse and ambiguous. There have also been a number of hypotheses involving corporate concentration and the media. For example, Warwick and Craig suggested that the existing pattern of media concentration, interlocking ownerships and dependence on advertising may produce a "climate of thought which either positively promotes or at least does not challenge the privileged position of the upper class in Canada". Chapter 14, "Corporate Influence", discussed corporate involvement in government decision-making, the issues of access to public authorities and the influence arising from it, corporate contributions to political parties and charitable organizations, concerns about bribery and corruption, the role of advertising, and particularly of advocacy advertising, and corporate influence on public opinion through ownership of print or broadcast media.

Many discussions of the social implications of corporate concentration propose some variant of a hypothesis that Warwick and Craig stated as follows: "By promoting greater technological refinements, mechanization, and industrialization, corporate concentration leads to an increasing alienation of the work force". Another hypothesis is that "corporation concentration, along with the growth of other large institutions, increases a sense of powerlessness by producing a greater dependence of employees on centralized decision-making". In Chapter 15, "Business Size and Working Conditions", we looked at issues related to employment, including alienation and power and influence in the work environment.

These four chapters cover many of the social consequences of corporate concentration which fall within our mandate. In looking at other possible social consequences raised in the briefs or hearings, we found that the relationships involved are often so complex that it has not yet been possible to determine, compile or analyse systematically the relevant data with which to test them.

We therefore decided that we should search for principles against which the validity of the basic idea of corporate social responsibility could be evaluated. Any such principles that we could find or formulate would also serve as standards against which to judge examples of particular activities that might illustrate the existence or lack, and the boundaries, of corporate social responsibility and the conclusions to which we or others might come. Our ambition in this chapter, therefore, is not to make definitive and certainly not authoritative pronouncements on social responsibility but rather to contribute to the development of an approach that might usefully assist and guide further study and action.

It soon became apparent that the social "implications" described to us are seldom consequences of corporate concentration as such. Usually, there is at most only a tenuous connection between a social problem and the size of a corporation or the concentration of the industry in which it operates. Rather, most of the social consequences we have heard about are outgrowths of an industrial society. While the economic activity of that society is largely conducted through corporations, many of them in concentrated industries, the consequences about which so much concern was expressed flow more from the fact and nature of industrial activity than from the characteristics of the firms that conduct it.

We concluded, therefore, that we had to consider the social implications not of corporate concentration but of an industrial economy. That conclusion led us, inevitably, into the whole debate over corporate social responsibility. We read much of the literature that has been produced on the subject. As might be expected, much of what we heard in our hearings is discussed in these writings. We think we can make a better contribution to the discussion of social responsibility in Canada if we draw on this literature as well as on the evidence that was produced for us.

The Meaning and Origins of "Corporate Social Responsibility"

The notion of corporate social responsibility springs from the premise that business exists to serve not only the economic needs of its shareholders, customers and employees, but also the wider economic and social needs of the society in which it operates. The public now expects more than an adequate supply of goods and services, and demands that business meet these additional expectations. Thus the corporation is seen as having a responsibility, over and above its economic one, to concern itself with and to devise or help to devise solutions to the social problems (many of which it has helped to create) that exist in the society of which it is a part.

The kinds of issues encompassed within the idea of corporate social responsibility can be grouped into three broad categories. First are the things that are intrinsically bound up with a firm's regular business activity: equal opportunity for employment and promotion, occupational health and safety and the quality of working life in general. The second set of issues is slightly outside regular business operations; in economic terminology they are described as "externalities", and include pollution, product safety and reliability and the social effect of plant locations, closings and layoffs. The third category is more clearly external to the firm, and comprises social problems of the larger society, which flow only indirectly, if at all, from business operations, but which business is or arguably should be interested in alleviating. Examples of things in this third class are urban decay, poverty in general and regional disparities.

Such a classification of social problems is a useful and even a necessary step towards their analysis and resolution. However, some of the proponents of corporate social responsibility group these quite different types of social problems together as issues that they feel business should address. We think that this kind of undifferentiated approach is more apt to confuse than to clarify.

It seems obvious to us that the kind of response that might reasonably be expected from corporations will not be the same for every social problem. Indeed, the proper response to some of them may be no response at all. We found that the classification outlined above helped our understanding and we use it in the discussion that follows.

A demand for something more than the technological and economic benefits that the business system has traditionally supplied reflects, implicitly, a belief that material progress measured solely by the output of goods and services is not enough. With some, it goes further, to a disenchantment with material goods themselves and the industrial system that produces them. Our impression is that the latter group is very much a minority; few seem to be willing to forsake the material benefits of a technological and industrial society in favor of the "simple life". Most advocates of corporate social responsibility do not eschew the products of the business system. On the contrary, they want, if not an absolute increase in the existing benefits, a more equitable distribution of them, and they want the social costs of that production to be reduced. Thus, the advocates of social responsibility do not want business to produce social benefits in place of material ones, but in addition to them, in part by reducing the social costs of the economic system as it presently operates.

It is probably no accident that the movement for corporate social responsibility developed its momentum principally during the 1960s and early 1970s, a period characterized by an unprecedented level of material affluence in most of the western world. If concern for the non-material aspects of life arises after a certain level of material comforts are enjoyed by the majority of the population, the demand for increased corporate social responsibility may tend to lessen if economic abundance is reduced, or even if it ceases to increase. it is possible, therefore, that pressure for changes in the social environment in which business operates, and which influences and is influenced by it, will wax and wane with the fortunes of the economy. In addition, pressures for different kinds of results within the broad rubric of social responsibility will interact with and influence one another, particularly as people come to see that the attainment of one desirable goal may be at the cost of another one no less desirable. In short, the ideas embraced within the notion of corporate social responsibility will be as fluid as society itself: they cannot be captured and dealt with once and for all.

However, social responsibility did not become an issue solely because society concluded that the economy had reached the point at which "social" goals had become affordable. In large part, the absolute amount of industrial production that occurred in the 1960s and 1970s made visible some of the social costs that had always been there. In addition, the discovery and invention of new materials and processes were seen, often long after the event, to carry with them many new hazards, not only to the users but to the makers of the products.

Finally, the idea of corporate social responsibility flowered during a time when many of society's other institutions were also being subjected to critical examination. Governments at all levels, organized religion, the education system and the professions, for example, have been attacked from within and without in recent years. Like business, these institutions are also being forced to justify themselves.

The Critics

Fundamentally, there are two criticisms of the idea of corporate social responsibility, and both deserve to be taken seriously. One flatly denies the legitimacy of the idea of social responsibility and says that corporations have no business, let alone an obligation, to concern themselves with anything other than business. The corporation is an economic institution, the argument goes, and it operates in a competitive market economy. Altruism and social statesmanship are held by these critics to be incompatible with competitive economics. The only responsibility of business is to manage efficiently, and within the law, the resources that come under its control. It does this by responding to the signals from the market place, not by making its own value judgments as to what is or is not good for society. Indeed, business is irresponsible if it does not concentrate its energies on doing the one thing for which it is equipped and needed, the pursuit of profit. As Ben W. Lewis put it in "Economics by Admonition" (*American Economic Review,* 1959):

> Economic decisions must be right as society measures right rather than good as benevolent individuals construe goodness. An economy is a mechanism designed to

pick up and discharge the wishes of society in the management of its resources; it is not an instrument for the rendering of gracious music by kindly disposed improvisers.

The argument certainly has a cold-blooded ring to it. It implies strongly that, if business is not exactly an immoral pastime, the market system and the people in it are at best amoral. In a sense this is true; in an "efficient market" the prize will go to the seller who offers the best combination of price, quality and service to a buyer who is presumed to be interested in nothing else. The impersonal nature of the modern marketplace also tends to suppress non-economic considerations, and the more distance there is between the producer and the consumer of a product, the more impersonal the relationship becomes. When the actors in the market, or some of them, are anonymous corporate organizations, and when the products on sale are complex assemblies of components produced by thousands of unknown hands, it is impossible for a buyer to bring moral considerations to bear on his choice, even if he wants to do so. On the other hand, it could be argued in reply that the nature of modern markets demonstrates the need for some concept of social responsibility.

The second argument is a political one. It says that businessmen are not competent to undertake the obligations of social responsibility and, worse, that it would be positively dangerous if they were allowed to do so. The proponents of this view argue that businessmen have no particular knowledge that would allow them to define social objectives in an acceptable way and, indeed, that their outlook may well be too narrow. The proper job of corporate management is to maximize profits for its shareholders. It is quite another thing to allow such a group to apply that view to non-economic matters and it is positively dangerous to allow such a powerful and influential group as corporation management, however benevolent its proclaimed intentions, to intrude where it does not belong. The critics say that social development is a task for legitimate public institutions, functioning in the open and formally accountable to society as a whole. The corporate conscience, they argue, is a self-interested conscience, not to be relied upon to achieve the common good.

Moreover, the argument goes, because corporate social responsibility is such an elusive concept, there are not and cannot be standards by which to evaluate and control it. It is ironic, these critics say, that those who have worried so much about the problem of controlling private economic power desire business to be the new dispenser of social goods. Social responsibility, they say, is a rationalization for freedom from effective social control of the corporate sector. They point out that the exercise of power by a narrowly selected and self-appointed minority, operating without clearly defined, democratically selected and legally enforceable standards is the essence of authoritarianism.

The corollary of this, the argument continues, is that the present and generally effective standard for judging managerial performance—profitability will be diluted and eventually destroyed. Corporate social responsibility will sabotage the market mechanism and distort the allocation of resources.

The "balance of interests" idea clouds the whole process and replaces standards with sentiments. The destruction of standards penalizes excellence and benefits the second-rate.

Finally, the argument concludes, business cannot have any significant social involvement until it frees itself from the domination of shareholders and the market. There can be no responsibility without authority. If business is to assume wider obligations it will necessarily have to equip itself with correspondingly wider powers. The inevitable next step will be for business to demand an equal voice with government in determining the direction of public policy.

The Commission's Assessment

Our reflections on the things we heard and read about corporate social responsibility led us to several very general conclusions, which it will be helpful to express at this point because the somewhat more specific recommendations we make later are influenced by them.

First, it is beyond argument that society expects business to be humane as well as efficient. Business will and should continue to be, first and foremost, an economic activity, but it is not true to say that the business corporation is an economic organization *only*. The corporation will have to temper its commercial judgments with a consideration of the social impact of those judgments. While this has always been true (because there has never been a time when business was totally immune from the society surrounding it), the relative importance of social consequences is greater now than it was in the past.

Second, and at the same time, the importance of costs to a business corporation will not recede. This point is not made as an excuse or as a device to deprecate the importance of social responsibility. It will not serve the cause of social responsibility, however, to pretend that a business corporation has an inexhaustible store of resources, or that it can command whatever it needs to discharge any responsibility that may be imposed on it. On the contrary, a business corporation must obtain its resources in a competitive marketplace, and it will not be able to do so unless it can meet the tests of that market. The capital and other markets make *economic* judgments, not social ones. As long as this is so (and the broad direction of public policy is to intensify market competition), the ability of a corporation to incur costs that will not be recovered in sales and profits will be restrained.

This is not to say that social responsibility necessarily translates into increased costs and foregone profits. There are a number of examples of corporations who undertook what they considered to be entirely socially motivated programs to find that they brought important economic benefits in their train. For instance, efforts to improve product and work-place safety have brought about reduced insurance costs and fewer working days lost through sickness and injury. Reviews of hiring practices to comply with legislative and other pressures to reduce discrimination have led to improvements in the overall personnel function.

It is all too easy to extrapolate from such happy examples a general conclusion that every reduction or elimination of a social problem improves the health, harmony, efficiency and general well-being of society, and that there is therefore no conflict between economics and social responsibility. While this proposition may be true in an overall sense, it is useless as a guide to specific decisions and actions.

The disappointing truth is that the economy does not operate as a harmonious and integrated whole, and the costs and benefits of social responsibility do not necessarily go hand in hand. The costs of leaving social problems unresolved are largely endured outside the production system, and the benefits from their resolution will also be enjoyed, for the most part, outside that system. A business corporation operates within a narrower and sometimes ruthless economic framework. Appeals to the market for resources with which to carry out a social responsibility are likely to receive a chilly response, however generally beneficient the undertaking might be. Even where the corporation might reasonably expect to benefit itself from a social expenditure, that benefit, no less than the benefits to society at large, may be long deferred.

No one should be surprised, therefore, if business managers concentrate their attention on the matter of costs when social responsibility is mentioned. Social responsibility usually increases the costs of goods and services, at least in the short run, so that, however unconsciously, the market will determine how much social responsibility there will be. A business manager's conscience and actions will always be confined by that knowledge, and so, indeed, must a politician's.

This will be a disagreeable finding only to those advocates of corporate social responsibility who place an absolute value on their cause. But resources are not unlimited; the necessity to make choices means that some wants will always be unsatisfied, some desires unfulfilled. The business managers, concern with the monetary and other costs of social responsibility may well be excessive at times, but that attitude can bring a healthy and necessary measure of discipline into the choices that society will make.

There is one more point, which applies with particular force in the Canadian economy. The choices we make in Canada among economic and social values will not always be the same as those that others will make. Our choices reflect themselves in the prices of the goods and services we sell. As we have already discovered, Canada has no ability to sell products in international markets irrespective of cost. Since, in comparison with most other industrial countries, Canada's economy depends disproportionately on international trade, it follows that Canadian producers are even more constrained by market forces than are those in other countries. At the same time, Canadians demand as high a level of material and non-material benefits from their economy as any other in the world, and probably higher than those most other people expect. To an important extent, the Canadian economy will be only as responsive to social demands as others outside this country will allow it to be.

EXPECTATIONS AND RESPONSES

We move now to a discussion, in slightly more specific terms, of what society may legitimately expect from corporations in terms of social responsibility, and how we think corporations should respond. Society's values are continuously changing, and thus the burden of relieving (or of not relieving) various harmful or otherwise undesirable effects for which corporations may in part be responsible will be in constant flux among corporations and the society in which they operate. It is not that long ago that a vista of smoking factory chimneys signalled prosperity: "Where there's muck there's money." The same scene today attracts condemnation. Other examples of this kind of change in public attitude are given by R. W. Ackerman and R. A. Bauer in *Corporate Social Responsiveness: The Modern Dilemna* [sic] (1976):

> Well within the memory of the older of the two authors, women were criticized for "taking a job that a man needs." Disposable containers were desirable until quite recently. Cheap and profligate (we can afford it!) use of energy was eulogized. Plastics were a triumph of our civilization rather than nonbiodegradable solid waste. In the market place, the doctrine of let the buyer beware has been replaced by the doctrine of let the seller beware. Employers were only recently forbidden by law to keep records of the race of their employees. Now it is required in order to develop affirmative action plans. One could go on, but we believe the point is made.

This phenomenon suggests to us first, that, whatever obligations business managers may have to respond to social change, they should not be expected always to be at the forefront of change. Although a business corporation may innovate in economic matters, in the social field it is probably better suited to meet challenges than to foresee and lead social change. Our conclusion in this respect is also, in part, a recognition of the force behind one of the critical arguments we summarized earlier in this chapter.

Second, society should be careful about the *kinds* of social obligations it asks business to asume, and business should be equally cautious in accepting them. In particular, we suggest that social problems within the third category we described earlier, that is those that lie essentially outside business activity, should normally not be treated as things to which corporations can respond (except perhaps through traditional philanthrophy). Put another way, business should properly be concerned only with things that are direct consequences of economic activity; it should not undertake external "good works". The line between the two will not be easy to draw, but a recognition that there is a line should help to develop attainable objectives.

That the warning is apposite is shown by the experience of corporations in the United States. According to what we have read, many of the more innovative and ambitious social action programs, such as the establishment of businesses in the ghettos and other schemes of urban redevelopment, were generally unsuccessful. Of course, we do not know all the details of those programs, and the reasons for their apparent failure are no doubt many and varied. Nevertheless, it would be folly to ignore the findings of those who have studied and commented upon them.

Most of these attempts originated in the late 1960s, at a time when social criticism of all kinds was at a peak. There was a popular argument that the skills of business people could be deployed in almost any field of activity and to the solution of almost any problem. Not a few business leaders joined the chorus. While to some the projects were probably little more than public relations exercises with nothing substantive behind them, many no doubt believed sincerely that they could supply the talent and energy that was lacking in government and elsewhere.

At all events, disillusion resulted when business so often failed to solve problems outside its experience and ability. In addition, the widespread assumption that the problems of economic growth and universal affluence had been mastered was shattered in the 1970s, and with it many of the ambitious programs of social reform to which business was expected to commit itself.

We ventured the opinion earlier that business should follow but not necessarily lead in social change. It is equally important that it not respond to every demand or follow every trend; there may indeed be times when it should actively resist. In our judgment, business should resist both the pressure and the temptation to be drawn into assuming responsibility for matters connected only tenuously, if at all, with its prime economic function.

This process of analysis will be assisted, and arid doctrinal debate avoided, if social responsibility is not approached in the abstract. Rather, specific instances of things alleged to be consequences of corporate activity should be analyzed carefully. The examination should try to determine, first, whether the phenomenon in question is truly a consequence of corporate activity, or whether it is more properly a consequence or by-product of some broader aspect of life in which a corporation is only coincidentally involved. Most things will probably not fall neatly into one category or another, but if a rational distinction is not made between primary and secondary causes the prescription chosen is likely to be ineffective. For example, there may be a sufficiently close connection between industrial pollution and a corporation's activity to support a conclusion that the corporation has a responsibility to reduce the pollution. In contrast, it would probably not be correct to conclude that a corporation manufacturing automobiles is responsible for traffic congestion, even though there might be no congestion if that corporation and others like it had not produced automobiles.

Even when a consequence with some undesirable attributes has been identified, however, and even if it is possible to say that corporate activity is the cause, there is a difficult question of how bad that thing is. Absolute judgments will rarely be possible. Invariably, the ill will be found on analysis to be part of the cost of something else. No one can be in favor of hazardous products, for example, but there is probably nothing that cannot be dangerous if it is improperly used. Equally, there will be few industrial processes that are absolutely free from danger to those engaged in them. If the products in question are generally desired (and they would not be produced if there was no one willing to buy them), then there will necessarily be some danger to those who produce and use them, and perhaps to others as well.

Although the corporation producing the products may be said to have a responsibility to reduce the dangers, that responsibility cannot be taken to the point where the corporation could guarantee them to be absolutely safe. Even the degree of safety that could be demanded would be a question of judgment as to how the costs of the danger, and the cost of remedying it, will be shared among those concerned. Judgments like this have always been made, but often in no particularly systematic way, by the corporation, its employers, its customers and the wider society, possibly but not necessarily through government. The idea of social responsibility implies that judgments like this should be made with more understanding, but it is not only corpations that should sharpen their perceptions.

Our conclusion that corporations should not be expected to concern themselves actively with matters basically outside the area of impact of their own operations is consistent also with the record of corporate success in social responsibility. According to those who have analyzed U.S. experience, the best and most lasting results are obtained when social objectives can be integrated into the corporation's usual commercial activities. For one thing, social demands are less dependent upon the consciences and less susceptible to the motivations of individual managers when they become part of the regular operations of the firm. Once social responsibilities become routine, they cease to be regarded as external. They are discharged as a matter of course, not as occasional and *ad hoc* responses to passing pressures.

This kind of operational integration is most likely to occur when corporate managers see that there is really no valid distinction between the economic and the social issues with which the manager is asked to concern himself. They are different aspects of the same activity. The motivation behind a decision to do a particular thing may well be exclusively economic or exclusively social, but the reason becomes irrelevant once the activity is under way. After that the *consequences* of the activity acquire the dominating importance, and those consequences will be both economic and social.

While it is true that the business corporation may find it easier to ignore the social consequences of its decisions (because the machinery for enforcing social demands is more diverse and less immediate in its effect than the marketplace), this is largely a problem of identification and timing. We stress the point that social responsibility should be seen in terms of the consequences or effects of business decisions. For one thing this perspective is the one most likely to appear relevant and legitimate to corporate management. Corporations are not being asked to undertake novel, ill-defined and apparently irrelevant sideshows. Instead, they are merely asked to consider *fully* the effects of what they are already doing, and to treat the social effects of their decisions as seriously as they do the economic ones.

Another advantage of this realistically confined approach to social responsibility is that it blends with the kinds of organizational skills that one might expect to find in a modern, well-managed corporation. Alert corporate managers are accustomed to scanning the environment for changing consumer values; scanning it for other emerging social demands is really not much different.

Equally, the implementation of a new social policy is an organizational problem not unlike those that must be solved when any new policy is adopted.

Conclusions

Society and corporations themselves have agreed that corporations have a social responsibility. The task before the scholars and the corporate executives alike is to give meaning to that ambiguous phrase. In the opening section of this chapter we declared that we did not intend to provide a series of prescriptions showing how business corporations in Canada should meet their social responsibilities. Instead, we have attempted to discover and describe what social responsibility is and to develop a framework for its analysis, development and application.

We have spoken about the corporate responsibility to develop techniques to recognize and respond to social issues, but we have offered no specific guidance as to how a corporation might best do this. The deficiencies in our own knowledge and understanding make that impossible. More than that, we do not think any social commentator can provide specific answers to problems that will arise differently in each corporation, and with which each must deal in its own way. Even if it were possible to provide categorical advice to a particular corporation at a defined time, the constantly changing mix and balance of social values would soon render the advice useless.

There are, however, two particular kinds or techniques of corporate response on which we will essay a comment or two. Finally, we will offer a few thoughts on the place of law in corporate social responsibility.

Codes of Behavior

Suggestions have been made from time to time that statements of good corporate social behavior should be formulated, perhaps by corporations themselves, or perhaps by the government. The intent behind these suggestions is at first sight perfectly reasonable. They would supply corporations with a measure of guidance and they would also provide a bench mark against which the public could monitor corporate performance. The idea of a kind of behavioral or ethical code also recognizes that not all social responsibility can be expressed in law, that, for a variety of reasons, the law can lay down only a minimum standard, which corporations should be encouraged to surpass.

We can see little reason to encourage the idea that codes of behavior will contribute positively to corporate social responsibility. Our pessimism derives partly from how we see the nature of social responsibility and partly from the limitations inherent in behavioral codes generally.

For the reasons we have tried to explain above, the most we should realistically expect corporate social responsibility to mean is that corporations will consider the social as well as the economic consequences of their decisions. If they do this, the decisions they make will result in a balance of economic and social benefits and costs. A code of behavior in general terms is of little use as a guide to specific decisions.

To be useful, a statement would have to go much further and spell out exactly how and to what extent this or that social consequence would influence every conceivable business decision. This kind of prediction and prescription is impossible. A corporation cannot predict in advance how it will weigh different economic factors against one other, let alone how it would treat the host of social consequences that might also be involved in the decision. It should be remembered that a business decision is never a contest between economic benefits and costs on the one hand and social ones on the other. The economic factors, especially the short-run and long-term ones, will often pull in different directions, and the social consequences will be even more difficult to identify and evaluate.

We illustrate this with two striking examples of the kind of difficult conflicts that can occur. In one case, a company made determined efforts to hire people belonging to minority groups, believing that they had been the victims of previous discriminatory personnel policies. When economic conditions required some reduction in the work force, the seniority principle (particularly since it was embodied in a collective agreement) operated to undo much of what had been achieved. In another case involving a layoff of staff, the trade union criticized the corporation for imposing on its employees the consequences of economic restraint while it continued to support charitable organizations with donations.

These examples illustrate how social consequences may be less at war with economic ones than with each other, and how impossible it would be to lay down a "right" answer in advance in a code of behavior. They also illustrate how a corporation's decisions may be confined or even determined by the view that someone else, such as a trade union, takes of *its* economic and social responsibilities.

Further, a code of social responsibility cannot be a useful monitoring or enforcement tool unless it can be expressed with the kind of precision that is required in a law. A code of ethics differs from a law only in its source and in the kind of sanctions that are available to enforce it. It cannot differ in the clarity of the things it defines or the conduct it commands and proscribes. If it does, it suffers from all the disabilities of a law containing the same flaws.

Codes of ethics and good practice are useful in professional organizations because they apply to a relatively small group of people who have undergone a uniform course of training in a comparatively narrow and fairly well-defined discipline. The kinds of professional situations dealt with in those codes arise naturally out of the activity the practitioners commonly pursue. There is usually little scope for argument about the relative values of the things that professional codes encourage or prohibit, because those values are shared by most of the members of the profession and, indeed, are the reason the profession exists. This internal cohesion permits, in turn, formal disciplinary machinery to enforce professional standards.

However, professional codes tend to break down around the edges of the professions' normal and settled activity. They are weak, for example, in dealing with questions of competence when the activity in respect of which a practitioner's competence is at issue is not a routine one. Also, it is often difficult to determine how far a professional code of ethics should reach; to what extent the non-professional side of a person's life should be governed by the ethical standards of the profession to which he belongs.

These considerations compel us to doubt the utility of any kind of code of ethical behavior for business or corporations and, in particular, to discourage the idea that they can contribute in any important way to social responsibility.

Social Reporting

The idea that business corporations have social as well as economic responsibilities has been accompanied, quite naturally, by the belief that corporations should provide information about the social impact of their business decisions to those who are affected by them. Social information is to social performance as financial information is to economic performance.

The analogy is useful but it should not be taken too far. Although, as we showed in an earlier chapter, the boundaries of financial reporting are still being debated, there is nevertheless fairly wide agreement on what financial information is, and the techniques for its dissemination have been refined over many years. Things are far different with social reporting. Corporations are not able to determine the range of their impact on society or the depth of that impact on the different groups within it. In addition, corporations and all the other elements in society are constantly changing and readjusting to one another. In this unending process of action and reaction there can never be agreement about the effect that one element of society has on another. All this makes it exceedingly difficult to decide what information will be useful in evaluating a corporation's social performance. Moreover, the social impact of what a corporation does not do may be at least as important as what it does. We do not think it will ever be possible to devise systems to measure the social impact of business decisions that even approximate financial accounting systems.

Although it would be unwise to encourage unrealistic expectations for corporate social reporting, the subject is still in its infancy and there should be continuous progress in this area, as there has been in financial disclosure. Work on social reporting is going forward, and the study that is being given to it will gradually develop techniques and standards for both the discovery of social information and its disclosure. An increasing number of corporations comment in their annual reports on things that seem to them to be of general concern. It is easy to criticize these reports for the one-sided and self-serving statements that many of them contain, but many corporations are making conscientious and useful efforts to respond to the need for information about their activities. As more corporate managers come to realize the significance of social information in economic decision-making, and as they recognize the effect of those decisions on the lives of individuals, so they will come to accept and meet the legitimate demands for information that the public needs to make proper judgments about private enterprise. We are satisfied that this is happening.

SOCIAL ACCOUNTING

There is one particular development within the concept of social reporting—social accounting—upon which we will comment in more specific terms. This school of social reporting takes as its point of departure the undisputed fact that the social consequences of a firm's decisions create costs that fall largely outside the corporation and its systems of measurement. These costs are external to the firm. The task of social responsibility is therefore one of accounting; how to "internalize" those real costs that now go unrecorded and thus unnoticed. The argument implies that the measurement of a firm's social responsibility is the amount of increased costs (and, in consequence, foregone profits) that would be identified by such a system of accounting. The idea is attractive because it promises the comfort of certainty in an area that is infuriatingly vague.

We think, however, that the notion of social responsibility through better accounting, though superficially appealing, is fundamentally misconceived. For one thing, a conscious application of some amount of corporate profits to the relief of social ills would do little, if only because there are not enough corporate profits in aggregate to make any difference. Another drawback to the accounting approach is that it implies that all benefits are worth their costs or, conversely, that all benefits cost what they are worth. The art of accounting, even when it is employed in the traditional sense, subsumes a great many assumptions, estimates and predictions, and one of its faults is that it creates an illusion of objectivity and precision. The quantification of value judgments inherent in the idea of social accounting would increase this effect and send both accounting and corporate social responsibility down a false trail.

Concentrating attention on those actions that a firm might undertake out of foregone profits distracts attention from the social impact of what the firm does in its main line of business. Furthermore, social responsibility through special programs, which is what the idea of foregone profits implies, will never be more than a small part of a firm's activities. It is the overall effect of the firm's operations that is important.

Social accounting gives special credits for consciously incurred social costs. This is only possible, of course, when special social projects are undertaken, but even here the idea breaks down. One critic gave an example of a bank that developed a program for lending to "minority entrepreneurs". Once the loan managers had learned how to manage these special loans and the program was running smoothly, it was transferred into the bank's regular operations. After that time it would have been difficult and pointless to assign overhead costs to those special loans because they were no longer special. In short, at the point when the program was successfully institutionalized into the regular operations of the bank, social accounting would cease to recognize the social responsibility of the program.

Social accounting will often have such bizarre effects. It is easy enough to identify the cost of pollution control and equipment, for example, but how can the cost of pollution control be determined when a process that does not pollute is installed? Suppose also that a process is more efficient as well as pollution-free or less dangerous to the employees using it. Should there be some kind of a charge to regular operations to offset a social responsibility credit? If so, how could it be rationally determined?

The fact is that there is usually no practical way of isolating and quantifying social costs, and no sound basis for matching those costs against anticipated future benefits. Social accounting can mean nothing unless this is done. The danger of social accounting is that firms will be led into making unsupportable estimates and tortured assumptions to provide the material for social accounting statements. Reality would be distorted and made meaningless by technique.

SOCIAL AUDIT

We conclude this discussion with a brief word on the "social audit". The notion of a social audit was perhaps a natural by-product of the idea of social accounting, and therefore suffers from the limitations inherent in an attempt to assign objective criteria to subjective phenomena. More generally, an audit implies an appraisal or assessment of performance against defined standards, to enable or assist the judgment of conduct and results. The concept of an audit may be useful in helping a corporation to evaluate the adequacy of the means by which people at various levels in the corporation identify and respond to social issues. It may also be employed to test the effectiveness of the responses a corporation makes to the social issues it has attempted to deal with. As such, the social audit is a management tool, valuable in assessing the attainment by management of objectives set by management. This is not, however, the context in which the word audit is normally used. In the customary sense, an audit of a corporation assesses results against externally established standards. As we explained above, objective standards for corporate social responsibility are a long way in the future and, until then, the social audit should be understood for what it is. Analogies with the usual financial audit will mislead and disappoint.

The Place of the Law

In Canada and elsewhere the law has already addressed most of the things commonly thought to fall within corporate social responsibility. Pollution, working conditions, product safety, racial and other kinds of discrimination, advertising and many other social as well as economic manifestations of industrial and commercial activity have been regulated by legislation. Before that, some were even subject, however peripherally, to common law. To the extent that the law invades or takes over an area of social responsibility, conscience is replaced with obligation and discretion is displaced by coercion. Indeed, the debate over corporate social responsibility is in large measure a discussion of whether and how far corporate conduct should go beyond the requirements of the law. Much of the criticism of corporations for failing to fulfill their social responsibilities could equally be taken, therefore, as a criticism of governments that have failed in their responsibilities to enact and enforce effective laws.

A decision to enact a law is, of course, a political one, which is presumed to reflect a significant body of public opinion demanding the action that the law set forth. Public opinion is filtered through the political and bureaucratic branches of government before it is responded to, however, and it may be distorted in the process by their biases and internal needs. For these and other reasons, including counter pressures from those who may expect to bear the burdens of the law, and a possibly incomplete understanding of the problem and the implications of a legal response to it, the law in its operation sometimes falls short of what those promoting it expect to see.

As a general rule, though, it is safe to say that the law will impose social responsibility when government becomes convinced that a substantial part of the public believes that the subject of the legislation is too important to be left to the whims of corporate conscience, or when the results of legislative inaction are judged to be intolerable. With some kinds of social problems there may be little or no action without law, and little scope for advance beyond it. The law, in short, will occupy the whole field. This is most likely to be true when the costs that corporations will incur are competitively significant. The outstanding example of this is probably pollution control. In some industries, the processes of pollution control are so costly that one firm, however much it may wish to install them, cannot do so and remain in business unless its competitors also take the same decision. In these circumstances, nothing significant will happen until the law compels all the competing firms in the industry to assume the additional costs of the (legislated) social responsibility.

Legislation can augment a firm's ability to enforce compliance with social obligations by focusing responsibility on particular individuals within the firm. Many corporate functions are widely decentralized, for example, and beyond the observation and control of senior management. Thus, the state licenses many people, such as airline pilots and taxi cab drivers, in an attempt to ensure technical competence and honest dealing. In cases like this, legislative or regulatory sanctions can be applied directly against the individual whose performance is inadequate, whether or not his employer chooses or is able to take remedial or disciplinary action. Some government inspection services (e.g., of the seaworthiness of ships' lifeboats) exist as much because of management's inability to ensure compliance with desired standards of social responsibility as because of its unwillingness to do so.

Action by the state to enforce social responsibility through law can create further problems because legal action can have secondary social and economic consequences, just as voluntary corporate action can. This is one reason why a legal solution to a social problem frequently seems not to go far enough. For example, a truly effective pollution law, even if it falls evenly on all the domestic producers it is directed at, may make the domestic industry uncompetitive vis-à-vis foreign suppliers. The government may be content with a second-best law, or may elect for lax enforcement of a good law, so as not to destroy the industry and those whose livelihood depends upon it. Again, because there are economies of scale in pollution control as in other industrial processes, and also because the firms in an industry may have varying abilities to adapt their plants to it, the full enforcement of an ideal pollution law may lead to the closure of some businesses and thus an increase in industrial concentration. The demands on governments are considerably more numerous and diverse than they are on even the largest corporations, and governments have many more social responsibilities to balance and discharge. For these reasons, there are real limits to what we should expect from the law.

It is obvious that we cannot promulgate any rules or principles to say when the law should act in an area of corporate social responsibility. That point will be determined by the political process. About all that can be said with certainty is that the law will act too soon in the judgment of some and too late for others.

We want to close with some observations on the application of law to corporate organizations, because we believe that this is a question that has been neglected too long by legal scholars and social activists alike. It is apparent that the traditional legal weapons are often inadequate to deal with corporate social conduct or misconduct, and that as social responsibility is legislated the law will also have to fashion new enforcement techniques.

We take no credit for the ideas that follow. Rather, they are developed in a book by Christopher D. Stone, *Where the Law Ends: The Social Control of Corporate Behavior* (1975). Stone explains the basic but frequently overlooked fact of organizations: that they tend to develop a life of their own distinct from those they comprise. Also individuals in an organization tend to develop a loyalty to the organization, which can both undermine and override their personal moral judgments. Conduct that would be reprehensible in an individual can, in the context of an organization, take on a different coloration and be justified as serving the greater good. Conscience, in a world of giant corporations, is a less reliable check on conduct than it would be in a world of individuals and small organizations, and, correspondingly, there is a larger burden on the law to implement social control.

Second, the traditional legal sanction of imprisonment cannot be applied to organizations as such, and the threat of a fine, even if it is significant to the corporation's profits (which it rarely is) will, for a variety of reasons that Stone describes, often not provoke an alteration in the conduct of the people in the organization. Moreover there are numerous reasons why legislatures and courts will shrink from imposing financial penalties that might really hurt a corporation. Most obviously, a corporate wrong is always a misdeed by one or more individuals, and a punishment severe enough to be felt by the corporation may have damaging consequences for all sorts of innocent people to whom the corporation's health and survival is vital.

Equally difficult problems surround any attempt by the law to strike at responsible individuals within the corporation. First, there are all the difficulties in proving the necessary guilty intent or even negligence on the part of individuals engaged in large organizations and taking part in complex industrial processes. It is often the case that no one person in a corporation possesses all the knowledge that would have allowed him to prevent a result that, once it has occurred, is clearly harmful. Many of the horror stories about dangerous products can be traced to this lack. Second, few individuals would be able to bear the financial penalties in fines or damages that might be appropriate in comparison with the harm caused by their conduct. Stone adds the important point that, even where a blameworthy individual within a corporation can be singled out and dealt with adequately, this may not necessarily change the conduct of the corporation, because it is in the nature of organizations to make particular individuals dispensable.

All this is by way of prelude to Stone's argument for an additional and different kind of legal trust:

> ...to steer corporations we cannot continue to rely as heavily as we do on threats posed to the organization as a whole, allowing the corporation to adjust to the law's threats as "it" sees fit, according to "its" calculus of profits and losses; nor even to trust to threats aimed at key individuals in order to induce them to institute the changes they see fit. It isn't that these strategies should be abandoned. But what we shall have to do, increasingly, is augment them with a new approach. The society shall have to locate certain specific and critical organizational variables, and, where feasible, reach into the corporation to arrange them as it itself deems appropriate. In other words, if we can first clarify what ideal internal configurations of authority and information flow would best ameliorate the problem of, say, corporate pollution. . . the society might then consider programs aimed at mandating such ideal internal configurations directly. Thus, what I have in mind is a legal system that, in dealing with corporations, moves toward an increasingly direct focus on the *processes of corporate decision-making*, at least as a supplement to the traditional strategies that largely await upon the corporate *acts*. Instead of treating the corporation's inner processes as a "black box," to be influenced only indirectly through threats laid about its environment like traps, we need more straightforward "intrusions" into the corporation's decision structure and processes than society has yet undertaken.

Stone then goes on to develop a number of ideas for legal reform, which we will not attempt to describe here. We do not agree with all of them, for example, his variants of the "public director" idea, which we touched on in Chapter 12. The thread running through all his suggestions, however, is the need to give the law more of a preventive cast, as opposed to a merely punitive or remedial one. This is a particularly necessary reorientation in areas such as pollution and product and work-place safety, where the need is to gather and evaluate information systematically during the stages of a product's development. He also advances some ideas based on a parole analogy for demonstrated corporate misconduct, and different techniques of supervision and inspection in especially dangerous industries.

There is much in Stone's book that will be unsettling and even frightening to corporate managers. Nevertheless, he has had more practical things to say about corporate social responsibility than anyone else we came across. We close this chapter with the hope that our brief exposition of some of his ideas will stimulate study and debate by lawmakers and others interested in social responsibility.

Chapter 17

The Regulated Sector and the Regulatory Process

Introduction

An examination of corporate concentration in Canada cannot ignore the special features of the regulated sector of the economy. For one thing, the regulated sector in Canada is large relative to the total economy compared, for example, with the United States, where it comprises approximately 17% of the gross national product (GNP). Second, regulation often has the effect of increasing concentration in an industry, even when that is not necessarily intended. Even when it does not increase concentration, regulation may have in its price-setting function, the same anticompetitive effects as a monopoly or an oligopoly. In this chapter we have focussed more on the nature and effects of regulatory processes than on the regulated corporations themselves.

Some definitional preliminaries are in order at this point. We make a distinction between direct regulation and qualitative regulation. The latter embraces a vast array of qualitative standards, which extend across all industries and, indeed, all of society. Health, sanitation and product-safety regulations, hours-of-work laws and zoning by-laws are a few examples out of thousands that affect almost everybody. Regulation of this kind may affect economic and other activity profoundly, but it does not have its roots in the particular structure within which a country's economic activity is organized.

In this chapter we will discuss what we call direct regulation, that is that framework of laws and agencies, including Crown corporations, that bear directly on pricing and resource allocation. Direct regulation in this sense takes two forms. First, there are those industries that are subject to regulatory boards that concern themselves primarily with prices, profits and adequacy of service. For example, railways, electricity, gas and telephone utilities, banks, pipelines, trucking, airlines, taxicabs, broadcasting, securities and insurance are all subject to controls of this general kind. Even in these industries, however, the focus of the regulation varies. The prices, profits and levels of service of railways and telephone companies are subject to close scrutiny but, in the insurance, banking and securities industries, the regulatory authorities are interested in financial soundness and integrity and do not control prices and profits, at least not directly. In broadcasting, the chief concern of the regulators seems to be the adequacy of service and, in some senses, programming. A second form of direct regulation is self-regulation. The professions and much of

395

agriculture operate under legislative umbrellas that give these groups broad powers to control quality, supply and prices. Direct regulation of either kind can take place at the local, provincial or federal level.

For our purposes we are not interested in the particular aspects of a regulated industry's activities which attract the most attention from the regulatory authority, nor with the governmental level at which the regulation takes place. Rather we are concerned with what is common to all regulated industries (though the emphasis given to it by the regulators varies from one to another): that entry to the industries is often restricted and prices and output are controlled. As a result regulated industries are often sheltered from competition. Controls on entry into an industry tend to increase concentration in that industry, and thus make direct regulation relevant to us.

In addition to increasing concentration as such, and even when concentration does not increase, direct regulation can have many of the same effects as any other restrictive practice. Direct regulation, indeed, is a sanctioned restrictive practice. Restrictions on entry to a regulated industry can entrench existing producers and inhibit the efficient allocation of resources. Regulation can also impose significant costs in technical and administrative time devoted to complying with the regulatory process, "X-inefficiency" (i.e. management slack) allowed by reduced competition, economically unjustified price discrimination, sluggish application of new technology and unresponsiveness to the needs and demands of consumers. Thus regulation may tolerate and even create what would otherwise be condemned.

Despite its importance to the Canadian economy, direct regulation has received little critical scrutiny. It is difficult to analyze and assess in a Canadian context the costs and benefits, the structural consequences and the possible alternatives to the various instruments by which governments control economic activity through direct regulation. Nevertheless, the research commissioned and the submissions and testimony received by the Commission have led us to some conclusions, the chief one of which is that a more stringent examination should be made of the regulatory process in Canada. The importance of economic regulation to the Canadian economy and to individual Canadians is too great to permit the lack of critical study and assessment of the effectiveness and efficiency of economic regulation to continue. Governments and academics should act to fill this information gap so that an intelligent debate can begin on the role of economic regulation in Canada. In this chapter, we have restricted ourselves to the questions implicit in our mandate: whether the public interest is adequately safeguarded against the potential misuse of power in a regulated environment, the accountability of direct regulatory agencies to the legislative process and the role of consumers in the regulatory mechanism.

Why Regulation?

Government may decide for many reasons to intervene in the market and regulate industries. For example, certain industries have economic characteristics that qualify them as "natural monopolies": a single supplier will have lower unit costs than would a group of competing suppliers, either because of economies of scale or because of high fixed costs of capital installations.

In other instances the market for one reason or another may not allocate to the industry the amount of resources desired by society. The size of the project or its risk of technological failure may be too high to attract private investment (e.g., in energy development). The free market may lead to unacceptable price fluctuations (e.g., in agricultural products). Some industries are thought to be so important to the country that their adequate and proper functioning must be ensured by government; communications and transport are examples of this.

These traditional economic reasons sometimes merge with social or political goals such as subsidizing service to particular groups (urban transit), regional development (rail and air transport), regional planning (electric power), preservation of the family farm (marketing boards), use and upgrading of natural resources (energy boards), and the maintenance of cultural and political integrity (communications). Often the non-economic reasons may well be more important than the economic ones.

Regulation and regulated industries cannot be analyzed from a purely economic standpoint because many of the regulators' decisions are not based on economics, and are not particularly intended to achieve efficiency either in the use of existing resources or in the allocation of resources to an industry. Usually regulation involves social and political questions at least as much as economic ones. Regulation often is put in place, therefore, when the free market system fails to achieve the allocation of resources desired by the public. The lack of a single or dominant criterion by which to evaluate many regulated industries leads to serious problems of accountability and control.

However, while direct regulation may protect the public from discriminatory pricing, monopolistic profits or economic inefficiencies, it may also inflict these on the public. In the next section of this chapter we outline some of the criticisms that are made of direct regulation.

Before turning to those criticisms, however, a word should be said about the particular significance of regulation in Canada. In one form or another the state has probably always played a comparatively larger economic role in Canada than it has in other countries in similar stages of development. Canada has a large territory and one, moreover, that is exceedingly difficult and expensive to develop. The population is very small relative to the size of the territory it occupies. In Canada the intervention of government may well be necessary to marshal the economic resources needed to develop and unify the country. For example this was true for the building of the Canadian Pacific Railway and has continued to be true for transport of all kinds. Canadians live beside a neighbor who is economically and culturally vigorous and powerful. The natural north-south pull of economic and cultural forces has been resisted with a complex network of tariffs, subsidies and other forms of economic control, which have made the Canadian economy a highly artifical one. Moreoever, the importance of foreign investment and foreign trade in the Canadian economy, and the tendency in some other countries for governments to take a prominent part in economic activity, all require a higher level of state intervention in the Canadian economy than might otherwise be necessary. A high level of state intervention may well be the *sine qua non* of Canadian nationhood.

We think it is important to emphasize this point here because most of the criticisms of government regulation discussed in the next section have emerged in the United States. Although detailed studies of those criticisms would no doubt show they are qualitatively applicable in Canada too, the degree to which they are valid in this country is apt to be less than may be true in the United States. The thread running through these criticisms is that regulation tends toward economic inefficiency. However, so long as Canada continues to exist in defiance of economics, economics must often take second place to considerations that are not measurable in terms of economic efficiency.

Criticism of Direct Regulation

The expansion of direct regulation as an instrument of government policy has made the costs and benefits of regulation both more obvious and more important. The steady increase of state intervention in the private sector of the economy has generated, particularly in the United States, a corresponding interest in deregulation. The advocates of deregulation say that regulation is too often ineffectual, inflexible and expensive relative to the benefits derived from it. They argue for outright deregulation of some industries and, at the least, for freer entry and more competition in regulated industries. The following points are commonly made in support of this general proposition:

1. Direct regulation as an instrument to prevent the earning of monopoly profits may be self-defeating or futile. The regulated company may frustrate the regulators by reducing the quality of service, or profits may be concealed through "creative" accounting for valuations and expenses.

2. If regulated firms are permitted rates of return exceeding their cost of capital, they have an incentive to overinvest in plant and equipment. On the other hand, if their returns are held down they may be unable to provide adequate levels of service.

3. Restrictive regulation may leave regulated firms with little incentive to innovate. As a consequence, technological change and rate of growth in productivity may be slower in regulated industries than it would otherwise be.

4. Many regulatory efforts focus on profits because inefficiency and costs are much more difficult to regulate. But a small inefficiency induced by regulation may offset what is gained by controlling profits. This X-inefficiency may become a pervasive problem in the regulated industry, since management has little incentive to increase its efficiency and often has a considerable incentive not to do so. Regulation in Canada has seldom

involved a close examination of costs, other than depreciation. Thus, a regulatory agency will frequently focus on whether a 9.8% or 10.1% rate of return on investment is appropriate, and not on costs in general: "... most consumers would rather pay $1 for a long distance call, 20 cents of which represented a monopoly profit ... than $1.10, all of which was cost."

5. Pricing may be more concerned with the winning of political support than with economic efficiency.

6. The regulatory process may discourage innovative pricing and reduce price flexibility.

7. Direct regulation may create problems later if the government decides to deregulate an industry. This problem arises when the restrictions imposed by the regulatory agency on entry into the industry create a substantial market value in the licence to do business.

8. Economic regulation presents two cross-subsidization possibilities. The first is the subsidization of some customers by the overcharging of others. The second involves the regulated company that engages in both regulated and non-regulated activities, but uses some of the same resources in the provision of both kinds of activity and incurs joint costs. The possibility exists for unfair competition against the competitors in the unregulated sector.

9. It is frequently alleged that firms in some regulated industries have become so large that effective cost analysis is impracticable and effective regulation is not possible.

10. The costs of administering regulatory programs may exceed the benefits. The regulatory process is not a free good, and it may be extremely expensive.

11. The regulatory boards often complain that they are chronically under-financed because they lack a political constituency.

12. There may be a natural human tendency for regulators at some point to abjure their regulatory role and to adopt a role of "promoting the health of the industry".

13. Concern exists that regulatory commissions may be "captured" as a result of bureaucratic symbiosis and the tendency for individuals on staffs of regulating agencies to move on to employment with the regulated firms. Individuals may accept employment with commissions in just such antici-pation. This has been a chronic problem in the United States.

14. There is a tendency for a regulatory board, once created, to become immortal. Conditions at some point in the past may have justified the establishment of a regulatory board; however, new technologies or eco-nomic or institutional changes may have eliminated the need for continued regulation.

15. While private interests can foresee and calculate the impact of regulatory policies, individual consumers typically do not do so collectively. Producers might be expected to incur lobbying, legal and related expenses to obtain

price increases, but consumers are not as likely to organize since the impact of an increase in the price of the regulated commodity or service is often small for each individual consumer. As a consequence, producers may appear at a hearing represented by a large and expert staff while consumers go under-represented or not represented at all.

16. Concern has been expressed over the lack of political accountability of regulatory commissions that make essentially political decisions establishing priorities in the use of resources. The lack of political accountability is a source of concern under a parliamentary system.

In recent years many economists and legal scholars have looked with increasing skepticism at the traditional arguments for direct regulation. Some suggest that direct regulation has not usually been introduced to prevent the use of monopoly power and to protect the public interest but, rather, has been introduced to entrench the market positions of those firms already established in the industry and to protect them from competition by new firms. This observation emerges from re-examination of the decisions of many regulatory agencies and the histories of the interest groups that supported their establishment and that have opposed the dismantling of the agencies.

Many observers of the regulated sector have noted that often regulated firms have demonstrated a preference for regulation rather than for competition, once they have become used to the regulatory process. The Director of Research and Investigation under the Combines Investigation Act, in his appearance before this Commission, reflected the attitudes of many economists and political scientists when he said: "Other scholars point out that however much business may resist the direct regulation initially, firms frequently learn very quickly to prefer the comfort of a regulated environment, to the cold winds and rough blows of competition." Michael Trebilcock, a Canadian commentator on regulatory law, in his brief to the Commission observed that: "It has been demonstrated time and again that both theoretically and empirically these regimes are a direct response to industry pressure for reduced competition, in effect for legalized cartelization."

Conclusions

It is not possible to do anything more with so general a list of observations than to say that they appear to raise valid points that deserve serious investigation. They justify, it seems to us, a critical study of at least some of the major instruments of state intervention. Further generalizations about the regulated sector as a whole would not be useful, although some valuable principles about the aims and techniques of regulation may emerge from a study of particular cases.

We were not able to do the kind of study that we think the subject deserves, but we were given many examples of things that suggest to us that much of the regulatory apparatus in Canada has developed without coherent principles and has continued without any fundamental re-examination of the objectives it seeks to achieve. There is also widespread discontent with the practices of many regulatory bodies.

While there is therefore good reason to think that regulation in Canada could be improved, the evidence does not permit us to make specific recommendations. In particular, we are not able to endorse the conclusions of many in the United States who say, for example, that steps should be taken to deregulate many industries. Firm judgments like this may be more satisfying and even more popular than our conclusion, but we think they would be premature in Canada. Again, it is wrong to suggest, as does one of the criticisms listed above, that concern on the part of the regulators for the health of an industry is necessarily in conflict with the regulatory role. Regulation is rarely a simple question of policing against wrongdoing. In varying degrees, regulators are concerned with the best possible operation of the industry within their jurisdiction, and they are therefore drawn into a role that goes beyond the control of abuses. It is hard to imagine, for example, that the importance of capital markets to the national well-being is not very much in the minds of those who regulate the banks and other financial institutions. The continued health of these organizations should be a proper concern of the regulators and, indeed, it is the reason there is regulation.

Furthermore, criticism of direct regulation is becoming more vocal at a time when the economy is less than robust. If, in the past, unwarranted hopes have been placed in the efficacy of schemes of economic regulation, the current spate of economic difficulties may be generating an excessive disenchantment with government intervention.

We can illustrate, and perhaps justify, our caution by reference to one aspect of regulation, which seems to have attracted more attention in Canada than any other. In recent years there has been much discussion about the level of public participation in the proceedings of regulatory tribunals, and several of our witnesses also spoke about it. The argument for public participation in regulatory decision-making is that regulatory proceedings cannot lead to decisions that are truly in the public interest unless all significant interests are well represented. If some important groups are chronically under-represented, material considerations could be excluded from the deliberations of the regulatory boards. The under-representation of consumer and environmental interests is a particular concern. Since in many cases of regulatory control the consumer interest makes up a large portion of the public interest that regulation is intended to serve, the lack of representation or under-representation of this group in the regulatory process is a serious problem.

J. S. Grafstein of the Canadian Transport Commission has commented that:

> the regulatory policy has not cast its net wide enough to examine the effects of transport policies of carriers' activities on the consumer. In massive rate hearings ... "the public interest intervenors" rarely have the resources of regulated corporations. This imbalance would change if an independent office ... a "Consumer Advocate"—were built into the regulatory process.

William Stanbury has noted that:

> ... Stigler is not alone when he remarks, "I know of no historical example of a viable, continuing, broad-based consumer political lobby". This is despite the fact that the aggregate gains or losses to consumers resulting from the actions of regulatory agencies often greatly exceed the direct benefits or losses to the regulated firms ...
>
> Any voluntary scheme will fail if each individual rationally pursues his own self interest. As Leone points out ... "despite public acceptance of the 'product' of public interest advocacy, few are willing to pay the costs of 'production'. He concludes that "the resource constraint ultimately will end the current round of public interest advocacy".
>
> The staffs of the regulatory commission have not lived up to their mandate; the commissioners have become "judges" in cases where the "defendant" (consumer) is unrepresented; and consumers themselves cannot voluntarily organize to represent their interests. Is it surprising that one hears a call for an institutionalized consumer advocate financed by government?

The chronic under-representation of consumer groups at regulatory hearings is largely the consequence of two interlocking factors: (1) In a democratic society, a highly concerned minority, whose members are willing to switch their political support over an issue, wields power disproportionate to its size. Consumer protection, however, is such a diffuse issue that most voters are not willing to switch their vote over some general need for increased consumer representation before regulatory boards. Hence, there is little incentive for government to provide either access or money to such an effort. (2) Consumer protection in any form is a "public good" once it has been put in place; repeated use will not diminish it and exclusion from its benefits is not possible (or desired). Hence there is a "free rider" problem. There is little incentive for the individual consumer to finance any consumer intervention at a regulatory hearing since he will benefit equally whether he has contributed or not.

The general problem of organization of interests is exacerbated by practical problems encountered in the regulatory process. In addressing this problem, a report of the Canadian Consumer Council draws attention to the following:

1. there are problems of public notice;
2. the failure of many boards to be required explicitly within their legislative mandates to consider the consumer interest frequently results in no consideration;
3. the standing of public interest groups to initiate judicial review of a board's decisions varies widely and is frequently unrecognized in law;
4. consumer groups lack information and expertise;
5. the heterogeneity of the consumer interests, rooted in differences in geography, occupation and age, can cause conflicts in objectives;
6. information on the criteria used by regulatory boards may not be accessible: in some instances, decisions are published without reasons and transcripts are not made available.

The problems associated with the unrepresentativeness of regulatory proceedings result chiefly from the length and cost of regulatory hearings. The complex nature of many regulatory matters, such as rates, demands expertise in understanding the issues as well as time to participate in usually lengthy hearings and money to prepare submissions and provide alternative expert witnesses. This often results in limited participation by groups other than the regulated. If regulators are to fulfill their mandates to protect and represent the public interest, then representation and participation by interests other than the regulated must be encouraged and facilitated. Wider public participation will provide regulators a broader range of facts and perspectives relevant to their responsibilities. Moreover, given the significance of the decisions of regulatory bodies for Canadians, care must be taken, on grounds of equity, to ensure that those affected are represented in the regulatory process. The competition of viewpoints that could result from wider representation of interests before regulatory agencies can be salutary for both the results of the regulatory process and, equally important, public confidence in that process.

Our difficulty with this line of argument is not that the points made are not valid, but that it begs the broader and more fundamental question of how the machinery of economic regulation is to be made accountable and responsive to the public it is intended to serve. We think the arguments for public participation put too much emphasis on the adjudicative processes of regulatory tribunals. They are attempts to make the process fair and they assume that better substantive decisions will flow from (and will justify the cost of) more broadly based hearings. There is an unarticulated analogy with proceedings in the courts of law, which, whatever their other failings, usually ensure that all affected parties are represented. The analogy overlooks the fact that courts are usually called upon to resolve narrowly defined *disputes*, within the framework of existing law. Regulatory tribunals, in contrast, are primarily concerned with *making* law, and they resolve disputes only incidentally and as a kind of by-product of that larger function.

The more important question is therefore how to design the lawmaking process that is necessarily delegated to regulatory boards by Parliament and the legislatures, so that the views of the public are made known to the regulators. It is not obvious to us, for example, that the litigation process, however representative it is made, is always or even usually the best route to good regulation. The danger of the bias that the consumer advocacy movement gives to the regulatory process is that the lawmaking functions of regulatory boards may be distracted by factors that are important to the contestants but only marginally relevant to the formulation of policy. Economic regulation is fundamentally a problem of government. It is not an industrial problem, nor is it basically a means of resolving controversies between opposing interest groups. It is for this reason that we are unwilling to endorse unreservedly those who plead for a more comprehensive system of support for consumer and environmental representation before regulatory tribunals.

Changes in Canada's apparatus of economic regulation would certainly require an examination of many aspects of parliamentary government itself. It is hardly necessary to say that an inquiry of this kind goes well beyond the brief given to us. The scope of such an inquiry can be seen by posing a few of the many questions that come to mind. For example, is there any acceptable way of reconciling the principle of regulatory independence with political control? Should government be able to overrule, direct or otherwise interfere with the decisions of independent regulatory boards exercising powers given them by Parliament and, if so, on what grounds? To what extent and in what manner should such executive interference be subject to the supervision of Parliament? What should be the proper scope of interest group participation in the regulatory rule-making process, and how can this be both assured and controlled? How often, in what way and in what respects should regulatory boards be accountable to the legislatures that create them? Is Parliament able to examine critically the policies and decisions of regulatory boards (remembering that it is already widely criticized for its inability to monitor regular government activity). Is it realistic to expect legislators to be interested in doing so? The answers to these questions may not be the same in all areas of economic regulation.

We therefore end where we began. Direct regulation often contributes to industrial concentration and the economic inefficiencies that tend to accompany it. At the same time, the various schemes of direct regulation exist because they were thought to be necessary to achieve other economic and social objectives. The problem is that many of these schemes seem to have been put in place, or at any rate continued, without a conscious assessment of their costs and benefits, including an awareness of their consequences for the efficiency of the overall economy, and their implications for democratic government. We can do little more here than point this out, and express the hope that a proper assessment of direct regulation will begin.

Chapter 18
General Conclusions

As we said in Chapter 1, the notion of corporate power has three inter-mixed strands, economic, political and social. Although, for purposes of analysis, we have made a broad distinction between economic power on the one hand and social and political power on the other, in fact these blend together so subtly that it is not possible to make judgments about one or the other separately. The purpose of this chapter is to collect in one place the major conclusions we reached during our analysis.

CONCENTRATION, SCALE AND COMPETITION

We discovered, first of all, that those corporations that can be considered large in Canada are in general small in comparison with large corporations elsewhere in the world. Moreover, over the last 15 or 20 years, many of Canada's largest corporations have declined in size relative to those operating in the same industries in other countries.

We looked at corporate concentration in terms of both aggregate concentration (the proportion of overall economic activity accounted for by the largest firms) and industrial concentration (the proportion of the activity in a particular industry accounted for by the largest firms in that industry). By both measures, concentration is higher in Canada than it is elsewhere. However, aggregate concentration in Canada has probably declined since the beginning of the century, and since about the mid-1960s there has been little change in the levels of either aggregate or industrial concentration.

In several countries, the largest firms in an industry have been encouraged to merge to increase their international competitiveness. If, as seems to be true in many industries, large size is necessary for efficient operations and to compete in international markets, efforts in Canada to reduce corporate concentration by limiting the size of firms will further reduce the competitiveness of Canadian firms in world markets. Equally, if Canadian firms can and do expand to world size, there may well be a significant increase in corporate concentration in Canada.

On the assumption that large Canadian firms, particularly those that sell in international markets, will attempt to expand in response to the pull of what

405

they will probably see as natural and imperative economic forces, and given that the price of this expansion will probably be further concentration in some sectors of the Canadian economy, an important policy choice is posed. A judgment has to be made as to whether public policy should encourage, discourage or be neutral toward the growth of large corporations. This judgment requires, in turn, a decision about the advantages of corporate size in an industrial economy.

It is a commonplace that many Canadian manufacturers tend to be small, unspecialized and inefficient by international standards. They survive in the small Canadian market behind a variety of tariff and non-tariff barriers to trade and have erected barriers to entry in many industries to protect themselves from further competition. Frequently they are not able to penetrate overseas markets for manufactured products. This oversimplified but basically accurate description of the Canadian economy is the basis for the argument commonly heard that Canadian producers can become more competitive only if they expand to efficient size. We examined the evidence on the relationship between size and efficiency and discovered that we disagreed with the emphasis this research has placed on plant-level economies of scale.

Canadian plants are not, in general, markedly smaller than those in other countries in many industries, and, for the most part, Canadian industry's cost disadvantages are not occasioned by inadequate scale at the plant level. Diversity of production *within* Canadian plants is a far more significant factor. In addition, the small size of *firms* (not plants) often creates diseconomies in finance, marketing, management and, particularly, risk-taking ability and research and development. While we therefore agree with the argument that the efficiency of the Canadian economy should be improved by policies favoring the growth of firms to efficient scale, we emphasize that the desired growth is that of firms and that greater rationalization of product lines must occur within their plants in order to realize economies of large-scale production.

The conclusions developed so far point in the direction of increased corporate concentration in Canada or, at any rate, no reduction in its present high level. That being so, the next question is whether the threat to market competition inherent in corporate concentration, a threat which is at least as real as the advantages from increased efficiency, can be mitigated. We believe that an adequate competition law is an essential instrument of a public policy that wants to preserve the advantages of market competition in an oligopolistic economy.

Accordingly, we agree in principle with the general direction of the proposals for reform of the competition law contained in Bill C-13, presently before Parliament. We think, however, that the Bill's provisions dealing with "joint monopolization" reach too far. Instead, an approach that attacks what is known as "conscious parallelism plus" will be fairer and more effective in countering restrictive market practices.

MERGERS

We also think that the merger provisions in Bill C-13 are misguided. Our research shows that industrial concentration has not increased over the last 15 years, a period that included the merger wave of the mid-1960s. The merger provisions in Bill C-13 are unnecessarily elaborate and expensive, given the small dimensions of the problem with which they are intended to deal. They will introduce an unacceptable degree of risk and uncertainty into Canada's economic environment. We prefer a law that deals sternly but surely with anticompetitive actions (including the building of barriers to entry) that may arise after a merger has been completed, rather than a law that operates on the basis of predictions about future actions.

Our study of conglomerate corporations revealed that their diversification has probably not increased concentration within industries and may even have increased competition. There are some indications that conglomerate diversification has decreased the overall efficiency of the firms involved, as measured by return on assets, and that investors in highly diversified firms have received lower-than-average returns. In theory, diversified firms have a greater ability than other firms to engage in a variety of anticompetitive practices (predatory pricing, cross-product subsidization, tied selling, etc.) but we have found only a few instances in which they have exercised this power. We conclude that the proposed competition law can deal with these problems adequately. Similarly, we see no need for special legislation affecting conglomerate mergers.

The attempted Power-Argus merger was important, not because of its potential effect on competition within industries (which we think would have been minor) but because the prominence of the parties in the economy made their actions significant to the public. Transactions this spectacular will always demand inquiry. We think that conglomerate mergers of this kind should first be analyzed under the competition law, but if (as in Power-Argus) there are no significant competitive implications, or none that could not be dealt with under the competition law, there may still be overriding reasons of public policy that will compel intervention by the state. We do not think it is possible to establish in advance legislative criteria by which unique cases like a Power-Argus merger can be assessed. If the state intervenes to prevent or dissolve a merger like Power-Argus, the decision to do so must be a political one, to be taken by government and Parliament in the light of the circumstances as they see them at the time.

FOREIGN DIRECT INVESTMENT

The kind of conflicting considerations that bear on the corporate concentration problem are highlighted when they are examined in conjunction with the phenomenon of foreign direct investment in Canada. Foreign direct investment is high in Canada, but its level has remained stable over the past several years and may even be declining in size relative to the economy as a whole. The several studies that have been made of foreign direct investment in recent years have illuminated the matter well, and the benefits and costs of this investment have been debated at length. It is clear that foreign investment has been an important stimulus to the development of the Canadian economy. However, this investment has probably exacerbated such problems as the truncation of research and development and the ability of Canadian firms to export. Although it is difficult to measure the effect of foreign direct investment on corporate concentration in Canada, it may have helped to sustain the level of concentration in some industries by making it more difficult for domestic firms to enter and survive in them and by importing into Canada the oligopolistic structure of industries abroad, particularly those in the United States. On the other hand, foreign investment has probably introduced increased competition and innovation in some industries.

Foreign investment was not our direct concern; we were interested in it only insofar as it relates to corporate concentration. Parliament has taken steps, notably through the Foreign Investment Review Act, to try to achieve the best possible balance of advantages and disadvantages from foreign investment in the future. We have no recommendations for substantive changes in the regulatory machinery that is now in place because we think the present laws are adequate to deal with foreign direct investment.

We are confident that those administering the Foreign Investment Review Act are conscious of the benefits of foreign investment to Canada and give them adequate consideration when reviewing investment proposals governed by that Act. Those who administer the competition law should also bear in mind that the growth of domestic firms, even at the cost of an increase in concentration, will offset, in part, both the proportion of the economy under foreign control and some of the undesirable consequences of foreign investment.

BANKING

We have been able to discover no economies of scale in banking that necessitate the current large size of banks and the oligopolistic structure of the industry. While there is no conclusive evidence that banks are earning monopoly profits, further consolidation among the major banks should not be allowed. The oligopolistic structure of the industry has led to overbranching and some lack of efficiency. We would encourage further entry into the industry and would allow other financial institutions to expand their services into personal loans and loans to small businesses. This extension should include foreign banks, but with the restrictions that they operate under the Bank Act and that they not be permitted to act as agents for their parent corporations abroad in securing underwriting business.

SMALLER BUSINESS

A healthy small and medium-sized business sector can offset the effects of high concentration in some industries, although stimulation or encouragement of small business will not fundamentally transform Canada's industrial structure, and many industries in Canada will continue to be dominated by large, capital-intensive firms. Nevertheless smaller businesses can increase competition in some industries and have beneficial social effects. They have demonstrated their ability to innovate and to sustain market competition when they are given a reasonable chance to grow.

Unfortunately, there are some major impediments to the development of a vigorous and effective smaller business sector in the Canadian economy. Many of the barriers to entry and impediments to the growth of small firms which are inherent in an economy characterized by large firms and a high level of foreign ownership are largely irremovable. However, some of these obstacles can be overcome by an intelligent use of the competition law.

TAXATION

The other serious problem hampering business generally, and smaller business in particular, is the scarcity of investment capital. This problem exists as a consequence of domestic institutional factors, which are difficult, but not impossible, to change. The problem is important because the prosperity of Canadians cannot be assured unless the proportion of the gross national product that is invested in the private sector is increased. We think this increase can come only from corporate investment. We have concluded that returns from business investment in Canada in recent years have simply been too low to attract the needed investment. The tax structure influences investment profoundly, as we discovered when we looked at the amount of Canadians' savings that flow into tax shelters of different kinds. For the most part these savings are not invested in the private sector, particularly not in equity securities. We do not think that minor adjustments in the tax laws or subsidies will be effective in generating the large amount of investment capital that Canada will require in the coming years. We therefore sought a solution that would be likely to improve the overall Canadian business and investment climate significantly. Ideally, something is required that will have a positive and direct effect on production costs and price competitiveness and that will also stimulate equity investment.

We think that the kind of solution required probably lies in far-reaching tax changes, and we suggested two areas, capital gains taxation and the timing of the taxation of business income, as candidates for critical review and possible reform. We are well aware of the difficulties that tax relief of the kind and magnitude embraced within these suggestions would create. However, the economic problems that have become visible over the past few years are so serious that we believe drastic, uncomfortable and even painful remedies are required. The problem of corporate concentration is small in comparison and cannot be dealt with in any event unless the more serious problems of productivity, inflation and inadequate investment are solved.

CORPORATE CONTROL

Our study of corporate governance and control did not lead us to conclude that major changes were needed in the existing pattern of legislation. However, we do suggest a number of steps that corporations could take to strengthen and diversify their boards of directors and thus improve public confidence in them. We believe that corporations, especially large corporations, have to overcome a deep-rooted and widespread public suspicion about their motives and an increasing public impatience with their bureaucratic insensitivity. There is no single answer to this problem, and certainly none that can be provided by the state through legislation. Indeed, government is one of the worst offenders.

Large corporations cannot overcome negative public attitudes toward them unless they can show, credibly, that their decisions take into account the social as well as the economic consequences of their actions on society as a whole. This is not a task that can be left to advertising and public relations. One of the most effective steps corporations could take, we think, would be to leaven their boards of directors with more people whose backgrounds are not in corporate business. People like this may provide the corporation with points of view it would not otherwise have and they may inspire more public trust in corporate decisions.

CORPORATE DISCLOSURE

As corporate actions have been seen to have widespread social consequences, so also has the importance of public trust in the integrity of business become important to the corporation. Public suspicions about business are often based on misunderstanding, but business itself must bear some of the blame for this. Once again, there is no easy way to overcome this problem, but fuller and better disclosure of business information is certainly necessary before the public can make more informed judgments about what business does.

Our recommendations on corporate disclosure therefore attempt both to expand the kind of corporate information that is made public and to reduce the cost and burden of supplying it. The latter objective will require a good deal of rationalization of data gathering by all governments and, we think, review and control mechanisms to check and discipline the insatiable appetite that governments have for information.

CORPORATE INFLUENCE

Many Canadians are profoundly concerned with what they think is the considerable power that large corporations have to influence official decisions and public opinion. We found little evidence to support this fear. Recent reforms of the election laws may help to reduce suspicions of improper or disproportionate corporate influence, but, in our judgment, safeguards against improper influence must be found within the processes of government.

Another aspect of the power of corporations is their ability to influence the public through advertising. Deceptive advertising can be dealt with under existing legislation. The Canadian Radio-Television and Telecommunications Commission (CRTC) may be able to produce regulations for advocacy advertising that will help to ensure a balanced presentation of viewpoints on public issues, but we see no way to ensure that corporate advertising does not lead consumers and others to make unwise choices. Advertising is essential to the operation of a market economy and an important aspect of competition. Exaggeration, bad taste and the other objectionable features of much advertising seem to be inevitable in a competitive market system, although government policies can have some moderating influence. Ultimately, however, the only effective defence against the persuasive arts of advertisers or anyone else is a critical sense in the public mind.

There are latent dangers in concentrated ownership of the mass media. Competition law may be a useful check on this kind of concentration occasionally, but there are no practical legislative or regulatory instruments available or in prospect to deal with this problem comprehensively. The CRTC has the legal power to control the ownership of broadcasting outlets but it is apparent that their decisions are much more heavily influenced by other considerations. We recommend that the CRTC be empowered to prevent the owners of broadcasting stations from also owning newspapers and other print media that circulate in the same market.

WORKING CONDITIONS

Our examination of the relationship between business size and working conditions revealed that there was little if any correlation between the size of the firm and health and safety standards, discrimination, and job satisfaction in the work place. There is some evidence that larger firms pay higher total compensation than small firms do. The available data in this area is extremely fragmentary, however, and much more research will be necessary before confident conclusions can be drawn.

CORPORATE SOCIAL RESPONSIBILITY

Our study of corporate social responsibility led us to several conclusions about the meaning and direction of the idea that corporations should consider and assume some responsibility for the social consequences of their activities. We decided, first, that the social implications of business with which people are concerned are inherent in an industrial system and, in general, have little to do with corporate concentration. We also concluded that there is no longer any serious question about whether business corporations should take into account the social implications of their decisions. Clearly, the public will insist that they do.

Social responsibility is therefore largely a matter of awareness on the part of business that social considerations are factors in business decisions no less legitimate than economic ones. There must, however, be an understanding on the part of the public of the kind of corporate responses that it may reasonably expect and, no less important, of what it should not expect, because action taken by business out of a feeling of social responsibility has costs as well as benefits. Social consequences are limitless in their range and variety, and we have made no attempt to prepare a comprehensive catalogue of them. Moreover, their significance one to the other changes constantly, both because the relative values that people attach to things change and because varying internal and external political and economic influences impose constraints on the ability of business to deliver particular results. All this makes it impossible for us to pronounce explicitly about either the kinds of social obligations that corporations should recognize or the manner in which they should respond to them.

We were struck by the extent to which public opinion in Canada has shifted during the course of this Commission's work. When we began our work the pressures on business to recognize and discharge social obligations, even at some economic cost, were much more insistent than they are as we complete our *Report*. The decline in business activity during this time and concern about rising unemployment seem to have brought forth a greater realization that corporate social responsibility has an economic price that is paid by those who depend on corporations for their livelihood and those who consume the goods they produce.

Social reporting should gradually extend and deepen understanding of corporate social responsibility, although we doubt that disclosure of social information will ever attain the degree of objectivity that has been realized in financial disclosure. The law, too, has a role to play in defining and enforcing social responsibility but it is often ill-adapted to the task. We think that the kind of interventionist legal techniques that Christopher Stone describes in his book *Where the Law Ends: The Social Control of Corporate Behavior* (see our Chapter 16) are only just over the horizon. Stone suggests that increasingly the law will have to act positively to influence decision-making within corporations to ensure that corporate decisions are made in accordance with the desires of society, rather than in reaction to prohibitions and penalties instituted as a result of social problems caused by corporate decisions. Whether these suggestions are adopted in Canada will depend very much on how business responds, and is seen to respond, to the social consequences of its activities, including its ability to dispel the climate of suspicion and hostility that has surrounded it in recent years.

REGULATED INDUSTRIES

Our penultimate chapter contained a brief discussion of the regulated sector of the economy and the regulatory process. Regulation in Canada has grown piecemeal, in response to particular problems and needs as they appeared. It is now a haphazard collection of laws and machinery by which the state attempts to direct business activity for a variety of ill-coordinated economic and social objectives. The subject of regulation is relevant to our work, not only because many regulated industries tend to be concentrated and insulated from competition but also because regulatory mechanisms are frequently created to accomplish social objectives. The difficult task of reconciling economic and social objectives is seen most clearly in the regulated industries, and is an additional reason why we urge that there be an adequate study of the regulatory process.

A study of economic regulation in Canada must be made against the broader backdrop of Canadian nationhood because we believe that this is the real justification for government intervention in economic affairs. The fundamental issue is the proper spheres of public and private economic power in Canada. The answer to this question lies largely outside economic analysis; it has more to do with the kind of country and government Canadians want.

*   *   *

In summary, the influences that have shaped the Canadian economy have made a high degree of concentration inevitable. If changes occur they are likely to be in the direction of more rather than less concentration, chiefly because of international competitive influences. Public responses to concentration should recognize that profound and far-reaching changes are not practicable. The best mix of benefits and burdens should be sought through vigilance and the selective use of the appropriate instruments of public policy. While we have recommended a number of improvements, we conclude that no radical changes in the laws governing corporate activity are necessary at this time to protect the public interest.

APPENDIX A

Orders in Council

Order in Council
P.C. 1975-879

Certified to be a true copy of a Minute of a Meeting of the Committee of the Privy Council, approved by His Excellency the Governor General on the 22 April, 1975.

WHEREAS the Committee of the Privy Council have had before them a report from the Prime Minister representing that it is desirable to cause an inquiry to be made into and concerning the concentration of corporate power in Canada.

The Committee, therefore, on the recommendation of the Prime Minister, advise that Robert Broughton Bryce, Esquire, of the City of Ottawa in the Province of Ontario, be appointed a Commissioner under Part I of the Inquiries Act to inquire into, report upon, and make recommendations concerning:

(a) the nature and role of major concentrations of corporate power in Canada;
(b) the economic and social implications for the public interest of such concentrations; and
(c) whether safeguards exist or may be required to protect the public interest in the presence of such concentrations.

The Committee further advise that the Commissioner

1. may exercise all the powers conferred upon him by section 11 of the Inquiries Act and be assisted to the fullest extent by government departments and agencies;
2. may adopt such procedure and methods as he may from time to time deem expedient for the proper conduct of the inquiry and sit at such times and in such places in Canada as he may decide from time to time;
3. may engage the services of such counsel, staff, clerks and technical advisers as he may require at rates of remuneration and reimbursement to be approved by the Treasury Board; and
4. shall report to the Governor in Council with all reasonable despatch, and file with the Privy Council Office the papers and records of the Commission as soon as reasonably may be after the conclusion of the inquiry.

CERTIFIED TO BE A TRUE COPY—COPIE CERTIFIÉE CONFORME

P. M. Pitfield

CLERK OF THE PRIVY COUNCIL—LE GREFFIER DU CONSEIL PRIVÉ

Order in Council
P.C. 1975-999

Certified to be a true copy of a Minute of a Meeting of the Committee of the Privy Council, approved by His Excellency the Governor General on the 1 May, 1975.

WHEREAS pursuant to Order in Council P.C. 1975-879 of 22nd April, 1975, Robert Broughton Bryce, Esquire, was appointed a Commissioner under Part I of the Inquiries Act with the duties and powers set out therein.

AND WHEREAS the Committee of the Privy Council have had before them a report from the Acting Prime Minister that it is desirable to appoint two additional Commissioners to act with Mr. Bryce.

Therefore, the Committee of the Privy Council, on the recommendation of the Acting Prime Minister, advise that Pierre Nadeau, Esquire, of Montreal, Quebec, and R. W. V. Dickerson, Esquire, of Vancouver, British Columbia, be appointed Commissioners under Part I of the Inquiries Act with the same duties and powers as set out in Order in Council P.C. 1975-879 of 22nd April, 1975.

The Committee further advise that Robert Broughton Bryce, Esquire, be appointed Chairman of the said Commission and that the Commission be known as the Royal Commission on Corporate Concentration.

CERTIFIED TO BE A TRUE COPY—COPIE CERTIFIÉE CONFORME
P. M. Pitfield
CLERK OF THE PRIVY COUNCIL—LE GREFFIER DU CONSEIL PRIVÉ

APPENDIX B
Briefs

Abitibi Paper Company Ltd.
Alberta Federation of Labour
The Alberta Gas Trunk Line Company Limited
Alberta New Democratic Party
Allen, Nelson
Andrewes, Peter J.
Archer, Anthony M.
Argus Corporation Limited
Armstrong, Donald E.
Asper, I. H.
Associated Grocers Limited and Alberta Grocers Wholesale Ltd.
Association of Canadian Venture Capital Companies
Atlantic Provinces Economic Council

Bank of British Columbia
The Bank of Nova Scotia
Bell Canada
Berg, K.
Berman, Joseph
Bertrand, Robert J., Director of Investigation and Research, Combines Investigation
    Act, Department of Consumer and Corporate Affairs
Better Business Bureau of Canada
Blachford, H. L.
Bouvier, P. Émile
Bradfield, Michael
Brascan Limited
Broadbent, J. Edward (M.P.), Leader of the New Democratic Party
Burchill, C. S.

CAE Industries Ltd.
Calgary Chamber of Commerce
Canada Cement Lafarge Ltd.
Canadian Association of Social Workers

The Canadian Bankers' Association
The Canadian Chamber of Commerce
The Canadian Chemical Producers' Association
Canadian Corporate Management Company Limited
The Canadian Council on Social Development
Canadian Export Association
Canadian Fertilizer Institute
Canadian Imperial Bank of Commerce
Canadian Industries Limited
Canadian Institute of Public Real Estate Companies
The Canadian Life Insurance Association
The Canadian Manufacturers' Association
Canadian Pacific Limited
Canadian Pulp and Paper Association
Cantlie, Ronald B.
Capon, Frank
Carniol, Ben
Caves, Richard E.
Centrale des Syndicats Démocratiques
Charlottetown Chamber of Commerce
Chodos, Robert
Christian Labour Association of Canada and CJL Foundation
Christie, R. E.
Committee for an Independent Canada
Communist Party of Canada
Communist Party of Canada, Northwestern Ontario Branch
Community Planning Association of Canada, Newfoundland Division
Conseil du Patronat du Québec
Consolidated-Bathurst Limited
Consumers' Association of Canada
Cooperative Union of Canada
Corporate Research Group
The Council of Canadian Filmmakers
Crow, Stanley
Cubberley, David J., and Keyes, John

Digiacomo, Gordon
Dobie, John C.
Domtar Limited
Downtown Action
Du Pont of Canada Limited
Duff, Huntly

Edmonton, City of
Edmonton Chamber of Commerce
Elliott, G. Clarence
Energy Probe

Famous Players Limited
Formula Growth Limited
Forster, Victor W.

Fournier, Pierre
Franklin, John
Fredericton Chamber of Commerce

Gardner, Philip L.
Genstar Limited
Grandy, J. F.
Great Canadian Oil Sands Limited
The Great-West Life Assurance Company
Green, Jerry
Grovum, O. W.
Gutstein, Donald, and Henderson, William

Hahlo, H. R.
Halifax Board of Trade
Hartle, Douglas G.
Harvie, Donald
Haskell, H. John
Heisey, Alan
Hincks, Alan
Hovsepian, John
Hudson's Bay Oil and Gas Company Limited
Huntington, Ron (M.P.)

Imasco Limited
Imperial Oil Limited
Indal Limited
Independent Gasoline Retailers Group of Manitoba
Investment Dealers Association of Canada
The Investors Group

Jannock Corporation Limited

King, E. W.
Kudelka, John

John Labatt Limited
Laurentide Financial Corporation Ltd.
Leighton, David S. R.
Leshchyshen, Bob
The Life Underwriters Association of Canada
Locke, W. F.
The London Chamber of Commerce
The Loram Group of Companies
Lorimer, James

MacMillan Bloedel Limited
Maher, E. D.
Malcolm, D., Deveaux, E. L., Hambling, S.

Marchant, C. K.
McCain Foods Limited
McLeod, William E.
Medwin, Bernard
Merrill, Wilson E.
Miller, Danny
Mokkelbost, Per B.
The Molson Companies Limited
Moussally, Sergieh F.
Mucha, Kenneth

Narver, John C.
National Association of Independent Building Materials' Distributors
National Association of Tobacco Confectionery Distributors
National Farmers Union, District 1, Region 1 (P.E.I.)
Neave, Edwin H.
New Democratic Party, Office of the Leader, Nova Scotia
Newfoundland and Labrador Federation of Municipalities
Nickerson, Dave
Norcen Energy Resources Limited
Northern Electric Company, Limited

Ontario, Government of
Ontario Anti-Poverty Organization, Thunder Bay Branch
The Ontario Milk Marketing Board
The Ottawa Board of Trade

Parr, Philip C.
Patton, Donald J.
Pelletier, Judy
Placer Development Limited
Pollock, Ian F.
Porter Land Ltd.
Power Corporation of Canada, Limited
Puxley, H. L.

Redpath Industries Limited
Reed Paper Ltd.
Richard, J. G.
Robertson, Struan
Robinson, A.
Robinson, H. Lukin
Rothmans of Pall Mall Canada Limited
The Royal Bank of Canada
Rubin, Ken
Hugh Russel Limited

SNC Enterprises Limited
St. John's Oxfam Committee

Saint-Pierre, Jacques
Sales, Arnaud
Scherer, F. M.
Shell Canada Limited
Sinclair, George
Smith, Dorothy E.
Sopha, Elmer
Steel Company of Canada, Limited
Sudbury Mine, Mill & Smelter Workers' Union, Local 598
Systems Dimensions Limited

Tabusintac Fishermen's Association
Taskforce on the Churches and Corporate Responsibility
Tasso, André J.
Thermex Manufacturing Limited
Thompson, Gordon L.
Thorne, R. R.
Thunder Bay Chamber of Commerce
The Toronto-Dominion Bank
The Toronto Society of Financial Analysts
TransCanada Pipelines Limited
Trebilcock, Michael J.
Twaits, William O.

United Church of Canada
United Electrical, Radio and Machine Workers of America
United Steelworkers of America

Wahn, Ian G.
Warnock Hersey International Limited
Warwick, Donald P., and Craig, John G.
George Weston Limited
Winestock, Samuel
The Winnipeg Supply & Fuel Company, Limited
Winter, John R.
Wrigley, Leonard

Yellowknife Chamber of Commerce

APPENDIX C

Witnesses

November 3, 1975, Ottawa

Corporate Research Group
Represented by:
James Lorimer
Robert Chodos
James Laxer
Clayton Ruby

Robert J. Bertrand, Director of Investigation and Research, Combines Investigation Act, Department of Consumer and Corporate Affairs
Assisted by:
R. Davidson
Mr. D. DeMelto
W. P. McKeown

New Democratic Party
Represented by:
J. Edward Broadbent
R. Levesque
D. O'Hagen
R. Weese

November 4, 1975, Ottawa

Richard E. Caves
Ken Rubin

Committee for an Independent Canada
Represented by:
David Treleaven

November 13, 1975, Vancouver

Donald Gutstein and William Henderson

Laurentide Financial Corporation Ltd.
Represented by:
Eugene Lindberg and Paul Paine

November 14, 1975, Vancouver

John C. Narver

November 17, 1975, Calgary

The Alberta Gas Trunk Line Company Limited
Represented by:
Robert S. Blair
Robert L. Pierce
Dianne Narvik

Ben Carniol

Associated Grocers Limited and Alberta Grocers Wholesale Ltd.
Represented by:
Wayne D. Smith and R. H. Cherot

November 18, 1975, Calgary

Hudson's Bay Oil and Gas Company Limited
Represented by:
D. C. Jones and L. B. Bannicke

November 20, 1975, Winnipeg

The Investors Group
Represented by:
Robert H. Jones
Donald J. McDonald
Andrew S. Jackson
Phillip E. Newman
D. Carl Bjarnason
Donald E. Rettie

Genstar Limited
Represented by:
James Unsworth
A. A. Franck
A. A. MacNaughton
R. J. Turner

The Winnipeg Supply & Fuel Company, Limited
Represented by:
Neil W. Baker

November 21, 1975, Winnipeg

The Great-West Life Assurance Company
Represented by:
J. W. Burns
II. W. B. Manning
G. W. Dominy
H. E. Harland

I. H. Asper

December 8, 1975, Montreal

Du Pont of Canada Limited
Represented by:
Robert J. Richardson
Franklin S. McCarthy
Henry J. Hemens
Donald A. S. Ivison
Anthony D. Amery

Conseil du Patronat du Québec
Represented by:
Charles Perreault
Roger Ranger
Ghislain DuFour
Michel Vastel
Jean-Claude LeBlanc

Canadian Industries Limited
Represented by:
Eric L. Hamilton
Christopher Hampson
David Braide
Russell Allgood
Pierre Daviault

December 9, 1975, Montreal

The Molson Companies Limited
Represented by:
James T. Black
Davis Lakie
Andrew G. McCaughey
Kenneth A. F. Gates

Frank Capon

December 10, 1975, Montreal

Power Corporation of Canada, Limited
Represented by:
Paul Desmarais
Jean Parisien
Peter Curry

December 11, 1975, Montreal

Canadian Pacific Limited
Represented by:
Ian Sinclair
Paul Nepveu
Don Maxwell

Domtar Limited
Represented by:
A. D. Hamilton
Stewart Kerr
James Smith

December 15, 1975, Toronto

Argus Corporation Limited
Represented by:
John A. McDougald
Donald A. McIntosh
A. Bruce Matthews
Harry H. Edmison

Jerry Green

The Life Underwriters Association of Canada
Represented by:
D. Roughton
R. Kaylar

December 16, 1975, Toronto

Donald P. Warwick and John G. Craig
David J. Cubberley and John Keyes

December 17, 1975, Toronto

James Lorimer
Robert Chodos
Peter Newman

January 12, 1976, Toronto

Hugh Russel Limited
Represented by:
Peter Foster
J. Mark O'Sullivan

Indal Limited
Represented by:
Walter E. Stracey
Dermot G. Coughlan
Murray Maynard
Clayton Wilson
Norman McKnight

United Steelworkers of America
Represented by:
William Mahoney
Peter Warrian
Kenneth Waldie
Paul Brennan
Gordon Milling
Michael Fenwick (for Lynn Williams)
Jean Gérin-Lajoie

Communist Party of Canada
Represented by:
Alfred Dewhurst
William Kashtan
Richard Orlandini

January 13, 1976, Toronto

MacMillan Bloedel Limited
Represented by:
G. B. Currie
D. W. Timmins

Canadian Institute of Public Real Estate Companies
Represented by:
A. E. Diamond
E. A. Goodman
B. Ghert

The Canadian Chamber of Commerce
Represented by:
G. E. Pearson
R. Booth
D. Braide
D. Armstrong
D. Lank

January 14, 1976, Toronto

The Steel Company of Canada, Limited
Represented by:
J. P. Gordon
J. D. Allan
N. J. Brown
R. E. Heneault
J. W. Younger

The Canadian Bankers' Association
Represented by:
Michael A. Harrison
T. S. Dobson
R. M. MacIntosh
J. Allan Boyle
R. D. Fullerton
J. H. Perry

January 16, 1976, Montreal

Consolidated-Bathurst Limited
Represented by:
W. I. M. Turner, Jr.
T. J. Wagg
T. O. Stangeland

Canadian Pulp and Paper Association
Represented by:
Howard Hart
David Wilson
Gordon Minnes

The Royal Bank of Canada
Represented by:
Earle McLaughlin
Thomas Dobson
Donald Wells
Ralph Sultan

January 20, 1976, Toronto

Norcen Energy Resources Limited
Represented by:
F. C. Bovey
C. Spencer Clark
Marilyn Trueblood

Canadian Corporate Management Company Limited
Represented by:
Walter L. Gordon
V. N. Stock
J. A. McKee

Shell Canada Limited
Represented by:
C. W. Daniel
C. F. Williams
D. W. Manzel
T. B. O. McKeag

January 21, 1976, Toronto

Abitibi Paper Company Ltd.
Represented by:
Thomas Bell
Ian McGibbon
James Baillie

The Toronto-Dominion Bank
Represented by:
Allan Lambert
Richard M. Thomson
Alan B. Hockin

April 13, 1976, Montreal

Bell Canada
Represented by:
Jean de Grandpré
Or Tropea
John Farrell

Formula Growth Limited
Represented by:
John W. Dobson
Ian A. Soutar

Pierre Fournier

April 14, 1976, Montreal

Donald E. Armstrong
Assisted by:
Manfred Fr. Kets De Vries
Peter H. Friesen
Danny Miller

Imasco Limited
Represented by:
Paul Paré
Jean-Louis Mercier
George Ross

April 27, 1976, Toronto

Joseph Berman
Assisted by:
Ed Waitzner
Morris Wayman

John Crispo

The Council of Canadian Filmmakers
Represented by:
Sandra Gathercole
John Rocca
Kirwan Cox

April 28, 1976, Toronto

John Labatt Limited
Represented by:
P. N. T. Widdrington
Bruce Brighton
Dean Kitts

Taskforce on the Churches and Corporate Responsibility
Represented by:
Thomas Anthony
Reginald McQuaid
Renate Pratt
Tony Clarke
John Swaigen

April 29, 1976, Toronto

William O. Twaits
C. K. Marchant

May 4, 1976, Toronto

Stanley M. Beck
Canadian Imperial Bank of Commerce
Represented by:
Russel E. Harrison
Donald Fullerton
David A. Lewis

May 5, 1976, Toronto

Michael J. Trebilcock

The Toronto Stock Exchange
Represented by:
J. R. Kimber
Lester Lowe
Hugh J. Cleland

Douglas G. Hartle

May 6, 1976, Toronto

Edwin H. Neave
Assisted by:
James C. Ellert
W. Thomas Hodgson
William G. Leonard
John C. Wiginton

Imperial Oil Limited
Represented by:
J. A. Armstrong
Douglas MacAllan
Donald Eldon

May 12, 1976, Ottawa

The Canadian Chemical Producers' Association
Represented by:
A. J. Foote
Bruce MacDonald
D. I. W. Braide
D. S. Herskowitz
E. L. Weldon
J. H. Childs

Ron Huntington (M.P.)
Assisted by:
Paul Parlé
Elmer McKay (M.P.)

Richard Humphrys

Canadian Transport Commission
Represented by:
Guy Roberge
Anne Carver
Konrad Studnicki-Gizbert
Peter Wallis

May 13, 1976, Ottawa

Frederick M. Scherer

Redpath Industries Limited
Represented by:
Neil M. Shaw
K. Barnes

May 14, 1976, Ottawa

Consumers' Association of Canada
Represented by:
Jim O'Grady
Maryon Brechin
Ruth Lotzker
Ron Cohen
Nola Wade
Cathy Lesiack
Robert Kerton
Robert Olley

James F. Grandy

May 17, 1976, Halifax

Halifax Board of Trade
Represented by:
Galen Duncan
David Henniger

Struan Robertson

New Democratic Party, Office of the Leader, Nova Scotia
Represented by:
Marty Dolan

Mike Marshall

Alan Ruffman

Atlantic Provinces Economic Council
Represented by:
P. E. Gunther and W. A. Jenkins

Michael Bradfield

Donald J. Patton

Shaun Twomey

Judy Pelletier

Howard Crosbie

David Barrett

Judy Wouk

Jim Lotz

United Fishermen's Association of Nova Scotia
Represented by:
Paul Hanson

Dougall MacFarland

Martha MacDonald and Julia McMahon

Susan Mayo

Robert Manuge

May 18, 1976, Charlottetown

Charlottetown Board of Trade
Represented by:
Ed Goss

Grove MacMillian

C. M. McLean

Robert Lippers

Leo Deveau

J. J. Revell

National Farmers Union, District 1, Region 1 (P.E.I.)
Represented by:
Urban Laughlin

Mr. McQuigan

Mary Boyd

May 19, 1976, Fredericton

J. G. Richard
R. R. Thorne
June Parr
Philip Aitken

McCain Foods Limited
Represented by:
Mr. Morris

S. Hambling, E. L. Deveaux, D. Malcolm

Fredericton Chamber of Commerce
Represented by:
Edward Mayer

Roland White
Sidney Pobihushchy

May 20, 1976, St. John's

S. A. Neary

Community Planning Association of Canada, Newfoundland Division
Represented by:
Sean O'Dea

New Democratic Party, Newfoundland
Represented by:
Gerald Panting

Robert Sexty

St. John's Oxfam Committee
Represented by:
J. Williams

Newfoundland and Labrador Federation of Municipalities
Represented by:
William Titford

St. John's Board of Trade
Represented by:
Andrew Crichton

June 2, 1976, Ottawa

Brascan Limited
Represented by:
J. H. Moore
E. C. Freeman-Attwood

Famous Players Limited
Represented by:
George P. Destounis
Robert Grainger
Larry Pilon

June 3, 1976, Ottawa

Association of Canadian Venture Capital Companies
Represented by:
Paul Lowenstein
Gerald Sutton
Michael Pik
Ernest Mercier

Government of Ontario
Represented by:
The Honourable W. Darcy McKeough

June 15, 1976, Sherbrooke

P. Émile Bouvier

Confédération des Syndicats Démocratiques
Represented by:
P.-E. D'Alpé

Gaston Durocher
H. R. Hahlo
David Jones

June 16, 1976, Trois-Rivières

Association des consommateurs du Canada
Represented by:
Pauline Valentine
Michel Richard

Cercle des économistes de la Mauricie
Represented by:
Marcel Therrien

Association des détaillants en alimentation régionaux de la Mauricie
Represented by:
George Charette

Association des consommateurs provinciale
Represented by:
Pauline Boileau

Association des consommateurs
Represented by:
Jeanne Bergeron

June 17, 1976, Quebec

Arnaud Sales
Jacques St-Pierre
Guy Charest
Gilberte Parent

C.E.Q.
Represented by:
Guy Charbonneau

Paul Mackcy
Pierre Bédard
Neddley Pruno
Jacqueline Blanchet

June 21, 1976, Windsor

Canadian Human Rights Party
Represented by:
Joseph Crouchman

Windsor and District Labour Council
Represented by:
Edward Baillargeon

Maud Hermann

Windsor Chamber of Commerce
Represented by:
Milton Grant
Stanley Martin
Robert Richardson
Valerie Kaurak

Gordon Thompson
Thomas Roden
Richard Barrett

June 22, 1976, London

Mr. Monroe

June 23, 1976, Sudbury

Elmer Sopha
Fred Hackett

Sudbury Mine, Mill & Smelter Workers' Union, Local 598
Represented by:
Roy Scranton

William McLeod

Sudbury and District Chamber of Commerce
Represented by:
Ronald Meredith

Charles Hews
Mel Young

June 28, 1976, Victoria

Barbara Mitcham

Consumers' Association of Canada
Represented by:
Bobbie Rose

C. S. Burchill
Nelson Allen
Wilson Merrill
Elmer McKeown
Rick Palmer
Herbert J. Bruch
L. Ryan
Catherine Palmer
David Chadwick
Robert Willis
John Postmar

June 29, 1976, Prince George

Peter Roach
Pat Snider
Ron Surgenor

July 8, 1976, Chicoutimi

Camille Girard
Laval Gagnon
Sergieh F. Moussally
Gérard Talbot
F.-R. Thériault

September 7, 1976, Regina

Sharon and Terry Russel
Samuel Winestock
Steven Heeren
Donald Mitchell

September 8, 1976, Edmonton

Edmonton Chamber of Commerce
Represented by:
John Barry
E. R. Baxter

New Democratic Party, Alberta
Represented by:
A. McEachern

The Automotive Retailers Association of Alberta
Represented by:
Perley Vail and Des Achilles

Alberta Federation of Labour
Represented by:
Harry Kostiuk
Warren Carogata

The National Automotive Trades Association
Represented by:
Mr. Dixon

Richard Cook
Dennis Marryat
Denis Goodale
Frank Riddell
David Leadbetter
Raymond Pallard
Joseph Pallard

September 9, 1976, Yellowknife

The Northwest Territories Legislative Assembly
Represented by:
Dave Nickerson, Member for Yellowknife-North

Yellowknife Chamber of Commerce
Represented by:
Grant Hinchey

Consumers' Association of Canada, Yellowknife
Represented by:
Diane Lonegan
Donna Lang

September 13, 1976, Thunder Bay

Ontario Anti-Poverty Organization, Thunder Bay Branch
Represented by:
Simon Hoad

Louis Pelletier

Thunder Bay Chamber of Commerce
Represented by:
Jack Masters

Frederick J. Anderson, Lakehead University

Communist Party of Canada, Northwestern Ontario Branch
Represented by:
Phil Harris

Carl Rose
Paul McRae, M.P.

APPENDIX D

Research Studies

The research we undertook has been grouped under four headings: corporate background reports; corporate case studies; technical reports and economic studies; and social implications studies. The studies in each category published by the Commission are described below. The number attached to each study is for publication and ordering purposes and does not reflect the sequence in which the studies were undertaken or completed.

Corporate Background Reports

The first part of our mandate requires us to "inquire into... the nature and role of major concentrations of corporate power in Canada". One of our first actions was to commission a number of historical studies by financial analysts on the structure, financing and growth of large diversified Canadian enterprises. These studies are based largely on information that has been publicly available at one time or another but that has not previously been drawn together and analyzed in one place. They were prepared with the knowledge and cooperation of the companies involved. The series was coordinated for us by Charles B. Loewen of Loewen, Ondaatje, McCutcheon & Co. Ltd., an investment firm in Toronto.

Argus Corporation Limited, by Harry T. Seymour (RCCC Study No. 1). Background to Argus Corporation Limited, interlocks with other companies, major long-term investments, unrealized initiatives by the company and growth and financial performance.

Brascan Limited, by E. Roy Birkett (RCCC Study No. 2). Background to Brascan Limited, including history of John Labatt Limited, Jonlab Investments Limited and other related companies; comments on methods of buying and selling Canadian companies.

The Cadillac Fairview Corporation Limited, by Ira Gluskin (RCCC Study No. 3). The historical background of the company, its financial performance and rate of return, its share of various markets, operations of different divisions, diversification, and a comparison with other public real estate companies.

Canada Development Corporation, by Michael R. Graham (RCCC Study No. 4). The political origins of CDC, its objectives and operating policies, current perspectives, the motivation for various mergers and acquisitions, including Texasgulf, and the effects of the acquisitions on the companies, the industries, the investors and Canada.

Canadian Pacific Investments Limited, by Terrance K. Salman (RCCC Study No. 5). History of the company, its relationship to Canadian Pacific Limited and its financial performance; major acquisitions of the company; profiles of the 13 main subsidiaries.

Domtar Limited, by Murray Savage (RCCC Study No. 6). History of the company, its acquisitions and divestitures, its relationship with Argus Corporation and external relations.

The Molson Companies Ltd., by Michel G. Perreault (RCCC Study No. 8). The brewing operations of Molson, Molson's acquisition policy, with case studies of four acquisitions, its financial structure and performance and its use of human resources.

Noranda Mines Limited, by Patrick J. Mars (RCCC Study No. 9). History of the company since 1945, its corporate structure, methods employed in acquisitions and takeovers, unsuccessful acquisitions and financial performance.

Power Corporation of Canada, Limited, by C. J. Hodgson, J. E. Douville, Norman Heimlich and Nicholas Majendie (RCCC Study No. 10). Corporate acquisitions and investments, financial performance and ownership structure, including the role of Nordex, Gelco, subsidiaries and affiliates.

Rothmans of Pall Mall Canada Limited and Carling O'Keefe Limited, by Robert G. Shoniker (RCCC Study No. 11). The relationship of Rothmans of Pall Mall with Carling O'Keefe; the histories and acquisitions program of each company; the involvement of Argus Corporation in Canadian Breweries Limited.

George Weston Limited, by D. Tigert (RCCC Study No. 12). The corporate structure and financial history of George Weston Limited and Loblaw Companies Limited, their competitive position in each market and the acquisition program from 1928 to 1975.

Corporate Case Studies

Three of our studies relate to large but not diversified corporations, and their economic and social impacts. One of these firms, Alcan Aluminium, is a major Canadian refining and manufacturing company with almost equal shares of domestic and foreign ownership and with extensive overseas operations. A second, IBM Canada, is the Canadian element of a large multinational company, foreign-owned and in a high-technology industry. A third, MacMillan Bloedel Limited, is a large resource-based company, primarily Canadian-owned and controlled and selling largely in the export market. A fourth study, *The Irving Companies,* looks at an example of regional concentration. The companies were selected to illustrate the diverse nature, role and implications of such large business units in Canada. The reports were prepared by professional economists.

Alcan Aluminium Limited, by Isaiah A. Litvak and Christopher J. Maule (RCCC Study No. 13). The historical evolution of Alcan, the Canadianization of its operations, its corporate strategy and structure including diversification, integration, and international operations; the corporate impact on Canada.

IBM Canada Ltd., by Marcel Côté, Yvan Allaire and Roger-Émile Miller (RCCC Study No. 14). The history and development of IBM and IBM Canada; the market power of IBM in data processing products, including demand growth, market share, and segmentation; organizational structure and management principles, political power and social responsibility.

The Existence and Exercise of Corporate Power: A Case Study of MacMillan Bloedel Ltd., By R. Schwindt (RCCC Study No. 15). The Pacific Northwest forest products sector, supply and demand, industry structure and conduct, the economics of the company and its component industries, corporate structure and strategy and the economic and social implications of company operation.

The Irving Companies (RCCC Study No. 16). The study on the Irving group of companies discusses the size, scope, strategy and structure of an ownership-linked group of companies that constitute a significant regional concentration of ownership in Canada.

Technical Reports and Economic Studies

A third series of our studies used economic, mathematical and statistical analysis to draw conclusions from available aggregate and sectoral data. The first study undertaken attempted to measure quantitatively the relationship between the size or other dimensions of corporate structure and corporate economic performance. A second analyzed some of the relationships among corporate size, diversification and financing. A third was a statistical analysis of the patterns of ownership and interlocking personnel of corporate complexes, measuring the effects of different definitions of control on industrial concentration ratios. Other studies followed as different issues arose from briefs, hearings and our own deliberations.

Enterprise Structure and Corporate Concentration, by Stephen D. Berkowitz, Yehuda Kotowitz and Leonard Waverman (RCCC Study No. 17). The effects of changing enterprise definitions on concentration ratios, using ownership ties, directorship, officership and executive board ties.

Corporate Dualism and the Canadian Steel Industry, by Isaiah A. Litvak and Christopher J. Maule (RCCC Study No. 19). Competitive aspects of corporate dualism, the specific case of dualism in the Canadian steel industry and the effect of dualism on competition.

Notes on the Economies of Large Firm Size, by D. G. McFetridge and L. J. Weatherley (RCCC Study No. 20). Statistical analysis of the various economic advantages that may be related to corporate size; economies of scale in marketing, financial activity, the cost of raising capital, efficiency in the disposition of capital, risk-taking, progressiveness, export ability and management functions.

Reciprocal Buying Arrangements: A Problem in Market Power? by W. T. Stanbury (RCCC Study No. 24). Survey of the Canadian and U.S. literature and empirical evidence on reciprocal buying arrangements, including a review of the contested cases in the United States.

Studies in Canadian Industrial Organization, by Richard E. Caves, Michael E. Porter, A. Michael Spence, John T. Scott and André Lemelin (RCCC Study No. 26). A series of studies on comparative market structures, diversification in manufacturing industries, the sources of concentration, market power and the cost of capital, market performance and industrial efficiency. The studies share a common origin in a large, integrated data set of variables on the manufacturing and distribution sectors and for firms in Canada and the United States.

Corporate Concentration and the Canadian Tax System, by Stikeman, Elliott, Tamaki, Mercier & Robb (RCCC Study No. 28). Some of the ways in which the Canadian income tax system may encourage or discourage corporate concentration, including tax concessions, investment tax credit, capital cost allowance, consolidation of returns, designated surplus, dividend stripping and rollover provisions.

Economies of Scale in Manufacturing: A Survey, by Donald J. Lecraw (RCCC Study No. 29). A survey of the economies of scale available to Canadian manufacturers at the product, multiproduct plant, multiplant and firm levels. It summarizes the theoretical literature and describes the evidence on these economies of scale for firms in Canada.

Concentration Levels and Trends in the Canadian Economy, 1965-73, by Christian Marfels (RCCC Study No. 31). Overall and aggregate concentration in the Canadian economy in eight divisions of the economy and in manufacturing, mining and logging industries; a comparison of Canadian concentration levels and trends with those in other countries.

Conglomerate Mergers, by Donald J. Lecraw and Donald N. Thompson (RCCC Study No. 32). Economic aspects of the growth of conglomerate firms in Canada: their structure, acquisition patterns, the efficiency of conglomerate firms and the role of conglomerates in fostering or inhibiting competition.

Mergers and Acquisitions in Canada, by Steven Globerman (RCCC Study No. 34). The theoretical motives for mergers, empirical evidence on mergers and acquisitions in Canada, primary and secondary merger consequences and alternative approaches to merger policy.

Social Implications Studies

Eight of the studies we are publishing relate to the social implications of corporate concentration. Far less Canadian literature exists in the social area than in the economic; readers could certainly think of literally dozens of other studies that might have been undertaken. The studies listed cover a sampling of areas that we felt to be important, and which served as a general indication of the degree to which there were major unresolved problems in the social area. As an indication of the diversity involved, one of the first studies undertaken was on Canadian requirements for disclosure of corporate information; the second was a study of the concept of social responsibility as it has developed thus far in Canada; the third was a study of recent changes in Canadian laws regarding political contributions and the role of corporations as a source of funding for political parties.

Corporate Disclosure, by John A. Kazanjian (RCCC Study No. 18). An analysis of existing requirements for corporate disclosure under provincial regulation, federal regulation, and U.S. securities regulation; the corporate justification for limiting disclosure and various proposals for expanding corporate disclosure.

Corporate Social Performance in Canada, by R. Terrance Mactaggart (RCCC Study No. 21). The concept of corporate social responsibility as it is perceived and practised by managers of large corporations, its probable evolution and its impact to date on Canadian corporate practice.

Party, Candidate and Election Finance, by Khayyam Z. Paltiel (RCCC Study No. 22). The traditional pattern of Canadian political party finance, federal and provincial election expense legislation, the control of political financing in other jurisdictions.

La Presse, by Yvan Allaire, Roger-Émile Miller and Paul Dell'Aniello (RCCC Study No. 23). The relationship and the forms of power and control that exist between Power Corporation and *La Presse*.

Personnel Administration in Large and Middle-Sized Canadian Businesses, by Victor V. Murray and David E. Dimick (RCCC Study No. 25). Comparison of a number of dimensions of employee relations practices in ten large enterprises, with ten middle-sized enterprises in the same industries in Canada.

Organization Size and Alienation, by John W. Gartrell (RCCC Study No. 27). The relationship between organization size and alienation based on survey results from two large cross-sectional studies, one carried out in Canada and one in the United States.

The Social Characteristics of One-Industry Towns in Canada, by Alex Himelfarb (RCCC Study No. 30). The general consequences of a community's dependence on a single or dominant industry: a review of the literature in Canada.

Organization Size as a Factor Influencing Labour Relations, by T. H. White (RCCC Study No. 33). A literature review and data analysis on the relationship between corporate size and labor relations, using variables of commitment to organization, labor relations climate and job satisfaction.

APPENDIX E
Staff

Senior Officers

Yves Bériault, Assistant Counsel
Serge Bourque, Executive Secretary
Martin H. Freedman, Counsel
Tony P. Going, Executive Assistant to the Chairman
Richard M. Hofer, Assistant Secretary
Donald J. Lecraw, Chief Economist
Donald N. Thompson, Director of Research

Senior Adviser

Robert T. Morgan

Research Consultants

Richard E. Caves
Steven Globerman
D. Craig McKie
Victor V. Murray
Gilbert B. Reschenthaler
William T. Stanbury
Leonard Wrigley

Editors

Louis P. Chabot
Claire Dumais-Sabourin
Elizabeth Ediger
Mary E. Gallant
Ruth E. Hood
J. Henriot Mayer
Jean Pouliot
Moyra Tooke

449

Staff

Diane Attfield
Paula Barry
Alice Bourdon
Nicole Comtois
Judy Chatfield
Helen Cutts
Norah Curley
Jane Davey
Madeleine deCarufel
Sushama Gera
Barbara Glover
Lise Gougeon
Louise Haines
Robert Haydon
Anne Hindley
Neera Huckvale
John Itty

Anita LaRose
Hélène Lamontagne
Nicole Leclerc
Barbara Michalos
Margaret Oughtred
Lorraine Parent
Sam Patayanikorn
George Pickering
Marianne Potts
Amrik Rakhra
Anne Redpath
Robert Rudd
Martha St. Pierre
Indu Sahni
Marie-Paule Scott
Jeffrey Shaffer
Margaret Twiss